STUDY GUIDE

AVI J. COHEN ◆ **HARVEY**

York University   *University of Regina*

ECONOMICS

CANADA IN THE GLOBAL ENVIRONMENT

FIFTH EDITION

MICHAEL PARKIN ◆ ROBIN BADE

PEARSON

Addison
Wesley

Toronto

ISBN 0-321-15439-8

Acquisitions Editor: Gary Bennett
Developmental Editor: Meaghan Eley
Production Editor: Marisa D'Andrea
Production Coordinator: Deborah Starks

3 4 5   07 06 05

Printed and bound in Canada.

PEARSON
Addison
Wesley

Contents

Acknowledgments

This fifth edition of the *Study Guide* has benefited from help and advice from many sources. Colleagues have helped raise the quality of our questions with suggestions and corrections—we would especially like to thank Robin Bade, Eric Kam (whose review of the fourth edition prompted many of the changes here), Keith MacKinnon, Michael Parkin, and especially David Grey. Various students have pointed out mistakes and ambiguities they found in using the *Study Guide*. Thanks to Lydia Bonanno, Jing Chang, Bing Chen, Jing Chen, Iryna Ivanova, Andrew Krupowicz, Lily Liu, Jason Pisarri, and Christine Sheepway for helping us in this area.

Harvey King dedicates this edition to Tracy for being so patient while I holed myself up in the study night after night. Avi Cohen dedicates this edition to Robert Cohen, my father, whose extraordinary qualities as a teacher make him my role model.

Harvey King
Avi Cohen
March 2003

Introduction

Before You Begin...

Our experience has taught us that what first-year economics students want most from a *Study Guide* is help in mastering course material in order to do well on examinations. We have developed this *Study Guide* to respond specifically to that demand. Using this *Study Guide* alone, however, is not enough to guarantee that you will do well in your course. In order to help you overcome the problems and difficulties that most first-year students encounter, we have some general advice on how to study, as well as some specific advice on how to best use this *Study Guide*.

Some Friendly Advice

The study of economics requires a different style of thinking than what you may encounter in other courses. Economists make extensive use of assumptions to break down complex problems into simple, analytically manageable parts. This analytical style, while not ultimately more demanding than the styles of thinking in other disciplines, feels unfamiliar to most students and requires practice. As a result, it is not as easy to do well in economics simply on the basis of your raw intelligence and high-school knowledge as it is in many other first-year courses. Many students who come to our offices are frustrated and puzzled by the fact that they are getting As and Bs in their other courses but only a C or worse in economics. They have not recognized that the study of economics is different and requires practice. In order to avoid a frustrating visit to your instructor after your first test, we suggest you do the following.

Don't rely solely on your high-school economics. If you took high-school economics, you will have seen the material on demand and supply which your instructor will lecture on in the first few weeks. Don't be lulled into feeling that the course will be easy. Your high-school knowledge of economic concepts will be very useful, but it will not be enough to guarantee high marks on exams. Your college or university instructors will demand much more detailed knowledge of concepts and ask you to apply them in new circumstances.

Keep up with the course material on a weekly basis. Read the appropriate chapter in the textbook before your instructor lectures on it. In this initial reading, don't worry about details or arguments you can't quite follow—just try to get a general understanding of the basic concepts and issues. You may be amazed at how your instructor's ability to teach improves when you come to class prepared. As soon as your instructor has finished covering a chapter, complete the corresponding *Study Guide* chapter. Avoid cramming the day before or even just the week before an exam. Because economics requires practice, cramming is an almost certain recipe for failure.

Keep a good set of lecture notes. Good lecture notes are vital for focusing your studying. Your instructor will only lecture on a subset of topics from the textbook. The topics your instructor covers in a lecture should usually be given priority when studying. Also give priority to studying the figures and graphs covered in the lecture.

Instructors do differ in their emphasis on lecture notes or the textbook, so early on in the course ask which is more important in reviewing for exams— lecture notes or the textbook. If your instructor answers that both are important, then ask the following, typically economic question: at the margin, which will be more beneficial—spending an extra hour re-reading your lecture notes or an extra hour re-reading the textbook? This question assumes that you have read each textbook chapter twice (once before lecture for a general understanding, and then later for a thorough understanding); that you have prepared a good set of lecture notes; and that you have worked through all of the problems in the appropriate *Study Guide* chapters. By applying this style of analysis to the problem of efficiently allocating your study time, you are already beginning to think like an economist!

Use your instructor and/or teaching assistants for help. When you have questions or problems with course material, come to the office to ask questions. Remember, you are paying for your education and instructors are there to help you learn. We are often amazed at how few students come to see us during office hours. Don't be shy. The personal contact that comes from one-on-one tutoring is professionally gratifying for us as well as (hopefully) beneficial to you.

Form a study group. A very useful way to motivate your studying and to learn economics is to discuss the course material and problems with other students. Explaining the answer to a question out loud is a very effective way of discovering how well you understand the question. When you answer a question only in your head, you often skip steps in the chain of reasoning without realizing it. When you are forced to explain your reasoning aloud, gaps and mistakes quickly appear, and you (with your fellow group members) can quickly correct your reasoning. The true/false and explain questions in the *Study Guide* and the critical thinking questions at the end of each textbook chapter are good study-group material. You might also get together after having worked the *Study Guide* problems, but before looking at the answers, and help each other solve unsolved problems.

Work old exams. One of the most effective ways of studying is to work through exams your instructor has given in previous years. Old exams give you a feel for the style of question your instructor may ask, and give you the opportunity to get used to time pressure if you force yourself to do the exam in the allotted time. Studying from old exams is not cheating, as long as you have obtained a copy of the exam legally. Some institutions keep old exams in the library, others in the department or at the student union. Upper-year students who have previously taken the course are usually a good source as well. Remember, though, that old exams are a useful study aid only if you use them to understand the reasoning behind each question. If you simply memorize answers in the hopes that your instructor will repeat the identical question, you are likely to fail. From year to year, instructors routinely change the questions or change the numerical values for similar questions.

Use the Parkin–Bade Web site. In addition to the *Study Guide*, we believe this resource is worth using for the valuable help it will provide in mastering course material and doing well on examinations. However, don't just take our word for it—ask students who have used it for their opinions.

The Parkin–Bade Web site (www.pearsoned.ca/parkin) includes online diagnostic quizzes with feedback, Economics in Action (an integrated tutorial, quizzing, and graphing tool that makes curves shift and graphs come to life), answers to odd-numbered end-of-chapter problems, daily Economics in the News updates, Economic Links, and an online Office Hours feature that enables you to get help by email from Robin Bade.

Using the *Study Guide*

You should only attempt to complete a chapter in the *Study Guide* after you have read the corresponding textbook chapter and listened to your instructor lecture on the material. Each *Study Guide* chapter contains the following sections.

Key Concepts This first section is a one- to two-page summary, in point form, of all key definitions, concepts, and material from the textbook chapter. The summary is organized using the same major section headings from the textbook chapter. Key terms from the textbook appear in bold. This section is designed to focus you quickly and precisely on the core material that you must master. It is an excellent study aid for the night before

an exam. Think of it as crib notes that will serve as a final check of the key concepts you have studied.

Helpful Hints When you encounter difficulty in mastering concepts or techniques, you will not be alone. Many students find certain concepts difficult and often make the same kinds of mistakes. We have seen these common mistakes often enough to have learned how to help students avoid them. The hints point out these mistakes and offer tips to avoid them. The hints focus on the most important concepts, equations, and techniques for problem solving. They also review crucial graphs that appear on every instructor's exams. We hope that this section will be very useful, since instructors always ask exam questions designed to test these possible mistakes in your understanding.

This section sometimes includes extra material that your instructor may add to the course, but is not in textbook chapters. An example of extra material is the discussion in Chapter 2 of absolute advantage in producing a single good. This extra material is marked with the symbol ℮ for extra, and may be skipped if your instructor does not cover it. The symbol ℮ is used in the *Study Guide* to identify questions and answers based on extra material.

Self-Test This will be one of the most useful sections of the *Study Guide*. The questions are designed to give you practice and to test skills and techniques you must master to do well on exams. There are plenty of the multiple-choice questions (25 for each chapter) that you are most likely to encounter on course tests and exams. There are other types of questions, described below, each with a specific pedagogical purpose. Questions (and answers) based on extra material covered in the Helpful Hints are marked with ℮ so that you can easily skip them if your instructor does not assign the extra material. Before we describe the three parts of the Self-Test section, here are some general tips that apply to all parts.

Use a pencil to write your answers in the *Study Guide*. This will allow you to erase your mistakes and have neat, completed pages from which to study. Draw graphs wherever they are applicable. Some questions will ask explicitly for graphs; many others will not but will require a chain of reasoning that involves shifts of curves on a graph. *Always draw the graph.* Don't try to work through the reasoning in your head—you are much more likely to make mistakes that way. Whenever you draw a graph, even in the margins of the *Study Guide*, label the axes. You may think that you can keep the labels in your head, but you will be confronting many different graphs with many different variables on the axes. Avoid confusion and label. As an added incentive, remember that on exams where graphs are required, instructors will deduct marks for unlabelled axes.

Do the Self-Test questions as if they were real exam questions, which means do them *without looking at the answers.* This is the single most important tip we can give you about effectively using the *Study Guide* to improve your test and exam performance. Struggling for the answers to questions that you find difficult is one of the most effective ways to learn. The athletic adage—no pain, no gain—applies equally well to studying. You will learn the most from right answers you had to struggle for and from your wrong answers and mistakes. Only after you have attempted all the questions should you look at the answers. When you finally do check the answers, be sure to understand where you went wrong and why the right answer is correct.

If you want to impose time pressure on yourself to simulate the conditions of a real exam, allow two minutes for each true/false and multiple-choice question. The short answer problems vary considerably in their time requirements, so it is difficult to give time estimates for them. However, we believe that such time pressure is probably *not* a good idea for *Study Guide* questions. A state of mind of relaxed concentration is best for work in the *Study Guide.* Use old exams if you want practice with time pressure, or use the Part Wrap Up Midterm Examinations (see description on page x).

There are many questions in each chapter, and it will take you somewhere between two and five hours to answer all of them. If you get tired (or bored), don't burn yourself out by trying to work through all of the questions in one sitting. Consider breaking up your Self-Test over two (or more) study sessions.

The three parts of the Self-Test section are:

True/False and Explain These questions test basic knowledge of chapter concepts and your ability to apply the concepts. Some challenge your understanding, to see if you can identify mistakes in statements using basic concepts. These questions will quickly identify gaps in your knowledge and are useful to answer out loud in a study group. There are 15 of these questions, organized using the same major section headings from the textbook. The Test Bank that your instructor will likely use to make up tests and exams also contains, for the first time, true/false questions like those in the Self-Test.

When answering, identify each statement as *true* or *false.* Explain your answer in one sentence. The space underneath each question is sufficient for writing your answer.

Multiple-Choice These more difficult questions test your analytical abilities by asking you to apply concepts to new situations, manipulate information, and solve numerical and graphical problems.

This is the most frequently used type of test and exam question, and the Self-Test contains 25 of them

organized using the same major section headings from the textbook. Your instructor's Test Bank contains all of the *Study Guide* multiple-choice questions, numerous questions that closely "parallel" the *Study Guide* questions, plus many similar questions.

Read each question and all five choices carefully before you answer. Many of the choices will be plausible and will differ only slightly. You must choose the one *best* answer. A useful strategy in working these questions is first to eliminate any obviously wrong choices and then to focus on the remaining alternatives. Be aware that sometimes the correct answer will be "none of the above choices is correct." Don't get frustrated or think that you are dim if you can't immediately see the correct answer. These questions are designed to make you work to find the correct choice.

Short Answer Problems The best way to learn to do economics is to do problems. Problems are also a popular type of test and exam question—practice them as much as possible! Each Self-Test concludes with ten short answer, numerical, or graphical problems, often based on economic policy issues. In many chapters, this is the most challenging part of the Self-Test. It is also likely to be the most helpful for deepening your understanding of the chapter material. We have, however, designed the questions to teach as much as to test. We have purposely arranged the parts of each multipart question to lead you through the problem-solving analysis in a gradual and sequential fashion, from easier to more difficult parts.

Problems that require critical thinking are marked with the symbol ⓒ , to alert you to the need for extra time and effort. These ⓒ symbols give you the same indication you would have on a test or exam from the number of marks or minutes allocated to a problem.

Answers The Self-Test is followed by answers to all questions. But do not look at an answer until you have attempted a question. When you do finally look, use the answers to understand where you went wrong and why the right answer is correct.

Each true/false and multiple-choice answer includes a brief, point-form explanation to suggest where you might have gone wrong and the economic reasoning behind the answer. At the end of each answer are page numbers in the textbook where you can go to find a more complete explanation. Answers to critical thinking questions are marked with ⓒ to indicate why you might have struggled with that question! (We purposely did not mark which true/false and multiple-choice questions were critical thinking, to stay as close as possible to a real test or exam format. In an exam, all multiple-choice questions, for example, are worth the same number of marks, and you have no idea which questions are the more difficult ones requiring critical thinking.)

The detailed answers to the short answer problems should be especially useful in clarifying and illustrating typical chains of reasoning involved in economic analysis. Answers to critical thinking problems are marked with ⊕ . If the answers alone do not clear up your confusion, go back to the appropriate sections of the textbook. If that still does not suffice, go to your instructor's or teaching assistants' office, or to your study-group members, to get help and clarification.

Part Wrap Up Problem and Midterm Examination Every few chapters, at the end of each of the ten parts of the textbook, you will find a special problem (and answer). These multipart problems draw on material from all chapters in the part, and emphasize policy and real-world questions (for example, the impact of cigarette smuggling on tax revenues). These wrap up problems will help you integrate concepts from different chapters that may seem unconnected, but that are actually related. We often design exam questions similar to these problems.

Each Part Wrap Up also contains a Midterm Examination, consisting of four or more multiple-choice questions from each chapter in the textbook part. The midterm is set up like a real examination or test, with a scrambled order and a time limit for working the questions. Like the other multiple-choice questions in the *Study Guide*, there are answers with point-form explanations as well as page numbers in the textbook where you can go to find more complete explanations.

If you effectively combine the use of the textbook, the *Study Guide*, the Parkin–Bade Web site, and all other course resources, you will be well prepared for exams. Equally importantly, you will also have developed analytical skills and powers of reasoning that will benefit you throughout your life and in whatever career you choose.

Do You Have Any Friendly Advice For Us?

We have attempted to make this *Study Guide* as clear and as useful as possible, and to avoid errors. No doubt, we have not succeeded entirely, and you are the only judges who count in evaluating our attempt. If you discover errors, or if you have other suggestions for improving the *Study Guide*, please write to us. In future editions, we will try to acknowledge the names of all students whose suggestions help us improve the *Study Guide*. Send your correspondence or email to either of us:

Professor Avi J. Cohen
Department of Economics
Vari Hall, York University
Toronto, Ontario M3J 1P3
avicohen@yorku.ca

Professor Harvey B. King
Department of Economics
University of Regina
Regina, Saskatchewan S4S 0A2
Harvey.King@uregina.ca

Should the Study of Economics Be Part of Your Future?

by Robert Whaples (Wake Forest University) and
Harvey King (University of Regina)

Should You Take More Economics Courses?

Soon you will learn about supply and demand, utility and profit maximization, employment and unemployment. Before, however, let's take a moment to look to the future.

- Should you take more classes or maybe even major in economics?

- What about graduate school in economics?

Economists generally assume that people try to make rational choices to maximize their own well-being. The purpose of this chapter is help you make that rational maximizing choice by providing low-cost information. Let us assess the benefits and see whether they outweigh the costs of studying economics.

Benefits from Studying Economics

Knowledge, Enlightenment, and Liberation

As John Maynard Keynes, a famous British economist, said, "The ideas of economists ... both when they are right and when they are wrong, are more powerful than is commonly understood. Indeed the world is ruled by little else. Practical men, who believe themselves to be quite exempt from any intellectual influences, are usually the slaves of some defunct economist." Studying economics is a liberating and enlightening experience. You don't want to be the slave of a defunct economist, do you? Liberate yourself. It's better to bring your ideas out in the open, to confront and understand them, rather than to leave them buried.

Knowledge, Understanding, and Satisfaction

Many of the most important problems in the world are economic. Studying economics gives you a practical set of tools to understand and solve them. Every day, on television and in the newspapers, we hear and read about big issues such as economic growth, inflation, unemployment, health care reform, welfare reform, the environment, and the transition away from Communism. Your introduction to economics will let you watch the news or pick up a newspaper and better understand these issues. As an added bonus, economics helps you understand smaller, more immediate concerns, such as: How much Spam should I buy? Is skipping class today a good idea? Should I put my retirement funds in government bonds or in the stock market? After all, as George Bernard Shaw put it, "Economy is the art of making the most of life." Mick Jagger, who dropped out of the London School of Economics, complains that he "can't get no satisfaction." Maybe he should have studied more economics. The economic way of thinking will help you maximize your satisfaction.

Career Opportunities

All careers are not equal. While the wages in many occupations have not risen much lately, the wages of "symbolic analysts" who "solve, identify, and broker problems by manipulating symbols" are soaring.[1] These people "simplify reality into abstract images that can be rearranged, juggled, experimented with, communicated to other specialists, and then, eventually, transformed back into reality." Their wages have been rising as the globalization of the economy increases the demand for their insights and as technological developments (especially computers) have enhanced their productivity. Economists are the quintessential symbolic analysts as we manipulate ideas about abstractions such as supply and demand, cost and benefits, and equilibrium. You can think of your training in economics as an exercise regimen, a workout for your brain.

You will use many of the concepts you will learn in introductory economics during your career, but it is the practice in abstract thinking that will really pay off. In fact, most economics majors do not go on to become economists. They enter fields that use their analytical abilities, including business, management, insurance, finance, real estate, marketing, law, education, policy analysis, consulting, government, planning, and even medicine, journalism, and the arts.

A recent survey of 100 former economics majors at one university included all of these careers. If you want to verify that economics majors graduate to successful and rewarding careers, just ask your professors or watch what happens to economics majors from your school as they graduate.

Statistics from the 1996 Canadian census (the most recent available at the time of writing) show that economics majors earn a healthy salary. Table 1 shows the average yearly earnings for selected occupations, with those occupations that generally require a reasonable understanding of economics highlighted in italics.

TABLE 1   AVERAGE YEARLY EARNINGS, FULL-YEAR, FULL-TIME WORKERS (BOTH SEXES), 1995 (TOP 15 OCCUPATIONS, PLUS SELECTED OTHERS)

Occupation	Average Yearly Earnings
Judges	$126,246
Specialist physicians	$123,976
General practitioners and family physicians	$107,620
Dentists	$102,433
Senior managers – Goods production, etc.	$99,360
Senior managers – Financial, etc.	*$99,117*
Lawyers and Quebec notaries	*$81,617*
Senior managers – Trade, etc.	$79,200
Primary production managers	$76,701
Securities agents, investment dealers, and traders	*$75,911*
Petroleum engineers	$72,543
Chiropractors	$68,808
Engineering and science managers	$68,235
University professors*	*$68,195*
Senior managers – health, education, social services, etc.	*$68,187*
Financial managers in administrative services	*$61,779*
Managers in financial services	*$59,113*
Government managers in economic analysis, etc.	*$58,695*
Economists and economic policy researchers and analysts	*$58,578*
Economic development officers and marketing researchers	*$49,793*
Average income, all occupations	$37,556

*Clearly, not *all* professors require an understanding of economics! The point is that becoming a professor is a high-paying option for an economics major.

Source: Statistics Canada, "1996 Census: Sources of income, earnings and total income, and family income," *The Daily,* 12 May 1998.

We can also see that economics degrees do well by examining data on entry-level wages (*Source: Job Futures, Part 2: Career Outlooks for Graduates,* Human Resources and Development Canada, accessed at http://jobfutures.ca). In 1998, the average starting salary for a B.A. in economics was $31,500. Although this is lower than degrees in engineering ($39,200) or computing science, it is higher than the starting salary for a B.A. in humanities (English degrees earned $27,600, French degrees $29,500), or for a B.A. in the other social sciences (psychology degrees earned $28,000, sociology degrees $27,800), or for a B.Sc. in many of the sciences (physics degrees earned $31,600, biology degrees $27,400). In addition, employment rates for economics B.A.s were higher than average, and salaries grew over the first five years at a higher-than-average rate.

You might like to consider graduate school in economics—the entry-level wage for an M.A. in economics was roughly $42,100 in 1998.

The Costs of Studying Economics

Since the "direct" costs of studying economics (tuition, books, supplies) aren't generally any higher or lower than the direct costs of other courses, indirect costs will be the most important of the costs to studying economics.

Forgone Knowledge

If you study economics, you can't study something else. This forgone knowledge could be very valuable.

Time and Energy

Economics is a fairly demanding major. Although economics courses do not generally take as much time as courses in English and history (in which you have to read a lot of long books) or anatomy and physiology (in which you have to spend hours in the lab and hours memorizing things), they do take a decent amount of time. In addition, some people find the material "tougher" than most subjects because memorizing is not the key. In economics (like physics), analyzing and solving are the keys.

Grades

As Table 2 shows, grades in introductory economics courses are generally lower than grades in some other majors, including other social sciences and the humanities. On the other hand, grades in economics are similar to grades in some sciences and math.

TABLE **2** AVERAGE GRADES AND GRADE DISTRIBUTION IN INTRODUCTORY COURSES AT SEVEN ONTARIO UNIVERSITIES

Department	Mean Grade*	% (A + B)	% (D + F)
Music	3.02	72.1	9.7
English	2.76	64.0	9.4
French	2.69	61.1	12.4
Philosophy	2.54	57.6	15.3
Biology	2.52	54.5	19.7
Sociology	2.51	52.8	14.2
Political Science	2.49	55.6	14.1
Psychology	2.40	48.4	20.6
Physics	2.38	46.1	28.4
Mathematics	2.19	44.4	33.9
Chemistry	2.18	42.9	30.9
Economics	2.18	41.6	30.7

*A = 4, B = 3, C = 2, D = 1, F = 0.

Source: Paul Anglin and Ronald Meng, "Evidence on Grades and Grade Inflation at Ontario's Universities," *University of Windsor Working Paper,* Nov. 1999. Used with permission.

Caveat Emptor (Buyer Beware): Interpreting Your Grades Is Not Straight Forward

High grades provide direct satisfaction to most students, but they also act as a signal about the student's ability to learn the subject material. Unfortunately, because the grade distribution is not uniform across departments, you may be confused and misled by your grades. You may think that you are exceptionally good at a subject because of a high grade, when in fact nearly everyone gets a high grade in that subject. The important point here is that you should be informed about your own school's grade distribution. Just because you got a B in economics and an A in history does not necessarily mean that your comparative advantage is in learning history rather than economics. Everyone—or virtually everyone—may receive an A in history. Earning a B or a C in economics could mean that it is the best major for you because high grades are much harder to earn in economics. It is fun to have a high GPA in college, but maximizing GPA should not be your goal. Maximizing your overall well-being is probably your goal, and this might be obtained by trading off a tenth or so of your GPA for a more rewarding major—perhaps economics.

Potential Side Effects from Studying Economics

Studying economics has some potential side effects. We're not sure whether they are costs or benefits and will let you decide.

Changing Ideas About What Is Fair

One study compared students at the beginning and end of the semester in an introductory economics course.[2] It found that by the end of the semester, significantly more of the students thought that the functioning of the market is "fair." This was especially true for female students. The results were consistent across a range of professors who fell across the ideological spectrum.

For example, the proportion of students who regarded it as unfair to increase the price of flowers on a holiday fell almost in half. The proportion that favoured government control over flower prices, rather than market determination, fell by over 60 percent. The study argues that these responses do not reflect changes in deep values, but instead represent the discovery of previous inconsistencies and their modification in the light of new information learned during the semester.

Changing Behaviour

Many people believe that the study of economics changes students' values and behaviour. Some think that it changes them for the worse. Others disagree. In particular, it is argued that economics students become more self-interested and less likely to cooperate, perhaps because they spend so much time studying economic models, which often assume that people are self-interested. For example, one study reports experimental evidence that economics students are more likely than nonmajors to behave self-interestedly in prisoners' dilemma games and ultimatum bargaining games.[3]

This need not mean that studying economics will change you, however. Another study compares beginning freshmen and senior economics students and concludes that economics students "are already different when they begin their study of economics."[4] In other words, students signing up for economics courses are already different; studying economics doesn't change them. However, there are reasons to question both of these conclusions, because it is not clear whether these laboratory experiments using economic games reflect reality. One experiment asked students whether they would return money that had been lost. It found that economics students were more likely than others to say that they would keep the cash.

However, what people say and what they do are sometimes at odds. In a follow-up experiment, this theory was tested by dropping stamped, addressed envelopes containing $10 in cash in different campus classrooms. To return the cash, the students had only to seal the envelopes and mail them. The results were that 56 percent of the envelopes dropped in economics classes were returned, while only 31 percent of the envelopes dropped in history, psychology, and business classes were sent in.[5] Perhaps economics students are less selfish than others!

Obviously, no firm conclusions have been reached about whether or how studying economics changes students' behaviour.

Cost Versus Benefits

Suppose that you've weighed the costs and benefits of studying economics and you've decided that the benefits are greater than or equal to the costs. Obviously, then, you should continue to take economics courses. If you can't decide whether the benefits outweigh the costs, then you should probably collect more information—especially if it is good but inexpensive. In either case, read the rest of this section.

The Economics Major

The study of economics is like a tree. The introductory microeconomics and macroeconomics courses you begin with are the tree's roots. Most colleges and universities require that you master this material before you go on to any other courses. The way of thinking, the language, and the tools that you acquire in the introductory course are usually reinforced in intermediate microeconomics and macroeconomics courses before they are applied in more specialized courses that you take. The intermediate courses are the tree's trunk. Among the specialized courses that make up the branches of economics are econometrics (statistical economics), financial economics, labour economics, resource economics, international trade, industrial organization, public finance, public choice, economic history, the history of economic thought, mathematical economics, current economic issues, and urban economics. The branches of the tree vary from department to department, but these are common. It will pay to check your school calendar and discuss these courses with professors and other students.

Graduate School In Economics

Preparing for Graduate School in Economics

You can prepare for graduate school in economics by taking several math classes. This would probably include one year of calculus plus a couple of courses in probability and statistics and linear/matrix algebra. Ask your advisor about the particular courses to take at your university. In addition, the mathematical economics and econometrics courses in the economics department are essential. (*Helpful hint:* Even if you aren't going to graduate school, these mathematical courses can be valuable to you, just as more economics courses can be valuable for nonmajors.)

If your school offers graduate level economics courses, you might want to sit in on a few to get accustomed to the flavour of graduate school.

Most graduate programs require strong grades in economics, a good score on the Graduate Record Examination (GRE) for U.S. schools, and solid letters of recommendations. It is a good idea to get to know a few professors very well and to go above and beyond what is expected so that they can write glowing letters about you.

Financing Graduate School

Unlike some other graduate and professional degree programs, you probably won't need to pile up a massive amount of debt while pursuing an M.A. or Ph.D. in economics. Most graduate programs hire their economics graduate students as teaching or research assistants. Teaching assistants begin by grading papers and running review sessions and can advance to teaching classes on their own. Research assistants generally do data collection, statistical work, and library research for professors and often jointly write papers with them. Most assistantships will pay for tuition and provide you with enough money to live on.

Where Should You Apply?

The best graduate school for you depends on a lot of things, especially your ability level, geographical location, areas of research interests, and, of course, financing. You should talk with your professors about ability level and areas of research. In addition, for U.S. schools there are informative articles that give overall departmental rankings and rankings by subfield. See especially John Tschirhart, "Ranking Economics Department in Areas of Expertise," *Journal of Economic Education,* Spring 1989, and Richard Dusansky and Clayton J. Vernon, "Rankings of U.S. Economics Departments," *Journal of Economic Perspectives,* vol. 12, no. 1, Winter 1998, pp. 157–70.

What You Will Do in Graduate School

Most students who go on to graduate school do only an M.A. These degrees typically take one year for the non-thesis route and about two years for the thesis route. Course work will include 2–4 courses in economic theory, plus 4–6 courses in specific subfields.

Most Ph.D. programs in economics begin with a year of theory courses in macroeconomics and microeconomics. After a year you will probably take a series of tests to show that you have mastered this core theory. If you pass these tests, in the second and third year of courses you will take more specialized subjects and perhaps take lengthy examinations in a couple of subfields. After this you will be required to write a dissertation—original research that will contribute new knowledge to one of the fields of economics. These stages are intertwined with work as a teaching and/or research assistant, and the dissertation stage can be quite drawn out. In the social sciences the median time that it takes for a student to complete the Ph.D. degree is about 7.5 years.[6] Be aware that a high percentage (roughly 50 percent) of students do not complete their doctoral degree.

What Is Graduate School Like?

Graduate school in economics comes as a surprise to many students. The material and approach are distinctly different from what you will learn as an undergraduate. The textbooks and journal articles you will read in graduate school are often very theoretical and abstract. A good source of information is sitting in on courses or reading the reflections of recent students. See especially *The Making of an Economist* by Arjo Klamer and David Colander (Boulder, Colo.: Westview Press, 1990).

The Committee on Graduate Education in Economics (COGEE) undertook an important review of graduate education in economics and reported its findings in the September 1991 issue of the *Journal of Economic Literature*. COGEE asked faculty members, graduate students, and recent Ph.D.s to rank the most important skills needed to be successful in the study of graduate economics. At the top of the list were analytical skills and mathematics, followed by critical judgment, the ability to apply theory, and computational skills. At the bottom of the list were creativity and the ability to communicate. If you are interested in economic issues but do not have the characteristics required by graduate economics departments, there are other economics-related fields to consider, such as graduate school in public policy. Many economics majors go to business schools to obtain an MBA and are often better prepared than students who have undergraduate degrees in business.

Economics Reading

If you decide to make studying economics part of your future, or if you're hungry for more economics, you should immediately begin reading the economic news and books by economists. Life is short. Why waste it watching TV?

The easiest way to get your daily recommended dose of economics is to keep up with current economic events. Here are a few sources to pick up at the newsstand, bookstore, or library over your summer or winter break.

The Globe and Mail *or the* National Post

Many undergraduates subscribe to *The Globe and Mail* or the *National Post* at low student rates. Join them! Not only are these well-written business newspapers, but they also have articles on domestic and international news, politics, the arts, travel, and sports, as well as lively editorial pages. Reading one of these papers is one of the best ways to tie the economics you are studying to the real world and to prepare for your career.

Magazines and Journals

The Economist, a weekly magazine published in England, is available at a student discount rate. Pick up a copy at your school library and you will be hooked by its informative, sharp writing. *Business Week* is also well worth the read.

Also recommended are *Challenge* magazine and *The Public Interest,* two quarterlies that discuss economic policy, as well as *Policy Options,* a bimonthly publication of the Institute for Research on Public Policy. Finally, there is the *Journal of Economic Perspectives,* which is published by the American Economic Association and written to be accessible to undergraduate economics students.

Books by Economists

Robert Whaples recently asked a group of economics professors (members of the Teach-Econ computer discussion list) the following question: "A bright, enthusiastic student who has just completed introductory economics comes up to you, the professor, and asks you to recommend an economics book for reading over the summer. What do you suggest?"

Here is what they suggested that you, the bright, enthusiastic student, should read:

Top Choices

Milton Friedman, *Capitalism and Freedom.*

Robert Heilbroner, *The Worldly Philosophers: The Lives, Times, and Ideas of the Great Economic Thinkers.*

Steve Landsburg, *The Armchair Economist: Economics and Everyday Life.*

Other Good Choices

Alan Blinder, *Hard Heads, Soft Hearts: Tough-Minded Economics for a Just Society.*

Patrick Luciani, *Economics Myths: Making Sense of Canadian Policy Issues.*

Paul Krugman, *Peddling Prosperity: Economic Sense and Nonsense in the Age of Diminished Expectations.*

Hernando deSoto, *The Mystery of Capital: Why Capitalism Triumphed in the West and Failed Everywhere Else.*

David Friedman, *Hidden Order: The Economics of Everyday Life.*

Russell Roberts, *The Choice: A Parable of Free Trade and Protectionism.*

In addition, Adam Smith's *The Wealth of Nations* is a must read for every student of economics. Written in 1776, it is the most influential work of economics ever. Its insights are still valuable today.

Endnotes

1. This term is used by Robert Reich in *The Work of Nations.* The quote is from p. 178.

2. Robert Whaples, "Changes in Attitudes about the Fairness of Free Markets among College Economics Students," *Journal of Economic Education,* Vol. 26, no. 4, Fall 1995.

3. Robert H. Frank, Thomas Gilovich, and Dennis T. Regan, "Does Studying Economics Inhibit Cooperation?' *Journal of Economic Perspectives,* Vol. 7, no. 2, Spring 1993, pp. 159-171.

4. John R. Carter and Michael D. Irons, "Are Economists Different, and If So, Why?" *Journal of Economic Perspectives,* Vol. 5, no. 2, Spring 1991, pp. 171-177.

5. "Economics Students Aren't Selfish, They're Just Not Entirely Honest," *Wall Street Journal,* January 18, 1995, B1.

6. See Ronald Ehrenberg, "The Flow of New Doctorates," *Journal of Economic Literature,* Vol. 30, June 1992, pp. 830–875. If breaks in school attendance are included, this climbs to 10.5 years. Of course, some students attend only part time, and most have some kind of employment while completing their degrees.

What Is Economics?

Definition of Economics

All economic questions arise from **scarcity**.

◆ Because wants exceed the resources available to satisfy them, we cannot have everything we want and must make choices.

◆ **Economics** is the social science that studies the choices people make to cope with scarcity.

   • **Microeconomics** studies choices of individuals and businesses.
   • **Macroeconomics** studies national and global economies.

Three Big Microeconomic Questions

Three questions summarize microeconomic choices:

◆ What **goods and services** are produced and in what quantities?

◆ How are goods and services produced?

◆ For whom are goods and services produced?

The **factors of production** used to produce goods and services are:

◆ **land** (shorthand for all natural resources) which earns **rent**.

◆ **labour** (includes **human capital**—knowledge and skills from education, training, experience) which earns **wages**.

◆ **capital** (machinery) which earns **interest**.

◆ **entrepreneurship** which earns **profit**.

Three Big Macroeconomic Questions

Three questions summarize macroeconomic analysis:

◆ What determines the **standard of living**?

◆ What determines the **cost of living**?

◆ Why does our economy fluctuate (What causes the **business cycle**)?

The cost of living depends on prices.

◆ **Inflation** is a rising cost of living.

◆ **Deflation** is a falling cost of living.

The Economic Way of Thinking

A choice is a **tradeoff**—we give up one thing to get something else—and the **opportunity cost** of any action is the highest-valued alternative forgone. Opportunity cost is the single most important concept for making choices.

Microeconomic tradeoffs:

◆ "what," "how" and "for whom" tradeoffs.

◆ the **big tradeoff**—between equality and efficiency. Government redistribution using taxes and transfers weaken incentives, so a more equally shared pie results in a smaller pie.

Macroeconomic tradeoffs:

◆ standard of living tradeoffs between current consumption and higher future standard of living.

◆ **output-inflation tradeoff**—government policy to increase output increases inflation; the tradeoff for policy to lower inflation is lower output.

We make choices in small steps, or at the **margin**, and choices are influenced by **incentives**.

◆ Economic choices are made by comparing the *additional* benefit—**marginal benefit**—and *additional* cost—**marginal cost**—of a small increase in an activity. If marginal benefit exceeds marginal cost, we choose to increase the activity.

◆ By choosing only activities that bring greater benefits than costs, we use our scarce resources in the way that makes us as well off as possible.

◆ Given a change in incentives—inducements to take particular actions—we can predict how choices will change by looking for changes in marginal benefit and marginal cost.

Economics: A Social Science

Economics, as a social science, distinguishes between

◆ *positive* statements—statements about what *is*, that can be tested by checking them against the facts.

◆ *normative* statements—statements about what *ought* to be, that depend on values and cannot be tested.

Economic science attempts to understand the economic world and is concerned with positive statements. Economists try to discover positive statements that are consistent with observed facts by

◆ observation and measurement.

◆ building **economic models**—abstract, simplified representations of the real world with two components:

  • *Assumptions* about what is essential versus inessential detail.
  • *Predictions* that can be tested by comparison with observed facts.

◆ testing economic models to develop **economic theories**—generalizations for understanding economic choices and economic performance.

Useful economic models and theories isolate important economic forces and disentangle cause and effect. This requires

◆ *ceteris paribus* assumptions to hold other things equal to isolate the effects of one force at a time.

◆ avoiding errors of reasoning including the

  • fallacy of composition—the false statement that what is true of the parts is true of the whole, or what is true of the whole is true of the parts.
  • *post hoc* fallacy—the false claim that event *a* caused event *b* just because event *a* occurred first.

Economists agree on a wide range of questions about how the economy works.

HELPFUL HINTS

1 The definition of economics (explaining the choices we make using limited resources to try to satisfy unlimited wants) leads us directly to two important economic concepts—choice and opportunity cost. If wants exceed resources, we cannot have everything we want and therefore must make *choices* among alternatives. In making a choice, we forgo other alternatives, and the *opportunity cost* of any choice is the highest-valued alternative forgone.

2 Marginal analysis is a fundamental tool economists use to predict people's choices. The key to understanding marginal analysis is to focus on *additional*, rather than total, benefits and costs. For example, to predict whether or not Taejong will eat a fourth Big Mac, the economist compares Taejong's *additional* benefit or satisfaction from the fourth Big Mac with its *additional* cost. The total benefits and costs of all four Big Macs are not relevant. Only if the marginal benefit exceeds the marginal cost will Taejong eat a fourth Big Mac.

3 In attempting to understand how and why something works (for example, an airplane, a falling object, an economy), we can try to use description or theory. A description is a list of facts about something. But it does not tell us which facts are essential for understanding how an airplane works (the shape of the wings) and which facts are less important (the colour of the paint).

Scientists use theory to abstract from the complex descriptive facts of the real world and focus only on those elements essential for understanding. Those essential elements are fashioned into models—highly simplified representations of the real world.

In physics and some other natural sciences, if we want to understand the essential force (gravity) that causes objects to fall, we use theory to construct a simple model, then test it by performing a controlled experiment. We create a vacuum to eliminate less important forces like air resistance.

Economic models are also attempts to focus on the essential forces (competition, self-interest) operating in the economy, while abstracting from less important forces (whims, advertising, altruism). Unlike physicists, economists cannot easily perform controlled experiments to test their models. As a result, it is difficult to conclusively prove or disprove a theory and its models.

4 Models are like maps, which are useful precisely because they abstract from real-world detail. A map that reproduced all of the details of the real world (street lamps, fireplugs, electric wires) would be useless. A useful map offers a simplified view, which is carefully selected according to the purpose of the map. Remember that economic models are not claims that the real world is as simple as the model. Models claim to capture the simplified effect of some real force operating in the economy. Before drawing conclusions about the real economy from a model, we must be careful to consider whether, when we reinsert all of the real-world complexities the model abstracted from, the conclusions will be the same as in the model.

5 The most important purpose of studying economics is not to learn what to think about economics but rather *how* to think about economics. The "what"—the facts and descriptions of the economy—can always be found in books. The value of an economics education is the ability to think critically about economic problems and *to understand how* an economy works. This understanding of the essential forces governing how an economy works comes through the mastery of economic theory and model-building.

S E L F - T E S T

True/False and Explain

Definition of Economics

1 Economics explains how we use unlimited resources to satisfy limited wants.

2 Economics studies the choices people make to cope with scarcity and the institutions that influence and reconcile choices.

Three Big Microeconomic Questions

3 In economics, the definition of "land" includes nonrenewable resources but excludes renewable resources.

4 In economics, the definition of "capital" includes financial assets like stocks and bonds.

5 Entrepreneurs bear the risks arising from the business decisions they make.

6 The richest 20 percent of individuals earn almost half of total income in Canada.

Three Big Macroeconomic Questions

7 "For whom are goods and services produced?" is one of the big macroeconomic questions.

8 Deflation brings a rising value of the dollar.

9 Production and jobs shrink in a recession.

The Economic Way of Thinking

10 When the opportunity cost of an activity increases, the incentive to choose that activity increases.

11 Tradeoffs and opportunity costs are the key concepts for understanding the economic way of thinking.

Economics: A Social Science

12 A positive statement is about what is, while a normative statement is about what will be.

13 Economics is not a science since it deals with the study of willful human beings and not inanimate objects in nature.

14 *Ceteris paribus* means "after this, therefore because of this."

15 Observers are correct in noting that economists disagree on most questions.

Multiple-Choice

Definition of Economics

1 The fact that human wants cannot be fully satisfied with available resources is called the problem of

a opportunity cost.
b scarcity.
c normative economics.
d what to produce.
e who will consume.

2 The problem of scarcity exists

a only in economies with government.
b only in economies without government.
c in all economies.
d only when people have not optimized.
e now, but will be eliminated with economic growth.

3 Scarcity differs from poverty because

a resources exceed wants for the rich.
b wants exceed resources even for the rich.
c the rich do not have to make choices.
d the poor do not have any choices.
e the poor do not have any wants.

4 The branch of economics that studies the choices of individual households and firms is called

a macroeconomics.
b microeconomics.
c positive economics.
d normative economics.
e home economics.

5 Microeconomics studies all of the following *except* the

a decisions of individual firms.
b effects of government safety regulations on the price of cars.
c global economy as a whole.
d prices of individual goods and services.
e effects of taxes on the price of beer.

6 Macroeconomic topics would *not* include the

a reasons for a decline in the price of orange juice.
b reasons for a decline in average prices.
c effect of interest rates on national economic growth.
d effect of the government budget deficit on total employment.
e determination of national income.

Three Big Microeconomic Questions

7 The three big microeconomic questions

a all arise from scarcity.
b describe the scope of microeconomics.
c are about goods and services.
d describe choices we make.
e are all of the above.

8 The three big microeconomic questions about goods and services include all of the following *except*

a *what* to produce.
b *why* produce.
c *how* to produce.
d *with what* factors of production to produce.
e *who* gets what is produced.

9 All of the following are resources *except*

a natural resources.
b tools.
c entrepreneurship.
d government.
e land.

10 The knowledge and skill obtained from education and training is

a labour.
b human capital.
c physical capital.
d entrepreneurship.
e technological know-how.

11 Which statement about incomes earned by factors of production is *false*?

a Land earns rent.
b Natural resources earn rent.
c Labour earns wages.
d Capital earns profit.
e Entrepreneurship earns profit.

Three Big Macroeconomic Questions

12 During an inflation, the cost of living is _____ and the value of the dollar is _____.

a rising; rising
b rising; falling
c rising; constant
d falling; rising
e falling; falling

13 The correct order for the phases of the business cycle following an expansion are

a trough, recession, peak.
b trough, peak, recession.
c recession, trough, peak.
d peak, trough, recession.
e peak, recession, trough.

The Economic Way of Thinking

14 When the government chooses to use resources to build a dam, those resources are no longer available to build a highway. This illustrates the concept of

a a market.
b macroeconomics.
c opportunity cost.
d an output-inflation tradeoff.
e the big tradeoff.

15 The big tradeoff is between

a taxes and transfers.
b equality and efficiency.
c current consumption and a higher future standard of living.
d guns and butter.
e output and inflation.

16 Renata has the chance to either attend an economics lecture or play tennis. If she chooses to attend the lecture, the value of playing tennis is

a greater than the value of the lecture.
b not comparable to the value of the lecture.
c equal to the value of the lecture.
d the opportunity cost of attending the lecture.
e zero.

17 Which of the following sayings best describes opportunity cost?

a "Make hay while the sun shines."
b "Money is the root of all evil."
c "Boldly go where no one has gone before."
d "There's no such thing as a free lunch."
e "Baseball has been very good to me."

18 Marginal benefit is the

a total benefit of an activity.
b additional benefit of a decrease in an activity.
c additional benefit of an increase in an activity.
d opportunity cost of a decrease in an activity.
e opportunity cost of an increase in an activity.

19 Monika will choose to eat a seventh pizza slice if

a the marginal benefit of the seventh slice is greater than its marginal cost.
b the marginal benefit of the seventh slice is less than its marginal cost
c the total benefit of all seven slices is greater than their total cost.
d the total benefit of all seven slices is less than their total cost.
e she is training to be a Sumo wrestler.

Economics: A Social Science

20 A positive statement is

a about what ought to be.
b about what is.
c always true.
d capable of evaluation as true or false by observation and measurement.
e **b** and **d**.

21 Which of the following is a positive statement?

a Low rents will restrict the supply of housing.
b High interest rates are bad for the economy.
c Housing costs too much.
d Owners of apartment buildings ought to be free to charge whatever rent they want.
e Government should control the rents that apartment owners charge.

22 A normative statement is a statement regarding

a what is usually the case.
b the assumptions of an economic model.
c what ought to be.
d the predictions of an economic model.
e what is.

23 Which of the following statements is/are normative?

a Scientists should not make normative statements.
b Warts are caused by handling toads.
c As compact disc prices fall, people will buy more of them.
d If income increases, sales of luxury goods will fall.
e None of the above.

24 An economic model is tested by
  a examining the realism of its assumptions.
  b comparing its predictions with the facts.
  c comparing its descriptions with the facts.
  d the Testing Committee of the Canadian Economic Association.
  e all of the above.

25 The Latin term *ceteris paribus* means
  a "Innocent until proven guilty."
  b "Fallacies are composed."
  c "Compositions are fallacious."
  d "The whole is not the sum of the parts."
  e "If all other relevant things remain the same."

Short Answer Problems

1 What is meant by scarcity, and why does the existence of scarcity mean that we must make choices?

2 If all people would only economize, the problem of scarcity would be solved. Agree or disagree and explain why.

3 Ashley, Doug, and Mei-Lin are planning to travel from Halifax to Sydney. The trip takes one hour by airplane and five hours by train. The air fare is $100 and train fare is $60. They all have to take time off from work while travelling. Ashley earns $5 per hour in her job, Doug $10 per hour, and Mei-Lin $12 per hour.

Calculate the opportunity cost of air and train travel for each person. Assuming they are all economizers, how should each of them travel to Sydney?

4 Suppose the government builds and staffs a hospital in order to provide "free" medical care.
  a What is the opportunity cost of the free medical care?
  b Is it free from the perspective of society as a whole?

ct 5 Branko loves riding the bumper cars at the amusement park, but he loves the experience a little less with each successive ride. In estimating the benefit he receives from the rides, Branko would be willing to pay $10 for his first ride, $7 for his second ride, and $4 for his third ride. Rides actually cost $5 apiece for as many rides as Branko wants to take. This information is summarized in Table 1.1.

TABLE 1.1

Ride	1st	2nd	3rd
Marginal benefit	10	7	4
Marginal cost	5	5	5

  a If Branko chooses by comparing total benefit and total cost, how many rides will he take?
  b If Branko chooses by comparing marginal benefit and marginal cost, how many rides will he take?
  c Is Branko better off by choosing according to total or marginal benefit and cost? Explain why.

ct 6 Assume Branko's benefits are the same as in Short Answer Problem **5**. Starting fresh, if the price of a bumper car ride rises to $8, how many rides will Branko now take? Explain why.

7 Indicate whether each of the following statements is positive or normative. If it is normative (positive), rewrite it so that it becomes positive (normative).
  a The government ought to reduce the size of the deficit in order to lower interest rates.
  b Government imposition of a tax on tobacco products will reduce their consumption.

8 Consider the following paradox. If one farmer has a bumper crop, her income increases. On the basis of the experience of the individual farmer, you predict that, in general, bumper crops cause rising farm incomes. But when all farmers have bumper crops, the excess supply causes prices to fall drastically and farm income actually decreases. What error in reasoning ruined your prediction? Explain.

9 Suppose we examine a model of plant growth that predicts that, given the amount of water and sunlight, the application of fertilizer stimulates plant growth.
  a How might you test the model?
  b How is the test different from what an economist could do to test an economic model?

ct 10 Suppose your friend, who is a history major, claims that economic theories are useless because the models on which they are based are so unrealistic. He claims that since the models leave out so many descriptive details about the real world, they can't possibly be useful for understanding how the economy works. How would you defend your decision to study economic theory?

A N S W E R S

True/False and Explain

1 **F** Limited resources and unlimited wants. (2)
2 **T** This is the full definition of Economics—the institutional aspect is often omitted for brevity. (2)
3 **F** "Land" includes all natural resources, whether nonrenewable (oil) or renewable (forests). (4)
4 **F** "Capital" consists of physical equipment like tools and buildings used in production. (4)
5 **T** Entrepreneurs earn profits in return for organizing labour, land, and capital. (4)
6 **T** See Figure 1.4 (5).
7 **F** "For whom" is one of the big microeconomic questions. (5)
8 **T** Deflation decreases prices and the cost of living, so each dollar buys more goods and services. (7)
9 **T** Recessions are downturns in economic activity. (8)
10 **F** Incentive decreases because activity is now more expensive. (11)
11 **T** Scarcity requires choice, choice involves tradeoffs, and tradeoffs involve opportunity cost. (9-11)
12 **F** Normative statements are about what *ought* to be. (12)
13 **F** Science not defined by subject, but by method of observation, measurement, and testing of theoretical models. (12–13)
14 **F** *Ceteris paribus* means "other things being equal." Other quote is *post hoc ergo propter hoc*. (13–14)
15 **F** There is agreement on a wide range of (mostly positive) questions. (14)

Multiple-Choice

1 **b** Definition. (2)
2 **c** With infinite wants and finite resources, scarcity will never be eliminated. (2)
3 **b** Poverty is a low level of resources. But wants exceed resources for everyone, necessitating choice. (2)
4 **b** Definition. (2)
5 **c** Macroeconomic topic. (2)
6 **a** Price of individual good is a microeconomic topic. (2)
7 **e** Microeconomics explains individual and business choices about goods and services created by scarcity. (3–5)
8 **b** *Why* is not one of the three questions. (3–5)
9 **d** Government is a social institution. (4)

10 **b** Definition. (4)
11 **d** Capital earns interest. (4–5)
12 **b** Definition of inflation is rising cost of living; rising prices means each $1 buys fewer goods and services. (7)
13 **e** Expansion ends at a peak, recession begins and then ends at a trough (lowest point). (8)
14 **c** Highway is forgone alternative. (9–11)
15 **b** Greater equality (using taxes and transfers) reduces efficiency by weakening incentives. **c**, **d**, and **e** are other tradeoffs. (9–10)
16 **d** Choosing lecture means its value > tennis. Tennis = (highest-valued) forgone alternative to lecture. (9, 11)
17 **d** Every choice involves a cost. (11)
18 **c** Definition; **e** is marginal cost, **b** and **d** are nonsense. (11)
19 **a** Choices are made at the margin, when marginal benefit exceeds marginal cost. (11)
20 **e** Definition. (12)
21 **a** While **a** may be evaluated as true or false, other statements are matters of opinion. (12)
22 **c** Key word for normative statements is *ought*. (12)
23 **a** Key word is *should*. Even statement **b** is positive. (12)
24 **b** Assumptions not realistic descriptions; are simplified representations of world. (12–13)
25 **e** Definition. **a**, **b**, and **c** are nonsense. **d** is fallacy of composition. (13)

Short Answer Problems

1 Scarcity is the universal condition that human wants always exceed the resources available to satisfy them. The fact that goods and services are scarce means that individuals cannot have all of everything they want. It is therefore necessary to choose among alternatives.

2 Disagree. If everyone economized, then we would be making the best possible use of our resources and would be achieving the greatest benefits or satisfaction possible, given the limited quantity of resources. But this does not mean that we would be satisfying all of our limitless needs. The problem of scarcity can never be "solved" as long as people have infinite needs and finite resources for satisfying those needs.

3 The main point is that the total opportunity cost of travel includes the best alternative value of travel time as well as the train or air fare. The total costs of train and air travel for Ashley, Doug, and Mei-Lin are calculated in Table 1.2.

TABLE **1.2**

Traveller	Train	Plane
Ashley		
(a) Fare	$ 60	$100
(b) Opportunity cost of travel time at $5/hr	$ 25	$ 5
Total cost	**$ 85**	**$105**
Doug		
(a) Fare	$ 60	$100
(b) Opportunity cost of travel time at $10/hr	$ 50	$ 10
Total cost	**$110**	**$110**
Mei-Lin		
(a) Fare	$ 60	$100
(b) Opportunity cost of travel time at $12/hr	$ 60	$ 12
Total cost	**$120**	**$112**

On the basis of the cost calculation in Table 1.2, Ashley should take the train, Mei-Lin should take the plane, and Doug could take either.

4 a Even though medical care may be offered without charge ("free"), there are still opportunity costs. The opportunity cost of providing such health care is the highest-valued alternative use of the resources used in the construction of the hospital, and the highest-valued alternative use of the resources (including human resources) used in the operation of the hospital.

b These resources are no longer available for other activities and therefore represent a cost to society.

5 a If Branko rides as long as total benefit is greater than total cost, he will take 3 rides.

Total benefit (cost) can be calculated by adding up the marginal benefit (cost) of all rides taken. Before taking any rides, his total benefit is zero and his total cost is zero. The first ride's marginal benefit is $10, which when added to 0 yields a total benefit of $10. The first ride's marginal cost is $5, which when added to zero yields a total cost of $5. Total cost is greater than total benefit, so Branko takes the first ride. For the first and second rides together, total benefit is $17, which is greater than total cost of $10. For all 3 rides together, total benefit is $21, which is greater than total cost of $15.

b If Branko compares the marginal benefit of each ride with its marginal cost, he will only take 2 rides. He will take the first ride because its marginal benefit ($10) is greater than its marginal cost ($5). After the first ride, he will still choose to take the second ride because its marginal benefit ($7) is greater than its marginal cost ($5). But he will quit after the second ride. The third ride would add a benefit of $4, but it costs $5, so Branko would be worse off by taking the third ride.

c The marginal rule for choosing will make Branko better off. It would be a mistake to pay $5 for the third ride when it is only worth $4 to Branko. He would be better off taking that final $5 and spending it on something (the rollercoaster?) that gives him a benefit worth at least $5.

You will learn much more about applying marginal analysis to choices like Branko's in Chapters 2 and 5.

6 If the price of a bumper car rises to $8, Branko now takes only 1 ride. He will take the first ride because its marginal benefit ($10) is greater than its marginal cost ($8). After the first ride, he will quit. The marginal benefit of the second ride ($7) is now less than its marginal cost ($8).

7 a The given statement is normative. The following is positive: If the government reduces the size of the deficit, interest rates will fall.

b The given statement is positive. The following is normative: The government ought to impose a tax on tobacco products.

8 The paradox is an example of the fallacy of composition—the (false) statement that what is true of the parts is true of the whole. We cannot always generalize from the parts to the whole, and the prediction that bumper crops cause rising incomes for all farmers is a false generalization from the parts to the whole.

9 a The prediction of the model can be tested by conducting the following controlled experiment and carefully observing the outcome. Select a number of plots of ground of the same size that have similar characteristics and are subject to the same amount of water and sunlight. Plant equal quantities of seeds in all the plots. In some of the plots apply no fertilizer and in some of the plots apply (perhaps varying amounts of) fertilizer. When the plants have grown, measure the growth of the plants and compare the growth of the fertilized plots and the unfertilized plots. If plant growth is greater in fertilized plots, we provisionally accept the model and the theory on which it is based. If plant growth is not greater in fertilized plots, we discard the theory (model), or modify its assumptions. Perhaps the effective use of fertilizer requires more water.

Then construct a new model that predicts that, given more water (and the same amount of sunlight), fertilized plants will grow larger than equivalently watered unfertilized plants. Test that model and continue modifying assumptions until predictions are consistent with the facts.

b Economists cannot easily perform such controlled experiments and instead must change one assumption at a time in alternative models and compare the results. Then differences in outcomes can only be tested against variations in data that occur naturally in the economy. This is a more difficult and less precise model-building and testing procedure than exists for the controlled fertilizer experiment.

10 A brief answer to your friend's challenge appears in Helpful Hint **3**. Models are like maps, which are useful precisely because they abstract from real-world detail. A useful map offers a simplified view, which is carefully selected according to the purpose of the map. No mapmaker would claim that the world is as simple as her map, and economists do not claim that the real economy is as simple as their

models. What economists claim is that their models isolate the simplified effect of some real forces (like optimizing behaviour) operating in the economy, and yield predictions that can be tested against real-world data.

Another way to answer your friend would be to challenge him to identify what a more realistic model or theory would look like. You would do well to quote Milton Friedman (a Nobel Prize winner in economics) on this topic: "A theory or its 'assumptions' cannot possibly be thoroughly 'realistic' in the immediate descriptive sense. ... A completely 'realistic' theory of the wheat market would have to include not only the conditions directly underlying the supply and demand for wheat but also the kind of coins or credit instruments used to make exchanges; the personal characteristics of wheat-traders such as the color of each trader's hair and eyes, ... the number of members of his family, their characteristics, ... the kind of soil on which the wheat was grown, ... the weather prevailing during the growing season; ... and so on indefinitely. Any attempt to move very far in achieving this kind of 'realism' is certain to render a theory utterly useless."

From Milton Friedman, "The Methodology of Positive Economics," in *Essays in Positive Economics (Chicago: University of Chicago Press,* 1953), p. 32.

Appendix: Graphs in Economics

Graphing Data

Graphs represent quantity as a distance. On a two-dimensional graph,

- horizontal line is *x-axis*.
- vertical line is *y-axis*.
- intersection (0) is the *origin*.

Main types of economic graphs:

- **Time-series graph**—shows relationship between time (measured on *x*-axis) and other variable(s) (measured on *y*-axis). Reveals variable's level, direction of change, speed of change, and **trend** (general tendency to rise or fall).
- **Cross-section graph**—shows level of a variable across different groups at a point in time.
- **Scatter diagram**—shows relationship between two variables, one measured on *x*-axis, the other measured on *y*-axis. Correlation between variables does not necessarily imply causation.

Misleading graphs often break the axes or stretch/compress measurement scales to exaggerate or understate variation. Always look closely at the values and labels on axes before interpreting a graph.

Graphs Used in Economic Models

Graphs showing relationships between variables fall into four categories:

- **Positive (direct) relationship**—variables move together in same direction: upward-sloping.
- **Negative (inverse) relationship**—variables move in opposite directions: downward-sloping.

- Relationships with a maximum/minimum:
  - Relationship slopes upward, reaches a maximum (zero slope), and then slopes downward.
  - Relationship slopes downward, reaches a minimum (zero slope), and then slopes upward.
- Unrelated (independent) variables—one variable changes while the other remains constant; graph is vertical or horizontal straight line.

The Slope of a Relationship

Slope of a relationship is change in value of variable on *y*-axis divided by change in value of variable on *x*-axis.

- Δ means "change in."
- Formula for slope is $\Delta y/\Delta x$ = rise/run.
- Straight line (**linear relationship**) has constant slope.
  - A positive, upward-sloping relationship has a positive slope.
  - A negative, downward-sloping relationship has a negative slope.
- Curved line has varying slope, which can be calculated
  - *at a point*—by drawing straight line tangent to the curve at that point and calculating slope of the line.
  - *across an arc*—by drawing straight line across two points on the curve and calculating slope of the line.

Graphing Relationships Among More Than Two Variables

Relationships among more than two variables can be graphed by holding constant the values of all variables except two. This is done by making a *ceteris paribus* assumption—"other things remain the same."

HELPFUL HINTS

1 Throughout the text, relationships among economic variables will almost invariably be represented and analyzed graphically. An early, complete understanding of graphs will greatly facilitate your mastery of the economic analysis of later chapters. Avoid the common mistake of assuming that a superficial understanding of graphs will be sufficient.

2 If your experience with graphical analysis is limited, this appendix is crucial to your ability to readily understand later economic analysis. You will likely find significant rewards in occasionally returning to this appendix for review. If you are experienced in constructing and using graphs, this appendix may be "old hat." Even so, you should skim it and work through the Self-Test in this *Study Guide*.

3 Slope is a *linear* concept since it is a property of a straight line. For this reason, the slope is constant along a straight line but is different at different points on a curved (nonlinear) line. For the slope of a curved line, we actually calculate the slope of a straight line. The text presents two alternatives for calculating the slope of a curved line: (1) slope at a point and (2) slope across an arc. The first of these calculates the slope of the *straight line* that just touches (is tangent to) the curve at a point. The second calculates the slope of the *straight line* formed by the arc between two points on the curved line.

4 A straight line on a graph can also be described by a simple equation (see Text Mathematical Note, pages 28–29). The general form for the equation of a straight line is

$$y = a + bx$$

If you are given such an equation, you can graph the line by finding the *y*-intercept (where the line intersects the vertical *y*-axis), finding the *x*-intercept (where the line intersects the horizontal *x*-axis), and then connecting those two points with a straight line:

To find the *y*-intercept, set $x = 0$.

$$y = a + b(0)$$

$$y = a$$

To find the *x*-intercept, set $y = 0$.

$$0 = a + bx$$

$$x = -a/b$$

Connecting these two points (($x = 0$, $y = a$) and ($x = -a/b$, $y = 0$)) or (0, a) and ($-a/b$, 0) allows you to graph the straight line. For any straight line with the equation of the form $y = a + bx$, the slope of the line is b. Figure A1.1 illustrates a line where b is a *negative* number, so there is a *negative* relationship between the variables x and y.

FIGURE **A1.1**

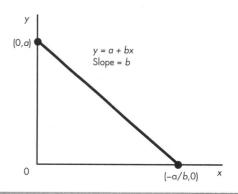

To see how to apply this general equation, consider this example:

$$y = 6 - 2x$$

To find the *y*-intercept, set $x = 0$.

$$y = 6 - 2(0)$$

$$y = 6$$

To find the *x*-intercept, set $y = 0$.

$$0 = 6 - 2x$$

$$x = 3$$

Connecting these two points, (0, 6) and (3, 0), yields the line in Figure A1.2.

FIGURE **A1.2**

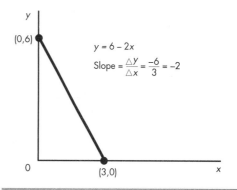

The slope of this line is −2. Since the slope is negative, there is a negative relationship between the variables *x* and *y*.

S E L F - T E S T

True/False and Explain

Graphing Data

1 A time-series graph shows the level of a variable across different groups at a point in time.

2 A graph with a break in the axes must be misleading.

3 If a scatter diagram shows a clear relationship between variables x and y, then x must cause y.

Graphs Used in Economic Models

4 If the graph of the relationship between two variables slopes upward (to the right), the graph has a positive slope.

5 The graph of the relationship between two variables that are in fact unrelated is always vertical.

6 In Figure A1.3, the relationship between y and x is first negative, reaches a minimum, and then becomes positive as x increases.

FIGURE **A1.3**

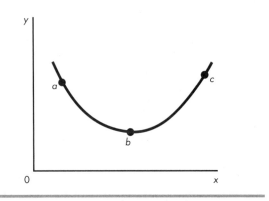

7 In Figure A1.3, the value of x is a minimum at point b.

The Slope of a Relationship

8 In Figure A1.3, the slope of the curve is increasing as we move from point b to point c.

9 In Figure A1.3, the slope of the curve is approaching zero as we move from point a to point b.

10 The slope of a straight line is calculated by dividing the change in the value of the variable measured on the horizontal axis by the change in the value of the variable measured on the vertical axis.

11 For a straight line, if a small change in y is associated with a large change in x, the slope is large.

12 For a straight line, if a large change in y is associated with a small change in x, the line is steep.

13 The slope of a curved line is not constant.

Graphing Relationships Among More Than Two Variables

14 *Ceteris paribus* means "other things change."

15 Relationships between three variables can be displayed on a two-dimensional graph.

Multiple-Choice

Graphing Data

1 Figure A1.4 is a time-series graph. The horizontal axis measures _____ and the vertical axis measures _____.

a time; the variable of interest
b time; slope
c the variable of interest in one year; the variable of interest in another year
d the variable of interest; time
e slope; time

FIGURE **A1.4**

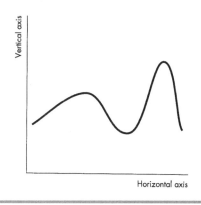

2 The tendency for a variable to rise or fall over time is called its

a slope.
b trend.
c y-coordinate.
d level.
e correlation.

3 Which type of graph can mislead?

a Time-series graphs only.
b Cross-section graphs only.
c Scatter diagrams only.
d Graphs with correlations between variables only.
e Any of the above.

Graphs Used in Economic Models

4 From the data in Table A1.1, it appears that

a x and y have a negative relationship.
b x and y have a positive relationship.
c there is no relationship between x and y.
d there is first a negative and then a positive relationship between x and y.
e there is first a positive and then a negative relationship between x and y.

TABLE **A1.1**

Year	x	y
2000	6.2	143
2001	5.7	156
2002	5.3	162

5 If variables x and y move up and down together, they are said to be

a positively related.
b negatively related.
c conversely related.
d unrelated.
e trendy.

6 The relationship between two variables that move in opposite directions is shown graphically by a line that is

a positively sloped.
b relatively steep.
c relatively flat.
d negatively sloped.
e curved.

The Slope of a Relationship

7 In Figure A1.5 the relationship between x and y as x increases is

a positive with slope decreasing.
b negative with slope decreasing.
c negative with slope increasing.
d positive with slope increasing.
e positive with slope first increasing then decreasing.

FIGURE **A1.5**

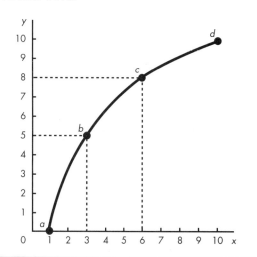

8 What is the slope across the arc between *b* and *c* in Figure A1.5?

a 1/2
b 2/3
c 1
d 2
e 3

9 In Figure A1.5, consider the slopes of arc *ab* and arc *bc*. The slope at point *b* is difficult to determine exactly, but it must be

a greater than 5/2.
b about 5/2.
c between 5/2 and 1.
d about 1.
e less than 1.

10 In Table A1.2, suppose that *w* is the independent variable measured along the horizontal axis. The slope of the line relating *w* and *u* is

a positive with a decreasing slope.
b negative with a decreasing slope.
c positive with an increasing slope.
d negative with a constant slope.
e positive with a constant slope.

TABLE **A1.2**

w	2	4	6	8	10
u	15	12	9	6	3

11 Refer to Table A1.2. Suppose that *w* is the independent variable measured along the horizontal axis. The slope of the line relating *w* and *u* is

a +3.
b −3.
c −2/3.
d +3/2.
e −3/2.

12 In Figure A1.6, if household income increases by $1,000, household expenditure will

a increase by $1,333.
b decrease by $1,333.
c remain unchanged.
d increase by $1,000.
e increase by $750.

FIGURE **A1.6**

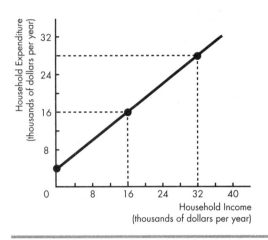

13 In Figure A1.6, if household income is zero, household expenditure is

a 0.
b −$4,000.
c $4,000.
d $8,000.
e impossible to determine from the graph.

14 In Figure A1.6, if household expenditure is $28,000, household income is

a $36,000.
b $32,000.
c $28,000.
d $25,000.
e none of the above.

15 At all points along a straight line, slope is

a positive.
b negative.
c constant.
d zero.
e none of the above.

16 What is the slope of the line in Figure A1.7?

a 2
b 1/2
c 3
d 1/3
e −3

FIGURE **A1.7**

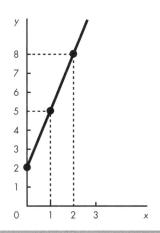

17 If the line in Figure A1.7 were to continue down to the *x*-axis, what would the value of *x* be when *y* is zero?

a 0
b 2
c 2/3
d –2/3
e –3/2

18 If the equation of a straight line is $y = 6 + 3x$, then the slope is

a –3 and the *y*-intercept is 6.
b –3 and the *y*-intercept is –2.
c 3 and the *y*-intercept is 6.
d 3 and the *y*-intercept is –2.
e 3 and the *y*-intercept is –6.

19 If the equation of a straight line is $y = 8 - 2x$, then the slope is

a –2 and the *x*-intercept is –4.
b –2 and the *x*-intercept is 4.
c –2 and the *x*-intercept is 8.
d 2 and the *x*-intercept is –4.
e 2 and the *x*-intercept is 4.

Graphing Relationships Among More Than Two Variables

20 To graph a relationship among more than two variables, what kind of assumption is necessary?

a normative
b positive
c linear
d independence of variables
e *ceteris paribus*

21 Given the data in Table A1.3, holding income constant, the graph relating the price of strawberries (vertical axis) to the purchases of strawberries (horizontal axis)

a is a vertical line.
b is a horizontal line.
c is a positively sloped line.
d is a negatively sloped line.
e reaches a minimum.

TABLE **A1.3**

Weekly Family Income ($)	Price per Box of Strawberries ($)	Number of Boxes Purchased per Week
300	$1.00	5
300	$1.25	3
300	$1.50	2
400	$1.00	7
400	$1.25	5
400	$1.50	4

22 Given the data in Table A1.3, suppose family income decreases from $400 to $300 per week. Then the graph relating the price of strawberries (vertical axis) to the purchases of strawberries (horizontal axis) will

a become negatively sloped.
b become positively sloped.
c shift rightward.
d shift leftward.
e no longer exist.

23 Given the data in Table A1.3, holding price constant, the graph relating family income (vertical axis) to the purchases of strawberries (horizontal axis) is a

a vertical line.
b horizontal line.
c positively sloped line.
d negatively sloped line.
e positively or negatively sloped line, depending on the price that is held constant.

24 In Figure A1.8, *x* is

a positively related to *y* and negatively related to *z*.
b positively related to both *y* and *z*.
c negatively related to *y* and positively related to *z*.
d negatively related to both *y* and *z*.
e greater than *z*.

FIGURE **A1.8**

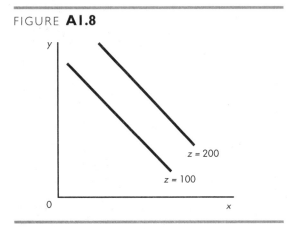

25 In Figure A1.8, a decrease in the value of z will cause, *ceteris paribus*,

a   a decrease in the value of x.
b   an increase in the value of x.
c   an increase in the value of y.
d   no change in the value of y.
e   no change in the value of x.

Short Answer Problems

1 Consider the data in Table A1.4.
a   Draw a time-series graph for the interest rate.
b   Draw a time-series graph for the inflation rate.
c   Draw a scatter diagram for the inflation rate (horizontal axis) and the interest rate (vertical axis).
d   Would you describe the general relationship between the inflation rate and the interest rate as positive, negative, or unrelated?

TABLE **A1.4**

Year	Inflation Rate (%)	Interest Rate (%)
1970	5.4	6.4
1971	3.2	4.3
1972	3.4	4.1
1973	8.3	7.0
1974	11.8	7.9
1975	6.7	5.8
1976	4.9	5.0
1977	6.5	5.3
1978	8.6	7.2
1979	12.3	10.0

2 Draw a graph of variables x and y that illustrates each of the following relationships:
a x and y move up and down together.
b x and y move in opposite directions.

c   as x increases y reaches a maximum.
d   as x increases y reaches a minimum.
e x and y move in opposite directions, but as x increases y decreases by larger and larger increments for each unit increase in x.
f y is unrelated to the value of x.
g x is unrelated to the value of y.

3 What does it mean to say that the slope of a line is $-2/3$?

4 Compute the slopes of the lines in Figure A1.9(a) and (b).

FIGURE **A1.9**

(a)

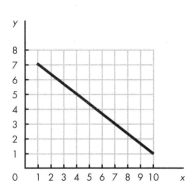

(b)

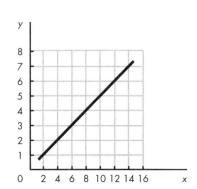

5 Draw each of the following:
a   a straight line with slope -10 and passing through the point $(2, 80)$
b   a straight line with slope 2 and passing through the point $(6, 10)$

6 The equation for a straight line is $y = 4 - 2x$.
a   Calculate: the y-intercept; the x-intercept; the slope.
b   Draw the graph of the line.

7 Explain two ways to measure the slope of a curved line.

8 Use the graph in Figure A1.10 to compute the slope
  a across the arc between points *a* and *b*.
  b at point *b*..
  c at point *c*, and explain your answer.

FIGURE **A1.10**

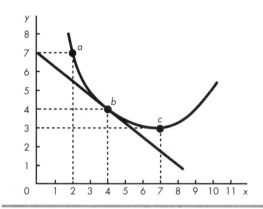

9 How do we graph a relationship among more than two variables using a two-dimensional graph?

10 In Table A1.5, *x* represents the number of umbrellas sold per month, *y* represents the price of an umbrella, and *z* represents the average number of rainy days per month.
  a On the same diagram, graph the relationship between *x* (horizontal axis) and *y* (vertical axis) when *z* = 4, when *z* = 5, and when *z* = 6. On average, it rains six days per month. This implies a certain average relationship between monthly umbrella sales and umbrella price. Suppose that the "greenhouse effect" reduces the average monthly rainfall to four days per month. What happens to the graph of the relationship between umbrella sales and umbrella prices?
  b On a diagram, graph the relationship between *x* (horizontal axis) and *z* (vertical axis) when *y* = $10 and when *y* = $12. Is the relationship between *x* and *z* positive or negative?
  c On a diagram, graph the relationship between *y* (horizontal axis) and *z* (vertical axis) when *x* = 120 and when *x* = 140. Is the relationship between *y* and *z* positive or negative?

TABLE **A1.5**

Umbrellas Sold per Month (x)	Price per Umbrella (y)	Average Number of Rainy Days per Month (z)
120	$10	4
140	$10	5
160	$10	6
100	$12	4
120	$12	5
140	$12	6
80	$14	4
100	$14	5
120	$14	6

ANSWERS

True/False and Explain

  1 **F** Definition of a cross-section graph. Time-series graph shows relationship between time (on *x*-axis) and other variable(s) (on *y*-axis). (18)
  2 **F** Breaks in the axes may be misleading, or may bring information into clearer view. (20)
  3 **F** *x* and *y* are correlated, but correlation does not guarantee causation. (20)
  4 **T** Upward-sloping curves/lines have positive slopes. (20–21)
  5 **F** Graph of unrelated variables may be vertical or horizontal. (23)
  6 **T** Arc *ab* would have negative slope, arc *bc* positive slope. (22–26)
  7 **F** Value of *y* is minimum at point *b*. (22–23)
  8 **T** Curve becomes steeper, meaning Δy increasing faster than Δx, so slope increasing. (24–26)
  9 **T** At *b*, tangent has slope = 0, since $\Delta y = 0$ along horizontal line through *b*. (24–26)
  10 **F** Slope = (Δ variable on vertical (*y*) axis)/(Δ variable on horizontal (*x*) axis). (24–25)
  11 **F** Large slope means large Δy associated with small Δx. (24–25)
  12 **T** Steep line has large slope, meaning large Δy associated with small Δx. (24–25)
  13 **T** Slope of straight line is constant. (24–25)
  14 **F** "Other things remain constant." Only variables being studied are allowed to change. (26)
  15 **T** See text Figure A1.12. A *ceteris paribus* assumption holds one variable constant, allowing other two variables to be plotted in two dimensions. (26–27)

Multiple-Choice

 1 **a** Time is measured on the *x*-axis and the variable in which we are interested on the *y*-axis. (18)
 2 **b** Definition. (18)
 3 **e** Any type of graph can mislead with breaks in the axes or stretched/compressed measurement scales. (20)
 4 **a** Higher values *x* (6.2) associated with lower values *y* (143). (20–22)
 5 **a** Definition. (20–22)
 6 **d** Graph may be steep, flat, or curved, but must have negative slope. (21–22)
 7 **a** Slope of arc *ab* = +2.5. Slope of arc *bc* = +1. (24–26)
 8 **c** $\Delta y = 3(8 - 5)$; $\Delta x = 3(6 - 3)$. (25–26)
 9 **c** 5/2 is slope of *ab*, while 1 is slope of *bc*. (25–26)
10 **d** As *w* increases, *u* increases. $\Delta u/\Delta w$ is constant. (24–26)
11 **e** Between any two points, $\Delta u = 3$, $\Delta w = -2$. (24–26)
12 **e** Slope $(\Delta y/\Delta x) = 3/4$. If Δx (Δ household income) = \$1,000, then Δy (Δ household expenditure) = \$750. (24–26)
13 **c** Where the line intersects the household expenditure (*y*) axis. (24–26)
14 **b** From \$28,000 on vertical (expenditure) axis, move across to line, then down to \$32,000 on horizontal (income) axis. (24–26)
15 **c** Along straight line, slope may or may not be **a**, **b**, or **d**. (24–25)
16 **c** Between any two points, $\Delta y = 3$ and $\Delta x = 1$. (24–25)
ct 17 **d** Equation of line is $y = 2 + 3x$. Solve for *x*-intercept (set $y = 0$). (24–26, 28–29)
18 **c** Use formula $y = a + bx$. Slope = *b*, *y*-intercept = *a*. (24–26, 28–29)
19 **b** Use formula $y = a + bx$. Slope = *b*, *x*-intercept = $-a/b$. (24–26, 28–29)
20 **e** Must hold constant other variables to isolate relationship between two variables. (26–27)
21 **d** Look either at data in top 3 rows (income = 300) or data in bottom 3 rows (income = 400). Higher price associated with lower purchases. (26–27)
ct 22 **d** At each price, fewer boxes will be purchased. (26–27)
ct 23 **c** For $P = 1$, two points on line are (5 boxes, \$300) and (7 boxes, \$400). Same relationship for other prices. (26–27)
24 **c** Increased *y* causes decreased *x* holding *z* constant. Increased *z* causes increased *x* holding *y* constant. (26–27)
ct 25 **a** Decreased *z* causes decreased *x* holding *y* constant. Decreased *z* causes decreased *y* holding *x* constant. (26–27)

Short Answer Problems

 1 **a** A time-series graph for the interest rate is given in Figure A1.11(a).
    b A time-series graph for the inflation rate is given in Figure A1.11(b).
    c The scatter diagram for the inflation rate and the interest rate is given in Figure A1.11(c).
    d From the graph in Figure A1.11(c), we see that the relationship between the inflation rate and the interest rate is generally positive (upward-sloping).

FIGURE **A1.11**

(a)

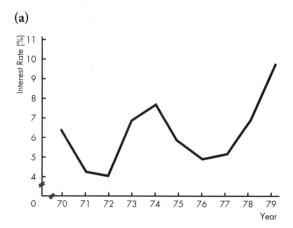

(b)

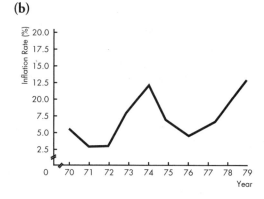

(c)

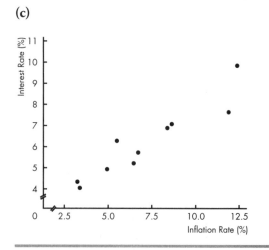

2 Figures A1.12(a) through (g) illustrate the desired graphs.

FIGURE **A1.12**

(a)

(b)

(c)

(d)

(e)

(f)

(g)

3 The negative sign in the slope of –2/3 means that there is a negative relationship between the two variables. The value of 2/3 means that when the variable measured on the vertical axis decreases by 2 units (the rise or Δy), the variable measured on the horizontal axis increases by 3 units (the run or Δx).

4 To find the slope, pick any two points on a line and compute $\Delta y/\Delta x$. The slope of the line in Figure A1.9(a) is –2/3, and the slope of the line in Figure A1.9(b) is 1/2.

5 a The requested straight line is graphed in Figure A1.13(a). First plot the point (2, 80). Then pick a second point whose y-coordinate decreases by 10 for every 1 unit increase in the x-coordinate, for example, (5, 50). The slope between the two points is –30/3 = –10.

b The requested straight line is graphed in Figure A1.13(b). First plot the point (6, 10). Then pick a second point whose y-coordinate decreases by 2 for every 1 unit decrease in the x-coordinate, for example, (5, 8). The slope between the two points is –2/–1 = 2.

FIGURE **A1.13**

(a)

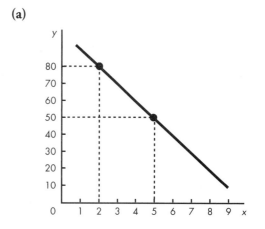

(b)

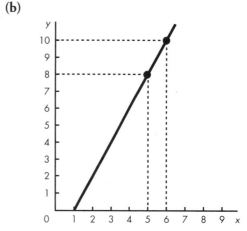

6 a To find the y-intercept, set $x = 0$.

$$y = 4 - 2(0)$$
$$y = 4$$

To find the x-intercept, set $y = 0$.

$$0 = 4 - 2x$$
$$x = 2$$

The slope of the line is –2, the value of the "b" coefficient on x.

b The graph of the line is shown in Figure A1.14.

FIGURE **A1.14**

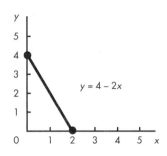

FIGURE **A1.15**

(a)

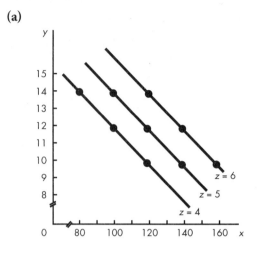

(b)

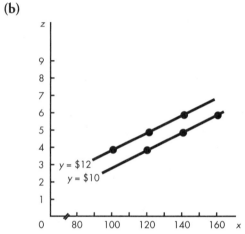

(c)

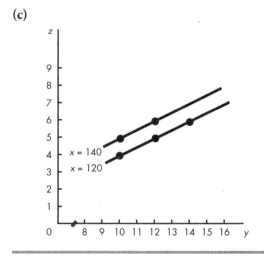

7 The slope of a straight line can be measured at a point or across an arc. The slope at a point is measured by calculating the slope of the straight line that is tangent to (just touches) the curved line at the point. The slope across an arc is measured by calculating the slope of the straight line that forms the arc.

8 a The slope across the arc between points a and b is $-3/2$.
b The slope at point b is $-3/4$.
c The slope at point c is zero because it is a minimum point. Nearby a minimum point the slope changes from negative to positive and must pass through zero, or no slope, to do so.

9 To graph a relationship among more than two variables, we hold all of the variables but two constant, and graph the relationship between the remaining two. Thus, we can graph the relationship between any pair of variables, given the constant values of the other variables.

10 a The relationships between x and y for $z = 4, 5$, and 6 are graphed in Figure A1.15(a). If the average monthly rainfall drops from 6 days to 4 days, the curve representing the relationship between umbrella sales and umbrella prices will shift from the curve labelled $z = 6$ to $z = 4$.
b The relationships between x and z when y is $10 and when y is $12 are graphed in Figure A1.15(b). The relationship between x and z is positive.
c The relationships between y and z when $x = 120$ and when $x = 140$ are graphed in Figure A1.15(c). The relationship between y and z is positive.

Chapter 2

The Economic Problem

Production Possibilities and Opportunity Cost

The **production possibility frontier** (*PPF*)

- is the boundary between unattainable and attainable production possibilities.
- shows maximum combinations of outputs (goods and services) that can be produced with given resources and technology.

PPF characteristics:

- Points on *PPF* represent **production efficiency**—more of one good cannot be produced without producing less of another good.
- Points inside *PPF* are inefficient—attainable, but not maximum combinations of outputs; they represent unused or misallocated resources.
- Points on *PPF* are preferred to points inside *PPF*.
- Points outside *PPF* are unattainable.
- Choosing among efficient points on *PPF* involves an *opportunity cost* and a *tradeoff*.

*PPF*s are generally bowed outward (concave), reflecting increasing opportunity costs as more of a good is produced.

- *PPF* is bowed outward because resources are not equally productive in all activities (nonhomogeneous). Resources most suitable for a given activity are the first to be used.
- Bowed-out-shaped *PPF* represents increasing opportunity cost—opportunity cost of good increases as its quantity produced increases.
- In moving between two points on *PPF* more good *X* can be obtained only by producing less good *Y*.

Opportunity cost on *PPF* of additional *X* is amount of *Y* forgone.

- No opportunity cost in moving from point inside *PPF* to point on *PPF*.

Using Resources Efficiently

To choose among points on *PPF*, compare

- **marginal cost**—opportunity cost of producing one more unit of a good.
  - marginal cost curve slopes upwards because of *increasing opportunity cost.*
- **marginal benefit**—benefit (measured in willingness to forgo other goods) from consuming one more unit of a good. Depends on a person's **preferences**—likes and dislikes.
  - **marginal benefit curve** slopes downwards because of *decreasing marginal benefit.*

We choose a point on *PPF* of **allocative efficiency**

- where we produces the goods and services valued most highly.
- where marginal benefit = marginal cost.

Economic Growth

Economic growth is the expansion of production possibilities—an outward shift of *PPF*.

- *PPF* shifts from changes in resources or technology.
- **Capital accumulation** and **technological change** shift *PPF* outward—economic growth.
- Opportunity cost of increased goods and services in future (economic growth through capital accumulation and technological progress) is decreased consumption today.

Gains from Trade

Production increases if people *specialize* in the activity in which they have a comparative advantage.

◆ Person has **comparative advantage** in producing a good if she can produce at lower opportunity cost than anyone else.

◆ When each person specializes in producing a good at which she has comparative advantage and exchanges for other goods, there are gains from trade.

◆ Specialization and exchange allow consumption (not production) at points outside *PPF*.

◆ Person has **absolute advantage** if, using the same quantity of resources, she can produce more goods than anyone else.

   • Absolute advantage is irrelevant for specialization and gains from trade.
   • Even a person with an absolute advantage gains by specializing in activity in which she has a comparative advantage and trading.

◆ **Dynamic comparative advantage** results from specializing in an activity, **learning-by-doing**, and over time becoming the producer with the lowest opportunity cost.

The Market Economy

Trade is organized using the social institutions of

◆ **property rights**—governing ownership, use, and disposal of resources, goods, and services.

◆ **markets**—coordinating buying and selling decisions through price adjustments.

H E L P F U L   H I N T S

1 This chapter reviews the absolutely critical concept of opportunity cost—the best alternative forgone—that was introduced in Chapter 1. Opportunity cost is a *ratio*. A very helpful formula for opportunity cost, which works well in solving problems, especially problems that involve moving up or down a production possibility frontier (*PPF*), is:

$$\text{Opportunity Cost} = \frac{\text{Give Up}}{\text{Get}}$$

Opportunity cost equals the quantity of goods you must give up divided by the quantity of goods you will get. This formula applies to all *PPF*s, whether they are bowed out as in Text Figure 2.1 or linear as in Text Figure 2.7. To illustrate, look again at the bowed-out *PPF*.

FIGURE **2.1**

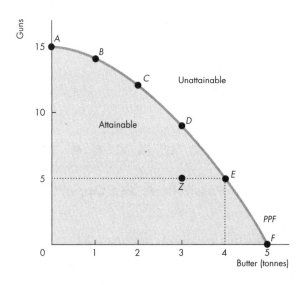

First, consider an example of moving down the *PPF*. In moving from *C* to *D*, what is the opportunity cost of an additional (tonne of) butter? This economy must give up 3 guns (12 − 9) to get 1 butter (3 − 2). Substituting into the formula, the opportunity cost is:

$$\frac{3 \text{ guns}}{1 \text{ butter}} = 3 \text{ guns per butter}$$

Next, consider an example of moving up the *PPF*. In moving from *D* to *C*, what is the opportunity cost of an additional gun? We must give up 1 (tonne of) butter (3 − 2) to get 3 guns (12 − 9). Substituting into the formula, the opportunity cost is:

$$\frac{1 \text{ butter}}{3 \text{ guns}} = \frac{1}{3} \text{ butter per gun}$$

Opportunity cost is always measured in the units of the forgone good.

2 Opportunity cost can also be related to the slope of the *PPF*. As we move down between any two points on the *PPF*, the opportunity cost of an additional unit of the good on the horizontal axis is:

$$|\text{slope of } PPF|$$

The slope of the *PPF* is negative, but economists like to describe opportunity cost in terms of a positive quantity of forgone goods. Therefore, we must use the absolute value of the slope to calculate the desired positive number.

As we move up between any two points on the *PPF*, the opportunity cost of an additional unit of the good on the vertical axis is:

$$\left| \frac{1}{\text{slope of } PPF} \right|$$

This is the *inverse* relation we saw between possibilities *C* and *D*. The opportunity cost of an additional butter (on the horizontal axis) between *C* and *D* is 3 guns. The opportunity cost of an additional gun (on the vertical axis) between *D* and *C* is 1/3 butter.

3 All points on a *PPF* achieve productive efficiency in that they fully employ all resources. But how do we pick a point on the *PPF* and decide *what* combination of goods we want? The *PPF* provides information about resources and *costs*. But choosing what goods we want also requires information about *benefits*.

This choice, like all economic choices, is made at the margin. To decide what goods we want, compare the marginal cost (*MC*) and marginal benefit (*MB*) of different combinations. Marginal cost is the opportunity cost of producing one more unit. The marginal cost of producing more of any good increases as we move along the *PPF*. Marginal benefit is the benefit received from consuming one more unit. Marginal benefit decreases as we consume more of any good.

If the marginal cost of a good exceeds the marginal benefit, we decrease production of the good. If the marginal benefit exceeds the marginal cost, we increase production. When marginal cost equals marginal benefit for every good, we have chosen the goods that we value most highly. The decision rule of *MB* = *MC* yields an *efficient* allocation of resources.

Text Figure 2.4 is crucial for explaining all economic decisions. Make sure you spend time on it even though it may be hard to fully understand. You will understand Text Figure 2.4 better after we spend time in future chapters elaborating the concepts of marginal cost and marginal benefit.

4 The guns and butter production possibility frontier assumes that resources are *not* equally productive in all activities. Resources with such differences are also called nonhomogeneous resources. As a result of this assumption, opportunity cost increases as we increase the production of either good. In moving from possibility *C* to *D*, the opportunity cost per unit of butter is 3 guns. But in increasing gun production from *D* to *E*, the opportunity cost per unit of butter increases to 4 guns. In producing the first 1 tonne of butter, we use the resources best suited to butter production. As we increase butter production, however, we must use resources that are less well suited to butter production—hence increasing opportunity cost. A parallel argument accounts for the increasing opportunity cost of increasing gun production.

It is also possible to construct an even simpler model of a *PPF* that assumes resources are equally productive in all activities, or homogeneous resources. As a result of this assumption, opportunity cost is constant as we increase production of either good. Constant opportunity cost means that the *PPF* will be a straight line (rather than bowed out). As you will see in some of the following exercises, such a simple model is useful for illustrating the principle of comparative advantage, without having to deal with the complications of increasing opportunity cost.

ⓔ **5** The text defines absolute advantage as a situation where one person has greater productivity than another in the production of all goods. We can also define *absolute advantage in the production of one good*. In comparing the productivity of two persons, this narrower concept of absolute advantage can be defined in terms of either greater output of the good per unit of resource inputs or fewer resource inputs per unit of output. It is useful to understand these definitions of absolute advantage only to demonstrate that absolute advantage has no role in explaining specialization and trade. The gains from trade depend only on differing comparative advantages. People have a comparative advantage in producing a good if they can produce it at lower opportunity cost than others.

6 This chapter gives us our first chance to develop and use economic models. It is useful to think about the nature of these models in the context of the general discussion of models in Chapter 1. For example, one model in this chapter is a representation of the production possibilities in the two-person and two-good world of Tom and Nancy. The model abstracts greatly from the complexity of the real world in which there are billions of people and numerous different kinds of goods and services. The model allows us to explain a number of phenomena that we observe in the world such as specialization and exchange.

The model also has some implications or predictions. For example, countries that devote a larger proportion of their resources to capital accumulation will have more rapidly expanding production possibilities. The model can be subjected to "test" by comparing these predictions to the facts we observe in the real world.

S E L F - T E S T

True/False and Explain

Production Possibilities and Opportunity Cost

Refer to the production possibility frontier (*PPF*) in Figure 2.2 for Questions **1** to **4**.

FIGURE **2.2**

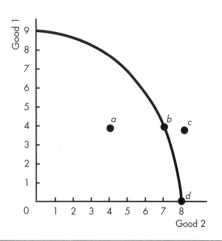

 I Point *a* is not attainable.

 2 The opportunity cost of increasing the production of good 2 from 7 to 8 units is 4 units of good 1.

 3 Point *c* is not attainable.

 4 In moving from point *b* to point *d*, the opportunity cost of increasing the production of good 2 equals the absolute value of the slope of the *PPF* between *b* and *d*.

Using Resources Efficiently

 5 The marginal cost of the 4th gun is the cost of producing all 4 guns.

 6 The marginal benefit of good *X* is the amount of good *Y* a person is willing to forgo to obtain one more unit of *X*.

 7 The principle of decreasing marginal benefit states that the more we have of a good, the *less* we are willing to pay for an additional unit of it.

 8 All points on a *PPF* represent both production efficiency and allocative efficiency.

Economic Growth

 9 Economic growth, by shifting out the *PPF*, eliminates the problem of scarcity.

 10 In a model where capital resources can grow, points on the *PPF* that have more consumption goods yield faster growth.

Gains from Trade

 11 With specialization and trade, a country can produce at a point outside its *PPF*.

 12 Canada has no incentive to trade with a cheap-labour country like Mexico.

 13 Nadim definitely has a comparative advantage in producing skateboards if he can produce more than Elle.

The Market Economy

14 The incentives for specialization and exchange do not depend on property rights but only on differing opportunity costs.

15 Price adjustments coordinate decisions in goods markets but not in factor markets.

Multiple-Choice

Production Possibilities and Opportunity Cost

1 If Harold can increase production of good X without decreasing the production of any other good, then Harold

a is producing on his *PPF*.
b is producing outside his *PPF*.
c is producing inside his *PPF*.
d must have a linear *PPF*.
e must prefer good X to any other good.

2 The bowed-out (concave) shape of a *PPF*

a is due to the equal usefulness of resources in all activities.
b is due to capital accumulation.
c is due to technological change.
d reflects the existence of increasing opportunity cost.
e reflects the existence of decreasing opportunity cost.

3 The economy is at point b on the *PPF* in Figure 2.3. The opportunity cost of producing one more unit of X is

a 1 unit of Y.
b 20 units of Y.
c 1 unit of X.
d 8 units of X.
e 20 units of X.

FIGURE **2.3**

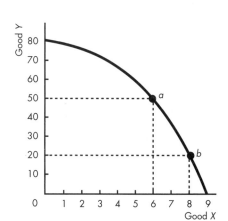

4 Refer to the *PPF* in Figure 2.3. Which of the following statements is *false*?

a Resources are not equally productive in all activities.
b Points inside the frontier represent unemployed resources.
c Starting at point a, an increase in the production of good Y will shift the frontier out.
d The opportunity cost of producing good Y increases as production of Y increases.
e Shifts in preferences for good X or good Y will not shift the frontier.

5 Refer to Figure 2.4, which shows the *PPF* for an economy without discrimination operating at maximum efficiency. If discrimination against women workers is currently occurring in this economy, the elimination of discrimination would result in a(n)

a movement from a to b.
b movement from b to c.
c movement from a to c.
d outward shift of the *PPF*.
e inward shift of the *PPF*.

FIGURE **2.4**

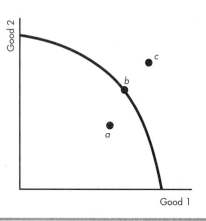

Suppose a society produces only two goods—hockey sticks and maple leaves. Three alternative combinations on its *PPF* are given in Table 2.1. Use the information in Table 2.1 to answer Questions **6** and **7**.

TABLE **2.1**   PRODUCTION POSSIBILITIES

Possibility	Units of Hockey Sticks	Units of Maple Leaves
a	3	0
b	2	3
c	0	9

6 In moving from combination *c* to combination *b*, the opportunity cost of producing one additional hockey stick is

a   2 maple leaves.
b   1/2 maple leaves.
c   6 maple leaves.
d   1/6 maple leaves.
e   3 maple leaves.

7 According to this *PPF*

a   resources are equally productive in all activities.
b   a combination of 3 hockey sticks and 9 maple leaves is attainable.
c   a combination of 3 hockey sticks and 9 maple leaves would not employ all resources.
d   the opportunity cost of producing hockey sticks increases as more hockey sticks are produced.
e   the opportunity cost of producing hockey sticks decreases as more hockey sticks are produced.

Using Resources Efficiently

8 The marginal benefit curve for a good

a   shows the benefit a firm receives from producing one more unit.
b   shows the amount a consumer is willing to pay for one more unit.
c   is upward-sloping.
d   is bowed out.
e   is none of the above.

9 With increasing production of food, its marginal benefit

a   increases and marginal cost increases.
b   increases and marginal cost decreases.
c   decreases and marginal cost increases.
d   decreases and marginal cost decreases.
e   decreases and marginal cost is constant.

10 Suppose the *PPF* for skirts and pants is a straight line. As the production of skirts increases, the marginal benefit of skirts

a   increases and marginal cost is constant.
b   is constant and marginal cost increases.
c   decreases and marginal cost decreases.
d   decreases and marginal cost increases.
e   decreases and marginal cost is constant.

11 With allocative efficiency, for each good produced, marginal

a   benefit equals marginal cost.
b   benefit is at its maximum.
c   benefit exceeds marginal cost by as much as possible.
d   cost exceeds marginal benefit by as much as possible.
e   cost is at its minimum.

Economic Growth

12 The *PPF* for wine and wool will shift if there is a change in

a   the price of resources.
b   the unemployment rate.
c   the quantity of resources.
d   preferences for wine and wool.
e   all of the above.

13 A movement *along* a given *PPF* will result from
a   technological change.
b   change in the stock of capital.
c   change in the labour force.
d   all of the above.
e   none of the above.

14 The opportunity cost of pushing the *PPF* outward is

a capital accumulation.
b technological change.
c reduced current consumption.
d the gain in future consumption.
e all of the above.

15 In general, the higher the proportion of resources devoted to technological research in an economy, the

a greater will be current consumption.
b faster the *PPF* will shift outward.
c faster the *PPF* will shift inward.
d closer it will come to having a comparative advantage in the production of all goods.
e more bowed out the shape of the *PPF* will be.

16 Refer to the *PPF* in Figure 2.5. A politician who argues that "if our children are to be better off, we must invest now for the future" is recommending a current point like

a *a.*
b *b.*
c *c.*
d *d.*
e *e.*

FIGURE **2.5**

17 Refer to the *PPF* in Figure 2.5. The statement that "unemployment is a terrible waste of human resources" refers to a point like

a *a.*
b *b.*
c *c.*
d *d.*
e *e.*

Gains from Trade

In an eight-hour day, Andy can produce either 24 loaves of bread or 8 kilograms of butter. In an eight-hour day, Rolfe can produce either 8 loaves of bread or 8 kilograms of butter. Use this information to answer Questions **18** and **19**.

© **18** Which of the following statements is *true*?

a Andy has an absolute advantage in butter production.
b Rolfe has an absolute advantage in butter production.
c Andy has an absolute advantage in bread production.
d Andy has a comparative advantage in butter production.
e Rolfe has a comparative advantage in bread production.

19 Andy and Rolfe

a can gain from exchange if Andy specializes in butter production and Rolfe specializes in bread production.
b can gain from exchange if Andy specializes in bread production and Rolfe specializes in butter production.
c cannot gain from exchange.
d can exchange, but only Rolfe will gain.
e can exchange, but only Andy will gain.

20 Mexico and Canada produce both oil and apples using labour only. A barrel of oil is produced with 4 hours of labour in Mexico and 8 hours of labour in Canada. A bushel of apples is produced with 8 hours of labour in Mexico and 12 hours of labour in Canada. Canada has

a an absolute advantage in oil production.
b an absolute advantage in apple production.
c a comparative advantage in oil production.
d a comparative advantage in apple production.
e none of the above.

21 In Portugal, the opportunity cost of a bale of wool is 3 bottles of wine. In England, the opportunity cost of 1 bottle of wine is 3 bales of wool. Given this information,

a England has an absolute advantage in wine production.
b England has an absolute advantage in wool production.
c Portugal has a comparative advantage in wine production.
d Portugal has a comparative advantage in wool production.
e no trade will occur.

22 To gain from comparative advantage, countries must not only trade, they must also

a save.
b invest.
c engage in research and development.
d engage in capital accumulation.
e specialize.

23 Learning-by-doing is the basis of

a absolute comparative advantage.
b dynamic comparative advantage.
c intellectual property rights.
d financial property rights.
e none of the above.

The Market Economy

24 Trade is organized using the social institutions of
a real property rights.
b financial property rights.
c intellectual property rights.
d markets.
e all of the above.

25 Markets
1 enable buyers and sellers to get information.
2 are defined by economists as geographical locations where trade occurs.
3 coordinate buying and selling decisions through price adjustments.

a 1 only
b 3 only
c 1 and 3 only
d 2 and 3 only
e 1, 2, and 3

Short Answer Problems

I Why is a *PPF* negatively sloped? Why is it bowed out?

2 Suppose that an economy has the *PPF* shown in Table 2.2.

TABLE **2.2** PRODUCTION POSSIBILITIES

Possibility	Maximum Units of Butter per Week	Maximum Units of Guns per Week
a	200	0
b	180	60
c	160	100
d	100	160
e	40	200
f	0	220

a On graph paper, plot these possibilities, label the points, and draw the *PPF*. (Put guns on the *x*-axis.)
b If the economy moves from possibility *c* to possibility *d*, the opportunity cost *per unit of guns* will be how many units of butter?
c If the economy moves from possibility *d* to possibility *e*, the opportunity cost *per unit of guns* will be how many units of butter?
d In general terms, what happens to the opportunity cost of guns as the output of guns increases?
e In general terms, what happens to the opportunity cost of butter as the output of butter increases? What do the results in parts **d** and **e** imply about resources?
f If (instead of the possibilities given) the *PPF* were a straight line joining points *a* and *f*, what would that imply about opportunity costs and resources?
g Given the original *PPF* you have plotted, is a combination of 140 units of butter and 130 units of guns per week attainable? Would you regard this combination as an efficient one? Explain.
h Given the original *PPF*, is a combination of 70 units of butter and 170 units of guns per week attainable? Does this combination achieve productive efficiency? Explain.

3 If the following events occurred (each is a separate event, unaccompanied by any other event), what would happen to the *PPF* in Short Answer Problem **2**?
a A new, easily exploited, energy source is discovered.
b A large number of skilled workers immigrate into the country.
c The output of butter increases.
d A new invention increases output per person in the butter industry but not in the guns industry.
e A new law is passed compelling workers, who could previously work as long as they wanted, to retire at age 60.

4 The Borg produce only two goods—cubes and transwarp coils—and want to decide where on their *PPF* to operate. Table 2.3 shows the marginal benefit and marginal cost of cubes, measured in the number of transwarp coils per cube.

TABLE **2.3**

Borg Cubes	Marginal Benefit	Marginal Cost
1	12	3
2	10	4
3	8	5
4	6	6
5	4	7
6	2	8

a If the Borg are efficient (and they are!), what quantity of cubes will they produce?

b If the Borg were to produce one more cube than your answer in **a**, why would that choice be inefficient?

5 Suppose the country of Quark has historically devoted 10 percent of its resources to the production of new capital goods. Use *PPF* diagrams like Text Figure 2.6 on page 41 to compare the consequences (costs and benefits) of each of the following:

a Quark continues to devote 10 percent of its resources to the production of capital goods.

b Quark begins now to permanently devote 20 percent of its resources to the production of capital goods.

6 Lawyers earn $200 per hour while secretaries earn $15 per hour. Use the concepts of absolute and comparative advantage to explain why a lawyer who is a better typist than her secretary will still specialize in doing only legal work and will trade with the secretary for typing services.

7 France and Germany each produce both wine and beer, using a single, homogeneous input—labour. Their production possibilities are:

- France has 100 units of labour and can produce a maximum of 200 bottles of wine or 400 bottles of beer.

- Germany has 50 units of labour and can produce a maximum of 250 bottles of wine or 200 bottles of beer.

a Complete Table 2.4.

TABLE **2.4**

	Bottles Produced by 1 Unit of Labour		Opportunity Cost of 1 Additional Bottle	
	Wine	Beer	Wine	Beer
France				
Germany				

Use the information in part **a** to answer the following questions.

b Which country has an absolute advantage in wine production?

c Which country has an absolute advantage in beer production?

d Which country has a comparative advantage in wine production?

e Which country has a comparative advantage in beer production?

f If trade is allowed, describe what specialization, if any, will occur.

8 Tova and Ron are the only two remaining inhabitants of the planet Melmac. They spend their 30-hour days producing widgets and woggles, the only two goods needed for happiness on Melmac. It takes Tova 1 hour to produce a widget and 2 hours to produce a woggle, while Ron takes 3 hours to produce a widget and 3 hours to produce a woggle.

a For a 30-hour day, draw an individual *PPF* for Tova, then for Ron.

b What does the shape of the *PPF*s tell us about opportunity costs? about resources?

c Assume initially that Tova and Ron are each self-sufficient. Define self-sufficiency. Explain what the individual consumption possibilities are for Tova, then for Ron.

d Who has an absolute advantage in the production of widgets? of woggles?

e Who has a comparative advantage in the production of widgets? of woggles?

f Suppose Tova and Ron each specialize in producing only the good in which she/he has a comparative advantage (one spends 30 hours producing widgets, the other spends 30 hours producing woggles). What will be the total production of widgets and woggles?

g Suppose Tova and Ron exchange 7 widgets for 5 woggles. On your *PPF* diagrams, plot the new point of Tova's consumption, then of Ron's consumption. Explain how these points illustrate the gains from trade.

9 The Netsilik and Oonark families live on the Arctic coast, west of Hudson Bay. They often go fishing and hunting for caribou together. During an average working day, the Netsiliks can, at most, either catch 6 kilograms of fish or kill 6 caribou. The Oonarks can either catch 4 kilograms of fish or kill 4 caribou.

a Assuming linear *PPF*s, draw each family's *PPF* on the same diagram. Put fish on the horizontal axis and caribou on the vertical axis.

b Complete Table 2.5.

TABLE **2.5**

	Opportunity Cost of 1 Additional	
	Fish (kg)	Caribou
Netsiliks		
Oonarks		

c Which family has a comparative advantage in catching fish? in hunting caribou?

d Can specialization and trade increase the total output of fish and caribou produced by the two families? Explain.

10 Explain the interdependence that exists between households and firms in Text Figure 2.10 on page 47.

A N S W E R S

True/False and Explain

1 **F** Attainable but not an efficient point. (34–35)
2 **T** Moving from *b* to *d*, production good 1 decreases by 4 units. (35–36)
3 **T** Outside *PPF.* (34–35)
ⓔ **4** **T** See Helpful Hint **2**. (35–36)
5 **F** Marginal cost is *additional* cost of producing the 4th gun alone. (37)
6 **T** Marginal benefit is also the amount a person is willing to pay for one more unit, but payment in money ultimately represents an opportunity cost in goods forgone. (38)
7 **T** The more we have of a good, the smaller is the marginal benefit and hence the willingness to pay for it. (38)
8 **F** All points represent productive efficiency (efficient use of resources). But allocative

efficiency only occurs at the single point (combination of goods) that we prefer above all others (where *MB* = *MC*). (39)

9 **F** Cost of growth is forgone current consumption. (40)
10 **F** Points with capital goods yield faster growth. (40–41)
11 **F** Can *consume* at point outside *PPF*. (43–44)
12 **F** Mutually beneficial trade depends on comparative advantage, not absolute advantage. (45)
13 **F** Nadim has absolute advantage in skateboard production, but without information about opportunity costs, we don't know if he has comparative advantage. (45)
14 **F** Property rights are prerequisite for specialization and exchange. (46)
15 **F** Price adjustments coordinate buying and selling decisions in all markets. (46–47)

Multiple-Choice

1 **c** For 0 opportunity cost, must be unemployed resources. (34–35)
2 **d** **a** would be true if *un*equal resources; **b** and **c** shift *PPF*. (36)
3 **b** To increase quantity *X* to 9, must decrease quantity *Y* from 20 to 0. (35–36)
ⓒⓣ **4** **c** Increased production *Y* moves up *along PPF*. (34–36)
5 **a** Discrimination causes underemployment of resources. Women not allowed to produce up to full abilities. (34–36)
6 **e** Give up 6 maple leaves to get 2 hockey sticks: 6/2 = 3 maple leaves per hockey stick. (35–36)
ⓒⓣ **7** **a** Constant opportunity cost means resources equally productive for producing all goods—see Helpful Hint **4**. (34–36)
8 **b** Benefits apply to consumers; curve is downward-sloping. (38)
9 **c** Principles of diminishing marginal benefit and increasing marginal cost. (37–39)
ⓒⓣ **10** **e** Diminishing marginal benefit, but linear *PPF* means constant opportunity and marginal costs. (37–39)
11 **a** Whenever *MB* ≠ *MC*, efficiency improves by reallocating resources to produce more goods with high marginal benefits, causing a decrease in their marginal benefit and increase in marginal cost. (39)
12 **c** Only changes in resources or technology shift *PPF*. (40)
ⓒⓣ **13** **e** **a**, **b**, and **c** all shift *PPF*. (40–41)
14 **c** **a** and **b** cause outward shift PPF, not opportunity cost; **d** effect of outward shift *PPF*. (40–41)

15 b Technological change shifts *PPF* outward at cost of current consumption. (40–41)

16 a Producing more capital goods now, shifts *PPF* outward in future. (40–41)

17 d Points inside *PPF* represent unemployed resources, whether labour, capital, or land. (34–35, 40–41)

ⓔ **18 c** Andy produces 3 loaves bread per hour; Rolfe produces 1 loaf per hour—see Helpful Hint **5**. (42–45)

19 b Andy has comparative advantage (lower opportunity cost) bread, Rolfe has comparative advantage butter production. (42–45)

ⓒⓣ **20 d** Opportunity cost oil in bushels of apples—Canada 2/3, Mexico 1/2. Opportunity cost apples in barrels of oil—Canada 3/2, Mexico 2. (42–45)

21 c Opportunity cost wine in bales of wool—Portugal 1/3, England 3. Opportunity cost wool in bottles of wine—Portugal 3, England 1/3. (42–45)

22 e Gains from trade require specialization based on comparative advantage. **a – d** may increase productivity and absolute advantage, not necessarily comparative advantage. (42–45)

23 b Definition. (45)

24 e Property rights and markets keys to trade. (46)

25 c 2 is the ordinary meaning of markets, not the economist's definition. (46)

Short Answer Problems

1 The negative slope of the *PPF* reflects opportunity cost: in order to have more of one good, some of the other must be forgone.

It is bowed out because the existence of resources not equally productive in all activities creates increasing opportunity cost as we increase the production of either good.

2 a The graph of the *PPF* is given in Figure 2.6.

FIGURE **2.6**

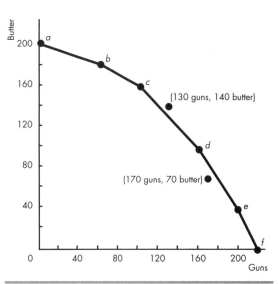

b In moving from *c* to *d*, in order to gain 60 units of guns, we must give up 160 – 100 = 60 units of butter. The opportunity cost per unit of guns is

$$\frac{60 \text{ units butter}}{60 \text{ units guns}} = 1 \text{ unit butter per unit of guns}$$

c In moving from *d* to *e*, in order to gain 40 units of guns, we must give up 100 – 40 = 60 units of butter. The opportunity cost per unit of guns is:

$$\frac{60 \text{ units butter}}{40 \text{ units guns}} = 1.5 \text{ unit butter per unit of guns}$$

d The opportunity cost of producing more guns increases as the output of guns increases.

e Likewise, the opportunity cost of producing more butter increases as the output of butter increases. Increasing opportunity costs imply that resources are not equally productive in gun and butter production; that is, they are nonhomogeneous.

f Opportunity costs would always be constant, regardless of the output of guns or butter. The opportunity cost per unit of guns would be

200/220 = 10/11 units of butter

The opportunity cost per unit of butter would be

220/200 = 1.1 units of guns

Constant opportunity costs imply that resources are equally productive in gun and butter production; that is, they are homogeneous.

g This combination is outside the *PPF* and therefore is not attainable. Since the economy cannot produce this combination, the question of efficiency is irrelevant.

h This combination is inside the *PPF* and is attainable. It is inefficient because the economy could produce more of either or both goods without producing less of anything else. Therefore some resources are not fully utilized.

3 a Assuming that both goods require energy for their production, the entire *PPF* shifts out to the northeast as in Figure 2.7(a).

b Assuming that both goods use skilled labour in their production, the entire *PPF* shifts out to the northeast.

c The *PPF* does not shift. An increase in the output of butter implies a movement along the *PPF* to the left, not a shift of the *PPF* itself.

d The new invention implies that for every level of output of guns, the economy can now produce more butter. The *PPF* swings to the right, but remains anchored at point *f* as in Figure 2.7(b).

e The entire *PPF* shifts in towards the origin.

FIGURE **2.7**

(a)

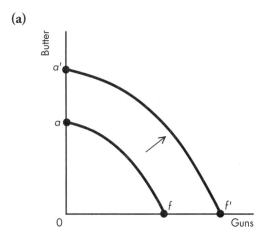

(b)

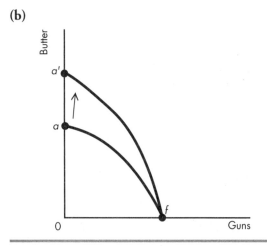

4 a At the efficient quantity of output, marginal benefit = marginal cost. The Borg will produce 4 cubes (*MB* = *MC* = 4 transwarp coils/cube).

b At 5 cubes, marginal benefit = 4 and marginal cost = 7. Since *MC* > *MB*, the Borg could get better use from their resources by shifting production out of cubes and into transwarp coils.

5 a The situation for Quark is depicted by Figure 2.8. Suppose Quark starts on *PPF* 1. If it continues to devote only 10 percent of its resources to the production of new capital goods, then it is choosing to produce at a point like *a*. This will shift the *PPF* out in the next period, but only to the curve labelled 2 (where, presumably, Quark will choose to produce at point *b*).

FIGURE **2.8**

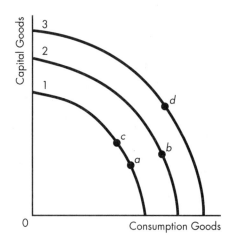

b Starting from the same initial *PPF*, if Quark now decides to increase the resources devoted to the production of new capital to 20 percent, it will be choosing to produce at a point like *c*. In this case, next period's *PPF* will shift further—to curve 3, and a point like *d*, for example.

Thus in comparing points *a* and *c*, we find the following costs and benefits: point *a* has the benefit of greater present consumption but at a cost of lower future consumption; point *c* has the cost of lower present consumption, but with the benefit of greater future consumption.

6 The lawyer has an absolute advantage in producing both legal and typing services relative to the secretary. Nevertheless, she has a comparative advantage in legal services, and the secretary has a comparative advantage in typing. To demonstrate these comparative advantages, we can construct Table 2.6 of opportunity costs.

TABLE **2.6**

	Opportunity Cost of 1 Additional Hour ($)	
	Legal Services	Typing
Lawyer	200	200
Secretary	>200	15

Consider first the lawyer's opportunity costs. The lawyer's best forgone alternative to providing 1 hour of legal services is the $200 she could earn by providing another hour of legal services. If she provides 1 hour of typing, she is also forgoing $200 (1 hour) of legal services. What would the secretary have to forgo to provide 1 hour of legal services? He would have to spend 3 years in law school, forgoing 3 years of income in addition to the tuition he must pay. His opportunity cost is a very large number, certainly greater than $200. If he provides 1 hour of typing, his best forgone alternative is the $15 he could have earned at another secretarial job.

Thus Table 2.6 shows that the lawyer has a lower opportunity cost (comparative advantage) of providing legal services, and the secretary has a lower opportunity cost (comparative advantage) of providing typing services. It is on the basis of comparative advantage (not absolute advantage) that trade will take place from which both parties gain.

7 a The completed table is shown here as Table 2.4 Solution.

TABLE **2.4** SOLUTION

	Bottles Produced by 1 Unit of Labour		Opportunity Cost of 1 Additional Bottle	
	Wine	Beer	Wine	Beer
France	2	4	2.0 beer	0.50 wine
Germany	5	4	0.8 beer	1.25 wine

b Germany, which can produce more wine (5 bottles) per unit of input, has an absolute advantage in wine production.

c Neither country has an absolute advantage in beer production, since beer output (4 bottles) per unit of input is the same for both countries.

d Germany, with the lower opportunity cost (0.8 beer), has a comparative advantage in wine production.

e France, with the lower opportunity cost (0.5 wine), has a comparative advantage in beer

production.

f The incentive for trade depends only on differences in comparative advantage. Germany will specialize in wine production and France will specialize in beer production.

8 a The individual *PPF*s for Tova and Ron are given by Figure 2.9(a) and (b) respectively.

FIGURE **2.9**

(a)

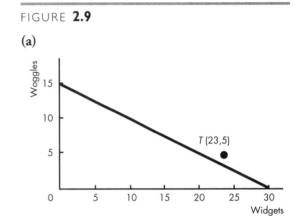

(b)

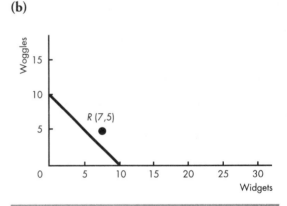

b The linear shape of the *PPF*s tells us that opportunity costs are constant along each frontier and that resources are homogeneous.

These linear *PPF*s with constant opportunity costs abstract from the complexity of the real world. The world generally has increasing opportunity costs, but that fact is not essential for understanding the gains from trade, which is the objective of this problem. Making the model more complex by including increasing opportunity costs would not change our results, but it would make it more difficult to see them.

c Individuals are self-sufficient if they consume only what they produce. This means there is no trade. Without trade, Tova's (maximum) consumption possibilities are exactly the same as her production possibilities—points along her *PPF*. Ron's (maximum) consumption possibilities are likewise the points along his *PPF*.

d Tova has an absolute advantage in the production of both widgets and woggles. Her absolute advantage can be defined either in terms of greater output per unit of inputs or fewer inputs per unit of output. A comparison of the *PPF*s in Figure 2.9 shows that, for given inputs of 30 hours, Tova produces a greater output of widgets than Ron (30 versus 10) and a greater output of woggles than Ron (15 versus 10). The statement of the problem tells us equivalently that, per unit of output, Tova uses fewer inputs than Ron for both widgets (1 hour versus 3 hours) and woggles (2 hours versus 3 hours). Since Tova has greater productivity than Ron in the production of all goods (widgets and woggles), we say that overall she has an absolute advantage.

e Tova has a comparative advantage in the production of widgets, since she can produce them at lower opportunity cost than Ron (1/2 woggle versus 1 woggle). On the other hand, Ron has a comparative advantage in the production of woggles, since he can produce them at a lower opportunity cost than Tova (1 widget versus 2 widgets).

f Tova will produce widgets and Ron will produce woggles, yielding a total production between them of 30 widgets and 10 woggles.

g After the exchange, Tova will have 23 widgets and 5 woggles (point *T*). Ron will have 7 widgets and 5 woggles (point *R*). These new post-trade consumption possibility points lie outside Tova's and Ron's respective pre-trade consumption (and production) possibilities. Hence trade has yielded gains that allow the traders to improve their consumption possibilities beyond those available with self-sufficiency.

9 a The *PPF*s of the Netsiliks and Oonarks are shown in Figure 2.10.

FIGURE **2.10**

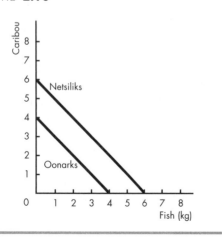

b The completed table is shown here as Table 2.5 Solution.

TABLE **2.5** SOLUTION

	Opportunity Cost of 1 Additional	
	Fish (kg)	**Caribou**
Netsiliks	1 caribou	1 kg fish
Oonarks	1 caribou	1 kg fish

c Neither family has a comparative advantage in catching fish since the opportunity cost of fish is the same (1 caribou) for each family. Similarly, neither family has a comparative advantage in hunting caribou since the opportunity cost of a caribou is the same (1 kg fish) for each family.

d Gains from specialization and trade are due to the existence of comparative advantage. In this case, no family has a comparative advantage in either fishing or hunting, so there are no gains from specialization and trade.

To illustrate the absence of gains, suppose that initially each family devoted half of its time to each activity. Then suppose that the Netsiliks specialized completely in catching fish and the Oonarks specialized completely in hunting caribou. Production before and after specialization is shown in Table 2.7.

TABLE **2.7**

	Before Specialization		After Specialization	
	Fish (kg)	**Caribou**	**Fish (kg)**	**Caribou**
Netsiliks	3	3	6	0
Oonarks	2	2	0	4
Total Production	5	5	6	4

Compare the total production of both commodities before and after specialization. Specialization has increased the total production of fish by 1 kilogram, but it has also led to a decrease in the total production of caribou by 1. There are no clear gains in consumption from specialization and trade.

10 Firms depend on households for the supply of factors of production. In exchange, households depend on firms for income. Households use that income to buy goods and services from firms, while firms depend on the money they get from household purchases to purchase more factors of production in the next period and renew the circular flow.

Understanding the Scope of Economics

PROBLEM

The economy is a mechanism that allocates scarce resources among competing uses. But how do those allocation decisions get made? In the Canadian economy, markets are the primary institutions that coordinate individual decisions through price adjustments.

Suppose, for simplicity, the Canadian economy produced only two outputs—child-care services and televisions. The production possibility frontier (*PPF*) for the economy appears in Figure P1.1 below. The economy is operating at point *a*, producing Q^0_{cc} units of child-care services and Q^0_{tv} televisions.

FIGURE **P1.1**

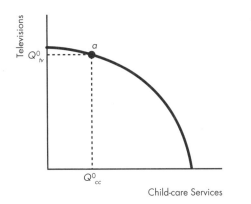

a What does the bowed-out (concave) shape of the *PPF* imply about resources? opportunity costs?

b As more women enter the labour force, there is increased demand for child-care services. As a result, the price and quantity of child-care services both increase. At the same time, the demand for televisions falls (perhaps to save money to pay for the additional child-care

services). As a result, the price and quantity of televisions both decrease.

On the *PPF* in Figure P1.1, label as point *b* a new combination of child-care services and televisions reflecting the changes in demand.

c Explain how the economy came to produce these new quantities in response to the changing demands of households.

d What determines the distance of the *PPF* from the origin? What determines the precise point on the *PPF* at which the economy operates? What is the true cost of moving from point *a* to point *b* on the *PPF*?

MIDTERM EXAMINATION

You should allocate 30 minutes for this examination (15 questions, 2 minutes per question). For each question, choose the one *best* answer.

1 A *PPF* shows that

a there is a limit to the production of any one good.

b to produce more of one good, we must produce less of another good.

c there are limits to total production with given resources and technology.

d all of the above are true.

e none of the above is true.

2 The graph showing the level of a variable across different groups at a point in time is a

a   linear graph.
b   time-series graph.
c   cross-section graph.
d   misleading graph.
e   scatter diagram.

Suppose a society produces only two goods—guns and butter. Three alternative combinations on its *PPF* are given in Table P1.1. Use the information in Table P1.1 to answer Questions **3** and **4**.

TABLE **P1.1**   PRODUCTION POSSIBILITIES

Possibility	Units of Butter	Units of Guns
a	8	0
b	6	1
c	0	3

3 In moving from combination *b* to combination *c*, the opportunity cost of producing *one* additional unit of guns is

a   2 units of butter.
b   1/2 unit of butter.
c   6 units of butter.
d   1/6 unit of butter.
e   3 units of butter.

4 According to this *PPF*

a   a combination of 6 butter and 1 gun would not employ all resources.
b   a combination of 0 butter and 4 guns is attainable.
c   resources are equally productive in all activities.
d   the opportunity cost of producing guns increases as more guns are produced.
e   the opportunity cost of producing guns decreases as more guns are produced.

5 Which of the following is a normative statement?

a   Pollution is an example of an external cost.
b   Pollution makes people worse off.
c   Firms that pollute should be forced to shut down.
d   Pollution imposes opportunity costs on others.
e   None of the above.

6 The graph of the relationship between two variables that are negatively related

a   is horizontal.
b   slopes upward to the right.
c   is vertical.
d   slopes downward to the right.
e   is linear.

7 In Figure P1.2, the slope of the line is

a   1.50.
b   1.25.
c   1.00.
d   0.75.
e   0.50.

FIGURE **P1.2**

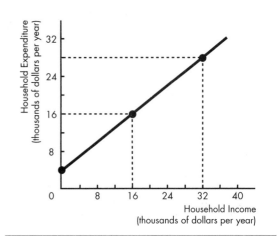

8 Other things being equal, which of the following statements is correct?
   1 If unemployment increases, the opportunity cost of attending university decreases.
   2 If men generally earn more than women in the labour market, the opportunity cost of attending university is higher for men than for women.

a   1 only
b   2 only
c   1 and 2
d   neither 1 nor 2
e   impossible to judge without additional information

9 The economy is at point *b* on the *PPF* in Figure 1.3. The opportunity cost of increasing the production of *Y* to 50 units is

a   2 units of *X*.
b   6 units of *X*.
c   8 units of *X*.
d   20 units of *Y*.
e   30 units of *Y*.

FIGURE **P1.3**

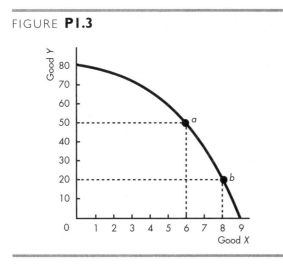

14 If variables *x* and *y* move in opposite directions, they are said to be
a positively related.
b negatively related.
c intimately related.
d unrelated.
e siblings.

15 *Ceteris paribus* is a Latin term meaning
a "After this, therefore because of this."
b "What is true of the parts is true of the whole."
c "What is true of the parts is *not* true of the whole."
d "Other things being equal."
e "Your place or mine."

10 Because productive resources are scarce, we must give up some of one good in order to acquire more of another. This is the essence of the concept of
a specialization.
b monetary exchange.
c comparative advantage.
d absolute advantage.
e opportunity cost.

11 The scarcity of resources implies that the *PPF* is
a bowed inward (convex).
b bowed outward (concave).
c positively sloped.
d negatively sloped.
e linear.

12 If additional units of any good can be produced at a constant opportunity cost, the *PPF* is
a bowed inward (convex).
b bowed outward (concave).
c positively sloped.
d perfectly horizontal.
e linear.

13 Marginal cost is the
a total cost of an activity.
b additional benefit of a decrease in an activity.
c additional benefit of an increase in an activity.
d opportunity cost of a decrease in an activity.
e opportunity cost of an increase in an activity.

ANSWERS

Problem

a The bowed-out shape of the *PPF* implies that resources are not equally productive in all activities; they are nonhomogeneous. With nonhomogeneous resources, there are increasing opportunity costs as production increases of either child-care services or televisions.
b See Figure P1.1 Solution.

FIGURE **P1.1** SOLUTION

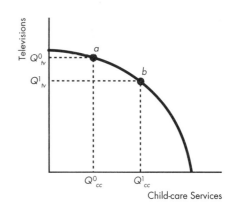

c The increased demand for child-care services puts upward pressure on the price of child-care services, making it more profitable to produce them. The higher price serves as a signal to firms to shift additional resources to producing child-care services.

Those additional resources come from the television market. The decreased demand for televisions puts downward pressure on the price of televisions, making it less profitable to produce them. The lower price serves as a signal to firms to shift resources to more profitable uses (in child-care).

Thus the market economy responds to the changing demands of households by reallocating resources into child-care services from television production. Prices are the signals that coordinate the demand decisions of households with the resource allocation decisions of firms. The market—operating through a combination of price signals, self-interest, and competition—acts like an "invisible hand" to guide resources to the uses that households desire.

d The distance of the *PPF* from the origin is determined by the quantities of resources and the technology in the economy. The *PPF* shows maximum combinations of outputs (goods and services) that can be produced with given resources and technology.

The precise point on the *PPF* at which the economy operates (for example, the combination at point *a* of child-care services and televisions) is determined by the demands of households.

The true cost of moving from point *a* to point *b* is the televisions that must be forgone as scarce resources are shifted to produce more child-care services. In other words, the true cost of additional child-care is an opportunity cost—forgone televisions.

Midterm Examination

1 **d** **a** and **b** show scarcity, **c** shows opportunity cost. (34–36)

2 **c** Definition. Example is a bar chart. (18–20)
3 **e** Give up 6 butter to get 2 guns: 6/2 = 3 butter per gun. (34–36)
4 **d** Opportunity cost gun between *a* and *b* = 2 butter; between *b* and *c* = 3 butter. *a* on *PPF*, *b* outside *PPF*. (34–36)
5 **c** **a** is a true statement (definition); **d** and **b** are positive statements that can be tested. (12–13)
6 **d** As *x* increases, *y* decreases. (21–22)
7 **d** For example, using points (0, 4) and (16, 16): $\Delta y = 12$ (16 − 4), $\Delta x = 16$ (16 − 0). (24–25)
8 **c** Unemployment decreases expected average income from working. Higher opportunity cost for men may not be fair, but is a fact. (11)
9 **a** To move from *b* to *a*, quantity *X* decreases from 8 to 6. (35–36)
10 **e** Definition. (35–36)
11 **d** Scarcity implies opportunity cost, which involves a negative relationship—to get more of *X* you must give up *Y*. (34–36)
12 **e** Constant opportunity cost yields constant slope *PPF*. (36, 42)
13 **e** Definition; **c** is marginal benefit, **b** and **d** are nonsense. (11, 37)
14 **b** Definition. (21–22)
15 **d** Definition; **a** is *post hoc ergo propter hoc*. (13–14)

Chapter 3

Demand and Supply

KEY CONCEPTS

Markets and Prices

Competitive market—many buyers and sellers so no one can influence prices.

Relative price of a good is

◆ its *opportunity cost*—the other goods that must be forgone to buy it.

◆ ratio of its *money price* to the money price of another good.

◆ determined by demand and supply.

Demand

The **quantity demanded** of a good is the amount consumers plan to buy during a given time period at a particular price. The **law of demand** states: "Other things remaining the same, the higher the price of a good, the smaller the quantity demanded." Higher price reduces quantity demanded for two reasons:

◆ *Substitution effect*—with an increase in the relative price of a good, people buy less of it and more of substitutes for the good.

◆ *Income effect*—with an increase in the relative price of a good and unchanged incomes, people have less money to spend on all goods, including the good whose price increased.

The **demand curve** represents the inverse relationship between quantity demanded and price, *ceteris paribus*. The demand curve also is a willingness-and-ability-to-pay curve, which measures marginal benefit.

◆ A change in price causes movement along the demand curve. This is called a **change in the quantity demanded**. The higher the price of a good, the lower the quantity demanded.

◆ A shift of the demand curve is called a **change in demand**. The demand curve shifts from changes in

  • prices of related goods.
  • expected future prices.
  • income.
  • population.
  • preferences.

◆ Increase in demand—demand curve shifts rightward.

◆ Decrease in demand—demand curve shifts leftward.

◆ For an increase in

  • price of a **substitute**—demand shifts rightward.
  • price of a **complement**—demand shifts leftward.
  • expected future prices—demand shifts rightward.
  • income (**normal good**)—demand shifts rightward.
  • income (**inferior good**)—demand shifts leftward.
  • population—demand shifts rightward.
  • preferences—demand shifts rightward.

Supply

The **quantity supplied** of a good is the amount producers plan to sell during a given time period at a particular price. The **law of supply** states: "Other things remaining the same, the higher the price of a good, the greater the quantity supplied." Higher price increases quantity supplied because marginal cost increases with increasing quantities. Price must rise for producers to be willing to increase production and incur higher marginal cost.

The **supply curve** represents the positive relationship between quantity supplied and price, *ceteris paribus*. The supply curve is also a minimum-supply-price curve, showing the lowest price at which a producer is willing to sell another unit.

- A change in price causes movement along the supply curve. This is called a **change in the quantity supplied**. The higher the price of a good, the greater the quantity supplied.

- A shift of the supply curve is called a **change in supply**. The supply curve shifts from changes in

  - prices of productive resources.
  - prices of related goods produced.
  - expected future prices.
  - number of suppliers.
  - technology.

- Increase in supply—supply curve shifts rightward.

- Decrease in supply—supply curve shifts leftward.

- For an increase in

  - prices of productive resources—supply shifts leftward.
  - price of a *substitute in production*—supply shifts leftward.
  - price of a *complement in production*—supply shifts rightward.
  - expected future prices—supply shifts leftward.
  - number of suppliers—supply shifts rightward.
  - technology—supply shifts rightward.

Market Equilibrium

The **equilibrium price** is where the demand and supply curves intersect, where quantity demanded equals quantity supplied.

- Above the equilibrium price, there is a surplus (quantity supplied > quantity demanded), and price will fall.

- Below the equilibrium price, there is a shortage (quantity demanded > quantity supplied), and price will rise.

- Only in equilibrium is there no tendency for the price to change. The **equilibrium quantity** is the quantity bought and sold at the equilibrium price.

Predicting Changes in Price and Quantity

For a single change *either* in demand *or* in supply, *ceteris paribus*, when

- demand increases, P rises and Q increases.
- demand decreases, P falls and Q decreases.
- supply increases, P falls and Q increases.
- supply decreases, P rises and Q decreases.

When there is a simultaneous change *both* in demand *and* supply, we can determine the effect on either price

or quantity. But without information about the relative size of the shifts of the demand and supply curves, the effect on the other variable is ambiguous. *Ceteris paribus*, when

- both demand and supply increase, P may rise/fall/remain constant and Q increases.

- both demand and supply decrease, P may rise/fall/remain constant and Q decreases.

- demand increases and supply decreases, P rises and Q may rise/fall/remain constant.

- demand decreases and supply increases, P falls and Q may rise/fall/remain constant.

HELPFUL HINTS

1 When you are first learning about demand and supply, think of specific examples to help you understand how to use the concepts. For example, in analyzing complementary goods, think about hamburgers and french fries; in analyzing substitute goods, think of hamburgers and hot dogs. This will reduce the "abstractness" of the economic theory and make concepts easier to remember.

2 The statement that "price is determined by demand and supply" is a shorthand way of saying that price is determined by all of the factors affecting demand (prices of related goods, expected future prices, income, population, preferences) and all of the factors affecting supply (prices of productive resources, prices of related goods produced, expected future prices, number of suppliers, technology). The benefit of using demand and supply curves is that they allow us to systematically sort out the influences on price of each of these separate factors. Changes in the factors affecting demand shift the demand curve and move us up or down the given supply curve. Changes in the factors affecting supply shift the supply curve and move us up or down the given demand curve.

Any demand and supply problem requires you to sort out these influences carefully. In so doing, *always draw a graph*, even if it is just a small graph in the margin of a true/false or multiple-choice problem. Graphs are a very efficient way to "see" what happens. As you become comfortable with graphs, you will find them to be effective and powerful tools for systematically organizing your thinking.

Do not make the common mistake of thinking that a problem is so easy that you can do it in your head, without drawing a graph. This mistake will cost you dearly on examinations. Also, when you do draw a graph, be sure to label the axes. As the course progresses, you will encounter many graphs with different variables on the axes. It is easy to become confused if you do not develop the habit of labelling the axes.

3 Another very common mistake among students is failing to *distinguish* correctly between *a shift in a curve* and *a movement along a curve*. This distinction applies both to demand and to supply curves. Many questions in the Self-Test are designed to test your understanding of this distinction, and you can be sure that your instructor will test you heavily on this. The distinction between "shifts in" versus "movements along" a curve is crucial for systematic thinking about the factors influencing demand and supply, and for understanding the determination of equilibrium price and quantity.

Consider the example of the demand curve. The quantity of a good demanded depends on its own price, the prices of related goods, expected future prices, income, population, and preferences. The term "demand" refers to the relationship between the price of a good and the quantity demanded, holding constant all of the other factors on which the quantity demanded depends. This demand relationship is represented graphically by the demand curve. Thus, the effect of a change in price on quantity demanded is already reflected in the slope of the demand curve; the effect of a change in the price of the good itself is given by a movement along the demand curve. This is referred to as a **change in quantity demanded**.

On the other hand, if one of the other factors affecting the quantity demanded changes, the demand curve itself will shift; the quantity demanded *at each price* will change. This shift of the demand curve is referred to as a **change in demand**. The critical thing to remember is that a change in the price of a good will not shift the demand curve; it will only cause a movement along the demand curve. Similarly, it is just as important to distinguish between shifts in the supply curve and movements along the supply curve.

To confirm your understanding, consider the effect (draw a graph!) of an increase in household income on the market for compact discs (CDs). First note that an increase in income affects the demand for CDs and not supply. Next we want to determine whether the increase in income causes a shift in the demand

curve or a movement along the demand curve. Will the increase in income increase the quantity of CDs demanded even if the price of CDs does not change? Since the answer to this question is yes, we know that the demand curve will shift rightward. Note further that the increase in the demand for CDs will cause the equilibrium price to rise. This price increase will be indicated by a movement along the supply curve (an increase in the quantity supplied) and will not shift the supply curve itself.

Remember: It is shifts in demand and supply curves that cause the market price to change, not changes in the price that cause demand and supply curves to shift.

4 When analyzing the shifts of demand and supply curves in related markets (for substitute goods like beer and wine), it often seems as though the feedback effects from one market to the other can go on endlessly. To avoid confusion, stick to the rule that each curve (demand and supply) for a given market can shift a maximum of *once*. (See Short Answer Problems **4** and **6** for further explanation and examples.)

5 The relationships between price and quantity demanded and supplied can be represented in three equivalent forms: demand and supply schedules, curves, and equations. Text Chapter 3 illustrates schedules and curves, but demand and supply equations are also powerful tools of economic analysis. The Mathematical Note to Chapter 3 provides the general form of these equations. The purpose of this Helpful Hint and the next is to further explain the equations and how they can be used to determine the equilibrium values of price and quantity.

Figure 3.1 presents a simple demand and supply example in three equivalent forms: (a) schedules, (b) curves, and (c) equations. The demand and supply schedules in (a) are in the same format as Text Figure 3.7. The price-quantity combinations from the schedules are plotted on the graph in (b), yielding linear demand and supply curves. What is new about this example is the representation of those curves by the equations in (c).

If you recall (Chapter 1 Appendix) the formula for the equation of a straight line ($y = a + bx$), you can see that the demand equation is the equation of a straight line. Instead of y, P is the dependent variable on the vertical axis, and, instead of x, Q_D is the independent variable on the horizontal axis. The intercept on the vertical axis a is +5, and the slope b is −1. The supply equation is also linear and graphed in the same way, but with Q_S as the independent variable. The supply curve intercept on the vertical axis is +1, and the slope is +1. The negative slope of the demand curve reflects the law of demand, and the positive slope of the supply curve reflects the law of supply.

You can demonstrate the equivalence of the demand schedule, curve, and equation by substituting various values of Q_D from the schedule into the demand equation, and calculating the associated prices. These combinations of quantity demanded and price are the coordinates (Q_D, P) of the points on the demand curve. You can similarly demonstrate the equivalence of the supply schedule, curve, and equation.

FIGURE **3.1**

(a) Demand and Supply Schedules

Price ($)	Q_D	Q_S	Shortage (–)/ Surplus (+)
1	4	0	–4
2	3	1	–2
3	2	2	0
4	1	3	+2
5	0	4	+4

(b) Demand and Supply Curves

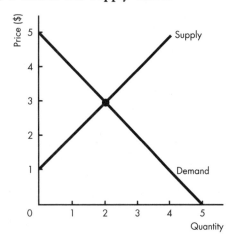

(c) Demand and Supply Equations

Demand: $P = 5 - 1Q_D$
Supply: $P = 1 + 1Q_S$

The demand and supply equations are very useful for calculating the equilibrium values of price and quantity. As the schedules and curves both show, two things are true in equilibrium: (1) the price is the same for consumers (the highest price they are willing to pay for the last unit) and producers (the lowest price they are willing to accept for the last unit) and (2) the quantity demanded equals the quantity supplied, so that there are no surpluses or shortages. In terms of the demand and supply equations, this means that, *in equilibrium,*

(1) the price in both equations is the same. We will denote the equilibrium price as P^*.
(2) $Q_D = Q_S$ = the equilibrium quantity bought and sold. We will denote the equilibrium quantity as Q^*.

In equilibrium, the equations become

Demand: $P^* = 5 - 1Q^*$
Supply: $P^* = 1 + 1Q^*$

These equilibrium equations constitute a simple set of simultaneous equations. Since there are two equations (demand and supply) and two unknowns (P^* and Q^*), we can solve for the unknowns.

Begin the solution by setting demand equal to supply:

$$5 - 1Q^* = 1 + 1Q^*$$

Collecting like terms, we find

$$4 = 2Q^*$$
$$2 = Q^*$$

Once we have Q^* (equilibrium quantity), we can solve for the equilibrium price using either the demand or the supply equations. Look first at demand:

$$P^* = 5 - 1Q^*$$
$$P^* = 5 - 1(2)$$
$$P^* = 5 - 2$$
$$P^* = 3$$

Alternatively, substituting Q^* into the supply equation yields the same result:

$$P^* = 1 + 1Q^*$$
$$P^* = 1 + 1(2)$$
$$P^* = 1 + 2$$
$$P^* = 3$$

Once you have solved for Q^*, the fact that substituting it into either the demand or the supply equation yields the correct P^* provides a valuable check on your calculations. If you make a mistake in your calculations, when you substitute Q^* into the demand and supply equations, you will get two different prices. If that happens, you know to recheck your calculations. If you get the same price when you substitute Q^* into the demand and supply equations, you know your calculations are correct.

6 Economists have developed the convention of graphing quantity as the independent variable (on the horizontal *x*-axis) and price as the dependent variable (on the vertical *y*-axis), and the foregoing equations reflect this. Despite this convention, economists actually consider real-world prices to be the independent variables and quantities the dependent variables. In that case, the equations would take the form

Demand: $Q_D = 5 - 1P$
Supply: $Q_S = -1 + 1P$

You can solve these equations for yourself to see that they yield exactly the same values for P^* and Q^*. (*Hint:* First solve for P^* and then for Q^*.) Whichever form of the equations your instructor may use, the technique for solving the equations will be similar and the results identical.

S E L F - T E S T

True/False and Explain

Markets and Prices

1 In a competitive market, every single buyer and seller influences price.

2 The relative price of of good is the other goods that must be forgone to buy it.

3 A good's relative price can fall even when its money price rises.

Demand

4 The law of demand tells us that as the price of a good rises, demand decreases.

5 The demand curve is a willingness-and-ability-to-pay curve that measures marginal cost.

6 Hamburgers and fries are complements. If Burger Bar reduces the price of fries, the demand for hamburgers increases.

7 A decrease in income always shifts the demand curve leftward.

Supply

8 A supply curve shows the maximum price at which the last unit will be supplied.

9 If *A* and *B* are substitutes, an increase in the price of *A* always shifts the supply curve of *B* leftward.

10 When a cow is slaughtered for beef, its hide becomes available to make leather. Thus beef and leather are substitutes in production.

11 If the price of beef rises, there will be an increase in both the supply of leather and the quantity of beef supplied.

Market Equilibrium

12 When the actual price is above the equilibrium price, a shortage occurs.

Predicting Changes in Price and Quantity

13 If the expected future price of a good increases, there will always be an increase in equilibrium price and a decrease in equilibrium quantity.

14 Suppose new firms enter the steel market. *Ceteris paribus*, the equilibrium price of steel will always fall and the quantity will rise.

15 Suppose the demand for personal computers increases while the cost of producing them decreases. The equilibrium quantity of personal computers will rise and the price will always fall.

Multiple-Choice

Markets and Prices

1 A relative price is

a the ratio of one price to another.
b an opportunity cost.
c a quantity of a "basket" of goods and services forgone.
d determined by demand and supply.
e all of the above.

Demand

2 If an increase in the price of good *A* causes the demand curve for good *B* to shift leftward, then

a *A* and *B* are substitutes in consumption.
b *A* and *B* are complements in consumption.
c *A* and *B* are complements in production.
d *B* is an inferior good.
e *B* is a normal good.

3 Which of the following could *not* cause an increase in demand for a commodity?

a an increase in income
b a decrease in income
c a decrease in the price of a substitute
d a decrease in the price of a complement
e an increase in preferences for the commodity

4 Some sales managers are talking shop. Which of the following quotations refers to a movement along the demand curve?

a "Since our competitors raised their prices our sales have doubled."
b "It has been an unusually mild winter; our sales of wool scarves are down from last year."
c "We decided to cut our prices, and the increase in our sales has been remarkable."
d "The Green movement has sparked an increase in our sales of biodegradable products."
e none of the above.

5 If Hamburger Helper is an inferior good, then, *ceteris paribus*, a decrease in income will cause

a a leftward shift of the demand curve for Hamburger Helper.
b a rightward shift of the demand curve for Hamburger Helper.
c a movement up along the demand curve for Hamburger Helper.
d a movement down along the demand curve for Hamburger Helper.
e none of the above.

6 A decrease in quantity demanded is represented by a

a rightward shift of the supply curve.
b rightward shift of the demand curve.
c leftward shift of the demand curve.
d movement upward and to the left along the demand curve.
e movement downward and to the right along the demand curve.

7 Which of the following "other things" are *not* held constant along a demand curve?

a income
b prices of related goods
c the price of the good itself
d preferences
e all of the above

Supply

8 The fact that a decline in the price of a good causes producers to reduce the quantity of the good supplied illustrates

a the law of supply.
b the law of demand.
c a change in supply.
d the nature of an inferior good.
e technological improvement.

9 A shift of the supply curve for rutabagas will be caused by

a a change in preferences for rutabagas.
b a change in the price of a related good that is a substitute in consumption for rutabagas.
c a change in income.
d a change in the price of rutabagas.
e none of the above.

10 If a resource can be used to produce either good *A* or good *B*, then *A* and *B* are

a substitutes in production.
b complements in production.
c substitutes in consumption.
d complements in consumption.
e normal goods.

11 Which of the following will shift the supply curve for good *X* leftward?

a a decrease in the wages of workers employed to produce *X*
b an increase in the cost of machinery used to produce *X*
c a technological improvement in the production of *X*
d a situation where quantity demanded exceeds quantity supplied
e all of the above

12 Some producers are chatting over a beer. Which of the following quotations refers to a movement along the supply curve?

a "Wage increases have forced us to raise our prices."
b "Our new, sophisticated equipment will enable us to undercut our competitors."
c "Raw material prices have skyrocketed; we will have to pass this on to our customers."
d "We anticipate a big increase in demand. Our product price should rise, so we are planning for an increase in output."
e "New competitors in the industry are causing prices to fall."

13 If an increase in the price of good *A* causes the supply curve for good *B* to shift rightward, then

a *A* and *B* are substitutes in consumption.
b *A* and *B* are complements in consumption.
c *A* and *B* are substitutes in production.
d *A* and *B* are complements in production.
e *A* is a factor of production for making *B*.

Market Equilibrium

14 If the market for Twinkies is in equilibrium, then

a Twinkies must be a normal good.
b producers would like to sell more at the current price.
c consumers would like to buy more at the current price.
d there will be a surplus.
e equilibrium quantity equals quantity demanded.

15 The price of a good will tend to fall if

a there is a surplus at the current price.
b the current price is above equilibrium.
c the quantity supplied exceeds the quantity demanded at the current price.
d all of the above are true.
e none of the above is true.

16 A surplus can be eliminated by

a increasing supply.
b government raising the price.
c decreasing the quantity demanded.
d allowing the price to fall.
e allowing the quantity bought and sold to fall.

17 A shortage is the amount by which quantity

a demanded exceeds quantity supplied.
b supplied exceeds quantity demanded.
c demanded increases when the price rises.
d demanded exceeds the equilibrium quantity.
e supplied exceeds the equilibrium quantity.

Predicting Changes in Price and Quantity

18 Which of the following will definitely cause an increase in the equilibrium price?

a an increase in both demand and supply
b a decrease in both demand and supply
c an increase in demand combined with a decrease in supply
d a decrease in demand combined with an increase in supply
e none of the above

19 Coffee is a normal good. A decrease in income will

a increase the price of coffee and increase the quantity demanded of coffee.
b increase the price of coffee and increase the quantity supplied of coffee.
c decrease the price of coffee and decrease the quantity demanded of coffee.
d decrease the price of coffee and decrease the quantity supplied of coffee.
e cause none of the above.

20 An increase in the price of Pepsi (a substitute for coffee) will

a increase the price of coffee and increase the quantity demanded of coffee.
b increase the price of coffee and increase the quantity supplied of coffee.
c decrease the price of coffee and decrease the quantity demanded of coffee.
d decrease the price of coffee and decrease the quantity supplied of coffee.
e cause none of the above.

21 A technological improvement lowers the cost of producing coffee. At the same time, preferences for coffee decrease. The *equilibrium quantity* of coffee will

a rise.
b fall.
c remain the same.
d rise or fall depending on whether the price of coffee falls or rises.
e rise or fall depending on the relative shifts of demand and supply curves.

22 Since 1980, there has been a dramatic increase in the number of working mothers. Based on this information alone, we can predict that the market for child-care services has experienced a(n)

a increase in demand.
b decrease in demand.
c increase in quantity demanded.
d decrease in quantity supplied.
e increase in supply.

23 If *A* and *B* are complementary goods (in consumption) and the cost of a resource used in the production of *A* decreases, then the price of

a both *A* and *B* will rise.
b both *A* and *B* will fall.
c *A* will fall and the price of *B* will rise.
d *A* will rise and the price of *B* will fall.
e *A* will fall and the price of *B* will remain unchanged.

24 The demand curve for knobs is $P = 75 - 6Q_D$ and the supply curve for knobs is $P = 35 + 2Q_S$. What is the equilibrium price of a knob?

a $5
b $10
c $40
d $45
e none of the above

25 The demand curve for tribbles is $P = 300 - 6Q_D$. The supply curve for tribbles is $P = 20 + 8Q_S$. If the price of a tribble was set at $120, the tribble market would experience

a equilibrium.
b excess demand causing a rise in price.
c excess demand causing a fall in price.
d excess supply causing a rise in price.
e excess supply causing a fall in price.

Short Answer Problems

1 Explain the difference between wants and demands.

2 The price of personal computers has continued to fall even in the face of increasing demand. Explain.

3 A tax on crude oil would raise the cost of the primary resource used in the production of gasoline. A proponent of such a tax has claimed that it will not raise the price of gasoline using the following argument. While the price of gasoline may rise initially, that price increase will cause the demand for gasoline to decrease, which will push the price back down. What is wrong with this argument?

4 Brussels sprouts and carrots are substitutes in consumption and, since they can both be grown on the same type of land, substitutes in production too. Suppose there is an increase in the demand for brussels sprouts. Trace the effects on price and quantity traded in both the brussels sprout and carrot markets. [Keep in mind Helpful Hint **4**.]

5 The information given in Table 3.1 is about the behaviour of buyers and sellers of fish at the market on a particular Saturday.

TABLE **3.1** DEMAND AND SUPPLY SCHEDULES FOR FISH

Price (per fish)	Quantity Demanded	Quantity Supplied
$0.50	280	40
$1.00	260	135
$1.50	225	225
$2.00	170	265
$2.50	105	290
$3.00	60	310
$3.50	35	320

a On graph paper, draw the demand curve and the supply curve. Be sure to label the axes. What is the equilibrium price?
b We will make the usual *ceteris paribus* assumptions about the demand curve so that it does not shift. List five factors that we are assuming do not change.
c We will also hold the supply curve constant by assuming that five factors do not change. List them.
d Explain briefly what would happen if the price was initially set at $3.00.

e Explain briefly what would happen if the price was initially set at $1.00.

f Explain briefly what would happen if the price was initially set at $1.50.

6 The market for wine in Canada is initially in equilibrium with supply and demand curves of the usual shape. Beer is a close substitute for wine; cheese and wine are complements. Use demand and supply diagrams to analyze the effect of each of the following (separate) events on the equilibrium price and quantity in the Canadian wine market. Assume that all of the *ceteris paribus* assumptions continue to hold except for the event listed. For both equilibrium price and quantity you should indicate in each case whether the variable rises, falls, remains the same, or moves ambiguously (may rise or fall).

a The income of consumers falls (wine is a normal good).

b Early frost destroys a large part of the world grape crop.

c A new churning invention reduces the cost of producing cheese.

d A new fermentation technique is invented that reduces the cost of producing wine.

e A new government study is published that links wine drinking and increased heart disease.

f Costs of producing both beer and wine increase dramatically.

7 A newspaper reported that "Despite a bumper crop of cherries this year, the price drop for cherries won't be as much as expected because of short supplies of plums and peaches."

a Use a demand and supply graph for the cherry market to explain the effect of the bumper crop alone.

b On the same graph, explain the impact on the cherry market of the short supplies of plums and peaches.

8 Table 3.2 lists the demand and supply schedules for cases of grape jam.

TABLE **3.2** DEMAND AND SUPPLY SCHEDULES FOR GRAPE JAM PER WEEK

Price (per case)	Quantity Demanded (cases)	Quantity Supplied (cases)
$70	20	140
$60	60	120
$50	100	100
$40	140	80
$30	180	60

a On the graph in Figure 3.2, draw the demand and supply curves for grape jam. Be sure to properly label the axes. Label the demand and supply curves D_0 and S_0 respectively.

FIGURE **3.2**

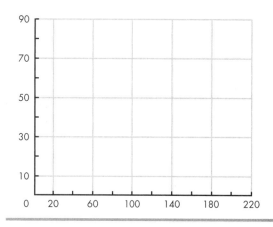

b What are the equilibrium price and quantity in the grape jam market? On your diagram, label the equilibrium point *a*.

c Is there a surplus or shortage at a price of $40? How much?

d The demand and supply schedules can also be represented by the following demand and supply equations:

Demand: $P = 75 - 0.25 Q_D$
Supply: $P = 0.5 Q_S$

Use these equations to solve for the equilibrium quantity (Q^*); equilibrium price (P^*). [*Hint*: Your answers should be the same as those in **8b**.]

e Suppose the population grows sufficiently that the demand for grape jam increases by 60 cases per week at every price.

i Construct a table (price, quantity demanded) of the new demand schedule.

ii Draw the new demand curve on your original graph and label it D_1.

iii Label the new equilibrium point *b*. What are the new equilibrium price and quantity?

iv What is the new demand equation? [*Hints*: What is the new slope? What is the new price-axis intercept?]

9 The demand equation for dweedles is

$$P = 8 - 1 Q_D$$

The supply equation for dweedles is

$$P = 2 + 1 Q_S$$

where P is the price of a dweedle in dollars, Q_D is the quantity of dweedles demanded, and Q_S is the quantity of dweedles supplied. The dweedle market is initially in equilibrium and income is $300.

a What is the equilibrium quantity (Q^*) of dweedles?

b What is the equilibrium price (P^*) of a dweedle?

c As a result of an increase in income to $500, the demand curve for dweedles shifts (the supply curve remains the same). The new demand equation is

$$P = 4 - 1Q_D$$

Use this information to calculate the new equilibrium quantity of dweedles; calculate the new equilibrium price of a dweedle.

d On the graph in Figure 3.3, draw and label: (1) the supply curve, (2) the initial demand curve, (3) the new demand curve.

e Are dweedles a normal or inferior good? How do you know?

FIGURE **3.3**

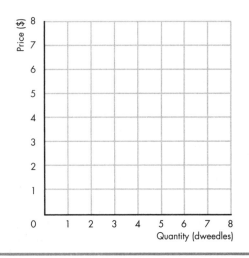

10 The demand equation for flubits is

$$P = 80 - 2Q_D$$

The supply equation for flubits is

$$P = 50 + 1Q_S$$

where P is the price of a flubit in dollars, Q_D is the quantity of flubits demanded, and Q_S is the quantity of flubits supplied. Assume that there are no changes in *ceteris paribus* assumptions.

a If the price of flubits was set at $56, calculate the exact surplus or shortage of flubits.

b Explain the adjustment process that will bring the situation above to equilibrium.

c What is the equilibrium quantity (Q^*) of flubits?

d What is the equilibrium price (P^*) of a flubit?

e Now assume that as a result of technological advance, the supply curve for flubits shifts (the demand curve remains the same). The new supply equation is

$$P = 20 + 1Q_S$$

Use this information to calculate the new equilibrium quantity of flubits; calculate the new equilibrium price of a flubit.

ANSWERS

True/False and Explain

1 F No single buyer or seller influences price. (60)

2 T Relative price is an opportunity cost. (60)

ⓒ **3 T** If money prices of other goods rise even more, a good's relative price falls. If price of gum rises from $1 to $2, but price of coffee rises from $1 to $4, opportunity cost of pack of gum falls from 1 to 0.5 coffee forgone. (60)

4 F As price rises, quantity demanded decreases. (61)

5 F Measures marginal benefit. (62)

6 T Combined meal of hamburger and fries now cheaper. (63)

ⓒ **7 F** Leftward shift for normal good, rightward shift for inferior good. (64)

8 F Supply curve shows minimum price at which last unit supplied. (67)

ⓒ **9 F** True if A and B substitutes in production, but false if substitutes in consumption. (68–69)

ⓒ **10 F** Beef and leather complements in production because produced together of necessity. (67–68)

11 T For complements in production, higher price for one good causes increased quantity supplied and increase in supply other good. (68–69)

12 F At $P >$ equilibrium P, there is surplus (quantity supplied > quantity demanded). (70–71)

13 F Higher expected future prices cause rightward shift demand and leftward shift supply. Price rises, but Δ quantity depends on relative magnitude shifts. (63–64, 68, 75)

14 T Increased number of firms causes rightward shift supply leading to fall in price and increased quantity. (73)

15 F Quantity will increase but Δ price depends on relative magnitude shifts in demand and supply. (75)

Multiple-Choice

1 **e** Definitions. (60)

2 **b** For example, higher-price fries causes decreased demand for hamburgers. (63)

ct **3** **c** Both income answers could be correct if commodity were normal (**a**) or inferior (**b**). (63–64)

4 **c** Other answers describe shifts of demand curve. (63–65)

5 **b** Changes in income shift demand curve rather than causing movement along demand curve. (64)

6 **d** Decreased quantity demanded is movement up along demand curve. Could also be caused by leftward shift supply. (64–65)

ct **7** **c** "Other things" shift demand curve. Only price can change along fixed demand curve. (65)

8 **a** Question describes movement down along supply curve. (66–67)

ct **9** **e** Answers **a**, **b**, and **c** shift demand, while **d** causes movement along supply curve. (67–69)

10 **a** Definition of substitute in production. (67–68)

11 **b** Higher price productive resource shifts supply leftward. (67–68)

12 **d** Other answers describe shifts of supply curve. (68–69)

13 **d** Definition of complements in production. Price changes related goods in consumption shift demand. (67–68)

14 **e** At equilibrium price, plans producers and consumers match; quantity demanded = quantity supplied. (70–71)

15 **d** All answers describe price above equilibrium price. (70–71)

16 **d** Other answers make surplus (excess quantity supplied) larger. (70–71)

17 **a** Shortage is horizontal distance between demand and supply curves at price below equilibrium price. (70–71)

18 **c** Answers **a** and **b** have indeterminate effect on price, while **d** causes lower price. (74–75)

19 **d** Demand shifts leftward. (72–73)

20 **b** Demand shifts rightward. (72–73)

21 **e** Supply shifts rightward, demand shifts leftward, price definitely falls. (75)

22 **a** More working mothers increases preferences for child care, causing increased demand for child-care services. (72–75)

ct **23** **c** Supply *A* shifts rightward causing lower-price *A*. This increases demand for *B*, causing higher price of *B*. (72–75)

ct **24** **d** See Helpful Hint **5**. Set demand equal to supply, solve for $Q^* = 5$. Substitute $Q^* = 5$ into either demand or supply equation to solve for P^*. (78–79)

ct **25** **b** At $P = \$120$, $Q_D = 30$, and $Q_S = 12.5$. Excess demand so price will rise. (71, 78–79)

Short Answer Problems

1 Wants are our unlimited desires for goods and services without regard to our ability or willingness to make the sacrifices necessary to obtain them. The existence of scarcity means that many of those wants will not be satisfied. On the other hand, if we demand something, then we want it, can afford it, and have made a definite plan to buy it. Demands reflect decisions about which wants to satisfy.

2 Due to the tremendous pace of technological advance, not only has the demand for personal computers been increasing, but the supply has been increasing as well. Indeed, supply has been increasing much more rapidly than demand, which has resulted in falling prices. Thus *much* (but not all) of the increase in sales of personal computers reflects a movement down along a demand curve rather than a shift in demand.

ct **3** This argument confuses a movement along an unchanging demand curve with a shift in the demand curve. The proper analysis is as follows. The increase in the price of oil (the primary resource in the production of gasoline) will shift the supply curve of gasoline leftward. This will cause the equilibrium price of gasoline to increase and thus the quantity demanded of gasoline will decrease. Demand itself will not decrease—that is, the demand curve will not shift. The decrease in supply causes a movement along an unchanged demand curve.

4 The answer to this question requires us to trace through the effects on the two graphs in Figure 3.4: (a) for the brussels sprout market and (b) for the carrot market. The sequence of effects occurs in order of the numbers on the graphs.

Look first at the market for brussels sprouts. The increase in demand shifts the demand curve rightward from D_0 to D_1 (1), and the price of brussels sprouts rises. This price rise has two effects (2) on the carrot market. Since brussels sprouts and carrots are substitutes in consumption, the demand curve for carrots shifts rightward from D_0 to D_1. And, since brussels sprouts and carrots are substitutes in production, the supply curve of carrots shifts leftward from S_0 to S_1. Both of these shifts in the carrot market raise the price of carrots, causing feedback effects on the brussels sprout market. But remember the rule (Helpful Hint **4**) that each curve (demand and supply) for a given market can shift a maximum of *once*. Since the demand curve for brussels sprouts has already shifted, we can only shift the supply curve from S_0 to S_1 (3) because of the substitutes in production relationship. Each curve in each market has now shifted once and the analysis must stop. We can predict that the net effects are increases in the equilibrium prices of both brussels sprouts and carrots, and indeterminate changes in the equilibrium quantities in both markets.

FIGURE **3.4**

(a) Brussel Sprout Market

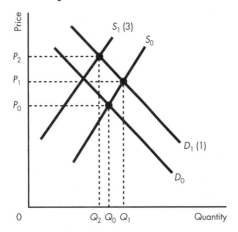

(b) Carrot Market

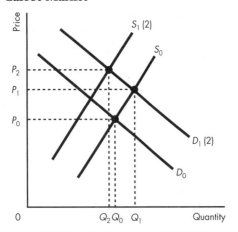

FIGURE **3.5**

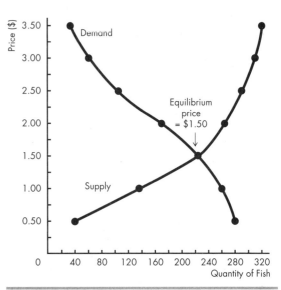

b Prices of related goods; expected future prices; income; population; preferences.

c Prices of productive resources; prices of related goods produced; expected future prices; number of suppliers; technology.

d At a price of $3.00, quantity supplied (310) exceeds quantity demanded (60). Fish sellers find themselves with surplus fish. Rather than be stuck with unsold fish (which yields no revenue), some sellers cut their price in an attempt to increase the quantity of fish demanded. Competition forces other sellers to follow suit, and the price falls until it reaches the equilibrium price of $1.50, while quantity demanded increases until it reaches the equilibrium quantity of 225 units.

e At a price of $1.00, the quantity demanded (260) exceeds the quantity supplied (135)—there is a shortage. Unrequited fish buyers bid up the price in an attempt to get the "scarce" fish. As prices continue to be bid up as long as there is excess demand, quantity supplied increases in response to higher prices. Price and quantity supplied both rise until they reach the equilibrium price ($1.50) and quantity (225 units).

f At a price of $1.50, the quantity supplied exactly equals the quantity demanded (225). There is no excess demand (shortage) or excess supply (surplus), and therefore no tendency for the price or quantity to change.

5 a The demand and supply curves are shown in Figure 3.5. The equilibrium price is $1.50 per fish.

6 The demand and supply diagrams for parts **a** to **e** are shown in Figure 3.6.

FIGURE **3.6**

(a)

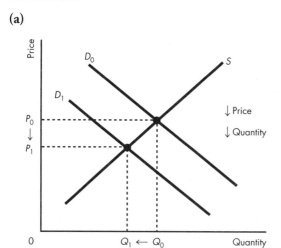

(b)

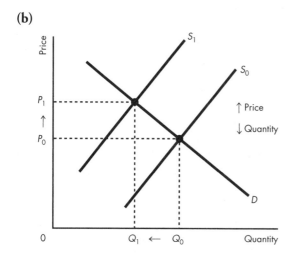

(c)

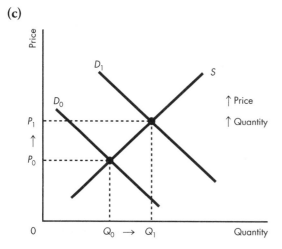

(d)

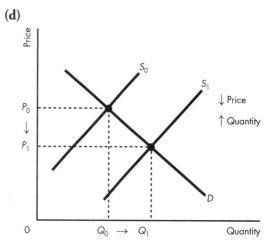

(e)

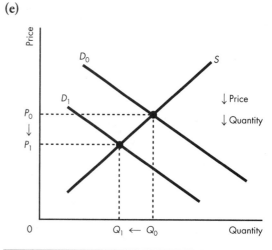

f Questions like this require the examination of two separate but related markets—the beer and wine markets. Since this kind of question often causes confusion for students, Figure 3.7 gives a more detailed explanation of the answer.

Look first at the beer market. The increase in the cost of beer production shifts the supply curve of beer leftward from S_0 to S_1. The resulting rise in the price of beer affects the wine market since beer and wine are substitutes (in consumption).

Turning to the wine market, there are two shifts to examine. The increase in beer prices causes the demand for wine to shift rightward from D_0 to D_1. The increase in the cost of wine production shifts the supply curve of wine leftward from S_0 to S_1. This is the end of the analysis, since the question only asks about the wine market. The final result is a rise in the equilibrium price of wine and an ambiguous change in the quantity of wine. Although the diagram shows $Q_1 = Q_0$, Q_1 may be $\geq$ or $\leq Q_0$.

FIGURE **3.7**

(a) Beer Market

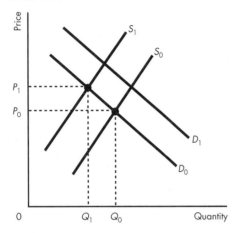

(b) Wine Market

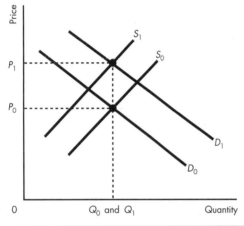

Many students rightfully ask, "But doesn't the rise in wine prices then shift the demand curve for beer rightward, causing a rise in beer prices and an additional increase in the demand for wine?" This question, which is correct in principle, is about the dynamics of adjustment, and these graphs are only capable of analyzing once-over shifts of demand or supply. We could shift the demand for beer rightward, but the resulting rise in beer prices would lead us to shift the demand for wine a *second time*. In practice, stick to the rule that each curve (demand and supply) for a given market can shift a maximum of *once*.

7 a The demand and supply curves for the cherry market are shown in Figure 3.8.

FIGURE **3.8**

Cherry Market

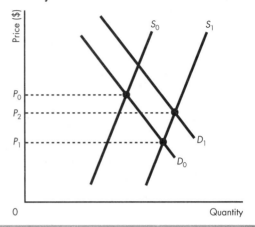

Suppose D_0 and S_0 represent the demand and supply curves for cherries last year. This year's bumper crop increases supply to S_1. Other things being equal, the price of cherries would fall from P_0 to P_1.

b But other things are not equal. Short supplies of plums and peaches (their supply curves have shifted leftward) drive up their prices. The increase in the prices of plums and peaches, which are substitutes in consumption for cherries, increases the demand for cherries to D_1. The net result is that the price of cherries only falls to P_2 instead of all the way to P_1.

8 a The demand and supply curves for grape jam are shown in Figure 3.2 Solution.

FIGURE **3.2** SOLUTION

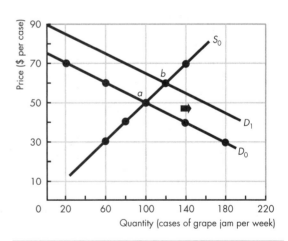

b The equilibrium is given at the intersection of the demand and supply curves (labelled point *a*). The equilibrium price is $50 per case and the equilibrium quantity is 100 cases per week.

c At a price of $40 there is a shortage of 60 cases per week.

d In equilibrium, the equations become:

Demand: $P^* = 75 - 0.25Q^*$
Supply: $P^* = 0.5Q^*$

To solve for Q^*, set demand equal to supply:

$$75 - 0.25Q^* = 0.5Q^*$$
$$75 = 0.75Q^*$$
$$100 = Q^*.$$

To solve for P^*, we can substitute Q^* into either the demand or supply equations. Look at demand first:

$$P^* = 75 - 0.25Q^*$$
$$P^* = 75 - 0.25(100)$$
$$P^* = 75 - 25$$
$$P^* = 50$$

Alternatively, substituting Q^* into the supply equation yields the same result:

$$P^* = 0.5Q^*$$
$$P^* = 0.5(100)$$
$$P^* = 50$$

e i Table 3.3 also contains the (unchanged) quantity supplied, for reference purposes.

TABLE **3.3** NEW DEMAND AND UNCHANGED SUPPLY SCHEDULES FOR GRAPE JAM PER WEEK

Price (per case)	Quantity Demanded (cases)	Quantity Supplied (cases)
$70	80	140
$60	120	120
$50	160	100
$40	200	80
$30	240	60

ii The graph of the new demand curve, D_1, is shown in Figure 3.2 Solution.

iii The new equilibrium price is $60 per case and the quantity is 120 cases of grape jam per week.

iv The new demand equation is $P = 90 - 0.25Q_D$. Notice that the slope of the new demand equation is the same as the slope of the original demand equation. An increase in demand of 60 cases at every price results in a rightward *parallel* shift of the demand curve.

Since the two curves are parallel, they have the same slope. The figure of 90 is the price-axis intercept of the new demand curve, which you can see on your graph. *Remember:* The demand equation is the equation of a straight line ($y = a + bx$)—in this case, $a = 90$.

If you want additional practice in the use of demand and supply equations for calculating equilibrium values of price and quantity, you can use the new demand curve equation together with the supply curve equation to calculate the answers you found in **e iii**.

9 In equilibrium, the equations become

Demand: $P^* = 8 - 1Q^*$
Supply: $P^* = 2 + 1Q^*$

a To solve for Q^*, set demand equal to supply:

$$8 - 1Q^* = 2 + 1Q^*$$
$$6 = 2Q^*$$
$$3 = Q^*$$

b To solve for P^*, we can substitute Q^* into either the demand or supply equations. Look first at demand:

$$P^* = 8 - 1Q^*$$
$$P^* = 8 - 1(3)$$
$$P^* = 8 - 3$$
$$P^* = 5$$

Alternatively, substituting Q^* into the supply equation yields the same result:

$$P^* = 2 + 1Q^*$$
$$P^* = 2 + 1(3)$$
$$P^* = 2 + 3$$
$$P^* = 5$$

c In equilibrium, the equations are

Demand: $P^* = 4 - 1Q^*$
Supply: $P^* = 2 + 1Q^*$

To solve for Q^*, set demand equal to supply:

$$4 - 1Q^* = 2 + 1Q^*$$
$$2 = 2Q^*$$
$$1 = Q^*$$

To solve for P^*, we can substitute Q^* into either the demand or supply equations. Look first at demand:

$$P^* = 4 - 1Q^*$$
$$P^* = 4 - 1(1)$$
$$P^* = 4 - 1$$
$$P^* = 3$$

Alternatively, substituting Q^* into the supply equation yields the same result:

$$P^* = 2 + 1Q^*$$
$$P^* = 2 + 1(1)$$
$$P^* = 2 + 1$$
$$P^* = 3$$

d The supply curve, initial demand curve, and new demand curve for dweedles are shown in Figure 3.3 Solution.

FIGURE **3.3** SOLUTION

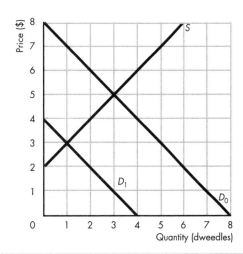

e Dweedles are an inferior good. An increase in income (from $300 to $500) caused a decrease in demand—the demand curve for dweedles shifted leftward.

10 a Substitute the price of $56 into the demand and supply equations to calculate the quantities demanded and supplied at that price. This is the mathematical equivalent of what you do on a graph when you identify a price on the vertical axis, move your eye across to the demand (or supply) curve, and then move your eye down to read the quantity on the horizontal axis.

Substituting into the demand equation, we find

$$P = 80 - 2Q_D$$
$$56 = 80 - 2Q_D$$
$$2Q_D = 24$$
$$Q_D = 12.$$

Substituting into the supply equation,

$$P = 50 + 1Q_S$$
$$56 = 50 + 1Q_S$$
$$6 = Q_S$$

Quantity demanded exceeds quantity supplied by 6 (12 − 6), so there is a shortage of 6 flubits.

b A shortage means the price was set below the equilibrium price. Competition between consumers for the limited number of flubits will bid up the price and increase the quantity supplied until we reach the equilibrium price and quantity.

c In equilibrium, the equations are

Demand: $P^* = 80 - 2Q^*$
Supply: $P^* = 50 + 1Q^*$

To solve for Q^*, set demand equal to supply:

$$80 - 2Q^* = 50 + 1Q^*$$
$$30 = 3Q^*$$
$$10 = Q^*$$

d To solve for P^*, substitute Q^* into the demand equation:

$$P^* = 80 - 2Q^*$$
$$P^* = 80 - 2(10)$$
$$P^* = 80 - 20$$
$$P^* = 60$$

You can check this answer yourself by substituting Q^* into the supply equation.

e The new equilibrium equations are

Demand: $P^* = 80 - 2Q^*$
Supply: $P^* = 20 + 1Q^*$

To solve for Q^*, set demand equal to supply:

$$80 - 2Q^* = 20 + 1Q^*$$
$$60 = 3Q^*$$
$$20 = Q^*$$

To solve for P^*, substitute Q^* into the supply equations:

$$P^* = 20 + 1Q^*$$
$$P^* = 20 + 1(20)$$
$$P^* = 20 + 20$$
$$P^* = 40$$

You can check this answer yourself by substituting Q^* into the demand equation.

Chapter 4

Elasticity

Price Elasticity of Demand

Price elasticity of demand (η) measures responsiveness of quantity demanded to change in price.

◆ η is units-free measure of responsiveness.

$$\eta = \left| \frac{\% \, \Delta \text{ quantity demanded}}{\% \, \Delta \text{ price}} \right| = \left| \frac{\Delta Q / Q_{ave}}{\Delta P / P_{ave}} \right|$$

◆ Elasticity is *not* equal to slope. Moving down along a linear demand curve, slope ($\Delta P / \Delta Q$) is constant but elasticity decreases as P_{ave} falls and Q_{ave} increases.

◆
When	*Demand Is*
$\eta = \infty$	**perfectly elastic** (horizontal)
$1 < \eta < \infty$	**elastic**
$\eta = 1$	**unit elastic**
$0 < \eta < 1$	**inelastic**
$\eta = 0$	**perfectly inelastic** (vertical)

Elasticity and **total revenue** ($P \times Q$)—the **total revenue test**:

◆
When Demand Is	*Price Cut Causes*
elastic ($\eta > 1$)	increased total revenue
unit elastic ($\eta = 1$)	no change total revenue
inelastic ($\eta < 1$)	decreased total revenue

Elasticity of demand depends on

◆ *closeness of substitutes*—closer substitutes for a good yield higher elasticity.

- Goods defined more narrowly have higher elasticity.
- Necessities generally have poor substitutes and inelastic demands.
- Luxuries generally have many substitutes and elastic demands.

◆ *proportion of income spent on good*—greater proportion of income spent on a good yields higher elasticity.

◆ *time elapsed since price change*—longer time elapsed yields higher elasticity.

- Short-run demand describes responsiveness to a change in price *before* sufficient time for all substitutions to be made.
- Long-run demand describes responsiveness to a change in price *after* sufficient time for all substitutions to be made.
- Short-run demand is usually less elastic than long-run demand.

More Elasticities of Demand

Cross elasticity of demand (η_x) measures the *responsiveness* of quantity demanded of good *A* to a change in price of good *B*.

◆ $\eta_x = \dfrac{\% \, \Delta \text{ quantity demanded good } A}{\% \, \Delta \text{ price good } B}$

◆
$\eta_x > 0$	Goods are substitutes
$\eta_x = 0$	Goods are independent
$\eta_x < 0$	Goods are complements

Income elasticity of demand (η_y) measures *responsiveness* of demand to change in income.

◆ $\eta_y = \dfrac{\% \, \Delta \text{ quantity demanded}}{\% \, \Delta \text{ income}}$

◆
When	*Demand Is*
$\eta_y > 1$	income elastic (normal good)
$0 < \eta_y < 1$	income inelastic (normal good)
$\eta_y < 0$	negative income elasticity (inferior good)

Elasticity of Supply

Elasticity of supply (η_s) measures *responsiveness* of quantity supplied to change in price.

♦ $\eta_s = \dfrac{\% \, \Delta \text{ quantity supplied}}{\% \, \Delta \text{ price}}$

♦
When	Supply Is
$\eta_s = \infty$	perfectly elastic (horizontal)
$1 < \eta_s < \infty$	elastic
$\eta_s = 1$	unit elastic
$0 < \eta_s < 1$	inelastic
$\eta_s = 0$	perfectly inelastic (vertical)

Elasticity of supply depends on

♦ *resources substitution possibilities*—the more common the productive resources used, the higher η_s.

♦ *time frame for supply decision*—the longer the time elapsed, from momentary to short-run to long-run supply, the higher η_s.

  • Momentary supply describes responsiveness of quantity supplied immediately following a price change.
  • Short-run supply describes responsiveness of quantity supplied to a price change when *some* technologically possible adjustments to production have been made.
  • Long-run supply describes responsiveness of quantity supplied to a price change when *all* technologically possible adjustments to production have been made.

HELPFUL HINTS

I   There are many elasticity formulae in this chapter, but they are all based on the same simple, intuitive principle—*responsiveness*. All of the demand and supply elasticity formulae measure the *responsiveness* (sensitivity) *of quantity* (demanded or supplied) to changes in something else. Thus percentage change in quantity is always in the numerator of the relevant formula. As you come to understand how quantity responds to changes in price, income, and prices of related goods, you will be able to work out each elasticity formula, even if you have temporarily forgotten it.

2   The complete formula (see Text Figure 4.2, page 85) for calculating the price elasticity of demand between two points on the demand curve is

$$\eta = \dfrac{\% \, \Delta \text{ quantity demanded}}{\% \, \Delta \text{ price}}$$

$$= \left| \left(\dfrac{\Delta Q}{Q_{ave}} \right) \Big/ \left(\dfrac{\Delta P}{P_{ave}} \right) \right|$$

The law of demand assures us that price and quantity demanded always move in opposite directions along any demand curve. Thus without the absolute value sign, the formula for the price elasticity of demand would yield a negative number. Because our main interest is in the *magnitude* of the response in quantity demanded to a change in price, for simplicity's sake we take the absolute value to guarantee a positive number. Whenever you see the often-used shorthand term, *elasticity* of demand, remember that it means the absolute value of the *price* elasticity of demand.

3   Elasticity is *not* the same as slope (although they are related). Along a straight-line demand curve the slope is constant, but the elasticity varies from infinity to zero as we move down the demand curve. To see why, look at the formula below, which is just a rearrangement of the elasticity formula in Helpful Hint **2**.

$$\eta = \left| \left(\dfrac{\Delta Q}{\Delta P} \right) \times \left(\dfrac{P_{ave}}{Q_{ave}} \right) \right|$$

The term in the first parentheses is simply the inverse of the slope. Since the slope is constant everywhere along a straight-line demand curve, so is the inverse of the slope. Consider, however, what happens to the term in the second parentheses as we move down the demand curve. At the "top" of the demand curve, P_{ave} is very large and Q_{ave} is very small, so the term in the second parentheses is large. As we move down the demand curve, P_{ave} becomes smaller and Q_{ave} becomes larger, so the term in the second parentheses falls in value. The net result is that the absolute value of the price elasticity of demand falls as we move down the demand curve.

4   One of the most practical and important uses of the concept of price elasticity of demand is that it allows us to predict the effect on total revenue of a change in price. A fall in price will increase total revenue if demand is elastic, leave total revenue unchanged if demand is unit elastic, and decrease total revenue if demand is inelastic. Because price and quantity demanded always move in opposite directions along a demand curve, a fall in price will cause an increase in

quantity demanded. Since total revenue equals price times quantity, the fall in price will tend to decrease total revenue, while the increase in quantity demanded will increase total revenue. The net effect depends on which of these individual effects is larger.

The concept of price elasticity of demand conveniently summarizes the net effect. For example, if demand is elastic, the percentage change in quantity demanded is greater than the percentage change in price. Hence, with a fall in price, the quantity effect dominates and total revenue will increase. If, however, demand is inelastic, the percentage change in quantity demanded is less than the percentage change in price. Hence, with a fall in price, the price effect dominates and total revenue will decrease.

5 Two other important elasticity concepts are the income elasticity of demand and the cross elasticity of demand.

Income elasticity of demand:

$$\eta_y = \frac{\% \ \Delta \ \text{quantity demanded}}{\% \ \Delta \ \text{income}}$$

$$= \left(\frac{\Delta Q}{Q_{ave}} \right) \bigg/ \left(\frac{\Delta Y}{Y_{ave}} \right)$$

Cross-elasticity of demand:

$$\eta_x = \frac{\% \ \Delta \ \text{quantity demanded good } A}{\% \ \Delta \ \text{price good } B}$$

$$= \left(\frac{\Delta Q^A}{Q^A_{ave}} \right) \bigg/ \left(\frac{\Delta P^B}{P^B_{ave}} \right)$$

Notice that these two elasticity formulas do *not* have absolute value signs and can take on either positive or negative values. While these formulae measure responsiveness, both the magnitude *and the direction* of the response are important. In the case of income elasticity of demand, the response of quantity demanded to an increase in income will be positive for a normal good and negative for an inferior good. In the case of cross elasticity of demand, the response of the quantity demanded of good A to an increase in the price of good B will be positive if the goods are substitutes and negative if the goods are complements.

In calculating an income elasticity or a cross elasticity, be alert to the fact that the *price of the good in the numerator* of the formula *is assumed constant.* Income elasticity measures the quantity response to a change in income, *ceteris paribus.* Cross elasticity measures the quantity response of good A to a change in the price of good B,

ceteris paribus. This means that we cannot simply read numerical values for calculating these elasticities from the equilibrium positions of a set of demand and supply curves. For example, when income increases, demand shifts rightward (for a normal good), and the new equilibrium quantity will also have a higher equilibrium price. To calculate income elasticity correctly, we compare the income and quantity demanded of the initial equilibrium with the new income and quantity demanded. To obtain the correct new quantity demanded, we must use the new demand curve, but must calculate the quantity demanded that would have prevailed at the *initial,* unchanged price. (See Short Answer Problems **9** and **10** for examples.)

SELF-TEST

True/False and Explain

Price Elasticity of Demand

1 The price elasticity of demand measures how responsive prices are to changes in demand.

2 Price elasticity of demand is constant along a linear demand curve.

3 If a decrease in supply causes total revenue to increase, then demand must be inelastic.

4 If a 9 percent increase in price leads to a 5 percent decrease in quantity demanded, total revenue has decreased.

5 If you like Pepsi Cola and Coca-Cola about the same, your demand for Pepsi is likely to be elastic.

6 The more narrowly we define a good, the more elastic its demand.

7 If your expenditures on toothpaste are a small proportion of your total income, your demand for toothpaste is likely to be inelastic.

8 The demand for gasoline is likely to become more inelastic with the passage of time after a price increase.

More Elasticities of Demand

9 An inferior good has a negative cross elasticity of demand.

10 If a 10 percent increase in the price of widgets causes a 6 percent increase in the quantity of woozles demanded, then widgets and woozles must be complements.

11 We would expect a negative cross elasticity of demand between hamburgers and hamburger buns.

Elasticity of Supply

12 Elasticity of supply equals the change in quantity supplied divided by the change in price.

13 A horizontal supply curve is perfectly elastic.

14 Goods produced with rare resources have a low elasticity of supply.

15 Supply is generally more inelastic in the long run than in the short run.

Multiple-Choice

Price Elasticity of Demand

1 There are two points on the demand curve for volleyballs, as shown in Table 4.1.

TABLE **4.1**

Price per Volleyball	Quantity Demanded
$19	55
$21	45

What is the elasticity of demand between these two points?

a 2.5
b 2.0
c 0.5
d 0.4
e none of the above

2 If the price elasticity of demand is 2, then a 1 percent decrease in price will

a double the quantity demanded.
b reduce the quantity demanded by half.
c increase the quantity demanded by 2 percent.
d reduce the quantity demanded by 2 percent.
e increase the quantity demanded by 0.5 percent.

3 If price elasticity of demand is zero, then as the price falls

a total revenue does not change.
b quantity demanded does not change.
c quantity demanded falls to zero.
d total revenue increases from zero.
e none of the above occurs.

4 A perfectly vertical demand curve has a price elasticity of

a zero.
b greater than zero but less than one.
c one.
d greater than one.
e infinity.

5 A union leader who claims that "higher wages increase living standards without causing unemployment" believes that the demand for labour is

a income elastic.
b income inelastic.
c perfectly elastic.
d perfectly inelastic.
e unit elastic.

6 Business people talk about price elasticity of demand without using the actual term. Which of the following statements reflect elastic demand for a product?

a "A price cut won't help me. It won't increase sales, and I'll just get less money for each unit that I was selling before."

b "I don't think a price cut will make any difference to my bottom line. What I may gain from selling more I would lose on the lower price."

c "My customers are real bargain hunters. Since I set my prices just a few cents below my competitors', customers have flocked to the store and sales are booming."

d "With the recent economic recovery, people have more income to spend and sales are booming, even at the same prices as before."

e None of the above.

7 A technological breakthrough lowers the cost of photocopiers. If the demand for photocopiers is price inelastic, we predict that photocopier sales will

a fall and total revenue will rise.

b fall and total revenue will fall.

c rise and total revenue will rise.

d rise and total revenue will fall.

e rise but changes in total revenue will depend on elasticity of supply.

8 A decrease in tuition fees will decrease the university's total revenue if the price elasticity of demand for university education is

a negative.

b greater than zero but less than one.

c equal to one.

d greater than one.

e less than the price elasticity of supply.

9 If the demand for orange juice is price elastic, then a severe frost that destroys large quantities of oranges will likely

a reduce the equilibrium price of juice, but increase total consumer spending on it.

b reduce the equilibrium quantity of juice as well as total consumer spending on it.

c reduce both the equilibrium quantity and the price of juice.

d increase the equilibrium price of juice as well as total consumer spending on it.

e increase the equilibrium price of juice, but leave total consumer spending on it constant.

10 If a 4 percent rise in the price of peanut butter causes total revenue to fall by 8 percent, then demand for peanut butter

a is elastic.

b is inelastic.

c is unit elastic.

d has an elasticity of 1/2.

e has an elasticity of 2.

11 Tina and Brian work for the same recording company. Tina claims that they would be better off by increasing the price of their CDs while Brian claims that they would be better off by decreasing the price. We can conclude that

a Tina thinks the demand for CDs has price elasticity of zero, and Brian thinks price elasticity equals one.

b Tina thinks the demand for CDs has price elasticity equal to one, and Brian thinks price elasticity equals zero.

c Tina thinks the demand for CDs is price elastic, and Brian thinks it is price inelastic.

d Tina thinks the demand for CDs is price inelastic and Brian thinks it is price elastic.

e Tina and Brian should stick to singing and forget about economics.

12 Given the relationship shown in Figure 4.1 between total revenue from the sale of a good and the quantity of the good sold, then

a this is an inferior good.

b this is a normal good.

c the elasticity of demand is zero.

d the elasticity of demand is infinity.

e the elasticity of demand is one.

FIGURE **4.1**

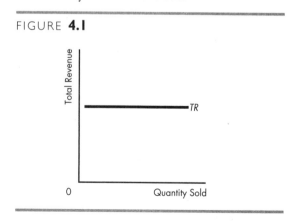

13 If the Jets decrease ticket prices and find that total revenue does not change, then the price elasticity of demand for tickets is

a zero.
b greater than zero, but less than one.
c equal to one.
d greater than one.
e inferior.

14 The fact that butter has margarine as a close substitute in consumption

a makes the supply of butter more elastic.
b makes the supply of butter less elastic.
c makes the demand for butter more elastic.
d makes the demand for butter less elastic.
e does not affect butter's elasticity of supply or demand.

15 A given percentage increase in the price of a good is likely to cause a larger percentage decline in quantity demanded

a the shorter the passage of time.
b the larger the proportion of income spent on it.
c the harder it is to obtain good substitutes.
d all of the above.
e none of the above.

More Elasticities of Demand

16 A negative value for

a price elasticity of supply implies an upward-sloping supply curve.
b cross elasticity of demand implies complementary goods.
c price elasticity of demand implies an inferior good.
d income elasticity of demand implies a normal good.
e income elasticity of demand implies an error in your calculation.

17 The cross elasticity of the demand for white tennis balls with respect to the price of yellow tennis balls is probably

a negative and high.
b negative and low.
c positive and high.
d positive and low.
e zero.

18 If a 10 percent increase in income causes a 5 percent increase in quantity demanded (at a constant price), what is the income elasticity of demand?

a 0.5
b −0.5
c 2.0
d −2.0
e none of the above

19 Luxury goods tend to have income elasticities of demand that are

a greater than one.
b greater than zero but less than one.
c positive.
d negative.
e first positive and then negative as income increases.

20 If a 4 percent decrease in income (at a constant price) causes a 2 percent decrease in the consumption of dweedles, then

a the income elasticity of demand for dweedles is negative.
b dweedles are a necessity and a normal good.
c dweedles are a luxury and a normal good.
d dweedles are an inferior good.
e **a** and **d** are true.

Elasticity of Supply

21 When price goes from $1.50 to $2.50, quantity supplied increases from 9,000 to 11,000 units. What is the price elasticity of supply?

a 0.4
b 0.8
c 2.5
d 4.0
e none of the above

22 Preferences for brussels sprouts increase. The price of brussels sprouts will not change if the price elasticity of

a demand is 0.
b demand is 1.
c supply is 0.
d supply is 1.
e supply is infinity.

23 A sudden end-of-summer heat wave increases the demand for air conditioners and catches suppliers with no reserve inventories. The momentary supply curve for air conditioners is

a perfectly elastic.

b perfectly inelastic.

c elastic.

d upward-sloping.

e horizontal.

24 The long-run supply curve is likely to be

a more elastic than momentary supply, but less elastic than short-run supply.

b less elastic than momentary supply, but more elastic than short-run supply.

c less elastic than both momentary and short-run supply curves.

d more elastic than both momentary and short-run supply curves.

e vertical.

25 Long-run elasticity of supply of a good is greater than short-run elasticity of supply because

a more substitutes in consumption for the good can be found.

b more complements in consumption for the good can be found.

c more technological ways of adjusting supply can be exploited.

d income rises with more elapsed time.

e the long-run supply curve is steeper.

Short Answer Problems

1 Why is elasticity superior to slope as a measure of the responsiveness of quantity demanded to changes in price?

2 In each of the following, compare the price elasticity of demand for each pair of goods and explain why the demand for one of the goods is more elastic than demand for the other.

a IBM personal computers before the development of other "clone" personal computers versus IBM personal computers after the production of such clones

b television sets versus matches

c electricity just after an increase in its price versus electricity two years after the price increase

d acetaminophen versus Tylenol-brand acetaminophen

3 Why does supply tend to be more elastic in the long run?

4 In Figure 4.2, which demand curve (D_A or D_B) is more elastic in the price range P_1 to P_2? Explain why. [*Hint:* Use the formula for price elasticity of demand.]

FIGURE **4.2**

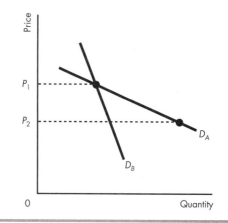

5 Consider the demand curve in Figure 4.3(a). A portion of the demand curve is also described by the demand schedule in Table 4.2.

FIGURE **4.3**

(a)

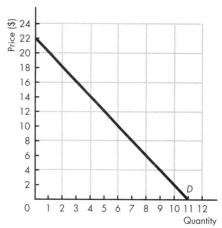

(b)

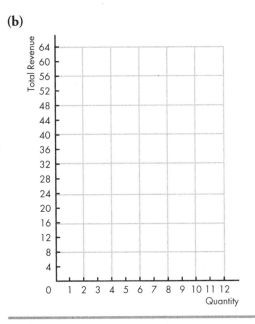

TABLE **4.2**

Price ($)	Quantity Demanded	Total Revenue
22	0	
20	1	
18	2	
16	3	
14	4	
12	5	
10	6	
8	7	
6	8	

Fill in the numbers for total revenue in the last column of Table 4.2, and graph your results on Figure 4.3(b). Describe the shape of the total revenue curve as quantity increases (price decreases).

6 Using the same information for the demand curve in Short Answer Problem **5**:

a Complete the second and third columns of Table 4.3: η (the price elasticity of demand) and ΔTR (the change in total revenue) as the price falls from the higher price to the lower price. Describe the relationship between elasticity and change in total revenue as price falls (moving down the demand curve).

TABLE **4.3**

ΔP ($)	η	ΔTR ($)	η'	$\Delta TR'$ ($)
16 — 14				
14 — 12				
12 — 10				
10 — 8				
8 — 6				

b Suppose income increases from $10,000 to $14,000, causing an increase in demand: at every price, quantity demanded increases by 2 units. Draw the new demand curve on Figure 4.3(a) and label it D'. Use this new demand curve to complete the last two columns of Table 4.3 for η' (the new price elasticity of demand) and $\Delta TR'$ (the new change in total revenue).

c Using the price range between $16 and $14, explain why D' is more inelastic than D.

d Calculate the income elasticity of demand, assuming the price remains constant at $12. Is this a normal or inferior good? Explain why you could have answered the question even without calculating the income elasticity of demand.

7 The demand equation for woozles is $P = 60 - 2Q_D$. The supply equation for woozles is $P = 32 + 5Q_S$, where P is the price of a woozle in dollars, Q_D is the quantity of woozles demanded, and Q_S is the quantity of woozles supplied.

a Calculate the price elasticity of demand for woozles between $Q_D = 4$ and $Q_D = 6$.

b Initially, the woozle market is in equilibrium with $P^* = 52$ and $Q^* = 4$. Then, the supply curve shifts (the demand curve remains constant) yielding a new equilibrium price of $P^* = 48$.

Using all of the relevant information above, show *two separate methods* for determining whether total revenue increases, decreases, or remains constant in moving from the initial equilibrium to the new equilibrium.

8 Suppose Jean loses his present job and his monthly income falls from $10,000 to $6,000, while his monthly purchases of grits increase from 200 to 400.

a Calculate his income elasticity of demand for grits.

b Are grits a normal or inferior good? Explain why.

9 The demand equation for tribbles is
$P = 50 - 1Q_D$. The supply equation for tribbles
is $P = 20 + 0.5Q_S$, where P is the price of a
tribble in dollars, Q_D is the quantity of tribbles
demanded, and Q_S is the quantity of tribbles
supplied. The tribble market is initially in
equilibrium, and income is $180.

a What is the equilibrium quantity (Q^*) of
tribbles?

b What is the equilibrium price (P^*) of a tribble?

c As a result of a decrease in income to $120, the
demand curve for tribbles shifts (the supply
curve remains the same). The new demand
equation is:

$$P = 110 - 1Q_D$$

Use this information to calculate the new
equilibrium quantity of tribbles; calculate the
new equilibrium price of a tribble.

d Calculate the income elasticity of demand for
tribbles. Are tribbles a normal or inferior good?
[*Hint*: In your calculation be sure to: (1) use the
information about the *initial* equilibrium
conditions (price, quantity, and income) and
(2) keep in mind that price is assumed *constant*
in calculating income elasticity. Only income
and quantity change.]

10 Table 4.4 gives the demand schedules for good A
when the price of good B (P_B) is $8 and $12.
Complete the last column of the table by
computing the cross elasticity of demand
between goods A and B for each of the three
prices of A. Are A and B complements or
substitutes?

TABLE **4.4** DEMAND SCHEDULES FOR
GOOD A

P_A	$P_B = \$8$ Q_A	$P_B = \$12$ Q'_A	η_x
$8	2,000	4,000	
$7	4,000	6,000	
$6	6,000	8,000	

A N S W E R S

True/False and Explain

1 **F** Responsiveness quantity demanded to ΔP.
(84)

2 **F** Slope constant; η falls as move down demand
curve. (87)

3 **T** Decreased S causes increased P and increased
total revenue, so demand inelastic. (88)

4 **F** (% increase P) > (% decrease Q), so total
revenue ($P \times Q$) increases. (88)

5 **T** Colas are substitutes for you. (89)

6 **T** With narrower definition, more substitutes.
(89)

7 **T** Lower proportion income spent on good,
more inelastic demand. (90)

8 **F** Elasticity increases with elapsed time. (90)

9 **F** Inferior good has negative income elasticity;
cross elasticity sign depends on whether
substitute or complement. (91–92)

10 **F** η_x positive so goods are substitutes. (91–92)

11 **T** η_x negative for complements. (91–92)

12 **F** η_s equals *percentage* change in quantity
supplied divided by *percentage* change in
price. (94)

13 **T** η_s = infinity. (95)

14 **T** η_s < 1. (95)

15 **F** Supply more elastic in long run. (96)

Multiple-Choice

1 **b** $|(-10/50)/(2/20)| = 2$. (85–86)

2 **c** $\eta = |(\% \Delta Q_D)/(\% \Delta P)| = |(1/5)/(1/10)| = 2$.
Q_D and P always inversely related on demand
curve. (85–86)

3 **b** Demand curve vertical so lower P does not
Δ quantity demanded. (86–87)

4 **a** Definition. (86–87)

5 **d** Labour demand curve would be vertical.
(86–87)

6 **c** Small fall P causes large increase quantity
demanded. **a** inelastic, **b** unit elastic, **d** on
income elasticity. (86–87)

7 **d** Rightward shift supply causes increased
quantity sold and lower P; with inelastic
demand causes decreased total revenue. (88)

8 **b** Lower P causes decreased total revenue when
η < 1. η never negative. (88)

9 **b** Decreased S causes decreased Q_D and higher
P. Since η > 1, higher P causes decreased
expenditure. (88)

ct **10** **a** If higher P causes decreased total revenue,
then η must be > 1. Must know (% ΔQ_D) to
precisely calculate η. (88)

11 **d** Better off means increased total revenue. By
definition of relation between higher P, η,
and total revenue. (88)

ct **12** **e** Note total revenue (*TR*) on y-axis. Since *TR*
constant as increased Q (and presumably
lower P), η = 1. **a**, **b** depend on η_y. (88)

13 **c** Total revenue test. (88)

14 c Closer substitutes yield higher elasticity demand. (89)

15 b η increases with increased proportion income spent on good. η increases when longer time passage and easier to obtain substitutes. (89–90)

16 b η_s and η never negative. η_y negative for inferior good. (91–92)

17 c Close substitutes so η_x positive and very elastic (high). (91)

18 a $\eta_y = (\% \Delta Q_D)/(\% \Delta$ income$) = 5/10 = 0.5$. (92)

19 a See answer to **20** below. **c** correct, but **a** best answer. (92–93)

20 b $\eta_y > 0$ so normal good. Necessities tend to have $\eta_y < 1$, while luxuries tend to have $\eta_y > 1$. (92–93)

21 a $\eta_s = (\% \Delta Q_S)/(\% \Delta P) = (2,000/10,000)/(1/2) = 0.4$. (94–95)

22 e Increased D causes no ΔP if supply curve horizontal ($\eta_s =$ infinity). (94–95)

23 b Definition. (96)

24 d Definition. Momentary supply curve most vertical. (96)

25 c Definition. **a, b, d** affect demand, not supply. Long-run supply curve flatter than short-run. (95–96)

Short Answer Problems

1 The slope of a demand curve tells us how much quantity demanded changes when price changes. However, the numerical value of the slope depends on the units we use to measure price and quantity and will change if the unit of measure is changed even though demand is unchanged. For example, if we change the unit of measure for quantity from tonnes to kilograms, the new slope of the (same) demand curve will be 1,000 times the old slope. On the other hand, elasticity gives a unit-free measure of the responsiveness of quantity demanded to price changes.

2 a The demand for IBM personal computers will be more elastic after the production of clone personal computers since there would then be more readily available substitutes.

b The demand for television sets will be more elastic since they will generally take a larger proportion of consumer income.

c The demand for electricity after the passage of two years will be more elastic since consumers will have more time to find substitutes for electricity, for example a gas stove.

d The demand for Tylenol is more elastic. There are far more substitutes for Tylenol (other brands of acetaminophen) than for acetaminophen in general.

3 Supply is more elastic in the long run because the passage of time allows producers to find better (more efficient) ways of producing that are not available in the short run. The responsiveness of production to an increase in price will increase as firms have time to discover and implement new technologies or to increase the scale of operation.

4 D_A is more elastic than D_B. To see why, look at the formula for price elasticity of demand:

$$\eta = \left| \frac{\% \Delta \text{ quantity demanded}}{\% \Delta \text{ price}} \right|$$

The percentage change in price is the same for the two demand curves. But the percentage change in quantity is greater for D_A. At P_1, the initial quantity demanded is the same for both demand curves (Q_1). With the fall in price to P_2, the increase in quantity demanded is greater for D_A (to Q_{2A}) than for D_B (to Q_{2B}). Therefore D_A is more elastic than D_B.

FIGURE **4.2** SOLUTION

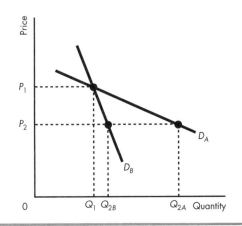

5 The numbers for total revenue are shown in Table 4.2 Solution. The total revenue curve is shown in Figure 4.3(b) Solution. The total revenue curve first increases (at a diminishing rate—its slope is decreasing as we move up the curve), then reaches a maximum between $Q = 5$ and $Q = 6$, and then decreases. We will encounter this pattern of changing total revenue again in studying monopoly in Chapter 12.

TABLE **4.2** SOLUTION

Price ($)	Quantity Demanded	Total Revenue
22	0	0
20	1	20
18	2	36
16	3	48
14	4	56
12	5	60
10	6	60
8	7	56
6	8	48

FIGURE **4.3(a)** SOLUTION

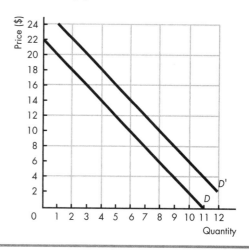

FIGURE **4.3(b)** SOLUTION

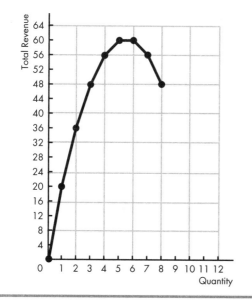

6 a The completed columns of Table 4.3 are shown here. The second and third columns of the table show that as price falls, total revenue increases when demand is elastic; total revenue remains constant when demand is unit elastic; total revenue falls when demand is inelastic.

TABLE **4.3** SOLUTION

ΔP ($)	η	ΔTR ($)	η′	ΔTR′ ($)
16 — 14	2.14	+8	1.36	+4
14 — 12	1.44	+4	1.00	0
12 — 10	1.00	0	0.73	−4
10 — 8	0.69	−4	0.53	−8
8 — 6	0.47	−8	0.37	−12

b The new demand curve is labelled D′ in Figure 4.3(a) Solution. The last two columns of the table have been completed on the basis of the new demand curve.

c Since they are parallel, D′ and D have exactly the same slope. Thus we know that for a given change in price, the change in quantity demanded will be the same for the two curves. However, elasticity is determined by *percentage* changes, and the percentage change in quantity demanded is different for the two curves, although the percentage change in price will be the same. For a given percentage change in price, the percentage change in quantity demanded will always be less for D′. For example, as the price falls from $16 to $14 (a 13 percent change), the quantity demanded increases from 5 to 6 units along D′, but from 3 to 4 along D. The percentage change in quantity demanded is only 18 percent along D′ and 29 percent along D. Since the percentage change in price is the same for both curves, D′ is more inelastic than D.

d Income increases from $10,000 to $14,000. At a constant price of $12, the increase in income, which shifts out the demand curve to D′, increases the quantity consumers will demand from 5 units to 7 units. Substituting these numbers into the formula for the income elasticity of demand yields

$$\eta_y = \left(\frac{\Delta Q}{Q_{ave}}\right) \Big/ \left(\frac{\Delta Y}{Y_{ave}}\right)$$

$$= \left(\frac{2}{6}\right) \Big/ \left(\frac{4,000}{12,000}\right) = +1$$

The income elasticity of demand is a positive number, since both ΔQ and ΔY are positive. Therefore this is a normal good. We already knew that from the information in part **b**, which stated that the demand curve shifted rightward with an increase in income. If this were an inferior good, the increase in income would have shifted the demand curve leftward and the income elasticity of demand would have been negative.

7 a In order to calculate price elasticity of demand, we need to know two points (each point a combination of price and quantity demanded) on the demand curve. We only are given the quantity demanded coordinate of each point. By substituting $Q_D = 4$ and $Q_D = 6$ into the demand equation, we can solve for the two price coordinates:

At $Q_D = 4$; $P = 60 - 2(4) = 52$
At $Q_D = 6$; $P = 60 - 2(6) = 48$

These price and quantity demanded coordinates can now be substituted into the formula for the price elasticity of demand:

$$\eta = \left| \left(\frac{\Delta Q}{Q_{ave}}\right) \middle/ \left(\frac{\Delta P}{P_{ave}}\right) \right|$$

$$= \left| \left(\frac{-2}{5}\right) \middle/ \left(\frac{4}{50}\right) \right| = 5$$

b One method is simply to compare total revenue ($P \times Q$) at each equilibrium:

- *Initial equilibrium:*
  Total revenue = ($P \times Q$) = (52 × 4) = 208.

- *New equilibrium:*
  If $P^* = 48$, Q^* can be calculated by substituting P^* into the demand equation:

$$48 = 60 - 2Q^*$$
$$2Q^* = 12$$
$$Q^* = 6$$

So total revenue = ($P \times Q$) = (48 × 6) = 288. In moving from the initial to the new equilibrium, total revenue has increased.

A second method is to use the information from part **a** on the price elasticity of demand. We know that between $Q_D = 4$ and $Q_D = 6$ on the demand curve, demand is elastic. These two points correspond to the initial equilibrium and, after the shift of the supply curve, the new equilibrium. Since demand here is elastic, we know that the fall in price from $P = 52$ to $P = 48$ will increase total revenue.

8 a Using the formula for income elasticity of demand:

$$\eta_y = \left(\frac{\Delta Q}{Q_{ave}}\right) \middle/ \left(\frac{\Delta Y}{Y_{ave}}\right)$$

$$= \left(\frac{200 - 400}{\frac{1}{2}(200 + 400)}\right) \middle/ \left(\frac{10,000 - 6,000}{\frac{1}{2}(10,000 + 6,000)}\right)$$

$$= \left(\frac{-200}{300}\right) \middle/ \left(\frac{4,000}{8,000}\right) = -\frac{4}{3}$$

b Grits are an inferior good because the income elasticity of demand is negative.

9 a The initial equilibrium quantity (Q^*) of tribbles is 20. (Refer to *Study Guide* Chapter 3 if you need help in solving demand and supply equations.)

b The initial equilibrium price (P^*) of a tribble is $30. (Refer to *Study Guide* Chapter 3 if you need help in solving demand and supply equations.)

c The new equilibrium quantity of tribbles is 60. The new equilibrium price of a tribble is $50.

d At the initial income of $180 and price of $30, the quantity of tribbles demanded is 20. In order to find the new quantity demanded at income of $120, we have to use the new demand equation. But since *price* is assumed constant in calculating income elasticity, we have to substitute $P = 30$ into the new demand equation to get the appropriate new quantity. It would be *incorrect* to use the new equilibrium quantity, because that quantity corresponds to a *different price* ($50).

$$P = 110 - 1Q_D$$
$$30 = 110 - 1Q_D$$
$$Q_D = 80$$

We now have appropriate information about the initial quantity demanded (20) and income ($180), and about the new quantity demanded (80) and income ($120). Substituting this information into the formula for income elasticity of demand yields

$$\eta_y = \left(\frac{\Delta Q}{Q_{ave}}\right) \middle/ \left(\frac{\Delta Y}{Y_{ave}}\right)$$

$$= \left(\frac{-60}{50}\right) \middle/ \left(\frac{60}{150}\right) = -3$$

Since the income elasticity of demand for tribbles is negative, tribbles are an inferior good.

10 The cross elasticities of demand between A and B are listed in Table 4.4 Solution. Since the cross elasticities are positive, we know that A and B are substitutes.

TABLE **4.4** SOLUTION
DEMAND SCHEDULES FOR GOOD A

	$P_B = \$8$	$P_B = \$12$	
P_A	Q_A	Q'_A	η_x
$8	2,000	4,000	1.67
$7	4,000	6,000	1.00
$6	6,000	8,000	0.71

Efficiency and Equity

Efficiency: A Refresher

Efficient allocation:

◆ Efficient allocation produces goods and services most highly valued.

◆ Efficient allocation cannot produce more goods and services without giving up more highly valued goods and services.

Marginal benefit—maximum amount a person is willing to pay for one more unit of a good or service.

◆ Principle of decreasing marginal benefit—marginal benefit decreases as quantity consumed increases.

Marginal cost—opportunity cost of producing one more unit of a good or service.

◆ Principle of increasing marginal cost—marginal cost increases as quantity produced increases.

An efficient allocation of resources occurs only when marginal benefit equals marginal cost.

Value, Price, and Consumer Surplus

Value is what consumers are willing to pay; price is what consumers actually pay.

◆ Demand curve is a marginal benefit curve.

  • marginal benefit = value = maximum willing to pay for additional unit.

◆ **Consumer surplus** is the value of a good minus its price. It is the triangular area under the demand curve, but above market price (see Text Figure 5.3, page 107).

Cost, Price, and Producer Surplus

Opportunity cost is what producers pay; price is what producers receive.

◆ Supply curve is a marginal cost curve.

  • marginal cost = minimum producers must receive to produce additional unit.

◆ **Producer surplus** is the price of a good minus its opportunity cost of production.

◆ Producer surplus is the triangular area below market price, but above the supply curve (see Text Figure 5.5, page 109).

Is the Competitive Market Efficient?

In competitive equilibrium

◆ marginal benefit = marginal cost.

◆ resource allocation is efficient.

◆ sum of consumer surplus and producer surplus is maximized.

Obstacles to efficient resource allocation:

◆ Price ceilings, price floors, taxes, subsidies, quotas (Ch. 6).

◆ *Monopolies*—firms that restrict output and raise price (Ch. 12).

  • Monopolies create **deadweight loss**—total social loss of consumer surplus and producer surplus below efficient levels.

◆ *Public goods*—consumed simultaneously by all, even if they don't pay for it (Ch. 16).

  • Competitive markets produce less than the efficient quantity of public goods because of the free-rider problem.

◆ *External costs*—costs not borne by producer but by others (Ch. 18).

  • Competitive markets produce too large a quantity of goods and services that have external costs.

◆ *External benefits*—benefits not accruing to buyer of a good but to others (Ch. 18).

  • Competitive markets produce too small a quantity of goods and services that have external benefits.

Is the Competitive Market Fair?

Ideas about fairness divide into two approaches:

◆ Fair results—there should be equality of incomes.

  • **Utilitarianism**—result should be "greatest happiness for the greatest number." Requires income transfers from rich to poor.
  • Income transfers create the "**big tradeoff**" between efficiency and fairness. Transfers use scarce resources and weaken incentives, so a more equally shared pie results in a smaller pie.
  • Modified utilitarianism—after incorporating costs of income transfers, result should make the poorest person as well off as possible.

◆ Fair rules—people in similar situations should be treated similarly:

  • **Symmetry principle.**
  • Equality of opportunity.
  • Requires property rights and voluntary exchange.

HELPFUL HINTS

1 This chapter provides important tools for analyzing economic policies. Policy analysis involves judgements of efficiency and fairness (or equity). The concepts of consumer and producer surplus allow us to evaluate efficiency—efficient outcomes maximize the sum of consumer and producer surplus. Efficiency is a positive concept. The outcomes of different policies can be measured and compared objectively (at least in principle) to see which is more efficient.

Fairness is another important aspect of any economic policy. Fairness is a normative concept, depending on value judgements about which reasonable people can differ. But policy makers must make decisions, and it is helpful to be explicit about what ideas of fairness are used

to judge policy. The two main normative ideas developed in this chapter are fair results and fair rules.

2 There are two ways to interpret or "read" a demand curve—as a demand curve and as a marginal benefit curve. Both readings are correct, but each provides slightly different information. You can see the two readings in Text Figure 5.2 on page 106.

The first reading (a) starts with price. For a given price, the demand curve tells us the quantity demanded. Pick a price on the vertical axis. To find quantity demanded, we go "over" to the demand curve and "down" to the quantity axis. This is the standard demand curve of Chapter 3.

The second reading (b) starts with quantity. For a given quantity, the demand curve tells us the maximum price people are willing to pay. Pick a quantity on the horizontal axis. To find the maximum price people are willing to pay, we go "up" to the demand curve and "over" to the price axis. This is a reading of the demand curve as a marginal benefit curve. For a given quantity, the marginal benefit curve tells us the value (equals the maximum price people are willing to pay) of that unit of the good.

We read a demand curve "over and down." But we read a marginal benefit curve "up and over." Each reading is helpful, depending on the problem you are trying to solve or the issue you are trying to analyze. If you get stuck with a demand or marginal benefit curve problem, you may not be using the most suitable reading. Try reading the curve both ways and see which one is most helpful.

3 As with the demand curve, there are two ways to interpret or "read" a supply curve—as a supply curve and as a marginal cost curve. Both readings are correct, but each provides slightly different information. You can see the two readings in Text Figure 5.4 on page 108.

The first reading (a) starts with price. For a given price, the supply curve tells us the quantity supplied. Pick a price on the vertical axis. To find quantity supplied, we go "over" to the supply curve and "down" to the quantity axis. This is the standard supply curve of Chapter 3.

The second reading (b) starts with quantity. For a given quantity, the supply curve tells us the minimum price producers are willing to accept. Pick a quantity on the horizontal axis. To find the minimum price producers are willing to accept, we go "up" to the supply curve and "over" to the price axis. This is a reading of the supply curve as a marginal cost curve. For a given quantity, the marginal cost curve tells us the opportunity cost of producing that unit of the good.

Thus we read a supply curve "over and down," while we read a marginal cost curve "up and over." Each reading is helpful, depending on the problem you are trying to solve or the issue you are trying to analyze. If you get stuck with a supply or marginal cost curve problem, you may not be using the most suitable reading. Try reading the curve both ways and see which one is most helpful.

4 Once you understand the demand curve as a marginal benefit curve and the supply curve as a marginal cost curve, the concepts of consumer surplus and producer surplus follow directly. Consumer surplus is the difference between the maximum amount people are willing to pay and the price actually paid. At any price, consumer surplus for the market is the area below the demand (marginal benefit) curve but above the horizontal line at market price. Producer surplus is the difference between the minimum amount producers are willing to accept and the price actually received. At any price, producer surplus for the market is the area above the supply (marginal cost) curve but below the horizontal line at market price.

5 An efficient allocation of resources occurs at the quantity of output that maximizes the sum of consumer surplus and producer surplus. That sum is maximized at the quantity where marginal benefit (MB) equals marginal cost (MC). To see why the $MB = MC$ condition signals maximum efficiency, consider outputs less than and greater than the efficient quantity of output.

If output is less than the efficient quantity (to the left), MB is greater than MC. Resources are creating more value (MB) than they cost (MC). By shifting more resources into production of this good and out of production of other goods where MB is only equal to or less than MC, total benefit will increase.

Similarly, if output is greater than the efficient quantity (to the right), MC is greater than MB. Resources cost more (MC) than the value (MB) that they are creating. By shifting more resources out of production of this good and into production of other goods where MB is at least equal to or greater than MC, total benefit will increase.

Only at the output where $MB = MC$ are total benefits at a maximum, and no reallocation

of resources can increase the sum of consumer surplus and producer surplus.

6 Fairness is a normative issue. But note that the tradeoff between economic efficiency and fairness (the "big tradeoff") is a positive issue. Income transfers to achieve fairness norms have real impacts on economic output due to administrative costs and incentive effects. The loss of output and reduced efficiency can be measured. Even though fairness has a cost, policy makers may still come to the conclusion that improved fairness or equity is worth the loss in efficiency. That is the normative issue.

True/False and Explain

Efficiency: A Refresher

1 As more of a good is consumed, its marginal benefit decreases.

2 An efficient allocation of resources occurs when marginal benefit is maximized.

3 If marginal cost exceeds marginal benefit, then production should be decreased.

Value, Price, and Consumer Surplus

4 The value of a good is its consumer benefit.

5 Consumer surplus is the value of a good minus the price paid for it.

6 Consumer surplus equals the area above the demand curve, but below market price.

Cost, Price, and Producer Surplus

7 A supply curve indicates the quantity of other goods and services that buyers must forgo to produce one more unit.

8 The opportunity cost of producing a given quantity of a good is the area under the supply curve.

9 Producer surplus is the opportunity cost of producing a good minus its price.

Is the Competitive Market Efficient?

10 Adam Smith's "invisible hand" suggests that competitive markets send resources to their highest valued use.

11 Markets always use resources efficiently.

12 Deadweight loss is a loss to consumers and a gain to producers.

Is the Competitive Market Fair?

13 Utilitarianism is an example of a fair results idea.

14 If we think of the total income of a society as a pie, a more equally shared pie results in a larger pie.

15 In economic life, the symmetry principle translates into equality of outcomes.

Multiple-Choice

Efficiency: A Refresher

1 In an efficient allocation of resources
a goods and services people value most are produced.
b we cannot produce more of a good without giving up a more highly valued good.
c marginal benefit equals marginal cost.
d all of the above are true.
e none of the above are true.

2 The marginal benefit of a good is
a the maximum amount a person is willing to pay for an additional unit.
b the minimum amount a person is willing to pay for an additional unit.
c equal to marginal cost.
c greater than marginal cost.
e less than marginal cost.

3 The marginal cost of a service is
a the opportunity cost of the first unit produced.
b the maximum price producers must receive to induce them to supply an additional unit of the service.
c the value of all alternatives forgone.
d increasing with increased output.
e decreasing with increased output.

4 At current output, the marginal benefit of Furbys is greater than marginal cost. To achieve an efficient allocation,
1 Furby output must increase.
2 Furby output must decrease.
3 the marginal benefit of Furbys will rise.
4 the marginal cost of Furbys will fall.
a 1 and 3
b 1 and 4
c 2 and 3
d 2 and 4
e 1 only

Value, Price, and Consumer Surplus

5 The maximum price a consumer is willing to pay for a good is known as the
a consumer surplus.
b value of a good.
c relative price of a good.
d money price of a good.
e marginal cost of a good.

6 Consumer surplus is the

a difference between the maximum price consumers are willing to pay and the minimum price producers are willing to accept.
b difference between the value of a good and the price paid for the good.
c total value to consumers of a good.
d area under the demand curve.
e total amount paid for the good.

7 Consider the demand curve in Figure 5.1. What is the value of the first unit of the good?

FIGURE **5.1**

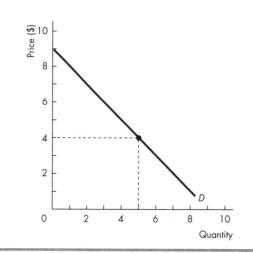

a $10
b $9
c $8
d $5
e $4

8 Consider the demand curve in Figure 5.1. If the price of the good is $4, what is the total consumer surplus?

a $32.50
b $25.00
c $20.00
d $12.50
e none of the above.

Cost, Price, and Producer Surplus

9 A supply curve is

a a marginal cost curve.
b a minimum supply-price curve.
c an opportunity cost of production curve.
d all of the above.
e none of the above.

10 Producer surplus is the

a difference between the maximum price consumers are willing to pay and the minimum price producers are willing to accept.
b difference between producers' revenues and opportunity costs of production.
c opportunity cost of production.
d area under the supply curve.
e total amount paid for the good.

11 Consider the demand and supply curves in Figure 5.2. Which area in the diagram indicates the opportunity cost of production?

a *abc*
b *aec*
c *ebc*
d 0*bcd*
e 0*ecd*

FIGURE **5.2**

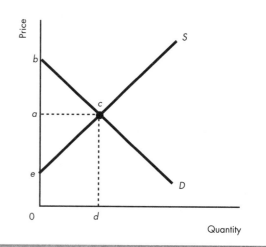

12 Consider the demand and supply curves in Figure 5.2. Which area in the diagram indicates producer surplus?

a *abc*
b *aec*
c *ebc*
d 0*bcd*
e 0*ecd*

Is the Competitive Market Efficient?

13 If production is not at an efficient level, which of the following *must* be true?

a marginal benefit exceeds marginal cost.
b marginal cost exceeds marginal benefit.
c production will increase.
d production will decrease.
e none of the above.

14 In competitive equilibrium, which of the following statements is *false*?

a marginal benefit equals marginal cost.
b willingness to pay equals opportunity cost.
c the sum of consumer surplus and producer surplus is maximized.
d deadweight loss is maximized.
e resources are used efficiently to produce goods and services that people value most highly.

15 If resources are allocated efficiently,

a consumer surplus exceeds producer surplus.
b producer surplus exceeds consumer surplus.
c the sum of consumer surplus and producer surplus is maximized.
d marginal benefit is maximized.
e marginal cost is minimized.

16 Markets may not achieve an efficient allocation of resources when there are

a public goods.
b external benefits.
c monopolies.
d subsidies.
e all of the above.

17 The overproduction of a good means that

a deadweight loss has been eliminated.
b the sum of consumer surplus and producer surplus is greater than the sum for an efficient allocation.
c marginal cost exceeds marginal benefit.
d marginal benefit exceeds marginal cost.
e this is a public good.

18 Deadweight loss is

a borne entirely by consumers.
b gained by producers.
c the social loss from inefficiency.
d not a problem with overproduction.
e all of the above.

19 Consider the demand and supply curves in Figure 5.3. Which area in the diagram indicates the deadweight loss from underproduction?

a *eacf*
b *acd*
c *abd*
d *bcd*
e *kaci*

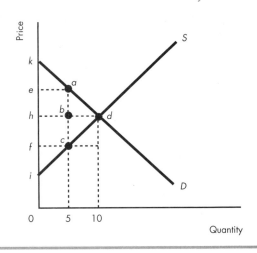

FIGURE **5.3**

20 Consider the demand and supply curves in Figure 5.3. Which area in the diagram indicates the loss in consumer surplus from underproduction?

a *eacf*
b *acd*
c *abd*
d *bcd*
e *kaci*

Is the Competitive Market Fair?

21 Which of the following applies to the *results* principle of fairness?

a symmetry principle.
b equality of opportunity.
c the big tradeoff.
d protection of private property.
e purely voluntary exchange.

22 A principle of fairness that emphasizes equality of opportunity is

a fair results.
b fair rules.
c fair incomes.
d utilitarianism.
e modified utilitarianism.

23 According to the "big tradeoff,"

a income transfers reduce efficiency.
b efficiency requires income transfers.
c a more equally shared pie results in a larger pie.
d property rights and voluntary exchange insure equality of opportunity.
e income transfers should make the poorest person as well off as possible.

24 According to John Rawls' modified utilitarianism, income should be redistributed until

a incomes are equal.
b opportunities are equal.
c the poorest person is as well off as possible.
d the poorest person is as well off as possible, after incorporating the costs of income transfers.
e the big tradeoff is eliminated.

25 Economists tend to

a agree about efficiency and about fairness.
b agree about efficiency but disagree about fairness.
c disagree about efficiency but agree about fairness.
d be more agreeable than philosophers about fairness.
e be more disagreeable than philosophers about fairness.

Short Answer Problems

Figure 5.4 shows the market for champagne. Note that the demand curve is also a marginal benefit curve, and the supply curve is also a marginal cost curve. Use this information to answer Questions 1–5.

FIGURE **5.4**   THE CHAMPAGNE MARKET

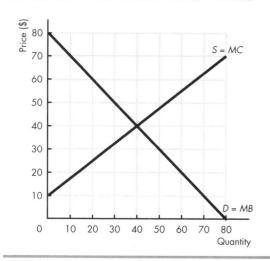

1 a If the price of a bottle of champagne is $60, what is the quantity demanded? the quantity supplied?
b At the price of $60, is there a shortage or a surplus of champagne? Explain the forces that will move the market towards equilibrium.

2 a If the quantity sold of champagne is 20 bottles, what is the marginal benefit of the 20th bottle to consumers? the marginal cost to producers?
b At the quantity of 20 bottles, what is the relationship between the value of the 20th bottle of champagne and the value of the resources forgone to make it? Explain the forces that will move the market towards an efficient allocation of resources.

3 Suppose the champagne market in Figure 5.4 is in equilibrium.
a Calculate the consumer surplus.
b Calculate the producer surplus.
c What is the sum of consumer surplus and producer surplus?
d What is the condition for economic efficiency?

4 Suppose now that that there is underproduction in the champagne market in Figure 5.4 and output is restricted to 20 bottles.
a List three kinds of obstacles to efficiency that might cause underproduction.
b Calculate the deadweight loss.
c What is the sum of consumer surplus and producer surplus?
d How does the sum compare to the sum in Problem **3c**? Is the output of 20 bottles efficient?

5 Suppose instead that there is overproduction in the champagne market and output increases to 60 bottles.
a List one kind of obstacle to efficiency that might cause overproduction.
b Calculate the deadweight loss.
c What is the sum of consumer surplus and producer surplus?
d How does the sum compare to the sum in Problem **3c**? Is the output of 60 bottles efficient?

6 a Define deadweight loss.
b Who gains from deadweight loss? Who loses?
c Explain how a policymaker would use the concept of deadweight loss to decide between two alternative economic policies.
d What other issue would the policymaker have to consider in her decision?

ⓒ **7** There appears to be a contradiction between the Chapter 1 claim that the basic economic problem is scarcity and the Chapter 5 claim that there can be a problem of "overproduction." When the basic problem is that there is too little to meet our wants, how can there be too much of a good?

8 Ideas about fairness divide into two groups—fair results and fair rules.

  a What is the basic principle of fair results ideas? What is the basic principle of fair rules ideas?

  b What is utilitarianism? Explain why it is a fair results or fair rules idea.

9 Why is there a "big tradeoff" between fairness and efficiency?

⊕ 10 Suppose two political parties are vying for your vote in an upcoming election. The "Rights" advocate a more privatized health care system, where the market sets the price for medical services and individuals pay more of their own bills. The "Lefts" advocate more government subsidies in health care, that would extend free coverage to preventative dental care and prescription drugs.

  a As an intelligent and economically informed citizen, use the concepts of efficiency and fairness (equity) to evaluate the likely pros and cons of each party's policy.

  b Which policy would you likely support? What does this say about your personal valuation of efficiency versus equity?

A N S W E R S

True/False and Explain

1 **T** Principle of decreasing marginal benefit. (104)

2 **F** Efficiency requires $MB = MC$ and maximizes the sum of consumer and producer surplus. (104–105)

3 **T** By shifting resources to other uses where marginal benefit is at least equal to marginal cost, sum of consumer and producer surpluses increases. (105)

4 **F** Value = MB. (106)

5 **T** Definition. (107)

6 **F** Area under the demand curve, but above market price. (107)

7 **F** Other goods and services that *sellers* must forgo. (108)

8 **T** That area sums opportunity cost of production for each unit of good produced. (109)

9 **F** Price of a good minus its opportunity cost of production. (109)

10 **T** Competitive markets are "led by an invisible hand" to promote efficient resource use which benefits all. (111)

11 **F** Not when obstacles to efficiency like monopoly, public goods, external costs, external benefits. (111–112)

12 **F** Social loss borne by entire society. (112)

13 **T** For utilitarianism, only equality of results is fair, bringing "the greatest happiness for the greatest number." (114)

14 **F** A more equally shared pie results in a smaller pie because of the "big tradeoff" between efficiency and fairness. (115)

15 **F** The symmetry principle—treat others as you would like to be treated—translates into equality of *opportunity*. (116)

Multiple-Choice

1 **d** All characteristics of efficiency. (104–105)

2 **a** Definition. Relation to MC depends if allocation is efficient or not. (104–105)

3 **d** Principle of increasing marginal cost; MC = value of *best* alternative forgone. (104–105)

4 **e** With increasing Q, MB must fall and MC rise. (105)

5 **b** Value = marginal benefit. (106)

6 **b** Definition. Area under demand curve but above market price. (106–107)

7 **c** From $Q = 1$, go up to demand curve to read over to maximum price willing to pay. (106)

8 **d** Area of triangle $(1/2\,ba)$ below demand and above $P = 4$. (107)

9 **d** All definitions of supply curve. (108–109)

10 **b** Definition. Area below market price but above supply curve. (109)

11 **e** Area below supply curve. (109)

12 **b** Area below market price but above supply curve. (109)

13 **e** If production below efficient level, **a** and **c** true; if production above efficient level, **b** and **d** true. (110)

14 **d** No deadweight loss. All other answers are definitions of competitive equilibrium. (110)

15 **c** Definition where marginal benefit equals marginal cost. No other necessary relation between consumer and producer surplus. (110)

16 **e** All change quantity produced above (**d**) or below (**a**, **b**, **c**) efficient quantity. (111–112)

17 **c** Deadweight loss reduces sum of consumer and producer surplus. (113)

18 **c** Borne by consumers and producers when underproduction or overproduction. (112–113)

19 **b** Decrease in consumer and producer surplus compared to efficient quantity (10) of production. (112–113)

20 c Area subtracted from consumer surplus at efficient quantity (10) of production (*hkd*). (112–113)

21 c Other answers apply to *rules* principle of fairness. (114–116)

22 b Other answers apply to *results* principle of fairness. (114–116)

23 a Tradeoff between equity (which requires income transfers) and efficiency. (115)

24 d Rawls' idea incorporates the effects of the big tradeoff in trying to redistribute income more equally, but not totally equally. (115)

25 b Efficiency is a positive issue; fairness is a normative issue. (114)

Short Answer Problems

1 a Quantity demanded is 20 bottles; quantity supplied is approximately 67 bottles. We find these quantities by starting with the price of $60 and reading "over" to each curve and "down" to the quantity.

b There is a surplus because quantity supplied exceeds quantity demanded. Producers have excess supplies, so they will cut prices rather than be stuck with unsold goods. Quantity demanded will increase as price falls, until we end up at the equilibrium price of $40/bottle and the equilibrium quantity of 40 bottles.

2 a Marginal benefit is $60; marginal cost is $25. We find these values by starting with the quantity of 20 bottles and reading "up" to each curve and "over" to the marginal benefit and cost (measured in prices).

b The 20th bottle of champagne is valued by consumers at $60, but uses only $25 worth of resources to make. With marginal benefit exceeding marginal cost, consumers would happily pay more than $25 for an additional bottle of champagne and will bid up the price. Producers will increase the quantity supplied until the market reaches the equilibrium price of $40/bottle and the equilibrium quantity of 40 bottles. Producers increase champagne output by transferring resources from other uses. Resources, which were being used elsewhere to create value just equal to their cost, are now being used more efficiently in that they create more value in champagne production than their cost.

3 a Consumer surplus is the triangular area under the demand curve but above the horizontal line at the market price of $40. The formula for the area of a triangle is 1/2(base)(altitude), so consumer surplus = 1/2(40)(40) = 800.

b Producer surplus is the triangular area above the supply curve but below the horizontal line at the market price of $40. Producer surplus = 1/2(40)(30) = 600.

c The sum of consumer and producer surplus is 800 + 600 = 1,400.

d Economic efficiency occurs when the sum of consumer surplus and producer surplus is maximized. Is this specific outcome efficient? We can't be sure if 1,400 is a maximum until we compare other situations in the champagne market.

4 a Price ceilings, taxes, quotas, and monopoly all might cause output to be restricted.

b Deadweight loss is the decrease in consumer surplus and producer surplus that results from an inefficient level of production. It is equal to the triangular area between the demand and supply curves from quantity = 20 to quantity = 40. Deadweight loss = 1/2(35)(20) = 350.

c The new sum of consumer and producer surplus is the original amount of 1,400 minus the deadweight loss: 1,400 – 350 = 1,050.

d The sum of consumer and producer surplus (1,050) is less than the equilibrium sum in Problem **2c** at an output of 40 bottles. Since an efficient output maximizes the sum of consumer and producer surplus, the output of 20 bottles is not efficient.

5 a Subsidies to producers increase the quantity produced.

b Deadweight loss is equal to the triangular area between the demand and supply curves from quantity = 40 to quantity = 60. Deadweight loss = 1/2(35)(20) = 350. (It is just a coincidence that this deadweight loss from overproduction happens to be equal to the deadweight loss from underproduction. In general these losses are not necessarily equal.)

c The new sum of consumer and producer surplus is the original amount of 1,400 minus the deadweight loss: 1,400 – 350 = 1,050.

d The sum of consumer and producer surplus (1,050) is less than the equilibrium sum in Problem **3c** at an output of 40 bottles. Since an efficient output maximizes the sum of consumer and producer surplus, the output of 60 bottles is not efficient.

6 a Deadweight loss is the decrease in consumer surplus and producer surplus that results from an inefficient level of production.

b No one gains from deadweight loss. It is a social loss borne by the entire society—consumers and producers.

c A policymaker would choose the most efficient policy—the one with the smallest deadweight loss.

d Fairness or equity would be the other consideration in deciding between alternative policies.

© **7** Because wants *in general* exceed the resources available to satisfy them, we cannot have everything we want and must make choices. This basic problem leads to economizing behaviour—choosing the best or optimal use of available resources. But *specific* wants can be satisfied. Each of us has relatively limited wants, for example, for salt, for heat in our houses during the winter, or for nail clippers. If these or other goods are produced beyond the point where the marginal benefit equals the marginal cost, there is a problem of overproduction.

Overproduction is a problem because the resources could be *better used* to produce different goods that could meet still-unsatisfied wants. The money invested in excessive salt production could be diverted to health research to find a cure for cancer, or to schools to allow more demands for education to be satisfied. Because wants *in general* are unlimited, producing too much of a good to satisfy a *specific* want actually prevents us from making optimal use of available resources. So the ideas of scarcity and overproduction are not contradictory. In fact, overproduction of a *specific* good is a problem precisely because there is a problem of scarcity in satisfying wants *in general.*

8 a Fair results ideas are based on the principle that results are most important, and that the fairest economic result is equal incomes for all. Fair rules ideas are based on the symmetry principle—that people in similar situations should be treated similarly. This principle translates into equality of opportunity in economic life.

b Utilitarianism is based on the principle that the fairest system is one where incomes are equal. Utilitarians argue that transferring income from the rich to the poor will result in "the greatest happiness for the greatest number," since the marginal benefit of an additional dollar to the poor person is greater than the benefit to the rich person. Only at equal incomes for all is total social benefit at a maximum. Since utilitarianism focuses on equal incomes or results, it is a fair results idea.

9 If greater fairness means increasing the equality of income, it can only be achieved by income redistribution. The income of some must be taxed in order to pay for the transfer payments and administrative costs of a redistribution policy. However, there are incentive effects that reduce the total amount of income available to be distributed.

If productive activities such as work are taxed, there will be a tendency to reduce time spent in those activities. Furthermore, any redistribution program requires the use of resources to administer it and thus leave fewer resources for other productive activities. Thus we arrive at the insight: A more equally shared pie results in a smaller pie.

© **10 a** The "Rights" market-oriented health care policy likely is more efficient. It requires less government administration, and would probably allow lower taxes because less is being spent by government and more by private individuals. With lower taxes, incentives to work might increase, and the size of the economic pie might be larger.

With lower government subsidies, the price of health care to individuals will rise. Health care may become unaffordable to some members of society, so the "Rights" policy may be less fair from a "fair results" perspective. From a "fair rules" perspective, the "Rights" policy is fair as long as everyone faces the same opportunities.

The "Lefts" subsidized health care policy likely is less efficient because it would require subsidies to health care providers and require more government administration and higher taxes to pay for the policy. With higher taxes, incentives to work might decrease, and the size of the economic pie might be smaller. On the other hand, with a healthier population, productivity might increase because fewer work days would be lost to illness. So the net effect on efficiency is unclear.

More health care services will become available to a greater number of people, so the "Lefts" policy may be fairer from a fair results perspective. From a fair rules perspective, the "Lefts" policy may be less fair if, to pay for the policy, individuals with higher incomes are taxed more than those with lower incomes.

b There is obviously no single correct answer to this question. The important thing is to think explicitly about your personal valuation of efficiency versus equity, and which idea of fairness appeals most to you.

Chapter 6

Markets in Action

Housing Markets and Rent Ceilings

In an unregulated housing market

◆ shortages cause rising rents, economizing on space, and increased quantity supplied (short run).

◆ in the long run, building activity shifts supply rightward, rents fall, and the housing stock increases.

In a regulated housing market

◆ a **rent ceiling** (a **price ceiling** applied to rents) makes it illegal to raise rents.

◆ housing stocks are lower than in an unregulated market both in short and long run. No incentive to economize on space or build new housing.

◆ shortages cause excess demand and

  • **search activity** (time spent looking for someone with whom to do business).
  • **black markets** (illegal markets where prices exceed ceilings).

Unregulated markets allocate housing resources efficiently, while rent ceilings create inefficiencies (deadweight loss) without necessarily improving equity.

The Labour Market and the Minimum Wage

A **minimum wage** (a **price floor** applied to wages) makes it illegal to hire labour below a specified wage.

◆ Minimum wages create excess supply of labour (unemployment) and lower the quantity of labour demanded and hired.

◆ Unemployed workers willing to work at a lower wage spend more time searching for work.

Taxes

Sales tax shifts up supply curve by vertical distance equal to amount of tax. Who pays tax depends on elasticities of supply and demand.

Supply elasticity and tax division:

◆ Perfectly inelastic supply—sellers pay all.

◆ More inelastic supply—sellers pay more.

◆ More elastic supply—buyers pay more.

◆ Perfectly elastic supply—buyers pay all.

Demand elasticity and tax division:

◆ Perfectly inelastic demand—buyers pay all.

◆ More inelastic demand—buyers pay more.

◆ More elastic demand—sellers pay more.

◆ Perfectly elastic demand—sellers pay all.

Sales tax decreases quantity produced and consumed, creating deadweight loss.

Markets for Illegal Goods

Penalizing dealers for selling illegal goods increases cost of selling goods and decreases supply. Penalizing buyers for consuming illegal goods decreases willingness to pay and decreases demand.

◆ When (sellers' penalties > buyers' penalties), Q decreases, P rises.

◆ When (sellers' penalties < buyers' penalties), Q decreases, P falls.

◆ Taxing (decriminalized) goods can achieve the same consumption levels as prohibition.

Stabilizing Farm Revenue

Demand for most farm products is inelastic, creating large variations in farm revenue.

◆ Poor harvest (decreased S) causes rising P, increased total revenue.

◆ Bumper harvest (increased S) causes falling P, decreased total revenue.

Farm prices are stabilized through speculation by inventory holders, who buy at low prices and sell at high prices, reducing price fluctuations.

Farm stabilization agencies (**farm marketing boards**) also limit price fluctuations by setting

◆ price floors, which increase market price and surpluses.

◆ **quotas** (quantity restrictions on production), which increase market price and decrease Q grown.

◆ **subsidies** (payments by governments to producers), which increase supply and decrease market price (but farmers receive market price plus subsidy).

Farm marketing boards are inefficient and redistribute income from consumers to farmers. The equity of the redistribution is a normative question.

H E L P F U L   H I N T S

I In the real world we frequently observe market regulation by governments in the form of price constraints so it is important to study the effects of such regulation. Another benefit of studying government regulation is to obtain an understanding of how markets work when, by contrast, the government does *not* affect the normal operation of markets.

Whenever something disturbs an equilibrium in an unregulated (free) market, the desires of buyers and sellers are brought back into balance by price movements. If prices are controlled by government regulation, however, the price mechanism can no longer serve this purpose. Thus *balance* must be restored in some other way. In the case of price ceilings, black markets are likely to arise. If black markets cannot develop because of strict enforcement of price ceilings, then demanders will be forced to bear the costs of increased search activity, waiting in line, or something else.

2 This chapter discusses government price constraints in three specific markets: rental housing, labour, and farm products. The basic principles, however, can be generalized to other markets.

In any market with a legal price ceiling set below the market-clearing price, we will observe excess quantity demanded, because price cannot increase to eliminate it. As a consequence, the marginal benefit of the last unit of the good available will exceed the controlled price. Demanders are willing to engage in costly activities up to the marginal benefit of that last unit (search activity, waiting lines, and black market activity) in order to obtain the good.

Furthermore, if price is allowed to increase in response to a decrease in supply or an increase in demand, there are incentive effects for suppliers to produce more and demanders to purchase less (movements along the supply and demand curves). Indeed, it is the response to these incentives that restores equilibrium in markets with freely adjusting prices. If the price cannot adjust, these price-induced incentive effects do not have a chance to operate. In the case of rent ceilings, the inability of rents (price) to rise means that: (1) there is no inducement to use the current stock of housing more intensively in the short run and (2) there is no incentive to construct new housing in the long run. Similarly, the effects on any market in which a minimum price (price floor) is set above the market-clearing (equilibrium) price will be similar to those discussed in the text for the labour market under minimum wage or price floors in agricultural markets.

3 The division of the burden of a tax is also called tax incidence. Who pays a sales tax imposed on producers depends on the elasticities of demand and supply. The general principles of tax incidence are
• more inelastic demand—consumers pay more.
• more elastic demand—producers pay more.
• more inelastic supply—producers pay more.
• more elastic supply—consumers pay more.

True/False and Explain

Housing Markets and Rent Ceilings

1 In an unregulated housing market, higher rents increase the short-run quantity of housing supplied.

2 When rents in an unregulated housing market rise due to a decrease in supply, people who are unable to pay the higher rents will not get housing.

3 If a rent ceiling exceeds people's willingness to pay, search activity and black markets will increase.

The Labour Market and Minimum Wage

4 In an unregulated labour market, a decrease in the demand for labour causes the wage rate to rise.

5 An increase in the minimum wage will reduce the number of workers employed.

6 Most economists believe that raising the minimum wage has no effect on unemployment.

7 Minimum wage laws increase the amount of time people spend searching for work.

Taxes

8 The more elastic demand is for a product, the larger the fraction of a sales tax paid by consumers.

9 A sales tax always creates deadweight loss.

10 The deadweight loss from a sales tax equals the tax revenue collected by government.

Markets for Illegal Goods

11 The statement "If we legalize and tax drugs, tax revenues could be used to finance more drug education programs" is normative.

12 If penalties are imposed on both sellers and buyers in a market for prohibited goods, the price may rise, fall, or remain constant, while the quantity bought always decreases.

Stabilizing Farm Revenues

13 Suppose the supply curve for corn fluctuates widely but the demand curve is stable. The price of corn will fluctuate more if demand is elastic rather than inelastic.

14 Inventory holders sell goods when price is higher than the forecasted future price.

15 A subsidy paid to producers shifts the demand curve for a good rightward.

Multiple-Choice

Housing Markets and Rent Ceilings

1 The short-run supply curve for rental housing is positively sloped because

a the supply of housing is fixed in the short run.
b the current stock of buildings will be used more intensively as rents rise.
c the cost of constructing new buildings increases as the number of buildings increases.
d the cost of constructing new buildings is about the same regardless of the number of buildings in existence.
e new buildings will be constructed as rents rise.

2 Rent ceilings imposed by governments

a keep rental prices below the unregulated market price.
b keep rental prices above the unregulated market price.
c keep rental prices equal to the unregulated market price.
d increase the stock of rental housing.
e increase the intensity of use of the current stock of rental housing.

3 A price ceiling set below the equilibrium price will result in

a excess supply.
b excess demand.
c the equilibrium price.
d an increase in supply.
e a decrease in demand.

4 Which of the following is *not* a likely outcome of rent ceilings?

a a black market for rent-controlled housing
b long waiting lists of potential renters of rent-controlled housing
c a short-run shortage of housing
d black market prices below the rent ceiling prices
e increased search activity for rent-controlled housing

The Labour Market and the Minimum Wage

5 If the minimum wage is set at $2 per hour in Figure 6.1, what is the level of unemployment in millions of hours?

a 50
b 40
c 20
d 10
e 0

FIGURE **6.1**

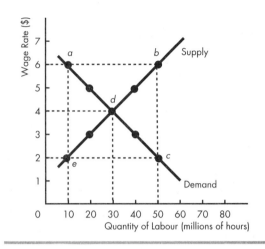

6 In Figure 6.1, if the minimum wage is set at $6 per hour, what is the level of unemployment in millions of hours?

a 50
b 40
c 20
d 10
e 0

7 In Figure 6.1, if the minimum wage is set at $6 per hour, what is the area of deadweight loss?

a *abd*
b *bcd*
c *cde*
d *ade*
e 0

Taxes

8 Figure 6.2 shows the market for frisbees before and after a sales tax is imposed. The sales tax on each frisbee is

a $0.40.
b $0.60.
c $1.00.
d $5.60.
e $6.60.

FIGURE **6.2**

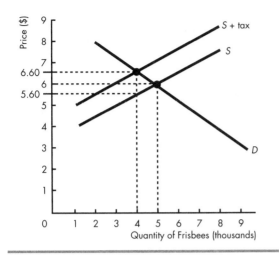

9 Refer to Figure 6.2. For each frisbee, the sellers' share of the tax is

a $0.40.
b $0.60.
c $1.00.
d $5.60.
e $6.60.

10 Refer to Figure 6.2. For each frisbee, the buyers' share of the tax is

a $0.40.
b $0.60.
c $1.00.
d $5.60.
e $6.60.

11 Refer to Figure 6.2. Government revenue from the tax is

a $4,000.
b $5,000.
c $22,400.
d $26,400.
e $30,000.

12 From Figure 6.2 we can deduce that between 4,000 and 5,000 units, the demand for frisbees is

a inelastic.
b unit elastic.
c elastic.
d more elastic than the supply (S) of frisbees.
e soaring.

13 If the price of a good is not affected by a sales tax, then

a supply is perfectly elastic.
b demand is perfectly elastic.
c elasticity of supply is greater than elasticity of demand.
d elasticity of demand is greater than elasticity of supply.
e none of the above.

Markets for Illegal Goods

14 If enforcement is aimed at sellers of a prohibited good,

a price and quantity bought will decrease.
b price and quantity bought will increase.
c price will increase and quantity bought will decrease.
d price will decrease and quantity bought will increase.
e price change will be uncertain and quantity bought will decrease.

15 Which of the following statements about prohibited goods is *true*?

a Taxes are more effective in changing preferences than prohibition.
b Prohibition is more effective in generating revenue than an equivalent tax.
c Taxes and penalties cannot be set so as to yield equivalent outcomes.
d Taxes generate revenues, while prohibition generates more enforcement expenses.
e None of the above is true.

Stabilizing Farm Revenue

16 A momentary supply curve is

a elastic since price is fixed.
b relatively more elastic than a short-run supply curve.
c relatively inelastic, since yields are known but sales are not.
d inelastic since output is fixed.
e as ephemeral as gossamer wings.

17 With inventory speculation, a bumper crop of barley will

a decrease farm revenue, while a poor harvest will increase farm revenue.

b increase farm revenue, while a poor harvest will decrease farm revenue.

c decrease farm revenue as will a poor harvest.

d increase farm revenue as will a poor harvest.

e do none of the above.

18 Which of the following combinations would generally yield the greatest price fluctuation?

a large supply shifts and inelastic demand

b large supply shifts and elastic demand

c large supply shifts and perfectly elastic demand

d small supply shifts and inelastic demand

e small supply shifts and elastic demand

19 With inventory speculation

a prices stabilize but farm revenue does not.

b prices do not stabilize but farm revenue does.

c bumper crops bring decreased total revenue.

d poor harvests bring increased total revenue.

e **c** and **d**.

20 Figure 6.3 illustrates the short-run demand and supply curves in the wheat bran market. If the Wheat Marketing Board sets a quota of 50 million bushels, the market-clearing price of a bushel of wheat bran is

a $1.00.

b $3.00.

c $5.00.

d two scoops of raisins.

e none of the above.

FIGURE **6.3**

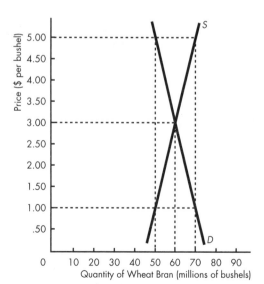

21 Refer to Figure 6.3. With the quota of 50 million bushels, farmers have an incentive to

a decrease output because the market-clearing price is below cost of production.

b decrease output because there is a surplus at the market-clearing price.

c increase output because the market-clearing price is above cost of production.

d increase output because there is a shortage at the market-clearing price.

e stick to the quota.

22 Refer to Figure 6.3. Suppose the marketing board develops a new kind of subsidy called a direct payment plan. Farmers are told, "We will guarantee you $5 per bushel, but everything you produce at this price must be sold on the market for whatever buyers will pay; then we will give you (at taxpayers' expense) the difference between the market price and $5 per bushel." How many bushels of wheat bran will be sold?

a 20 million

b 50 million

c 60 million

d 70 million

e none of the above

23 Refer to Figure 6.3. The amount of taxpayers' money that the marketing board pays to farmers in Question **22** is

a zero.

b $70 million.

c $250 million.

d $280 million.

e $350 million.

24 European Union (EU) countries have been accumulating butter and cheese mountains and wine lakes. These surpluses are consistent with

a floor prices for agricultural products that are below market prices.

b floor prices for agricultural products that are above market prices.

c ceiling prices for agricultural products that are below market prices.

d ceiling prices for agricultural products that are above market prices.

e quotas for agricultural products.

25 An agricultural subsidy

a shifts the supply curve rightward.

b benefits consumers by lowering product prices.

c benefits farmers by raising the price they receive.

d imposes major costs on taxpayers.

e does all of the above.

Short Answer Problems

I Suppose that the market for rental housing is initially in long-run equilibrium. Use graphs to answer the following:

a Explain how an unregulated market for rental housing would adjust, if there is a sudden significant increase in demand. What will happen to rent and the quantity of units rented in the short run and in the long run? Be sure to discuss the effect on incentives (in both the short and the long run) as the market-determined price (rent) changes.

b Now explain how the market would adjust to the increase in demand, if rent ceilings are established at the level of the initial equilibrium rent. What has happened to supplier incentives in this case?

2 The demand for and supply of gasoline are given in Table 6.1.

a What are the equilibrium price and quantity of gasoline?

TABLE **6.1**

Price ($ per litre)	Quantity Demanded (millions of litres per day)	Quantity Supplied (millions of litres per day)
1.40	8	24
1.30	10	22
1.20	12	20
1.10	14	18
1.00	16	16
0.90	18	14

b Suppose that the quantity of gasoline supplied suddenly declines by 8 million litres per day at every price. Construct a new table of price, quantity demanded, and quantity supplied, and draw a graph of the demand curve and the initial and new supply curves. Assuming that the market for gasoline is unregulated, use either your table or graph to find the new equilibrium price and quantity of gasoline.

c How has the change in price affected the behaviour of demanders? the behaviour of suppliers?

3 Suppose that the government imposes a price ceiling of $1 per litre of gasoline at the same time as the decrease in supply reported in Short Answer Problem **2b**.

a What is the quantity of gasoline demanded? quantity supplied?

b What is the quantity of gasoline actually sold?

c What is the excess quantity of gasoline demanded?

d For the last litre of gasoline sold, what is the marginal benefit? marginal cost?

e Is this an efficient outcome? Explain.

4 Governments tend to place high sales taxes (often called "sin" taxes) on liquor and cigarettes. Aside from moral and health reasons, why are these goods chosen as a source of tax revenue?

5 The Ministry of Treasury has been authorized to levy a $0.15 per unit excise (sales) tax on one of two goods—comic books or dog biscuits. As a summer student at the Ministry, you are given an assignment by the Director of Taxes, Dr. More. You must choose the good that meets two objectives: (1) it will yield the greatest tax revenue and (2) the major burden of the tax will fall on consumers. Ministry researchers have estimated the supply and demand curves (without the tax) for each market. The comic book market is shown in Figure 6.4 and the dog biscuit market in Figure 6.5. The following questions will help you complete your assignment.

FIGURE **6.4**   COMIC BOOK MARKET

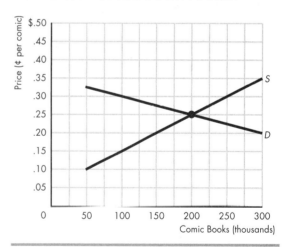

a For the comic book market, shift the appropriate curve to reflect the tax and draw it on Figure 6.4. Label the curve either "*S + tax*" or "*D + tax*." Identify the new equilibrium price and quantity. Compare the total expenditure in the original and new equilibriums.

b Calculate the total tax revenue collected, and indicate it as an area on Figure 6.4.

c How much of the tax is paid by consumers? by producers?

FIGURE **6.5** DOG BISCUIT MARKET

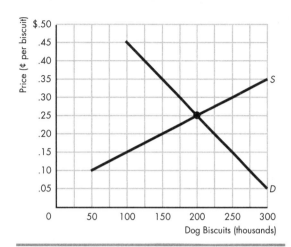

d Now perform the same analysis on the dog biscuit market. Shift the appropriate curve to reflect the tax and draw it on Figure 6.5. Label the curve either "*S + tax*" or "*D + tax*." Identify the new equilibrium price and quantity. Compare the total expenditure in the original and new equilibriums.

e Calculate the total tax revenue collected, and indicate it as an area on Figure 6.5.

f How much of the tax is paid by consumers? by producers?

g What is your recommendation to Dr. More? Explain.

(ct) **6** Dr. More was pleased with your excise tax recommendation in Short Answer Problem **5**, but you can't stop wondering about his comment, "Hmm, I thought you would do it the other way." If you haven't already figured out to what he was referring, the following questions will help.

a For the comic book market, calculate the elasticity of demand between the original and new equilibrium points. Is demand elastic or inelastic?

b Perform the same calculation for the dog biscuit market. Is demand elastic or inelastic?

c What do you know about demand elasticities that would have allowed you to complete your assignment "the other way" and predict which market would yield maximum tax revenue, and which market would place most of the tax burden on consumers?

7 After spending so much time on Dr. More's tax assignment in Short Answer Problems **5** and **6**, you realize you have one last chance to impress the boss. While your previous tax assignment had two important policy objectives—maximum tax revenue and appropriate tax burden—no one asked you about the relative efficiency loss of a tax on comic books versus dog biscuits. If the policy objective is to minimize deadweight loss, which good do you recommend be taxed?

8 Suppose the Nudist Party wins the next federal election because all the clothed citizens forgot to vote. The Nudists pass a law making clothes illegal. Unfortunately for the Nudists, the police don't take the law seriously (where would officers pin their badges?) and put almost no effort into enforcement. Use a diagram to explain why the black market price of now illegal clothes will be close to the unregulated market equilibrium price.

9 The supply of fruit is subject to unpredictable fluctuations. Why does the price of fresh fruit fluctuate much more than the price of canned fruit?

(ct) **10** Figure 6.6 shows the demand curve in the market for grinola seeds. Grinola is difficult to grow—simply a frown from a farmer in the field causes the seeds to develop split ends, which makes them worthless. As a result, grinola harvests fluctuate widely.

FIGURE **6.6** DEMAND FOR GRINOLA

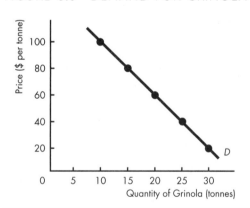

a If there are no inventory speculators in the grinola market, what will the market price be when momentary supply is 25 tonnes? 20 tonnes? 15 tonnes?

b Suppose inventory speculators discover that grinola can be stored easily and enter the market looking for a profit. They forecast an expected price of $60 per tonne. Explain what happens when the momentary supply is 25 tonnes. Identify the amount the inventory speculators buy or sell, the quantity bought by consumers, and the market price.

c Repeat the analysis in part **b** for a momentary supply of 20 tonnes.

d Repeat the analysis in part **b** for a momentary supply of 15 tonnes.

e What has happened to price fluctuations in the grinola market?

f Inventory speculators don't operate out of the goodness of their hearts. Have they made a profit in grinola? Explain your calculation.

ANSWERS

True/False and Explain

1 T Higher rents create incentives to use current buildings more intensively. (124)

2 T At equilibrium rent, all who can afford housing get it, but not necessarily those who need housing. (124–125)

3 F Ceiling is above market price so search activity won't increase and black markets won't arise. (125–126)

4 F Leftward shift demand causes wage rate to fall. (128–129)

5 T Raising the minimum wage decreases quantity labour demanded. (128–129)

6 F Exceptions are economists Card and Krueger. (130)

7 T Compared to unregulated market, increased job search by labour in excess supply at minimum wage. (129–130)

8 F More elastic demand means more substitutes available and consumers better able to escape tax by not buying. (132)

ct **9 F** Usually true; false if demand or supply perfectly inelastic. (134)

10 F See Text Figure 6.9. Tax revenue and deadweight loss come from lost surplus, but not equal. (134)

ct **11 F** Positive statement; can be verified by observation. (135–136)

ct **12 T** Effect on P depends on relative magnitude of penalties. (135–136)

13 F Fluctuate more if demand inelastic. (137–138)

14 T Compared to forecasted prices, sell at high prices and buy at low prices. (138–139)

15 F Shifts supply rightward. (140–141)

Multiple-Choice

1 b **c**, **d**, and **e** refer to long run. (124–125)

2 a Definition. **d** and **e** result of higher rent in unregulated market. (125–126)

3 b Draw graph. No Δ *ceteris paribus* assumptions, so no shift supply or demand. (125–127)

4 d Black market prices will be above ceiling. (126–127)

ct **5 e** Floor below equilibrium P doesn't prevent market from reaching equilibrium. (129–130)

6 b Quantity supplied (50) > quantity demanded (10). (129–130)

7 d Half of loss is consumer surplus, half is producer surplus. (129–130)

8 c Equals the vertical distance between the two supply curves. (131–132)

9 a Original P = $6, new P = $6.60. Sellers pay $1 tax and get $0.60 more from buyers, so sellers pay $0.40. (131–133)

10 b See previous answer. (131–133)

11 a $1 per frisbee × 4,000 units sold. (131–134)

ct **12 c** Rise in P ($6 to $6.60) decreases total revenue ($30,000 to $26,400). **d** wrong: η = 2.3 and η_s = 3.2. (131–134)

13 b **a** would raise P by full amount tax. **c** and **d** affect P but amounts uncertain. (132–133)

14 c Supply shifts leftward as penalties are added to other costs. (135–136)

15 d Reverse taxes and prohibition to make **a** and **b** true. (135–136)

16 d Definition. (137)

17 b Price remains constant so total revenue is positively correlated with output. (137–139)

18 a Draw graphs to see. (137–138)

19 a Quantities (and revenues) still fluctuate. **c** and **d** true if reverse decrease and increase. (137–139)

20 c Where momentary supply curve at 50 million bushels intersects demand. (139–141)

ct **21 c** Farmers receiving $5 but willing to supply this quantity at (their cost of) $1. (139–141)

ct **22 d** Quantity supplied at P = $5. (139–141)

ct **23 d** 70 million bushels sell for $1 per bushel. Taxpayers make up difference of $4 per bushel × 70 million. (139–141)

24 b Floor above market P creates excess supply. (139–141)

25 e Definition. (140–141)

Short Answer Problems

1 a Figure 6.7 corresponds to an unregulated market for rental housing. The initial demand, short-run supply, and long-run supply curves are D_0, SS_0, and LS respectively. The market is initially in long-run equilibrium at point a corresponding to rent R_0 and quantity of rental units Q_0. Demand then increases to D_1, creating excess quantity demanded of $Q_2 - Q_0$ at the initial rent. In the short run, in an unregulated market, rent will rise to R_1 to clear the markets and the equilibrium quantity of housing rented is Q_1 (point b). Note that as the rent rises, the quantity of rental housing supplied increases (a movement from point a to point b along supply curve SS_0) as the existing stock of housing is used more intensively. Also the quantity of housing demanded decreases (a movement from point c to point b along demand curve D_1). Together, these movements eliminate the excess quantity demanded. The higher rent also provides an incentive to construct new housing in the long run. This is illustrated by the shift in the supply curve from SS_0 to SS_1. Finally, a new long-run equilibrium is achieved at point c, with rent restored to its original level and the number of units rented equal to Q_2.

FIGURE **6.7**

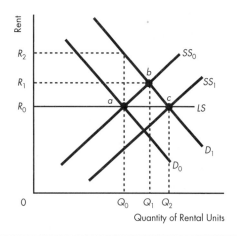

b We can also use Figure 6.7 to discuss the behaviour of a market with a rent ceiling set at R_0. Start in the same long-run equilibrium at point a. Once again we observe an increase in demand from D_0 to D_1. In this case, however, the rent cannot rise to restore equilibrium. There will be no incentive to use the existing stock of housing more intensively in the short run or to construct new housing in the long run. The quantity of rental housing supplied will remain

at Q_0. Since the last unit of rental housing is valued at R_2, but rent is fixed at R_0, demanders of rental housing will be willing to bear additional costs up to $R_2 - R_0$ (in the form of additional search activity or illegal payments) in order to obtain rental housing.

2 a The equilibrium price of gasoline is $1 per litre, since at that price the quantity of gasoline demanded is equal to the quantity supplied (16 million litres per day). The equilibrium quantity of gasoline is 16 million litres per day.

b The new table and graph are shown in Table 6.2 and Figure 6.8.

TABLE **6.2**

Price	Quantity Demanded (millions of litres per day)	Quantity Supplied (millions of litres per day)
1.40	8	16
1.30	10	14
1.20	12	12
1.10	14	10
1.00	16	8
0.90	18	6

FIGURE **6.8**

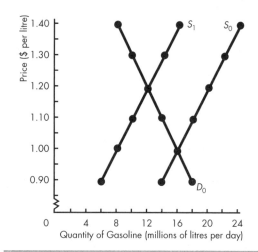

The new equilibrium price is $1.20 per litre, since at that price the quantity of gasoline demanded equals the new quantity supplied (12 million litres per day). The new equilibrium quantity is 12 million litres of gasoline per day.

c The increase in price has caused the quantity of gasoline demanded to decrease by 4 million litres per day (from 16 to 12 million). Given the new supply curve S_1, the increase in price from $1 to $1.20 per litre increases the quantity of gasoline supplied by 4 million litres per day (from 8 to 12 million).

3 a At the ceiling price of $1, quantity demanded is 16 million litres per day, quantity supplied is 8 million litres per day.

b The quantity of gasoline actually sold is 8 million litres per day. When, at a given price, quantity demanded and quantity supplied differ, whichever quantity is *less* determines the quantity actually sold.

c The excess quantity of gasoline demanded is 8 million litres per day.

d The marginal benefit of the 8-millionth litre per day of gasoline sold is $1.40. You can obtain this answer from your graph by imagining a vertical line from the quantity 8 million litres up to where it intersects the demand curve at $1.40. The demand curve is also a marginal benefit curve, showing the highest price consumers are willing to pay for each additional litre.

   The marginal cost of the 8-millionth litre per day of gasoline sold is $1. The imaginary vertical line from the quantity 8 million litres intersects the supply curve S_1 at $1. The supply curve is also a marginal cost curve, showing the minimum producers must receive to produce an additional litre.

e Since marginal benefit ($1.40) > marginal cost ($1), the outcome is *not* efficient. The sum of consumer and producer surplus could be increased by allowing the price to rise, which would shift more resources into production of this good and out of production of other goods where marginal benefit is only equal to or less than marginal cost.

4 Because alcohol and nicotine are addictive, the demands for liquor and cigarettes are relatively inelastic. When liquor and cigarette prices are increased by "sin" taxes, the percentage fall in quantity demanded is less than the percentage increase in price. Thus total revenue increases as does tax revenue. To raise a fixed amount of revenue, it takes a much smaller per-unit tax on goods with inelastic demand than on goods with elastic demand. Inelastic demand also means, *ceteris paribus*, that a greater portion of the tax is borne by consumers rather than producers.

5 a See Figure 6.4 Solution. In the comic book market, the supply curve shifts up vertically by an amount equal to the tax ($0.15). The original equilibrium price is $0.25 and quantity is 200,000. The new equilibrium price is $0.30 and quantity is 100,000. Total expenditure has decreased, from $50,000 ($0.25 × 200,000) to $30,000 ($0.30 × 100,000).

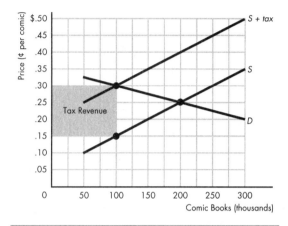

FIGURE **6.4** SOLUTION
COMIC BOOK MARKET

b Total tax revenue is $0.15 per comic book × 100,000 units sold = $15,000 and is indicated by the shaded area on Figure 6.4 Solution.

c As a result of the tax, the price to consumers has gone up by $0.05 (from $0.25 to $0.30). Consumers' share of the tax burden is $5,000 ($0.05 × 100,000). Producers pay the $0.15 tax to government, but only get back $0.05 of it from consumers. Therefore producers' share of the tax burden is $10,000 ($0.10 × 100,000).

d See Figure 6.5 Solution. In the dog biscuit market, the supply curve shifts up vertically by an amount equal to the tax ($0.15). The original equilibrium price is $0.25 and quantity is 200,000. The new equilibrium price is $0.35 and quantity is 150,000. Total expenditure has increased, from $50,000 ($0.25 × 200,000) to $52,500 ($0.35 × 150,000).

FIGURE **6.5** SOLUTION
DOG BISCUIT MARKET

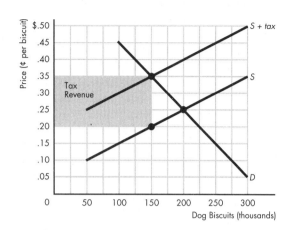

e Total tax revenue is $0.15 per dog biscuit ×
150,000 units sold = $22,500 and is indicated
by the shaded area on Figure 6.5 Solution.

f As a result of the tax, the price to consumers has
gone up by $0.10 (from $0.25 to $0.35).
Consumers' share of the tax burden is $15,000
($0.10 × 150,000). Producers pay the $0.15 tax
to government, and get back $0.10 of it from
consumers. Therefore producers' share of the tax
burden is $7,500 ($0.05 × 150,000).

g You confidently recommend to Dr. More that the
Ministry tax dog biscuits. An excise tax on dog
biscuits meets both objectives: (1) it will raise
more tax revenue than a tax on comic books
($22,500 versus $15,000) and (2) it will place
more of the tax burden on consumers. In the dog
biscuit market, consumers will pay $15,000,
which is 67 percent of the tax burden. In the
comic book market, consumers will pay only
$5,000, which is 33 percent of the tax burden.

6 You are kicking yourself because you forgot that
there is a relationship between elasticity of
demand and both (1) a change in total revenue
for a (tax-induced) increase in price, and (2)
whether consumers or producers bear more of
the burden of a tax.

a For the comic book market, the elasticity of
demand calculation is

$$\eta = \left| \left(\frac{\Delta Q}{Q_{ave}} \right) \middle/ \left(\frac{\Delta P}{P_{ave}} \right) \right|$$

$$= \left| \left(\frac{100 - 200}{150} \right) \middle/ \left(\frac{.30 - .25}{.275} \right) \right|$$

$$= \left| \left(\frac{-.667}{.182} \right) \right| = 3.67$$

Demand is elastic.

b For the dog biscuit market, the elasticity of
demand calculation is

$$\eta = \left| \left(\frac{\Delta Q}{Q_{ave}} \right) \middle/ \left(\frac{\Delta P}{P_{ave}} \right) \right|$$

$$= \left| \left(\frac{150 - 200}{175} \right) \middle/ \left(\frac{.35 - .25}{.30} \right) \right|$$

$$= \left| \left(\frac{-.286}{.333} \right) \right| = 0.86$$

Demand is inelastic.

c You forgot that an increase in price increases
total expenditure when demand is inelastic, and
decreases total expenditure when demand is
elastic. Thus you could have used elasticity data
to predict that expenditure would increase in the
dog biscuit market. An increase in expenditure is
not the same as an increase in tax revenue, but if
more money is being spent, there is more to be
spent on taxes. You also forgot that the more
inelastic demand is, the more of a tax consumers
pay.

If you had thought of the elasticity approach
without prompting, good for you! Dr. More will
be calling on you again for advice. If you didn't
think of it, time to return to Drs. Parkin and
Bade for a refresher.

7 Deadweight loss can be calculated from Figure
6.4 Solution and Figure 6.5 Solution. The loss is
area of the triangle bordered by the 3 black dots.
For comic books, the triangle has a base of $0.15
and altitude of 100,000, so the area = 1/2*ba*
= 1/2($0.15)(100,000) = $7,500.

For dog biscuits, the triangle has a base of
$0.15 and altitude of 50,000, so the area =
1/2*ba* = 1/2($0.15)(100,000) = $3,750.

Once again, your recommendation is to tax
dog biscuits. Dr. More is impressed—you are
offered full-time employment!

8 The clothing market is illustrated in Figure 6.9.
The demand curve is *D* and the supply curve is
S. The equilibrium price is P_c and the quantity is
Q_c. Since police enforcement is lax, the cost of
breaking the law (*CBL*) is very small for both
buyers and sellers. Thus the curves that
incorporate *CBL* are very close to the original
demand and supply curves. The intersection of
D − *CBL* and *S* + *CBL* yields a new equilibrium
price identical to the original price (the price
may be slightly higher or lower depending on
the relative magnitude of the shifts of demand
and supply) and a new equilibrium quantity
(Q_p) only slightly less than the original quantity.

FIGURE **6.9**

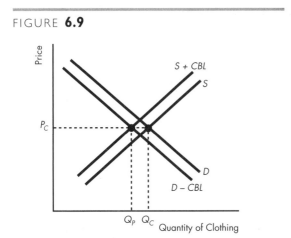

9   The key difference between the two goods is that most fresh fruit cannot be stored effectively while canned fruit is stored easily. Without storage, inventory speculation is difficult, and fresh fruit prices fluctuate widely with variations in the momentary supply curve. Since canned fruit can be stored, inventory holders operate to make the supply of canned fruit perfectly elastic at the inventory holders' expected price. Thus supply-induced price fluctuations for canned fruit are eliminated. Canned fruit prices can still fluctuate if the inventory holders' expected price changes.

ct **10**   Refer to Figure 6.6 Solution.

FIGURE **6.6**   SOLUTION
GRINOLA MARKET

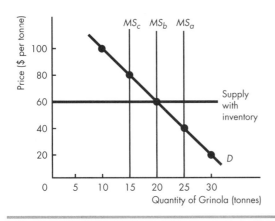

a   When momentary supply is 25 tonnes, $P = \$40$. When momentary supply is 20 tonnes, $P = \$60$. When momentary supply is 15 tonnes, $P = \$80$.

b   The forecasted future price is $60. When momentary supply is 25 tonnes, the market price of $40 would be below the forecasted future price, so speculators buy grinola to store. They start buying at $40, but their added demand pushes up the price until it quickly

reaches $60. The speculators buy 5 tonnes, paying somewhere between $40 and $60 per tonne. Consumers buy the remaining 20 tonnes, and the final market price is $60.

c   In this case, the forecasted future price and the market price are identical ($60), so speculators take no action. The market price is $60.

d   The forecasted future price is $60. When momentary supply is 15 tonnes, the market price of $80 would be above the forecasted future price so speculators sell grinola from their inventories. They start selling at $80, but their added supply pushes down the price until it quickly reaches $60. The speculators sell 5 tonnes, receiving somewhere between $80 and $60 per tonne. Consumers buy 20 tonnes (15 from producers and 5 from speculators), and the final market price is $60.

e   Price fluctuations for consumers have been largely eliminated, since, regardless of the momentary supply, the market price moves quickly to $60.

f   It is likely that the inventory speculators have made a profit. In part **b**, they bought 5 tonnes at a price somewhere between $40 and $60 per tonne. Therefore they spent between $200 and $300. They made no transactions in part **c**. In part **d**, they sold 5 tonnes at a price somewhere between $80 and $60 per tonne. Therefore they earned between $400 and $300. Their net profit is somewhere between a maximum of $200 ($400 – $200) and a minimum of zero ($300 – $300).

Understanding How Markets Work

PROBLEM

The finance minister has asked your boss at the finance department, Dr. Ina Lastic, to estimate the effects of levying a $24-per-carton tax on cigarettes. Dr. Lastic predicts that the tax will raise significant tax revenues (at least $30 million) because cigarette demand is inelastic.

Unfortunately, Dr. Lastic is unaware of a recent study you read in the *Globe and Mail* about past tax increases that found "Ottawa has not received the entire tax windfall it expected from increased cigarette levies because of growing tobacco smuggling."

She has asked you to perform the following detailed analysis for her predictions. The demand and supply curves (without taxes) for cigarettes are given in Figure P2.1. The before-tax price is $28 per carton, and the before-tax quantity is 2.25 million cartons per year.

a Draw the new "S + tax" curve on Figure P2.1.
b According to Dr. Lastic's predictions, what is the after-tax equilibrium price? equilibrium quantity?
c Calculate her predicted tax revenues.
d Check to see if Dr. Lastic's claim that the demand for cigarettes is inelastic is correct by calculating η between the before-tax equilibrium and the after-tax equilibrium. Was she right?

FIGURE **P2.1** CANADIAN CIGARETTE MARKET

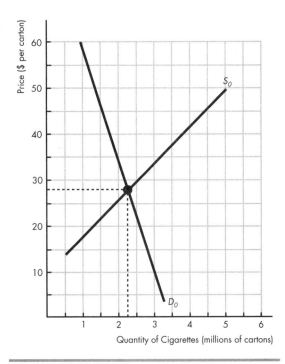

e Dr. Lastic gets high marks for economics so far. Nonetheless, you respectfully point out that her revenue prediction is wrong because she hasn't taken into account the effects of smuggling. Showing an uncharacteristic willingness to stretch herself, she replies, "I'm listening. What's *your* prediction of tax revenue?"

Here's your chance to impress the boss. You know that the supply curve of cigarettes in the United States is the same as the before-tax supply curve in Canada. You have estimated the cost of breaking the law (*CBL*) to suppliers at $16 per carton and risk to consumers of buying smuggled cigarettes is so small that their *CBL* is effectively zero. Use this information to answer the following questions.

i Draw and label any appropriate new curve(s) on Figure P2.1.

ii What is *your* prediction of the after-tax price of a carton of cigarettes? the quantity of cigarettes sold legally? the quantity of smuggled cigarettes sold illegally? [*Hint:* the price of legal and illegal cigarettes will be equal because they are perfect substitutes.]

iii What is your prediction of tax revenue?

MIDTERM EXAMINATION

You should allocate 32 minutes for this examination (16 questions, 2 minutes per question). For each question, choose the one *best* answer.

1 The magnitude of *both* the elasticity of demand and the elasticity of supply depends on

a the resource substitution possibilities.
b the proportion of income spent on a good.
c the time elapsed since the price change.
d the technological conditions of production.
e none of the above factors.

2 If an increase in price causes a decrease in total revenue, price elasticity of demand is

a negative.
b zero.
c greater than zero but less than one.
d equal to one.
e greater than one.

3 Inventory holders

a sell goods from inventory when price is less than the forecasted future price.
b buy goods to put into inventory when price is greater than the forecasted future price.
c make the market supply curve perfectly elastic at the price forecasted by inventory holders.
d do all of the above.
e do none of the above.

4 The proportion of a sales tax paid by consumers will be greater the more

1 elastic is demand.
2 inelastic is demand.
3 elastic is supply.
4 inelastic is supply.

a 2 only
b 1 and 3
c 1 and 4
d 2 and 3
e 2 and 4

5 The "big tradeoff" is between

a efficiency and fairness.
b fair results and fair rules.
c equality of income and equality of opportunity.
d the symmetry principle and utilitarianism.
e consumer surplus and producer surplus.

6 If both demand and supply increase, then equilibrium price

a will rise and quantity will increase.
b will fall and quantity will increase.
c could rise or fall and quantity will increase.
d will rise and quantity could either increase or decrease.
e will fall and quantity could either increase or decrease.

7 If turnips are an inferior good, then, *ceteris paribus*, a rise in the price of turnips will cause

a a decrease in the demand for turnips.
b an increase in the demand for turnips.
c a decrease in the supply of turnips.
d an increase in the supply of turnips.
e none of the above.

8 In Figure P2.2, if the minimum wage is set at $6 per hour, what is the level of unemployment in millions of hours?

a 50
b 40
c 20
d 10
e 0

FIGURE **P2.2**

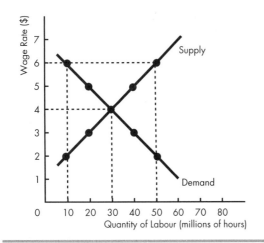

9 A demand curve is

a a consumer surplus curve.
b a marginal benefit curve.
c a minimum-willingness-to-pay curve.
d all of the above.
e none of the above.

10 If a 10 percent increase in income causes a 10 percent decrease in the consumption of widgets (at a constant price),

a the price elasticity of demand for widgets equals 1.
b the income elasticity of demand for widgets is negative.
c the income elasticity of demand for widgets equals 1.
d widgets are a normal good.
e none of the above is true.

11 A price floor set below the equilibrium price results in

a excess supply.
b excess demand.
c the equilibrium price.
d an increase in supply.
e a decrease in demand.

12 When there is underproduction of a good,

a the sum of consumer surplus and producer surplus is greater than the sum for an efficient allocation.
b the sum of consumer surplus and producer surplus is less than the sum for an efficient allocation.
c deadweight loss is less than for an efficient allocation.
d consumer surplus only is lost.
e producer surplus only is lost.

13 A decrease in the price of X from \$6 to \$4 causes an increase in the quantity of Y demanded (at the current price of Y) from 900 to 1,100 units. What is the cross elasticity of demand between X and Y?

a 0.5
b –0.5
c 2
d –2
e **a** or **b**, depending on whether X and Y are substitutes or complements

14 A decrease in quantity supplied is represented by a

a movement down the supply curve.
b movement up the supply curve.
c leftward shift of the supply curve.
d rightward shift of the supply curve.
e rightward shift of the demand curve.

15 At current output, the marginal benefit of shoehorns is less than marginal cost. To achieve an efficient allocation,

1 shoehorn output must increase.
2 shoehorn output must decrease.
3 the marginal benefit of shoehorns will rise.
4 the marginal cost of shoehorns will rise.

a 1 and 3
b 1 and 4
c 2 and 3
d 2 and 4
e 1 only

16 Farmland can be used to produce either cattle or corn. If the demand for cattle increases then

a demand for corn will increase.
b supply of corn will increase.
c demand for corn will decrease.
d supply of corn will decrease.
e **b** and **c**.

ANSWERS

Problem

a See Figure P2.1 Solution. Ignore the curve $S + CBL$ for now.

FIGURE **P2.1** SOLUTION
CANADIAN CIGARETTE MARKET

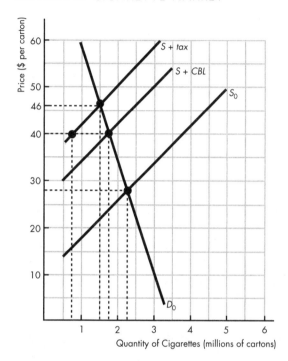

b The after-tax equilibrium price is $46 per carton. The after-tax equilibrium quantity is 1.5 million cartons per year.

c Tax revenue is 1.5 million cartons × $24 per carton = $36 million per year.

d $\eta = \left| \dfrac{\dfrac{\Delta Q}{Q_{ave}}}{\dfrac{\Delta P}{P_{ave}}} \right|$

$\eta = \left| \dfrac{\dfrac{-.75}{1.875}}{\dfrac{18}{37}} \right| = \dfrac{.4}{.486} = .82$

The demand curve is inelastic ($\eta < 1$) between the two equilibrium points. Dr. Lastic's predictions about tax revenue (without smuggling) and elasticity were correct.

e i See Figure P2.1 Solution. Since the *CBL* to consumers is zero, the demand curve does not shift. The smugglers' supply curve is $S + CBL$.
ii Since consumers can buy cigarettes from smugglers at a price of $40 per carton, no one is willing to buy at the higher legal price of $46. The legal price is bid down to $40. At that price, legal suppliers will supply 0.75 million cartons, and total market demand is 1.75 million cartons. Smugglers supply the difference, 1 million cartons.
iii Tax revenue is 0.75 million cartons × $24 per carton = only $18 million per year.

Dr. Lastic is impressed. She says, "When I studied economics, we were taught that illegal activities were the business of law enforcement officials, not economists. What you have shown is that almost any activity can be analyzed from an economic perspective. Well done. Let's draft our reply to the minister."

Midterm Examination

1 **c** **a, d** affect η_s only. **b** affects η only. (89–90, 95–96)
2 **e** Total revenue test. (88–89)
3 **c** **a** and **b** would be true if reversed "less" and "greater." (138–139)
4 **d** Definition. (131–133)
5 **a** Definition. (115)
6 **c** Rightward shifts demand and supply must increase equilibrium quantity, but effect on price indeterminate. (74)
7 **e** Rise in *P* causes movement along demand curve. (61–65)
8 **b** Quantity supplied (50) > quantity demanded (10). (128–130)
9 **b** Also a *maximum* willingness to pay curve. (106–107)
10 **b** $\eta_y = (\% \Delta Q_D)/(\% \Delta \text{ income}) = -10/10 = -1$; widgets inferior good. (92)
11 **c** Draw graph. Floor doesn't prevent *P* rising from excess demand. (129–130)
12 **b** Deadweight loss reduces both consumer and producer surplus relative to an efficient allocation. (112–113)
13 **b** $\eta_x = (\% \Delta Q^Y_D)/(\% \Delta P^X) = (200/1{,}000)/(-2/5) = -0.5$. (91)
14 **a** Illustration of law of supply. (66–69)
15 **c** With decreasing *Q*, *MB* must rise and *MC* fall. (105)
16 **d** Cattle and corn substitutes in production. Increased demand for cattle raises price of cattle, causing decreased supply corn. (67–68)

Chapter 7

Utility and Demand

KEY CONCEPTS

Household Consumption Choices

Household consumption choices are determined by

◆ consumption possibilities.

  • Income and prices (P) of goods and services are given.
  • Budget line marks boundary between affordable (points on line or inside) and unaffordable (outside line) choices.

◆ preferences—likes and dislikes based on utility.

Utility is benefit or satisfaction from consumption.

◆ **Total utility** (TU) is total benefit or satisfaction from consumption of goods and services. Increased consumption increases total utility.

◆ **Marginal utility** (MU) is Δ total utility from one-unit increase in quantity good consumed. MU positive, but due to **diminishing marginal utility**, decreases as consumption good increases.

Maximizing Utility

Consumers strive for utility maximization—maximum attainable benefit.

◆ Given income and the prices of goods and services, **consumer equilibrium** occurs when consumer allocates income in way that maximizes total utility.

◆ Total utility is maximized when all income is spent and **marginal utility per dollar spent** is equal for all goods. For substitute goods movies (M) and pop (P), this occurs when

$$\frac{MU_M}{P_M} = \frac{MU_P}{P_P}$$

The power of marginal analysis for predicting economic choices stems from a simple rule—if the marginal gain from an action exceeds the marginal loss, take the action.

◆ The rule applied to the utility maximization example is—if the marginal utility per dollar spent on movies exceeds the marginal utility per dollar spent on pop, buy more movies and less pop.

◆ The marginal gain from more movies exceeds the marginal loss from less pop.

Predictions of Marginal Utility Theory

Ceteris paribus, if P_M falls, Q_M consumed increases (movement down along demand curve for movies); also causes leftward shift demand curve for pop.

Ceteris paribus, if P_P rises, Q_P consumed decreases (movement up along demand curve for pop); also causes rightward shift demand curve for movies.

Movies and pop normal goods. *Ceteris paribus*, increased income causes increased consumption movies and pop (rightward shifts both demand curves).

Marginal utility theory allows us to derive and predict the above results which, in Chapter 3, were just *assumptions* about consumer demand.

Individual and market demand:

◆ Individual demand—relationship between quantity demanded and price for single individual.

◆ **Market demand**—sum of individual demands; relationship between total quantity demanded and price.

◆ Market demand curve—horizontal sum of individual demand curves.

Marginal utility helps explain elasticity. When price falls and quantity consumed increases, if

◆ marginal utility diminishes slowly, demand for good is elastic (close substitutes).

◆ marginal utility diminishes rapidly, demand for good is inelastic (poor substitutes).

Efficiency, Price, and Value

Value is related to total utility or consumer surplus. Price is related to marginal utility. Distinction between total utility and marginal utility resolves diamond-water paradox.

◆ Diamonds, though less useful (low *TU* and small consumer surplus) than water, have higher price (high *MU*).

◆ Water more useful (high *TU* and large consumer surplus), but has lower price (low *MU*).

HELPFUL HINTS

1 Utility is a very useful abstract concept that allows us to think more clearly about consumer choice. Do not be concerned that arbitrary units are used to measure utility. The only important basis for marginal utility theory is that you can judge whether the additional satisfaction per dollar spent on good *X* is greater or less than the additional satisfaction per dollar spent on *Y*. If it is greater, then you decide to consume an additional unit of *X*. How much greater is irrelevant for the decision.

2 The marginal utility per dollar spent on good *X* can be written as MU_X/P_X, where MU_X is the marginal utility of the last unit of *X* consumed and P_X is the price of a unit of good *X*. The consumer equilibrium (utility-maximizing) condition for goods *X* and *Y* can be written

$$\frac{MU_X}{P_X} = \frac{MU_Y}{P_Y}$$

This implies that, in consumer equilibrium, the ratio of marginal utilities will equal the ratio of prices of the two goods:

$$\frac{MU_X}{MU_Y} = \frac{P_X}{P_Y}$$

This result is often useful.

3 If an individual is not in consumer equilibrium, then the preceding equation is not satisfied. For example, consider spending all of your income on a consumption plan where

$$\frac{MU_X}{P_X} > \frac{MU_Y}{P_Y}$$

or, equivalently,

$$\frac{MU_X}{MU_Y} > \frac{P_X}{P_Y}$$

Since P_X and P_Y are given, this means that MU_X is "too large" and MU_Y is "too small." Total utility can be increased by increasing consumption of *X* (and thereby decreasing MU_X due to the principle of diminishing marginal utility) and decreasing consumption of *Y* (and thereby increasing MU_Y due to diminishing marginal utility).

4 Text Table 7.7 on page 162 is a good review device.

SELF-TEST

True/False and Explain

Household Consumption Choices

1 All points inside a consumer's budget line are unaffordable.

2 The principle of diminishing marginal utility means that as consumption of a good increases, total utility increases but at a decreasing rate.

Maximizing Utility

3 A household is maximizing utility if the marginal utility per dollar spent is equal for all goods and all its income is spent.

4 If the marginal utilities from consuming two goods are not equal, the consumer cannot be in equilibrium.

5 If the marginal utility per dollar spent on good X exceeds the marginal utility per dollar spent on good Y, total utility will increase by increasing consumption of X and decreasing consumption of Y.

Predictions of Marginal Utility Theory

6 When the price of good X rises, the marginal utility from the consumption of X decreases.

7 When income decreases, the marginal utility derived from a good will always increase.

8 The market demand curve is the horizontal sum of all individual demand curves.

9 The market demand curve is formed by adding the willingness to pay for each individual at each price.

10 If the marginal utility from a good diminishes rapidly as more is consumed, the good has close substitutes.

11 As quantity consumed increases, marginal utility diminishes more for goods with inelastic demands than for goods with elastic demands.

Efficiency, Price, and Value

12 In consumer equilibrium, price equals marginal benefit for the last unit consumed.

13 A demand curve describes the quantity demanded at each price when marginal utility is maximized.

14 Consumer surplus for relatively cheap goods like water will be relatively low.

15 If a shift in supply decreases the price of a good, consumer surplus increases.

Multiple-Choice

Household Consumption Choices

1 A household's consumption choices are determined by
a prices of goods and services.
b income.
c preferences.
d all of the above.
e **a** and **b** only.

2 Total utility equals
a the sum of the marginal utilities of each unit consumed.
b the area below the demand curve but above the market price.
c the slope of the marginal utility curve.
d the marginal utility of the last unit divided by price.
e the marginal utility of the last unit consumed multiplied by the total number of units consumed.

3 Total utility is always
a greater than marginal utility.
b less than marginal utility.
c decreasing when marginal utility is decreasing.
d decreasing when marginal utility is increasing.
e increasing when marginal utility is positive.

4 According to the principle of diminishing marginal utility, as consumption of a good increases, total utility
a decreases and then eventually increases.
b decreases at an increasing rate.
c decreases at a decreasing rate.
d increases at an increasing rate.
e increases at a decreasing rate.

Maximizing Utility

5 If a consumer is in equilibrium, then

a total utility is maximized given the consumer's income and the prices of goods.

b marginal utility is maximized given the consumer's income and the prices of goods.

c marginal utility per dollar spent is maximized given the consumer's income and the prices of goods.

d the marginal utility of each good will be equal.

e none of the above is true.

6 Suppose that Ally spends her entire income of $10 on law books and miniskirts. Law books cost $2 and miniskirts cost $4 (see Table 7.1). The marginal utility of each good is independent of the amount consumed of the other good.

TABLE **7.1**   ALLY'S MARGINAL UTILITY

	Marginal Utility	
Quantity	Law Books	Miniskirts
1	12	16
2	10	12
3	8	8
4	6	4

If Ally is maximizing her utility, how many miniskirts does she buy?

a 0
b 1
c 2
d 3
e 4

7 If potato chips were free, individuals would consume

a an infinite quantity of chips.

b the quantity of chips at which total utility from chips falls to zero.

c the quantity of chips at which marginal utility from chips falls to zero.

d zero chips, since this equates marginal utility and price.

e none of the above.

8 In consumer equilibrium, a consumer equates the

a total utility from each good.

b marginal utility from each good.

c total utility per dollar spent on each good.

d marginal utility per dollar spent on each good.

e total income spent on each good with total utility from each good.

9 Samir consumes apples and bananas and is in consumer equilibrium. The marginal utility of the last apple is 10 and the marginal utility of the last banana is 5. If the price of an apple is $0.50, then what is the price of a banana?

a $0.05
b $0.10
c $0.25
d $0.50
e $1.00

10 If Ms. Petersen is maximizing her utility in the consumption of goods A and B, which of the following statements must be *true*?

a $MU_A = MU_B$

b $\dfrac{MU_A}{P_A} = \dfrac{MU_B}{P_B}$

c $\dfrac{MU_A}{P_B} = \dfrac{MU_B}{P_A}$

d $TU_A = TU_B$

e $\dfrac{TU_A}{P_A} = \dfrac{TU_B}{P_B}$

11 Squid costs $2 per kilogram and octopus costs $1 per kilogram. Jacques buys only octopus and gets 10 units of utility from the last kilogram he buys. Assuming that Jacques has maximized his utility, his marginal utility, in units, from the first kilogram of squid must be

a more than 10.
b less than 10.
c more than 20.
d less than 20.
e zero.

12 If Soula is maximizing her utility and two goods have the same marginal utility, she will

a buy only one.
b buy equal quantities of both.
c be willing to pay the same price for each.
d get the same total utility from each.
e do none of the above.

13 Suppose that Madonna spends her entire income of $6 on purple nail polish and leather outfits. Nail polish costs $1 per unit and outfits cost $2 per unit (see Table 7.2). The marginal utility of each good is independent of the amount consumed of the other good.

TABLE **7.2** MADONNA'S MARGINAL UTILITY

| | Marginal Utility | |
Quantity	Nail Polish	Outfits
1	8	16
2	6	12
3	4	10
4	3	6

If Madonna is maximizing her utility, what is her *total* utility?

a 19
b 28
c 38
d 42
e none of the above

14 Sergio is maximizing his utility in his consumption of beer and bubblegum. If the price of beer is greater than the price of bubblegum, then we know with *certainty* that

a Sergio buys more beer than bubblegum.
b Sergio buys more bubblegum than beer.
c the marginal utility of the last purchased beer is greater than the marginal utility of the last purchased bubblegum.
d the marginal utility of the last purchased bubblegum is greater than the marginal utility of the last purchased beer.
e the marginal utilities of the last purchased beer and bubblegum are equal.

Predictions of Marginal Utility Theory

15 Bikes and roller blades are substitutes. Marginal utility theory predicts that when the price of bikes increases, the quantity demanded of bikes

a decreases and the demand curve for roller blades shifts rightward.
b decreases and the demand curve for roller blades shifts leftward.
c decreases and the demand curve for roller blades will not shift.
d increases and the demand curve for roller blades shifts rightward.
e increases and the demand curve for roller blades shifts leftward.

16 Which of the following is *not* a prediction of marginal utility theory?

a Other things remaining the same, the higher the price of a good, the lower the quantity demanded.
b Other things remaining the same, the higher the price of a good, the higher the consumption of substitutes for that good.
c Other things remaining the same, the lower the price of a good, the lower the consumption of substitutes for that good.
d the law of demand
e diminishing marginal utility

17 Chuck and Barry have identical preferences but Chuck has a much higher income. If each is maximizing his utility,

a they will have equal total utilities.
b Chuck will have lower total utility than Barry.
c Chuck will have lower marginal utility than Barry for each normal good consumed.
d Chuck will have higher marginal utility than Barry for each normal good consumed.
e they will have equal marginal utilities for each normal good consumed.

18 The relative prices of beer to back bacon are 2:1. If Bob's current consumption is at a level where $MU_{BEER}/MU_{BACK\ BACON}$ is 1:2, then to achieve maximum utility Bob must

a consume more beer and less back bacon.
b not change his current consumption of beer and back bacon.
c consume less beer and more back bacon.
d increase the price of beer.
e consume twice as much beer and one-half as much back bacon.

19 Broomhilda is initially maximizing her utility in her consumption of goods X and Y. The price of good X doubles, *ceteris paribus*. For Broomhilda to once again maximize her utility, her *quantity* of X consumed must

a rise until the marginal utility of X has doubled.
b fall to one-half its previous level.
c fall until the marginal utility of X has doubled.
d fall until the marginal utility of X falls to one-half its previous level.
e yield infinite bliss.

20 Beverly is currently in consumer equilibrium. An increase in her income will

a increase her total utility.
b decrease her total utility.
c increase her marginal utility of all goods.
d decrease her marginal utility of all goods.
e increase her consumption of all goods.

21 Market demand is the
a sum of the prices that each individual is willing to pay for each quantity demanded.
b sum of the quantities demanded by each individual at each price.
c sum of the consumer surplus of each individual.
d difference between the maximum amount each individual is willing to pay for a good and the market price.
e difference between the market price and the maximum amount each individual is willing to pay for a good.

22 If marginal utility diminishes slightly when price falls and quantity consumed increases, then the good has
1 elastic demand.
2 inelastic demand.
3 close substitutes.
4 poor substitutes.
a 1 and 3
b 1 and 4
c 2 and 3
d 2 and 4
e 1 only

Efficiency, Price, and Value

23 The value of a good relates to
a total utility while price relates to consumer surplus.
b consumer surplus while price relates to total utility.
c marginal utility while price relates to consumer surplus.
d marginal utility while price relates to total utility.
e total utility while price relates to marginal utility.

24 Bill and Ted consume 15 chocolate bars each at the current price. If Bill's demand curve is more elastic than Ted's demand curve,
a Bill's willingness to pay for the 15th chocolate bar is greater than Ted's.
b Ted's willingness to pay for the 15th chocolate bar is greater than Bill's.
c Bill's consumer surplus is greater than Ted's.
d Ted's consumer surplus is greater than Bill's.
e Bill's consumer surplus equals Ted's.

25 The high price of diamonds relative to the price of water reflects the fact that, at typical levels of consumption,
a the total utility of water is relatively low.
b the total utility of diamonds is relatively high.
c the marginal utility of water is relatively high.
d the marginal utility of diamonds is relatively low.
e none of the above is true.

Short Answer Problems

1 Explain why the consumer equilibrium condition and the principle of diminishing marginal utility imply the law of demand.

2 Consider the following information for a consumer who is trying to allocate her income between goods X and Y so as to maximize utility. The price of X is $2 and the price of Y is $1 per unit. When all income is spent, the marginal utility of the last unit of X is 20 and the marginal utility of the last unit of Y is 16.
a Why is the consumer not in equilibrium?
b To increase utility, which good should this consumer consume more of and which less of?

3 A consumer is initially maximizing his utility in the consumption of goods A and B so that

$$\frac{MU_A}{P_A} = \frac{MU_B}{P_B}$$

The price of A then rises as a result of the shift in supply shown in Figure 7.1.

FIGURE **7.1**

Use the above condition for utility maximization to explain how the consumer will move to a new utility-maximizing equilibrium. Show the connection between your explanation and the change on the diagram.

4 Tables 7.3 and 7.4 give Amy's utility from the consumption of popcorn and candy bars during a week.

TABLE **7.3** AMY'S UTILITY FROM POPCORN

Bags of Popcorn	Total Utility	Marginal Utility
1	20	
2	36	
3	50	
4		12
5	72	
6	80	

TABLE **7.4** AMY'S UTILITY FROM CANDY BARS

Number of Candy Bars	Total Utility	Marginal Utility
1	14	
2	26	
3		10
4	44	
5	51	
6	57	

a Complete the tables.

b Suppose the price of a bag of popcorn is $1 and the price of a candy bar is $0.50. Given the information in Tables 7.3 and 7.4, complete Table 7.5 where *MU/P* means marginal utility divided by price, which is equivalent to marginal utility per dollar spent.

TABLE **7.5** AMY'S *MU/P*

Bags of Popcorn	*MU/P*	Number of Candy Bars	*MU/P*
1		1	
2		2	
3		3	
4		4	
5		5	
6		6	

5 Amy's weekly allowance is $4. Using your answers to Short Answer Problem **4** above, answer the following if Amy spends her entire allowance on popcorn and candy.

  a How much popcorn and how many candy bars will Amy consume each week if she maximizes her utility?

b Show that the utility maximum condition is satisfied.

c What is total utility?

d If, instead, Amy consumed 3 bags of popcorn and 2 candy bars, explain why she would not be maximizing her utility using figures both for total utility and for the terms *MU/P*.

6 Suppose that Amy's preferences remain as they were in Short Answer Problem **4**, but the price of a candy bar doubles to $1.

a Construct a new table (similar to Table 7.5) of *MU/P* for popcorn and candy bars.

b Amy's allowance continues to be $4. After the price change, how much popcorn and how many candy bars will she consume each week?

c Are popcorn and candy bars substitutes or complements for Amy? Why?

d On the basis of the information you have obtained, draw Amy's demand curve for candy bars.

e Suppose that both bags of popcorn and candy bars continue to sell for $1 each, but now Amy's allowance increases to $6 per week.
   i How many candy bars and bags of popcorn will Amy choose to consume per week under the new situation?
   ii Are popcorn and candy bars normal goods? Why or why not?

7 Suppose that Andre Agassi spends his entire income of $8 on razors and toy tennis rackets (see Table 7.6). The price of a razor is $2 and the price of a tennis racket is $4. The marginal utility of each good is independent of the amount consumed of the other good.

TABLE **7.6** ANDRE'S MARGINAL UTILITY

	Marginal Utility	
Quantity	Razors	Rackets
1	20	36
2	18	32
3	16	20
4	8	16

a If Andre is maximizing his utility, how many units of each good should he purchase?

b If Andre's income rises to $24, how many units of each good should he purchase?

c Using the information above, calculate Andre's income elasticity of demand for razors.

8 Suppose that Igor maximizes his utility by spending his entire income on bats and lizards (see Table 7.7). The marginal utility of each good is independent of the amount consumed of the other good.

TABLE **7.7** IGOR'S MARGINAL UTILITY

Quantity	Marginal Utility	
	Bats	Lizards
1	20	45
2	18	40
3	16	25
4	8	20

Igor's income is $16. The price of a bat is $2, and he buys 3 bats. If the marginal utility of the last lizard he buys is 40, calculate the price of a lizard using two separate methods.

9 Table 7.8 gives the demand schedules for broccoli for three individuals: Tom, Jana, and Ted.

TABLE **7.8** INDIVIDUAL DEMAND FOR BROCCOLI

Price ($ per kilogram)	Quantity Demanded (kilograms per week)		
	Tom	Jana	Ted
0.50	10	4	10
0.75	9	2	7
1.00	8	0	4
1.25	7	0	1

a Calculate the market demand schedule.
b On a single diagram, draw the individual demand curves for Tom, Jana, and Ted, as well as the market demand curve.

ⓒ **10** An apparent paradox that bothers many people is that although child-care workers are usually paid low salaries, it is often said that "they have the most important job in the world." Use economic reasoning to resolve this paradox.

ANSWERS

True/False and Explain

1 **F** Points on and inside budget line are affordable; points outside are unaffordable. (154)
2 **T** Because *MU* positive but diminishing. (155)
3 **T** Rules for maximizing total utility. (157)
4 **F** If prices unequal, then marginal utilities unequal in consumer equilibrium. (157–159)
ⓒ **5** **T** Increased consumption *X* causes decreased MU_X. Decreased consumption *Y* causes increased MU_Y. Moves ratios *MU/P* towards equality. (157–159)
6 **F** Rising *P* causes decreased *Q* and increased *MU*. (159–161)
ⓒ **7** **F** True for normal good; may be false for inferior good. (162)
8 **T** Definition. (163)
9 **F** Adding the quantities demanded by each individual at each price. (163)
10 **F** Goods with inelastic demands (poor substitutes) have faster diminishing marginal utility. (164)
ⓒ **11** **T** For given Δ*P*, small increase in quantity of good (Δ*Q*) restores consumer equilibrium, so demand inelastic. (164)
12 **T** Consumer on demand curve = willingness-to-pay curve. (164–165)
13 **F** When *total* utility maximized. (164–165)
14 **F** Since many units consumed, many earlier units have willingness to pay > price. (164–165)
15 **T** With fall in price and increased quantity consumed, more units with willingness-to-pay > price. (164–165)

Multiple-Choice

1 **d** Consumption possibilities (constraints) and preferences. (154)
2 **a** **b** is consumer surplus. For **c**, *MU* = slope *TU* curve. **d** and **e** nonsense. (154–155)
3 **e** *TU* increasing when *MU* positive, whether *MU* decreasing or increasing. *TU* may be ⋛ *MU*. (154–155)
ⓒ **4** **e** Because marginal utility is positive but diminishing with increased consumption. (155–156)
5 **a** Consumers maximize *TU*. **c** and **d** wrong because *MU/P* equal for *TU* maximization. (157–159)
6 **b** Buys 1 miniskirt (*MU/P* = 16/4) and 3 books (*MU/P* = 8/2). (157–159)

ⓒⓣ **7 c** Maximizes *TU*. With fewer chips, *MU* still positive, so *TU* could increase. With more, *MU* turns negative so *TU* would decrease. (157–159)

8 d Definition. *MU/P* key to utility maximization. (157–159)

9 c Solve $10/0.5 = 5/P_{BANANA}$ for P_{BANANA}. (157–159)

10 b Definition. (157–159)

ⓒⓣ **11 d** For octopus, $MU_O/P_O = 10$. For squid, $MU_S/2$ would need to be < 10, so MU_S must be < 20. (157–159)

12 c From maximum condition of equal *MU/P*. No necessary relation between *MU* and quantity or *TU*. (157–159)

13 d Buys 2 polish and 2 outfits. $TU = 8 + 6 + 16 + 12$. (157–159)

ⓒⓣ **14 c** From maximum condition of equal *MU/P*. No necessary relation between *MU* and quantity. (157–159)

15 a See text discussion. (159–161)

16 e Diminishing *MU* is *assumption* of theory. (159–162)

17 c Chuck consumes greater quantities of each good, so *MU* lower. (162)

18 c To equalize *MU/P* must increase MU_{BEER} and decrease $MU_{BACK\ BACON}$. **d** wrong because no control over prices. (159–162)

19 c From maximum condition of equal *MU/P*. No necessary relation between *MU* and quantity consumed. (159–161)

ⓒⓣ **20 a** For inferior goods, consumption may decrease and *MU* increase. (162)

21 b See text discussion. (163)

22 a Goods with elastic demands (close substitutes) have slower diminishing marginal utility. (164)

23 e Value relates to total utility and consumer surplus; price relates to marginal utility. (164–165)

24 d Ted's steeper demand curve means greater willingness to pay for previous units. Willingness to pay for last unit equal. (164–165)

25 e For diamonds: *TU* relatively low, *MU* relatively high. For water: *TU* relatively high, *MU* relatively low. (164–165)

Short Answer Problems

1 Suppose we observe an individual in consumer equilibrium consuming X_0 units of good *X* and Y_0 units of good *Y*, with the prices of *X* and *Y* given by P_X and P_Y respectively. This means that at consumption levels X_0 and Y_0, the marginal utility per dollar spent on *X* equals the marginal utility per dollar spent on *Y*. Now let the price of *X* increase to P^1_X. The marginal utility per dollar spent on *X* declines and thus is now less than the marginal utility per dollar spent on *Y*. To restore equilibrium, our consumer must increase the marginal utility of *X* and decrease the marginal utility of *Y*. From the principle of diminishing marginal utility we know that the only way to do this is to decrease the consumption of *X* and increase the consumption of *Y*. This demonstrates the law of demand since an increase in the price of *X* has been shown to require a decrease in the consumption of *X* to restore consumer equilibrium.

2 a This consumer is not in equilibrium because the marginal utility per dollar spent is not the same for goods *X* and *Y*. The marginal utility per dollar spent on *X* is $MU_X/P_X = 20/2 = 10$, which is less than the marginal utility per dollar spent on *Y*: $MU_Y/P_Y = 16$.

b To equate the marginal utilities per dollar spent (and thus increase utility), this consumer should increase consumption of *Y* and decrease consumption of *X*. The principle of diminishing marginal utility implies that this will decrease the marginal utility of *Y* and increase the marginal utility of *X*.

3 When the price of *A* rises, *ceteris paribus*:

$$\frac{MU_A}{P_A} < \frac{MU_B}{P_B}$$

The consumer is no longer in equilibrium. In order to restore the equality in the equilibrium condition, the consumer must change his consumption to make MU_A rise and MU_B fall. (The consumer cannot change the prices of *A* and *B*.) Since marginal utility diminishes with increases in quantity consumed, the consumer must decrease consumption of *A* and increase consumption of *B*. Decreased consumption of *A* moves the consumer up to the left on the demand curve, from the initial intersection of *D* and S_0 to the new intersection of *D* and S_1. In the new consumer equilibrium, equality will be restored in the equilibrium condition.

4 a The tables are completed in Table 7.3 Solution and Table 7.4 Solution.

TABLE **7.3** SOLUTION
AMY'S UTILITY FROM POPCORN

Bags of Popcorn	Total Utility	Marginal Utility
1	20	20
2	36	16
3	50	14
4	62	12
5	72	10
6	80	8

TABLE **7.4** SOLUTION
AMY'S UTILITY FROM CANDY BARS

Number of Candy Bars	Total Utility	Marginal Utility
1	14	14
2	26	12
3	36	10
4	44	8
5	51	7
6	57	6

b The table is completed in Table 7.5 Solution.

TABLE **7.5** SOLUTION
AMY'S *MU/P*

Bags of Popcorn	MU/P	Number of Candy Bars	MU/P
1	20	1	28
2	16	2	24
3	14	3	20
4	12	4	16
5	10	5	14
6	8	6	12

5 a 2 bags of popcorn and 4 candy bars.
b The utility maximum condition is satisfied, since Amy spends all of her income ($4), and the marginal utility per dollar spent is the same for popcorn and candy bars (16).
c Total utility is the utility from the consumption of 2 bags of popcorn (36) plus the utility from the consumption of 4 candy bars (44) = 80.
d If Amy consumed 3 bags of popcorn and 2 candy bars, total utility would be 76, which is less than 80, the total utility from the consumption of 2 bags of popcorn and 4 candy bars. For the combination of 3 bags of popcorn

and 2 candy bars, *MU/P* for popcorn is 14 while *MU/P* for candy bars is 24. Since *MU/P* is not the same for both goods, this combination does not meet the condition for utility maximization.

6 a See Table 7.9.

TABLE **7.9** AMY'S *MU/P*

Bags of Popcorn	MU/P	Number of Candy Bars	MU/P
1	20	1	14
2	16	2	12
3	14	3	10
4	12	4	8
5	10	5	7
6	8	6	6

b 3 bags of popcorn and 1 candy bar. Amy spends all of her income ($4) and the marginal utility per dollar spent is the same for popcorn and candy bars (14).
c Popcorn and candy bars are substitutes for Amy, since an increase in the price of a candy bar causes an increase in the demand for popcorn.
d Amy's demand curve for candy bars is given in Figure 7.2. Two points on the demand curve have been identified: when the price of a candy bar is $1, one candy bar will be demanded, and when the price is $0.50, 4 candy bars will be demanded. The demand curve is a line through these two points.

FIGURE **7.2**

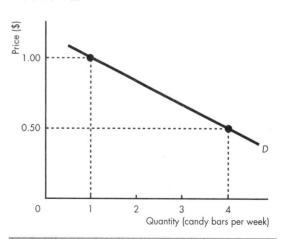

e i Now, Amy will choose to consume 4 bags of popcorn and 2 candy bars (instead of 3 bags of popcorn and 1 candy bar). Amy spends all of her income ($6) and the marginal utility per dollar spent is the same for popcorn and candy bars (12).

ii Popcorn and candy bars are both normal goods for Amy, since the increase in income (allowance) leads to increases in the demand for both goods.

7 a The utility-maximizing combination of goods is shown in Table 7.10.

TABLE **7.10** ANDRE'S *MU/P*

| Quantity | MU/P | |
	Razors	Rackets
1	10	9
2	9	8
3	8	5
4	4	4

Andre should purchase 2 razors and 1 racket. Andre spends all of his income ($8), and the marginal utility per dollar spent is the same for razors and rackets (9).

b Andre should purchase 4 razors and 4 rackets. He spends all of his income ($24), and the marginal utility per dollar spent is the same for razors and rackets (4).

c The income elasticity of demand for razors is

$$\eta_y = \frac{\dfrac{\Delta Q}{Q_{ave}}}{\dfrac{\Delta Y}{Y_{ave}}} = \frac{\dfrac{4-2}{\frac{1}{2}(4+2)}}{\dfrac{24-8}{\frac{1}{2}(24+8)}} = \frac{\dfrac{2}{3}}{\dfrac{16}{16}} = \frac{2}{3}$$

8 There are two methods for calculating the price of a lizard. One method is based on the fact that Igor spends all of his income on bats and lizards. This means that

$$Y = P_B Q_B + P_L Q_L$$

where Y = income, P_B = the price of a bat, Q_B = the quantity of bats purchased, P_L = the price of a lizard, and Q_L = the quantity of lizards purchased. We know Y = 16, P_B = 2, Q_B = 3, and if the marginal utility of the last lizard is 40, then Q_L = 2. Substituting these values, we can solve for P_L.

$$16 = 2(3) + P_L(2)$$
$$10 = P_L(2)$$
$$5 = P_L$$

The second method uses the condition for utility maximization:

$$\frac{MU_B}{P_B} = \frac{MU_L}{P_L}$$

We know that MU_L = 40, P_B = 2, and if Igor buys 3 bats MU_B = 16. Substituting these values, we can solve for P_L.

$$\frac{16}{2} = \frac{40}{P_L}$$
$$80 = 16P_L$$
$$5 = P_L$$

9 a The market demand schedule is obtained by adding the quantities demanded by Tom, Jana, and Ted at each price (see Table 7.11).

TABLE **7.11** MARKET DEMAND SCHEDULE FOR BROCCOLI

Price ($ per kilogram)	Quantity Demanded (kilograms per week)
0.50	24
0.75	18
1.00	12
1.25	8

b Figure 7.3 illustrates the individual demand curves for Tom, Jana, and Ted as well as the market demand curve.

FIGURE **7.3**

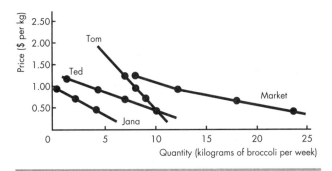

10 While most parents place a high value on child-care services, many child-care workers are willing to provide those services. While the total utility provided by the services of child-care workers is high, the marginal utility of those (abundantly supplied) services is low.

Chapter 8

Possibilities, Preferences, and Choices

KEY CONCEPTS

Consumption Possibilities

Budget line shows limits to household consumption, given income, and prices of goods and services. Consider example of movies (horizontal axis) and pop (vertical axis).

◆ Budget equation is

$$Q_P = \frac{Y}{P_P} - \frac{P_M}{P_P} Q_M$$

◆ Magnitude of slope of budget equation (P_M/P_P) equals **relative price** of movies in terms of pop.

◆ Intercepts measure household's **real income** in movies (x-intercept) and pop (y-intercept).

◆ Higher P_M yields steeper budget line, fixed pop-intercept.

◆ Higher P_P yields flatter budget line, fixed movie-intercept.

◆ Higher Y yields rightward parallel shift budget line.

Preferences and Indifference Curves

Indifference curve maps household preferences, joining combinations goods giving equal satisfaction.

◆ Indifference curves generally slope downward and bow towards the origin (convex).

◆ Indifference curves farther from the origin represent higher levels of satisfaction.

◆ Indifference curves never intersect.

◆ **Marginal rate of substitution** (*MRS*) is magnitude of slope of indifference curve—rate at which household gives up good *y* (pop) for additional unit good *x* (movies) and remains indifferent (remains on same indifference curve).

◆ **Diminishing marginal rate of substitution** is tendency for *MRS* to diminish as move down along an indifference curve. Accounts for bowed-towards-the-origin shape of indifference curves.

- More substitutability between goods yields straighter indifference curves.
- Less substitutability between goods yields more tightly curved indifference curves.

Predicting Consumer Behaviour

Given income and prices of goods, household allocates income to maximize satisfaction. Household chooses best-affordable point, which is on budget line and on highest possible indifference curve. At the best-affordable point,

◆ household spends all its income and achieves maximum possible satisfaction.

◆ budget line and indifference curve are tangent and have same slope—*MRS* equals the relative price.

Price effect is Δ consumption resulting from Δ price of a good. Price effect = substitution effect + income effect.

◆ **Substitution effect**—Δ consumption resulting from Δ price accompanied by (hypothetical) Δ income leaving household indifferent between initial and new situations. For normal and inferior goods, substitution effect of falling price is increased consumption.

◆ **Income effect**—Δ consumption resulting from (hypothetically) restoring original income but keeping prices constant at new level. For normal goods, income effect of (hypothetically) increased income is increased consumption. For inferior goods, (hypothetically) increased income yields decreased consumption.

♦ The downward-sloping demand curve is a consequence of the consumer choosing his best-affordable combination of goods. The demand curve can be derived from the price effect—by tracing the best-affordable quantity of a good as its price changes.

For normal goods, substitution and income effects work in same direction, so falling price yields increased consumption.

For inferior goods, substitution and income effects work in opposite directions, but net effect of falling price usually yields (smaller) increased consumption.

Work-Leisure Choices

The labour supply curve is a consequence of the consumer choosing a utility-maximizing allocation of time between labour and leisure.

♦ An *income-time budget line* and indifference curves describe constraints and preferences for the choice between labour (income) and leisure.

♦ A rising wage changes the slope of the budget line yielding

• substitution effects—more time spent labouring.
• income effects—more income for consuming more of all normal goods, including leisure.

♦ The labour supply curve is

• upward-sloping when substitution effect > income effect.
• backward-bending when income effect > substitution effect.

HELPFUL HINTS

1 The consumer's basic problem is to do the best given her constraints. These constraints, which limit possible choices, depend on income and the prices of goods and are represented graphically by the budget line. Doing the best means finding the most preferred outcome consistent with those constraints. In this chapter, preferences are represented graphically by indifference curves.

Graphically, the consumer problem is to find the highest indifference curve attainable given the budget line. To make graphical analysis easier, we examine choices between only two goods, but the same principles apply in the real world to many choices, including the choice between labour and leisure.

2 The budget equation for pop and movies on text page 173 is

$$Q_P = \frac{Y}{P_P} - \frac{P_M}{P_P} Q_M$$

This is the type of straight-line equation ($y = a + bx$) that we discussed in Chapter 1 appendix. The differences are that Q_P is the dependent variable (instead of y) and Q_M is the independent variable (instead of x). We can use the budget equation to graph the budget line by finding the Q_P-intercept (where the line intersects the vertical Q_P axis), finding the Q_M intercept (where the line intersects the horizontal Q_M axis), and then connecting those two points with a straight line.

To find the Q_P-intercept, set $Q_M = 0$.

$$Q_P = \frac{Y}{P_P} - \frac{P_M}{P_P} (0)$$

$$Q_P = \frac{Y}{P_P}$$

To find the Q_M-intercept, set $Q_P = 0$.

$$0 = \frac{Y}{P_P} - \frac{P_M}{P_P} Q_M$$

$$\frac{P_M}{P_P} Q_M = \frac{Y}{P_P}$$

$$Q_M = \frac{Y}{P_M}$$

The Q_P-intercept, $Q_P = Y/P_P$, is the consumer's real income in terms of pop. It tells us how much pop could be purchased if all income was spent on pop. The Q_M-intercept, $Q_M = Y/P_M$, is the consumer's real income in terms of movies. It tells us how many movies could be purchased if all income was spent on movies. These intercepts provide an easy method for drawing a budget line. Each of the two endpoints (the intercepts) is just income divided by the price of the good on that axis. Connecting those endpoints with a straight line yields the budget line.

The slope of the budget line provides additional information for the consumer's choice. The magnitude (absolute value) of the slope equals the relative price (or opportunity cost) of movies in terms of pop. In other words, the magnitude of the slope equals the number of units of pop it takes to buy one movie. More generally, the magnitude of the slope of the budget line (P_X/P_Y) equals the relative price (or opportunity cost) of the good on the horizontal *x*-axis in terms of the good on the vertical *y*-axis; or the number of units of vertical-axis goods it takes to buy one unit of the horizontal-axis good.

ⓔ **3** The marginal rate of substitution (*MRS*) is the rate at which a consumer gives up good *Y* for an additional unit of good *X* and still remains indifferent (on the same indifference curve). The *MRS* equals the magnitude of the slope of the indifference curve, $\Delta Q_Y/\Delta Q_X$.

Because indifference curves are bowed towards the origin (convex), the magnitude of the slope and hence the *MRS* diminish as we move down an indifference curve. The diminishing *MRS* means that the consumer is willing to give up less of good *Y* for each additional unit of good *X*. As the consumer moves down an indifference curve, she is coming to value good *Y* more and value good *X* less. This is easily explained by the principle of diminishing marginal utility, which underlies the following equation.

$$\text{Marginal rate} \atop \text{of substitution} = \frac{MU_X}{MU_Y}$$

At the top of the indifference curve, the consumer is consuming little *X* and much *Y*, so the marginal utility of $X\,(MU_X)$ is high and the marginal utility of $Y\,(MU_Y)$ is low. Moving down the curve, as the quantity of *X* consumed increases, MU_X decreases; and as the quantity of *Y* consumed decreases, MU_Y increases. Thus the principle of diminishing marginal utility provides an intuitive understanding of why the *MRS* diminishes as we move down an indifference curve.

ⓔ **4** At the consumer's best-affordable point, the budget line is just tangent to the highest-affordable indifference curve, so the magnitude of the slope of the budget line equals the magnitude of the slope of the indifference curve. Combining the information from Helpful Hint **2** (the magnitude of the slope of the budget line equals P_X/P_Y) and Helpful Hint **3**

(the magnitude of the slope of the indifference curve equals MU_X/MU_Y) yields

$$\frac{P_X}{P_Y} = \frac{MU_X}{MU_Y}$$

Rearranging terms yields

$$\frac{MU_X}{P_X} = \frac{MU_Y}{P_Y}$$

This is the equation for utility maximization from Chapter 7. You can now see why the budget equation/indifference curve analysis of consumer choice developed here complements the marginal utility analysis of Chapter 7.

5 Understanding the distinction between the income and substitution effects of a change in the price of a good is often challenging for students. Consider a decrease in the price of good *A*. This has two effects that will influence the consumption of *A*. First, the decrease in the price of *A* will reduce the relative price of *A*, and, second, it will increase real income. The substitution effect is the answer to the question: How much would the consumption of *A* change as a result of the relative price decline if we also (hypothetically) reduce income by enough to leave the consumer indifferent between the new and original situations? The income effect is the answer to the question: How much more would the consumption of *A* change if we (hypothetically) restore the consumer's real income but leave relative prices at the new level?

SELF-TEST

True/False and Explain

Consumption Possibilities

1 The graph of a budget line will be bowed towards the origin.

2 At any point on a budget line, all income is spent.

3 *Ceteris paribus*, an increase in the price of goods means that real income falls.

4 An increase in income causes a leftward parallel shift of the budget line.

Preferences and Indifference Curves

5 We assume that more of any good is preferred to less of the good.

6 Higher indifference curves represent higher levels of income.

7 The principle of the diminishing marginal rate of substitution explains why indifference curves are bowed towards the origin.

8 Perfect substitutes will have L-shaped indifference curves.

Predicting Consumer Behaviour

9 At the best-affordable consumption point of movies and pop, the marginal rate of substitution equals the ratio of the price of movies to the price of pop.

10 When the relative price of a good decreases, the income effect always leads to increased consumption of the good.

11 The law of demand can be derived from an indifference curve model by tracing the impact on quantity demanded of an increase in price.

12 When the price of an inferior good falls, the substitution effect increases consumption and the income effect decreases consumption.

Work-Leisure Choice

13 An income-time budget line describes preferences for income versus leisure.

14 When the labour supply curve is upward-sloping, the substitution and income effects work in the same direction.

15 When the labour supply curve is backward-bending, the income effect dominates the substitution effect.

Multiple-Choice

Consumption Possibilities

1 Which of the following statements best describes a consumer's budget line?
a the amount of each good a consumer can purchase
b the limits to a consumer's set of affordable consumption choices
c the desired level of consumption for the consumer
d the consumption choices made by a consumer
e the set of all affordable consumption choices

2 Real income is measured in
a monetary units.
b price units.
c units of satisfaction.
d units of indifference.
e units of goods.

3 Consider the budget line and indifference curve in Figure 8.1. If the price of good *X* is $2, what is the price of good *Y*?
a $0.37
b $0.67
c $1.50
d $2.67
e impossible to calculate without additional information

FIGURE **8.1**

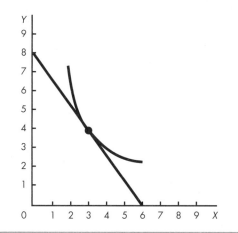

4 The budget line depends on

a income only.
b prices only.
c income and prices.
d preferences only.
e preferences and prices.

5 Bill consumes apples and bananas. Suppose Bill's income doubles and the prices of apples and bananas also double. Bill's budget line will

a shift left but not change slope.
b remain unchanged.
c shift right but not change slope.
d shift right and become steeper.
e shift right and become flatter.

6 The initial budget equation for pop and movies is $Q_P = 20 - 4Q_M$, and the price of pop (P_P) is $5. If the price of pop falls to $4, which of the following is the new budget equation?

a $Q_P = 25 - 2Q_M$
b $Q_P = 25 - 4Q_M$
c $Q_P = 25 - 5Q_M$
d $Q_P = 20 - 5Q_M$
e none of the above

7 Zarina's income allows her to afford 3 tomatoes and no toothbrushes, or 2 toothbrushes and no tomatoes. The relative price of toothbrushes (price toothbrush/price tomato) is

a 2/3.
b 3/2.
c 6/1.
d 1/6.
e impossible to calculate without additional information.

8 If the price of the good measured on the vertical axis increases, the budget line will

a become steeper.
b become flatter.
c shift leftward but parallel to the original budget line.
d shift rightward but parallel to the original budget line.
e shift leftward and become steeper.

9 If income increases, the budget line will

a become steeper.
b become flatter.
c shift leftward but parallel to the original budget line.
d shift rightward but parallel to the original budget line.
e shift parallel but leftward or rightward depending on whether a good is normal or inferior.

Preferences and Indifference Curves

10 The shape of an indifference curve depends on

a the prices of goods.
b household income.
c the substitutability between goods for the household.
d the level of satisfaction for the household.
e all of the above.

11 In general, as a consumer moves down an indifference curve, increasing consumption of good X (measured on the horizontal axis),

a more of Y must be given up for each additional unit of X.
b a constant amount of Y must be given up for each additional unit of X.
c less of Y must be given up for each additional unit of X.
d the relative price of Y increases.
e the relative price of Y decreases.

12 Which of the following statements is *false*?

a Indifference curves are negatively sloped.
b A preference map consists of a series of nonintersecting indifference curves.
c Indifference curves are bowed out from the origin.
d The marginal rate of substitution is the magnitude of the slope of an indifference curve.
e The marginal rate of substitution increases with movement up an indifference curve.

13 In moving down along an indifference curve, the marginal rate of substitution (*MRS*) for complements will

a increase faster than the *MRS* for substitutes.
b increase more slowly than the *MRS* for substitutes.
c be relatively constant.
d decrease faster than the *MRS* for substitutes.
e decrease more slowly than the *MRS* for substitutes.

14 If two goods are perfect substitutes, then their

a indifference curves are positively sloped straight lines.
b indifference curves are negatively sloped straight lines.
c indifference curves are L-shaped.
d marginal rate of substitution is zero.
e marginal rate of substitution is infinity.

Predicting Consumer Behaviour

15 Which of the following statement(s) about Figure 8.2 is/are *true*?

a Point *s* is preferred to point *q*, but *s* is not affordable.
b Points *q* and *r* yield the same utility, but *q* is more affordable.
c Point *t* is preferred to point *q*, but *t* is not affordable.
d Points *q* and *s* cost the same, but *q* is preferred to *s*.
e All of the above statements are true.

FIGURE **8.2**

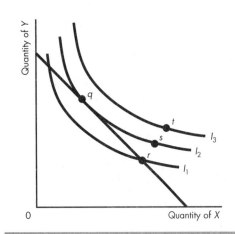

16 For a rise in price, the substitution effect

a always increases consumption.
b increases consumption for normal goods only.
c decreases consumption for normal goods only.
d decreases consumption for inferior goods only.
e does none of the above.

17 The initial budget line labelled *RS* in Figure 8.3 would shift to *RT* as a result of a(n)

a rise in the price of good *X*.
b fall in the price of good *X*.
c decrease in preferences for good *X*.
d rise in the price of good *Y*.
e increase in real income.

FIGURE **8.3**

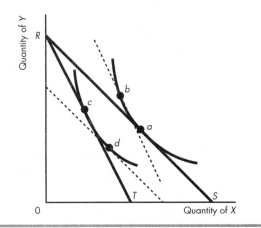

18 When the initial budget line labelled *RS* in Figure 8.3 shifts to *RT*, the substitution effect is illustrated by the move from point

a *a* to *b*.
b *a* to *c*.
c *a* to *d*.
d *b* to *d*.
e *d* to *c*.

19 When the initial budget line labelled *RS* in Figure 8.3 shifts to *RT*, the income effect is illustrated by the move from point

a *a* to *b*.
b *a* to *c*.
c *a* to *d*.
d *b* to *c*.
e *b* to *d*.

20 If the price of good *X* (measured on the horizontal axis) falls, the substitution effect is represented by a movement to a

a higher indifference curve.
b lower indifference curve.
c steeper part of the same indifference curve.
d flatter part of the same indifference curve.
e flatter part of a higher indifference curve.

21 When Clark Gable took off his shirt in *It Happened One Night*, he was not wearing an undershirt. As a result, men's undershirt sales plummeted. *Ceteris paribus*, we can conclude that men's undershirt

a preferences changed when prices changed.
b preferences changed when income changed.
c choices changed when preferences changed.
d choices changed when prices changed.
e choices changed when income changed.

22 When the price of an inferior good falls, the

1 income and substitution effects both move quantity demanded in the same direction.
2 income and substitution effects move quantity demanded in opposite directions.
3 income effect is usually larger than the substitution effect.
4 substitution effect is usually larger than the income effect.

a 1 and 2
b 1 and 4
c 2 and 3
d 2 and 4
e none of the above

Work-Leisure Choices

23 The opportunity cost of an hour of leisure is

a $0.
b the value of time spent watching television.
c the hourly wage rate.
d the income effect.
e the substitution effect.

24 Over the past century, the quantity of labour supplied has fallen as wages have increased because the

a income and substitution effects both increased leisure.
b income and substitution effects both decreased leisure.
c income effect decreasing leisure dominated the substitution effect increasing leisure.
d income effect increasing leisure dominated the substitution effect decreasing leisure.
e substitution effect increasing leisure dominated the income effect decreasing leisure.

25 When the substitution effect dominates the income effect, the labour supply curve is

a positively sloped.
b horizontal.
c negatively sloped.
d vertical.
e shifting rightward.

Short Answer Problems

1 Why is an indifference curve negatively sloped?

2 Explain why it is logically impossible for indifference curves to intersect each other, by comparing points *a*, *b*, and *c* in Figure 8.4.

FIGURE **8.4**

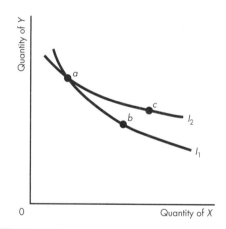

3 Helpful Hint **3** establishes that the

$$\text{Marginal rate of substitution} = \frac{\text{Marginal utility of movies}}{\text{Marginal utility of pop}}$$

As we move down an indifference curve, use the principle of diminishing marginal utility to explain why the marginal rate of substitution diminishes.

ⓒ **4**   For normal goods,

- an increase in income causes an *increase in demand* (demand curve shifts to the right).
- the income effect (due to a decrease in price) causes an *increase in quantity demanded.*

Explain why these two statements are or are not contradictory. Be sure to define clearly any important concepts.

5   Jan and Dan both like bread and peanut butter and have the same income. Since they face the same prices, they have identical budget lines. Currently, Jan and Dan consume exactly the same quantities of bread and peanut butter; they have the same best-affordable consumption point. Jan, however, views bread and peanut butter as close (though not perfect) substitutes, while Dan considers bread and peanut butter to be quite (but not perfectly) complementary.

a   On the same diagram, draw a budget line and representative indifference curves for Jan and Dan. (Measure the quantity of bread on the horizontal axis.)

b   Now, suppose the price of bread declines. Graphically represent the substitution effects for Jan and Dan. For whom is the substitution effect greater?

ⓒ **6**   Figure 8.5 illustrates a consumer's indifference map for food and clothing.

FIGURE **8.5**

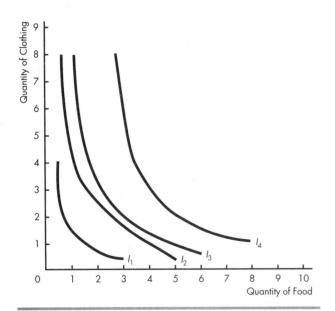

a   i   Initially, the price of a unit of clothing is $P_C = \$1$ and the price of a unit of food is $P_F = \$1.50$. If income is $Y = \$9$, draw the consumer's budget line on Figure 8.5 and label the best-affordable point as point *a*. What is the quantity of food consumed?

ii   What is the equation of the budget line in terms of P_C, P_F, and Y? What is the equation of the budget line in numerical terms? Express the magnitude (absolute value) of the slope of the budget line as a ratio of P_C and P_F.

iii   At point *a*, what is the value of the marginal rate of substitution (or equivalently, MU_F/MU_C)?

iv   Use your answers in parts **ii** and **iii** to derive the formula for utility maximization. Explain.

b   If P_F increases to $3 per unit while income and P_C remain unchanged, draw the new budget line and label the new best-affordable point as point *b*. What is the new quantity of food consumed?

c   If P_F increases again to $4.50 per unit while income and P_C remain unchanged, draw the corresponding budget line and label the best-affordable point as point *c*. What is the quantity of food consumed?

d   On a separate graph, plot and draw the demand curve for food that corresponds to points *a*, *b*, and *c*. Be sure to clearly label the axes.

e   Suppose prices remain at their initial values ($P_C = \$1$, $P_F = \$1.50$) but income falls to $3. Draw the new budget line and label the best-affordable point as point *z*. What is the quantity of food consumed? Is food a normal or inferior good? Explain. On your demand curve graph from part **d**, plot point *z* and roughly sketch a demand curve corresponding to the new income level.

7   Sharon, a fitness fanatic, plays squash and takes aerobics classes at her health club. Squash courts rent for $2 per hour and aerobics classes are $1 per hour. Sharon has decided to spend $12 per week for fitness activities. Figure 8.6 illustrates several indifference curves for squash and aerobics on Sharon's preference map.

FIGURE **8.6**

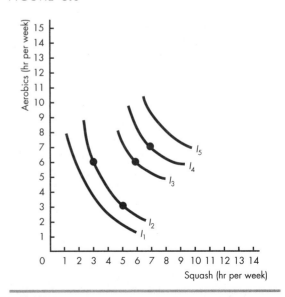

a How many hours of squash and aerobics will Sharon consume at her best-affordable point?
b Suppose that squash rentals fall to $1 per hour.
i How many hours of squash and aerobics will Sharon now consume? What is the increase in her hours of squash?
ii Of the total increase in hours of squash, how many hours are due to the substitution effect of the price fall?
iii Of the total increase in hours of squash, how many hours are due to the income effect of the price fall?
c On a separate graph, plot two points on Sharon's demand curve for squash and draw her straight-line demand curve.
d The price of squash continues to be $1 but Sharon's fitness budget increases to $14. How many hours of squash and aerobics will Sharon now consume?

8 Ms. Muffet consumes both curds and whey. The initial price of curds is $1 per unit, and the price of whey is $1.50 per unit. Ms. Muffet's initial income is $12.
a What is the relative price of curds?
b Derive Ms. Muffet's budget equation and draw her budget line on a graph. (Measure curds on the horizontal axis.)
c On your graph, draw an indifference curve so that the best-affordable point corresponds to 6 units of curds and 4 units of whey.
d What is the marginal rate of substitution of curds for whey at this point?
e Show that any other point on the budget line is inferior.

9 Given the initial situation described in Short Answer Problem **8**, suppose Ms. Muffet's income now increases.
a Illustrate graphically how the consumption of curds and whey are affected if both goods are normal. (Numerical answers are not necessary. Just show whether consumption increases or decreases.)
b Draw a new graph showing the effect of an increase in Ms. Muffet's income if whey is an inferior good.

10 Return to the initial circumstances described in Short Answer Problem **8**. Now, suppose the price of curds doubles to $2 a unit, while the price of whey remains at $1.50 per unit and income remains at $12.
a Draw the new budget line.
b Why is the initial best-affordable point (label it point *r*) no longer the best-affordable point?

c Using your graph, show the new best-affordable point and label it *t*. What has happened to the consumption of curds?
d Decompose the effect on the consumption of *X* into the substitution effect and the income effect. On your graph, indicate the substitution effect as movement from point *r* to point *s* (which you must locate) and indicate the income effect as movement from point *s* to point *t*.

ANSWERS

True/False and Explain

1 **F** Budget lines straight. Indifference curves bowed towards origin. (172–173)
2 **T** Expenditure = income along budget line. (172–173)
3 **T** Real income = income/price goods. (173)
4 **F** Rightward parallel shift. (174)
5 **T** See text discussion. (175–176)
6 **F** Represent higher levels satisfaction. (175–176)
7 **T** See text discussion. (176–177)
8 **F** True for perfect complements. (177–178)
9 **T** Budget line tangent to indifference curve. (178–179)
10 **F** True for normal, false for inferior goods. (181–182)
11 **T** See text discussion. (179–180)
12 **T** Income effect decreases consumption—higher real income means household can afford to buy higher quality (normal) goods instead. (181–182)
13 **F** Describes *constraints* on income (labour) versus leisure choice. (182–183)
14 **F** Higher wages cause substitution effect of more labour and income effect of more leisure, but substitution effect dominates. (182–183)
15 **T** At higher wage, use increased real income to consume more leisure, dominating the substitution effect of more labour supplied. (182–183)

Multiple-Choice

1 **b** **a** should be combinations of goods; **c** about indifference curves; **d** about best-affordable point; **e** includes area inside budget line. (172–173)
2 **e** Quantity goods household can buy. (173)

3 **c** Income = $12 ($2 × 6 units X), so price Y = $12/8 units Y. (172–174)

4 **c** See text discussion. Indifference curves depend on preferences. (172–173)

5 **b** Numerators and denominators of both intercepts double, so intercepts do not change. (173–174)

ⓒ **6** **c** From $Q_P = (Y/P_P) - (P_M/P_P)Q_M$. If P_P = $5, then Y = $100 and P_M = $20. Then recalculate Q_P equation for P_P = $4. (173–174)

ⓒ **7** **b** (3 × price tomato) = (2 × price toothbrush). Divide both sides equation by price tomato and by 2. (172–174)

8 **b** y-intercept shifts down, x-intercept unchanged. (173–174)

9 **d** Increased income does not change slope but increases x- and y-intercepts. (173–174)

10 **c** Budget line depends on **a** and **b**. At any level satisfaction, indifference curve could be any shape. (175–178)

11 **c** Due to diminishing MRS. **d** and **e** wrong since relative price relates to budget line, not indifference curve. (175–178)

12 **c** Indifference curves bow in towards the origin. (175–178)

ⓒ **13** **d** MRS always diminishing moving down indifference curve. Complements have more tightly curved indifference curves. (177–178)

14 **b** With constant slope = 1. (177–178)

15 **c** t on higher indifference curve, but outside budget line. s and q yield same utility so **a**, **d** wrong. q preferred to r so **b** wrong. (178–179)

16 **e** For rising price, substitution effect always decreases consumption for both normal and inferior goods. (181–182)

17 **a** With same income, less X can be purchased. **c** relates to indifference curves. Increase in real income is move from point b to c. (179–180)

18 **a** Budget line with new prices tangent to original indifference curve. (181–182)

19 **d** Hypothetically restore original income (reverse the increase in real income) but keep prices constant at new level. (181–182)

ⓒ **20** **d** New budget line flatter and drawn tangent to same indifference curve. (181–182)

21 **c** Gable's influence caused decreased preference for undershirts. Combined with unchanged prices and incomes, caused decreased consumption. (178–182)

ⓒ **22** **d** See text discussion. (181–182)

23 **c** Forgone hourly wage from working. (182–183)

24 **d** Higher wages increase opportunity cost of leisure and cause substitution of time away from leisure; higher wages increase income

causing (greater) income effect towards leisure. (182–183)

25 **a** See Text Figure 8.10. Negatively sloped (backward-bending) when income effect dominates. (182–183)

Short Answer Problems

1 An indifference curve tells us how much the consumption of one good must increase as the consumption of another good decreases in order to leave the consumer indifferent (no better or worse off). It is negatively sloped because the goods are both desirable. As we decrease the consumption of one good, in order to not be made worse off, consumption of the other good must increase. This implies a negative slope.

2 The explanation takes the form of a proof by contradiction. Since points a and b are on the same indifference curve (I_1), the consumer is indifferent between them. Since points a and c are on the same indifference curve (I_2), the consumer is also indifferent between them. If the consumer is indifferent between a and b and between a and c, this implies an indifference between b and c. But indifference between points b and c is logically impossible, because we assume that more of any good is preferred to less of that good. Since point c has more of both good X and good Y than point b, the consumer cannot be indifferent between b and c. Indifference between b and c contradicts the assumption that more is preferred to less. Hence indifference curves cannot intersect.

ⓔ **3** As we move down an indifference curve for pop and movies, such as in Text Figure 8.4 on page 176, we increase the quantity of movies consumed and decrease the quantity of pop consumed. As movie consumption increases, each additional movie yields lower marginal utility because of the principle of diminishing marginal utility. Thus the value of the numerator on the right-hand side of the equation below decreases.

$$\text{Marginal rate of substitution} = \frac{\text{Marginal utility of movies}}{\text{Marginal utility of pop}}$$

As pop consumption decreases, each previous pop consumed yields higher marginal utility. Thus, the value of the denominator on the right-hand side of the equation increases. The combined effect of a decrease in the numerator and an increase in the denominator is that the ratio MU_{MOVIES}/MU_{POP} falls as we move down an indifference curve, corresponding to a diminishing marginal rate of substitution on the left-hand side of the equation.

4 These statements appear to be contradictory because an increase in income leads, in the first statement, to a shift of the demand curve but, in the second statement, to a movement along the demand curve. The reason the statements are *not* contradictory has to do with a crucial distinction between *nominal* income and *real* income.

The first statement (an *increase* in income causes an increase in *demand* [demand curve shifts rightward]) describes how an increase in *nominal* income shifts the demand curve. *Nominal* income is measured in dollars.

The second statement (the income effect [due to a decrease in price] causes an increase in *quantity demanded*) describes how an increase in *real* income causes a movement along the stationary demand curve.

Real income is measured in purchasing power, or the quantities of goods that nominal income can buy. When the price of a good decreases, your *real* income goes up because you can now purchase more of that good with the same, unchanged, *nominal* income. Because *nominal* income is unchanged in the second statement, the demand curve does not shift. But because *real* income has increased, the decrease in price leads to an increase in *quantity demanded*.

5 a Initially, Jan and Dan are at point c on the budget line labelled AB in Figure 8.7. Jan's indifference curve is illustrated by I_J. Note that her indifference curve is close to a straight line, reflecting the fact that bread and peanut butter are close substitutes. On the other hand, since Dan considers bread and peanut butter to be complementary, his indifference curve, I_D, is more tightly curved.

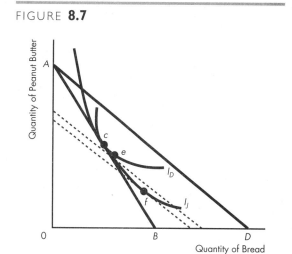

FIGURE **8.7**

b If the price of bread declines, the budget line will become flatter, such as the line labelled AD in Figure 8.7. In order to measure the substitution effect, find the point on the original indifference curve that has the same slope as the new budget line. Since Dan's indifference curve is more sharply curved, it becomes flatter quite rapidly as we move away from point c. Thus the substitution effect is quite small, from c to point e. Since Jan's indifference curve is almost a straight line, the substitution effect must be much larger, from c to point f.

6 The consumer's budget line is shown in Figure 8.5 Solution.

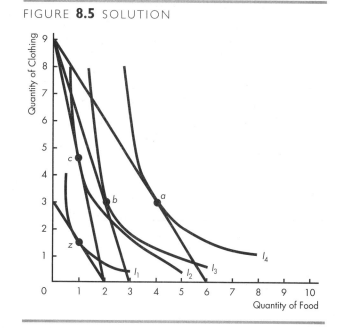

FIGURE **8.5** SOLUTION

a i 4 units of food.

ii The consumer's budget is given by

$$P_C Q_C + P_F Q_F = Y$$

To obtain the budget equation, follow the calculation procedure on text page 173. Divide by P_C to obtain

$$Q_C + \frac{P_F}{P_C} Q_F = \frac{Y}{P_C}$$

Subtract $(P_F/P_C)Q_F$ from both sides to obtain

$$Q_C = \frac{Y}{P_C} - \frac{P_F}{P_C} Q_F$$

To obtain the budget equation in numerical terms, substitute in the values $P_C = \$1$, $P_F = \$1.50$, and $Y = \$9$.

$$Q_C = \frac{9}{1} - \frac{1.50}{1} Q_F$$

The magnitude (absolute value) of the slope of the budget line is 3/2, which is the ratio of P_F/P_C. Note that this price ratio cannot be read directly off the graph, since the axes measure quantities, not prices.

iii The marginal rate of substitution at point *a* is defined as the magnitude of the slope of the indifference curve at point *a*. Since the slope of the indifference curve at point *a* is equal to the slope of the tangent at *a*, and since the budget line is tangent at *a*, the magnitude of the slope of the indifference curve is 3/2. This magnitude is equivalent to MU_F/MU_C.

iv The magnitude of the slope of the budget line is P_F/P_C and the magnitude of the slope of the indifference curve at *a* is MU_F/MU_C. Since the two magnitudes are equal, $P_F/P_C = MU_F/MU_C$ or $MU_F/P_F = MU_C/P_C$.

b See Figure 8.5 Solution: 2 units of food.
c See Figure 8.5 Solution: 1 unit of food.
d The demand curve for food is shown in Figure 8.8.

FIGURE **8.8**

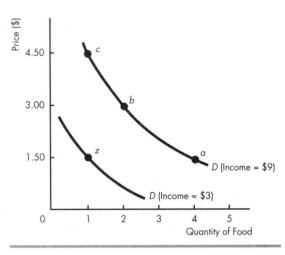

e See Figure 8.5 Solution. 1 unit of food. Food is a normal good because a *decrease* in income (with prices constant) causes a decrease in food consumption (from 4 units to 1 unit). See Figure 8.8 for the new demand curve (income = $3).

7 a In order to find Sharon's best-affordable point, draw the budget line in Figure 8.6 Solution. The initial budget line is labelled *AB* and Sharon's best-affordable point is point *c* on indifference curve I_2. Thus Sharon consumes 3 hours of squash and 6 hours of aerobics per week.

FIGURE **8.6** SOLUTION

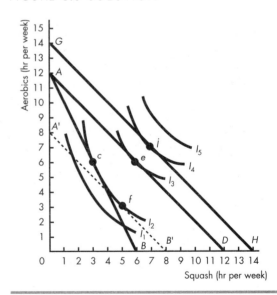

b If the price of squash falls to $1, the budget line becomes *AD*.
i Now Sharon's best-affordable point is point *e* on indifference curve I_3. This corresponds to consumption of 6 hours of squash and 6 hours

of aerobics per week. Her squash consumption has increased by 3 hours.

ii To measure the substitution effect, shift the new budget line leftward in parallel fashion until it is tangent to the indifference curve I_2, where Sharon was before the fall in the price of squash. In effect, budget line $A'B'$ removes the increase in real income due to the price fall in order to isolate the substitution effect of the price fall on Sharon's consumption of squash. Point f is what Sharon would have consumed at the new prices if her income fell just enough to return her to her original indifference curve. The substitution effect of the fall in the price of squash is the movement from initial point c to point f, which is an increase in squash hours consumed of 2 (from 3 to 5 hours).

iii To measure the income effect, shift the budget line $A'B'$ rightward in parallel fashion until it is tangent to the indifference curve I_3, where Sharon was before we hypothetically reduced her real income. In effect, this shift isolates the income effect by restoring the increase in real income due to the price fall while keeping prices constant at their new values. The income effect of the fall in the price of squash is the movement from point f to point e, which is an increase in squash hours consumed of 1 (from 5 to 6 hours).

The results are summarized in Table 8.1.

TABLE **8.1**   PRICE EFFECT FROM FIGURE 8.6 SOLUTION

Effect	Move from Point	Δ Hours Squash
Substitution effect	c to f	2
+ Income effect	f to e	1
= Price effect	c to e	3

c In parts **a** and **b**, income spent on fitness was constant at $12 and the price of aerobics was constant at $1 per hour. When the price of squash was $2 per hour, Sharon wanted to consume 3 hours of squash and when the price of squash was $1, Sharon wanted to consume 6 hours of squash. This gives us two points on Sharon's demand curve for squash, which are labelled a and b in Figure 8.9. Drawing a line passing through these points allows us to obtain her straight-line demand curve, labelled D.

FIGURE **8.9**

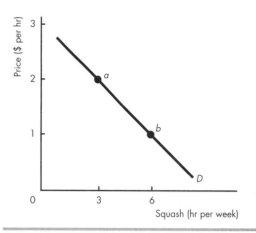

d When Sharon's fitness budget increases to $14, the budget line shifts right to the line labelled GH in Figure 8.6 Solution. Sharon's best-affordable point is now at j, which corresponds to 7 hours of squash and 7 hours of aerobics consumed per week.

8 a The relative price of curds is the price of curds divided by the price of whey:

$$\$1.00/\$1.50 = 2/3$$

b Let P_C = the price of curds, P_W = the price of whey, Q_C = quantity of curds, Q_W = quantity of whey, and Y = income. The budget equation, in general form, is

$$Q_W = \frac{Y}{P_W} - \frac{P_C}{P_W} Q_C$$

Since P_C = $1, P_W = $1.50, and Y = $12, Ms. Muffet's budget equation is specifically given by

$$Q_W = 8 - 2/3 \, Q_C$$

The graph of this budget equation, the budget line, is given by the line labelled AB in Figure 8.10.

FIGURE **8.10** CURDS & WHEY NORMAL GOODS

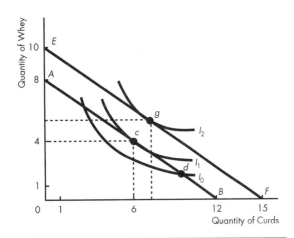

FIGURE **8.11** WHEY AS INFERIOR GOOD

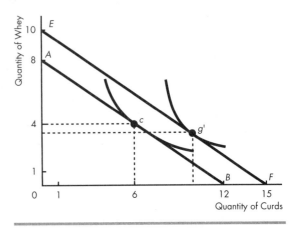

c If the best-affordable point corresponds to 6 units of curds and 4 units of whey, then the relevant indifference curve must be tangent to (just touch) the budget line AB at c, which is indifference curve I_1.

d The marginal rate of substitution is given by the magnitude of the slope of the indifference curve at point c. We do not know the slope of the indifference curve directly, but we can easily compute the slope of the budget line. Since, at point c, the indifference curve and the budget line have the same slope, we can obtain the marginal rate of substitution of curds for whey. Since the slope of the budget line is –2/3, the marginal rate of substitution is 2/3. For example, Ms. Muffet is willing to give up 2 units of whey in order to receive 3 additional units of curds and still remain indifferent.

e Since indifference curves cannot intersect each other and since indifference curve I_1 lies everywhere above the budget line (except at point c), we know that every other point on the budget line is on a lower indifference curve. For example, point d lies on indifference curve I_0. Thus every other point on the budget line is inferior to point c.

9 a An increase in income will cause a parallel rightward shift of the budget line, for example to EF in Figure 8.10. If both curds and whey are normal goods, Ms. Muffet will move to a point like g at which the consumption of both goods has increased.

b If whey is an inferior good, then its consumption will fall as income rises. This is illustrated in Figure 8.11. Once again the budget line shifts from AB to EF, but Ms. Muffet's preferences are such that her new consumption point is a point like g' where the consumption of whey has actually declined.

10 a Ms. Muffet's initial budget line is AB and the initial best-affordable point is r in Figure 8.12. Note that point r in Figure 8.12 is the same as point c in Figure 8.10. The new budget line following an increase in the price of curds to $2 (income remains at $12) is AH.

FIGURE **8.12**

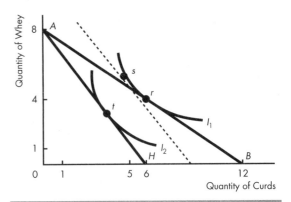

b After the price increase, point r is no longer the best-affordable point, since it is no longer even affordable.

c The new best-affordable point (labelled t in Figure 8.12) indicates a decrease in the consumption of curds.

d The substitution effect of the increase in the price of curds is indicated by the movement from r to s in Figure 8.12. This gives the effect of the change in relative prices while keeping Ms. Muffet on the same indifference curve. The income effect is indicated by movement from s to t.

Part 3 Wrap Up

Understanding Households' Choices

PROBLEM

Michael spends his income on only two goods—food and medicine. The indifference map and budget line in Figure P3.1 show different combinations of food and medicine that Michael prefers given different incomes. The combinations can also be described as the points *a* to *f* in Table P3.1. Use this information to answer the following questions.

FIGURE **P3.1**

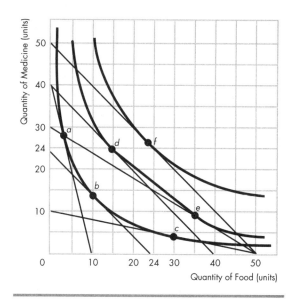

Quantity of Medicine (units)

Quantity of Food (units)

TABLE **P3.1**

Point	Quantity of Food (units)	Quantity of Medicine (units)
a	3	28
b	10	14
c	30	4
d	15	25
e	35	9
f	23	27

a Assume Michael's income is $300 and the price of food is $6 per unit. Using the information in Table P3.1, derive the coordinates (combinations of price and quantity) of three points on Michael's demand curve for medicine. Record the points in Table P3.2.

TABLE **P3.2** MICHAEL'S DEMAND CURVE FOR MEDICINE

Price ($)	Quantity (units)

b Now assume Michael's income is $600, the price of food is $12 per unit, and the price of medicine is $20 per unit. At Michael's best affordable point (consumer equilibrium), what is the ratio of $MU_{FOOD}/MU_{MEDICINE}$?

c Starting from Michael's best affordable point in part **b**, suppose the price of medicine then falls to $12 per unit and we want to separate the substitution and income effects of the price change.

i The substitution effect moves Michael from point _____ to point _____ (fill in the blanks).
ii The income effect moves Michael from point _____ to point _____ (fill in the blanks).

d Define the substitution effect and explain how your answer to part **c i** illustrates the substitution effect *alone*.

e Define the income effect and explain how your answer to part **c ii** illustrates the income effect *alone*.

f Is medicine a normal or inferior good for Michael? Explain your answer.

MIDTERM EXAMINATION

You should allocate 20 minutes for this examination (10 questions, 2 minutes per question). For each question, choose the one *best* answer.

1 Marginal utility equals
a total utility divided by price.
b total utility divided by the total number of units consumed.
c the slope of the total utility curve.
d the inverse of total utility.
e the area below the demand curve but above market price.

2 A consumer maximizes his utility by purchasing 2 units of good X at \$5/unit and 3 units of good Y at \$7/unit. What is the ratio of the marginal utility of X to the marginal utility of Y?
a 5/7
b 7/5
c 2/3
d 3/2
e 10/21

3 A change in the price of the good measured on the horizontal (x) axis changes which aspect(s) of the budget equation?
a slope and y-intercept
b slope and x-intercept
c x- and y-intercepts but not slope
d slope only
e none of the above

4 Which of the following statements about the budget line is *false*? The budget line
a divides affordable from unaffordable consumption points.
b is based on fixed prices.
c is based on fixed income.
d is based on fixed quantities.
e constrains consumer choices.

5 Suppose good X is measured on the horizontal axis and good Y on the vertical axis. The marginal rate of substitution is best defined as the
a relative price of good X in terms of good Y.
b relative price of good Y in terms of good X.
c rate at which a person will give up good Y to get more of good X and remain indifferent.
d rate at which a person will give up good X to get more of good Y and remain indifferent.
e slope of the budget line.

6 When the price of a good changes, the change in consumption that leaves the consumer indifferent is called the
a utility effect.
b substitution effect.
c income effect.
d price effect.
e inferior effect.

7 Shelley is maximizing her utility in her consumption of mink coats and Porsches. If the marginal utility of her last purchased mink coat is twice the marginal utility of her last purchased Porsche, we know with certainty that
a Shelley buys twice as many mink coats as Porsches.
b Shelley buys twice as many Porsches as mink coats.
c Shelley buys more Porsches than mink coats, but we do not know how many more.
d the price of a mink coat is twice the price of a Porsche.
e the price of a Porsche is twice the price of a mink coat.

8 The difference between the value of a good and its price is known as
a excess demand.
b excess supply.
c consumer surplus.
d consumer excess.
e marginal utility.

9 A change in income changes which aspect(s) of the budget equation?

a slope and y-intercept only

b slope and x-intercept only

c x- and y-intercepts but not slope

d slope only

e none of the above

10 When the price of a normal good rises, the income effect

a increases consumption of the good and the substitution effect decreases consumption.

b decreases consumption of the good and the substitution effect increases consumption.

c and the substitution effect both increase consumption of the good.

d and the substitution effect both decrease consumption of the good.

e is always larger than the substitution effect.

ANSWERS

Problem

a If Michael spends his entire income of $300 on food (at $6 per unit), he can buy 50 units of food. This gives us the quantity-of-food intercept of his budget line. There are three alternative budget lines with that intercept. If Michael can also buy 50 units of medicine with $300, the price of a unit a medicine must be $6. That budget line is tangent to the highest indifference curve at point f, where Michael would consume 27 units of medicine. So one point on Michael's demand curve for medicine is (price = $6, quantity = 27 units). The other two points in Table P3.2 Solution (points e and c in Figure P3.1) can be derived in the same way.

TABLE **P3.2** SOLUTION
MICHAEL'S DEMAND CURVE FOR MEDICINE

Price ($)	Quantity (units)
6	27
10	9
30	4

b At the best affordable point (see Chapter 7's Helpful Hint **2**, page 95)

$$MU_{FOOD}/MU_{MEDICINE} = P_{FOOD}/P_{MEDICINE}$$

Since $P_{FOOD}/P_{MEDICINE} = 12/20$,

$$MU_{FOOD}/MU_{MEDICINE} = 12/20 = 3/5.$$

c i The substitution effect moves Michael from point e to point d.

ii The income effect moves Michael from point d to point f.

d The substitution effect is the effect of a change in price on the quantity bought when the consumer (hypothetically) remains indifferent between the original and new situation.

In moving from point e to point d, the new price of medicine is reflected in the budget line tangent to the indifference curve at point d. This budget line eliminates the increase in real income that resulted from the decrease in the price of medicine. Michael is indifferent between the original (point e) and the new situation (point d) since both are on the same indifference curve.

e The income effect is the change in consumption resulting from (hypothetically) restoring the consumer's original income but keeping prices constant at new level.

In moving from point d to point f, the prices of medicine (and food) stay constant at their new level, but Michael's real income is (hypothetically) restored to what it would have been as a result of the fall in the price of medicine.

f Medicine is a normal good for Michael because the income effect is positive—consumption of medicine increases from 25 to 27 units between points d and f.

Midterm Examination

1 c $MU = \Delta$ total utility/Δ quantity. (155–156)

2 a Quantities irrelevant. Ratio of MUs must be equal to ratio prices. (157–158)

3 b See Chapter 8 Helpful Hint **2** and analyze ΔP_M (movies on horizontal axis). (172–174)

4 d Quantities vary along budget line. (154)

5 c Definition. **a** and **b** relate to slope budget line. MRS = **e** only at best affordable point. (176)

6 b Definition. (181)

7 d From maximum condition of equal MU/P. No necessary relation between MU and quantity. (157–159)

8 c See Text Figure 7.7. (164–165)

9 c See Chapter 8 Helpful Hint **2**. Δ income (Y) does not change slope (P_M/P_F) but does Δ intercepts (Y/P_M) and (Y/P_F). (172–174)

10 d Both work in same direction. Rising P causes decreased quantity consumed. (181–182)

Chapter 9

Organizing Production

The Firm and Its Economic Problem

A **firm** is an institution that hires and organizes factors of production to produce and sell goods and services. Firm's goal is profit maximization.

Accountants' costs and profits:

◆ Accounting costs = explicit costs + conventional depreciation

◆ Accounting profit = revenues − (explicit costs + conventional depreciation)

Opportunity costs of production consist of explicit costs (paid in money) and implicit costs (opportunities forgone but not paid in money). A firm's major implicit costs are

◆ **implicit rental rate**—opportunity cost of using its own capital. Equals **economic depreciation** (change in market value of capital) + forgone interest.

◆ cost of owner's resources—(wage income forgone) + normal profit. **Normal profit** is the expected return to *entrepreneurial ability* and is part of a firm's opportunity costs of production. Normal profit is the average profit in industry.

Economists' costs and profits:

◆ *Opportunity costs* = explicit costs + implicit costs

◆ **Economic profit** = revenues − (explicit costs + implicit costs)

◆ Because normal profit is part of implicit costs, economic profit (when positive) is over and above normal profit.

◆ Opportunity cost and economic profit are the key to correctly predicting firm behaviour.

Limits to profit maximization are:

◆ **technology** constraints—available resources and technology.

◆ information constraints—limited information and uncertainty about firm's workforce, potential customers, and competitors.

◆ market constraints—limited demand for firm's output; marketing efforts of competitors.

Technology and Economic Efficiency

Technological efficiency—using least inputs to produce given output.

Economic efficiency—least cost of producing given output.

Information and Organization

Firms organize production by using

◆ **command systems** based on a managerial hierarchy.

◆ **incentive systems** to overcome problems of limited information and uncertainty.

With limited information, the **principal-agent problem** arises when *agents* (those employed by others) do not act in the best interests of the *principals* (employers of the agents).

◆ Strategies for coping with the principal-agent problem and inducing agents to act in the best interests of the principals include ownership, incentive pay, and long-term contracts.

◆ To cope with limited information and uncertainty, firms have devised different forms of business organization:

• *sole proprietorship*—single owner with unlimited liability

- *partnership*—two or more owners with unlimited liability
- *corporation*—owned by limited-liability stockholders

Markets and the Competitive Environment

Types of market structure

- **Perfect competition**—many firms; identical products; easy entry of new firms.

- **Monopolistic competition**—many firms; slightly differentiated products (**product differentiation**); easy entry.

- **Oligopoly**—few firms; identical or differentiated products; some barriers to entry.

- **Monopoly**—single firm; product with no close substitutes; high barriers to new entry.

Market structure of most industries lies between extremes of perfect competition and monopoly.

- To evaluate competitiveness of a market, economists use two measures of industrial concentration:

  - **four-firm concentration ratio**—percentage of industry sales made by largest four firms.
  - **Herfindahl-Hirschman Index** (HHI)—sum of squared market shares of 50 largest firms in industry.

- High concentration ratios usually indicate low degree competition.

- Problems with concentration ratios:

  - national, but many industries regional/global.
  - no indication of entry barriers and turnover.
  - firms operate in other industries.

Markets and Firms

Firms coordinate economic activity when they perform task more efficiently than markets. Firms often have advantages of

- lower **transactions costs**—costs arising from finding someone with whom to do business.

- **economies of scale**—lower unit cost of producing good as output rate increases.

- **economies of scope**—lower unit cost from producing range of goods and services.

- economies of team production—individuals in production process specializing in mutually supportive tasks.

HELPFUL HINTS

1 In this chapter, we again meet our old friend opportunity cost. Here we look at the costs firms face and examine the differences between *opportunity cost* measures used by economists and *accounting cost* measures. Opportunity cost, which is the relevant cost concept for economic decisions, includes *explicit* and *implicit costs*. Important examples of implicit costs include economic depreciation, the owner's forgone interest and forgone wages, and normal profits. Accounting cost includes only explicit, out-of-pocket costs, and conventional depreciation. These differences in cost measures between accountants and economists also lead to the following differences in profit measures.

Economists
Opportunity costs = Explicit costs + Implicit costs
Economic profit = Revenues – (Explicit costs + Implicit costs)

Accountants
Accounting costs = Explicit costs + Conventional depreciation
Accounting profit = Revenues – (Explicit costs + Conventional depreciation)

Implicit costs, which economists include but accountants exclude, are the key difference between economists' and accountants' measures of cost and profit. Accounting profit does *not* subtract normal profits or other implicit costs, so accounting profit is generally greater than economic profit.

Because normal profit is part of implicit costs, economic profit is profit over and above normal profit. If we think of normal profit as average profit, economic profit is *above-average* profit. Economic profit is a signal to firms that they are earning a greater return on investment than could be earned on average elsewhere in the economy.

Economic profit can also be negative if revenues are less than opportunity costs. As we will see in Chapter 11, such an *economic loss* is a signal to firms that they are earning a lower return on investment than could be earned on average elsewhere.

2 The difference between *technological efficiency* and *economic efficiency* is critical since economic decisions are made only on the basis of economic efficiency. Technological efficiency is an engineering concept and occurs when the

firm produces a given output using the least inputs. There is no consideration of input costs. Economic efficiency occurs when the firm produces a given output at least cost. All technologically efficient production methods are not economically efficient. But all economically efficient methods are also technologically efficient. Competition favours firms that choose economically efficient production methods, and penalizes firms that do not.

3 This chapter introduces four types of market structure—perfect competition, monopolistic competition, oligopoly, and monopoly. These market structures will not mean that much to you now, but you are about to learn more about them in Chapters 11–13. Pay attention to Table 9.6 (page 208), which summarizes the characteristics of the different market structures and gives you a sense how the structures differ. As you study each market structure in the following chapters, refer back to Table 9.6 to put it in perspective.

S E L F - T E S T

True/False and Explain

The Firm and Its Economic Problem

1 The goal of the firm is to maximize market share.

2 Normal profit is the expected return for supplying entrepreneurial ability.

3 Implicit costs include economic profit.

4 A firm's opportunity cost of using its own machine is lower than if it had rented the machine.

Technological and Economic Efficiency

5 Economically efficient production methods use relatively less of higher-cost resources and relatively more of lower-cost resources.

6 An economically efficient production process can become economically inefficient if the relative prices of inputs change.

7 All economically efficient production methods are also technologically efficient.

Information and Organization

8 Giving corporate managers stock in their companies is a strategy for coping with a principal-agent problem.

9 In a principal-agent relationship between the stockholders and managers of Scotiabank, the stockholders are agents and the managers are principals.

10 Owners of a corporation have limited liability.

Markets and the Competitive Environment

11 Product differentiation gives a monopolistically competitive firm some monopoly power.

12 A high concentration ratio always indicates a low degree of competition.

13 Concentration ratios measure barriers to entry in a market.

Markets and Firms

14 Outsourcing is an example of firm coordination of economic activity.

15 Markets will coordinate economic activity in situations where there are economies of scale.

Multiple-Choice

The Firm and Its Economic Problem

1 Abdul operates his own business and pays himself a salary of $20,000 per year. He refused a job that pays $30,000 per year. What is the opportunity cost of Abdul's time in the business?
a $10,000
b $20,000
c $30,000
d $50,000
e zero

2 Economic profit is revenues minus
a explicit costs.
b implicit costs.
c opportunity costs.
d accounting costs.
e (explicit costs + conventional depreciation).

3 The rate of interest is 10 percent per year. You invest $50,000 of your own money in a business and earn *accounting* profit of $20,000 after one year. *Ceteris paribus*, what is your *economic* profit?
a $20,000
b $15,000
c $5,000
d $2,000
e −$15,000

4 In general,
  1 opportunity cost is greater than accounting cost.
  2 opportunity cost is less than accounting cost.
  3 economic profit is greater than accounting profit.
  4 economic profit is less than accounting profit.
a 1 only
b 1 and 3
c 1 and 4
d 2 and 3
e 2 and 4

5 A profit-maximizing firm is constrained by
a demand for its product.
b limited resources.
c available technology.
d limited information.
e all of the above.

Technology and Economic Efficiency

6 In Table 9.1, which method(s) of making a photon torpedo is/are technologically efficient?
a 1 only
b 2 only
c 3 only
d all of the above
e 1 and 3 only

TABLE **9.1** THREE METHODS OF MAKING ONE PHOTON TORPEDO

Method	Labour	Capital
1	5	10
2	10	7
3	15	5

Quantities of Inputs

7 Refer to Table 9.1. If the price of labour is $10 per unit and the price of capital is $20 per unit, which method(s) is/are economically efficient?
a 1 only
b 2 only
c 3 only
d all of the above
e 1 and 3 only

8 Which of the following statements is *true*?
a All technologically efficient methods are also economically efficient.
b All economically efficient methods are also technologically efficient.
c Technological efficiency changes with changes in relative input prices.
d Technologically efficient firms will be more likely to survive than economically efficient firms.
e None of the above.

9 The business people are still talking over coffee. Which of their statements below describes *economic* efficiency?

a "The new production process we've installed uses less capital and labour than the old one."

b "The new assembly line has higher capital costs, but the fall in workers' hours has lowered overall costs."

c "The costs per unit fell dramatically as we increased the length of our production runs."

d "Despite the higher costs of negotiating the contracts, hiring the cleaning firm is much cheaper than using our own staff."

e "The computer servicing people we hired work well as an integrated problem-solving group."

10 To produce a unit of output, Alphaworks uses 10 hours of labour and 5 kilos of material, Betaworks uses 5 hours of labour and 10 kilos of material, and Gammaworks uses 10 hours of labour and 10 kilos of material. If labour costs $10/hour and material costs $5/kilo, which firm(s) is/are economically efficient?

a Alphaworks only

b Betaworks only

c Gammaworks only

d Alphaworks and Betaworks

e Alphaworks and Gammaworks

Information and Organization

11 Firms organize production using

a command systems only.

b incentive systems only.

c command and incentive systems.

d market systems only.

e principal-agent systems only.

12 The possibility that an employee may not work hard is an example of the

a limited liability problem.

b principal-agent problem.

c transactions cost problem.

d technological efficiency problem.

e partnership problem.

13 Firm strategies for coping with the principal-agent problem are

a ownership, incentive pay, and long-term contracts.

b proprietorship, partnership, and the corporation.

c economies of scale, scope, and team production.

d technology, information, and the market.

e none of the above.

14 A firm that has two or more owners with joint unlimited liability is

a a proprietorship.

b a partnership.

c a conglomerate.

d a corporation.

e none of the above.

15 What is a *disadvantage* of a corporation relative to a proprietorship or partnership?

a owners have unlimited liability

b profits are taxed twice as corporate profits and stockholders' dividends.

c high cost of capital

d perpetual life

e none of the above

16 The majority of business revenues are accounted for by

a proprietorships.

b partnerships.

c corporations.

d cooperatives.

e not-for-profit organizations.

Markets and the Competitive Environment

17 The most extreme *absence* of competition is

a perfect competition.

b monopolistic competition.

c product differentiation.

d oligopoly.

e monopoly.

18 A market structure where a small number of firms compete is

a perfect competition.

b monopolistic competition.

c product differentiation.

d oligopoly.

e monopoly.

19 Product differentiation is an important feature of the market structure of

a perfect competition.

b monopolistic competition.

c oligopoly.

d monopoly.

e all of the above.

20 The four-firm concentration ratio measures the share of the largest four firms in total industry

a profits.
b sales.
c cost.
d capital.
e none of the above.

21 Which of the following statements is *false*? Concentration ratios

a are national measures, but firms in some industries operate in regional markets.
b are national measures, but firms in some industries operate in global markets.
c tell us nothing about barriers to entry in the industry.
d tell us nothing about how sales vary among firms in the industry.
e have difficulty classifying multi-product firms by industry.

Markets and Firms

22 Which of the following statements is *false*?

a Firms and markets are institutions for coordinating economic activity.
b Firms organize productive resources in order to produce goods and services.
c Firms sell goods and services.
d Technologically efficient firms can eliminate scarcity.
e Firms use command systems to organize production.

23 Firms coordinate economic activity more efficiently than markets when firms have

a lower transactions costs.
b economics of scale.
c economies of scope.
d economies of team production.
e all of the above.

24 Economies of scale exist when

a transactions costs are high.
b transactions costs are low.
c hiring additional inputs does not increase the price of inputs.
d the cost of producing a unit of output falls as the output rate increases.
e the firm is too large and too diversified.

25 A firm with lower unit cost from producing a wider range of goods and services has economies of

a transactions costs.
b scale.
c scope.
d team production.
e market coordination.

Short Answer Problems

1 A year ago, Frank, the bricklayer, decided to start a business manufacturing doll furniture. Frank has two sisters; Angela is an accountant and Edith is an economist. (Both sisters are good with numbers, but Edith doesn't have enough personality to be an accountant.) Each of the sisters computes Frank's cost and profit for the first year using the following information.

1 Frank took no income from the firm. He has a standing offer to return to work as a bricklayer for $30,000 per year.
2 Frank rents his machinery for $9,000 a year.
3 Frank owns the garage in which he produces, but could rent it out at $3,000 per year.
4 To start the business, Frank used $10,000 of his own money and borrowed $30,000 at the market rate of interest of 10 percent per year.
5 Frank hires one employee at an annual salary of $20,000.
6 The cost of materials during the first year is $40,000.
7 Frank's entrepreneurial abilities are worth $14,000.
8 Frank's revenue for his first year is $100,000.

a Set up a table indicating how Angela and Edith would compute Frank's cost. Ignore any depreciation. What is Frank's cost as computed by Angela? by Edith?
b What is Frank's profit (or loss) as computed by Angela? by Edith?

2 According to your roommate, it is always more economically efficient to produce wheat using some machinery than using only labour. Suppose that there are two technologically efficient methods of producing one tonne of wheat.

• Method 1 requires 20 machine hours plus 20 hours of labour.
• Method 2 requires 100 hours of labour.

Country *A* has a highly developed industrial economy, while country *B* is less developed. In country *A* the price of an hour of labour (the wage rate) is $8, while the wage rate in country *B* is $4. The price of a machine hour is $20 in both countries. Which method is economically efficient in country *A*? in country *B*? Explain.

3 Consider countries *A* and *B* described in Short Answer Problem **2**.
 a What wage rate in country *B* would make the two methods equally efficient in country *B*?
 b What price of a machine hour would make the two methods equally efficient in country *A*?

4 Explain why an economically efficient production method must be technologically efficient.

5 The standard tip in a restaurant is 15 percent. Restaurants could raise their prices 15 percent, set a no-tipping policy, and pay servers the extra 15 percent. Use principal-agent analysis to explain why most restaurants prefer tipping.

6 The annual sales for firms in the Canadian thingamabob industry are reported in Table 9.2.

TABLE **9.2**   THINGAMABOB INDUSTRY SALES

Firm	Sales ($)
Things 'R' Us	500
ThingMart	400
The Thing Club	350
Thingmania	250
All other firms	13,500

 a Calculate the four-firm concentration ratio for the thingamabob industry.
 b How competitive is the industry according to the ratio?

7 The U.S. yadayada industry consists of only five firms, whose markets shares are reported in Table 9.3.

TABLE **9.3**   YADAYADA INDUSTRY MARKET SHARE

Firm	Market Share (%)
Jerry's Yadayadas	30
Elaine's Yadayadas	40
George's Yadayadas	20
Kramer's Yadayadas	5
Neuman's Yadayadas	5

 a Calculate the Herfindahl-Hirschman Index for the yadayada industry.

 b How competitive is the industry according to the index?

8 Considering the geographical scope of markets, how might a concentration ratio *understate* the degree of competitiveness in an industry? How might it *overstate* the degree of competitiveness?

9 a List and describe briefly the four types of market structure.
 b For each of the four types of market structure, what, in general terms, is the value of the four-firm concentration ratio?

10 Markets and firms are alternative ways of coordinating economic activity that arise because of scarcity. Why do both firms and markets exist?

ANSWERS

True/False and Explain

 1 **F** Maximize profit. (196)
 2 **T** Definition. (197)
 3 **F** Implicit costs include normal profit. (196–197)
 4 **F** Opportunity cost equal for ownership or rental. Explicit cost lower for ownership. (196–197)
 5 **T** That achieves lowest per-unit cost. (199–200)
 6 **T** Technological efficiency does not change with price changes, but economic efficiency can. (199–200)
 7 **T** But reverse is false—technological efficiency does not guarantee economic efficiency. (199–200)
 8 **T** Makes managers' (agents) incentives same as shareholders' (principal). (201–202)
 9 **F** Stockholders' (principals) profits depend on job done by managers (agents). (201–202)
 10 **T** Liability only for value of investment. Sole proprietorship has unlimited liability. (202–203)
 11 **T** Firm is sole producer of differentiated version of good. (205)
 12 **F** Often true, but depends on geographical scope market, barriers to entry, and multi-product firms. (206–209)
 13 **F** Small town with 4 restaurants has high concentration ratio but low entry barriers. (206–209)
 14 **F** Example of market coordination. (210–211)

15 F Firms more efficient if economies of scale. (210–211)

Multiple-Choice

1 c Forgone income. (196–197)
2 c Definition. (196–197)
3 b Economic profit = accounting profit – implicit costs = $20,000 – (0.10 × $50,000). (196–197)
4 c See formulas in Helpful Hint **1**. (196–197)
5 e Technology, information, and market constraints. (198)
6 d No method has more of one input and same amount of other input, compared with alternative method. (199–200)
7 b 2 costs $240 while 1 and 3 cost $250. (199–200)
8 b **c** true for economic efficiency. Reverse of **d** true. (199–200)
9 b Lowest cost. **c** describes economies of scale. **d** and **e** describe market coordination of production. (199–200)
10 b Costs are Alphaworks = $125, Betaworks = $100, Gammaworks = $150. (199–200)
11 c Principal-agent solutions are part of incentive system. (201–202)
12 b See text discussion. (201–202)
13 a All create incentives for agent to work in interests of principal. **b** lists types of business organization, **c** lists advantages of firms over markets, **d** lists constraints on firms. (202)
14 b Definition. (202–203)
15 b See Text Table 9.4; **d** advantage, **a** and **c** disadvantages proprietorship and partnership. (203)
16 c See Text Figure 9.1. (204)
17 e Monopoly is least competition, perfect competition is the most. (205–206)
18 d Definition. (205–206)
19 b Many firms producing slightly differentiated products. (205–206)
20 b Definition. (206)
21 d Concentration ratios measure sales by size of firm. (207–209)
22 d Scarcity can never be eliminated. (210–211)
23 e See text discussion. (210–211)
24 d See text discussion. (210–211)
25 c Definition. (211)

Short Answer Problems

1 a Table 9.4 gives the cost as computed by Angela and Edith. The item numbers correspond to the item numbers in the problem.

TABLE **9.4**

Item Number	Angela's Accounting Computation (accounting cost)	Edith's Economic Computation (opportunity cost)
1.	$0	$30,000
2.	9,000	9,000
3.	0	3,000
4.	3,000	4,000
5.	20,000	20,000
6.	40,000	40,000
7.	0	$14,000
Total Cost	$72,000	$120,000

b Revenue is $100,000. Angela's accounting computation of profit uses this formula:

Accounting profit = Revenues – Explicit costs
= $100,000 – $72,000
= $28,000

Edith's economic computation of profit uses this formula:

Economic profit = Revenues – Opportunity costs
= $100,000 – $120,000
= –$20,000 (an economic loss)

2 Both production methods are technologically efficient. The economically efficient production method has the lower cost of producing a tonne of wheat. In country A, the price of an hour of labour is $8 and the price of a machine hour is $20. The cost of producing a tonne of wheat is $560 using method 1 and $800 using method 2. Therefore method 1 is economically efficient for country A.

The price of an hour of labour is $4 in country B, and thus it will face different costs of producing a tonne of wheat. Under method 1, the cost will be $480 but under method 2, which uses only labour, the cost will be $400. So method 2 is economically efficient for country B.

The reason for this difference is that economic efficiency means producing at lowest cost. If the relative prices of inputs are different in two countries, there will be differences in the relative costs of production using alternative methods. Therefore your roommate is wrong.

3 a If the wage rate in country B were to increase to $5 an hour, then production of a tonne of wheat would be $500 under either method. How did we obtain this answer? Express the cost under method 1 (C_1) and the cost under method 2 (C_2) as follows:

$$C_1 = 20P_m + 20P_h$$
$$C_2 = 100P_h$$

where P_m is the price of a machine hour and P_h is the price of an hour of labour (the wage rate). We are given that $P_m = \$20$ and asked to find the value of P_h that makes the two methods equally efficient; the value of P_h that makes $C_1 = C_2$. Thus we solve the following equation for P_h:

$$20P_m + 20P_h = 100P_h$$
$$20(\$20) + 20P_h = 100P_h$$
$$\$400 = 80P_h$$
$$\$5 = P_h$$

b If the price of a machine hour is $32, production of a tonne of wheat would be $800 under either method in country A. This question asks: Given the wage rate of $8 ($P_h$) in country A, what value of P_m makes $C_1 = C_2$? Thus we solve the following equation for P_m:

$$20P_m + 20P_h = 100P_h$$
$$20P_m + 20(\$8) = 100(\$8)$$
$$20P_m = \$640$$
$$P_m = \$32$$

4 If a production method is economically efficient, then it is the least-cost method of producing a given level of output. Why does this imply that the method must also be technologically efficient—using the least inputs?

Try to imagine an economically efficient production method that is technologically *inefficient*. The method would *not* use the least inputs. No matter what the price of those inputs, there would always be a method that uses less inputs and therefore costs less. So a technologically inefficient method could *not* be economically efficient. Economic efficiency implies technological efficiency.

5 Restaurants face a classic principal-agent problem because servers may provide poor service to customers and drive away future business. Instead of having managers try to closely monitor each server, it is more efficient to delegate monitoring to customers. Customers tip on the basis of quality of service, creating an incentive for the server—the agent—to provide good service. This is exactly what the restaurant owner—the principal—wants.

6 a The four-firm concentration ratio is the percentage of the value of sales accounted for by the four largest firms in an industry. For thingamabobs, sales of the four largest firms are

500 + 400 + 350 + 250 = 1,500. Total industry sales are 1,500 + 13,500 = 15,000. So the ratio is 1,500/15,000 = 10 percent.

b Since a ratio of less than 40 percent indicates a competitive market, the thingamabob industry is very competitive.

7 a The Herfindahl-Hirschman Index, for an industry of fewer than 50 firms, is the square of the percentage market share of each firm. For the yadayada industry, the index is $30^2 + 40^2 + 20^2 + 5^2 + 5^2 = 2,950$.

b Since an index of greater than 1,800 indicates a concentrated market, the yadayada industry is very concentrated.

8 Concentration ratios are calculated from a national geographical perspective. If the actual scope of the market is not national, the concentration ratio will likely misstate the degree of competitiveness in an industry. If the actual market is global, the concentration ratio will understate the degree of competitiveness. A firm may have a concentration ratio of 100 as the only producer in the nation, but may face a great deal of international competition. When the scope of the market is regional, the concentration ratio will overstate the degree of competitiveness. The concentration ratio includes firms elsewhere in the nation that are not real competitors in the region.

9 a Perfect competition—many firms; identical products; easy entry of new firms. Monopolistic competition—many firms; slightly differentiated products; easy entry. Oligopoly—few firms; identical or differentiated products; some barriers to entry. Monopoly—single firm; product with no close substitutes; high barriers to new entry

b Perfect competition—close to 0 percent. Monopolistic competition—low. Oligopoly—high. Monopoly—100 percent.

10 As we saw in the example on text pages 210–211, car repair can be coordinated by the market or by a firm. The institution (market or firm) that actually coordinates will be the one that is more efficient. Where there are significant transactions costs, economies of scale, or economies of team production, firms are likely to be more efficient, and firms will dominate the coordination of economic activity. But the efficiency of firms is limited, and there are many circumstances where market coordination of economic activity dominates because it is more efficient.

Chapter 10
Output and Costs

KEY CONCEPTS

Decision Time Frames

Firm has two decision time frames.

- **Short run**—quantities of some resources fixed. Quantities of other resources are variable.

  - Fixed resources are called the firm's fixed *plant*—usually technology, buildings, capital, and management.
  - Variable resources—usually labour.
  - Short-run decisions are easily reversed.

- **Long run**—quantities of all resources variable.

  - **Sunk cost**—*past* cost of buying a new plant. Firm's decisions depend only on short-run cost of changing labour input and long-run cost of changing plant. Sunk costs are irrelevant.
  - Long-run decisions are *not* easily reversed.

Short-Run Technology Constraint

Short-run production described by

- **total product** curve (*TP*)—maximum attainable output with fixed quantity capital as quantity labour varies.

- **marginal product** curve (*MP*)—ΔTP resulting from one-unit increase variable input.

- **average product** curve (*AP*)—*TP* per unit variable input.

As increase variable input, *MP* increases (increasing marginal returns), reaches maximum, and then decreases (**diminishing marginal returns**). When *MP* > *AP*, *AP* increasing. When *MP* < *AP*, *AP* decreasing. When *MP* = *AP*, maximum *AP*.

- **Law of diminishing returns**—with given quantity fixed inputs, as firm uses more variable input, its *MP* eventually diminishes.

Short-Run Cost

Short-run cost curves determined by technology and prices of productive resources.

- **Total cost** (*TC*) = *TFC* + *TVC*

  - **Total fixed cost** (*TFC*)—cost of fixed inputs (including normal profit).
  - **Total variable cost** (*TVC*)—cost of variable inputs.

- **Marginal cost** (*MC*)—ΔTC resulting from one-unit increase in output.

- **Average total cost** (*ATC*) = *AFC* + *AVC*

  - **Average fixed cost** (*AFC*)—total fixed cost per unit output.
  - **Average variable cost** (*AVC*)—total variable cost per unit output.
  - *AFC* curve decreases constantly as output increases.
  - *AVC*, *ATC*, and *MC* curves are U-shaped.
  - As output increases, *MC* decreases, reaches minimum, and then increases.
  - When *MC* < *ATC*, *ATC* decreases. When *MC* > *ATC*, *ATC* increases. When *MC* = *ATC*, minimum *ATC*. Same relation *MC* and *AVC*.

Long-Run Cost

Long-run cost—cost of production when all inputs (capital and labour) adjusted to economically efficient quantities.

◆ *Production function*—relationship between maximum attainable output and quantities of all inputs—describes long-run costs.

Long-run average cost curve (*LRAC*)—a planning curve that tells the firm the plant size and quantity of labour to use at each output to minimize cost. Consists of the segments of different short-run *ATC* curves along which average total cost is lowest.

◆ In the long run, when all inputs increase by same percentage, increases in output can show three different returns to scale.

 • **Economies of scale** (increasing returns to scale)—percentage increase firm's output > percentage increase inputs. *LRAC* slopes downward.
 • **Constant returns to scale**—percentage increase firm's output = percentage increase inputs. *LRAC* horizontal.
 • **Diseconomies of scale** (decreasing returns to scale)—percentage increase firm's output < percentage increase inputs. *LRAC* slopes upward.

◆ **Minimum efficient scale**—smallest quantity of output yielding minimum *LRAC*.

HELPFUL HINTS

1 Be sure to understand how economists use the terms *short run* and *long run*. These terms do *not* refer to calendar time. Think of them as planning horizons. The short run is a planning horizon short enough that while some resources are variable, at least one resource cannot be varied but is fixed. The long run refers to a planning horizon that is long enough that all resources can be varied.

2 This chapter introduces many new concepts and graphs and may at first appear overwhelming. Don't get lost among the trees and lose sight of the forest. There is a simple and fundamental relationship between product curves and cost curves.

The chapter explains the short-run product curves and concepts of total product, marginal product, and average product. This is followed by the short-run cost function and concepts of total cost, marginal cost, average variable cost, and average total cost.

But all of these seemingly separate concepts are related to the *law of diminishing returns*. The law states that as a firm uses more of a variable

input, with a given quantity of fixed inputs, the marginal product of the variable input eventually diminishes. This law explains why the marginal product and average product curves eventually fall, and why the total product curve becomes flatter. When productivity falls, costs increase, and the law explains the eventual upward slope of the marginal cost curve. When marginal product falls, marginal cost increases.

The marginal cost curve, in turn, explains the U-shape of the average variable cost and average total cost curves. When the marginal cost curve is below the average variable (or total) cost curve, the average variable (or total) cost curve is falling. When marginal cost is above the average variable (or total) cost curve, the average variable (or total) cost curve is rising. The marginal cost curve intersects the average variable (or total) cost curve at the minimum point on the average variable (or total) cost curve.

Use the law of diminishing returns as the key to understanding the relationships between the many short-run concepts and graphs in the chapter. But all concepts and graphs are not equally important. Pay most attention to the unit-cost concepts and graphs—especially marginal cost, average variable cost, and average total cost—because these will be used the most in later chapters to analyze the behaviour of firms.

3 Be sure to thoroughly understand Figure 10.1 (Text Figure 10.5 on page 225). It is the most important graph in the chapter and one of the most important graphs in all of microeconomics.

FIGURE **10.1**

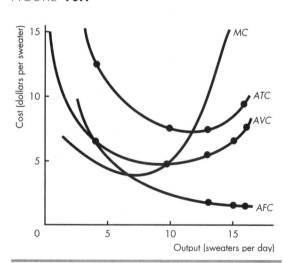

The curves for average total cost (*ATC*), average fixed cost (*AFC*), and average variable cost (*AVC*) are derived by taking the values for *TC, TFC,* and *TVC* and dividing by quantity of output. Since these are average values for a fixed quantity of output, they are plotted directly above the corresponding units of output.

On the other hand, marginal cost (*MC*) is the *change* in total cost (or equivalently, in total variable cost) resulting from a one-unit increase in output. It is plotted *midway* between the corresponding units of output. The *ATC, AVC,* and *MC* curves are crucially important. The *ATC* and *AVC* curves are both U-shaped. The *MC* curve is also U-shaped and intersects the *ATC* and *AVC* curves at their minimum points. The *MC* curve is below the *ATC* and *AVC* curves when *ATC* and *AVC* are falling, and above the *ATC* and *AVC* curves when they are rising. The less important *AFC* curve falls continuously as output increases.

4 You will probably draw a graph like the one in Figure 10.1 at least one hundred times in this course. Here are some hints on drawing the graph quickly and easily.

Be sure to label the axes: quantity of output (*Q*) on the horizontal axis and average cost on the vertical axis.

Draw an upward-sloping marginal cost curve, as shown here in Figure 10.2. The marginal cost curve can have a small downward-sloping section at first, but this is not important. Next, draw a shallow U-shaped curve that falls until it intersects the marginal cost curve, and then rises. Then pick a point further up the marginal cost curve. Draw another shallow U-shaped curve whose minimum point passes through your second point. Finally, label the curves.

Any time a test question (including those in the Self-Test) asks about these curves, *draw a graph* before you answer.

FIGURE **10.2**

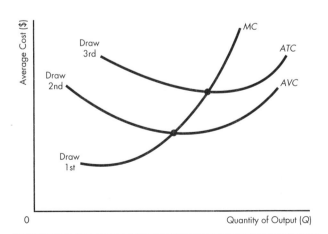

5 The later sections of the chapter explain long-run costs using a production function where both labour and capital inputs are variable. While diminishing returns is the key for understanding short-run costs, the concept of *returns to scale* is the key for understanding long-run costs. Returns to scale are the increase in output relative to the increase in inputs when all inputs are increased by the same percentage. Returns to scale can be increasing, constant, or decreasing, and correspond to the downward-sloping, horizontal, and upward-sloping sections of the long-run average cost curve.

S E L F - T E S T

True/False and Explain

Decision Time Frames

1 All resources are fixed in the short run.

2 The firm's short-run decisions are easily reversed.

3 The firm's long-run decisions depend on sunk costs.

Short-Run Technology Constraint

4 Given a fixed quantity of capital, if 2 additional labourers produce 15 additional units of output, the marginal product of labour is 15 units of output.

5 The law of diminishing returns implies that eventually the marginal product curve will be negatively sloped as the variable input increases.

6 Marginal product is measured by the slope of the total product curve.

7 The law of diminishing returns implies that we will not observe a range of increasing marginal returns.

8 If the marginal product of labour is greater than the average product of labour, average product is increasing.

Short-Run Cost

9 Average variable cost reaches its minimum at the same level of output at which average product is a maximum.

10 If average variable cost is decreasing, then marginal cost must be decreasing.

11 The average total cost curve always intersects the minimum point of the marginal cost curve.

Long-Run Cost

12 No part of any short-run average total cost curve can lie below the long-run average cost curve.

13 Economies of scale means that the long-run average cost curve is positively sloped.

14 If a firm can double its output by building a second plant identical to its first plant, there are constant returns to scale.

15 Minimum efficient scale occurs at the minimum point on the average total cost curve.

Multiple-Choice

Decision Time Frames

1 In economics, the short run is a time period in which
a one year or less elapses.
b all resources are variable.
c all resources are fixed.
d some resources are variable but some resources are fixed.
e all resources are variable but the technology is fixed.

2 Long-run decisions
a are not easily reversed.
b do not depend on sunk costs.
c involve changes in a firm's plant.
d can vary all resources of a firm.
e are all of the above.

Short-Run Technology Constraint

3 The average product of labour is
a the slope of the total product curve.
b the slope of the marginal product curve.
c the increase in total product divided by the increase in labour employed.
d the total product divided by the quantity of labour employed.
e none of the above.

4 When the marginal product of labour is less than the average product of labour,
a the average product of labour is increasing.
b the marginal product of labour is increasing.
c the total product curve is negatively sloped.
d the firm is experiencing diminishing returns.
e none of the above is true.

5 Refer to Figure 10.3 illustrating Swanky's short-run total product curve. Which of the following statements is *true*?
a Points above the curve are attainable and inefficient.
b Points below the curve are attainable and inefficient.
c Points below the curve are unattainable and inefficient.
d Points on the curve are unattainable and efficient.
e Points on the curve all have equal marginal products.

FIGURE **10.3**

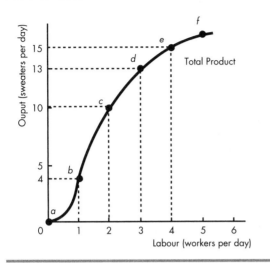

6 Refer to Figure 10.3 illustrating Swanky's short-run total product curve. Marginal product reaches a maximum when you add which labourer?

a 1st labourer
b 2nd labourer
c 3rd labourer
d 4th labourer
e 5th labourer

7 Which of the following statements by a restaurant owner refers to the law of diminishing returns?

a "The higher the quality of the ingredients we use, the higher the cost of producing each meal."
b "If we double the size of our premises and double everything else—kitchen staff, serving staff, equipment—we can increase the number of meals we serve, but not to double current levels."
c "We can increase the number of meals we serve by just adding more kitchen staff, but each additional worker adds fewer meals than the previous worker because traffic in the kitchen will get worse."
d "We can serve the same number of meals with fewer kitchen staff, but we would have to buy more labour-saving kitchen equipment."
e "We can serve the same number of meals with less kitchen equipment, but we would have to hire more kitchen staff."

Short-Run Cost

8 The vertical distance between the *TC* and *TVC* curves is

a decreasing as output increases.
b increasing as output increases.
c equal to *AFC*.
d equal to *TFC*.
e equal to *MC*.

9 Total cost is $20 at 4 units of output and $36 at 6 units of output. Between 4 and 6 units of output, marginal cost

a is less than average total cost.
b is equal to average total cost.
c is equal to average variable cost.
d is greater than average total cost.
e cannot be compared with any average cost without additional information.

10 Marginal cost is the amount that

a total cost increases when one more labourer is hired.
b fixed cost increases when one more labourer is hired.
c variable cost increases when one more labourer is hired.
d total cost increases when one more unit of output is produced.
e fixed cost increases when one more unit of output is produced.

11 A firm's fixed costs are $100. If total costs are $200 for one unit of output and $310 for two units, what is the marginal cost of the second unit?

a $100
b $110
c $200
d $210
e $310

12 If *ATC* is falling then *MC* must be

a rising.
b falling.
c equal to *ATC*.
d above *ATC*.
e below *ATC*.

13 Which of the following does *not* cause decreasing *ATC*?

a decreasing marginal cost
b decreasing average variable cost
c decreasing average fixed cost
d increasing marginal product
e increasing returns to scale

14 The average variable cost curve will shift up if

a there is an increase in fixed costs.
b there is a technological advance.
c the price of a variable input decreases.
d the price of a variable input increases.
e the price of output increases.

15 The marginal cost (*MC*) curve intersects the

a *ATC*, *AVC*, and *AFC* curves at their minimum points.
b *ATC* and *AFC* curves at their minimum points.
c *AVC* and *AFC* curves at their minimum points.
d *ATC* and *AVC* curves at their minimum points.
e *TC* and *TVC* curves at their minimum points.

16 According to the law of diminishing returns,

1 marginal productivity eventually rises.
2 marginal productivity eventually falls.
3 marginal cost eventually rises.
4 marginal cost eventually falls.

a 1 and 3
b 1 and 4
c 2 and 3
d 2 and 4
e 4 only

17 Average variable cost is at a minimum at the same output where

a average product is at a maximum.
b average product is at a minimum.
c marginal product is at a maximum.
d marginal product is at a minimum.
e marginal cost is at a minimum.

18 A rise in the price of a fixed input will cause a firm's

a average variable cost curve to shift up.
b average total cost curve to shift up.
c average total cost curve to shift down.
d marginal cost curve to shift up.
e marginal cost curve to shift down.

19 A technological advance will shift

1 *TP*, *AP*, and *MP* curves up.
2 *TP*, *AP*, and *MP* curves down.
3 *TC*, *ATC*, and *MC* curves up.
4 *TC*, *ATC*, and *MC* curves down.

a 1 and 3
b 1 and 4
c 2 and 3
d 2 and 4
e none of the above

Long-Run Cost

20 In the long run,

a only the plant size is fixed.
b all inputs are variable.
c all inputs are fixed.
d a firm must experience diseconomies of scale.
e none of the above is true.

21 The long-run average cost curve

a is a planning curve.
b identifies the cost-minimizing plant size and quantity of labour for each output level.
c is the relation between lowest attainable *ATC* and output when both plant size and labour are variable.
d consists of the segments of different short-run *ATC* curves along which average total cost is lowest.
e is all of the above.

22 Constant returns to scale means that as all inputs are increased,

a total output remains constant.
b average total cost remains constant.
c average total cost increases at the same rate as inputs.
d long-run average cost remains constant.
e long-run average cost rises at the same rate as inputs.

23 If all inputs are increased by 10 percent and output increases by less than 10 percent, it must be the case that

a average total cost is decreasing.
b average total cost is increasing.
c the *LRAC* curve is negatively sloped.
d there are economies of scale.
e there are diseconomies of scale.

24 Minimum efficient scale is the smallest quantity of output at which

a the *LRAC* curve reaches it lowest level.
b the *ATC* curve reaches its lowest level.
c the *AFC* curve reaches its lowest level.
d economies of scale begin.
e diminishing returns begin.

25 A firm will always want to increase its scale of plant if

a it persistently produces on the upward-sloping part of its short-run average total cost curve.
b it persistently produces on the downward-sloping part of its short-run average total cost curve.
c it is producing below minimum efficient scale.
d marginal cost is below average total cost.
e marginal cost is below average variable cost.

Short Answer Problems

1 Why must the marginal cost curve intersect the average total cost curve at the minimum point of the average total cost curve?

2 Explain the connection, if any, between the U-shape of the average total cost curve and (a) fixed costs, and (b) the law of eventually diminishing returns.

3 Use the concepts of marginal and average to answer the following question. Suppose the worst student at Hubertville High School transfers to Histrionic High School. Is it possible that the average grade-point of the students at each school rises? Explain.

4 What is the difference, if any, between diminishing returns and diseconomies of scale?

5 For a given scale of plant, Table 10.1 gives the total monthly output of golf carts attainable using varying quantities of labour.

TABLE **10.1** MONTHLY GOLF CART PRODUCTION

Labourers (per month)	Output (units per month)	Marginal Product	Average Product
0	0		
1	1		
2	3		
3	6		
4	12		
5	17		
6	20		
7	22		
8	23		

a Complete the table for the marginal product and average product of labour. (Note that marginal product should be entered *midway* between rows to emphasize that it is the result of *changing* inputs—moving from one row to the next. Average product corresponds to a fixed quantity of labour and should be entered on the appropriate row.)
b Label the axes and draw a graph of the total product curve (*TP*).
c On a separate piece of paper, label the axes and draw a graph of both marginal product (*MP*) and average product (*AP*). (Marginal product should be plotted *midway* between the corresponding units of labour, as in Text Figure 10.2(b) on page 221, while average product should be plotted directly above the corresponding units of labour, as in Text Figure 10.3 on page 222.)

6 Now let's examine the short-run costs of golf cart production. The first two columns of Table 10.1 are reproduced in the first two columns of Table 10.2. The cost of 1 labourer (the only variable input) is $2,000 per month. Total fixed cost is $2,000 per month.

TABLE **10.2** SHORT-RUN COSTS (MONTHLY)

L	Q	TFC ($)	TVC ($)	TC ($)	MC ($)	AFC ($)	AVC ($)	ATC ($)
0	0	2,000						
1	1							
2	3							
3	6							
4	12							
5	17							
6	20							
7	22							
8	23							

a Given this information, complete Table 10.2 by computing total fixed cost (*TFC*), total variable cost (*TVC*), total cost (*TC*), marginal cost (*MC*), average fixed cost (*AFC*), average variable cost (*AVC*), and average total cost (*ATC*). Your completed table should look like the table in Text Figure 10.5 on page 225, with marginal cost entered *midway* between the rows.

b Label the axes and draw the *TC, TVC,* and *TFC* curves on a single graph.

c Label the axes and draw the *MC, ATC, AVC,* and *AFC* curves on a single graph. Be sure to plot *MC midway* between the corresponding units of output.

7 Now suppose that the price of a labourer increases to $2,500 per month. Construct a table for the new *MC* and *ATC* curves (output, *MC, ATC*) for golf cart production. Label the axes and draw a graph of the new *MC* and *ATC* curves. What is the effect of the increase in the price of the variable input on these curves?

8 Return to the original price of labour of $2,000 per month. Now suppose that we double the quantity of fixed inputs so that total fixed costs also double to $4,000 per month. This increases the monthly output of golf carts for each quantity of labour as indicated in Table 10.3.

TABLE **10.3** NEW MONTHLY PRODUCTION OF GOLF CARTS

Labourers (per month)	Output (units per month)
0	0
1	1
2	4
3	10
4	19
5	26
6	31
7	34
8	36

a Construct a table for the new *MC* and *ATC* curves (output, *MC, ATC*). Label the axes and draw a graph of the new *MC* and *ATC* curves.

b What is the effect on these curves (compared with the original *MC* and *ATC* curves in Short Answer Problem **6c**) of an increase in "plant size"? Are there economies of scale?

c Draw the long-run average cost (*LRAC*) curve if these are the only two plant sizes available.

9 At a firm's minimum efficient scale of plant, long-run average cost is at its lowest level. Therefore, firms should always build plants at minimum efficient scale. Agree or disagree with this statement and explain your answer.

10 Figure 10.4 gives a sequence of short-run *ATC* curves numbered 1 through 7 corresponding to seven different plant sizes.

FIGURE **10.4**

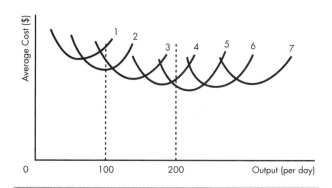

a Draw the long-run average cost curve on Figure 10.4.

b If the desired level of output is 100 units per day, what is the best plant size? (Give the number of the associated short-run *ATC* curve.) What if the desired level of output is 200 units per day?

ANSWERS

True/False and Explain

1 **F** Some resources fixed, some variable. (218)
2 **T** Firm can change output by changing quantity of labour hired. Long-run decisions not easily reversed. (218)
3 **F** Sunk costs are past costs and are irrelevant to all firm decisions about present or future. (218)
4 **F** $\Delta TP/\Delta L = 15/2 = 7.5$. (219–221)
5 **T** MP must eventually diminish with increasing L. (220–221)
6 **T** $\Delta TP/\Delta L$
7 **F** *Eventually* diminishing returns. MP can initially increase. (220–221)
8 **T** See Text Figure 10.3 and grade point discussion for intuition. (222)
⊕ 9 **T** $AVC = TVC/Q = WL/Q = W/(Q/L) = W/AP$. (226)
⊕ 10 **F** MC must be below AVC, but MC may be increasing or decreasing. (224–226)
11 **F** MC intersect minimum ATC. (224–225)
12 **T** $LRAC$ consists of lowest cost segments of all average total cost curves. (229–230)
13 **F** Negatively sloped; falling long-run average costs as output increases. (230)
14 **T** All inputs increase by 100% and output increases by 100%. (230–231)
15 **F** Smallest Q at which $LRAC$ curve is at minimum. ATC is short-run. (231)

Multiple-Choice

1 **d** Definition. (218)
2 **e** From definition of long run. (218)
3 **d** Definition. (219–221)
⊕ 4 **d** When $MP < AP$, MP is decreasing (diminishing returns), AP is decreasing, and TP is positively sloped. (219–221)
5 **b** Attainable but not maximum TP. (219–220)
6 **b** MP = slope TP curve = 6 for 2nd labourer. (219–221)
7 **c** MP decreases as restaurant uses more variable resource (labour). (221)
8 **d** $TC = TFC + TVC$. Distance constant. (223–224)
⊕ 9 **d** $MC = 16/2 = 8$. ATC is $5 at 4 units and $6 at 6 units. (223–225)
10 **d** Definition; **b** and **e** wrong because fixed costs don't change; **a** and **c** wrong because MC can also decrease and may be affected by costs other than labour. (224)

11 **b** Fixed costs irrelevant. $\Delta TC/\Delta Q = (\$310 - \$200)/(2 - 1)$. (223–224)
⊕ 12 **e** MC could be increasing or decreasing below ATC when ATC is decreasing. (224–225)
13 **e** Increasing returns to scale is long-run concept; ATC is short-run concept. (224–226)
14 **d** **a** and **e** don't affect AVC; **b** and **c** shift AVC down. (226–227)
15 **d** AFC always decreases, TC and TVC always increase. (224–226)
16 **c** Decreasing MP causes increasing MC. (224–226)
17 **a** AVC decreases as long as AP is increasing. See Text Figure 10.6. (226)
18 **b** Won't affect AVC or MC. (226–227)
19 **b** Productivity increases, costs decrease. (226–227)
20 **b** Definition. All returns to scale possible in long run. (218, 228)
21 **e** All definitions of $LRAC$. (229–230)
22 **d** $LRAC$ horizontal. (231)
23 **e** Definition. Since all resources variable, **a** and **b** irrelevant. (230–231)
24 **a** Definition of a long-run concept; **b**, **c**, **e** are short-run concepts; **d** would be correct if where economies of scale *end*. (231)
25 **a** Plant already too big in **b**; for **c**, sales may not justify a plant that big; **d** and **e** relate to short run. (228–231)

Short Answer Problems

1 The average total cost curve is U-shaped, first falling and then rising as output increases. When average total cost is falling, marginal cost must be less than average total cost, and when average total cost is rising, marginal cost must be greater than average total cost. Therefore the marginal cost curve must intersect the average total cost curve at its minimum point. In order for average total cost to fall, it must have been *pulled down* by a smaller increase in cost from the last unit of output. Therefore marginal cost is lower than average total cost. Similarly, when average total cost is rising, it must be that it has been *pulled up* by a higher marginal cost. When average total cost is at its minimum, it is neither falling nor rising, so marginal cost cannot be lower or higher than average total cost. Therefore, marginal cost must be equal to average total cost.

2 The U-shape of the average total cost (*ATC*) curve arises from the opposing forces of (a) spreading fixed costs over a larger output and (b) the law of eventually diminishing returns.

As output increases, fixed costs are spread over a larger output so average fixed cost (*AFC*) falls. Initially, as output increases, the marginal productivity of the variable resource rises, causing average variable cost (*AVC*) to fall. Falling *AVC*, together with falling *AFC*, causes average total cost (*ATC*) to fall, contributing to the downward-sloping portion of *ATC*. Eventually, as output increases, diminishing returns set in, marginal productivity falls, and *AVC* rises. Eventually, *AVC* rises more quickly than *AFC* falls, contributing to the upward sloping portion of *ATC*.

3 Yes, it is possible that the average grade-point of the students at each school rises. Think of the transferring student as the *marginal* student. If his grade-point average, although the lowest at Hubertville High, is higher than the *average* grade-point at Histrionic High, then the results are: the *average* grade-point at Hubertville High rises with the elimination of the lowest grade-point; and the average grade-point at Histrionic High rises because the transferring (*marginal*) student's grade-point pulls up the *average* grade-point.

4 The law of diminishing returns states that as a firm uses more of a variable input, with a given quantity of fixed inputs, the marginal product of the variable input eventually diminishes. Diseconomies of scale occur when a firm increases all of its inputs by an equal percentage, and this results in a lower percentage increase in output. Diminishing (marginal) returns is a short-run concept since there must be a fixed input. Diseconomies of scale is a long-run concept since all inputs must be variable.

5 a The completed Table 10.1 is shown here as Table 10.1 Solution.

TABLE **10.1** SOLUTION
MONTHLY GOLF CART PRODUCTION

Labourers (per month)	Output (units per month)	Marginal Product	Average Product
0	0		0
		·········· 1	
1	1		1.00
		·········· 2	
2	3		1.50
		·········· 3	
3	6		2.00
		·········· 6	
4	12		3.00
		·········· 5	
5	17		3.40
		·········· 3	
6	20		3.33
		·········· 2	
7	22		3.14
		·········· 1	
8	23		2.88

b Figure 10.5 gives the graph of the total product curve.

FIGURE **10.5**

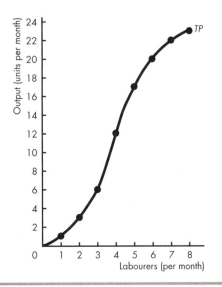

c Figure 10.6 gives the graphs of marginal product and average product.

FIGURE **10.6**

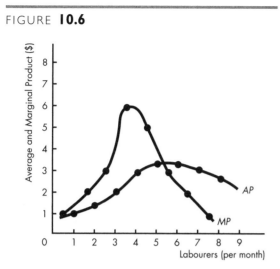

FIGURE **10.7**

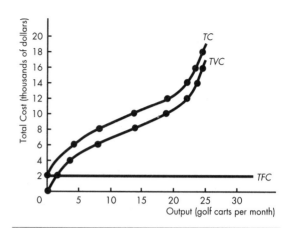

c The *MC, ATC, AVC,* and *AFC* curves are graphed in Figure 10.8.

6 a Completed Table 10.2 is given here as Table 10.2 Solution.

TABLE **10.2** SOLUTION
SHORT-RUN COSTS (MONTHLY)

L	Q	TFC ($)	TVC ($)	TC ($)	MC ($)	AFC ($)	AVC ($)	ATC ($)
0	0	2,000	0	2,000		—	—	—
					2,000			
1	1	2,000	2,000	4,000		2,000	2,000	4,000
					1,000			
2	3	2,000	4,000	6,000		667	1,333	2,000
					667			
3	6	2,000	6,000	8,000		333	1,000	1,333
					333			
4	12	2,000	8,000	10,000		167	667	833
					400			
5	17	2,000	10,000	12,000		118	588	706
					667			
6	20	2,000	12,000	14,000		100	600	700
					1,000			
7	22	2,000	14,000	16,000		91	636	727
					2,000			
8	23	2,000	16,000	18,000		87	696	783

b The *TC, TVC,* and *TFC* curves are graphed in Figure 10.7.

FIGURE **10.8**

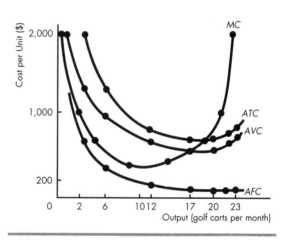

7 The new *MC* and *ATC* curves (and the associated table) for golf cart production are given in Figure 10.9. The original curves, MC_0 and ATC_0, are indicated for reference. The new curves are labelled MC_1 and ATC_1. Both curves have shifted up as a result of an increase in the price of labour.

FIGURE **10.9**

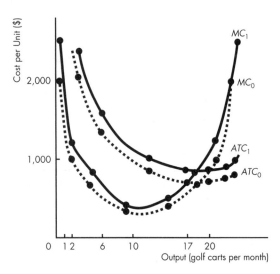

Output	MC ($)	ATC ($)
0		0
	2,500	
1		4,500
	1,250	
3		2,333
	833	
6		1,583
	417	
12		1,000
	500	
17		853
	833	
20		850
	1,250	
22		886
	2,500	
23		957

8 a The new *MC* and *ATC* curves (and the associated table) are given in Figure 10.10. The new curves are labelled MC_2 and ATC_2. The original curves, MC_0 and ATC_0, are indicated for reference.

FIGURE **10.10**

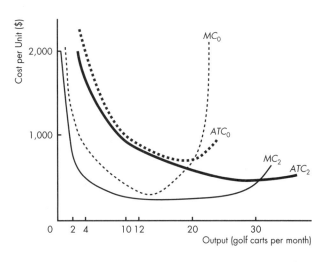

Output	MC ($)	ATC ($)
0		0
	2,000	
1		6,000
	667	
4		2,000
	333	
10		1,000
	222	
19		632
	286	
26		538
	400	
31		516
	667	
34		529

b The curves have shifted (generally) down and to the right as a result of increasing the plant size. There are economies of scale (increasing returns to scale) up to the level of output at which MC_2 intersects ATC_2 (approximately 32 units).

c The long-run average cost curve is indicated in Figure 10.10 by the heavy line tracing out the lowest short-run average total cost of producing each level of output. In this example, that happens to correspond entirely to ATC_2.

9 Disagree. To produce at minimum efficient scale, a firm must have a certain quantity of output. If demand for the firm's product does not justify that quantity of output, the firm with a minimum efficient scale plant may actually have higher short-run average total costs. Consider Text Figure 10.7. The minimum efficient scale plant has ATC_2. But if the firm is producing less than 9 units of output, average total cost would actually be lower with plant having ATC_1.

10 a The long-run average cost curve is indicated in Figure 10.4 Solution by the heavy scalloped-shaped curve tracing out the lowest short-run average cost of producing each level of output.

b For output of 100 units, the best plant size is associated with short-run average total cost curve 2. For output of 200 units, the best plant size is associated with short-run average total cost curve 5.

FIGURE **10.4** SOLUTION

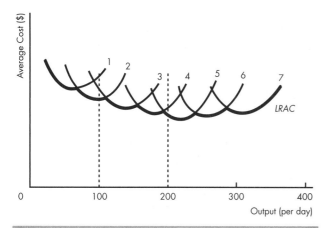

Chapter 11

Perfect Competition

Competition

Perfect competition is a model of market structure where the force of *competition* is extreme and firms have no *market power*. Assumptions include many firms; identical products; many buyers; free entry; no advantages for existing firms over new firms; complete information.

Perfect competition can arise when

◆ industry demand is *large* relative to the minimum efficient scale of a firm (smallest quantity of output yielding minimum *LRAC*).

◆ products of each firm are identical.

In perfect competition,

◆ each firm is a **price taker**.

◆ each firm faces a perfectly elastic demand curve at the market price.

Firm maximizes economic profit.

◆ Economic profit = total revenue – total cost (total cost includes normal profit).

◆ Normal profit = expected return to entrepreneurial ability.

◆ **Total revenue** (*TR*)—price (*P*) × quantity (*Q*).

  • Average revenue (*AR*)—*TR*/*Q*.
  • **Marginal revenue** (*MR*)—$\Delta TR/\Delta Q$.
  • In perfect competition, $AR = MR = P$.

The Firm's Decisions in Perfect Competition

In the short run, firm decides what quantity to produce or to shut down.

◆ Economic profit maximized at quantity where $MR = MC$:

  • If $MR > MC$, firm increases Q to increase economic profit.
  • If $MR < MC$, firm decreases Q to increase economic profit.

◆ Three possible short-run profit-maximizing outcomes:

  • $P (= AR = MR) > ATC$ yields economic profit.
  • $P (= AR = MR) = ATC$ yields zero economic profit (*break-even point* at minimum *ATC*; firm just earning normal profit).
  • $P (= AR = MR) < ATC$ yields economic loss (firm earning less than normal profit).

◆ For firm incurring economic loss:

  • If $P > AVC$, firm will continue to produce.
  • If $P < AVC$, firm will temporarily shut down.
  • **Shutdown point** at minimum *AVC*.

Perfectly competitive firm's supply curve is its *MC* curve above minimum *AVC*.

Short-run industry supply curve is horizontal sum of individual firm supply curves.

Output, Price, and Profit in Perfect Competition

Equilibrium market price and quantity determined by industry demand and supply curves.

In the short run

◆ perfectly competitive firms can make an economic profit, normal profit (zero economic profit), or incur an economic loss.

◆ the number of firms and their plant size are fixed.

In the long run, the number of firms in the industry and the plant size of each firm can adjust. Economic profit/loss are signals for firms to enter/exit the industry and cause reallocation of resources.

◆ Economic profit attracts new entry, causing a rightward shift of industry supply, causing falling *P* and the elimination of economic profit.

◆ Economic loss induces existing firms to exit, causing a leftward shift of industry supply, causing rising *P* and the elimination of economic loss.

In long-run competitive equilibrium

◆ *MR* = *P* = *MC*. Firms maximize short-run profit.

◆ *P* = minimum *ATC*. Economic profit is zero. No incentive for firms to enter or exit industry.

◆ *P* = minimum *LRAC*. Optimum plant size. No incentive for firm to change plant size.

Changing Tastes and Advancing Technology

For a permanent shift in demand

◆ decreased demand causes falling *P*, economic loss and exit, decreased industry supply, causing rising *P*. In the long run, enough firms exit so remaining firms earn normal profit.

◆ increased demand causes rising *P*, economic profit and entry, increased industry supply, causing falling *P*. In the long run, enough firms enter so economic profit is eliminated and firms earn normal profit.

The change in long-run equilibrium price from a permanent shift in demand depends on

◆ **external economies**—factors beyond control of firm that lower costs as industry output increases.

◆ **external diseconomies**—factors beyond control of firm that raise costs as industry output increases.

The shape of the **long-run industry supply curve** depends on existence of external economies or diseconomies. The long-run industry supply curve shows how industry quantity supplied varies as market price varies after all possible adjustments, including changes in plant size and number of firms. Shape may be

◆ horizontal for constant-cost industry.

◆ upward-sloping for increasing cost industry with external diseconomies.

◆ downward-sloping for decreasing cost industry with external economies.

New technology lowers costs, increases industry supply, causing falling *P*. New technology firms make economic profit and enter. Old technology firms incur economic loss and exit or switch to new technology. In the long run, all firms use new technology and earn zero economic profit (normal profit only).

Competition and Efficiency

Resource use is efficient when the most highly valued goods are produced; when no one can become better off without someone else becoming worse off; when marginal benefit equals marginal costs. Requires

◆ consumers are on their demand = marginal benefit curves, and are getting the most value from their resources.

◆ firms are on their supply = marginal cost curves, and are technologically efficient and economically efficient.

◆ equilibrium where price = marginal benefit = marginal cost. Maximum gains from trade (consumer surplus + producer surplus).

◆ no **external benefits**—benefits accruing to people other than buyer of good; no **external costs**—costs borne by people other than producer of good.

Perfect competition achieves efficient use of resources at the market equilibrium price and quantity if there are no external benefits and external costs.

Main obstacles to efficiency are monopoly, public goods, and external benefits and costs.

HELPFUL HINTS

I Although perfectly competitive markets are rare in the real world, there are three important reasons to develop a thorough understanding of their behaviour.

First, many markets closely approximate perfectly competitive markets. The analysis in this chapter gives direct and useful insights into the behaviour of these markets.

Second, the theory of perfect competition allows us to isolate the effects of competitive forces that are at work in *all* markets, even in those that do not match the assumptions of perfect competition.

Third, the perfectly competitive model serves as a useful benchmark for evaluating the relative efficiency of different market structures in subsequent chapters.

2 In the short run, a perfectly competitive firm cannot change the size of its plant—it has fixed inputs. The firm also is a price taker; it always sells at the market price, which it cannot influence. The only variable that the firm controls is its level of output. The short-run condition for profit maximization is to choose the level of output at which marginal revenue equals marginal cost. This is a general condition which, as we will see in subsequent chapters, applies to other market structures such as monopoly and monopolistic competition. Since for the perfectly competitive firm, marginal revenue is equal to price, this profit-maximizing condition takes a particular form; choose the level of output at which price is equal to marginal cost ($P = MC$).

3 Many students have trouble understanding why a firm continues to operate at the break-even point, where economic profit is zero. The key to understanding lies in the definition of which costs are included in the average total cost curve. Recall from Chapter 9 that the economist defines a firm's total costs as *opportunity costs*, which include both explicit costs and *implicit costs*.

Implicit costs include forgone interest, forgone rent, and forgone cost of the owner's resources. Owners supply their time, which could have been used to earn income elsewhere. Owners also supply entrepreneurial ability. Normal profit is the expected return to entrepreneurial ability and is part of a firm's implicit costs.

At the break-even point where total revenue equals total cost (or, equivalently, average revenue equals average total cost), the owners of the firm are still earning a return on their investment, time, and entrepreneurial ability, which is equal to the best return that they could earn elsewhere. That is the definition of opportunity cost—the best alternative forgone. As the phrase "normal profit" implies, this profit could normally be earned as a return to entrepreneurial ability, on average, in any other industry. At the break-even point, the firm is earning normal profit even though its economic profit (sometimes called "extra-normal," or "above-average," profit) is zero. In earning normal profit, the firm is earning just as much profit as it could anywhere else, and is therefore totally content to continue producing in this industry.

4 When the price of output falls below the break-even point, but is above the shutdown point, the firm will continue to produce even though it is incurring economic losses. In this price range, the firm is no longer earning normal profit and theoretically could earn more by switching to another industry. Nonetheless, the firm will continue to operate in the short run because switching has costs. In order to switch industries, the firm must shut down, which entails still paying its total fixed costs.

As long as price is above the shutdown point (minimum average variable cost), a firm will decide to produce since it will be covering total variable cost and part of total fixed cost. Its loss will be less if it continues to produce at the output where $P = MC$ than if it shuts down.

If price falls below the shutdown point, a firm that produces output will not only lose its total fixed costs, it will lose *additional* money on every unit of output produced, since average revenue is less than average variable cost. Thus when price is less than average variable cost, the firm will choose to minimize its loss by shutting down.

5 In the long run, fixed costs disappear, and the firm can switch between industries and change plant size without cost. Economic profit serves as the signal for the movement or reallocation of firm resources until long-run equilibrium is achieved. Firms will move out of industries with negative economic profit (economic loss) and into industries with positive economic profit. Only when economic profit is zero will there be no tendency for firms to exit or enter industries.

The fact that there are no restrictions on entry into the industry is what assures that economic profit will be zero and that firms will be producing at the minimum of their long-run average cost curves in long-run equilibrium.

6 In long-run equilibrium, three conditions are satisfied for each firm in an industry:
   i $MR = P = MC$. This implies that profits are maximized for each firm.
   ii $P = ATC$. This implies that economic profit is zero and each firm is just earning normal profit.
   iii $P =$ minimum $LRAC$. This implies that production takes place at the point of minimum long-run average cost.

True/False and Explain

Competition

1 A firm in a perfectly competitive industry cannot influence price.

2 The industry demand curve in a perfectly competitive industry is horizontal.

3 The objective of firms in a competitive industry is to maximize revenue.

The Firm's Decision in Perfect Competition

4 Firms will incur an economic loss in the long run but not the short run.

5 At prices below minimum average total cost, a firm will always shut down.

6 The supply curve of a perfectly competitive firm gives the quantities of output supplied at alternative prices as long as the firm earns economic profit.

Output, Price, and Profit in Perfect Competition

7 In long-run equilibrium, each firm in a perfectly competitive industry will choose the plant size associated with minimum long-run average cost.

8 Suppose a perfectly competitive industry is in long-run equilibrium when there is a substantial increase in total fixed costs. All firms will now incur economic losses and some firms will go out of business.

9 Suppose a perfectly competitive industry is in long-run equilibrium when there is an increase in demand. As new firms start entering the industry, the output of each existing firm will increase.

Changing Tastes and Advancing Technology

10 Suppose a perfectly competitive industry is in long-run equilibrium when there is a permanent increase in demand. In the short run, firms will earn an economic profit.

11 Suppose a perfectly competitive industry is in long-run equilibrium when there is a permanent decrease in demand. In the long run, firms will incur an economic loss.

12 In a perfectly competitive industry with external economies, the long-run industry supply curve is positively sloped.

Competition and Efficiency

13 Resource use is efficient as long as marginal benefit is greater than marginal cost.

14 Resource use is efficient as long as consumer surplus equals producer surplus.

15 A perfectly competitive industry will achieve efficiency if there are no external costs or external benefits.

Multiple-Choice

Competition

1 Which of the following is *not* a characteristic of a perfectly competitive industry?

a downward-sloping industry demand curve
b perfectly elastic demand curve for each individual firm
c each firm decides its quantity of output
d slightly differentiated products
e many firms each supplying a small fraction of industry supply

2 For perfect competition to arise it is necessary that industry demand be

a inelastic.
b elastic.
c perfectly elastic.
d large relative to the minimum efficient scale of a firm.
e small relative to the minimum efficient scale of a firm.

3 If a firm faces a perfectly elastic demand for its product, then

a it is not a price taker.
b it will want to lower its price to increase sales.
c it will want to raise its price to increase total revenue.
d its marginal revenue curve is equal to the price of the product.
e it will always earn zero economic profit.

The Firm's Decisions in Perfect Competition

4 In a perfectly competitive industry, the market price is \$10. An individual firm is producing the output at which $MC = ATC = \$15$. AVC at that output is \$10. What should the firm do to maximize its short-run profits?

a shut down
b expand output
c contract output
d leave output unchanged
e insufficient information to answer

5 In which of the following situations will a perfectly competitive firm earn economic profit?

a $MR > AVC$
b $MR > ATC$
c $ATC > MC$
d $ATC > AR$
e $AR > AVC$

6 In the price range below minimum average variable cost, a perfectly competitive firm's supply curve is

a horizontal at the market price.
b vertical at zero output.
c the same as its marginal cost curve.
d the same as its average variable cost curve.
e none of the above.

7 A firm in a perfectly competitive industry is maximizing its short-run profits by producing 500 units of output. At 500 units of output, which of the following *must be false*?

a $MC < AVC$
b $MC < ATC$
c $MC > ATC$
d $AR < ATC$
e $AR > AVC$

8 If a profit-maximizing firm in perfect competition is earning economic profit, then it must be producing a level of output where

a price is greater than marginal cost.
b price is greater than marginal revenue.
c marginal cost is greater than marginal revenue.
d marginal cost is greater than average total cost.
e average total cost is greater than marginal cost.

9 If a perfectly competitive firm in the short run is able to pay its variable costs and part, but not all, of its fixed costs, then it is operating in the range on its marginal cost curve that is anywhere

a above the break-even point.
b below the break-even point.
c above the shutdown point.
d below the shutdown point.
e between the shutdown and break-even points.

10 The short-run industry supply curve is

a the horizontal sum of the individual firms' supply curves.
b the vertical sum of the individual firms' supply curves.
c vertical at the total level of output being produced by all firms.
d horizontal at the current market price.
e none of the above.

11 The supply curve for an individual firm in a perfectly competitive industry is $P = 1 + 2Q_S$. If the industry consists of 100 identical firms, then what is industry supply when $P = 7$?

a 300
b 400
c 600
d 800
e none of the above

Output, Price, and Profit in Perfect Competition

12 Refer to Fact 11.1. If the price of fiddleheads last month was $15 per bag, Franklin

a should have shut down because total revenue did not cover total variable cost.
b incurred an economic loss of $135.
c earned zero economic profit.
d earned economic profit of $50.
e earned economic profit of $100.

FACT **11.1**

Franklin is a fiddlehead farmer. He sold 10 bags of fiddleheads last month, with total fixed cost of $100 and total variable cost of $50.

---

13 Refer to Fact 11.1. If fiddlehead prices fell to $10 per bag while production and cost figures remained the same, Franklin would

a shut down immediately.
b break even because total revenues just cover total fixed costs.
c be indifferent between producing and shutting down because his loss of $50 just covers total variable costs.
d continue producing despite his loss of $50.
e continue producing despite his loss of $100.

14 Refer to Fact 11.1. Suppose the price of fiddleheads is expected to stay at $10 per bag, and Franklin's production and cost figures are expected to stay the same. His total fixed cost consists entirely of rent on land, and his five-year lease on the land runs out at the end of the month. Should Franklin renew the lease?

a Yes, because total revenue will still cover total fixed cost.
b Yes, because total revenue will still cover total variable cost and a portion of total fixed cost.
c No, because total revenue must cover all costs for resources to remain in fiddlehead farming in the long run.
d No, because in the long run, zero economic profit is a signal to move resources out of fiddlehead farming.
e Insufficient information to answer.

15 The maximum loss for a firm in long-run equilibrium is

a zero.
b its total cost.
c its total variable cost.
d its average total cost.
e none of the above.

16 For a perfectly competitive firm in long-run equilibrium, which of the following is *not* equal to price?

a short-run average total cost
b short-run average variable cost
c short-run marginal cost
d long-run average cost
e average revenue

17 When economic profit is zero

a the product will not be produced in the short run.
b the product will not be produced in the long run.
c firms will leave the industry.
d revenues are not covering implicit costs.
e none of the above will occur.

Changing Tastes and Advancing Technology

18 A perfectly competitive industry is in short-run equilibrium with price below average total cost. Which of the following is *not* a prediction of the long-run consequences of such a situation?

a price will increase
b the output of the industry will increase
c firms will leave the industry
d the output of each remaining firm will increase
e economic profit will be zero

19 Figure. 11.1 illustrates the cost curves for a perfectly competitive firm. The current market price is $11 and the firm has the plant size shown by $SRAC_1$. The firm's short-run equilibrium output is

a 7 units.
b 9 units.
c 10 units.
d 17 units.
e 18 units.

FIGURE **11.1**

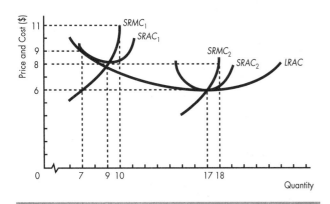

20 Refer to Figure. 11.1. The current market price is $11 and the firm has the plant size shown by *SRAC*₁. In the long run, the firm will

a exit from the industry.
b keep its current plant size, and other firms will enter the industry.
c keep its current plant size, and other firms will exit from the industry.
d increase its plant size, and other firms will enter the industry.
e increase its plant size, and other firms will exit from the industry.

21 Refer to Figure. 11.1. The long-run equilibrium price and quantity combination is

a $6 and 7 units.
b $6 and 17 units.
c $8 and 9 units.
d $8 and 18 units.
e $9 and 7 units.

22 If an industry experiences external economies as the industry expands in the long run, the long-run industry supply curve will

a be perfectly inelastic.
b be perfectly elastic.
c have a positive slope.
d have a negative slope.
e have allocative inefficiency.

23 Which of the following is *not* true of a new long-run equilibrium resulting from a new technology in a perfectly competitive industry?

a price will be lower
b industry output will be greater
c firm profits will be greater
d all firms in the industry will be using the new technology
e average total cost will be lower

Competition and Efficiency

24 A long-run equilibrium in a perfectly competitive industry would *not* be efficient if

a firms are price takers.
b new technologies are developed.
c there are external economies or external diseconomies.
d there are external costs or external benefits.
e there is free entry to the industry.

25 Resources are used efficiently when

a consumers are on their marginal benefit curves.
b firms are economically efficient.
c price = marginal benefit = marginal cost.
d there are no external benefits or external costs.
e there are all of the above.

Short Answer Problems

1 Why will a firm in a perfectly competitive industry choose *not* to charge a price either above or below the market price?

2 Why will economic profit tend to zero in long-run equilibrium in a perfectly competitive industry?

3 Table 11.1 gives the total cost structure for one of many identical firms in a perfectly competitive industry.

  a Complete the table by computing total variable cost, average total cost, average variable cost, and marginal cost at each level of output. [*Remember:* As in the problems in Chapter 10, marginal cost should be entered *midway* between rows.]

TABLE **11.1**

Quantity (units per day)	Total Cost ($)	Total Variable Cost ($)	Average Total Cost ($)	Average Variable Cost ($)	Marginal Cost ($)
0	12				
					...
1	24				
					...
2	32				
					...
3	42				
					...
4	54				
					...
5	68				
					...
6	84				

b Complete Table 11.2 by computing the profit (per day) for the firm at each level of output if the price of output is $9; $11; $15.

TABLE **11.2**

Quantity (units per day)	Profit P = $9	Profit P = $11	Profit P = $15
0			
1			
2			
3			
4			
5			
6			

c Consider the profit-maximizing output decision of the firm at alternative prices. How much will the firm produce if the price of output is $9? $11? $15? Explain each of your answers.

4 A firm will maximize profit if it produces every unit of output for which marginal revenue exceeds marginal cost. This is called the *marginal analysis* of profit maximization. Using marginal analysis, determine the profit-maximizing level of output for the firm in Short Answer Problem **3** when the price of output is $15. How does your answer here compare with your answer in **3c**?

5 This problem concerns a hypothetical pottery manufacturing firm that produces ceramic mugs for sale in a purely competitive market. With a plant of given size, the firm can turn out the quantities of ceramic mugs shown in Table 11.3, by varying the amount it uses of a single variable input, labour.

TABLE **11.3**

Number of Mugs	Labour-Hours (per day)
20	6.50
40	11.00
60	14.50
80	17.50
100	20.50
120	23.75
140	27.50
160	32.00
180	37.50
200	44.50
220	53.50
240	65.00
260	79.50
280	97.50

Suppose the firm can hire all the labour it would ever want at the going wage of $8 per labour-hour. The firm's total fixed costs are $64 per day.

a Draw a table showing output, total variable cost (*TVC*), total cost (*TC*), average variable cost (*AVC*), average total cost (*ATC*), and marginal cost (*MC*). [*Remember:* Marginal cost should be entered *midway* between rows of output.]

b On a graph with *Mugs (per day)* on the horizontal axis, draw the three "per-unit" cost curves, *AVC, ATC,* and *MC.* [Note that the marginal cost values from your table should be plotted on the graph *midway* between the corresponding units of output.]

c Consider (separately) the following alternative market prices that the firm might face:

P = $3.20, P = $2, P = $1.65, P = $1.40.

Assuming that the firm wants to maximize its profit, for *each* of the above prices, answer the following questions: Approximately how many mugs per day would the firm produce? How do you know? Is the firm making a profit at that price? And if so, approximately how much?

6 Suppose that the ceramic pottery mug industry consists of 60 firms, each identical to the single firm discussed in Short Answer Problem **5**. Table 11.4 represents some points on the industry demand schedule for ceramic pottery mugs.

TABLE **11.4**

Price ($)	Quantity Demanded
1.00	15,900
1.60	14,400
2.20	12,900
2.80	11,400
3.40	9,900
4.00	8,400
4.60	6,900
5.20	5,400
5.80	3,900
6.40	2,400
7.00	900

a On a new graph, draw the industry short-run supply curve. Draw the industry demand curve on the same graph.

b What is the short-run equilibrium price of ceramic pottery mugs?

c Is the ceramic pottery mug industry in long-run equilibrium? Explain your answer.

ct **7** A perfectly competitive industry has 100 identical firms in the short run, each of which has the short-run cost curves listed in Table 11.5.

TABLE **11.5**

Output (units)	Average Total Cost ($)	Average Variable Cost ($)	Marginal Cost ($)
11	20.5	13.1	
			12
12	19.8	13.0	
			14
13	19.3	13.1	
			16
14	19.1	13.3	
			18
15	19.0	13.6	
			20
16	19.1	14.0	
			22
17	19.2	14.5	
			24
18	19.5	15.0	
			26
19	19.8	15.6	
			28
20	20.3	16.2	
			30
21	20.7	16.9	

This short-run average total cost curve touches the long-run average cost curve at the minimum point on the long-run average cost curve as point *M* in Text Fig. 11.9 on page 249. The industry demand schedule is the same in the long and the short run. Table 11.6 represents some points on the demand schedule.

TABLE **11.6**

Price ($)	Quantity Demanded
11	3,200
13	3,000
15	2,800
17	2,600
19	2,400
21	2,200
23	2,000
25	1,800
27	1,600
29	1,400
31	1,200

a What is the quantity of output corresponding to the firm's break-even point? the shutdown point? Explain your answers.

b What is the short-run equilibrium price in this market? Show how you found your answer.

c What amount of profit or loss is being made by each firm at the short-run equilibrium price? Is this industry in long-run equilibrium at its present size? Why or why not?

d Exactly how many firms will exist in this industry in the long run? Explain your answer. How much economic profit will each firm earn in the long run?

8 Suppose we observe a perfectly competitive industry in a long-run equilibrium when there is a permanent decrease in demand for the industry's product. There are no external economies or diseconomies. How does the industry adjust to a new long-run equilibrium? What happens to price, quantity, firm profits, and the number of firms during the adjustment process?

9 Consider a perfectly competitive industry in long-run equilibrium. All firms in the industry are identical.

a Draw a two-part graph illustrating the long-run equilibrium for the industry—part (a) on the left—and for the typical firm—part (b) on the right. The graph of the firm should include the *MC*, *ATC*, *MR*, and *LRAC* curves. Assume that the *LRAC* curve is U-shaped as it is in Text Figure 11.9 on page 249. Label the equilibrium price P_0, the equilibrium industry quantity Q_0, and the output of the firm q_0.

b Now, suppose there is a decline in industry demand. Using your graphs from part **a**, show what happens to market price, firm output, firm profits, and industry equilibrium quantity in the short run (assume that the shutdown point is not reached).

Then show what happens to market price, firm output, firm profits, and industry equilibrium quantity in the long run (assume that there are no external economies or diseconomies). What has happened to the number of firms?

10 In a perfectly competitive industry with no external benefits or costs, suppose output is restricted to a quantity less than the equilibrium quantity. Explain why this level of output is inefficient.

ANSWERS

True/False and Explain

1 T Each firm is price taker. (238)
2 F Individual firm demand curve horizontal. Industry demand curve downward-sloping. (238–239)
3 F Maximize economic profit. (238)
4 F Losses in short run but not long run. (243–244)
ct 5 F True if $P <$ minimum *AVC*. False if $P >$ minimum *AVC* but $<$ minimum *ATC*. (243–244)
6 F As long as $P >$ minimum *AVC*. (244–245)
7 T Otherwise firm driven out of business by lower-cost firms. (248–249)
ct 8 T *ATC* shifts upward with no ΔMC. Economic losses cause exit. (247–248)
9 F As supply shifts rightward, price falls and output each existing firms decreases. (246–247)
10 T Price rises above *ATC*, creating economic profit. (250–251)
11 F Short-run economic losses cause firms to exit, shifting supply leftward, raising price until economic losses eliminated. (250–251)
12 F Negatively sloped. (251–252)
13 F Efficient when $MB = MC$. (254–255)
14 F Efficient when sum of consumer surplus and producer surplus maximized. (254–255)
15 T $P = MB = MC$ and maximum sum of consumer and producer surpluses. (254–255)

Multiple-Choice

1 d Identical products. (238–239)
2 d So there is room for many (efficient) firms in the industry. (238)
3 d Firm can increase Q without ΔP, so *MR* from additional $Q = P$. (238–239)
ct 4 c Draw graph. Firm should choose lower Q where $P = MC$. If *AVC* at current $Q = \$10$, minimum *AVC* must be $< \$10$, so new Q at $P >$ minimum *AVC*. (242–244)
5 b Since $MR = AR$, $AR > ATC$. Multiplying by Q yields $TR > TC$, so economic profit. (242–244)
6 b Firm stays shut down ($Q = 0$) until P reaches minimum *AVC*. (244)
ct 7 a **a** implies shutdown. Other answers possible with losses (**b, d**) or profits (**c, e**). (242–244)
8 d ($MC = P =$) $AR > ATC$. **a, b, c** not consistent with profit maximization. **e** implies losses. (242–244)
9 e If couldn't pay variable costs then below shutdown. If paying all variable and fixed costs then breaking even. (242–244)
10 a Definition. **c** is momentary supply curve. **d** is demand curve facing individual firm. (245)
11 a For one firm: $7 = 1 + 2Q_S$; $2Q_S = 6$; $Q_S = 3$. For 100 firms, $3 \times 100 = 300$. (245)
12 c Profit $= TR (\$15 \times 10) - TC (\$100 + \$50) = 0$. (246–247)
ct 13 d $TR (\$10 \times 10) - TC (\$100 + \$50) = -\$50$. Shutting down would bring bigger loss of $\$100$ (fixed costs). (246–247)
ct 14 c He is making long-run decision. **a, b** refer to short run. **d** false because *losses* are signal to move resources. (247–249)
15 a Definition long-run equilibrium includes zero economic profit. (247–249)
16 b Long-run equilibrium at intersection *ATC*, *MC*, and *LRAC* curves. (248–249)
17 e Product produced in short and long run, revenues exactly cover all costs (including implicit costs). (247–249)
18 b As firms exit, supply shifts left, decreasing industry Q and raising P. In response to higher P, remaining firms increase Q. (250–251)
19 c Choose Q where $P = MC$. (250–251)
20 d Economic profit attracts new entry, causing falling P and incentive to build larger, lower cost plant. (250–251)
21 b Long-run equilibrium at intersection *SRAC*, *MC*, and *LRAC* curves. (250–251)

22 d Because decreasing costs as industry Q increases. (251–253)

23 c In long-run equilibrium, economic profit always zero. (250–253)

24 d **a, e** conditions perfect competition. **b, c** affect shape long-run supply curve but not efficiency. (254–255)

25 e When no external benefits or external costs, **a** and **b** are true; **c** is the equilibrium between demand and supply. (254–255)

Short Answer Problems

1 If a firm in a perfectly competitive industry charged a price even slightly higher than the market price, it would lose all of its sales. Thus it will not charge a price above the market price. Since it can sell all it wants at the market price, it would not be able to increase sales by lowering its price. Thus it would not charge a price below the market price since this would decrease total revenue and profits.

2 In a perfectly competitive industry, the existence of positive economic profit will attract the entry of new firms, shifting the industry supply curve rightward, causing the market price to fall and firm profits to decline. This tendency will exist as long as there is positive economic profit. Similarly, the existence of economic losses will cause firms to exit from the industry, shifting the industry supply curve leftward, causing the market price to rise and firm profits to rise (losses to decline). This tendency will exist as long as losses are being incurred. Thus, the only point of rest in the long run (the only equilibrium) occurs when economic profits are zero.

3 a Completed Table 11.1 is shown here as Table 11.1 Solution.

TABLE **11.1** SOLUTION

Quantity (units per day)	Total Cost ($)	Total Variable Cost ($)	Average Total Cost ($)	Average Variable Cost ($)	Marginal Cost ($)
0	12	0	—	—	
					... 12
1	24	12	24.00	12.00	
					... 8
2	32	20	16.00	10.00	
					... 10
3	42	30	14.00	10.00	
					... 12
4	54	42	13.50	10.50	
					... 14
5	68	56	13.60	11.20	
					... 16
6	84	72	14.00	12.00	

b Completed Table 11.2 is given here as Table 11.2 Solution. The values for profit are computed as total revenue minus total cost, where total revenue is price times quantity and total cost is given in Table 11.1.

TABLE **11.2** SOLUTION

Quantity (units per day)	Profit $P = \$9$	Profit $P = \$11$	Profit $P = \$15$
0	−12	−12	−12
1	−15	−13	−9
2	−14	−10	−2
3	−15	**−9**	3
4	−18	−10	6
5	−23	−13	**7**
6	−30	−18	6

c If the price is $9, profit is maximized (actually loss is minimized) when the firm shuts down and produces zero units. If the firm chooses to produce, its loss will be at least $14, which is greater than the fixed cost loss of $12. If the price is $11, the firm is still unable to make a positive economic profit. The loss is minimized (at $9) if the firm produces 3 units. At this price, all of variable cost and part of fixed cost can be recovered. At a price of $15, the firm will maximize profit (at $7) at an output of 5 units per day.

4 The marginal analysis of profit maximization states that the firm should produce all units of output for which marginal revenue exceeds marginal cost. For a perfectly competitive firm, marginal revenue equals price, so (equivalently) the firm should produce every unit for which price exceeds marginal cost. If the price of output is $15, we can see from Table 11.2 Solution that the firm should produce 5 units. Since the marginal cost of moving from the 4th to the 5th unit ($14) is less than price ($15), the 5th unit should be produced. The marginal cost of moving to the 6th unit ($16), however, is greater than price. It should not be produced. The answer here is the same as the answer in **3c**.

5 a With only one variable input (labour), *AVC* (for any level of output) = (labour hours × wage rate). The requested table is Table 11.7.

TABLE **11.7**

Output (per day)	TVC ($)	TC ($)	AVC ($)	ATC ($)	MC ($)
0	0	64	—	—	
					... 2.60
20	52	116	2.60	5.80	
					... 1.80
40	88	152	2.20	3.80	
					... 1.40
60	116	180	1.93	3.00	
					... 1.20
80	140	204	1.75	2.55	
					... 1.20
100	164	228	1.64	2.28	
					... 1.30
120	190	254	1.58	2.12	
					... 1.50
140	220	284	1.57	2.03	
					... 1.80
160	256	320	1.60	2.00	
					... 2.20
180	300	364	1.67	2.02	
					... 2.80
200	356	420	1.78	2.10	
					... 3.60
220	428	492	1.95	2.24	
					... 4.60
240	520	584	2.17	2.43	
					... 5.80
260	636	700	2.45	2.69	
					... 7.20
280	780	844	2.79	3.01	

b The graph appears in Figure 11.2. It also illustrates the answers to part **c**.

FIGURE **11.2**

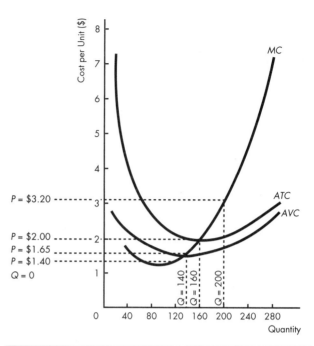

c In every case, at the profit-maximizing output, marginal revenue (which, for a price-taking firm in a perfectly competitive market, is the same as market price) is equal to marginal cost, provided that price is greater than average variable cost.

Profit "per unit of output" is the difference between average revenue (price) and average total cost at the level of output. Total profit is "per unit profit" × number of units of output. Economic profit might be zero or negative (a loss) and still be the best the firm can attain in the short run. The calculations of total profit at each price appear in Table 11.8.

TABLE **11.8**

Price ($)	Output Chosen	Per Unit Profit ($)	Total Profit ($)
3.20	200	1.10	220.00
2.00	160	0	0
1.65	140	−0.38	−53.20
1.40	0	0	−64.00

Note the following:

1. Marginal cost is $3.20 at approximately 200 units.

2. The per unit profit is $P - ATC$.

3. 160 units is the "break-even" level of output, where MC = minimum ATC and the firm is just covering all its opportunity costs.

4. At an output of 140 units, the firm continues to produce in the short run because it can more than cover its variable costs. If it produced zero units, its loss would be greater, $64, which is the amount of its fixed costs.

5. Any positive output increases losses when the price is below the shutdown price, which here is approximately $1.57. When price is less than minimum AVC, the firm would not only lose its fixed costs, it would also lose additional money on every unit it produced.

6 There are 60 identical price-taking firms. For every possible price (above minimum AVC of approximately $1.57), each firm will supply the quantity at which $P = MC$. We can derive (in Table 11.9) the industry supply schedule from the MC curve of an individual firm.

TABLE **11.9**

Price ($)	Quantity Supplied by I Firm	Quantity Supplied by 60 Firms
1.57	134	8,040
1.80	150	9,000
2.20	170	10,200
2.80	190	11,400
3.60	210	12,600
4.60	230	13,800
5.80	250	15,000
7.20	270	16,200

a The graph of the industry supply curve appears in Figure. 11.3, together with the industry demand curve.

FIGURE **11.3**

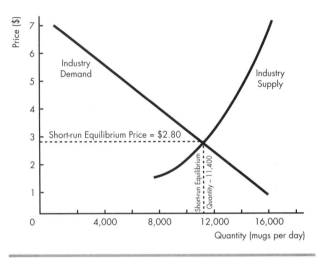

b The short-run equilibrium price is $2.80 (where a total of 11,400 mugs per day are supplied and sold; or 190 mugs per day supplied by each firm at MC of $2.80).

c At a price of $2.80 and output of 190, for each firm, $P > ATC$ where ATC = $2.06. So all existing firms are making an economic profit after covering all opportunity costs including a normal profit. (See Helpful Hint **3**.) The industry will attract new entrants because it offers more than normal profit. Even though the industry is in short-run equilibrium, it is *not* in long-run equilibrium because the number of firms has not "stabilized." New firms will enter the industry, the industry supply curve will shift rightward, and price will fall until no firm is making economic profit.

ⓒ **7 a** The break-even point occurs at 15 units of output. At this level of output, ATC is at its minimum ($19) and is equal to MC. Since the MC of moving from the 14th to the 15th unit is $18, and the MC of moving from the 15th to the 16th unit is $20, we can interpolate the MC exactly at 15 units as midway between $18 and $20, or as $19. The shutdown point occurs at 12 units of output. At this level of output, AVC is at its minimum ($13) and is equal to MC. The interpolated value of MC at exactly 12 units of output is midway between $12 and $14, or is $13.

b The short-run equilibrium price is $25. This is the price at which industry quantity supplied equals quantity demanded as shown in Table 11.10.

c At a price of $25, each firm produces 18 units of output. At 18 units, ATC is $19.50, so economic profit is being earned. The amount of profit is ($25 − $19.50 per unit =) $5.50 per unit. Total economic profit per firm is $5.50/unit × 18 units = $99. This means that new entrants will be attracted to the industry. We conclude that the industry is not in long-run equilibrium.

d Entry continues until economic profit is competed away, and all firms are operating at the minimum point of the *LRAC* curve (which, in this problem, is also the minimum point of the given short-run average total cost curve).

Minimum *ATC* for each firm occurs at 15 units of output, when *ATC* = *MC* = $19, so price in the long run must be $19. At a price of $19, consumers demand 2,400 units (from Table 11.10). It follows that when the industry is in long-run equilibrium, there must be 2,400 units/15 units per firm = 160 firms in the industry, each producing 15 units of output, at zero economic profit.

TABLE **11.10**

P = MC ($)	Quantity Supplied by 1 Firm	Quantity Supplied by 100 Firms	Quantity Demanded
13	12	1,200	3,000
15	13	1,300	2,800
17	14	1,400	2,600
19	15	1,500	2,400
21	16	1,600	2,200
23	17	1,700	2,000
25	**18**	**1,800**	**1,800**
27	19	1,900	1,600
29	20	2,000	1,400

8 The decrease in market demand causes the market price to fall. Since, in the initial long-run equilibrium, each firm was earning zero economic profit, the fall in price means that profits will fall and firms will now incur losses. Since the decrease in demand is permanent, these losses will induce some firms to leave the industry. This will shift the industry supply curve leftward, causing an increase in market price. The increasing price causes profits to increase for the remaining firms, so their losses will decline. The exit of firms continues until losses are eliminated. Costs have not been affected by the decrease in demand, so if there are no external economies or diseconomies, the price must continue rising until it reaches its original level in the new long-run equilibrium. The output of each firm will also equal its original level, but the equilibrium quantity at the industry level will be less because the number of firms has declined.

9 a A long-run equilibrium in a perfectly competitive industry is illustrated in Figure. 11.4.

Part (a) illustrates industry equilibrium at the intersection of industry demand (D_0) and industry supply (S_0): point *a*. The equilibrium industry quantity is labelled Q_0 and the equilibrium market price is labelled P_0.

Part (b) illustrates the situation for a single firm in long-run equilibrium. The firm is at point *a′*, the minimum point of both the short-run average total cost curve (*ATC*) and the long-run average cost curve (*LRAC*). The firm is producing the output labelled q_0 and earning zero economic profit.

FIGURE **11.4**

(a) Industry

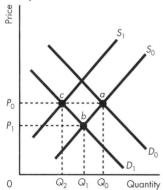

(b) Firm

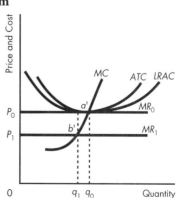

b The new short-run equilibrium is also illustrated in Figure 11.4. The decrease in demand shifts the market demand curve leftward, from D_0 to D_1. The new market equilibrium is at point b. The price has fallen from P_0 to P_1 and the industry equilibrium quantity has fallen from Q_0 to Q_1. The fall in price induces firms to reduce output as shown by the move from point d to point b' on the MC curve in part (b). Since P_1 is less than minimum ATC, firms are incurring losses in the new short-run equilibrium.

The new long-run equilibrium is also illustrated in Figure 11.4. With short-run losses, firms will exit from the industry in the long run. This causes the industry supply curve to shift leftward, causing the price to rise and thus reducing losses. Firms continue to leave until the industry supply curve has shifted enough to eliminate losses, from S_0 to S_1. This gives a new long-run industry equilibrium at point c and the price has returned to its initial level, P_0, but industry quantity has fallen to Q_2.

As firms exit and the market price rises, remaining firms will increase their output (moving up the MC curve from point b' to point d') and their losses will be reduced. When sufficient firms have left the industry, the price will have risen (returned) to P_0 and firms will have returned to point d' in part (b). At this point, each firm is again earning zero economic profit and firm output has returned to q_0. But, since there are now fewer firms, industry equilibrium quantity is less.

10 Refer to Text Figure 11.12 on page 255. If output is restricted to quantity Q_0, the value to consumers of an additional unit of the good is B_0, while producers would be willing to supply additional goods for any price at or above C_0. If more goods are produced and sold at any price in between V_0 and C_0, consumers will be better off because they value the goods more than the price paid, and producers will be better off because they receive a higher price than the minimum necessary to induce production. Consumers and producers could be made better off without making someone else worse off. Therefore at quantity Q_0, there are unrealized gains from trade (more consumer and producer surplus is possible), and this level of output is allocatively inefficient.

Chapter 12

Monopoly

Market Power

Monopoly is a model of market structure where the force of *competition* is absent and firms have extreme **market power**. Assumptions include industry with one supplier; no close substitutes; barriers to entry.

Monopoly can arise when

◆ no close substitutes for product.

◆ **barriers to entry**—constraints protecting firm from competition from potential new entrants.

• Legal barriers to entry—for a **legal monopoly**, competition and entry restricted by *public franchise, government licence, patent*, or *copyright*.
• Natural barriers to entry—a **natural monopoly** occurs when, due to economies of scale, one firm can supply the market at lower *ATC* than multiple firms can.

Price-setting strategies depend on type of monopoly:

◆ **Single-price monopoly**—must sell each unit of output at same price to all customers.

◆ **Price discrimination**—selling different units of output for different prices.

A Single-Price Monopoly's Output and Price Decision

Single-price monopoly charges same price for every unit output.

◆ Monopoly's demand curve is industry demand curve.

◆ Marginal revenue (*MR*) < price (*P*). To sell additional output, must lower *P* on *all* output.

◆ In moving down the monopoly's demand curve

• when total revenue (*TR*) increasing, *MR* positive, $\eta > 1$.
• when *TR* maximum, *MR* zero, $\eta = 1$.
• when *TR* decreasing, *MR* negative, $\eta < 1$.

◆ Monopoly's technology and costs like firm in perfect competition.

◆ Profit-maximizing monopoly chooses output at which *MR* = *MC*, charges maximum price consumers willing to pay (on demand curve).

◆ Monopoly never operates in inelastic range of demand curve. Monopoly has no supply curve.

◆ Monopoly can make economic profit even in long run because barriers prevent entry of new firms.

Single-Price Monopoly and Competition Compared

Output and price:

◆ Single-price monopoly *Q* < competitive *Q*.

◆ Single-price monopoly *P* > competitive *P*.

Efficiency:

◆ Single-price monopoly inefficient compared to efficiency of perfect competition. Monopoly prevents gains from trade: restricts output, captures some consumer surplus, but creates *deadweight loss*—total loss due to *consumer surplus* and *producer surplus* (revenue – opportunity cost production) below efficient levels.

◆ Social cost of monopoly greater than deadweight loss because of **rent seeking**—attempt to capture consumer surplus, producer surplus or economic profit.
• If no barriers to rent seeking, cost of resources used rent seeking = value monopoly profit (with no rent seeking), so no economic profit.

- Social cost of monopoly = deadweight loss + resources used rent-seeking.

Price Discrimination

Price discrimination (selling different units of output for different prices) converts consumer surplus into economic profit for the monopoly. Examples include charging lower per-unit price on large order than small; discriminating among groups with different average willingness-to-pay.

Price discrimination requires:

- ◆ Product cannot be resold.

- ◆ Charge lower P to lower willingness-to-pay group. Charge higher P to higher willingness-to-pay group.

Perfect price discrimination—different price for each unit sold; obtains maximum price each consumer willing to pay; converts *all* consumer surplus into economic profit.

- ◆ *MR* curve same as demand curve.

- ◆ Same output and efficiency (zero deadweight loss) of perfectly competitive industry, but

  - • all consumer surplus captured as economic profit.
  - • rent seeking occurs which could eliminate economic profit.

Monopoly Policy Issues

Gains from monopoly:

- ◆ Increased innovation and technological change (in some cases)

- ◆ Economies of scale (decreased *LRAC* through increased Q)

- ◆ Economies of scope (decreased *ATC* through increased range of goods produced)

Natural monopolies may be regulated to achieve gains from monopoly but avoid worst inefficiencies. Possible rules:

- ◆ **Marginal cost pricing rule**—set price equal to marginal cost. Maximizes total surplus and is efficient, but not viable because firm incurs economic loss.

- ◆ **Average cost pricing rule**—set price equal to average total cost. Firm earns normal profit only. Inefficient, but better outcome than unregulated monopoly.

HELPFUL HINTS

I   The opposite extreme of perfect competition is monopoly. While in perfect competition there are many firms that can decide only on quantity produced but not on price, a monopoly is a single firm with the ability to set both quantity and price. These differences create differences in the revenue situation facing the monopoly. The cost curves for the two market structures are assumed to be the same.

Because there is only one firm, the industry demand curve is also the firm demand curve. Facing a negatively sloped demand curve, if a single-price monopoly wants to sell one more unit of output, it must lower its price. This has two effects on revenue. First, the sale of an additional unit will increase revenue by the amount of the price. However, since the firm must also *drop the price on previous units*, revenue on these will decrease. The net change in revenue, the marginal revenue, will be less than price and the marginal revenue curve will lie below the demand curve.

Combining this new revenue situation with our familiar cost curves from Chapter 10 yields the important Text Figure 12.4(b), which is reproduced below as Figure 12.1. Notice the following points about this graph.

FIGURE **12.1** MONOPOLY OUTPUT & PRICE

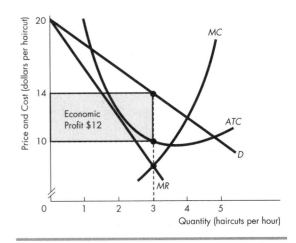

The profit maximization rule for a single-price monopoly is to find the quantity of output where $MR = MC$. This is the same rule that applies to a perfectly competitive firm.

For a perfectly competitive firm MR is also equal to price, so the intersection of MR and MC yields the profit-maximizing output and price. That is not true for the monopolist. MR is not equal to price, and once the profit-maximizing output is identified, the monopolist still has to set the price.

To find the profit-maximizing price, draw an imaginary vertical line up to the demand curve from the intersection of MR and MC. Then draw an imaginary horizontal line to the price axis to read the price.

Understanding what the vertical and horizontal distances of the economic profit area represent will make you less likely to make mistakes in drawing that area. The vertical distance is between the demand (or average revenue) curve and the average total cost curve. That distance measures average revenue minus average total cost, which equals average economic profit, or economic profit per unit. The horizontal distance is just the number of units produced. So the area of the rectangle (vertical distance × horizontal distance) = economic profit per unit × number of units = total economic profit. Do *not* make the mistake of drawing the vertical distance down to the intersection of MC and MR. That intersection has no economic meaning for the calculation of total economic profit.

2 There is an easy trick for drawing the marginal revenue curve corresponding to any linear demand curve. The price intercept (where $Q = 0$) is the same as for the demand curve, and the quantity intercept (where $P = 0$) is exactly *half* of the output of the demand curve. The marginal revenue curve is, therefore, a downward-sloping straight line whose slope is twice as steep as the slope of the demand curve.

3 Price discrimination can be profitable for a monopoly only if different consumer groups have different willingness-to-pay for the product. If such differences exist, the price-discriminating monopolist treats the groups as different markets. The profit maximization rule for a price-discriminating monopoly is to find the quantity of output where *MR in each market* = *MC*. Then, in each market, charge the maximum price the consumer group is willing to pay for that output (on demand curve). Different willingness-to-pay translates into different elasticities of demand between groups, yielding different prices in the two markets.

4 The absence of entry barriers into a perfectly competitive industry is the basis for the prediction that any short-run economic profit in perfect competition will be competed away in the long run. Conversely, the presence of entry barriers in monopoly is the basis for the prediction that monopoly profits can persist in the long run. However, when rent-seeking activity is taken into account, there may be no long-run economic profit, even in monopoly. Rent seeking is any activity aimed at obtaining existing monopoly rights or creating new monopoly rights. Competition among rent seekers bids up the cost of rent seeking until it just equals the value of the potential monopoly profits, leaving the rent-seeker-turned-monopolist with little or no economic profit.

SELF-TEST

True/False and Explain

Market Power

1 Monopoly can arise when there are close substitutes for a product.

2 If one firm can supply the market at a lower cost than multiple firms can, then there are natural barriers to entry.

3 Barriers to entry are essential to a monopoly.

A Single Price Monopoly's Output and Price Decision

4 Over the output range where total revenue is decreasing, marginal revenue is positive.

5 The supply curve of a monopoly firm is its marginal cost curve.

6 Once a single-price monopoly chooses its output, average revenue always equals price.

Single Price Monopoly and Competition Compared

7 A monopoly will always make economic profit.

8 In moving from perfect competition to single-price monopoly, part of the deadweight loss is due to a reduction in producer surplus.

9 Because of the existence of rent seeking, the social cost of monopoly is smaller than the deadweight loss.

10 When rent seeking is taken into account, economic profits from monopoly are guaranteed in the long run.

Price Discrimination

11 Price discrimination only works for goods that can be readily resold.

12 Price discrimination is an attempt by a monopolist to capture the producer surplus.

13 For a perfect price-discriminating monopolist, the demand curve is also the marginal revenue curve.

Monopoly Policy Issues

14 A monopoly industry with large economies of scale and scope may produce more output and charge a lower price than does a perfectly competitive industry.

15 If a regulator applies an average total cost pricing rule, a natural monopoly will earn normal profits only.

Multiple-Choice

Market Power

1 Which of the following is a *natural* barrier to the entry of new firms in an industry?
a licensing of professions
b economies of scale
c issuing a patent
d a public franchise
e all of the above

A Single-Price Monopoly's Output and Price Decision

2 In order to increase sales from 7 units to 8 units, a single-price monopolist must drop the price from $7 per unit to $6 per unit. What is marginal revenue in this range?
a $48
b $6
c $1
d –$1
e none of the above

3 If marginal revenue is negative at a particular output, then
a price must be negative.
b the monopolist should increase output.
c the elasticity of demand is less than 1 at that output.
d demand must be elastic at that output.
e the monopolist should shut down.

4 Four monopolists were overheard talking at an expensive restaurant. Which of their statements below is a correct strategy for maximizing profits?
a "In my company, we don't increase output unless we know that the larger output will raise total revenue."
b "I think cost minimization is the key to maximizing profits."
c "We try to make the most of our equipment by producing at maximum capacity."
d "I don't really keep close tabs on total profits, but I don't approve any business deal unless it increases my revenue more than it increases my costs."
e None of the above.

5 A profit-maximizing monopoly will never produce at an output level

a where it would incur economic losses.
b where marginal revenue is less than price.
c where average cost is greater than marginal cost.
d in the inelastic range of its demand curve.
e in the inelastic range of its marginal revenue curve.

6 If a single-price monopoly has shut down, then at the level of output where marginal cost and marginal revenue intersect, it *must be true* that

a marginal revenue is less than average variable cost.
b marginal cost is less than average variable cost.
c price is less than average variable cost.
d total revenue is less than total cost.
e all of the above are correct.

7 For the single-price monopoly shown in Figure 12.2, when profit is maximized, quantity is

a 3 and price is $3.
b 3 and price is $6.
c 4 and price is $4.
d 4 and price is $5.
e 5 and price is $4.

FIGURE **12.2**

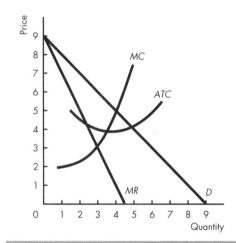

8 If the single-price monopoly shown in Figure 12.2 is maximizing profit, what is total economic profit?

a $3
b $4
c $6
d $9
e none of the above

9 A single-price monopolist will maximize profits if it produces the output where

a price equals marginal cost.
b price equals marginal revenue.
c marginal revenue equals marginal cost.
d average revenue equals marginal cost.
e average revenue equals marginal revenue.

10 If a profit-maximizing monopoly is producing an output at which marginal cost exceeds marginal revenue, it

a should raise price and lower output.
b should lower price and raise output.
c should lower price and lower output.
d is incurring losses.
e is maximizing profit.

11 A monopoly will go out of business in the short run if

a it is incurring an economic loss.
b *MR* is less than *AVC*.
c the price is less than *AVC*.
d the profit-maximizing level of output is in the elastic range of the demand curve.
e *MR* is less than *AR*.

Single-Price Monopoly and Competition Compared

12 Table 12.1 lists marginal costs for the XYZ firm. If XYZ sells 3 units at a price of $6 each, what is its producer surplus?

a $2
b $6
c $7
d $9
e $12

TABLE **12.1**

Quantity	Marginal Cost
1	2
2	3
3	4
4	5

13 Which of the following is true for a producing single-price monopolist but not for a producing perfect competitor?

a The firm maximizes profit by setting marginal cost equal to marginal revenue.

b The firm is a price-taker.

c The firm can sell any level of output at any price it sets.

d The firm's marginal cost is less than average revenue.

e None of the above.

14 Activity for the purpose of creating monopoly is

a called rent seeking.

b illegal in Canada.

c called price discrimination.

d called legal monopoly.

e costless.

15 Taking rent-seeking activity into account, the social cost of monopoly is equal to the

a deadweight loss from monopoly.

b monopoly profit.

c deadweight loss plus monopoly profit.

d deadweight loss minus monopoly profit.

e consumer surplus lost plus producer surplus lost.

16 Consider the industry demand curve in Figure 12.3. If the industry operates under perfect competition, which area in the diagram indicates consumer surplus?

a *aek*

b *dhk*

c *dik*

d *dih*

e none of the above

FIGURE **12.3**

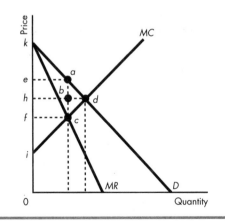

17 Consider the industry demand curve in Figure 12.3. If the industry operates under perfect competition, which area in the diagram indicates producer surplus?

a *aek*

b *dhk*

c *dik*

d *dih*

e none of the above

18 Consider the industry demand curve in Figure 12.3. Which area in the diagram indicates the deadweight loss from a single-price monopoly?

a *eacf*

b *acd*

c *abd*

d *bcd*

e none of the above

Price Discrimination

19 Which area in Figure 12.3 indicates the deadweight loss from a perfect price-discriminating monopoly?

a *eacf*

b *acd*

c *abd*

d *bcd*

e none of the above

20 A perfect price-discriminating monopoly

a has a demand curve which is also its average revenue curve.

b will maximize revenue.

c is assured of making a profit.

d will produce the quantity at which the marginal cost curve intersects the demand curve.

e will be allocatively inefficient.

21 When perfect price discrimination occurs, which of the following statements is *false*?

a Buyers cannot resell the product.

b The firm can distinguish between buyers.

c The firm sets prices.

d The firm captures consumer surplus.

e Efficiency is worse than with single-price monopoly.

22 The output of a (not perfect) price-discriminating monopoly will be

a less than a single-price monopoly.

b more than a single-price monopoly, but less than a perfectly competitive industry.

c the same amount as a perfectly competitive industry.

d more than a perfectly competitive industry.

e none of the above.

23 Many video stores charge a lower rental for Wednesday nights compared with weekends. This price discrimination is profitable only if the average willingness to pay for videos on Wednesdays is

a greater than the average willingness to pay for videos on weekends.

b less than the average willingness to pay for videos on weekends.

c positive and the average willingness to pay for videos on weekends is negative.

d negative and the average willingness to pay for videos on weekends is positive.

e equal to one.

Monopoly Policy Issues

24 A monopoly has economies of scope if

a average total cost declines as the firm's scale increases.

b average total cost declines as output increases.

c total profit declines as output increases.

d average total cost declines as the number of different goods produced increases.

e total profit declines as the number of different goods produced increases.

25 *Disadvantages* of monopoly include

a economies of scope.

b economies of scale.

c diffusion of technological advances.

d rent-seeking behaviour.

e all of the above.

Short Answer Problems

1 Why is marginal revenue less than price for a single-price monopoly?

2 A single-price monopoly is the only seller of skyhooks in the Canadian market. The firm's total fixed cost is $112 per day. Its total variable costs and total costs (both in dollars per day) are shown in Table 12.2.

a Complete the table by computing marginal cost, average variable cost, and average total cost. [*Remember:* Marginal cost should be entered *midway* between rows of output.]

TABLE **12.2**

Quantity	Total Variable Cost (TVC)	Total Cost (TC)	Marginal Cost (MC)	Average Variable Cost (AVC)	Average Total Cost (ATC)
9	135	247			
10	144	256			
11	155	267			
12	168	280			
13	183	295			
14	200	312			
15	219	331			
16	240	352			
17	263	375			
18	288	400			
19	315	427			
20	344	456			

b Table 12.3 lists some points on the demand curve facing the firm, as well as the total cost information from part **a**. Complete the table by copying your values for marginal cost from Table 12.2 and by computing total revenue, marginal revenue, and economic profit. [*Remember:* Marginal revenue, like marginal cost, should be entered *midway* between rows of output.]

What is the firm's profit-maximizing quantity of output? At what price will it sell skyhooks? What will be its total economic profit? Explain your answers.

TABLE **12.3**

Price (P)	Quantity Demanded (Q_D)	Total Revenue (TR)	Marginal Revenue (MR)	Total Cost (TC)	Marginal Cost (MC)	Economic Profit (TR–TC)
57	9			247		
56	10			256		
55	11			267		
54	12			280		
53	13			295		
52	14			312		
51	15			331		
50	16			352		
49	17			375		
48	18			400		
47	19			427		
46	20			456		

c On the graph in Figure 12.4, plot the demand curve and the *MR, AVC, ATC,* and *MC* curves corresponding to the data in parts **a** and **b**. Show the equilibrium output and the area of economic profit on your diagram.

FIGURE **12.4**

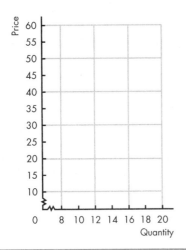

d The firm's cost curves are unchanged, but now consumer demand shifts. Table 12.4 lists some points on the new demand curve, as well as the total cost information from part **a**. Complete the table by copying your values for marginal cost from Table 12.2, and by computing the new

values for total revenue, marginal revenue, and economic profit.

TABLE **12.4**

Price (P)	Quantity Demanded (Q_D)	Total Revenue (TR)	Marginal Revenue (MR)	Total Cost (TC)	Marginal Cost (MC)	Economic Profit (TR–TC)
24.50	9			247		
24.00	10			256		
23.50	11			267		
23.00	12			280		
22.50	13			295		
22.00	14			312		
21.50	15			331		
21.00	16			352		
20.50	17			375		
20.00	18			400		
19.50	19			427		
19.00	20			456		
18.50	21			487		

What is the firm's new profit-maximizing quantity of output? At what price will it now sell skyhooks? What will be its total economic profit? Explain your answers.

e On the graph in Figure 12.5, plot the new demand curve and *MR* curve. Copy the *AVC, ATC,* and *MC* curves from Figure 12.4. Show the new equilibrium output and the area of economic profit on your diagram.

FIGURE **12.5**

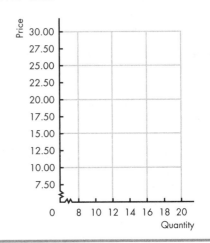

f Suppose demand falls even further so that the new demand curve equation is $P = 19 - 1/2Q_D$. On the graph in Figure 12.6, plot this demand curve and copy the *AVC* curve from Figure 12.4. Explain why the monopolist will shut down in the short run.

FIGURE **12.6**

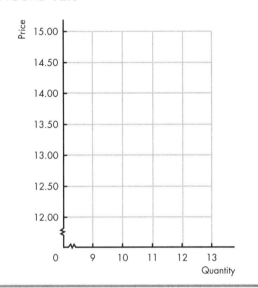

3 You are given the following information about an industry consisting of 100 identical firms.

The demand curve facing the industry is

$$P = 36 - 0.01Q$$

The marginal revenue curve facing the industry is

$$MR = 36 - 0.02Q$$

The marginal cost curve of an individual firm is

$$MC = -12 + 2Q$$

The horizontal sum of the marginal cost curves of all of the firms in the industry is

$$MC = -12 + 0.02Q$$

Use this information to answer the following questions.

a Suppose all 100 firms are controlled by a single-price monopolist. Calculate the profit-maximizing quantity of output for the monopolist. Calculate the price per unit of output that the monopolist will charge.

b Suppose instead that the 100 firms operate independently as a perfectly competitive industry. Calculate the short-run equilibrium quantity of output for the industry as a whole. Calculate the short-run equilibrium price for the industry.

c *Without* using your answer about industry output to part **b**, calculate the short-run equilibrium output per firm.

d Compare the monopoly price and quantity outcomes with the perfect competition price and quantity outcomes.

4 Explain why the output of a competitive industry will always be greater than the output of the *same* industry under single-price monopoly.

5 Before every Olympic Games, the International Olympic Committee (IOC) auctions off the rights to televise the Games to the highest bidder. NBC won the bid for the Summer 1996 Olympics, paying US$456 million. The television rights gave NBC a monopoly. Yet analysts (correctly) predicted that NBC would not make a profit. Their prediction was reasonable, since NBC failed to make a profit on similar telecasts of the 1988 and 1992 Olympics. The questions below will help to understand this apparent paradox.

a What kind of monopoly does NBC have?

b NBC earns revenue by selling airtime to commercial sponsors. Assume that NBC faces a normal, downward-sloping demand curve in selling 30-second commercial spots. Let's ignore for the moment the payment to the IOC and assume that marginal cost and average total cost of delivering the airtime are equal and constant. Draw a diagram representing NBC's profit-maximizing decision. Although you do not have enough information to calculate precise numbers, indicate generally the quantity of commercial spots sold and the price per commercial spot.

c On your diagram, indicate the area representing economic profit. If the analysts' predictions were correct, what is the value of this area?

d Why did NBC fail to realize this economic profit?

6 Barney's Bistro has two kinds of customers for lunch: stockbrokers and retired senior citizens. The demand schedules for lunches for the two groups are given in Table 12.5.

Barney has decided to price discriminate between the two groups by treating each demand separately and charging the price that maximizes profit in each of the two submarkets. Marginal cost and average total cost are equal and constant at $2 per lunch.

a Complete Table 12.5 by computing the total and marginal revenue associated with

TABLE **12.5**

Price (P)	Stockbrokers				Senior Citizens		
	Quantity Demanded (Q_D)	Total Revenue (TR_{SB})	Marginal Revenue (MR_{SB})		Quantity Demanded (Q_D)	Total Revenue (TR_{SC})	Marginal Revenue (MR_{SC})
8	0				0		
7	1				0		
6	2				0		
5	3				1		
4	4				2		
3	5				3		
2	6				4		
1	7				5		
0	8				6		

stockbroker demand (TR_{SB} and MR_{SB}) as well as the total and marginal revenue associated with senior citizen demand (TR_{SC} and MR_{SC}). [*Remember:* Marginal revenue should be entered *midway* between rows.]

b What are the profit-maximizing output and price for stockbrokers?

c What are the profit-maximizing output and price for senior citizens?

d What is total economic profit?

e Show that the total economic profit in part **d** is the maximum by comparing it with total economic profit if instead Barney served: 1 additional lunch *each* to stockbrokers and senior citizens; 1 less lunch *each* to stockbrokers and senior citizens.

f What is the consumer surplus for stockbrokers? for senior citizens? for all customers?

ct **7** The stockbrokers complain bitterly about Barney's discriminatory pricing policy, and threaten to bring bag lunches unless Barney charges a uniform price to all customers. Barney buckles under the pressure, and sits down with his calculator to figure out his profit-maximizing output and price as a single-price monopolist. Using the previous information in Short Answer Problem 7, can you figure it out for him *without* looking at the hints below? If not, answer these questions.

a Calculate Barney's demand schedule by adding up the quantity demanded by stockbrokers and senior citizens at each price. Construct a table similar to Table 12.5, with columns for price, quantity demanded, total revenue, and marginal revenue. (*Remember:* Marginal revenue should be entered *midway* between rows.)

b Marginal cost and average total cost remain unchanged at $2 per lunch. What are Barney's profit-maximizing output and price?

c What is Barney's total economic profit as a single-price monopolist? How does this compare with his total economic profit as a price-discriminating monopolist?

d What is the consumer surplus for all customers? How does this compare with the consumer surplus for all customers when Barney price discriminated?

ct **8** The price of the last unit sold and the quantity sold are exactly the same in an industry under perfect competition and under a perfect price-discriminating monopoly. Are consumers therefore indifferent between the two? Explain.

9 Figure 12.7 gives the demand, marginal revenue, and marginal cost curves for a certain industry. Your task is to illustrate how consumer and producer surplus are distributed under each of four ways of organizing the industry. In each case redraw any relevant part of Figure 12.7 and then (1) indicate the region of the graph corresponding to consumer surplus by drawing horizontal lines through it; (2) indicate the region corresponding to producer surplus by drawing vertical lines through it; and (3) indicate the region (if any) corresponding to deadweight loss by putting dots in the area.

a The industry consists of many perfectly competitive firms.

b The industry is a single-price monopoly.

c The industry is a price-discriminating monopoly charging two prices: P_1 and P_3.

d The industry is a perfect price-discriminating monopoly.

FIGURE **12.7**

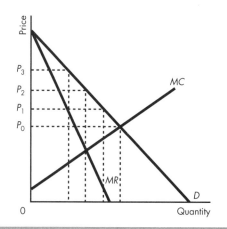

10 Under what circumstances would a monopoly be more efficient than a large number of competitive firms? Illustrate graphically such a situation where a monopoly produces more and charges a lower price than would be the case if the industry consisted of a large number of perfectly competitive firms.

A N S W E R S

True/False and Explain

1 F When there are *no* close substitutes. (262)
2 T Definition of natural monopoly. (262–263)
3 T Without barriers to entry, other firms will enter industry, creating competition. (262–263)
4 F *MR* is negative. (264–265)
5 F Monopolist has no supply curve. (266–267)
6 T Average of all (equal) prices of product = price. For any row in text Table 12.1, $AR = TR/Q = P$. (264–267)

7 F Monopoly no guarantee economic profit if rent seeking is costly enough. (268–271)
8 T Area below competitive price and above *MC* for reduced output. (268–270)
9 F Greater. Resources used in rent-seeking cost to society. (270–271)
10 F In equilibrium, economic profit may be totally eliminated by rent-seeking costs. (270–271)
11 F Can*not* be readily resold. (271–272)
12 F To capture consumer surplus and convert to economic profit. (271–272)
13 T Demand curve gives revenue for each successive unit sold (at different price). (273–274)
14 T Advantages of monopoly. (275–276)
15 T $P = AR = ATC$. Outcome inefficient because deadweight loss, but more efficient than unregulated monopoly. (276–277)

Multiple-Choice

1 b Others are legal barriers. (262–263)
2 d $TR (P = \$7) = \$7 \times 7 = \$49$. $TR (P = \$6) = \$6 \times 8 = \$48$. $MR = \Delta TR = \$48 - \$49$. (264–266)
3 c Monopolist should decrease output. Shutdown decision premature since monopolist can change price. (266–267)
4 d *MR-MC* comparisons are key. Revenue **a** and cost **b** are important, but must be *compared* for profitability. (266–267)
5 d *TR* would be decreased needlessly. Monopolist could decrease *Q* and raise *P* to increase *TR*. (264–267)
6 c **a**, **b** irrelevant comparisons marginal and average quantities. **d** true if $TR < TVC$. (264–267)
7 b *Q* where $MR = MC$. Highest *P* consumers will pay for 3 units. (266–267)
8 c $(AR - ATC) \times Q = (\$6 - \$4) \times 3$. (266–267)
9 c Rule for choosing output. (266–267)
10 a Draw graph. $Q_{current} > Q$ corresponding to $MR = MC$. (266–267)
11 c Shutdown rule same as perfect competition. (266–267)
12 d Sum of $(P - MC)$ for each unit output. (268–269)
13 d **a** true for both. **b** true competitor only. **c** false for both. (268–269)
14 a Definition. Activity has costs. (270–271)
15 c Monopoly profit = resources used rent seeking. (270–271)
16 b Area above price but below demand (willingness-to-pay). (268–270)
17 d Area below price but above *MC*. (268–270)

18 b Sum of lost producer (*bcd*) and consumer (*abd*) surplus compared to competitive outcome. (268–270)

19 e Deadweight loss is zero. (273–274)

⊕ 20 d Same outcome as perfectly competitive industry, so **e** wrong. *D = MR* so **a** wrong. Profit maximizing so **b** wrong. (273–274)

21 e Efficiency same as perfect competition. (273–274)

22 b **c** true for perfect price discrimination. (271–273)

23 b Charge lower price with higher η and higher price with lower η. (271–273)

24 d Definition. (275–276)

25 d Others are advantages. Rent seeking diverts resources that could be used productively. (275–277)

Short Answer Problems

1 In order to sell an additional unit of output, a monopoly must drop the price. This has two effects on revenue: one positive and equal to price, and the other negative. Marginal revenue is the net effect, which must be less than price. First, the additional unit sold at the new lower price adds an amount to revenue equal to the price. But, a single-price monopoly must also lower the price to previous customers who would have paid more. The net effect on marginal revenue is equal to the price minus the loss of revenue from lowering the price to previous customers. This difference must necessarily be less than price.

2 a Completed Table 12.2 is given here as Table 12.2 Solution.

TABLE **12.2** SOLUTION

Quantity	Total Variable Cost (TVC)	Total Cost (TC)	Marginal Cost (MC)	Average Variable Cost (AVC)	Average Total Cost (ATC)
9	135	247		15.00	27.44
			⋯ 9		
10	144	256		14.40	25.60
			⋯ 11		
11	155	267		14.09	24.27
			⋯ 13		
12	168	280		14.00	23.33
			⋯ 15		
13	183	295		14.08	22.69
			⋯ 17		
14	200	312		14.29	22.29
			⋯ 19		
15	219	331		14.60	22.07
			⋯ 21		
16	240	352		15.00	22.00
			⋯ 23		
17	263	375		15.47	22.06
			⋯ 25		
18	288	400		16.00	22.22
			⋯ 27		
19	315	427		16.58	22.47
			⋯ 29		
20	344	456		17.20	22.80

b Completed Table 12.3 is shown here as Table 12.3 Solution.

TABLE **12.3** SOLUTION

Price (P)	Quantity Demanded (Q_D)	Total Revenue (TR)	Marginal Revenue (MR)	Total Cost (TC)	Marginal Cost (MC)	Economic Profit (TR–TC)
57	9	513		247		266
			... 47		... 9	
56	10	560		256		304
			... 45		... 11	
55	11	605		267		338
			... 43		... 13	
54	12	648		280		368
			... 41		... 15	
53	13	689		295		394
			... 39		... 17	
52	14	728		312		416
			... 37		... 19	
51	15	765		331		434
			... 35		... 21	
50	16	800		352		448
			... 33		... 23	
49	17	833		375		458
			... 31		... 25	
48	18	864		400		464
			... 29		... 27	
47	**19**	**893**		**427**		**466**
			... 27		... 29	
46	20	920		456		464

Equilibrium output occurs where $MC = MR = 28$, $Q = 19$, $P = \$47$, economic profit = \$466 per day.

The profit-maximizing quantity of output occurs where marginal cost equals marginal revenue, at 19 units. The maximum price the firm can charge and still sell 19 units is \$47. This combination of quantity and price yields a total economic profit of \$466, which, as can be seen from the table, is the maximum possible profit.

c The requested diagram appears in Figure 12.4 Solution.

FIGURE **12.4** SOLUTION

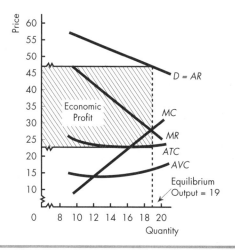

d Completed Table 12.4 is given here as Table 12.4 Solution.

TABLE **12.4** SOLUTION

Price (P)	Quantity Demanded (Q_D)	Total Revenue (TR)	Marginal Revenue (MR)	Total Cost (TC)	Marginal Cost (MC)	Economic Profit (TR–TC)
24.50	9	220.50		247		−26.50
			... 19.50		... 9	
24.00	10	240.00		256		−16.00
			... 18.50		... 11	
23.50	11	258.50		267		−8.50
			... 17.50		... 13	
23.00	12	276.00		280		−4.00
			... 16.50		... 15	
22.50	**13**	**292.50**		**295**		**−2.50**
			... 15.50		... 17	
22.00	14	308.00		312		−4.00
			... 14.50		... 19	
21.50	15	322.50		331		−8.50
			... 13.50		... 21	
21.00	16	336.00		352		−16.00
			... 12.50		... 23	
20.50	17	348.50		375		−26.50
			... 11.50		... 25	
20.00	18	360.00		400		−40.00
			... 10.50		... 27	
19.50	19	370.50		427		−56.50
			... 9.50		... 29	
19.00	20	380.00		456		−76.00

Equilibrium output occurs where $MC = MR = 16$, $Q = 13$, $P = \$22.50$, economic profit = −\$2.50.

The profit-maximizing quantity of output occurs where marginal cost equals marginal revenue, now at 13 units. The maximum price the firm can charge and still sell 13 units is $22.50. This combination of quantity and price yields a total economic profit of –$2.50 (an economic loss). As can be seen from the table, this is the minimum possible loss. The firm will continue to produce in the short run because this loss is less than its shutdown loss which would be $112, the amount of its fixed cost.

e The requested diagram appears in Figure 12.5 Solution.

FIGURE **12.5** SOLUTION

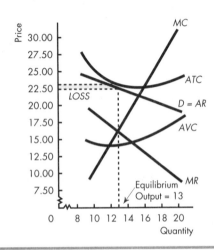

f The requested diagram appears in Figure 12.6 Solution. Since the demand curve is everywhere below the *AVC* curve, no matter what quantity of output the firm might produce, price will be less than *AVC*. This means that the firm will lose money on every unit produced in addition to losing its total fixed cost. The monopolist will minimize loss in this case by shutting down and losing just its fixed cost ($112).

FIGURE **12.6** SOLUTION

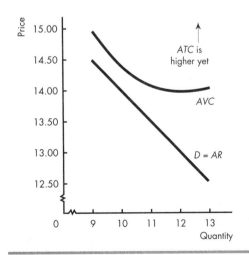

3 a The monopolist will choose the quantity of output where marginal revenue equals marginal cost. To calculate this quantity, set the equation for marginal revenue equal to the equation for industry marginal cost (since the monopolist controls all of the firms).

$$36 - 0.02Q = -12 + 0.02Q$$
$$48 = 0.04Q$$
$$1,200 = Q$$

To calculate the price that the monopolist will charge, substitute the quantity 1,200 into the demand equation. This is the mathematical equivalent of graphically, after finding the quantity corresponding to the intersection of *MC* and *MR*, moving your eye up to the demand curve to read the price.

$$P = 36 - 0.01Q$$
$$P = 36 - 0.01(1,200)$$
$$P = 36 - 12$$
$$P = 24$$

b The perfectly competitive industry's short-run equilibrium quantity of output occurs where industry demand intersects industry supply. Set the industry demand equation equal to the industry supply equation, which is the horizontal sum of the marginal cost curves of all firms in the industry.

$$36 - 0.01Q = -12 + 0.02Q$$
$$48 = 0.03Q$$
$$1,600 = Q$$

To calculate the short-run equilibrium price for the industry, we can substitute the quantity 1,600 into either the industry demand equation or the industry supply equation. Using the industry demand equation yields

$$P = 36 - 0.01Q$$
$$P = 36 - 0.01(1,600)$$
$$P = 36 - 16$$
$$P = 20$$

Using the industry supply equation yields the same result

$$P = -12 + 0.02Q$$
$$P = -12 + 0.02(1,600)$$
$$P = -12 + 32$$
$$P = 20$$

c If industry output is 1,600 units and there are 100 identical firms, then obviously the output per firm is 1,600 units/100 firms equals 16 units/firm. But the question specifically asks you *not* to use the information about industry output.

   The other way to calculate the short-run equilibrium output per firm is to substitute the equilibrium price of 20 into the individual firm's marginal cost curve, which is also its short-run supply curve.

$$P = -12 + 2Q$$
$$20 = -12 + 2Q$$
$$32 = 2Q$$
$$16 = Q$$

d The monopoly price ($24) is higher than the perfect competition price ($20) and the monopoly quantity of output (1,200) is lower than the perfect competition quantity of output (1,600).

4 A competitive industry will produce the level of output at which the industry marginal cost curve intersects the demand curve facing the industry. A single-price monopoly will produce at the level of output at which the industry marginal cost curve intersects the monopoly marginal revenue curve. Since the marginal revenue curve lies below the demand curve, this implies a lower level of output in the monopoly industry.

5 a NBC had a legal monopoly, based on a public franchise—an exclusive right granted to a firm to supply a good or service.

   b The requested diagram is shown in Figure 12.8. The quantity of commercial spots sold is Q_{CS} and the price is P_{CS}.

FIGURE **12.8**

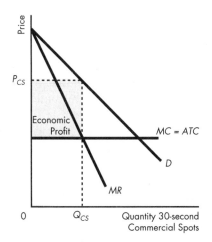

c The shaded rectangle above *ATC* and below P_{CS} in Figure 12.8 represents economic profit. That profit, which is based on costs that exclude the US$456 payment to the IOC, will be US$456 million if the analysts are correct.

d NBC fails to make an economic profit because of the costs of rent seeking. NBC had to compete for the monopoly rights to televise the Olympics. It makes sense for bidders to continue to offer a higher price for those rights up to the point where the price of the rights equals the value of the economic profit to be earned from owning them.

6 a The completed table is given in Table 12.5 Solution.

   b The profit-maximizing output for stockbrokers occurs when $MC = \$2 = MR_{SB}$. This is at 3 lunches and the price is $5 per lunch to stockbrokers.

   c The profit-maximizing output for senior citizens occurs when $MC = \$2 = MR_{SC}$. This occurs at 2 lunches and the price to senior citizens is $4 per lunch.

   d Total revenue is $15 from stockbrokers and $8 from senior citizens, or $23. Since average total cost is $2 per lunch, total cost is $2 × 5 lunches = $10. Thus total economic profit is $13.

   e If Barney served 1 additional lunch each to stockbrokers and senior citizens, that would make 4 lunches for stockbrokers (at $4 per lunch) and 3 lunches for senior citizens (at $3 per lunch). Since average total cost is $2 per lunch, the total cost is $2 × 7 lunches = $14. Total revenue is $16 from stockbrokers and $9 from senior citizens, or $25. Thus total economic profit is $11, less than the $13 in part **d**.

   If Barney served 1 less lunch each to stockbrokers and senior citizens, that would make 2 lunches for stockbrokers (at $6 per lunch) and 1 lunch for senior citizens (at $5 per lunch). Since average total cost is $2 per lunch, the total cost is $2 × 3 lunches = $6. Total revenue is $12 from stockbrokers and $5 from senior citizens, or $17. Thus total economic profit is $11, less than the $13 in part **d**.

   f The consumer surplus of stockbrokers is

$$(\$7 - \$5) + (\$6 - \$5) + (\$5 - \$5) = \$3$$

The consumer surplus of senior citizens is

$$(\$5 - \$4) + (\$4 - \$4) = \$1$$

The consumer surplus of all customers is

$$\$3 + \$1 = \$4$$

TABLE **12.5** SOLUTION

Price (P)	Stockbrokers				Senior Citizens			
	Quantity Demanded (Q_D)	Total Revenue (TR_{SB})	Marginal Revenue (MR_{SB})		Quantity Demanded (Q_D)	Total Revenue (TR_{SC})	Marginal Revenue (MR_{SC})	
8	0	0			0	0		
			 7				 0	
7	1	7			0	0		
			 5				 0	
6	2	12			0	0		
			 3				 5	
5	3	15			1	5		
			 1				 3	
4	4	16			2	8		
			.... −1				 1	
3	5	15			3	9		
			.... −3				.... −1	
2	6	12			4	8		
			.... −5				.... −3	
1	7	7			5	5		
			.... −7				.... −5	
0	8	0			6	0		

7 a The requested table is given as Table 12.6 Solution.

TABLE **12.6** SOLUTION

Price (P)	Quantity Demanded (Q_D)	Total Revenue (TR)	Marginal Revenue (MR)
8	0	0	
			 7
7	1	7	
			 5
6	2	12	
			 4
5	4	20	
			 2
4	6	24	
			 0
3	8	24	
			.... −2
2	10	20	
			.... −4
1	12	12	
			.... −6
0	14	0	

b The profit-maximizing output occurs when $MC = \$2 = MR$. This occurs halfway between a combination of 4 lunches at $5 per lunch, and 6 lunches at $4 per lunch. Either combination yields the same economic profit. Let's look at the combination of 6 lunches at $4 per lunch.

c Total revenue is $4 per lunch × 6 lunches = $24. Average total cost is $2 per lunch. Total cost is $2 × 6 lunches = $12. Thus total economic profit is $12.

Barney's economic profit as a single-price monopolist ($12) is less than his economic profit as a price-discriminating monopolist ($13).

d From the demand curves we can tell that there is 1 customer (stockbroker) who values lunch at $7, 1 customer (stockbroker) who values lunch at $6, 2 customers (stockbroker and senior) who value lunch at $5, and 2 customers (stockbroker and senior) who value lunch at $4. The consumer surplus for all customers is

$$1(\$7 - \$4) + 1(\$6 - \$4) + 2(\$5 - \$4) + 2(\$4 - \$4) = \$7$$

This consumer surplus without price discrimination ($7) is greater than consumer surplus with price discrimination ($4).

ⓒ **8** While the quantity sold and the price charged to the last customer are the same for perfect competition and a perfect price discriminator, the distribution of consumer surplus is not the same. Since a perfect price discriminator charges each customer the most she is willing to pay, there is no consumer surplus. Any consumer surplus that would have occurred under perfect competition now accrues to the monopoly. Consumers would like to obtain more consumer surplus, and therefore pay less for the same amount. Consequently, consumers prefer perfect competition.

9 a Under perfect competition, price equals marginal cost. The amount of consumer surplus is given by the area under the demand curve but above the price (P_0) while the amount of producer surplus is given by the area above the *MC* curve but below the price; see Figure 12.7 Solution (a).

b If the industry is a single-price monopoly, price will be greater than *MC* and output will be less than under competition. Consumer surplus is still given by the area under the demand curve but above the price (P_2), while producer surplus is given by the area above the *MC* curve but below the price up to the monopoly level of output. The remaining part of the large triangle is a deadweight loss—the amount of surplus under competition that is lost under a single-price monopoly; see Figure 12.7 Solution (b).

c Similar reasoning allows us to establish regions in Figure 12.7 Solution (c) corresponding to consumer surplus, producer surplus, and deadweight loss.

d Under perfect price discrimination, all of the potential surplus is captured by the producer and there is no deadweight loss (or consumer surplus). See Figure 12.7 Solution (d).

FIGURE **12.7** SOLUTION

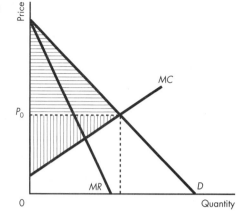

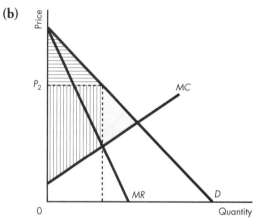

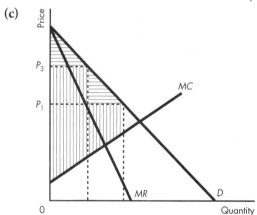

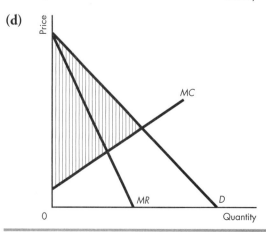

10   A monopoly would be more efficient than
perfect competition if the monopoly has
sufficient economies of scale and/or scope. Those
economies must be large enough that the
monopoly produces more than the competitive
industry and sells it at a lower price. Figure 12.9
illustrates such a situation. The important
feature is that the marginal cost curve for the
monopoly must not only be lower than the
supply curve of the competitive industry, but it
must also be sufficiently lower so that it
intersects the *MR* curve at an output greater
than *C* (the competitive output). Such a
situation could arise if there are extensive
economies of scale and/or scope.

FIGURE **12.9**

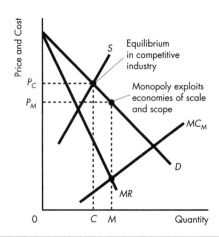

Chapter 13

Monopolistic Competition and Oligopoly

Monopolistic Competition

◆ **Monopolistic competition** is a model of market structure where many firms compete; there is **product differentiation** (firms make similar but slightly different products) giving firms some monopoly power; firms compete on product quality, price, and marketing; there is free entry and exit.

◆ Firm ignores other individual firms and collusion impossible because all have small market share.

◆ Firm faces downward-sloping demand curve.

◆ Marginal revenue curve ≠ demand curve.

◆ Firm can choose price and output.

Output and Price in Monopolistic Competition

Outcomes:
◆ Profit maximization: choose Q where $MC = MR$, charge highest possible price (on demand curve).

◆ Short-run economic profit possible, attract entry, causing leftward shift demand (and MR) curves facing each firm.

◆ Long-run economic profit = 0, $P = ATC$.

◆ ATC not at minimum. Firm has *excess capacity*, producing *below* **capacity output** where ATC = minimum.

◆ Inefficiency of monopolistic competition must be weighed against gain of greater product variety.

Product Development and Marketing

To restore economic profits, monopolistically competitive firms must continuously innovate and develop new products. New firms enter with similar products, compete away economic profits—the cycle continues.

Marketing expenditures on advertising and packaging (selling costs) are used to *create perception* of product differentiation even when actual product differences are small.

◆ Selling costs are fixed costs that increase total costs, but average total cost might decrease if output increases enough.

◆ Selling costs might increase demand for firm's product, but might also decrease demand by increasing competition.

Inefficiencies of monopolistic competition (selling costs and excess capacity) must be weighed against gain of greater product variety.

Oligopoly

Oligopoly is model of market structure where few firms compete and *strategically interact*. Firm considers effects of its actions on behaviour of others and actions of others on its own profit.

◆ *Kinked demand curve model* assumes if firm raises price, no firms follow, and if firm cuts price, all firms follow.

   • Result: each firm faces kinked demand curve, with kink at current P, Q.
   • Prediction: sticky prices—kink causes break in MR curve so MC curve can vary within break without affecting price or quantity.

◆ *Dominant firm oligopoly model* assumes one large firm with major cost advantage, many small firms.

- Predictions: large firm acts like monopoly, sets profit-maximizing price. Small firms take price, act like perfect competitors.

Oligopoly Games

Game theory analyzes strategic behaviour. Games have

- Rules—specify permissible actions by players.
- **Strategies**—actions such as raising or lowering price, output, advertising, or product quality.
- Payoffs—profits and losses of players. **Payoff matrix** shows payoffs for every possible action by each player.
- Outcome—determined by players' choices. In a **Nash equilibrium**, *A* takes best possible action given *B*'s action, and *B* takes best possible action given *A*'s action.

A "prisoners' dilemma" is a one-time, two-person game. Each player has a dominant strategy (unique best strategy independent of other player's action) of cheating, that is, confessing.

- Prisoners' dilemma yields a Nash equilibrium outcome that is *not* in the best interests of the players.

Duopoly is a model of market structure with two firms.

- In a duopoly game, each firm can *comply* with a **collusive agreement** to restrict output and raise price, or it can *cheat*.
- **Cartel**—group of firms in collusive agreement.
- In one-time price-fixing game, prisoners' dilemma solution occurs—each firm has dominant strategy of cheating, even though both firms would be better off if they could trust each other and comply.

Game theory can be used to analyze other choices for firms—how much to spend on research and development, on advertising, whether to enter or exit an industry.

Repeated Games and Sequential Games

In repeated game, other strategies can create **cooperative equilibrium** where each firm complies with collusive agreement and makes monopoly profits. Requires firms to punish cheating in previous period.

- *Tit-for-tat strategy*—taking same action other player took last period. Lightest punishment.
- *Trigger strategy*—cooperating until other player cheats, then cheating forever. Most severe punishment.

Game tree—shows decisions made at first and second stages of sequential game—can be used to analyze sequential entry-deterrence game. In a **contestable market** there are few firms but free entry and exit so existing firms face competition from *potential* entrants. Existing firms may use strategies of

- Set monopoly price, but risk entry of new firm.
- Set competitive price and earn normal profit to keep out a potential competitor.
- **Limit pricing**—set highest price that just inflicts loss on entrant. Compared to monopoly outcome, charge lower price and produce greater quantity in order to deter entry.

HELPFUL HINTS

1 Most industries are neither perfectly competitive nor pure monopolies; they lie somewhere between these two extremes. This does not mean that the last two chapters have been wasted. By examining firms under these extreme market structures, we now can discuss the wide range of industries between them in just one chapter.

The intermediate forms of market structure share many characteristics of perfect competition and/or monopoly. Consider the profit-maximizing rule of choosing the output where $MC = MR$. The rule applies not only in perfect competition and monopoly, but also in monopolistic competition, kinked demand curve, and dominant firm oligopoly models. Free entry leads to zero long-run economic profit in both perfect competition and monopolistic competition. The downward-sloping demand and marginal revenue curves of monopoly also apply to monopolistic competition, kinked demand curve, and dominant firm oligopoly models.

The extreme and unrealistic assumptions of models of perfect competition and monopoly allow us to isolate the impact of important forces like profit maximization and important constraints like competition and market demand. These forces and constraints also operate in more realistic market structures. But it was necessary to isolate these forces and constraints beforehand rather than attempt to immediately analyze "realistic" market structures like monopolistic competition and oligopoly, which would have been a confusing jumble of details and possible outcomes. It would have been like driving in a strange, large city without a road map.

2 In graphing a monopolistically competitive firm in long-run equilibrium, be sure that the *ATC* curve is tangent to the demand curve at the same level of output at which the *MC* and *MR* curves intersect. Also be sure that the *MC* curve intersects the *ATC* curve at the minimum point on the *ATC* curve.

3 This chapter uses elementary game theory to explain oligopoly. The prisoners' dilemma game illustrates the most important game theory concepts (rules, strategies, payoffs, outcome), which are then used in more complex game theory models like repeated and sequential games.

It is important to learn how to find the Nash equilibrium of a prisoners' dilemma–type game. Take the example of players *A* and *B*, where each player has to choose between two strategies—confess or deny. First set up the payoff matrix. Then look at the payoff matrix from *A*'s point of view. *A* does not know if *B* is going to confess or deny, so *A* asks two questions: (1) Assuming that *B* confesses, do I get a better payoff if I confess or deny? (2) Assuming that *B* denies, do I get a better payoff if I confess or deny?

If *A*'s best strategy is to confess, regardless of whether *B* confesses or denies, confessing is *A*'s dominant strategy. Next, look at the payoff matrix from *B*'s point of view. Let *B* ask the equivalent two questions, and find *B*'s dominant strategy. The combination of *A*'s dominant strategy and *B*'s dominant strategy comprises the Nash equilibrium outcome of the game.

4 The key insight of the prisoners' dilemma game is the *tension* between the Nash equilibrium outcome (where both players' best strategy is to confess because they can't trust each other) and the fact that both players could make themselves better off if only they would cooperate. All of the equilibrium situations we have examined up until now have been stable outcomes where all agents' self-interests (utility and profit) have been maximized. Remember, equilibrium is defined as a situation where there is no tendency to change. The Nash equilibrium of the prisoner's dilemma is different. Even though both players confess, their individual self-interests are not maximized. It is the additional possibility of strategic interaction (to trust or not to trust the other player) that creates the instability of outcomes.

The instability of outcomes in this simple game helps us to understand more complex market phenomena such as gasoline price wars.

When gasoline station owners trust each other, prices remain relatively high and profits are maximized. But there is always an incentive to cheat on a collusive agreement. Once cheating begins, trust breaks down and owners are driven to the equilibrium outcome where all owners cheat, prices fall, and profits are reduced. Eventually, reduced profits lead owners to take a chance on trusting each other again, since they figure it couldn't be worse than existing low prices and profits. All stations raise their prices, and the cycle begins again. This instability of price and profit outcomes stems from the cycle of trust and non-trust. In other words, instability arises from strategic interaction between station owners.

SELF-TEST

True/False and Explain

Monopolistic Competition

1 Barriers to entry give monopolistically competitive firms some monopoly power.

2 Product differentiation gives monopolistically competitive firms some monopoly power.

Output and Price in Monopolistic Competition

3 In monopolistic competition, short-run profits attract new entry, shifting each individual firm's demand curve rightward.

4 Free entry is the key characteristic of monopolistic competition that produces excess capacity.

5 When a monopolistically competitive industry is in long-run equilibrium, economic profit is zero and price equals minimum average total cost.

Product Development and Marketing

6 Firms in monopolistic competition must innovate continuously to enjoy economic profits.

7 Selling costs always increase average total costs.

8 Advertising by monopolistic competitors is never allocatively inefficient.

Oligopoly

9 The kinked demand curve model predicts that price and quantity will be sensitive to small cost changes.

10 An oligopolist will consider the reaction of other firms before it decides to cut its price.

Oligopoly Games

11 A Nash equilibrium occurs when A takes the best possible action given the action of B, and B takes the best possible action given the action of A.

12 If duopolists agree to collude, they can (jointly) make as much profit as a single monopoly.

13 For colluding duopolists in a nonrepeated game, the equilibrium is always for both firms to cheat.

Repeated Games and Sequential Games

14 For colluding duopolists in a repeated game, the equilibrium is always for both firms to cheat.

15 A limit pricing strategy sets the price that inflicts the highest loss on a new entrant.

Multiple-Choice

Monopolistic Competition

1 In monopolistic competition, firms
a can collude.
b strategically interact with other firms.
c have an element of monopoly power.
d face a kinked demand curve.
e do all of the above.

Output and Price in Monopolistic Competition

2 For a monopolistically competitive firm in long-run equilibrium,
a $P = MC$.
b $MC = ATC$.
c $AR = ATC$, but $P > MC$.
d $MC = AR$, but $ATC > AR$.
e none of the above is true.

3 Figure 13.1 represents a monopolistically competitive firm in short-run equilibrium. What is the firm's level of output?
a Q_1
b Q_2
c Q_3
d Q_4
e zero

FIGURE **13.1**

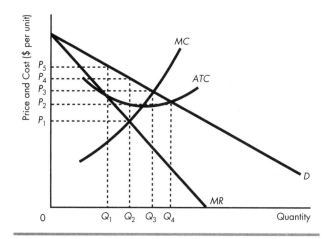

4 Figure 13.1 represents a monopolistically competitive firm in short-run equilibrium. What is the firm's economic profit *per unit*?

a $P_4 - P_2$

b $P_4 - P_1$

c P_4

d P_3

e none of the above

5 Figure 13.1 represents a monopolistically competitive firm in short-run equilibrium. In the long run,

a new firms will enter, and each existing firm's demand shifts leftward.

b new firms will enter, and each existing firm's demand shifts rightward.

c existing firms will leave, and each remaining firm's demand shifts leftward.

d existing firms will leave, and each remaining firm's demand shifts rightward.

e there will be no change from the short run.

6 Under monopolistic competition, long-run economic profit tends towards zero because of

a product differentiation.

b the lack of barriers to entry.

c excess capacity.

d inefficiency.

e downward-sloping demand curves facing each firm.

7 In the long run, a monopolistically competitive firm will earn the same economic profit as

a a monopolistically competitive firm in the short run.

b a member of a cartel.

c a pure price-discriminating monopolist.

d a perfectly competitive firm.

e none of the above.

8 Which of the following is true for perfect competition, monopolistic competition, and single-price monopoly?

a homogeneous product

b zero long-run economic profit

c short-run profit-maximizing quantity where $MC = MR$

d easy entry and exit

e none of the above

9 In the long run, the firm in monopolistic competition will

a face a perfectly elastic demand curve.

b produce more than the quantity that minimizes *ATC.*

c produce less than the quantity that minimizes *ATC.*

d produce the quantity that minimizes *ATC.*

e earn economic profit.

10 In the long run, a monopolistically competitive firm will produce the output at which price equals

a marginal cost.

b marginal revenue.

c average variable cost.

d average total cost.

e **b** and **d.**

11 Which of the following characteristics is *not* shared by single-price monopoly and monopolistic competition?

a firms face a downward-sloping demand curve

b profit-maximizing quantity where $MC = MR$

c equilibrium *ATC* above minimum *ATC*

d positive long-run economic profit

e positive long-run normal profit

Product Development and Marketing

12 Selling costs
a are variable costs that increase total cost.
b always increase demand for a firm's product.
c always decrease demand by increasing competition.
d always provide consumers with valuable services.
e include marketing expenditures on advertising and packaging.

Oligopoly

13 Which of the following statements about the sections of kinked demand curve in Figure 13.2 is *correct*?

a *AB* assumes new firms will enter the industry, while *BC* assumes no new firms will enter.
b *AB* assumes no new firms will enter the industry, while *BC* assumes new firms will enter.
c The kink between sections reflects market imperfections.
d *AB* assumes other firms will match a price increase, while *BC* assumes other firms will not match a price decrease.
e *AB* assumes other firms will not match a price increase, while *BC* assumes other firms will match a price decrease.

FIGURE **13.2**

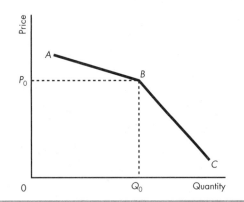

14 In the dominant firm model of oligopoly, the smaller firms act like

a oligopolists.
b monopolists.
c monopolistic competitors.
d perfect competitors.
e a cartel.

15 Each of the following is a characteristic of monopolistic competition. Which is *not* a characteristic of oligopoly?

a Each firm faces a downward-sloping demand curve.
b Firms are profit-maximizers.
c The sales of one firm will not have a significant effect on other firms.
d There is more than one firm in the industry.
e Firms set prices.

Oligopoly Games

16 Which of the following is *not* common to all games?

a rules
b collusion
c strategies
d payoffs
e the analysis of strategic interaction

17 In the prisoners' dilemma with players Art and Bob, each prisoner would be best off if

a both prisoners confess.
b both prisoners deny.
c Art denies and Bob confesses.
d Bob denies and Art confesses.
e none of the above is done.

18 If a duopoly with collusion maximizes profit,

a each firm must produce the same amount.
b each firm must produce its maximum output possible.
c industry marginal revenue must equal industry marginal cost at the level of total output.
d industry demand must equal industry marginal cost at the level of total output.
e total output will be greater than without collusion.

19 Table 13.1 gives the payoff matrix in terms of profit for firms *A* and *B*, when there are two strategies facing each firm: (1) charge a low price or (2) charge a high price. The equilibrium in this game (played once) is a Nash equilibrium, because

a firm *B* will reduce profit by more than *A* if both charge a lower price.
b firm *B* is the dominant firm.
c the best strategy for each firm does not depend on the strategy chosen by the other.
d there is no credible threat by either firm to punish the other if it breaks the agreement.
e all of the above are true.

TABLE **13.1**

		Firm B	
		Low Price	High Price
Firm A	Low Price	A: $2 B: $5	A: $20 B: −$15
	High Price	A: −$10 B: $25	A: $10 B: $20

20 Refer to the nonrepeated game in Table 13.1. In Nash equilibrium, what are firm *A*'s profits?

a −$10
b $2
c $10
d $20
e indeterminate.

21 Refer to the nonrepeated game in Table 13.1. If both firms could agree to collude, what would firm *A*'s profits be?

a −$10
b $2
c $10
d $20
e indeterminate.

22 The firms Trick and Gear form a cartel to collude to maximize profit. If this game is nonrepeated, the Nash equilibrium is

a both firms cheat on the agreement.
b both firms comply with the agreement.
c Trick cheats, while Gear complies with the agreement.
d Gear cheats, while Trick complies with the agreement.
e indeterminate.

Repeated Games and Sequential Games

23 Consider the same cartel consisting of Trick and Gear. Now, however, the game is repeated indefinitely and each firm employs a tit-for-tat strategy. The equilibrium is

a both firms cheat on the agreement.
b both firms comply with the agreement.
c Trick cheats, while Gear complies with the agreement.
d Gear cheats, while Trick complies with the agreement.
e indeterminate.

24 The equilibrium in Question **23** is called a

a credible strategy equilibrium.
b dominant player equilibrium.
c duopoly equilibrium.
d trigger strategy equilibrium.
e cooperative equilibrium.

25 Limit pricing refers to

a the highest price a monopolist can set.
b the highest price that just inflicts a loss on a potential entrant.
c a strategy used by entering firms in contestable markets.
d the price determined in a kinked demand curve model.
e none of the above.

Short Answer Problems

1 Consider a single firm in a monopolistically competitive industry in the short run. Using axes like those shown in Figure 13.3, draw a new graph for each of the following situations.

FIGURE **13.3**

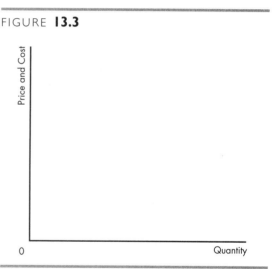

a The firm is making an economic profit.
b The firm is incurring a loss that will cause shutdown.
c The firm is incurring a loss, but is still producing.
d Starting from the situation in part **c**, explain what will happen in this industry and how your graph in part **c** will be affected. (No new graph required.)
e The firm is in long-run equilibrium.

ⓒ **2** Consider a monopolistically competitive industry in long-run equilibrium. Firm *A* in this industry attempts to increase profits by advertising.

  a On the graph in Figure 13.4, show what will happen in the short run as a result of the decision to advertise. Briefly explain your graph.

FIGURE **13.4**

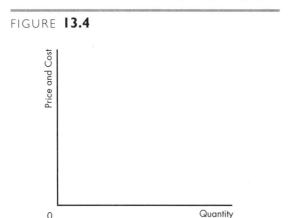

  b If the firm is successful in raising profits in the short run, what will happen in the long run?

3 Compare the advantages and disadvantages of perfect competition and monopolistic competition in terms of efficiency.

4 In monopolistic competition, will a single product innovation guarantee long-run economic profits? Explain.

5 Consider the case of two colluding duopolists in a nonrepeated game. In Nash equilibrium, will the firms comply or cheat on the agreement? Explain why.

6 How can a price war that eliminates profits be explained using game theory?

7 A small prairie town has two bakeries—Always Fresh and Never Stale. Transportation costs are high relative to the price of bread, so the bakeries do not get any out-of-town competition; the local bread industry is a duopoly. Always Fresh and Never Stale have the same cost curves, and each currently makes an annual profit of $2,000.

  Suppose that a new advertising service, Philomena's Flyers, starts up. If one bakery advertises in Philomena's Flyers, its annual profits will increase to $5,000, while the other bakery will lose $2,000. If both advertise, each will make a zero profit. If neither advertises, each bakery will continue to make an annual profit of $2,000.

  a Represent this duopoly as a game by identifying the players, strategies, and possible outcomes.
  b Construct the payoff matrix.
  c What is the Nash equilibrium outcome? Explain.

8 Figure 13.5(a) gives the identical average total cost (*ATC*) curve for Always Fresh and Never Stale. Figure 13.5(b) gives the town's market demand curve for bread and the firms' joint marginal cost curve. Suppose that the two

FIGURE **13.5**

(a) *ATC* Curve for Each Bakery

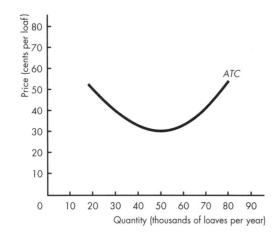

(b) Market Demand for Bread and Firm's Joint *MC* Curve

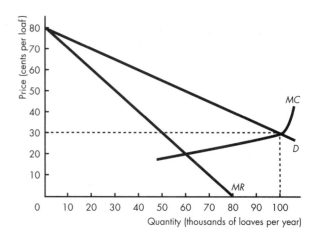

bakeries collude to maximize profit and agree to divide output equally for a single year.

a How much will each bakery produce and what price per loaf will they charge?

b What is each bakery's average total cost and profit?

ct **9** Now suppose that Never Stale convinces Always Fresh that demand has decreased and they must reduce their price by 10 cents per loaf in order to sell their agreed-upon quantity. Of course, demand has not decreased, but Always Fresh produces its agreed amount and charges 10 cents less per loaf. Never Stale, the cheater, also charges 10 cents less than before, but increases output sufficiently to satisfy the rest of demand at this price.

a How many loaves of bread does Never Stale produce?

b What is Always Fresh's average total cost and profit?

c What is Never Stale's average total cost and profit?

10 Return to the initial situation. The firms are preparing to enter into a *long-term* collusive agreement. Always Fresh credibly assures Never Stale that if Never Stale cheats in a repeated game, Always Fresh will undercut Never Stale's price as soon as the cheating is discovered. Would Never Stale want to cheat on the agreement now? Why or why not?

ANSWERS

True/False and Explain

1 **F** Free entry and exit in monopolistic competition. (284–285)

2 **T** Creates downward-sloping demand curve; some ability to raise price without sales going to zero. (284–285)

3 **F** New entry shifts individual firm demand (and marginal revenue) curves leftward. (286–287)

4 **F** Product differentiation creates downward-sloping demand tangent to *ATC* below full capacity output. (286–288)

5 **F** Zero economic profit, but $P >$ minimum *ATC*. (286–287)

6 **T** With existing products, new firms enter and compete away economic profits. (288–289)

7 **F** Selling costs are fixed costs that increase total costs, but if output increases enough, average total cost may decrease. (289–290)

ct **8** **F** Depends on information versus persuasion content of advertising and gains from increased product variety. (289–290)

9 **F** Insensitive to small cost changes. (291)

10 **T** Oligopoly involves strategic behaviour. (291, 295)

11 **T** Definition. (293–294)

12 **T** With collusion, act exactly like monopoly. (295–296)

13 **T** True for nonrepeated game but may be false for repeated game. (296–299)

ct **14** **F** Tit-for-tat strategy yields cooperative equilibrium in repeated game. (302–303)

15 **F** Sets highest price that just inflicts (smallest) loss, since any loss deters entry. (302–303)

Multiple-Choice

1 **c** All other answers describe oligopoly. (284–285)

ct **2** **c** Demand curve ($AR = P$) tangent to *ATC* and above *MC*. (286–287)

3 **b** Where $MC = MR$. (286–287)

ct **4** **a** At Q_2, $AR - ATC$. (286–287)

5 **a** With new entrants due to economic profit, industry demand divided among more firms so each firm's demand curve shifts leftward. (286–287)

6 **b** **a** and **e** create possibility of economic profit, **c** and **d** are outcomes, not forces leading to zero economic profit. (286–288)

7 **d** Zero economic profit. (286–288)

8 **c** **b** and **d** false for monopoly. **a** false for monopolistic competition. (284–288)

9 **c** Excess capacity at Q where demand tangent to downward slope *ATC*. (286–288)

10 **d** Where demand curve tangent to *ATC*. (286–288)

ct **11** **d** Zero long-run economic profit for monopolistic competition. (286–288)

12 **e** Selling costs are fixed costs that may increase or decrease demand, and may persuade consumers about exaggerated differences between products rather than provide valuable information. (289–290)

13 **e** *AB* more elastic than *BC* because price changes unmatched. (291)

14 **d** Dominant firm sets price, smaller firms take that price as given. (292)

ct **15** **c** Oligopoly involves interdependence between firms. (291–292)

16 **b** No collusion in prisoners' dilemma. (293–300)

17 b Doesn't happen because players cannot trust each other enough to collude. (293–294)
18 c See Text Figure13.9(b). (295–296)
19 c Dominant strategy for each. (298–299)
20 b Both firms charge low price. (298–299)
21 c Both firms charge high price. (298–299)
22 a Similar to prisoners' dilemma outcome. (295–299)
ⓒ **23 b** Cooperative equilibrium; each player responds rationally to credible threat of other. (301–302)
24 e Definition. (301–302)
25 b Definition. **c** would be true for existing firms. (302–303)

Short Answer Problems

1 a Figure 13.3 Solution (a) illustrates a monopolistically competitive firm making an economic profit in the short run. The important feature of the graph is that at the profit-maximizing output, price is greater than average total cost. Economic profit is the shaded area.

FIGURE **13.3** SOLUTION

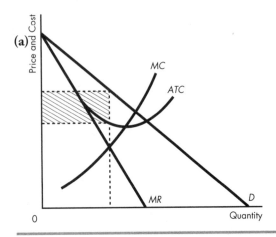

b Figure 13.3 Solution (b) illustrates a firm that will shut down in the short run since price is less than average variable cost at the profit-maximizing (loss-minimizing) level of output.

FIGURE **13.3** SOLUTION

(b)

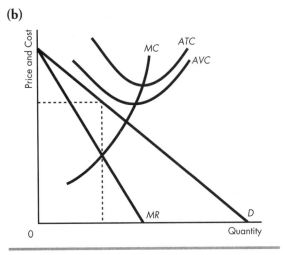

c Figure 13.3 Solution (c) illustrates a firm incurring a loss but continuing to produce. The loss is the shaded area. Note that, at the profit-maximizing output, price is less than ATC but greater than AVC.

FIGURE **13.3** SOLUTION

(c)

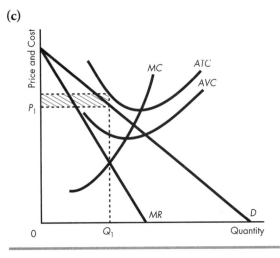

d Since firms are incurring a loss, firms will leave the industry. The demand curves facing each remaining firm will shift rightward as they each attract some customers of departing firms. As firms' demand curves shift rightward, losses are reduced. Firms continue to have an incentive to leave until losses are eliminated. Thus remaining firms' demand curves continue to shift until they are tangent to the ATC curve.

e Figure 13.3 Solution (d) illustrates a monopolistically competitive firm in long-run equilibrium. The demand curve facing the firm is tangent to the ATC curve at the profit-maximizing output. Thus the firm is making zero economic profit.

FIGURE **13.3** SOLUTION

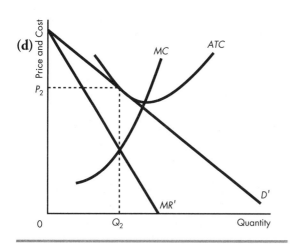

2 a Advertising will increase firm A's cost, but also increase demand (it hopes). If the increase in demand (revenue) is greater than the increase in cost, then firm A will increase its profit. Figure 13.4 Solution illustrates this situation. The initial curves are given by D_0, ATC_0, and MR_0.

Initially the firm is producing Q_0 and selling at price P_0 and making zero economic profit. Advertising, which is a fixed cost, raises the ATC curve to ATC_1 (MC does not shift), but also increases the demand and marginal revenue curves to D_1 and MR_1 respectively. The shift in the demand curve is sufficiently great that there is now positive economic profit at the new profit-maximizing level of output (Q_1). Economic profit is the shaded area.

FIGURE **13.4** SOLUTION

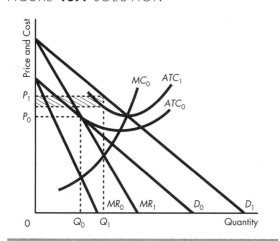

b Other firms will also begin to advertise to attempt to increase their profit (or recover lost profit). As all other firms advertise, the demand curve for our firm will shift back to the left as it loses some customers it gained. In the long run, once again, all firms will be making zero profit even after advertising.

3 The advantage of perfect competition is that it leads to production at minimum average total cost, while monopolistic competition leads to higher average total cost due to reduced output and high advertising expenditures.

The advantage of monopolistic competition is that it leads to greater product variety, which consumers value, while in a perfectly competitive industry there is a single, identical product produced by all firms. Monopolistic competition also leads to greater product innovation and, as a positive by-product of greater advertising, valuable information to consumers. Thus the loss in allocative efficiency and greater advertising costs (higher ATC) in monopolistic competition have to be weighed against the gains of greater product variety, greater product innovation, and more valuable information provided to consumers.

4 No. In the short run, a firm in monopolistic competition will earn economic profit because its downward-sloping demand curve gives it some price power. But in the long run, economic profit attracts new firms that make close substitutes for the product. With free entry, new firms compete away the economic profit. To restore economic profit, monopolistically competitive firms must continuously innovate and develop new products.

5 Each firm's best strategy is to cheat regardless of the strategy of the other firm. Call the firms A and B. Firm A knows that if firm B follows the collusive agreement, A can increase its profit by cheating. If firm B cheats, then firm A knows that it must also cheat to minimize its loss of profit. Thus cheating is the dominant strategy for firm A. It is also the dominant strategy for firm B, so the Nash equilibrium is both firms cheat.

6 Game theory explains price wars as the consequence of firms in a colluding industry responding to the cheating of a firm. If one firm cheats by cutting its price, then all other firms will cut their prices, and a price war will ensue. Once price has fallen sufficiently (perhaps to the zero profit level), firms will again have a strong incentive to rebuild their collusion.

7 a The players are Always Fresh and Never Stale. Each firm has two strategies: to advertise or not to advertise. There are four possible outcomes: (1) both firms advertise, (2) Always Fresh advertises but Never Stale does not, (3) Never Stale advertises but Always Fresh does not, and (4) neither firm advertises.

b The payoff matrix is given in Table 13.2. The entries give the profit earned by Always Fresh (*AF*) and Never Stale (*NS*) under each of the four possible outcomes.

TABLE **13.2**

		Never Stale	
		Advertise	Not Advertise
Always Fresh	Advertise	AF: 0 NS: 0	AF: $5,000 NS: −$2,000
	Not Advertise	AF: −$2,000 NS: $5,000	AF: $2,000 NS: $2,000

c First, consider how Always Fresh decides which strategy to pursue. If Never Stale advertises, Always Fresh can advertise and make zero profit or not advertise and make a $2,000 loss. Thus Always Fresh will want to advertise if Never Stale does.

If Never Stale does not advertise, Always Fresh can advertise and make a $5,000 profit or not advertise and make a $2,000 profit. Therefore Always Fresh will want to advertise whether Never Stale advertises or not. Never Stale will come to the same conclusion. The Nash equilibrium is that both firms advertise.

8 a The firms will agree to produce 30,000 loaves each and sell at a price of 50 cents per loaf. We determine this by noticing (Figure 13.5b) that the profit-maximizing (monopoly) output is 60,000 loaves for the industry ($MR = MC$ at 60,000) and the industry price is 50 cents per loaf. Since the firms have agreed to divide output equally, each will produce 30,000 loaves.

b From Figure 13.5(a) we determine that, at 30,000 loaves, each firm's average total cost is 40 cents per loaf. Since price is 50 cents per loaf, profit will be $3,000 for each firm.

9 a At the new price of 40 cents per loaf, total quantity demanded is 80,000 loaves. Since Always Fresh continues to produce 30,000 loaves, this means that Never Stale will produce the remaining 50,000 loaves demanded.

b Since Always Fresh continues to produce 30,000 loaves, its average total cost continues to be 40 cents per loaf. With the new price also at 40 cents, Always Fresh will make a zero economic profit.

c Never Stale has increased output to 50,000 loaves, which implies average total cost of 30 cents per loaf. Thus, given a price of 40 cents, Never Stale's economic profit will be $5,000.

10 Given that the agreement is long-term, Never Stale would almost surely not cheat. The reason is that, while Never Stale could increase short-term profit by cheating, it would lose much more future profit if Always Fresh retaliates in a repeated game.

The key point is that Never Stale's behaviour changes, not because cost or demand have changed, but rather because Always Fresh's behaviour has changed in the repeated game. In duopoly and oligopoly, the best strategy for any firm depends on the behaviour of other firms.

Understanding Firms and Markets

PROBLEM

FIGURE **P4.1**

(a) Industry

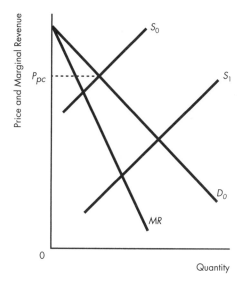

(b) Firm

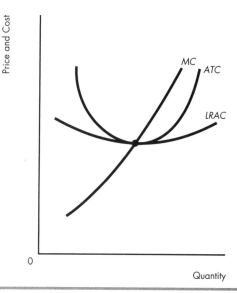

Despite significant differences between perfect competition, monopoly, and monopolistic competition, all of these market structures can be analyzed using the diagrams in Figure P4.1.

Figure P4.1(a) shows an industry in short-run equilibrium at the intersection of the demand (D_0) and supply (S_0) curves. Ignore for the moment the other supply curve (S_1) and the marginal revenue curve (MR). Long-run market demand is the same as short-run market demand. There are no external economies or diseconomies. Figure P4.1(b) shows the cost curves of one of many identical firms in the industry.

Let's first suppose this is a perfectly competitive (pc) industry.

a Describe the demand curve facing an individual firm; describe the marginal revenue curve.

b On Figure P4.1, identify and label the industry short-run equilibrium price (P_{pc}) (this is a giveaway!), output (Q_{pc}), and individual firm output (q_{pc}). Is each individual firm making a profit or loss? Explain.

c What happens in the long run? On Figure P4.1, identify and label the industry long-run equilibrium price (P^{LR}_{pc}), output (Q^{LR}_{pc}), and individual firm ouput (q^{LR}_{pc}).

Now suppose that the market in Figure P4.1(a) is supplied by a single-price monopolist (m) with a legal monopoly. S_1 is the monopolist's marginal cost curve. Ignore S_0 and part (b) of the figure.

d Describe the demand curve facing the monopolist; describe the supply curve of the monopolist.

e On Figure P4.1(a), identify and label the industry short-run equilibrium price (P_m) and output (Q_m).

f At Q_m, if the monopolist's average total cost is less than P_m, explain what happens in the long run. On Figure P4.1(a), identify and label the industry long-run equilibrium price (P^{LR}_m) and output (Q^{LR}_m).

g Compare the long-run allocative efficiency of this industry under monopoly versus under perfect competition. Identify any deadweight loss on the appropriate figure.

Finally, suppose that the industry in Figure P4.1(a) is supplied by many monopolistically competitive (*mc*) firms. The industry supply curve is S_0, and at price P_{pc}, each firm is in long-run equilibrium. Ignore S_1 and *MR*. Each firm has the cost curves in Figure P4.1(b), but produces a slightly differentiated product.

h Describe the demand curve facing an individual firm and draw it on Figure P4.1(b).

i On Figure P4.1(b), identify and label the long-run output (q_{mc}) for an individual monopolistically competitive firm. Describe one point that you can identify precisely on the marginal revenue curve facing an individual firm. Explain why this is a long-run equilibrium.

j Compare the long-run allocative efficiency of this industry under monopolistic competition versus under perfect competition. What consideration must be taken into account that is not taken into account for a monopoly?

MIDTERM EXAMINATION

You should allocate 48 minutes for this examination (24 questions, 2 minutes per question). For each question, choose the one *best* answer.

l The supply curve for a single-price monopoly is

a its marginal cost curve.

b its marginal cost curve above minimum average variable cost.

c its average variable cost curve.

d its marginal revenue curve.

e none of the above.

2 A successful price-discriminating firm must be able to

a prevent consumer resale.

b differentiate consumers with high price elasticity of demand and charge them low prices.

c differentiate consumers with low price elasticity of demand and charge them high prices.

d do all of the above.

e do none of the above.

3 Figure P4.2 represents a monopolistically competitive firm in short-run equilibrium. What is the firm's price?

a P_1

b P_2

c P_3

d P_4

e P_5

FIGURE **P4.2**

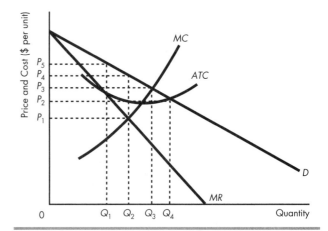

4 Figure P4.2 represents a monopolistically competitive firm in short-run equilibrium. In the long run, what is the firm's economic profit *per unit*?

a $P_4 - P_2$

b $P_4 - P_1$

c P_3

d P_2

e none of the above

5 For a single-price monopolist, which of the following statements is *false*?

a There is no unique one-to-one relationship between price and quantity supplied.
b For any output greater than zero, $MR < AR$.
c The industry demand curve is the monopolist's demand curve.
d The intersection of MR and MC provides all information necessary for identifying the profit-maximizing quantity and price.
e Total revenue is at a maximum where $MR = 0$.

6 A single-price monopoly never operates

a on an elastic portion of the demand curve.
b on a unit elastic portion of the demand curve.
c on an inelastic portion of the demand curve.
d at a quantity where marginal revenue is positive since total revenue is not at a maximum.
e under any of the above conditions.

7 In a perfectly competitive industry of 100 firms, the demand curve facing the individual firm is

a unit elastic.
b identical to the industry demand curve.
c 1/100 of the industry demand curve.
d one where $AR = MR$.
e none of the above.

8 If economic profits are being made by firms in a competitive industry, new firms will enter. This will shift

a the industry demand curve leftward, causing market price to fall.
b the industry demand curve rightward, causing market price to rise.
c the industry supply curve leftward, causing market price to rise.
d the industry supply curve rightward, causing market price to fall.
e none of the above curves.

9 The kinked demand curve model

a suggests that price will remain constant even with fluctuations in demand.
b suggests how the current price is determined.
c assumes that marginal revenue sometimes increases with output.
d assumes that competitors will match price cuts and ignore price increases.
e suggests none of the above.

10 In the prisoners' dilemma with players Art and Bob, the Nash equilibrium is

a both prisoners confess.
b both prisoners deny.
c Art denies and Bob confesses.
d Bob denies and Art confesses.
e indeterminate.

11 In a perfectly competitive industry, the market price is $5. An individual firm is producing the level of output at which marginal cost is $5 and is increasing, and average total cost is $25. What should the firm do to maximize its short-run profits?

a shut down
b expand output
c contract output
d leave output unchanged
e insufficient information to answer

12 The long-run competitive industry supply curve will be positively sloped if there are

a external economies.
b external diseconomies.
c no external economies or diseconomies.
d external costs.
e external benefits.

13 A perfectly competitive firm maximizes profit if

a marginal cost equals price and price is above minimum average variable cost.
b marginal cost equals price and price is above minimum average fixed cost.
c total revenue is at a maximum.
d average variable cost is at a minimum.
e average total cost is at a minimum.

14 The more perfectly a monopoly can price discriminate, the

a closer its output gets to the single-price monopoly output.
b more efficient is the outcome.
c more consumer surplus is converted to deadweight loss.
d more producer surplus is converted to deadweight loss.
e more producer surplus is captured as profit.

15 Selling costs in monopolistic competition

a shift up the average total cost curve.
b may be justified by the useful information provided to consumers.
c may not provide benefits that justify the increased opportunity cost.
d may attempt to increase product differentiation.
e do all of the above.

16 The construction cost of a building is $100,000. The conventional depreciation allowance is 5 percent per year. At the end of the first year the market value of the building is $80,000. For the first year, the depreciation cost is

a $20,000 to an accountant or an economist.
b $5,000 to an accountant or an economist.
c $5,000 to an accountant but $20,000 to an economist.
d $20,000 to an accountant but $5,000 to an economist.
e none of the above.

17 The marginal cost curve slopes upward because of

a diminishing marginal utility.
b diminishing marginal returns.
c technological inefficiency.
d economic inefficiency.
e none of the above.

18 In economics, the long run is a time frame in which

a one year or more elapses.
b all resources are variable.
c all resources are fixed.
d there is at least one fixed resource and at least one variable resource.
e all resources are variable but plant size is fixed.

19 A firm has $200 in explicit costs and sells the resulting output for $250. The normal rate of profit is 10 percent. Which of the following statements is *true*?

a Implicit costs are $25.
b Economic profits are $20.
c Economic profits are $50.
d Economic profits exceed accounting profits.
e Explicit costs exceed implicit costs.

20 If *AFC* is falling then *MC* must be

a rising.
b falling.
c above *AFC*.
d below *AFC*.
e none of the above.

21 If all inputs are increased by 10 percent and output increases by more than 10 percent, it must be the case that

a average total cost is decreasing.
b average total cost is increasing.
c the *LRAC* curve is positively sloped.
d there are economies of scale.
e there are diseconomies of scale.

22 In Table P4.1, which method(s) of making a medical hologram is/are technologically efficient?

a 1 only
b 2 only
c 3 only
d 1, 2, and 3
e 1 and 3 only

TABLE **P4.1**   THREE METHODS OF MAKING ONE MEDICAL HOLOGRAM

| | Quantities of Inputs ||
Method	Labour	Capital
1	5	10
2	10	15
3	15	5

23 Refer to Table P4.1. If the price of labour is $20 per unit and the price of capital is $10 per unit, which method(s) is/are economically efficient?

a 1 only
b 2 only
c 3 only
d 2 and 3 only
e 1 and 3 only

24 In a contestable market, the

a Herfindahl-Hirschman Index is always low.
b Herfindahl-Hirschman Index is always high.
c firm in the market earns large economic profits.
d firm in the market might play an entry deterrence game.
e firm in the market will not use a limit pricing strategy.

ANSWERS

Problem

a The individual firm's demand curve and marginal revenue curve is a horizontal line at P_{pc}.

b See Figure P4.1(b) Solution. Each firm is making economic profit because at output q_{pc}, price (P_{pc} = average revenue) is greater than average total cost.

c See Figure P4.1 Solution. In response to economic profit, new firms enter the industry, causing the industry supply curve to shift rightward until it reaches S_1. When price has fallen to P^{LR}_{pc}, economic profit has been eliminated and each firm is earning normal profit only.

FIGURE **P4.1** SOLUTION

(a) Industry

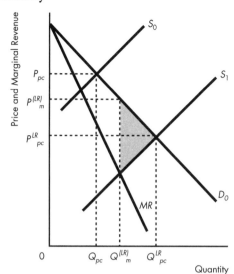

(b) Firm

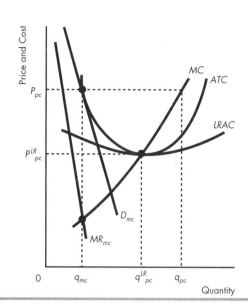

d The monopolist's demand curve is the industry demand curve D_0. The monopolist does not have a supply curve since she can choose a combination of price and quantity.

e See Figure P4.1(a) Solution.

f Even though the monopolist is earning economic profit, nothing happens in the long run because legal barriers prevent new entry. Long-run equilibrium price and output are the same as short-run price (P_m) and output (Q_m).

g Monopoly is less efficient than perfect competition, by the shaded area of deadweight loss indicated on Figure P4.1(a) Solution.

h See Figure P4.1(b) Solution. Since the firm is in long-run equilibrium, the downward-sloping demand curve must be tangent to the ATC curve at the equilibrium price P_{pc}.

i See Figure P4.1 Solution. A profit-maximizing firm chooses the output (q_{mc}) where MC intersects MR. Hence the MR curve must intersect MC at q_{mc}. This is a long-run equilibrium because the firm is earning zero economic profit, so no incentive for entry or exit.

j Under monopolistic competition, ATC is higher (P_{pc}) than under perfect competition (P^{LR}_{pc}), implying less efficiency. However, the loss in allocative efficiency of monopolistic competition must be weighed against the gain in increased product variety.

Midterm Examination

1 **e** Monopoly has no supply curve. (264–267)
2 **d** See text discussion. (271–273)

3 **d** Highest possible price to sell Q_2. (286–288)
4 **e** Long-run economic profit per unit = zero. (286–288)
ⓒ **5** **d** Need demand curve to identify price. (264–267)
6 **c** If demand is inelastic then $MR < 0$. But MR must always be > 0 to intersect (positive) MC. (264–265)
7 **d** Horizontal at market price. Infinite elasticity. (238–239)
8 **d** Economic profit/loss signal for supply shifts. Profit attracts entry new firms. (246–249)
9 **d** **a** true if fluctuation in MC. MR always decreases with increasing Q so **c** false. (291)
10 **a** Outcome of game. (293–294)
ⓒ **11** **e** Firm at Q where $P = MC$, but losing $ since $AR < ATC$. Need AVC information to determine if **a** or **d** correct. (242–245)
12 **b** Increasing costs as industry Q increases. (251–253)
13 **a** AFC irrelevant. Maximizing profit ≠ maximizing revenue. **d**, **e** might be true depending on P. (242–244)
14 **b** Perfect price discrimination has zero deadweight loss; all consumer surplus captured as profit. (273–274)
15 **e** Enhanced information and variety may or may not justify increased (opportunity) cost of selling costs. (289–290)
16 **c** Accountant's depreciation = (5 %) × $100,000. Economist's depreciation = Δ market value. (196–197)
17 **b** Diminishing marginal returns implies decreasing MP causing increasing MC. (224–226)

18 **b** Definition. All inputs and plant size variable. (218)

19 **e** Implicit costs = 0.10 ($200) = $20; economic profit = $25; accounting profit = $50. (196–197)

20 **e** *AFC* always falling; no necessary relation to *MC*. See Text Figure 11.5. (224–225)

21 **d** Definition downward sloping *LRAC*. Since all inputs variable, **a** and **b** irrelevant. (230–231)

22 **e** 2 uses more labour and more capital than 1. (199–200)

23 **a** 1 costs $200; 2 and 3 cost $350. (199–200)

24 **d** HHI may be high or low since measures actual, not potential competion. Firm may use entry deterrence or limit pricing and will not earn large profits. (302–303)

Chapter 14

Demand and Supply in Factor Markets

KEY CONCEPTS

Prices and Incomes in Competitive Factor Markets

Factors of production, or resources (labour, capital, land, entrepreneurship) are hired by firms to produce output.

Demand and supply in competitive factor markets for labour, capital, and land determine those factor prices (PF) (wages, interest, rent) and quantities (QF).

◆ Factor income = ($PF \times QF$).

◆ Factor price for entrepreneurship is normal profit. Economic profit/loss is residual income going to firm's owners.

Changes in demand and supply:

◆ Increased demand for factor increases PF, increases QF, and increases income.

◆ Decreased demand for factor decreases PF, decreases QF, and decreases income.

◆ Increased supply of factor decreases PF, increases QF, and increases income if $\eta_D > 1$; decreases income if $\eta_D < 1$.

◆ Decreased supply of factor increases PF, decreases QF, and decreases income if $\eta_D > 1$; increases income if $\eta_D < 1$.

Labour Markets

Demand for factors is a **derived demand**, stemming from demand for goods and services produced by a factor and driven by firms' profit-maximizing objective.

◆ **Marginal revenue product** (MRP) is extra revenue from employing one more unit of a factor.

  • $MRP = MP \times MR$
  • For a perfectly competitive firm, $MR = P_{output}$. So $MRP = MP$ (additional output produced by employing additional unit of factor) $\times P_{output}$.

Equivalent conditions for profit maximizing:

◆ Firm hires additional units of a factor up to quantity of

  • factor where $MRP = PF$. For labour (L), this is where MRP_L = wage rate.
  • output where $MR = MC$.

◆ Firm's demand curve for factor is identical to downward-sloping marginal revenue product curve of the factor.

◆ Firm's demand for labour curve (MRP_L curve) shifts

  • rightward if increased P_{output}.
  • rightward if technological change increases MP labour.
  • ambiguously if increased price other factors of production.

Market demand curve for labour is horizontal sum of quantities of labour demanded by all firms at each wage rate.

$$\text{Elasticity of demand for labour} = \left| \frac{\% \Delta \text{ quantity labour demanded}}{\% \Delta \text{ wage rate}} \right|$$

Demand for labour will be more elastic

◆ when production is more labour-intensive (wages a greater percentage of total cost).

◆ the greater the elasticity of demand for the final product.

◆ the greater the substitutability of capital for labour in the long run.

Supply of labour determined by households' decisions allocating time between labour supply (work) and leisure.

◆ Wage rate is *opportunity cost of leisure.*

◆ At wage rates above household's *reservation wage,* household supplies labour.

◆ *Substitution effect* from higher wage induces increased quantity labour supplied.

◆ *Income effect* from higher wage induces decreased quantity labour supplied.

◆ When wage rises, quantity labour supplied increases when substitution effect > income effect.

◆ Individual household labour supply curve is *backward-bending* when income effect > substitution effect.

Market supply of labour curve is horizontal sum of all household supply curves. Upward-sloping over normal range of wage rates.

◆ Supply of labour curve shift rightward if

• increased adult population.
• technological change or increased capital in home production.

Capital Markets

Capital markets coordinate household's saving decisions (supply of financial capital) and firm's investment decisions (demand for financial capital to buy physical capital equipment).

"Price of capital" determined by equilibrium of supply and demand in capital markets = real interest rate.

Demand for capital depends on future marginal revenue products of physical capital. Firms compare future marginal revenue products with present cost of capital.

◆ **Discounting** is conversion of future amount of money to its present value.

◆ **Present value** of future amount of money is amount that, if invested today, will grow as large as future amount, taking account of earned interest.

$$\text{Present value} = \frac{\text{Amount money available } n \text{ years}}{(1 + r)^n}$$

Firms decide whether or not to buy physical capital by evaluating net present value.

◆ **Net present value** (*NPV*) = future flow of marginal revenue product − purchase price.

◆ If net present value positive, firm buys capital good and increases profit.

◆ Higher interest rate lowers *NPV* and decreases quantity of capital firms demand (movement up along capital demand curve).

Market demand curve for capital shows relationship between quantity of capital demanded and the interest rate, *ceteris paribus.* Demand for capital shifts due to

◆ population growth—increases demand.

◆ technological change—increase demand for some types of capital, decreases demand for others.

Supply of capital determined by households' saving decisions. Households supply financial capital that firms use to buy physical capital equipment.

◆ Quantity of financial capital supplied determined by

• income—higher income yields higher saving.
• expected future income—when current income > expected future income, saving is higher.
• interest rate—higher interest rates yield higher saving.

Market supply of capital curve shows relationship between quantity of capital supplied and interest rate, *ceteris paribus.* Short-run supply inelastic. Long-run supply more elastic. Supply of capital shifts rightward due to

◆ increases in income or population.

◆ increases in middle-aged proportion of population.

Natural Resource Markets

Economists call all natural resources *land.*

◆ **Renewable natural resource** can be used repeatedly and not be depleted.

◆ **Nonrenewable natural resource** can only be used once and cannot be replaced.

Supply of renewable resources fixed and perfectly inelastic, so price determined by demand. But to individual competitive firm, supply of land perfectly elastic at market price.

Supply of nonrenewable natural resources depends on stock and flow supply.

◆ *Stock*—known quantity that exists at a given time. Perfectly inelastic.

◆ *Flow* supply—rate of use. Perfectly elastic at price equal to present value of expected price next period.

Because flow supply perfectly elastic, current period's price = present value next period's price.

◆ *Hotelling Principle*—price of natural resource expected to rise at rate = interest rate. But actual price may fluctuate from expected price because of unexpected technological change.

Income, Economic Rent, and Opportunity Cost

Economic rent is income received by factor owner above amount required to induce supply. Income required to induce supply is opportunity cost of factor of production.

◆ Total income = opportunity cost (area under supply curve) + economic rent (area above supply curve but below factor price).

◆ The more inelastic the supply of factor of production, the greater portion of its income is economic rent.

◆ Rent (price paid for services of land or a building) is distinct from economic rent (component of income of any factor of production).

HELPFUL HINTS

I Be careful to distinguish between the marginal revenue product of a factor of production and the marginal revenue of a unit of output. The marginal revenue product of a factor of production is calculated by multiplying marginal revenue and marginal product ($MRP = MR \times MP$). The intuition is this: marginal product tells us how much more output we receive from using more of a factor, and marginal revenue tells us how much more revenue we receive from selling each unit of that additional output. Therefore MP times MR tells us how much more revenue we receive (the MRP) from using more of the factor of production.

2 This chapter gives a broad overview of characteristics common to competitive markets for the factors of production labour, capital, and land. Profit-maximizing firms will hire each factor up to the point where marginal revenue product (MRP) is equal to the marginal cost (MC) of the factor. Since, in a competitive market, marginal cost is the price of the factor of production (PF), $MRP = PF$ in a competitive resource market.

3 The most important graph in this chapter appears in Text Figure 14.3, reproduced here as Figure 14.1. Using the example of Max's Wash 'n' Wax, the figure demonstrates that a firm's demand for labour curve is the same as its marginal revenue product curve of labour.

FIGURE **14.1**

(a)

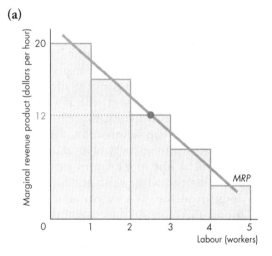

(a) Marginal revenue product

(b)

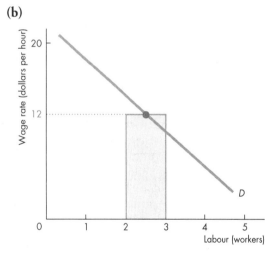

(b) Demand for labour

Part (a) shows the marginal revenue product curve (MRP) based on the numbers in Text Table 14.1 on page 318. Notice that the values for MRP are plotted midway between the labour inputs used in their calculation. For example, the MRP of moving from 0 to 1 labourer is 20, so the value of 20 on the MRP curve is plotted midway between 0 and 1 labourers.

Part (b) constructs Max's demand for labour by asking how much labour Max will hire at alternative wage rates. Since Max is a profit maximizer, he will hire labour up to the point where the marginal revenue product of labour is equal to the wage rate. For example, if the wage rate is $10 per hour, Max will hire 3 workers since marginal revenue product is $10 when 3 workers are hired. Other points on the labour demand curve can be obtained in similar fashion. The result is that the labour demand curve is the same as the MRP curve.

4   The concept of present value is essential in thinking about the value today of an investment or of future amounts of money. It gives us a method of comparing investments that have payments at different points in time. The intuition behind present value is a dollar today is worth more than a dollar in the future because today's dollar can be invested to earn interest. To calculate the value today of an amount of money that will be paid in the future, we must discount that future amount to compensate for the forgone interest. The present value of a future amount of money is the amount that, if invested today, will grow as large as the future amount, taking into account the interest that it will earn.

5   The profit-maximizing condition of hiring a factor of production until $MRP = PF$ must be adapted when a firm buys capital equipment. The reason is capital usually operates over more than one period and generates marginal revenue products distributed over time. The purchase price, however, must be paid now. In order to compare the purchase price (PF) with the stream of marginal revenue products, we must compute the present value of that stream.

In the case of capital equipment used over more than one period, the profit-maximizing condition becomes: buy an additional unit of capital as long as the present value of the stream of marginal revenue products is greater than the purchase price of the unit of capital. Since the net present value (NPV) of an investment is defined as the present value of the stream of marginal revenue products minus the purchase price of capital, an equivalent condition is: *buy capital equipment as long as its net present value is positive.*

SELF-TEST

True/False and Explain

Prices and Incomes in Competitive Factor Markets

1   Economic profit is the factor price of entrepreneurship.

2   An increase in the supply of labour always increases labour income.

Labour Markets

3   A firm's average revenue product curve is also its demand for labour curve.

4   Demand for labour is more elastic when demand for the final product is more inelastic.

5   A household supplies no labour at wage rates below its reservation wage.

6   A backward-bending supply of labour curve occurs when the income effect dominates the substitution effect.

Capital Markets

7   If the price of a unit of capital exceeds the present value of its marginal revenue product, a profit-maximizing firm should buy it.

8   If a household's current income is low compared with its expected future income, it will save very little.

9 The supply curve of capital is always highly elastic.

Natural Resource Markets

10 Natural resources can only be used once and cannot be replaced.

11 The market supply of a particular piece of land is perfectly elastic.

12 The Hotelling Principle states that the price of hotel stocks is expected to rise at a rate equal to the interest rate.

Income, Economic Rent, and Opportunity Cost

13 Economic rent is not the same thing as the rent you pay for an apartment.

14 If the supply of a factor of production is perfectly inelastic, its entire income is opportunity cost.

15 If Lloyd Robertson would be willing to read the news for $100,000 per year, and he is paid $2,100,000 per year to do so, he is earning economic rent of $2,000,000.

Multiple-Choice

Prices and Incomes in Competitive Factor Markets

1 Factor prices are wages for labour, rent for land,
a normal profit for capital, and interest for money.
b dividends for capital, and interest for money.
c interest for capital, and normal profit for entrepreneurship.
d interest for capital, and economic profit for entrepreneurship.
e economic profit for capital, and normal profit for entrepreneurship.

2 The supply of a factor of production is very elastic. An increase in demand for that factor results in a
a large increase in quantity supplied and small increase in price.
b small increase in quantity supplied and large increase in price.
c large increase in supply and small increase in price.
d small increase in supply and large increase in price.
e small increase in supply and small increase in price.

Labour Markets

3 An example of derived demand is the demand for
a sweaters derived by an economics student.
b sweaters produced by labour and capital.
c labour used in the production of sweaters.
d sweater brushes.
e none of the above.

4 A profit-maximizing firm will continue to hire units of a factor of production until the
a marginal cost of the factor equals its marginal product.
b marginal cost of the factor equals its average revenue product.
c average cost of the factor equals its marginal revenue product.
d marginal cost of the factor equals its marginal revenue product.
e factor's marginal revenue product equals zero.

5 A firm's marginal revenue product of labour curve is also its
a marginal cost curve for labour.
b labour demand curve.
c labour supply curve.
d output supply curve.
e average revenue curve.

6 If the price of its output falls, a perfectly competitive firm will employ
a less labour, causing the wage to fall.
b less labour, causing the marginal product of labour to rise.
c less labour, causing the marginal product of labour to fall.
d more labour, causing the marginal product of labour to rise.
e more labour, causing the marginal product of labour to fall.

7   A technological change that increases the marginal product of labour will shift the labour

a   demand curve leftward.
b   demand curve rightward.
c   supply curve leftward.
d   supply curve rightward.
e   supply and demand curves rightward.

8   The larger the proportion of total cost coming from labour, *ceteris paribus*, the

a   more elastic the demand for labour.
b   less elastic the demand for labour.
c   more elastic the supply of labour.
d   less elastic the supply of labour.
e   lower the demand for labour.

9   If the wage rate increases, the *substitution* effect will give a household an incentive to

a   raise its reservation wage.
b   increase leisure and decrease work.
c   increase work and decrease leisure.
d   increase both work and leisure.
e   decrease both work and leisure.

10   If the wage rate increases, the *income* effect will give a household an incentive to

a   raise its reservation wage.
b   increase leisure and decrease work.
c   increase work and decrease leisure.
d   increase both work and leisure.
e   decrease both work and leisure.

11   As the wage rate rises, a household will have a backward-bending labour supply curve if

a   the income effect reinforces the substitution effect.
b   the wage rate rises above the reservation wage.
c   the substitution effect dominates the income effect.
d   the income effect dominates the substitution effect.
e   leisure is an inferior good.

12   The labour supply curve facing the individual firm in a perfectly competitive labour market is

a   upward-sloping.
b   backward-bending.
c   first upward-sloping and then backward-bending as the wage increases.
d   vertical.
e   horizontal.

13   If the desire for leisure increased, the wage rate would

a   rise and employment would fall.
b   rise and employment would rise.
c   fall and employment would fall.
d   fall and employment would rise.
e   fall and employment may rise or fall.

Capital Markets

14   If the annual rate of interest is 10 percent, what is the present value of $100 received one year from now?

a $90.00
b $90.91
c $95.45
d $100.00
e $110.00

15   If the present value of $500 received one year from now is $463, what is the annual interest rate?

a   5 percent
b   8 percent
c   10 percent
d   20.8 percent
e   37 percent

16   The higher the rate of interest, the

a   higher the net present value of an investment.
b   lower the present value of the flow of marginal revenue products of an investment.
c   greater the quantity of capital demanded.
d   greater the marginal revenue product of capital.
e   lower the marginal revenue product of capital.

17   Firms will invest as long as net present value

a   exceeds the rate of interest.
b   equals the rate of interest.
c   is less than the rate of interest.
d   is positive.
e   is zero.

18   In the short run, a firm faces a supply of capital that is

a   elastic.
b   inelastic.
c   perfectly elastic.
d   perfectly inelastic.
e   backward bending.

19 The supply curve of capital shifts *rightward* if there is a(n)

a increase in the proportion of young households in the population.
b increase in the interest rate.
c decrease in the interest rate.
d increase in average household income.
e increase in the marginal revenue product of capital.

Natural Resource Markets

20 Which of the following is a nonrenewable natural resource?

a coal
b land
c water
d trees
e none of the above

21 If the market for a nonrenewable natural resource is currently in equilibrium, the price of the resource

a is equal to the marginal revenue product of the resource.
b is expected to rise at a rate equal to the interest rate.
c is expected to fall at a rate equal to the interest rate.
d will actually rise at a rate equal to the interest rate.
e will actually fall at a rate equal to the interest rate.

Income, Economic Rent, and Opportunity Cost

22 Economic rent is the

a price paid for the use of a hectare of land.
b price paid for the use of a unit of capital.
c income required to induce a given quantity of a factor of production to be supplied.
d income received above the amount required to induce a given quantity of a factor of production to be supplied.
e opportunity cost of a factor of production.

23 Consider the supply schedule of a factor of production given in Table 14.1. If 4 units are supplied at a price of $8 per unit, what is the opportunity cost of the factor of production?

a $8
b $12
c $20
d $32
e none of the above

TABLE **14.1**

Price of Factor ($)	Quantity of Factor Supplied
2	1
4	2
6	3
8	4
10	5

24 Consider the supply schedule of a factor of production given in Table 14.1. If 4 units of the factor are supplied at a price of $8 per unit, what is the economic rent?

a $8
b $12
c $20
d $32
e none of the above

25 The income of a factor of production in relatively inelastic supply will consist of

a opportunity cost only.
b economic rent only.
c more opportunity cost than economic rent.
d more economic rent than opportunity cost.
e equal amounts of opportunity cost and economic rent.

Short Answer Problems

1 Table 14.2 gives the total and marginal product schedules for a firm that sells its output and buys labour in competitive markets. Initially the price at which the firm can sell any level of output is $5 per unit and the wage rate at which it can purchase any quantity of labour is $15 per unit.

TABLE **14.2**

Quantity Labour (L)	Output (Q)	Marginal Product (MP$_L$)	P = $5		P = $3	
			Total Revenue (TR)	Marginal Revenue Product (MRP$_L$)	Total Revenue (TR)	Marginal Revenue Product (MRP$_L$)
0	0					
		... 12				
1	12					
		... 10				
2	22					
		... 8				
3	30					
		... 6				
4	36					
		... 4				
5	40					
		... 2				
6	42					

a Complete the first two blank columns in Table 14.2 by computing the *TR* and *MRP$_L$* corresponding to a price of output = $5.

b The marginal revenue product of labour (*MRP$_L$*) can be computed by either of the following formulas:

$$MRP_L = \Delta TR/\Delta L$$
$$MRP_L = MR \times MP_L$$

where ΔTR = the change in total revenue, ΔL = the change in labour, MR = marginal revenue, and MP_L = marginal product of labour. Show that these two formulas are equivalent for the case when the quantity of labour changes from 1 to 2 units.

c If the firm maximizes profit, what quantity of labour will it employ? How much output will it produce?

d If total fixed cost is $125, what is the amount of profit?

e What is its profit if the firm hires one more unit of labour than the profit-maximizing quantity? one less unit of labour than the profit-maximizing quantity?

f Draw a graph of the firm's demand for labour and the supply of labour to the firm and illustrate the profit-maximizing labour decision.

2 Now, suppose that the market demand for the output of the firm in Short Answer Problem **1** decreases, causing the price of output to decrease to $3 per unit. The total and marginal product schedules remain unchanged.

a Complete the last two blank columns in Table 14.2 by computing the *TR* and *MRP$_L$* corresponding to price of output = $3.

b If the wage remains at $15 per unit of labour, what is the profit-maximizing quantity of labour that the firm will hire? How much output will it produce?

c Total fixed cost continues to be $125. What is the amount of profit?

d Will the firm shut down in the short run? Explain.

e Draw a new graph of the firm's demand for labour and supply of labour and illustrate the new profit-maximizing labour decision.

3 The price of output for the firm in Short Answer Problem **2** remains at $3, but the wage now rises to $21 per unit of labour. The total and marginal product schedules remain unchanged.

a What happens to the demand curve for labour (the *MRP* of labour curve)?

b Under these circumstances, what is the profit-maximizing quantity of labour that the firm will employ? How much output will it produce?

c Total fixed cost continues to be $125. What is the amount of profit?

d Draw a graph of the firm's demand for labour and supply of labour and illustrate the new profit-maximizing labour decision.

ⓔ ⓒ 4 A perfectly competitive firm in long-run equilibrium produces flubits using only two factors of production—labour and capital. Each factor is sold in a perfectly competitive factor market. Labour costs $30 per unit and capital costs $50 per unit.

a Assuming the firm has hired the profit-maximizing quantity of capital in part **b** of this question, the marginal revenue product of labour curve is

$$MRP_L = 110 - 8/5 \ Q_L$$

where MRP_L is the marginal revenue product of labour and Q_L is the quantity (in units) of labour employed. How many units of labour does the firm employ?

b Assuming the firm has hired the profit-maximizing quantity of labour in part **a** of this question, the marginal revenue product of capital curve is

$$MRP_K = 125 - 75/40 \ Q_K$$

where MRP_K is the marginal revenue product of capital and Q_K is the quantity (in units) of capital employed. How many units of capital does the firm employ?

c The price of a flubit is $10.
  i How many flubits is the firm producing? [*Hint:* Remember that the firm is in long-run equilibrium]
  ii What is the marginal (physical) product of the 25th unit of labour hired?

ct 5 Using substitution and income effects, can you predict the effect on a household's quantity of labour supplied if the wage rate *decreases*? Explain.

ct 6 Why isn't the factor price for capital the price of the specific pieces of capital equipment that the firm buys?

ct 7 Larry's Lawn Care is considering the purchase of additional lawn mowers. These lawn mowers have a life of two years and cost $120 each. Marginal revenue products for each year are given in Table 14.3.

TABLE **14.3**

Number of Lawn Mowers	MRP in First Year	MRP in Second Year	NPV (r = 0.05)	NPV (r = 0.10)	NPV (r = 0.15)
1st	100	80			
2nd	80	64			
3rd	72	62			

a Complete Table 14.3 by computing net present values (*NPV*) if the interest rate is 5 percent (*r* = 0.05), 10 percent (*r* = 0.10), or 15 percent (*r* = 0.15).
b How many lawn mowers will Larry's Lawn Care purchase if the interest rate is 15 percent? 10 percent? 5 percent?
c Construct an approximate lawn mower demand curve for Larry's Lawn Care by graphically representing the three points identified in part **b** and drawing a curve through them.

8 Why does the quantity of capital demanded increase when the interest rate falls?

ct 9 *The Globe and Mail* reported that prices for hockey tickets for the Toronto Maple Leafs were the highest in the NHL. Are the prices of Toronto Maple Leafs tickets high because player salaries are high, or are player's salaries high because ticket prices are high? Explain.

10 Table 14.4 gives the market labour demand and supply schedules.

TABLE **14.4**

Wage Rate (dollars per hour)	Quantity of Labour Supplied (hours)	Quantity of Labour Demanded (hours)
0	0	240
1	20	200
2	40	160
3	60	120
4	80	80
5	100	40
6	120	0

a What is the equilibrium wage rate and the quantity of labour employed?
b What is the total amount of income received by labour in this market?
c Represent the market graphically. Identify the equilibrium wage and quantity of labour.
d Based on your graph from part **c**, how much of labour income is opportunity cost? How much is economic rent?
e Now suppose that the demand for labour increases by 60 hours at each wage rate.
  i What are the new equilibrium wage rate and quantity of labour?
  ii What is the new total amount of labour income?
  iii How much of this income is opportunity cost? How much is economic rent?

ANSWERS

True/False and Explain

1 F Normal profit. Economic profit is residual income to firm's owners, who may include the entrepreneur. (316)
2 F True if $\eta_D > 1$, false if $\eta_D < 1$. (316)
3 F Marginal revenue product curve is demand for labour curve. (319)
4 F Labour demand more elastic when product demand more elastic also. (322)
5 T Reservation wage minimum needed for labour supply. (322–323)
6 T Upward-sloping when substitution effect > income effect. (322–323)
7 F Reverse is true. (326–328)
8 T Saving for greater future consumption not sensible if expect to be better off in future anyway. (329–331)

ⓒ **9** **F** True for long run, false for short run. (330)
10 **F** False for renewable natural resources (true for nonrenewable). (331)
11 **F** Perfectly inelastic. (331–332)
12 **F** Definition applies to price of natural resources. (332–333)
13 **T** Economic rent is income received by any factor owner above amount required to induce supply. (334)
14 **F** Entire income is economic rent. (334–335)
15 **T** Excess of income over opportunity cost necessary to induce supply. (334–335)

Multiple-Choice

1 **c** Definition. (316)
2 **a** Movement up along flat supply curve. (316)
3 **c** Factor used as input to production. (317)
4 **d** Where supply curve of factor to firm (MC) intersects demand curve for factor (MRP). (318–320)
5 **b** Shows quantity labour demanded at each wage rate. (318–319)
ⓒ **6** **b** Labour demand curve shifts leftward. Labour supply curve horizontal to individual firm. Because of diminishing MP, *decreased* quantity L causes *rise* in MP. (320–321)
7 **b** At a given wage, firm will demand increased quantity of labour because MRP now higher (since MP has increased). (320–321)
8 **a** Higher wage causes greater increase in both total costs and product P, leading to greater decrease in both sales and labour hired. (322)
9 **c** Substitute work for leisure because opportunity cost leisure increases. (322–324)
10 **b** Consume more normal goods, including leisure, so working less. (322–324)
11 **d** Income and substitution effects work in opposite directions, so tendency to increase leisure and decrease work dominates. (322–324)
12 **e** Because firm small part of labour market, can buy as much labour as desired at market wage. (322–324)
13 **a** Labour supply would shift leftward. (322–324)
14 **b** $PV = \$100/(1 + 0.1)$. (326–327)
15 **b** $\$463 = \$500/(1 + r)$. Solve for r. (326–327)
16 **b** Reverse **a**, **c** true. r does not directly affect MRP capital, only its present value. (326–328)
17 **d** Present value exceeds purchase price of capital. **a**, **b**, and **c** are nonsense comparisons. (328)

18 **b** In any year, supply of savings small relative to existing capital stock, so even large changes in interest rate (and current savings rate) bring only small change in quantity capital supplied. (330)
19 **d** **a** causes leftward shift. **b** and **c** cause movement along supply curve. **e** shifts demand curve. (329–331)
20 **a** Others are renewable natural resources. (331)
21 **b** This is Hotelling Principle. For current equilibrium, *actual* future prices may or may not follow *expected* prices.(332–333)
22 **d** Definition. Price paid for land use is rent. (334–335)
23 **c** $\$2 + \$4 + \$6 + \$8$. (334–335)
ⓒ **24** **b** Total income ($\$32 = 4 \times \$8$) minus opportunity cost ($\$20$). (334–335)
25 **d** Draw graph with steep supply and compare areas above and below supply curve at equilibrium PF and QF. (334–335)

Short Answer Problems

1 a The completed columns for TR and MRP_L corresponding to a price of output = $5 are shown in Table 14.2 Solution. The values for TR come from multiplying the quantity of output by the price of output ($5). The values for MRP_L between any two quantities of labour come from dividing the change in TR by the change in quantity of labour, or by multiplying MR ($5) by MP_L.

TABLE **14.2** SOLUTION

Quantity Labour (L)	Output (Q)	Marginal Product (MP_L)	P = $5 Total Revenue (TR)	P = $5 Marginal Revenue Product (MRP_L)	P = $3 Total Revenue (TR)	P = $3 Marginal Revenue Product (MRP_L)
0	0		0		0	
		... 12		... 60		... 36
1	12		60		36	
		... 10		... 50		... 30
2	22		110		66	
		... 8		... 40		... 24
3	30		150		90	
		... 6		... 30		... 18
4	36		180		108	
		... 4		... 20		... 12
5	40		200		120	
		... 2		... 10		... 6
6	42		210		126	

b From part **a**, the formula $MRP_L = \Delta TR/\Delta L$ yields a marginal revenue product of labour of 50 when the quantity of labour changes from 1 to 2 units. To confirm that the second formula ($MRP_L = MR \times MP_L$) gives the same answer when the quantity of labour changes from 1 to 2 units, substitute in the values for MR ($5, the price of an additional unit of output) and MP_L (10 units of output). This yields the same marginal revenue product of labour as above; 5×10 units = $50.

c The firm maximizes profit by employing labour up to the point where the MRP of labour is equal to the marginal cost of labour (the wage rate). That point occurs at 5 units of labour. The MRP of moving from 4 to 5 units of labour is 20, and the MRP of moving from 5 to 6 units of labour is 10. In moving from 4 to 5 units, $MRP > MC$ so the firm should hire the 5th unit. But in moving from 5 to 6 units, $MRP < MC$, so the firm should not hire the 6th unit. Thus by interpolation, the MRP at exactly 5 units of labour is 15 (midway between 20 and 10). So when 5 units of labour are employed, the MRP of labour is equal to the wage rate ($15). Given that 5 units of labour are employed, the profit-maximizing output will be 40 units (from Table 14.2 Solution).

d To calculate profit, first calculate total revenue and then subtract total cost. Total revenue is $200 (40 units of output × $5 per unit) and total cost is also $200—sum of total variable (labour) cost of $75 (5 units of labour × $15 per unit) and total fixed cost of $125. Thus profit is zero.

e If the firm employs one more unit of labour (6 units), total revenue will be $210 (42 units of output × the $5 price). Total cost will be the $125 fixed cost plus $90 in total variable cost (6 units of labour × $15 wage rate) or $215. Thus profit will be negative $5 ($5 loss).

   If the firm employs one less unit of labour (4 units), total revenue will be $180 (36 units of output × the $5 price). Total cost will be the $125 fixed cost plus $60 in total variable cost (4 units of labour × $15 wage rate) or $185. Thus profit will be negative $5 ($5 loss).

f The graph of the firm's labour employment decision appears in Figure 14.2. The demand for labour is the firm's MRP_L curve which is labelled D_0 (D_1 will be discussed in Short Answer Problem **2**).

   Notice that the values for MRP are plotted midway between the corresponding quantities of labour. For example, MRP of 60 is plotted midway between 0 and 1 units of labour.

Since the firm purchases labour in a perfectly competitive labour market, the supply of labour to the firm is perfectly elastic at the market wage rate. The labour supply curve is labelled $W = 15. The profit-maximizing decision is at the intersection of these curves, and corresponds to a wage rate of $15 and a quantity of labour employed of 5 units.

FIGURE **14.2**

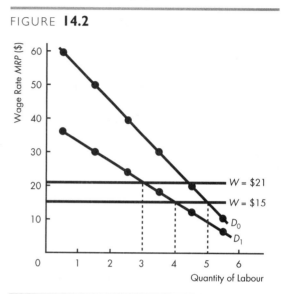

2 a The completed columns for TR and MRP_L corresponding to price of output = $3 are shown in Table 14.2 Solution. The values for TR come from multiplying the quantity of output by the price of output ($3). The values for MRP_L between any two quantities of labour come from dividing the change in TR by the change in quantity of labour, or by multiplying MR ($3) by MP_L.

b If the wage rate remains at $15, the profit-maximizing quantity of labour will fall to 4 units since MRP_L equals the wage rate at 4 units of labour. The MRP of moving from 3 to 4 units of labour is 18, and the MRP of moving from 4 to 5 units of labour is 12. Thus, by interpolation, the MRP at exactly 4 units of labour is 15 (midway between 18 and 12). Given that 4 units of labour are employed, the profit-maximizing output will be 36 units (from Table 14.2 Solution).

c Profit equals total revenue minus total cost. Total revenue is $108 (36 units of output × $3 per unit) and total cost is $185—sum of total variable (labour) cost of $60 (4 units of labour × $15 per unit) and total fixed cost of $125. Thus profit is –$77, or a loss of $77.

d The firm will not shut down since total revenue ($108) is enough to cover total variable cost

($60) and part of fixed cost. If the firm shut down, it would lose $125 of fixed cost rather than just $77.

e The graph of the firm's labour employment decision appears in Figure 14.2. The new demand for labour is given by the firm's new MRP_L curve, labelled D_1. The supply of labour has not changed; it continues to be horizontal at $15, the competitive market wage. The new profit-maximizing decision is at the intersection of these curves and corresponds to a wage rate of $15 and quantity of labour employed of 4 units.

3 a Since marginal revenue and the marginal product of labour are unaffected by a change in the wage rate, the demand curve for labour (the MRP of labour) will remain at D_1.

b If the wage rate rises to $21, the profit-maximizing quantity of labour will fall to 3 units since MRP_L equals the wage rate at 3 units of labour. Given that 3 units of labour are employed, the profit-maximizing output will be 30 units (from Table 14.2 Solution).

c Profit equals total revenue minus total cost. Total revenue is $90 (30 units of output × $3 per unit) and total cost is $188—sum of total variable (labour) cost of $63 (3 units of labour × $21 per unit) and total fixed cost of $125. Thus profit is –$98, or a loss of $98.

d See Figure 14.2. The relevant labour demand curve continues to be D_1, but the labour supply curve reflects the rise in the competitive wage rate; it is now horizontal at a wage rate of $21 (labelled $W = $21). The new profit-maximizing decision is at the intersection of these curves and corresponds to a wage rate of $21 and a quantity of labour employed of 3 units.

ⓔ ⓒⓣ **4 a** By assuming that the firm has already hired its capital, we know (in principle) fixed costs and can calculate the profit-maximizing quantity of the variable factor of production (labour) by setting the MRP_L equal to the wage rate ($30).

$$30 = 110 - 8/5\ Q_L$$
$$8/5\ Q_L = 80$$
$$Q_L = 50$$

b By assuming that the firm has already hired its labour, we can treat labour as the fixed cost and treat capital as the variable factor of production. Calculate the profit-maximizing quantity of the capital by setting the MRP_K equal to the cost of a unit of capital ($50).

$$50 = 125 - 75/40\ Q_K$$
$$75/40\ Q_K = 75$$
$$Q_K = 40$$

c i The fact that the firm is in long-run equilibrium provides the key to calculating the quantity of flubits produced. In long-run equilibrium, the firm earns zero economic profit, so total revenue is exactly equal to total cost.

We can calculate total cost by adding the costs of the (only) two factors of production. Labour cost is 50 units of labour × $30 per unit or $1,500. Capital cost is 40 units of capital × $50 per unit or $2,000. Total cost is therefore $3,500.

Total revenue must also be equal to $3,500. Since total revenue (TR) is just the price of output (P) times quantity sold (Q), we can calculate Q by substituting in the values we have for TR ($3,500) and P ($10).

$$TR = P \times Q$$
$$\$3,500 = \$10 \times Q$$
$$Q = 350$$

ii To calculate the marginal product of the 25th unit of labour, we begin by calculating the marginal *revenue* product of the 25th unit of labour. Substituting $Q_L = 25$ into the equation for MRP_L yields

$$MRP_L = 110 - 8/5\ (25)$$
$$= 110 - 40$$
$$= 70$$

One definition of the marginal revenue product of labour is the marginal product of labour (MP_L) times marginal revenue (MR) or $MRP_L = MP_L \times MR$. Rearranging to solve for MP_L yields

$$MP_L = MRP_L / MR$$

Substituting in the values for the marginal revenue product of the 25th unit of labour (70) and for MR (the price of output $10) yields

$$MP_L = 70/10$$
$$MP_L = 7$$

ⓒⓣ **5** No, we can't predict the effect on the household's quantity of labour supplied. If the wage rate decreases, the opportunity cost of leisure decreases and households will have a tendency to shift from work to leisure (the substitution effect), thereby *decreasing* the quantity of labour supplied. The lower wage also decreases the household's income and thus causes the household to reduce its demand for leisure and other normal goods (the income effect) thereby *increasing* the quantity of labour supplied.

Since the substitution and income effects work in opposite directions, the net effect on the quantity of labour supplied will depend on which effect dominates. If the household is on the upward-sloping part of its labour supply curve, the decrease in wages will decrease the quantity of labour supplied. But if the household is on the backward-bending part of its labour supply curve, the decrease in wages will increase the quantity of labour supplied.

ct **6** In general, factor prices represent the opportunity cost to the firm of *using* that factor. Wages are the cost of using labour and rent is the cost of using land. The cost of using a piece of capital equipment bought by the firm is the interest that must be paid (explicitly or implicitly) on the funds tied up in the purchase of the equipment. Capital equipment lasts for a long period of time. The cost of capital during any one period is not the purchase price of the equipment; it is the cost of the funds tied up in the equipment over the period.

ct **7 a** Completed Table 14.3 appears here as Table 14.3 Solution. *NPV* is calculated as the present value of the stream of marginal revenue products resulting from an investment, minus the cost of the investment. For lawn mowers with a two-year life, the *NPV* is calculated using the following equation:

$$NPV = \frac{MRP_1}{1 + r} + \frac{MRP_2}{(1 + r)^2} - P_L$$

In this equation, MRP_1 and MRP_2 are the marginal revenue products in the first and second years respectively, and P_L is the price of a lawn mower. The values of MRP_1 and MRP_2 are given in Table 14.3 for the first, second, and third lawn mowers and P_L is given as $120. The values for *NPV* given in Table 14.3 Solution are obtained by substituting these values into the above equation and evaluating the expression for alternative values of *r*, the interest rate.

TABLE **14.3** SOLUTION

Number of Lawn Mowers	MRP in First Year	MRP in Second Year	NPV (r = 0.05)	NPV (r = 0.10)	NPV (r = 0.15)
1st	100	80	47.80	37.02	27.45
2nd	80	64	14.24	5.62	–2.04
3rd	72	62	4.81	–3.31	–10.51

b If the interest rate is 15 percent, only one additional lawn mower will be purchased since the second lawn mower has negative net present value. If the interest rate is 10 percent, two lawn mowers will be purchased, and if the interest rate is 5 percent, three lawn mowers will be purchased.

c The approximate lawn mower demand curve is illustrated in Figure 14.3. The curve indicates that, at an interest rate of 15 percent, one lawn mower will be demanded. At an interest rate of 10 percent, two lawn mowers will be demanded and, at an interest rate of 5 percent, three lawn mowers will be demanded.

FIGURE **14.3**

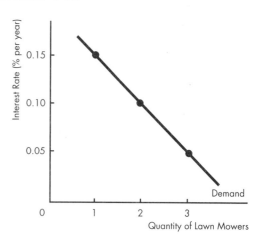

8 Profit-maximizing firms will demand capital as long as the present value of the stream of future marginal revenue product from the new capital exceeds the purchase price of the new capital; in other words, as long as its net present value is positive. Since a lower interest rate implies that the present value of any given future stream of marginal revenue product will be larger, the net present value will be positive for a *larger* number of additional capital goods and thus more capital will be purchased. Therefore the quantity of capital demanded increases as the interest rate falls.

ct **9** Player salaries are high because ticket prices are high. The full explanation combines demand and supply. The demand for NHL-calibre players is high, because team owners know that fans will pay high prices to see those players. The supply of talented NHL-calibre players is relatively inelastic, so, combined with the high demand, much of the income earned by NHL players is economic rent rather than payment for opportunity cost.

It is only because owners (who care about profits) know that they can charge high ticket prices (and television fees), that they compete against each other in bidding up the salaries of relatively scarce star players. That bidding for resources in relatively inelastic supply produces economic rents for the players.

10 a The equilibrium wage rate is $4 per hour and the quantity of labour employed is 80 hours.

  b Total income is $320 ($4 per hour × 80 hours).

  c The supply and demand curves for labour are given in Figure 14.4. The supply of labour is given by S_0 and the initial demand for labour is represented by D_0. The equilibrium occurs at the intersection of these two curves. You can see that the equilibrium wage is $4 per hour and the quantity of labour is 80 hours.

  d Given that the labour supply curve is a 45° line starting at the origin, half of income is opportunity cost (the area below the supply curve) and the other half is economic rent (the area above the supply curve). Since income is $320, each of these is $160.

  e i Each entry in the last column of Table 14.4 will increase by 60 units. The new equilibrium wage rate is $5 per hour and the new equilibrium quantity of labour is 100 hours. The new labour demand curve appears in Figure 14.4 as D_1.

  ii Total income is now $500 ($5 per hour × 100 hours).

  iii Once again the slope of the labour supply curve (which has not changed) implies that income is split evenly between opportunity cost and economic rent. Each will be equal to $250.

FIGURE **14.4**

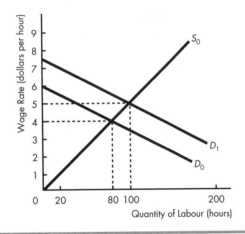

Appendix: Labour Unions

Market Power in the Labour Market

Labour unions are organized groups of workers.

◆ *Closed shop*—firms can hire only union members.
Union shop—firm can hire non-union members, but they must eventually join the union.
Open shop—employees not required to join union or pay union dues.

◆ **Rand Formula** requires all workers in a closed shop to pay union dues whether or not they join the union.

◆ *Collective bargaining*—process of negotiation between unions and employers.

Labour unions' objectives are increasing compensation, improving working conditions, and expanding job opportunities. Methods of achieving objectives include

◆ restricting supply of labour.

◆ increasing demand for union labour or making demand more inelastic by

- encouraging import restrictions.
- supporting minimum wage laws and immigration restrictions.
- increasing product demand.
- increasing marginal product of union members.

Monopsony—market structure in which there is a single buyer. Firm that is only employer in town is monopsonist in the labour market.

◆ To hire more labour, monopsonist must pay a higher wage. Marginal cost of labour curve (*MCL*) for monopsonist is upward-sloping and above and steeper than the market supply curve of labour.

◆ Profit-maximizing rule for monopsonist is to hire quantity of labour where *MCL* curve intersects *MRP* curve, then offer lowest wage for which labour will work (on supply curve).

◆ For monopsonist, employment and wage are lower than for competitive labour market. More elastic supply of labour means less *opportunity* for monopsony to cut wages, to reduce employment, or to increase economic profit.

Adding union to a monopsony labour market can create **bilateral monopoly**, in which wage determined by relative bargaining strength firm and union.

◆ Highest possible wage where *MCL* intersects *MRP*. Lowest possible wage is pure monopsony wage.

◆ Adding a minimum wage law to a monopsony labour market can actually increase wages and increase employment.

1 This appendix introduces the concept of a monopsonist, a firm that is the only buyer in a market, such as labour. The monopsonist faces an upward-sloping supply curve of labour. As a result, its marginal cost of labour curve (*MCL*) is different from the labour supply curve.

There is a close parallel between (a) the relationship between the labour supply curve and the *MCL* curve for the monopsonist and (b) the already familiar relationship (Chapter 12) between the demand curve and the marginal revenue curve (*MR*) for the monopolist. Both sets of relationships stem from the assumption of a single price for labour or output in the relevant market.

The monopolist, as the only seller in an output market, faces a downward-sloping demand curve. The marginal revenue from the sale of an additional unit of output is *less* than the selling price because the monopolist must *lower* the price on all previous units as well. Thus the *MR* curve lies *below* the demand curve for the single-price monopolist.

For the monopsonist in a labour market, the marginal cost of hiring an additional unit of labour is *higher* than the wage because the monopsonist must *raise* the wage on all previous units of labour as well. Thus the *MCL* curve lies *above* the supply of labour curve for the monopsonist.

Another way to think about this parallel is that the supply/*MCL* relationship (and the resulting wage versus *MRP* relationship) is just the demand/*MR* relationship (and the resulting price versus *MC* relationship) flipped upside-down.

SELF-TEST

True/False and Explain

Market Power in the Labour Market

1 A closed shop refers to a firm that is not operating because its workers are on strike.

2 Unions support minimum wage laws in part because they increase the cost of low-skill labour, a substitute for skilled union labour.

3 Most union workers earn about 40 percent more than nonunion workers in comparable jobs.

Monopsony

4 For a firm that is a monopsonist in the labour market, the supply curve of labour is the marginal cost of labour curve.

5 The more elastic labour supply is, the less opportunity a monopsonist has to make an economic profit.

6 In a monopsonistic labour market, the introduction of a minimum wage that is above the current wage will raise the wage but reduce employment.

7 In the case of bilateral monopoly in a labour market, the wage depends on the bargaining strength of the two traders.

Multiple-Choice

Market Power in the Labour Market

1 The Rand formula made
a collective bargaining compulsory.
b it compulsory for all workers in a partially unionized plant to pay union dues.
c binding arbitration legal.
d strikes and lockouts illegal under some circumstances.
e none of the above.

2 A working arrangement in which all workers must be members of the union before they can be hired by the firm is called a(n)
a open shop.
b closed shop.
c union shop.
d craft shop.
e professional association.

3 Which of the following would unions be *least* likely to support?
a increasing the legal minimum wage
b restricting immigration
c encouraging imports
d increasing demand for the goods their workers produce
e increasing the marginal product of union labour

4 A union is formed to restrict labour supply in a previously perfectly competitive labour market. If the union succeeds in raising the wage,

a employment will fall.
b employment will rise.
c employment will not change.
d the total wage bill will rise.
e the total wage bill will fall.

Monopsony

5 Figure A14.1 illustrates a monopsonist in the labour market (*MCL* = marginal cost of labour). The profit-maximizing wage rate and quantity of labour hired will be

a $4 per hour and 800 hours of labour.
b $4 per hour and 400 hours of labour.
c $7 per hour and 600 hours of labour.
d $9 per hour and 400 hours of labour.
e none of the above.

FIGURE **A14.1**

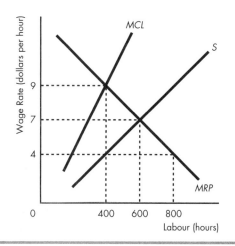

6 If the labour market illustrated in Figure A14.1 became competitive, the equilibrium wage rate and quantity of labour hired would be

a $4 per hour and 800 hours of labour.
b $4 per hour and 400 hours of labour.
c $7 per hour and 600 hours of labour.
d $9 per hour and 400 hours of labour.
e none of the above.

7 If a union forms to face the monopsonist in Figure A14.1, the situation is one of

a binding arbitration.
b derived demand.
c duopoly.
d collusive oligopoly.
e bilateral monopoly.

8 If a union and the monopsonist in Figure A14.1 agree to collective bargaining, the outcome will be an hourly wage

a of $7.
b between $4 and $7.
c between $4 and $9.
d between $7 and $9.
e of $9.

9 When compared with a competitive labour market with the same marginal revenue product and labour supply curves, a monopsonist labour market has a(n)

a lower wage and lower employment.
b lower wage and higher employment.
c higher wage and lower employment.
d higher wage and higher employment.
e indeterminate outcome.

10 If a strike or lockout occurs in a bilateral monopoly situation, it is usually because the

a demand for labour is relatively inelastic.
b demand for labour is relatively elastic.
c supply of labour is relatively inelastic.
d supply of labour is relatively elastic.
e union or firm has misjudged the bargaining situation.

11 For the monopsonist employer illustrated in Figure A14.2, the profit-maximizing wage rate and quantity of labour hired will be

a $9 per hour and 300 hours of labour.
b $8 per hour and 350 hours of labour.
c $8 per hour and 500 hours of labour.
d $7 per hour and 400 hours of labour.
e $6 per hour and 300 hours of labour.

FIGURE **A14.2**

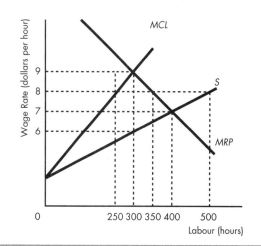

12 Suppose the government passes a minimum wage law that prohibits anyone from hiring labour at less than $8 per hour. In Figure A14.2, the marginal cost of labour (*MCL*) for the monopsonist

a is not affected.
b equals $8 only from 0 to 250 hours of labour.
c equals $8 only from 0 to 350 hours of labour.
d equals $8 only from 0 to 500 hours of labour.
e shifts up by a vertical distance of $8.

Short Answer Problems

1 Members of labour unions earn wages well above the minimum wage. Even so, why is it in the interest of a union to support increases in the legal minimum wage?

2 Initially we observe an industry facing a competitive labour market in which the supply of labour comes from two sources: domestic workers and foreign workers. All workers have similar skills. Also assume that the output of the industry competes with imported goods.

a In Figure A14.3, graphically represent the initial competitive labour market. Draw the labour demand and supply curves and identify the equilibrium wage rate and level of employment.

FIGURE **A14.3**

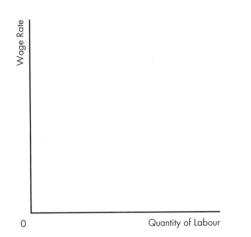

b Now suppose a union consisting of domestic workers is formed. Through its support a law is passed that prohibits firms from hiring foreign workers. What effect will this have on employment and the wage rate? Illustrate graphically using the graph in part **a**.

c Finally, the industry and union support the passage of a law that legally restricts imports that compete with industry output. Using the same graph, show the consequences for the wage rate and employment.

3 Pollutionless Paper is a pulp and paper mill that employs almost all of the labour in a small town in New Brunswick. The town's labour market, which approximates a monopsony, is illustrated in Figure A14.4, where *S* is the supply curve of labour, and *MRP* and *MCL* are Pollutionless Paper's marginal revenue product of labour and marginal cost of labour curves, respectively.

FIGURE **A14.4**

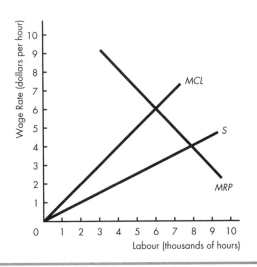

a If Pollutionless Paper is a profit-maximizing monopsonist, what wage rate will it pay and how much labour will it employ? What is the value of labour's *MRP* at this level of employment?

b If the town had a competitive labour market with the same *MRP* curve, what would the equilibrium wage rate and the level of employment be? Compare these outcomes with the monopsony outcomes in part **a**.

4 Consider the following alternatives for the labour market in Figure A14.4.

a Suppose the government imposes a minimum wage of $4 per hour. What wage rate will Pollutionless Paper pay and how much labour will it employ? Compare these outcomes with the monopsony outcomes in Short Answer Problem **3a**.

b Suppose there is no legal minimum wage, but the workers form a union. If the union tries to negotiate a higher wage rate while maintaining employment at the monopsony level, what is the maximum wage rate that Pollutionless Paper will be willing to pay? What is the minimum wage rate that the union will accept?

5 Consider the negotiations between Pollutionless Paper and the union in Short Answer Problem **4b**.

a What determines the wage rate that will actually be paid?

b If Pollutionless Paper and the union are equally strong and realize it, what will the wage rate likely be?

c If Pollutionless Paper and the union are equally strong, but the union mistakenly believes it is stronger, what is the likely outcome of negotiations?

d If Pollutionless Paper and the union are equally strong, but Pollutionless Paper mistakenly believes it is stronger, what is the likely outcome of negotiations?

ANSWERS

True/False and Explain

1 F Firm that can hire only union workers. (341)

2 T Increased price of substitute creates increased demand for union labour. (341–343)

3 F Union-nonunion wage differential in comparable jobs is 10 to 25 percent. (343–344)

4 F *MCL* curve is above supply curve of labour. (344–345)

ct **5 T** Greater η labour supply means smaller differences between *MCL* and wage. (344–345)

ct **6 F** Wages and employment both increase; true for competitive labour market. (344–346)

7 T See text discussion. (345–346)

Multiple-Choice

1 b See text discussion. (341)

2 b Definition. (341)

3 c Increasing imports substitutes for domestically produced goods, decreasing demand for domestic, union labour. (342–344)

4 a Leftward shift supply decreases employment. Impact on wage bill depends on elasticity of demand for labour. (342–343)

5 b *QL* where *MCL* intersects *MRP*. Firm pays lowest wage required for labour to supply that *QL* (on supply curve). (344–345)

6 c Where *S* intersects *MRP*. (344–345)

7 e Firm is only buyer of labour, union is only seller of labour. (345–346)

8 c Between minimum firm can achieve ($4) and maximum union can achieve ($9). (345–346)

9 a See Text Figure A14.3. (345–346)

10 e **a–d** may affect relative bargaining strength but do not cause strikes or lockouts. (345–346)

11 e *QL* where *MCL* intersects *MRP*. Firm pays lowest wage required for labour to supply that *QL* (on supply curve). (344–345)

ct **12 d** *MCL* horizontal at minimum wage until intersects *S*. Firm must then raise wage to get increased quantity supplied labour. (345–346)

Short Answer Problems

1 An increase in the minimum wage will increase the cost of hiring low-skill labour, which will tend to increase demand for high-skill labour which is a substitute.

2 a The initial competitive demand for labour and supply of labour curves are D_C and S_C respectively, in Figure A14.3 Solution (ignore the other curves for now). The equilibrium wage rate is W_C and the competitive equilibrium level of employment is QL_C.

FIGURE **A14.3** SOLUTION

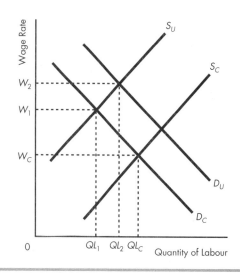

b If a law is passed prohibiting firms from hiring foreign workers, the labour supply curve (now under a union) will shift leftward (to S_U in Figure A14.3 Solution). This will raise the wage rate to W_1 and decrease the quantity of labour employed to QL_1.

c Restrictions on imports will increase demand for the product produced in the industry and thus increase the derived demand (*MRP*) of labour in the industry. In Figure A14.3 Solution this is a shift from D_C to D_U. The result is a further increase in the wage rate to W_2 and increase in employment to QL_2. Whether the quantity of labour hired now exceeds the initial competitive quantity depends on the magnitude of the shift in the labour demand curve.

3 **a** A profit-maximizing monopsonist will hire additional labour up to the point where *MCL* equals *MRP*. Referring to Figure A14.4, this means that Pollutionless Paper will hire 6,000 hours of labour. To hire that quantity of labour, the labour supply curve *S* tells us that the wage rate must be $3 per hour. This is less than the $6 per hour marginal revenue product of labour.

b In a competitive labour market, the wage rate would be $4 per hour and 8,000 hours of labour would be employed. The competitive labour market results in a higher wage rate and a higher level of employment than the monopsony outcomes.

4 **a** If the government establishes a minimum wage at $4 per hour, the marginal cost of labour to Pollutionless Paper becomes constant at $4 per hour (up to 8,000 hours of labour). Thus equating the marginal cost of labour and the marginal revenue product of labour leads to a wage rate of $4 and 8,000 hours of labour

employed. The addition of a minimum wage to the monopsony labour market results in a higher wage rate and a higher level of employment.

b The maximum wage rate Pollutionless Paper is willing to pay for 6,000 hours of labour is $6 per hour (the *MRP* of that amount of labour). The minimum wage rate that the union will accept for 6,000 hours of labour is $3 per hour (the supply price of that amount of labour).

5 **a** The wage rate that will actually be paid as the outcome of bargaining depends on the relative bargaining strengths of the firm and union. Bargaining strength depends on costs (from lockouts and strikes) that each side can inflict on the other if there is a failure to agree.

b Pollutionless Paper and the union will split the difference between $6 and $3 and agree on a wage rate of $4.50.

c If the union holds out for more than a $4.50 wage rate, Pollutionless Paper will likely lockout the workers.

d If Pollutionless Paper holds out for less than a $4.50 wage rate, the union will likely strike. When lockouts or strikes occur, it is usually because one side has misjudged the situation.

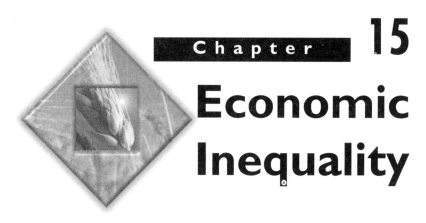

Chapter 15

Economic Inequality

Measuring Economic Inequality

Measures of economic inequality look at

- **market income**—wages, interest, rent and profit before paying income taxes.
- **total income**—market income + (cash payments to households by governments).
- **after-tax income**—total income – (tax payments by households to governments).

Distribution of after-tax household income in Canada in 1998 was positively skewed.

- *mode* (most common) income was $10,000–$14,999
- *median* income was $33,227
- *mean* income was $39,943

There is a great deal of inequality of income and wealth. The degree of inequality is measured by the Lorenz curve.

- The **Lorenz curve** for income (wealth) graphs the cumulative percentage of income (wealth) against the cumulative percentage of households.

- The 45° "line of equality" represents a hypothetically equal distribution of income (wealth).

- The farther the Lorenz curve from the line of equality, the more unequal the distribution.

- The distribution of wealth in Canada is even more unequal than the distribution of income.

Wealth is the *stock* of assets owned by an individual. Wealth includes *human capital* as well as financial assets. *Income* is the *flow* of earning received by an individual from his or her stock of wealth.

- Data used to construct wealth distributions do not include human capital and therefore overstate wealth inequalities.

- Distributions of annual income and wealth are more unequal than distributions of lifetime income and wealth.

- Even correcting for these factors, there are significant inequalities in distributions of income and wealth in Canada, with the income shares of the richest 20 percent of households rising since 1980.

Poverty exists when families cannot buy adequate food, shelter, and clothing.

- Poverty is a relative concept and is measured by the **low-income cutoff** (families spending 54.7 percent or more of their income on food, shelter, and clothing). In Canada, 14 percent of families have incomes below the low-income cutoff.

- Most important factors influencing poverty are source of income, household type, and sex and age of household head.

The Sources of Economic Inequality

Income inequality arises from differences in human capital, or skill differentials in labour markets.

- Demand—high-skilled labour has higher marginal revenue product (*MRP*) and demand curve than low-skilled labour. Vertical distance between demand curves = *MRP* of skill.

- Supply—high-skilled labour has more *human capital*, which is costly to acquire. Supply curve high-skilled labour is above supply curve low-skilled labour by vertical distance = compensation for cost of acquiring skill.

◆ Wages (equilibrium of demand and supply) higher for high-skilled labour.

Wage differentials between men and women can be partly explained by

- human capital differences—differences in schooling (mostly eliminated), work experience, and job interruptions (lessened recently).
- discrimination—results in lower wages and employment for those discriminated against.
- differences in degree of specialization—because of social conventions men have specialized in earning income, while women have divided their time between earning income and household activities (bearing and raising children and household chores).

Wealth inequality increases between generations because

- assets can be inherited but debt cannot.
- of *assortative mating* (marrying within one's own socioeconomic class).

Income Redistribution

Income is redistributed by governments through income taxes, income maintenance programs, and subsidized services.

◆ **Income taxes** can be

- **progressive**—marginal tax rate increases with higher-level income.
- **regressive**—marginal tax rate decreases with higher-level income.
- **proportional** (*flat-rate tax*)—marginal tax rate constant at all levels income.

◆ Income maintenance programs include social security, employment insurance, and welfare.

◆ Subsidized services (provision of goods and services below cost) such as education and health care services reduce inequality.

Income distribution *after taxes and benefits* redistributes income to the very poor considerably, reducing the inequality of the *market income* distribution.

Income redistribution creates a **big tradeoff** between equity and efficiency. Redistribution uses scarce resources and weakens incentives, so a more equally shared pie results in a smaller pie.

1 Statistics used to construct Lorenz curves do not always give an accurate picture of inequality. You should understand why a distribution of wealth that excludes the value of human capital gives a distorted picture relative to the distribution of income. You should also understand why the distribution of annual (static) income gives a distorted picture relative to the distribution of lifetime (dynamic) income. Finally, you should understand why the distribution of before-tax, before-benefits income gives a distorted picture relative to the distribution of after-tax, after-benefits income.

SELF-TEST

True/False and Explain

Measuring Economic Inequality

1 The farther is the Lorenz curve from the 45° line, the more equal the distribution of income.

2 In Canada, measured income is more equally distributed than measured wealth.

3 Wealth distribution data exclude human capital and thus *overstate* inequality.

4 Income is a stock of earnings.

5 The lifetime distribution of income is more equal than the annual distribution of income.

The Sources of Economic Inequality

6 Human capital is capital equipment constructed by human workers.

7 The demand for low-skilled workers is to the left of the demand for high-skilled workers.

8 The vertical distance between the labour supply curves for high-skilled and low-skilled workers is the marginal revenue product of the skill.

9 The larger the marginal revenue product of skill and the more costly it is to acquire, the smaller the wage differential between high-skilled and low-skilled workers.

10 Assortative mating makes the distribution of wealth more unequal over time.

Income Redistribution

11 Under a proportional income tax, total taxes rise as income rises.

12 Under a progressive income tax, the marginal tax rate does not change as income rises.

13 A regressive income tax redistributes income from the rich to the poor.

14 Compared with the market distribution of income, government taxes and benefits reduce the inequality of income distribution.

15 In general, reducing income inequality by redistributing income from the rich to the poor will lead to greater production of goods and services.

Multiple-Choice

Measuring Economic Inequality

1 Which diagram is used by economists to illustrate the distribution of income or wealth?

a Lorenz curve
b normal bell-shaped distribution
c Sophia Loren curve
d low-income cutoff curve
e none of the above

2 In Figure 15.1, the richest 20 percent of all households receive what share of all income?

a 10 percent
b 20 percent
c 30 percent
d 40 percent
e none of the above

FIGURE **15.1**

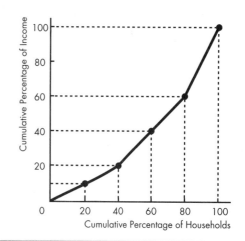

3 In Figure 15.1, the poorest 20 percent of all households receive what share of income?

a 10 percent
b 20 percent
c 30 percent
d 40 percent
e none of the above

4 In Figure 15.1, the middle 20 percent of all households receive what share of income?

a 10 percent
b 20 percent
c 30 percent
d 40 percent
e none of the above

5 The curve in Figure 15.1 represents the

a line of fairness.
b line of equality.
c learning curve.
d wage differential curve.
e Lorenz curve.

6 Consider the Lorenz curves in Figure 15.2. Which Lorenz curve corresponds to the greatest income *inequality*?

a *A*
b *B*
c *C*
d *D*
e impossible to tell without additional information

FIGURE **15.2**

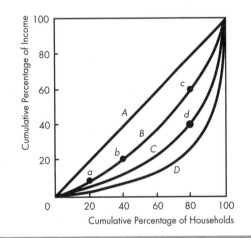

7 In Figure 15.2, what is curve *A* (a straight line) called?

a market distribution line
b line of equality
c fairness line
d low-income cutoff line
e none of the above

8 Which point in Figure 15.2 indicates that the richest 20 percent of households earn 40 percent of the income?

a *a*
b *b*
c *c*
d *d*
e none of the above

9 The distribution of *annual income*

a understates inequality because it does not take into account the household's stage in its life cycle.
b understates inequality because it does not take into account the distribution of human capital.
c overstates inequality because it does not take into account the household's stage in its life cycle.
d overstates inequality because it does not take into account the distribution of human capital.
e is an accurate measure of inequality.

10 The distribution of *wealth*

a understates inequality because it does not take into account the household's stage in its life cycle.
b understates inequality because it does not take into account the distribution of human capital.
c overstates inequality because it does not take into account the household's stage in its life cycle.
d overstates inequality because it does not take into account the distribution of human capital.
e is an accurate measure of inequality.

11 Which distribution would show the most *equality*?

a stock of financial wealth
b stock of human capital
c annual income
d lifetime income
e all show same degree of equality

12 Wealth differs from income in that

a income is a stock, wealth is a flow.
b wealth is derived from income.
c income is what you earn, wealth is what you own.
d income is what you own, wealth is what you earn.
e wealth is preferable to income.

13 The most important factor influencing the incidence of low income is

a source of income.
b sex of household head.
c age of household head.
d education of household head.
e geographical region.

The Sources of Economic Inequality

14 Refer to Figure 15.3. For any given quantity of labour employed,

a the elasticity of demand is lower for high-skilled workers than for low-skilled workers.
b wages will be lower for high-skilled workers than low-skilled workers.
c wages will be higher for high-skilled workers than low-skilled workers.
d the vertical distance between the curves is the compensation for the cost of acquiring skill.
e the vertical distance between the curves is the present value of human capital.

FIGURE **15.3**

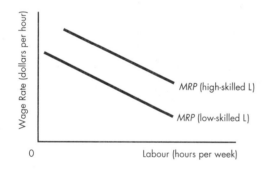

15 The vertical distance between the two supply curves in Figure 15.4

a is the compensation for the cost of acquiring skill.
b is the *MRP* of skill.
c is the result of discrimination against low-skilled workers.
d is the result of subsidies for high-skilled workers.
e will disappear if there is free entry in the high-skilled market.

FIGURE **15.4**

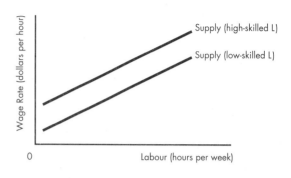

16 Refer only to the information in Figure 15.4. For any given wage rate, more hours of

a low-skilled labour will be demanded than high-skilled labour.
b high-skilled labour will be demanded than low-skilled labour.
c low-skilled labour will be supplied than high-skilled labour.
d high-skilled labour will be supplied than low-skilled labour.
e low-skilled labour will be supplied if the *MRP* of skill increases.

17 Which of the following is *not* a reason why the wage of high-skilled workers exceeds the wage of low-skilled workers?

a The market for high-skilled workers is more competitive than the market for low-skilled workers.
b The marginal revenue product of high-skilled workers is greater than that of low-skilled workers.
c The cost of training high-skilled workers is greater than the cost of training low-skilled workers.
d High-skilled workers have acquired more human capital than low-skilled workers.
e The demand curve for high-skilled workers lies to the right of the demand curve for low-skilled workers.

18 Wage differentials between males and females can be explained by

a educational differences.
b human capital differences.
c degree of specialization differences.
d discrimination.
e all of the above.

19 If discrimination takes the form of restricting a group's access to education and training, the effect on this group of workers will be to shift their

a *MRP* curve rightward and increase the wage.
b *MRP* curve leftward and decrease the wage.
c *MRP* curve rightward and decrease the wage.
d supply of labour curve up and decrease the wage.
e supply of labour curve down and decrease the wage.

20 Assortative mating means that

a poor men tend to marry rich women.
b rich men tend to marry rich women.
c rich men tend to marry poor women.
d same-sex marriages occur because "like attracts like."
e same-sex marriages are prohibited.

Income Redistribution

21 If the marginal tax rate increases as income increases, the income tax is defined as

a progressive.
b proportional.
c negative.
d regressive.
e excessive.

22 In Table 15.1, which tax plan is proportional?

a Plan *A*
b Plan *B*
c Plan *C*
d Plan *D*
e impossible to calculate without additional information

TABLE **15.1**

Current Market Income	Tax Payment Plan *A*	Tax Payment Plan *B*	Tax Payment Plan *C*	Tax Payment Plan *D*
0	0	0	0	200
1,000	100	100	200	200
2,000	200	400	200	200
4,000	400	1,600	200	200

23 In Table 15.1, which tax plan is progressive?

a Plan *A*
b Plan *B*
c Plan *C*
d Plan *D*
e impossible to calculate without additional information

24 Which of the following *reduces* the inequality of income or wealth relative to the market distribution?

a government payments to the poor
b a regressive income tax
c large inheritances
d assortative mating
e all of the above

25 Redistribution of income from the rich to the poor will lead to a reduction in total output. This is known as the

a market distribution.
b Robin Hood principle.
c inheritance principle.
d big tradeoff.
e capitalist dilemma.

Short Answer Problems

1 Consider the worlds of Vulcan and Klingon. The Vulcan Lorenz curve is given in Figure 15.5, and the Klingon income distribution data are given in Table 15.2.

FIGURE **15.5**

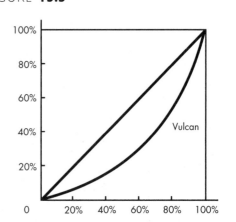

TABLE **15.2**   KLINGON INCOME
                 DISTRIBUTION

Household Income Rank	Percentage Share Total Income
Lowest 20%	10%
Second 20%	10%
Middle 20%	20%
Fourth 20%	30%
Highest 20%	30%

a Label the axes of Figure 15.5 and explain what the diagonal line represents.

b Using the data from Table 15.2, draw the Klingon Lorenz curve on Figure 15.5.

2 Chapter 5 describes two approaches to ideas about fairness—fair results and fair rules.

a Describe briefly each idea about fairness.

b Using only the information in Short Answer Problem **1**, which idea(s) about fairness can be used to judge Vulcan and Klingon? Which world is more fair according to the idea(s)?

3 Explain the differences and connections between the concepts of wealth and income.

4 Table 15.3 gives information regarding the distribution of income in an economy which generates $100 billion in total annual income.

TABLE **15.3**   TOTAL HOUSEHOLD INCOME

Percentage of Households	Total Income (billions of $)	Income Share (%)	Cumulative Percentage of Households	Cumulative Percentage of Income
Poorest 20%	5			
Second 20%	10			
Third 20%	15			
Fourth 20%	20			
Richest 20%	50			

a Complete the last three columns in Table 15.3.

b Draw the Lorenz curve for income in this economy and label it *A*.

5 Now suppose a progressive income tax is levied on the economy. The distribution of after-tax income is given in Table 15.4. We assume none of the revenue is redistributed to families in the economy. Note that total after-tax income is $71 billion.

TABLE **15.4**   AFTER-TAX HOUSEHOLD INCOME

Percentage of Households	After-Tax Income (billions of $)	After-Tax Income Share (%)	Cumulative Percentage of Households	Cumulative Percentage of After-Tax Income
Poorest 20%	5			
Second 20%	9			
Third 20%	12			
Fourth 20%	15			
Richest 20%	30			

a Complete Table 15.4.

b Draw the Lorenz curve for after-tax income on the same graph you used for Short Answer Problem **4b** and label it *B*.

c What effect has the progressive income tax had on inequality?

d What is the size of the "big tradeoff" in this case?

6 Finally, suppose that, in addition, the government redistributes all revenue so that the after-benefits (after-tax) income distribution is given in Table 15.5. For example, those in the poorest group receive benefits income of $10 billion so their after-benefits income becomes $15 billion.

TABLE **15.5**   AFTER-BENEFITS HOUSEHOLD
                 INCOME

Percentage of Households	After-Benefits Income Share (billions of $)	After-Benefits Income Share (%)	Cumulative Percentage of Households	Cumulative Percentage of After-Benefits Income
Poorest 20%	15			
Second 20%	16			
Third 20%	18			
Fourth 20%	20			
Richest 20%	31			

a Complete Table 15.5.

b Draw the Lorenz curve for after-benefits income on the same graph you used for Short Answer Problems **4b** and **5b** and label it *C*.

c What effect has income redistribution through benefits payments had on inequality?

7 Consider an economy consisting of 100 individuals who are identical in every way. Each lives to be 80 years of age and no older. Between birth and the age of 20 years they earn zero income; between the ages of 21 and 35 each earns an annual income of $30,000; between the ages of 36 and 50 each earns an annual income of $40,000; between the ages of 51 and 65 each receives an annual income of $60,000; and between the ages of 66 and 80 each receives an annual income of $20,000. At any given time there are 20 individuals in each of the five age groups. For simplicity, assume there are no bequests. This information is summarized in Table 15.6.

TABLE **15.6**   LIFETIME INCOME PATTERNS

Age Group (years)	Number in Age Group	Individual Annual Income ($)
0–20	20	0
21–35	20	30,000
36–50	20	40,000
51–65	20	60,000
66–80	20	20,000

a Draw the Lorenz curve for lifetime income in this economy and label it *A*.
b Draw the Lorenz curve for annual income in this economy and label it *B*.
c Which of these is a better measure of the inequality among individuals in this economy? Why?

8 Figure 15.6 shows the demand and supply of low-skilled and high-skilled labour. D_L and D_H are the demand curves for low-skilled and high-skilled workers respectively, and S_L and S_H are the supply curves for low-skilled and high-skilled workers respectively.

FIGURE **15.6**

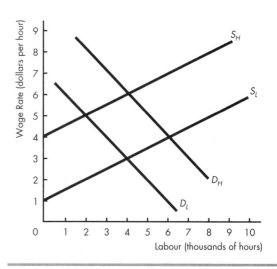

a What is the *MRP* of skill if 5,000 hours of each kind of labour are hired?
b What amount of extra compensation per hour is required to induce the acquisition of skill at the same level of hiring?
c What are the equilibrium wage and quantity of labour in the market for high-skilled labour?
d What are the equilibrium wage and quantity of labour in the market for low-skilled labour?

9 Suppose you are working for the Minister of Post-Secondary Education. She is constantly told by student groups that because university and college students have some of the lowest incomes in society, the government should make additional large income transfers to students. The Minister, who knows her economics, asks you to write up the economic arguments *against* the student groups' position. What are they? Can you think of any economic arguments in favour of society supporting larger transfers to students?

10 Why is there a "big tradeoff" between equity and efficiency?

ANSWERS

True/False and Explain

1 **F** More unequal. (349–351)
2 **T** Wealth distribution more unequal. (348–350)
3 **T** Human capital wealth is more equally distributed than financial wealth. (350–351)

4 F Income is a flow of earning from a stock of wealth. (350)
5 T Differences in life cyle stages make annual income more unequal. (351)
6 F Human capital is people's accumulated skills and knowledge. (354–356)
7 T Because the marginal revenue product of low-skilled workers is lower than that of high-skilled workers. (354–355)
8 F Vertical distance = compensation for cost of acquiring skill. (354–355)
9 F The larger the wage differential. (354–356)
10 T Wealthy people seek wealthy partners, increasing concentration of wealth. (358)
11 T Marginal tax rate constant, but total taxes increase. (359)
12 F Marginal tax rate rises with higher incomes. (359)
13 F From poor to rich. (359)
14 T See Text Figure 15.10. (360)
15 F Lower production due to the big tradeoff. (361)

Multiple-Choice

1 a Definition. (349–351)
2 d 100 percent – 60 percent of cumulative income. (348–351)
3 a 10 percent – 0 percent of cumulative income. (348–351)
4 b 40 percent – 20 percent of cumulative income. (348–351)
5 e Definition. (348–351)
6 d Curve farthest from 45° line. (348–351)
7 b Definition. (349–350)
8 c Moving from 80 percent to 100 percent of households (richest 20 percent) moves income from 60 percent to 100 percent of total (40 percent). (348–351)
ct **9 c** Human capital affects distribution of wealth, not income. (350–351)
ct **10 d** Life cycle biases distribution income, not wealth. (350–351)
11 d Lifetime income more equally distributed than annual income or than any wealth distribution in a given year. (350–351)
12 c Wealth is a stock, income a flow derived from wealth. (350)
13 a Longest vertical line in Text Figure 15.6. (352–353)
ct **14 c** Reverse **a** true. **d** applies to supply. **e** nonsense. (354–356)
15 a See Text Figure 15.7(b). (354–356)
16 c No demand curves on figure. Increased *MRP* skill shifts demand, not supply. (354–356)

17 a Wage differences not due to competitive differences. In any case, greater competitiveness would cause fall in high-skilled wages. (354–356)
18 e All can contribute to differentials. (355–358)
ct **19 e** Education and training would increase human capital and shift supply curve labour up. (354–358)
20 b Marriage within a socioeconomic class. (358)
21 a Definition. (359)
22 a Taxes are always 10 percent of income. (359)
23 b With higher income, tax rate increases from 0 percent, to 10 percent, to 20 percent, to 40 percent. (359)
24 a Others increase inequality. (359–361)
25 d See text discussion. (361)

Short Answer Problems

1 a See Figure 15.5 Solution. The diagonal line represents hypothetical income equality.
  b See Figure 15.5 Solution.

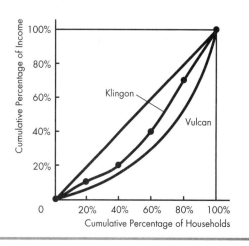

FIGURE **15.5** SOLUTION

2 a According to the fair results idea, there should be equality of incomes. According to the fair rules idea, there should be equality of opportunity.
  b Since we have information only on income outcomes and not on the processes or opportunities leading to those incomes, only the fair results idea can be used to judge Vulcan and Klingon. Since the Klingon Lorenz curve is closer to the line of equality, the Klingon world is more fair according to the fair results idea.

3 Wealth is the *stock* of assets owned by an individual, while income is the *flow* of earnings received by an individual. The concepts are connected in that an individual's income is the earnings that flow from her stock of wealth.

4 a Table 15.3 is completed as Table 15.3 Solution. The income share for each group of families is the total income of that group as a percent of total income in the economy ($100 billion). The cumulative percentage of income (last column) is obtained by adding the percentage income share of the group (from the third column) to the total percentage income share of all poorer groups of families.

TABLE **15.3** SOLUTION
TOTAL HOUSEHOLD INCOME

Percentage of Households	Total Income (billions of $)	Income Share (%)	Cumulative Percentage of Households	Cumulative Percentage of Income
Poorest 20%	5	5	20	5
Second 20%	10	10	40	15
Third 20%	15	15	60	30
Fourth 20%	20	20	80	50
Richest 20%	50	50	100	100

b The curve labelled *A* in Figure 15.7 is the Lorenz curve for total family income. This simply plots the values in the last two columns of Table 15.3 Solution.

FIGURE **15.7**

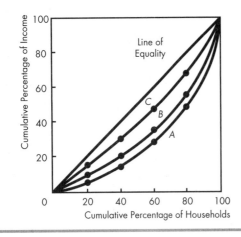

5 a Table 15.4 is completed as Table 15.4 Solution.

TABLE **15.4** SOLUTION
AFTER-TAX HOUSEHOLD INCOME

Percentage of Households	After-Tax Income (billions of $)	After-Tax Income Share (%)	Cumulative Percentage of Households	Cumulative Percentage of After-Tax Income
Poorest 20%	5	7	20	7
Second 20%	9	13	40	20
Third 20%	12	17	60	37
Fourth 20%	15	21	80	58
Richest 20%	30	42	100	100

b The curve labelled *B* in Figure 15.7 is the Lorenz curve for after-tax household income.

c The progressive income tax has reduced inequality by taking a larger percentage of income from higher income groups.

d The "big tradeoff" is the fact that a more equally shared pie results in a smaller pie. While the after-tax distribution is now more equal, total income has been reduced from $100 billion to $71 billion. The $29 billion loss is the cost of the big tradeoff, due to the costs of administering the redistribution program and the deadweight loss from weakened work incentives.

6 a Table 15.5 is completed as Table 15.5 Solution.

TABLE **15.5** SOLUTION
AFTER-BENEFITS HOUSEHOLD INCOME

Percentage of Households	After-Benefits Income Share (billions of $)	After-Benefits Income Share (%)	Cumulative Percentage of Households	Cumulative Percentage of After-Benefits Income
Poorest 20%	15	15	20	15
Second 20%	16	16	40	31
Third 20%	18	18	60	49
Fourth 20%	20	20	80	69
Richest 20%	31	31	100	100

b The curve labelled *C* in Figure 15.7 is the Lorenz curve for after-tax, after-benefits household income.

c Income redistribution through benefits payments has reduced inequality.

7 a Since each individual in the economy earns exactly the same lifetime income, the Lorenz curve for lifetime income coincides with the line of equality and is labelled *A* in Figure 15.8.

FIGURE 15.8

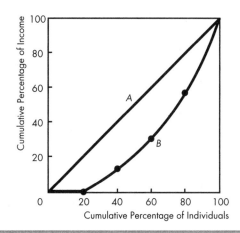

b The Lorenz curve for annual income is labelled *B* in Figure 15.8. It reflects that the poorest 20 percent of individuals, those aged 0–20 years, receive 0 percent of the annual income; the second-poorest 20 percent, 60–80 years, 13 percent; the third-poorest 20 percent, 21–35 years, 20 percent; the fourth-poorest 20 percent, 36–50 years, 27 percent; and the richest 20 percent, 51–65 years, 40 percent.

c The distribution of lifetime income is a better measure of the degree of inequality. In this imaginary economy all individuals are identical (equal), a fact reflected in equal lifetime incomes. The only reason annual income distribution in this economy is not equal is because individuals are at different stages of identical life cycles.

8 a The *MRP* of skill is the difference between the *MRP* of high-skilled versus low-skilled labour; the vertical distance between the demand curves for high-skilled and low-skilled labour. In Figure 15.6, the *MRP* of skill is $3 per hour when 5,000 hours of each kind of labour are employed.

b Since labour supply curves give the minimum compensation workers are willing to accept in return for supplying a given quantity of labour, the extra compensation for skill is the vertical distance between the supply curves of high-skilled and low-skilled labour. At 5,000 hours of employment for both kinds of labour, this is $3 per hour.

c In equilibrium in the market for high-skilled labour, the wage rate will be $6 per hour and employment will be 4,000 hours of labour. This occurs at the intersection of the D_H and S_H curves.

d In equilibrium in the market for low-skilled labour, the wage rate will be $3 per hour and employment will be 4,000 hours of labour. This occurs at the intersection of the D_L and S_L curves.

9 The request by students for more income transfers is related to many of the issues in this chapter. The first issue is the distribution of annual income versus lifetime income. Post-secondary students are relatively poor at this stage of their career, but can expect to earn far-above-average incomes for the rest of their lives. So on the basis of lifetime income (which is a more comprehensive measure than annual income), there is no good argument for transfers.

The reason behind these higher lifetime incomes is that post-secondary education is an investment in human capital for the individual paying the tuition. As an investment, the payoff comes later in life in the form of higher average incomes. Statistics show that the annual real rates of return (after allowing for inflation) for an investment in post-secondary education are 5 to 10 percent, a better return than almost any other investment you are likely to make (See text page 355).

Post-secondary students who will receive these high rates of return already receive transfers from government in the form of subsidized education. While tuition fees have been rising sharply over the past decade, in 2003 the average annual undergraduate university tuition in Ontario of $4,500 covered only a small fraction of the more than $18,000 it cost the government to supply that education.

Thus, from the material in this chapter there are many arguments *against* further income transfers to post-secondary students.

The most important argument in favour of further government support (subsidizes and transfers) for post-secondary education is that there are benefits to society as a whole from having a well-educated workforce and citizenry that are greater than the benefits to the individual receiving the education. This argument is developed in Chapters 16 and 18 in the discussion of public goods and positive externalities.

10   If greater equity means increasing the equality of income, it can only be achieved by income redistribution; the income of some must be taxed in order to make transfer payments to others. However, there are incentive effects that reduce the total amount of income available to be distributed.

If productive activities such as work are taxed, there will be a tendency to reduce time spent in those activities. Furthermore, any redistribution program would require resources to administer it and thus leave fewer resources for other productive activities. Thus we arrive at the insight: A more equally shared pie results in a smaller pie.

Part 5 Wrap Up

Understanding Factor Markets

PROBLEM

FIGURE **P5.1**   LABOUR MARKETS FOR PROGRAMMERS

(a) Left-Handed

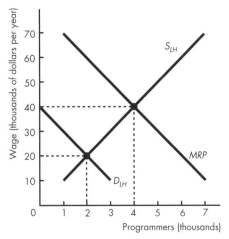

(b) Right-Handed

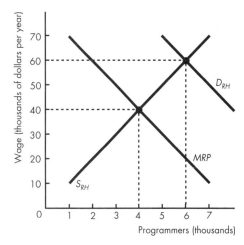

Suppose the computer software industry uses only two inputs—programmers (labour) and computers (capital). All programmers, whether left-handed or right-handed, have computer science degrees, are equally skilled and productive, and have the marginal revenue product (*MRP*) curve in Figure P5.1(a) and (b).

Software firms (run mostly by right-handers) discriminate against left-handed programmers, believing (wrongly) that left-handers are less productive than right-handers. Figure P5.1(a) shows the supply curve of left-handed programmers and firms' demand curve for left-handed programmers.

Software firms also discriminate in favour of right-handed programmers, believing (wrongly) that right-handers are more productive than left-handers. Figure P5.1(b) shows the supply curve of right-handed programmers and firms' demand curve for right-handed programmers.

a   What is the relationship between the wage and the marginal revenue product for left-handed programmers? for right-handed programmers?

b   Explain the competitive forces that would tend to eliminate this form of discrimination, even without government legislation.

c   If owners of firms are so strongly prejudiced against left-handers that they are willing to accept lower profits rather than employ left-handers, will competitive forces eliminate this discrimination?

d   The government introduces pay equity legislation, designed to equalize wages between left-handers and right-handers. The legislation includes an educational program to inform firms of the true and equal productivity of all programmers, regardless of their "handedness." If the program is successful, what will be the wage of programmers? the employment of left-handed programmers? the employment of right-handed programmers?

e   With equalized programmer wages, what is now the relationship between the wage and the marginal revenue product for left-handed programmers? for right-handed programmers? What other meaning does *pay equity* have besides paying different groups equal wages?

f   As a result of the pay equity legislation, what has happened to the *average* wage of programmers?

g   As a result of the pay equity legislation, what has happened to the average wage of *left-handed* programmers? Explain the impact on the decisions of left-handers to invest in human capital.

MIDTERM EXAMINATION

You should allocate 26 minutes for this examination (13 questions, 2 minutes per question). For each question, choose the one *best* answer.

l   Refer to Figure P5.2. If demand for a factor of production increases from D_0 to D_1, the *change* in the opportunity cost of using the resource is

a   area *ihfc*.
b   area *jcfk*.
c   area *0fk*.
d   area *0fh*.
e   none of the above

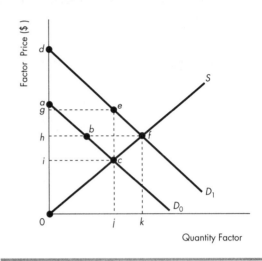

2   Household savings are larger when either current income is

a   low compared with expected future income or interest rates are high.
b   low compared with expected future income or interest rates are low.
c   high compared with expected future income or interest rates are high.
d   high compared with expected future income or interest rates are low.
e   above or below the reservation wage.

3   Wealth is the

a   large flow of income earned by the rich.
b   large stock of income available to the rich.
c   stock of assets owned by an individual.
d   flow of assets to an individual from labour.
e   flow of assets to an individual from capital.

4   Refer to Figure P5.3. For any given wage,

a   the elasticity of demand for high-skilled workers is greater than the elasticity of demand for low-skilled workers.
b   more high-skilled workers will be hired than low-skilled workers.
c   more low-skilled workers will be hired than high-skilled workers.
d   the horizontal distance between the curves is the compensation for the cost of acquiring skill.
e   the horizontal distance between the curves is the *MRP* of skill.

FIGURE **P5.3**

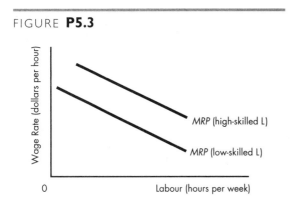

5 Consider the Lorenz curves in Figure P5.4. Which point indicates that the richest 20 percent of families earn 60 percent of the income?

a *a*
b *b*
c *c*
d *d*
e none of the above

FIGURE **P5.4**

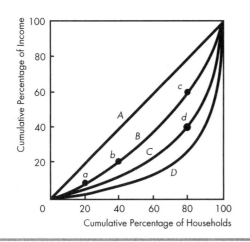

6 The demand curve for a factor of production will shift leftward as a result of a(n)

a decrease in the price of the factor.
b increase in the price of the factor.
c increase in technology.
d increase in the price of output.
e decrease in the price of output.

7 A profit-maximizing firm hires labour in a competitive labour market. If the marginal revenue product of labour is greater than the wage, the firm should

a increase the wage rate.
b decrease the wage rate.
c increase the quantity of labour it hires.
d decrease the quantity of labour it hires.
e diminish the marginal revenue product of labour.

8 For a monopsonist facing an upward-sloping supply curve of labour (*S*), the marginal cost of labour (*MCL*) curve

a intersects the *MRP* curve of labour at the equilibrium wage.
b is below and parallel to *S*.
c is identical to *S*.
d is above and parallel to *S*.
e is none of the above.

9 Suppose the government passes a minimum wage law that prohibits anyone from hiring labour at less than $8 per hour. In Figure P5.5, the monopsonist will hire

a 250 hours of labour.
b 300 hours of labour.
c 350 hours of labour.
d 400 hours of labour.
e 500 hours of labour.

FIGURE **P5.5**

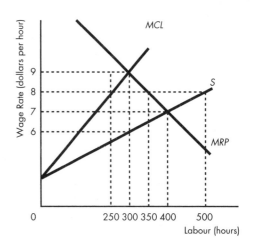

10 If the marginal tax rate decreases as income increases, the income tax is defined as

a progressive.
b proportional.
c negative.
d regressive.
e redistributive.

11 Which of the following is *not* part of an individual's stock of wealth?

a stock of assets
b flow of earnings
c human capital
d physical assets
e financial assets

12 If the net present value of a new machine is positive,

a the firm should not buy the machine.
b the present value of the machine's stream of marginal revenue products is greater than the purchase price.
c the present value of the machine's stream of marginal revenue products is less than the purchase price.
d **a** and **b**.
e **a** and **c**.

13 "A more equally shared pie results in a smaller pie" is the

a big tradeoff.
b Robin Hood principle.
c assortative mating principle.
d capitalist dilemma.
e socialist creed.

ANSWERS

Problem

a For the 2,000 left-handed programmers employed, the wage ($20,000 per year) is much less than the marginal revenue product of $60,000 per year. For the 6,000 right-handed programmers employed, the wage ($60,000 per year) is much more than the marginal revenue product of $20,000 per year.

b A nondiscriminating firm could earn higher profits by employing more left-handed programmers as long as their marginal revenue product exceeds the wage. Similarly, profits will increase by employing fewer right-handed programmers as long as their wage exceeds their

marginal revenue product. The competitive outcome would be a wage of $40,000 per year for every programmer, and employment of 4,000 left-handed and 4,000 right-handed programmers.

c No. Firms can continue to discriminate if they "pay" for the discrimination in the form of lower profits.

d A successful education program alters firms' beliefs about left-handed and right-handed programmers and moves the demand curves to the true *MRP* curves. The outcome will be the same as the competitive outcome—a wage of $40,000 per year for every programmer, and employment of 4,000 left-handed and 4,000 right-handed programmers.

e The wage is equal to the marginal revenue product for every programmer. Pay equity also means each labourer being paid an amount *equal* to the value of his or her marginal revenue product.

f Before legislation, the average yearly wage of programmers was a weighted (by employment) average of the wages of left-handers and right-handers.

$$\frac{(\$20,000 \times 2,000) + (\$60,000 \times 6,000)}{8,000} = \$50,000$$

After legislation, the average yearly wage has fallen to $40,000.

g The average yearly wage of left-handed programmers has increased from $20,000 to $40,000. This creates an incentive for more left-handers to invest in the necessary human capital (computer science degrees) to become programmers, increasing the quantity supplied of left-handed programmers.

Midterm Examination

1 b Increase in area under supply curve. (334–335)
2 c See text discussion. (329–330)
3 c Wealth is a stock of assets. Assets are stocks, not flows (**d**, **e**); income is a flow, not stock (**b**). (350–351)
4 b Reverse **a** true. **d** true for vertical distance between supply curves. **e** true for vertical distance between demand curves. (354–356)
5 d Moving from 80 percent to 100 percent of families (richest 20 percent) moves income from 40 percent to 100 percent of total (60 percent). (349–351)
6 e Lower price of output lowers *MR* which in turn lowers *MRP*. **a** and **b** move along curve, **c** and **d** shift curve rightward. (321)

7 **c** Hiring more labour increases profit since *MRP* > *MC*. **a** and **b** wrong because competitive firm can't change wage; **e** nonsense. (319–320)

ⓔ **8** **e** *MCL* is above, but not parallel to *S*. *MCL* intersects *S* at equilibrium *QL*, not wage. (344–346)

ⓔ **9** **c** New *MCL* flat at $8 until it hits *S* curve yielding *QL* where new *MCL* intersects *MRP*. (344–346)

10 **d** Definition. (359)

11 **b** Flow of earnings is *income* from individual's stock of wealth. (350–351)

12 **b** Definition. Firm should buy machine. (327–329)

13 **a** Tradeoff between equity and efficiency arises because redistribution uses scarce resources and weakens incentives. (361)

16
Public Goods and Taxes

KEY CONCEPTS

The Economic Theory of Government

Government economic activity attempts to correct

- **market failure**—failure of unregulated market to efficiently allocate resources. There are three cases:

  - **Public goods**—can be consumed simultaneously by everyone; no one can be excluded. Free-rider problem causes markets to produce less than the efficient quantity of public goods.
  - *Monopoly*—output restriction by monopolies and cartels and rent seeking prevent efficient allocation resources (Chapters 12, 17).
  - *Externalities*—external costs or benefits arising from economic activities that fall on people not participating in the transaction. Markets produce too many goods with negative externalities and too few goods with positive externalities (Chapter 18).

- economic inequality—an unregulated market economy produces an unequal distribution of income and wealth.

Public choice model analyses government as a political marketplace analogous to the economic marketplace. Actors are

- voters—consumers of political marketplace. Express their preferences by voting, lobbying, and campaign contributions.

- politicians—entrepreneurs in political marketplace. Objective is to get and stay elected. Votes to politicians are like economic profits to firms.

- bureaucrats—producers in political marketplace. Officials in government, hired by politicians. Objective is maximize budget of their department.

Political equilibrium—choices of voters, politicians, and bureaucrats are compatible, and no group can improve its position with a different choice.

Public Goods and the Free-Rider Problem

Pure public goods can be consumed simultaneously by everyone; no one can be excluded. They have two features:

- *Nonrival*—one person's consumption does not decrease amount available for another.

  - Opposite is *rival* good—one person's consumption decreases amount available for another (for example, a hot dog).

- *Nonexcludable*—no one can be excluded from consuming.

  - Opposite is *excludable* good—can exclude others from consuming (for example, cable television).

Public goods create **free riders** (someone who consumes without paying) and *free-rider problem*—no one has an incentive to pay for a public good.

- Efficient quantity of public good occurs where net benefit is maximized or where marginal benefit equals marginal cost of public good.

  - *Total benefit* is total $ value placed on public good.
  - *Net benefit* is total benefit – total cost.
  - *Marginal benefit* is increased total benefit from a unit increase in public good.
  - The economy's marginal benefit curve of a public good is the *vertical* sum of individual marginal benefit curves

- Private provision of a public good creates a free-rider problem and provides less than the efficient quantity of the good.

◆ Government provision can provide an efficient quantity of a public good, where politicians compete for votes of well-informed voters.

The quantity of government provision of a public good generally depends on political marketplace and actions of voters, politicians, and bureaucrats.

◆ Politicians follow **principle of minimum differentiation**—tendency for competitors to make themselves identical to appeal to maximum number voters/clients.

◆ Voters may be **rationally ignorant**—deciding *not* to acquire information because cost of acquisition > expected benefit. Then politicians, influenced by bureaucrats and special-interest lobbyists, may allow inefficient overprovision of a public good.

Types of Political Equilibrium:

◆ Public interest theory—predicts governments achieve efficiency because voters are fully informed.

◆ Public choice theory—predicts governments create inefficiency because voters are rationally ignorant.

Taxes

Government revenue comes from income taxes, social insurance taxes, sales taxes, property taxes, excise taxes.

Income taxes can be *progressive* (average tax rate rises with income), *proportional* (average tax rate constant), or *regressive* (average tax rate falls with income).

◆ **Average tax rate**—percentage of income paid in tax.

◆ **Marginal tax rate**—percentage of *additional dollar* of income paid in tax.

◆ Income tax shifts labour supply curve leftward—wages rise and employment decreases, creating deadweight loss. With progressive income tax, deadweight loss is larger for high-wage workers than for low-wage workers.

◆ Progressive income tax policy is prediction of *median voter* model—political parties pursue policies maximizing net benefit of median voter (who has low income).

• High-income voters prefer lower tax rates and fewer government benefits.
• Low-income voters prefer higher tax rates and greater benefits.

◆ Corporate profits tax is a tax on income from capital and economic profit. Decreases quantity of capital, decreasing productivity and labour income.

Social insurance taxes shift labour supply leftward (if paid by employees) or shift labour demand leftward (if paid by firms).

◆ Either way, outcome identical—wage rises and employment decreases, creating deadweight loss.

◆ Proportion of tax actually borne by employees and firm depends on elasticities of labour demand and labour supply, *not* on fractions stated in legislation.

GST and provincial sales taxes (discussed in Chapter 6) are regressive because lower income families pay a higher *percentage* of their income in sales taxes.

Property taxes finance **local public goods**—public goods consumed by local residents.

Excise tax is tax on sale of particular good.

◆ Tax on good shifts supply curve shifts leftward by vertical distance equal to amount of tax. Equilibrium *P* rises, equilibrium *Q* decreases, and deadweight loss is created.

◆ Size of deadweight loss depends on elasticity of demand. To minimize deadweight loss, governments place highest tax rates on goods with lowest elasticities of demand.

HELPFUL HINTS

I Economists judge the success of the market (or any other institution) in terms of efficiency. Efficiency means that the economy is producing all goods and services up to the point where marginal cost equals marginal benefit. At an efficient outcome, no one can be made better off without making someone else worse off.

When the market fails to achieve this "ideal" efficient outcome, we call it *market failure*. The market can fail by producing too little if the marginal benefit of the last unit exceeds the marginal cost. Or, the market can fail by producing too much if the marginal cost of the last unit exceeds the marginal benefit.

In this chapter (and in Chapters 17–18), we learn that governments can correct market failures, but can also create inefficiency. Since both markets and governments can fail, the relevant economic question in each case is: Which fails less?

2 All goods provided by the government are not necessarily public goods. A public good is defined by being *nonrival* and *nonexcludable*, not by whether or not it is publicly provided. For example, many communities provide swimming pools and residential garbage pickup. Neither of these is a pure public good despite the fact that each may be provided by the government. In other communities, the same services are provided by the private market.

3 The nonrival and nonexcludable properties of pure public goods imply that we obtain the marginal benefit curve for the economy as a whole differently than for private goods.

For a private good, to obtain the demand curve for the whole economy, we sum the individual marginal benefit (demand) curves *horizontally*. For example, at a price of $7, suppose Max demands 5 units of a private good, Lisa demands 5 units, and total demand is 10 units. Because the private goods are rival and excludable, the units Max consumes must be different from the units Lisa consumes, and therefore must be added together to get total market demand.

But for a public good, to obtain the economy's marginal benefit curve we sum the individual marginal benefit curves *vertically*. For example, for the fifth unit of a public good, suppose Max is willing to pay $7 and Lisa is willing to pay $7. Because public goods are nonrival and nonexcludable, both Max and Lisa can consume the fifth unit simultaneously. The total benefit from consuming the fifth unit is $7 + $7 = $14.

S E L F - T E S T

True/False and Explain

The Economic Theory of Government

1 Restriction of output by monopolies is an example of market failure.

2 The outcome resulting from the choices of voters, politicians, and bureaucrats is a political equilibrium.

3 Political equilibrium occurs only when there is no market failure.

Public Goods and the Free-Rider Problem

4 Goods supplied by government are defined as public goods.

5 The excludability feature of goods leads to the free-rider problem.

6 The existence of public goods gives rise to the free-rider problem.

7 The economy's marginal benefit curve for a public good is obtained by adding the marginal benefits of each individual at each quantity of provision.

8 The private market will produce much less than the efficient quantity of pure public goods.

9 According to public choice theory, not only is there possibility of market failure, there is also the possibility of "government failure."

10 Political parties tend to propose fundamentally different policies to give voters a clearer choice.

Taxes

11 The deadweight loss from an income tax is larger for low-wage workers than for high-wage workers.

12 The lobbying efforts of unions and employers determine the shares of an employment tax that each group actually pays.

13 Property taxes finance local public goods.

14 Excise taxes on goods create more deadweight loss when demand is more inelastic.

15 Excise taxes are most efficient on goods with many substitutes.

Multiple-Choice

The Economic Theory of Government

1 Government economic activity can attempt to correct

a free-rider problems.
b monopoly.
c externalities.
d economic inequality.
e all of the above.

2 In the public choice model of the political marketplace, politicians are the

a consumers.
b entrepreneurs.
c producers.
d firms.
e economists.

3 The public choice model

a argues that government policies move the economy towards efficiency.
b argues that politicians and bureaucrats are more concerned about the public interest than individuals in the private sector.
c argues that the public choices of government maximize net benefits.
d applies tools of economic analysis to analysis of government behaviour.
e applies tools of political analysis to analysis of economic markets.

Public Goods and the Free-Rider Problem

4 Governments provide pure public goods like national defence because

a governments are more efficient than private firms at producing such goods.
b of free-rider problems that result in underproduction by private markets.
c people do not value national defence very highly.
d of the potential that private firms will make excess profits.
e of external costs.

5 When a city street is not congested, it is like a(n)

a external good.
b internal good.
c rival good.
d private good.
e public good.

6 Which of the following goods is nonexcludable?

a city bus
b toll bridge
c lighthouse
d art museum
e all of the above

7 The quantity of public goods produced by an unregulated market tends to be

a less than the efficient quantity.
b equal to the efficient quantity.
c greater than the efficient quantity.
d that which maximizes total public benefit.
e that which maximizes net public benefit.

8 The market demand curve for a *private* good is obtained by summing the individual marginal

a cost curves horizontally.
b cost curves vertically.
c benefit curves horizontally.
d benefit curves vertically.
e benefit curves diagonally.

9 The economy's total demand curve for a *public* good is obtained by summing the individual marginal

a cost curves horizontally.
b cost curves vertically.
c benefit curves horizontally.
d benefit curves vertically.
e benefit curves diagonally.

10 The efficient scale of provision of a public good occurs where

a total benefit is at a maximum.
b total benefit is at a minimum.
c marginal benefit is at a maximum.
d marginal benefit minus marginal cost equals zero.
e marginal cost is at a minimum.

11 Refer to Figure 16.1 which shows the total cost and total benefit of proposals for building four different-sized high schools. The proposal with the largest net benefit is

a *A.*
b *B.*
c *C.*
d *D.*
e impossible to identify without additional information.

FIGURE **16.1**

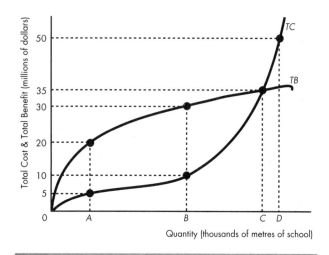

Quantity (thousands of metres of school)

12 Refer to Figure 16.1 which shows the total cost and total benefit of proposals for building four different-sized high schools. The proposal most likely to appeal to voters in an election is

a *A.*
b *B.*
c *C.*
d *D.*
e impossible to identify without additional information.

13 Refer to Figure 16.1 which shows the total cost and total benefit of proposals for building four different-sized high schools. The proposal that best meets the goals of the school district's bureaucrats is

a *A.*
b *B.*
c *C.*
d *D.*
e impossible to identify without additional information.

14 According to public choice theory, a voter will favour a candidate whose political program is

a perceived to offer the greatest personal benefit to the voter.
b best for the majority of the people.
c closest to allocative efficiency.
d favoured by the median voter.
e all of the above.

15 Competitors who make themselves identical to appeal to the maximum number of voters illustrate the principle of

a maximum differentiation.
b minimum differentiation.
c rational ignorance.
d nonrivalry.
e excludability.

16 Competition between two political parties will cause those parties to propose policies

a that are quite different.
b that are quite similar.
c of rational ignorance.
d that reduce the well-being of middle-income families and increase the well-being of the rich and the poor.
e that equate total costs and total benefits.

17 Rational ignorance

a results when the cost of information exceeds the benefits of having the information.
b allows special interest groups to exert political influence.
c combined with special-interest groups can yield inefficient provision of public goods.
d results in all of the above.
e results in none of the above.

18 If voters have similar views and are well informed, the quantity of national defence provided by the government will tend to be

a greater than the efficient quantity.
b less than the efficient quantity.
c the least costly quantity.
d the quantity that maximizes net benefit.
e the quantity that maximizes the Ministry of Defence budget.

Taxes

19 In general, a tax of $3 per unit on good *A* will shift the supply curve of *A* leftward by a vertical distance equal to

a $3 and increase the price of *A* by $3.
b $3 and increase the price of *A* by less than $3.
c $3 and increase the price of *A* by more than $3.
d more than $3 and increase the price of *A* by $3.
e less than $3 and increase the price of *A* by $3.

20 A tax causing a price increase creates deadweight loss consisting of lost

a consumer surplus.
b producer surplus.
c consumer surplus plus lost producer surplus.
d consumer surplus minus lost producer surplus.
e tax revenue from the decreased equilibrium quantity.

21 Figure 16.2 gives the demand and supply for imported cheese. If the government imposes a $3 tax per kilogram of imported cheese, price will increase by

a $3 to $7.
b $3 to $6.
c $2 to $6.
d $2 to $5.
e none of the above.

FIGURE **16.2**

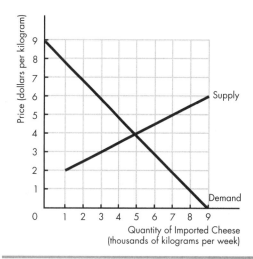

22 On any given spending issue subject to a vote, the median voter is the one who favours

a the least spending.
b the most spending.
c the efficient level of spending.
d the average level of spending.
e spending more than the level favoured by half the voters and less than the level favoured by half the voters.

23 Refer to Figure 16.3. Pre-tax consumer surplus is equal to triangle

a *gmc.*
b *gkc.*
c *mkc.*
d *dac.*
e *dbc.*

FIGURE **16.3**

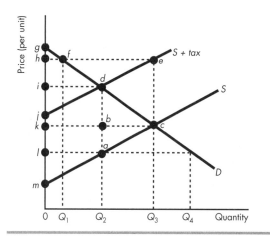

24 Refer to Figure 16.3. Pre-tax producer surplus is equal to triangle

a *gmc.*
b *gkc.*
c *mkc.*
d *dac.*
e *abc.*

25 Refer to Figure 16.3. Deadweight loss from the tax is equal to triangle

a *abc.*
b *dbc.*
c *dac.*
d *edc.*
e *gdj.*

Short Answer Problems

1 Briefly compare an equilibrium in a political market with an equilibrium in a market for goods and services.

2 Explain the *nonrival* and *nonexcludable* features of a pure public good.

3 What is the free-rider problem?

4 Heritage Apartments has 100 residents who are concerned about security. Table 16.1 gives the total cost of hiring a 24-hour security guard service as well as the marginal benefit to each of the residents.

TABLE **16.1**

Number of Guards	Total Cost per Day ($)	Marginal Benefit per Resident ($)	Marginal Benefit to All Residents ($)
1	300	10	
2	600	4	
3	900	2	
4	1,200	1	

a Why is a security guard a public good for the residents of Heritage Apartments?
b Why will zero guards be hired if each of the residents must act individually?
c Complete the last column of Table 16.1 by computing the marginal benefit of security guards to all of the residents together.

5 Now suppose that the residents form an Apartment Council that acts as a governing body to address the security issue.
a What is the optimal (allocatively efficient) number of guards? What is the net benefit at the optimal number of guards?
b Show that net benefit is less for either one less guard or for one more guard than for the optimal number of guards.
c How might the Apartment Council pay for the guards?

6 Two candidates are competing in an election for president of the Economics Club. The only issue dividing them is how much will be spent on the annual Economics Club party. It is well known that the seven voting members of the club (*A* through *G*) have the preferences in Table 16.2. These are strongly held preferences about exactly how much should be spent on the party.

TABLE **16.2** ECONOMICS CLUB PREFERENCES

Voting Member	Proposed Amount ($)
A	10
B	20
C	30
D	40
E	50
F	60
G	70

a How much will each candidate propose to spend?
b To demonstrate that your answer to part **a** is correct, consider the outcome of the following two contests.
   i Candidate 1 proposes the amount you gave in part **a** and candidate 2 proposes $1 less. Which candidate will win? Why?
   ii Candidate 1 proposes the amount you gave in part **a** and candidate 2 proposes $1 more. Which candidate will win? Why?
c Suppose the Sociology Club is also electing a president and the same single issue prevails. It is well known that the seven voting members of the Sociology Club have the following strongly held preferences regarding exactly how much should be spent on their party (see Table 16.3).

TABLE **16.3** SOCIOLOGY CLUB PREFERENCES

Voting Member	Proposed Amount ($)
T	0
U	0
V	0
W	40
X	41
Y	42
Z	43

How much will each of the two candidates propose in this case?

7 Explain why it may be rational for voters to be ignorant.

8 Table 16.4 gives three alternative income distributions for five individuals, *A* through *E*. Currently income is distributed according to distribution 1 (the first column of the table). Consider alternative proposed distributions 2 and 3, one at a time.

TABLE **16.4**

Individual	Distribution 1 ($)	Distribution 2 ($)	Distribution 3 ($)
A	0	200	150
B	200	300	250
C	400	350	450
D	700	600	600
E	1,000	850	850

a If distribution 2 is proposed as an alternative to distribution 1, will it have majority support? Why or why not?

b If distribution 3 is proposed as an alternative to distribution 1, will it have majority support? Why or why not?

9 Why does the imposition of an excise tax cause the supply curve of the taxed good to shift leftward?

10 Figure 16.4 gives the supply and demand for movie tickets in Ourtown. The market is initially in equilibrium (point *a*) with a price of $5 per ticket and 5,000 tickets sold per week. Suppose the town government establishes a new tax of $2 per movie ticket.

FIGURE **16.4**

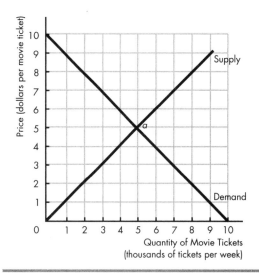

a Illustrate the effect of the new tax graphically. What will be the new equilibrium price and quantity?

b How much of the $2 tax is paid by consumers (in higher prices) and how much is paid by movie ticket sellers (in reduced revenue per ticket?)

c How much tax revenue will be collected each week?

d How much consumer surplus will be lost due to the tax? How much producer surplus will be lost? What is the deadweight loss of the tax?

ANSWERS

True/False and Explain

1 **T** Inefficient output. (374)

2 **T** Equilibrium outcome of political marketplace. (375)

3 **F** Occurs when neither voters, politicians nor bureaucrats can improve positions with a different choice. (375)

4 **F** By definition, public goods are *nonrival* and *nonexcludable*. But governments also supply swimming pools, which are rival and excludable goods (see Helpful Hint **2**). (376)

5 **F** Nonexcludability creates free-rider problem. (376)

6 **T** Nonexcludability means no incentive for anyone to pay. (376)

7 **T** See Helpful Hint **3**. (377)

8 **T** Because no accounting for external benefits. (378–379)

9 T Believe government agents act in own interest, not necessarily public interest. (381)

10 F Propose similar policies as vote-maximizing strategy appealing to median voter. (378–379)

11 F Larger for high-wage workers. (382–384)

12 F No matter what the shares assigned by law, who actually bears the tax depends on elasticities of demand and supply in labour market. (384–385)

13 T See text discussion. (385–386)

14 F Elastic demand creates more deadweight loss. (386–387)

15 F Least deadweight loss on goods with poor substitutes and inelastic demand. (386–387)

Multiple-Choice

1 e a–c are market failures, **d** is perceived to be unfair and needing government action. (374–375)

2 b Voters are consumers, bureaucrats are producers/firms. (375)

3 d Views government as political marketplace. (375)

4 b Would not be profitable for private firms. (376–379)

5 e Nonrival and nonexcludable. Congestion creates rivalry. (376)

6 c Can't prevent ships from seeing the light. (376)

7 a Private production unprofitable because of free-rider problem. (376–379)

8 c Because private goods rival and excludable, quantities consumed by each individual at each price are different and must be added to get total market demand. (377–399)

9 d Because public goods nonrival, can sum marginal benefit to each individual. See Text Figure 16.4. (377–399)

10 d Equivalent to maximum net benefit. (377–379)

11 b Largest *TB* − *TC*. (377–379)

12 b Maximizes net benefit. (377–381)

13 d Public choice theory assumes bureaucrats maximize budget (*TC*). (377–381)

14 a Voter, like consumer, assumed concerned only with own self-interest. (381)

15 b Definition of principle. (379)

16 b Vote maximizing by using principle of minimum differentiation. (379–381)

17 d **a** definition, **b**, **c** outcomes of rational ignorance. (380)

18 d Government will respond to demands of voters. (379–381)

19 b Draw graph. **a** true only for perfectly elastic supply. Other answers always false. (386–387)

20 c See text discussion. (386–387)

21 c Draw graph. Shift supply leftward by vertical distance of $3. (386–387)

22 e Median = exactly halfway between. (384)

23 b Area below demand, above market price. (386–387)

24 c Area above supply, below market price. (386–387)

25 c Lost consumer + producer surplus. (386–387)

Short Answer Problems

1 In both cases, equilibrium is a state of rest in the sense that no group has an incentive to change their choices. In equilibrium in an ordinary market for goods and services, neither demanders nor suppliers are able to make an exchange that will make them better off. Similarly, when a political market is in equilibrium, neither demanders (voters as consumers) nor suppliers (politicians as entrepreneurs, bureaucrats as producers) are able to make an alternative choice that will make them better off.

2 A good is nonrival if its consumption by one person does not reduce the amount available for others. Nonexcludable means that if the good is produced and consumed by one person, others cannot be excluded from consuming it as well.

3 The free-rider problem is the problem of unregulated markets producing too little of a pure public good because there is little incentive for individuals to pay for the good. The reason is that the person's payment will likely have no effect on the amount the person will be able to consume.

4 a A security guard is a public good because, in this case, it is nonrival and nonexcludable. It is nonrival because one resident's *consumption* of the security provided by a guard does not reduce the security of anyone else. It is nonexcludable because once a security guard is in place, all residents enjoy the increased security; none can be excluded.

b If each resident must act individually in hiring a security guard none will be hired because each resident receives only $10 in benefit from the first guard, which costs $300 per day.

c The entries in the last column of Table 16.1 Solution are obtained by multiplying the marginal benefit per resident by the number of residents, 100. This multiplication is the numerical equivalent of summing the individual marginal benefit curves vertically for each quantity of guards.

TABLE **16.1** SOLUTION

Number of Guards	Total Cost per Day ($)	Marginal Benefit per Resident ($)	Marginal Benefit to All Residents ($)
1	300	10	1,000
2	600	4	400
3	900	2	200
4	1,200	1	100

5 a If the Apartment Council hires each guard for whom the marginal benefit exceeds the marginal cost, they will hire the optimal number of guards. The marginal cost of each additional guard is $300. The marginal benefit of the first guard is $1,000, so he will be hired. Similarly, the marginal benefit of the second guard is $400, and she will be hired.

The marginal benefit of the third guard, however, is only $200, which is less than marginal cost. Therefore the efficient (optimal) number of guards is two. For two guards, the net benefit is $800: total benefit ($1,400) minus total cost ($600).

b For one guard, net benefit is $700: total benefit ($1,000) minus total cost ($300). For three guards, net benefit is also $700: total benefit ($1,600) minus total cost ($900). Thus the net benefit of $800 is greatest for two guards.

c The Apartment Council might pay for the guards by collecting a security fee of $6 per day from each of the 100 residents in order to hire two security guards.

6 a Each candidate will propose spending $40 since that is the preference of the median voter (voter *D*).

b i Candidate 1 will win because *D*, *E*, *F*, and *G* will vote for that candidate because $40 comes closer to matching their preferences than the $39 proposed by candidate 2. Only *A*, *B*, and *C* will vote for candidate 2.

ii Candidate 1 will win because *A*, *B*, *C*, and *D* will vote for that candidate while only *E*, *F*, and *G* will vote for candidate 2.

c Once again, the candidates will both propose spending $40 on the party since that is the preference of the median voter. Note that in this case, the median voter's view is not "average."

7 Most issues have only a small and indirect effect on most voters. In such cases it is irrational for a voter to spend much time and effort to become well informed because the additional cost would quickly exceed any additional benefit. Only if the voter is significantly and directly affected by an issue will it pay to become well informed. As a result, most voters will be rationally ignorant on any given issue.

8 a Only *A* and *B* are better off under distribution 2. Distribution 2 will receive the support of only *A* and *B* with *C*, *D*, and *E* opposed. Note that the median voter (*C*) is worse off under distribution 2.

b Distribution 3 will receive majority support since it makes the median voter better off. It will be supported by *A*, *B*, and *C* and opposed by *D* and *E*.

9 When an excise tax is imposed on a supplier, it raises the minimum price the supplier must receive to be willing to offer any given quantity for sale. This is nothing more than a leftward shift (decrease) in the supply curve. It is useful to think of a new excise tax as an increase in the cost of production.

10 a The new tax shifts the supply curve for movie tickets leftward by a vertical distance of $2 (the amount of the tax) between the two curves. In Figure 16.4 Solution, the new curve is labelled S_1. The new equilibrium (point *b*) price and quantity are $6 per ticket and 4,000 tickets per week respectively.

FIGURE **16.4** SOLUTION

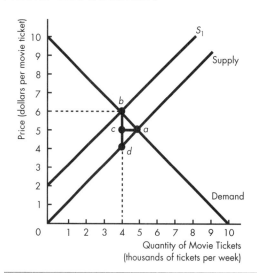

b Of the $2 tax, $1 is paid by consumers since the price of a ticket rises from $5 to $6, and $1 is paid by sellers, since the revenue per ticket they receive falls from $5 to $4.

c Total tax revenue will be $8,000 per week: $2 per ticket × 4,000 tickets sold.

d The loss of consumer surplus is given by the area of triangle *abc* in Figure 16.4 Solution and is equal to $500 (from the formula for the area of a right-angled triangle—area = 1/2 × base (*ac*) × height (*bc*) = 1/2 × 1,000 × $1). Similarly, the loss of producer surplus is given by the area of triangle *adc*, and is equal to $500. Thus the deadweight loss is $1,000, the sum of consumer and producer surplus.

Chapter 17

Competition Policy

Market Intervention

Forms of government intervention in monopolistic and oligopolistic markets:

◆ Regulation—rules determining prices, product standards, and entry conditions. *Deregulation*—removing rules.

◆ Public ownership—publicly owned firms are **Crown corporations**. **Privatization**—selling publicly owned corporation to private shareholders.

◆ **Anti-combine law**—makes some market behaviour (monopolistic practices) illegal.

Government intervention is designed to influence surpluses. Surpluses were defined in Chapter 5. To refresh your memory, total surplus represents combined gains from trade to consumers and producers; sum of *consumer surplus* and *producer surplus*.

◆ *Consumer surplus*—value of goods to consumers – price paid = area below demand curve and above market price.

◆ *Producer surplus*—total revenue – opportunity cost = area below market price and above supply curve.

Total surplus maximized under competition when *deadweight loss* = 0.

◆ Under monopoly, producer surplus increases, consumer surplus decreases and deadweight loss arises.

◆ Monopolistic practices create tension between consumer interests and producer interests. This tension is key to economic theory of regulation.

Economic Theory of Regulation

Economic theory of regulation part of broader theory of public choice (Chapter 16), but emphasizing government regulation.

◆ Demand for regulation increases with increased

  • consumer surplus per buyer.
  • number of buyers.
  • producer surplus per firm.
  • number of firms.

◆ Supply of regulation increases with increased

  • consumer surplus per buyer.
  • producer surplus per firm.
  • number of voters benefitted.

In political equilibrium, no interest group uses additional resources to press for changes in existing regulation, and no politicians find it worthwhile to offer different regulations. There are two theories of political equilibrium.

◆ **Public interest theory**—predicts regulations supplied to maximize total surplus and eliminate deadweight loss. Government acts in the public interest to eliminate waste and achieve allocative efficiency.

◆ **Capture theory**—predicts regulations supplied to maximize producer surplus and economic profit. Government "captured" by interests of producers.

Regulation and Deregulation

Government regulatory agencies set rules for prices, quantities, and market access.

Natural monopoly (Because of economies of scale, one firm can supply the market at lower *ATC* than multiple firms can) can be regulated with the following rules.

◆ **Marginal cost pricing rule**—set price equal to marginal cost. Maximizes total surplus, but not viable because firm incurs economic loss.

◆ **Average cost pricing rule**—set price equal to average total cost. May be most efficient even though deadweight loss.

◆ **Rate of return regulation**—set price to achieve target rate of return on capital.

  • Ideally, yields normal profit only; same outcome as average cost pricing rule.
  • But there is a problem of incentives for firm to inflate cost (of capital) to yield economic profit.

◆ Evidence mixed, but regulated natural monopolies seem to earn profits equal to or greater than average, supporting more predictions of capture theory than public interest theory.

Cartel (collusive agreement among firms in an oligopoly to restrict output and raise price) can be regulated with the following rules.

◆ Set price and quantity at competitive levels (intersection of industry demand and *MC* curves). Public interest theory outcome.

◆ Set price and quantity to maximize profit (highest price associated with quantity at intersection of industry *MC* and *MR* curves). Capture theory outcome.

◆ Evidence mixed, but regulated cartels seem to earn profits equal to or greater than average, supporting more of predictions of capture theory than public interest theory.

Public Ownership

Publicly owned corporations can be operated with the following objectives:

◆ Efficiency—set price equal to marginal cost and subsidize the economic loss. Maximizes consumer surplus.

◆ Budget maximization with marginal cost pricing—set price equal to marginal cost but pad production costs to maximum. Allocatively efficient, but maximizes producer benefits.

◆ Budget maximization at zero price—increase output until price falls to zero. Inefficient (deadweight loss), results in overproduction and maximizes producer benefits.

◆ Evidence suggests publicly owned firms will overproduce and be less efficient than private firms. Recent tendency to privatize publicly owned firms.

Anti-Combine Law

Competition Act of 1986 distinguishes between

◆ criminal actions (conspiracy to fix prices, bid-rigging, false advertising) dealt with by courts.

◆ noncriminal actions (mergers, abuse of market position, exclusive dealing) dealt with by Competition Tribunal.

Evidence suggests anti-combine laws have served the public interest.

HELPFUL HINTS

1 Figure 17.1 depicts revenue and marginal cost curves for an industry. Use this figure to think of regulation as determining the division of the potential total surplus (the area of triangle *abc*) among consumer surplus, producer surplus, and deadweight loss.

FIGURE **17.1**

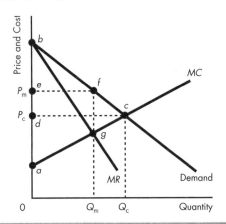

If the industry is perfectly competitive, then output will be Q_c and the market price will be P_c. Total surplus is maximized and is given by the area of triangle *abc*. Total surplus is equal to the sum of consumer surplus (triangle *dbc*) and producer surplus (triangle *adc*). There is no deadweight loss so efficiency is achieved.

If the industry is a profit-maximizing monopoly, output will be Q_m and the price will be P_m. In this case, total surplus is represented by the area of trapezoid *abfg*. Because of monopoly restriction of output, total surplus under monopoly is less than under competition. The difference is the deadweight loss from monopoly, the amount of total surplus that is lost when we go from competition to monopoly. The deadweight loss is given by the area of triangle *gfc*. Total surplus can be divided into consumer surplus (triangle *ebf*) and producer surplus (trapezoid *aefg*). Consumer surplus is quite small, but producer surplus is at a maximum.

Actual output is likely to be between these bounds. As output moves from Q_c to Q_m, consumer surplus decreases, while producer surplus and the deadweight loss both increase. If this industry is regulated, the public interest theory of intervention predicts output will be close to Q_c, while the capture theory of intervention predicts output closer to Q_m.

S E L F - T E S T

True/False and Explain

Market Intervention

1 Privatization is the process of converting a privately owned corporation into a Crown corporation.

2 Canada's anti-combine laws are used less vigorously than antitrust laws in the United States.

Economic Theory of Regulation

3 Politicians are more likely to supply regulation the greater the number of voters benefited.

4 In a political equilibrium, lobby groups stop lobbying.

5 Government intervention will always move the economy closer to efficiency.

6 According to the capture theory, government regulatory agencies eventually capture the profits of the industries they regulate.

Regulation and Deregulation

7 For a natural monopoly, marginal cost is always less than average total cost.

8 In practice, rate of return regulation is equivalent to marginal cost pricing.

9 Under rate of return regulation, firms can get closer to maximizing producer surplus if they inflate their costs.

10 Evidence of higher-than-normal rates of return for regulated natural monopolies matches the predictions of the capture theory.

11 Evidence that producers strongly support deregulation matches the predictions of the capture theory.

12 If industry prices and profits fall after deregulation, the regulation was likely serving the interest of consumers.

Public Ownership

13 An efficiently operated Crown corporation will maximize total surplus.

Anti-Combine Law

14 According to Canada's anti-combine laws, mergers and abuse of a dominant market position are criminal offences.

15 Anti-combine laws have helped achieve efficiency and serve the public interest.

Multiple-Choice

Market Intervention

1 Regulation refers to
a the discipline of the marketplace.
b rules administered by a government agency.
c selling a publicly owned corporation to private shareholders.
d cartelization of a competitive industry.
e the formation of monopolies.

2 The difference between the maximum amount consumers are willing to pay and the amount they actually do pay for a given quantity of a good is called
a government surplus.
b consumer surplus.
c producer surplus.
d total surplus.
e deadweight surplus.

3 Total surplus is maximized when
a marginal cost equals marginal revenue.
b marginal cost equals average total cost.
c price equals marginal cost.
d price equals average total cost.
e price equals average variable cost.

4 For a monopoly, producer surplus is maximized when
a marginal cost equals marginal revenue.
b marginal cost equals average total cost.
c price equals marginal cost.
d price equals average total cost.
e price equals average variable cost.

5 Allocative efficiency is achieved when
a consumer surplus is maximized.
b producer surplus is minimized.
c total surplus is maximized.
d total surplus is minimized.
e none of the above.

Economic Theory of Regulation

6 A large demand for intervention by *producers* results when there is a
a small consumer surplus per buyer.
b large consumer surplus per buyer.
c large number of buyers.
d small producer surplus per firm.
e large producer surplus per firm.

7 The supply of regulation increases with
a smaller consumer surplus per buyer.
b larger producer surplus per firm.
c smaller number of voters benefited.
d all of the above.
e none of the above.

8 The supply of economic regulation originates with
a monopolists.
b labour unions.
c fair trade associations.
d voters.
e politicians and bureaucrats.

9 In a political equilibrium,
a efficiency must be achieved.
b no one wants to change their proposals.
c firms will be making zero economic profit.
d all parties agree that the appropriate level of regulation has been achieved.
e all of the above are true.

10 Which of the following is consistent with the public interest theory of regulation?
a regulation of natural monopoly by setting price equal to marginal cost
b regulation of competitive industry to increase output
c regulation of airline industry by establishing minimum airfares
d regulation of agriculture by establishing barriers to exit from the industry
e none of the above

11 Which of the following is consistent with the capture theory of regulation?

a regulation of natural monopoly by setting price equal to marginal cost

b regulation of competitive industry to increase output

c regulation of airline industry by establishing minimum airfares

d regulation of agriculture by establishing barriers to exit from the industry

e none of the above

12 The public interest theory of regulation predicts that government regulation will

a maximize the interests of public officials.

b maximize total surplus.

c maximize producer surplus.

d minimize producer surplus.

e maximize consumer surplus.

Regulation and Deregulation

13 Which of the following is *not* a federal regulatory agency?

a Atomic Energy Control Board

b Canadian Radio-television and Telecommunications Commission

c Petro-Canada

d Canadian Transport Commission

e National Farm Products

14 Which of the following is *least* likely to be a *natural monopoly*?

a subway service

b electric utilities

c water and sewer service

d taxicab service

e cable TV service

15 A natural monopoly has

a low fixed cost and low marginal cost.

b low fixed cost and high marginal cost.

c high fixed cost and low marginal cost.

d high fixed cost and high marginal cost.

e high fixed cost and increasing marginal cost.

16 Figure 17.2 gives revenue and cost curves for an industry. This industry is a natural monopoly because

a one firm can supply the entire market at a lower price than can two or more firms.

b there are decreasing returns to scale over the entire range of demand.

c there are diseconomies of scale over the entire range of demand.

d even a single firm will be unable to earn a positive profit in this industry.

e all of the above are true.

FIGURE **17.2**

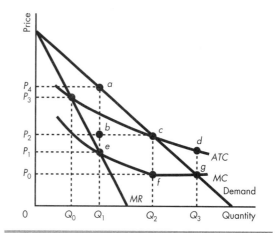

17 Consider the natural monopoly in Figure 17.2. If the firm is unregulated and operates as a private profit-maximizer, what output will it produce?

a 0, because the firm incurs economic losses when $P = MC$

b Q_0

c Q_1

d Q_2

e Q_3

18 Consider the natural monopoly in Figure 17.2. If regulators set a price just sufficient for the firm to earn normal profits, what output will it produce?

a 0, because the firm incurs economic losses when $P = MC$

b Q_0

c Q_1

d Q_2

e Q_3

19 Consider the natural monopoly in Figure 17.2. Total surplus is maximum when quantity is

a Q_0 and price is P_3.

b Q_1 and price is P_1.

c Q_1 and price is P_4.

d Q_2 and price is P_2.

e Q_3 and price is P_0.

20 Consider the natural monopoly in Figure 17.2. If regulators use a marginal cost pricing rule, what line segment gives the amount of subsidy (per unit of output) required to keep the monopolist in business?

a *ba*

b *ea*

c *fc*

d *gd*

e *eb*

21 Consider the natural monopoly in Figure 17.2. What region in the graph represents deadweight loss from an average cost pricing rule?

a *abc*

b *cdg*

c *cfg*

d *aeg*

e none of the above

22 A monopolist under rate of return regulation has an incentive to

a pad costs.

b produce more than the efficient quantity of output.

c charge a price equal to marginal cost.

d maximize consumer surplus.

e maximize shareholder profits.

Public Ownership

23 A Crown corporation may be

a operated to achieve economic efficiency.

b operated to maximize its budget.

c provincial.

d federal.

e all of the above.

24 A Crown corporation that maximizes its budget together with marginal cost pricing will

a produce the efficient level of output.

b produce more than the efficient level of output.

c produce less than the efficient level of output.

d maximize consumer surplus.

e minimize production cost.

Anti-Combine Law

25 Anti-combine laws attempt to

a support prices.

b establish Crown corporations.

c prevent monopoly practices.

d establish fair trade laws.

e regulate monopolies.

Short Answer Problems

1 Regulation of monopoly is necessary because of the tension between the public interest and the producer's interest. Explain.

2 In the regulation of natural monopoly, when would an average cost pricing rule be better than a marginal cost pricing rule?

3 Suppose the government tried to eliminate monopoly profit by taxing each unit of monopoly output.

a What effect would this policy have on the quantity a monopolist produces and the price it charges?

b What is the effect on economic efficiency?

4 The demand for Aerodisks, a disk made from a unique material that flies a considerable distance when thrown, is given by the equation

$$P = 10 - 0.01 Q_D$$

The corresponding marginal revenue (*MR*) equation is

$$MR = 10 - 0.02 Q$$

The Aerodisk Company is a natural monopoly. The firm's total fixed cost is $700 and the marginal cost is constant at $2 per disk. (*Note:* This implies that average variable cost is also constant at $2 per disk.) Suppose that the Aerodisk Company is *not* regulated.

a What will be the quantity sold and the price of an Aerodisk?

b How much is economic profit or loss?

c How much is producer surplus?

d How much is consumer surplus?

e How much is total surplus?

5 Now suppose that the Aerodisk Company becomes regulated and that the regulator uses a marginal cost pricing rule.
   a What will be the quantity sold and the price of an Aerodisk?
   b How much is economic profit or loss?
   c How much is producer surplus?
   d How much is consumer surplus?
   e How much is total surplus?

6 Suppose that the regulator of the Aerodisk Company uses an average cost pricing rule.
   a What will be the price of an Aerodisk and how many will be sold?
   b How much is economic profit or loss?
   c How much is producer surplus?
   d How much is consumer surplus?
   e How much is total surplus?

7 Since the Aerodisk Company will incur a loss under marginal cost pricing, the government must subsidize the production of Aerodisks for the firm to be willing to produce.
   a What is the total subsidy necessary under a marginal cost pricing rule to leave the firm with zero economic profit?
   b What is the amount of the deadweight loss associated with an average cost pricing rule?
   c Which pricing rule is superior?

8 Why is rate of return regulation equivalent to average cost pricing?

9 Figure 17.3 illustrates the industry demand, marginal revenue (*MR*) and marginal cost (*MC*) curves in an oligopoly. The industry is regulated.
   a What price and quantity are predicted by the public interest theory of regulation? Why?
   b What price and quantity are predicted by the capture theory of regulation? Why?
   c Can you explain why the firms in this industry might demand regulation?

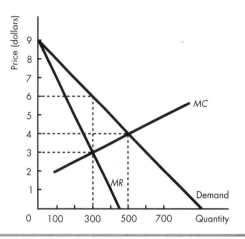

FIGURE **17.3**

10 During its 1999 attempt to take over both Air Canada and Canadian Airlines, the Onyx Corporation tried to advance its cause by taking out expensive multi-page advertisements in both national newspapers arguing that its proposal was in the "best interests of Canadians." Which theory of economic regulation does Onyx's actions support?

ANSWERS

True/False and Explain

1 **F** Privatization is selling a publicly owned corporation to private shareholders. (394)
2 **T** Test of guilt more stringent for Canadian laws. (394)
3 **T** Regulation then brings more votes to politicians. (394–395)
4 **F** Lobby groups continue to operate but do not find it worthwhile to *change* their quantity of lobbying. (395)
5 **F** True according to public interest theory, false according to capture theory. (394–396)
6 **F** Industry captures more of total surplus. (395–396)
7 **T** That's why *ATC* is always downward-sloping. (397–398)
8 **F** More like average cost pricing. (399–400)
9 **T** Increased costs yield increased profits. (400–401)
10 **T** Regulators act in interest of monopoly. (400–401)
11 **F** Matches public interest theory. (400–403)
12 **F** Serving producers. (401–403)
13 **T** Producing output where $P = MC$. (403–404)

14 F Noncriminal offences. Criminal offences include price-fixing, and false advertising. (406)

15 T See text discussion. (406–407)

Multiple-Choice

1 b See text discussion. (394)

2 b Definition; see Helpful Hint **1**. (394)

3 c Pricing rule for efficiency; see Helpful Hint **1**. (394)

4 a Pricing rule for monopoly profit maximization; see Helpful Hint **1**. (394)

5 c Sum of consumer surplus and producer surplus; see Helpful Hint **1**. (394)

6 e **b, c** increase demand by buyers. (394–395)

7 b Reverse **a, c** true. (395)

8 e Create legislation. (395)

9 b See text discussion. (395–396)

10 a Only option that increases allocative efficiency. (395–396)

11 c Helps airline firms, not consumers. (395–396)

12 b Achieve allocative efficiency. (395–396)

13 c Crown corporation. (396–397)

14 d No major economies of scale. (397–398)

15 c Yielding always downward-sloping *ATC*. (397–398)

16 a Definition natural monopoly. (397–398)

17 c Where $MC = MR$. (397–399)

18 d Where $P = ATC$. (397–399)

19 e Where $P = MC$. (397–399)

20 d To cover loss per unit of output. (398–399)

21 c See Text Figure 17.2. (398–400)

22 a To increase profits; see Text Figure 17.4. (399–400)

23 e See text discussion. (403–405)

24 a See Text Figure 17.6(b). (403–405)

25 c See text discussion. (406–407)

Short Answer Problems

1 It is in the public interest to achieve economic efficiency; to expand output to the level that maximizes total surplus. It is in the interest of the monopoly producer to restrict output in order to maximize producer surplus and thus monopoly profit.

   Since these interests are not the same, monopoly must be regulated to achieve efficiency. The public interest theory of regulation suggests that this principle guides regulation of monopoly industries.

2 An average cost pricing rule creates deadweight loss but so does a marginal cost pricing rule, through the need to impose a tax.

Since, for natural monopoly, marginal cost is less than average total cost, regulation using a marginal cost pricing rule requires the government to pay a subsidy for the firm to be willing to produce at all.

To pay that subsidy the government must levy a tax that imposes deadweight loss on the economy. If the deadweight loss associated with the tax (for example, the deadweight loss of the marginal cost pricing rule with its attendant subsidy) is greater than the deadweight loss of an average cost pricing rule, the average cost pricing rule is superior.

3 a Imposing a tax on each unit sold by a monopolist increases marginal cost. As a consequence the profit-maximizing monopolist will raise price and reduce the quantity produced.

   b The tax will certainly reduce the profit of the monopolist and may even eliminate it, but it will make the inefficiency due to monopoly even worse. This is illustrated in Figure 17.4. The curve *MC* is the marginal cost curve before the tax. An unregulated monopolist will produce amount Q_2, while the economically efficient output is Q_3. The tax, however, causes the monopolist to reduce output from Q_2 to Q_1, which moves the market outcome farther away from efficiency.

FIGURE **17.4**

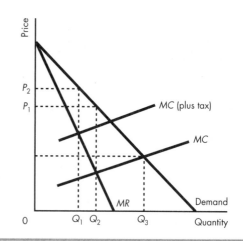

4 Figure 17.5 is helpful in answering questions about the Aerodisk market. It gives relevant revenue and cost curves for the Aerodisk Company.

FIGURE **17.5** AERODISK COMPANY

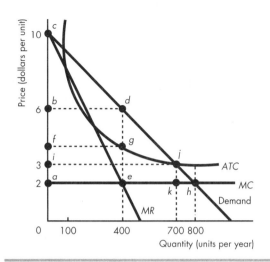

a In an unregulated market, the Aerodisk Company will choose output to maximize profit, where $MR = MC$. To calculate this output, set $MR = MC = 2$ and solve for Q:

$$10 - 0.02Q = 2$$
$$8 = 0.02Q$$
$$400 = Q$$

To calculate price, substitute $Q = 400$ into the demand equation:

$$P = 10 - 0.01Q_D$$
$$= 10 - 0.01(400)$$
$$= 10 - 4$$
$$= 6$$

400 Aerodisks will be produced and sold at a price of $6 each.

b To determine economic profit we first determine average total cost (ATC) when output (Q) is 400 units.

$$ATC = AFC + AVC$$
$$= (TFC/Q) + AVC$$
$$= (700/400) + 2$$
$$= 3.75$$

Therefore economic profit is the difference between price (average revenue) and ATC times the quantity sold. This is equal to $900 and is represented in Figure 17.5 by region *fbdg*.

c Producer surplus is the difference between the producer's revenue and the opportunity cost of production. Total revenue is $2,400 ($6 × 400 units) and total opportunity cost is $800 ($2 × 400 units). Thus producer surplus is $1,600. Graphically, producer surplus is the area of rectangle *abde* in Figure 17.5.

d Consumer surplus is the area in triangle *bcd* in Figure 17.5, $800.

e Total surplus is $2,400, the sum of producer and consumer surplus.

5 a Under a marginal cost pricing rule, the price of an Aerodisk is equal to marginal cost or $2. To calculate the quantity sold, substitute price into the demand equation:

$$P = 10 - 0.01Q_D$$
$$2 = 10 - 0.01Q_D$$
$$0.01Q_D = 8$$
$$Q_D = 800$$

b To determine economic profit or loss, we must first determine ATC when output is 800. Using the procedure in the previous problem we find at $Q = 800$, ATC is $2.875, which is greater than price by $0.875 (87.5¢). Therefore the Aerodisk Company will incur a loss of $700 ($0.875 × 800). Alternatively, since MC is constant, if price is set equal to MC which is equal to AVC, the total loss will be just TFC or $700.

c Producer surplus is zero. Note that profits = producer surplus − total fixed costs.

d Consumer surplus is the area of triangle *ach* in Figure 17.5, $3,200.

e Total surplus is $3,200 (a maximum).

6 a Computation of ATC at various levels of output allows us to determine the ATC curve crosses the demand curve when $Q = 700$ and $ATC = \$3$. Thus under an average cost pricing rule, the price of an Aerodisk is $3 and 700 units will be sold.

b Since price equals average total cost, economic profit is zero.

c Producer surplus is $700, area *aijh* in Figure 17.5. Note that profits = producer surplus − total fixed costs.

d Consumer surplus is $2,450, the area of triangle *ijc* in Figure 17.5.

e Total surplus is $3,150.

7 a The total subsidy equals the loss under marginal cost pricing. In Short Answer Problem **5b** we computed this to be $700.

b The deadweight loss from the average cost pricing rule is the loss of total surplus relative to the marginal cost pricing rule. We have computed total surplus under marginal cost pricing ($3,200) in Short Answer Problem **5e** and total surplus under average cost pricing ($3,150) in Short Answer Problem **6e**. The deadweight loss is the difference: $50.

c It depends on the size of the deadweight loss associated with the taxes required to cover the subsidy under the marginal cost pricing rule. If the deadweight loss from these taxes exceeds $50, then the average cost pricing rule has a smaller deadweight loss and is superior. If the deadweight loss is less than $50, then the marginal cost pricing rule is superior.

8 The key here is to recall that economic cost includes a normal rate of return. Because rate of return regulation sets a price that allows a normal rate of return, it is setting the price equal to average total cost.

9 a Public interest theory predicts that regulators set price and quantity to maximize total surplus. This means they choose quantity (and price) where *MC* is equal to demand. This corresponds to a quantity of 500 units and a price of $4 per unit.

b Capture theory predicts that regulators choose quantity and price to maximize the profit of the industry. This is the quantity a profit-maximizing monopolist would choose, 300 units, where *MC* = *MR*. The highest price that could be charged and still sell that quantity can be read from the demand curve: $6 per unit.

c Firms in the industry would demand regulation if the regulation increased profit to the industry. As we discovered in Chapter 13, cartels are unstable because there is always an incentive to

cheat on output restriction agreements and it is difficult to enforce the agreements. If, however, firms in an industry can get the government, through regulation, to enforce a cartel agreement, they will want to do it.

10 There is no single right answer to this question. Onyx's actions suggest that it was trying to influence the federal government to allow the takeover, by convincing Canadian citizens that a merged airline was in everyone's best interest. Obviously Onyx believed the takeover was in Onyx's interest, or it wouldn't have even tried. Since after the takeover there would have been only a single (monopoly) airline in Canada, the government would then have to provide some form of economic regulation. Because politicians respond to voters, if politicians believed that voters favoured the takeover, the politicians could support the takeover. Thus the advertisements, by swaying public opinion, were designed to ultimately influence the government/politicians. This line of reasoning is consistent with the capture theory.

On the other hand, the public interest theory suggests that any monopoly will be regulated in the public's best interest. For the airline monopoly to be approved in the first place (to take advantage of natural economies of scale), Onyx needed to convince the government (which would ultimately regulate its airline) that the takeover could work in the public interest.

18

Externalities

KEY CONCEPTS

Externalities in Our Lives

Externality is cost or benefit from production activities or consumption activities that affects people who are not part of the original activity. Externalities may be negative or positive.

◆ **Negative externality**—imposes external cost.

  • negative production externality (pollution).
  • negative consumption externality (tobacco smoke).

◆ **Positive externality**—provides external benefit.

  • positive production externality (honeybees pollinating nearby fruit orchard).
  • positive consumption externality (flu vaccination).

◆ Externalities create market failure (*in*efficiency). Markets overproduce goods/services with negative externalities and underproduce goods/services with positive externalities.

Negative Externalities: Pollution

Many people assume all pollution must be stopped. Economic analysis of pollution, however, evaluates costs and benefits to identify efficient amounts of pollution.

◆ **Marginal private cost** *(MC)*—cost of producing additional unit of good/service paid by producer.

◆ **Marginal external cost**—cost of producing additional unit of good/service that falls on people other than the producer.

◆ **Marginal social cost** *(MSC)*—*MC* incurred by entire society; *MSC* = *MC* + Marginal external cost.

FIGURE **18.1** GOOD WITH AN EXTERNAL COST

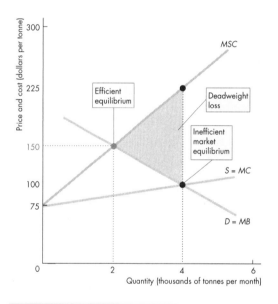

Figure 18.1 (text Figure 18.3) shows the marginal private cost curve, which is also the supply curve (*S* = *MC*), and the marginal social cost curve (*MSC*). For any quantity produced, marginal external cost = vertical distance between *S* = *MC* and *MSC* curves. Demand curve is same as marginal benefit curve (*D* = *MB*).

◆ Efficient equilibrium (where *D* = *MB* intersects *MSC*) takes into account all (private + external) costs.

◆ Private market equilibrium is inefficient (where *D* = *MB* intersects *S* = *MC*) because does not take into account marginal external cost.

◆ Private market equilibrium produces too much of good with external cost and creates deadweight loss (from *MSC* > *MB* for all units beyond efficient quantity).

Inefficiency from externalities can sometimes be reduced by establishing property rights.

♦ **Property rights**—legally established title to ownership, use, and disposal of factors of production and goods and services.

♦ **Coase theorem**—If property rights exist and **transactions costs** (opportunity costs of conducting transactions) are low, there will be no externalities and private transactions are efficient. Who has property rights will *not* affect the efficiency of the outcome.

Where property rights cannot be established or transactions costs are high, other government actions can achieve efficiency even with negative externalities.

♦ Taxes—to create incentive for producers to cut back negative externalities, government can impose **Pigovian tax** equal to external marginal cost.

  • This makes MSC curve the relevant MC curve for polluting producer's decision, yielding output where $MSC = MB$.

♦ Emission charges—set price per unit of pollution that polluter pays.

  • In practice, difficult to determine correct price.

♦ Marketable permits—each polluter given pollution limit (permit) that can be bought and sold.

  • Firms reducing pollution below their limit can sell "excess" reduction to other firms who then can pollute more. In competitive market for permits, price of permits = marginal external cost of pollution, yielding efficient outcome where $MSC = MSB$.

Positive Externalities: Knowledge

Knowledge from education and research creates private and social benefits.

♦ **Marginal private benefit** *(MB)*—benefit from additional unit of good/service received by consumer.

♦ **Marginal external benefit**—benefit from additional unit of good/service enjoyed by people other than the consumer.

♦ **Marginal social benefit** *(MSB)*—*MB* enjoyed by entire society; $MSB = MB +$ Marginal external benefit.

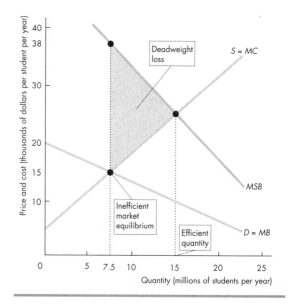

FIGURE **18.2** GOOD WITH AN EXTERNAL BENEFIT

Figure 18.2 (text Figure 18.7) shows the marginal private benefit curve, which is also the demand curve ($D = MB$), and the marginal social benefit curve (MSB). For any quantity consumed, marginal external benefit = vertical distance between $D = MB$ and MSB curves. Supply curve is same as marginal cost curve ($S = MC$).

♦ Efficient equilibrium (where MSB intersects $S = MC$) takes into account all (private + external) benefits.

♦ Private market equilibrium is inefficient (where $D = MB$ intersects $S = MC$) because does not take into account marginal external benefit.

♦ Private market equilibrium produces too little of good with external benefit and creates deadweight loss (from lost $MSB > MC$ for all units below efficient quantity).

Government actions to achieve efficiency even with positive externalities.

♦ **Public provision**—government provides the good/service (public education) and charges price below cost that equals marginal private benefit at the efficient quantity.

  • Additional cost paid by taxpayers, to yield total cost = $S = MC$.

♦ **Subsidies**—payment by government to private producers of goods/services.

  • If subsidy equal to external marginal benefit, supply curve becomes $S = MC -$ subsidy, yielding efficient equilibrium quantity.

♦ **Vouchers**—government-provided tokens to households for buying specified goods/services.

- Value of voucher = marginal external benefit, making *MSB* curve the market demand curve and yielding efficient equilibrium outcome.

◆ **Patents** and **copyrights**—provide creators of knowledge with **intellectual property rights** in their discoveries; help ensure creator profits.

- Patents and copyrights encourage development of new knowledge, but create temporary monopoly, so gains from increased knowledge must be balanced against loss from monopoly.

HELPFUL HINTS

1 A competitive market will produce the quantity of output at which marginal private cost is equal to marginal private benefit. The allocatively efficient quantity is the quantity at which marginal social cost is equal to marginal social benefit.

The difference between *marginal social cost* and *marginal private cost* is marginal external cost, and the difference between *marginal social benefit* and *marginal private benefit* is marginal external benefit.

In most economic activities, people who are not part of the original activity are not affected, so there are no external costs or benefits. This means private and social costs and benefits coincide and competitive markets are efficient. However, when third parties are affected, there are external costs or benefits and competitive markets are *not* efficient. Markets overproduce goods/services with external costs (negative externalities) and underproduce goods/services with external benefits (positive externalities).

2 Competitive markets with externalities are not efficient because some of the costs or benefits are *external*. If those costs or benefits could be *internalized* somehow, then the market would be efficient. There are two main approaches to internalizing externalities discussed in this chapter.

The first is to establish and strictly enforce property rights. Then costs imposed on people who are not part of the original activity can be recovered through the legal process and will be paid by those involved in the activity: the costs become internal (private).

The second approach to internalizing externalities is to tax activities that generate external costs and subsidize activities that generate external benefits. By charging a tax equal to the external costs, the entire cost becomes internal. Similarly, by paying a subsidy equal to the external benefits, the entire benefit becomes internal.

3 Figure 18.1 in Key Concepts shows the production of a good with a negative externality (pollution). Note that *the efficient level of pollution is not zero*—efficient Q is *not* $Q = 0$. Generally, costs saved by reducing pollution to zero are less than the benefits lost (benefits from consuming goods whose production created pollution as a by-product).

SELF-TEST

True/False and Explain

Externalities in Our Lives

1 Externalities arise only from production.

2 Flu vaccination is an example of a positive production externality.

3 A negative production externality imposes an external cost.

Negative Externalities: Pollution

4 If the production of a good involves no external cost, then marginal social cost is equal to marginal private cost.

5 If negative externalities exist, marginal social cost and marginal external cost are equivalent.

6 Externalities often arise from the absence of private property rights.

7 Assigning property rights always solves the problem of a negative externality.

8 Pigovian taxes creates incentives for producers to cut back negative externalities.

9 Firms with a low marginal cost of reducing pollution will buy marketable pollution permits.

10 When external costs are present, the private market produces more than the efficient level of output.

11 The efficient quantity of pollution is zero.

Positive Externalities: Knowledge

12 The existence of external benefits means that marginal social cost is greater than marginal private cost.

13 The private market equilibrium for goods with external benefits has deadweight loss, but the private market outcome with external costs has no deadweight loss because too many goods are produced.

14 Patents encourage invention and innovation.

15 Copyrights contribute to the development of knowledge so they have no economic cost.

Multiple-Choice

Externalities in Our Lives

1 An externality is a cost or benefit arising from an economic activity that falls on
a consumers but not producers.
b producers but not consumers.
c free riders.
d rivals.
e none of the above.

2 The production of too few goods with positive externalities is an example of
a market failure.
b government failure.
c producer sovereignty.
d consumer sovereignty.
e external costs.

3 Which of the following illustrates the concept of external cost?
a Bad weather reduces the size of the wheat crop.
b A reduction in the size of the wheat crop causes income of wheat farmers to fall.
c Smoking harms the health of the smoker.
d Smoking harms the health of nearby nonsmokers.
e Public health services reduce the transmission of disease.

Negative Externalities: Pollution

4 The income elasticity of demand for a better environment is
a negative.
b zero.
c positive.
d trendy.
e impossible to know without additional information.

5 Levels of acid rain caused by air pollution are
a less than efficient levels due to external costs.
b less than efficient levels due to external benefits.
c more than efficient levels due to external costs.
d more than efficient levels due to external benefits.
e decreasing the earth's average temperature.

6 Figure 18.3 shows demand for good *A* as well as the marginal private cost (*MC*) and marginal social cost (*MSC*) associated with production of good *A*. Production of the sixth unit of output generates an *external*

  a cost of $1.50.
  b cost of $3.00.
  c cost of $6.00.
  d benefit of $3.00.
  e benefit of $6.00.

FIGURE **18.3**

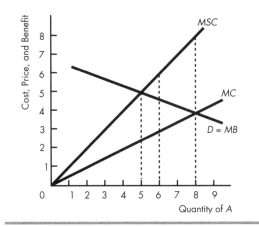

7 In Figure 18.3, how many units of good *A* will be produced in an unregulated market?

  a 0 units
  b 5 units
  c 6 units
  d 8 units
  e impossible to calculate without additional information

8 In Figure 18.3, what is the efficient quantity of good *A*?

  a 0 units
  b 5 units
  c 6 units
  d 8 units
  e impossible to calculate without additional information

9 At the current level of production of buckyballs, marginal social benefit is less than marginal social cost. To achieve allocative efficiency,

  a buckyballs should be taxed.
  b buckyballs should not be produced.
  c output of buckyballs should increase.
  d output of buckyballs should decrease.
  e property rights in buckyballs should be established.

10 The production of too many goods with negative externalities is an example of

  a redistribution.
  b consumer sovereignty.
  c producer sovereignty.
  d public failure.
  e market failure.

11 An externality is

  a the amount by which price exceeds marginal private cost.
  b the amount by which price exceeds marginal social cost.
  c the effect of government regulation on market price and output.
  d someone who consumes a good without paying for it.
  e a cost or benefit that arises from an activity but affects people not part of the original activity.

12 The marginal private cost curve (*MC*) is a positively sloped straight line starting at the origin. If marginal external costs per unit of output are constant, the marginal social cost curve is a positively sloped straight line

  a parallel to and above *MC*.
  b parallel to and below *MC*.
  c starting at the origin and above *MC*.
  d starting at the origin and below *MC*.
  e identical to *MC*.

13 A market economy tends to _____ goods with negative externalities and _____ goods with positive externalities.

  a overproduce; overproduce
  b overproduce; underproduce
  c underproduce; overproduce
  d underproduce; underproduce
  e produce; consume

14 Policies for correcting problems of negative externalities include all of the following *except*

  a emission charges.
  b patents.
  c quantitative limits.
  d Pigovian taxes.
  e marketable permits.

15 A battery acid producer pollutes the water upstream from nude swimmers belonging to the Polar Bear Club. If transactions costs are low, the quantity of pollution will be efficient

a   only if Ronald Coase is a member of the Polar Bear Club.

b   only if Ronald Coase is not a member of the Polar Bear Club.

c   only if water property rights are assigned to the producer.

d   only if water property rights are assigned to the Polar Bear Club.

e   if water property rights are assigned either to the producer or the Polar Bear Club.

16 Refer to Table 18.1. If the fertilizer market is perfectly competitive and unregulated, output (in tonnes) is

a   1.
b   2.
c   3.
d   4.
e   5.

TABLE **18.1**   CHEMICAL FERTILIZER MARKET

Output (tonnes)	Marginal Private Benefit ($)	Marginal Social Benefit ($)	Marginal Private Cost ($)	Marginal Social Cost ($)
1	140	140	50	80
2	120	120	60	90
3	100	100	70	100
4	80	80	80	110
5	60	60	90	120

17 Refer to Table 18.1. Fertilizer has a per-unit marginal external

a   cost of $100.
b   benefit of $100.
c   cost of $30.
d   benefit of $30.
e   cost of $0.

18 Refer to Table 18.1. The efficient output of fertilizer (in tonnes) is

a   1.
b   2.
c   3.
d   4.
e   5.

Positive Externalities: Knowledge

19 The marginal private benefit curve (*MB*) is a negatively sloped straight line. If marginal external benefits per unit of output are positive and decreasing with additional output, the marginal social benefit curve is a negatively sloped straight line

a   parallel to and above *MB*.
b   parallel to and below *MB*.
c   above and steeper than *MB*.
d   above and flatter than *MB*.
e   below and flatter than *MB*.

20 Figure 18.4 shows the demand curve for good *B*, the marginal social benefit (*MSB*) curve, and marginal private and social cost (*MC* = *MSC*) curve. How many units of good *B* will be produced and consumed in an unregulated market?

a   0
b   3
c   5
d   6
e   9

FIGURE **18.4**

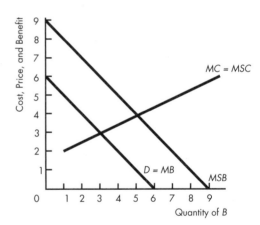

21 In Figure 18.4, what is the efficient quantity (in units) of good *B*?

a   0
b   3
c   5
d   6
e   9

22 In Figure 18.4, which of the following government policies would induce the market to achieve allocative efficiency?

a Tax the production of *B* at $3 per unit.
b Tax the production of *B* at $4 per unit.
c Provide vouchers for consumption of *B* at $1 per unit.
d Provide vouchers for consumption of *B* at $3 per unit.
e Provide vouchers for consumption of *B* at $4 per unit.

23 Policies to achieve allocative efficiency when there are external benefits include

a intellectual property rights.
b subsidies.
c public provision.
d all of the above.
e none of the above.

24 Knowledge, as a factor of production,

a displays diminishing marginal productivity.
b creates external costs.
c has costs totalling those paid to the patent holder.
d is encouraged by intellectual property rights.
e is all of the above.

25 When market failure occurs, government will act to reduce inefficiency. This is a prediction of a

a fair results theory of government behaviour.
b fair rules theory of government behaviour.
c public interest theory of government behaviour.
d public choice theory of government behaviour.
e rent-seeking theory of government behaviour.

Short Answer Problems

1 Your roommate is an environmentalist who is appalled at the economic concept of an "efficient" level of pollution. She argues that since everyone agrees pollution is "bad," society must work towards eliminating all pollution. How would you, as an economics major, convince her that it is not in society's best interests to eliminate all pollution?

2 The production of steel also produces pollution and generates external costs. Suppose government attempts to solve the problem by imposing a tax on steel producers. At the after-tax level of output, we observe the original marginal social cost curve is below the demand curve. Is the after-tax level of output efficient? If not, should steel production, and therefore pollution production, be increased or decreased?

3 Explain how a tax can be used to achieve efficiency in the face of external costs.

4 Two prairie pioneers, Jethro and Hortense, have adjacent fields. Because they get along so well and always work out any problems that arise, they have not bothered to put up a fence. Then one day Jethro buys a new pig, Babe. Babe sometimes wanders into Hortense's field and eats her corn. If Babe would only stay on Jethro's farm, he would eat valueless garbage. Suppose that Babe eats $500 worth of Hortense's corn per year (a negative externality imposed on Hortense) and that to build a fence between the farms costs $300. No property rights to keep animals off the fields have been established yet.

a If the property right is given to Jethro so Babe can continue to wander, will Hortense build a fence? Explain.
b If, instead, the property right is given to Hortense, so that she can charge Jethro for the corn Babe eats, will Jethro build a fence? Explain.
c Explain how this example illustrates the Coase theorem.

5 Lever Sisters Company produces Flatulost, a popular room deodorizer. Unfortunately, the production process releases sulfur dioxide into the atmosphere. The marginal private cost (*MC*) to Lever Sisters of producing Flatulost is

$$MC = 1Q_S.$$

The marginal social cost (*MSC*) is

$$MSC = 3/2Q_S$$

The demand curve for Flatulost (there are no external benefits) is

$$P = 12 - 1/2Q_D$$

Q_S is the quantity of Flatulost supplied, *P* is the price of Flatulost in dollars, and Q_D is the quantity demanded.

a In an unregulated market, what is the equilibrium quantity of Flatulost? the equilibrium price?
b To achieve allocative efficiency, what should be the equilibrium quantity of Flatulost? the equilibrium price?
c Compare the unregulated market quantity and price with the allocatively efficient quantity and price.
d The government wants to impose a tax on Flatulost to achieve the allocatively efficient quantity of output. What should the tax be?

6 Governments publicly provide education for free, or at least at a price (tuition) much less than cost. What is the economic argument that supports this policy?

7 The first two columns of Table 18.2 give the demand schedule for education in Hicksville, while the third column gives the marginal private cost. Since education generates external benefits, marginal social benefit given in the last column is greater than marginal private benefit.

TABLE **18.2** EDUCATION IN HICKSVILLE

Quantity (number of students)	Marginal Private Benefit ($)	Marginal Private Cost ($)	Marginal Social Benefit ($)
100	500	200	800
200	400	250	700
300	300	300	600
400	200	350	500
500	100	400	400
600	0	450	300

a Represent the data in Table 18.2 graphically.
b What equilibrium price and quantity would result if the market for education is unregulated?
c What is the allocatively efficient quantity of students in Hicksville?

8 In an attempt to address the inefficient level of education in Hicksville, the town council decides to publicly support schooling. The council offers a $200 voucher to each student who buys a year of education.
a Draw the new marginal private benefit curve, which includes the voucher, on your graph and label it MB_1.
b What are the approximate new equilibrium price and quantity?

9 The Hicksville town council increases the voucher to $400.
a Draw another marginal private benefit curve, which includes the voucher, on your graph and label it MPB_2.
b What are the approximate corresponding equilibrium price and quantity?
c What level of voucher will achieve the efficient quantity of education?

10 What are the benefits and costs of creating intellectual property rights for the creation of new knowledge?

ANSWERS

True/False and Explain

1 **F** Externalities can arise from production or consumption and be negative or positive. (414)
2 **F** Positive consumption externality. (414)
3 **T** Positive production or consumption externality provides external benefit. (414)
4 **T** $MSC = MC$ + marginal external cost. (417)
5 **F** $MSC = MC$ + marginal external cost. (417)
6 **T** Property rights allow recovery of (external) costs. (418–419)
7 **F** True if transactions costs low; false otherwise. (418–419)
8 **T** See text discussion. (420–421)
9 **F** Firms with low marginal cost of reducing pollution sell permits; firms with high marginal cost of reducing pollution buy. (420–421)
10 **T** Where MC (instead of MSC) intersects demand. (417–418)
11 **F** Efficient quantity where $D = MB$ intersects MSC production (including pollution). (417–418)
Ⓒ 12 **F** External benefits affect MSB, not MSC; $MSB = MB$ + Marginal external benefit. (421–423)
Ⓒ 13 **F** Both have deadweight loss; with external costs, deadweight loss is excess MSC over MB for units produced beyond efficient quantity. (417–418, 421–423)
14 **T** Intellectual property rights overcome positive externality problem of knowledge. (425)
15 **F** Copyrights are monopolies with associated inefficiencies; but benefits new knowledge presumed to outweigh costs of monopoly. (425)

Multiple-Choice

1 **e** Falls on people who are not part of original activity. (414)
2 **a** Markets fail to produce efficient quantity of goods with positive externalities. (413–414)
3 **d** Cost falls on people not part of original activity. (414)
4 **c** Better environment is normal good so $\eta y > 0$. (415)
5 **c** Market overproduction of good with negative externalities (external costs). (415–418)
6 **b** Vertical distance between MSC and MC at $Q = 6$. (417–419)
7 **d** Where MC intersects demand. (417–418)
8 **b** Where MSC intersects demand. (417–418)
9 **d** Draw graph. Don't know if positive, negative, or any externality. (417–423)

10 e Failure to achieve allocative efficiency because external costs not taken into account in private, market decisions. (417–419)
11 e Definition. (414–420)
12 a *MC* shifts leftward by vertical distance equal to marginal external cost per unit. (417)
13 b Outcomes of market failure. (418, 422–423)
14 b Patents correct problems of positive externalities. (420–421)
15 e This is the Coase theorem. (418–419)
16 d Where *MB* = *MC* = 80. (417–419)
17 c *MSC* – *MC* is constant in this example. (417–419)
18 c Where *MSB* = *MSC*. (417–419)
ⓒ **19 c** Similar to text Figure 18.6. (421–422)
20 b Where *MC* intersects demand. (421–423)
21 c Where *MC* intersects *MSB*. (421–423)
22 d Shift *MC* rightward by vertical distance between *MSB* and demand. (423–425)
23 d All move output to where *MSB* = *MSC*. (423–425)
24 d No diminishing marginal productivity; creates external benefits; patent monopoly creates loss from restricted use. (425)
25 c Public interest to achieve efficiency. (381, 423–425)

Short Answer Problems

ⓒ **1** We all want to eliminate pollution, *ceteris paribus*, but every action, including reducing pollution, has a cost. Once again, the key concept underlying the economic argument is opportunity cost. What is the opportunity cost of reducing pollution, or, what does society have to give up to achieve a pollution-free environment?

Small reductions in pollution are relatively inexpensive—eliminating lead from gasoline and paint, conserving energy to reduce output from coal-fired electrical plants, etc. But to eliminate all pollution would mean eliminating all cars and airplanes, outlawing all power except solar and hydroelectric power, shutting down most factories, etc. The cost of eliminating *all* pollution is enormous, and that additional cost is far greater than the additional benefits from further reductions in pollution. Therefore some level of pollution is efficient. Pollution is part of the opportunity cost of the benefits we receive from driving or flying instead of walking, from enjoying the comfort of air conditioning in hot weather, and from enjoying goods produced in factories. The efficient level of pollution balances the marginal social cost of the pollution against the marginal social benefit of the production and consumption associated with that level of pollution.

2 Since the marginal social cost curve is below the demand curve at the after-tax output, marginal social cost is less than marginal benefit. This means that the tax has been set too high; it has been set at a level in excess of the external cost. As a result, the after-tax level of steel production will be less than the efficient level. The level of steel production and pollution production should be increased by decreasing the amount of the tax.

3 The existence of external costs means that producers do not take into account all costs when deciding how much to produce. If a tax is levied that is exactly the amount of the external cost, the cost will no longer be external. As a result, the producer will take it into account and be induced to produce the efficient quantity.

4 a Hortense will build a fence. Although the fence costs $300 per year, it saves her the $500 in lost corn that Babe would otherwise eat.
b Jethro will build a fence. The $300 per year is less than the $500 per year he would now have to pay Hortense for Babe's wanderings.
c The Coase theorem states that if transactions costs are low and property rights are established, there are no externalities and an efficient outcome occurs regardless of who is assigned the property right. Because Jethro and Hortense can work out their problems amicably, transactions costs are low. The outcome of building a fence eliminates the negative externality of the wandering pig and occurs regardless of which pioneer is assigned the property right. The outcome is efficient because, for this one decision, the $300 cost to society of the fence is less than the $500 cost of consumed corn.

ⓔⓒ **5 a** In an unregulated market, the equilibrium quantity would be determined by the intersection of the supply (*MC*) and demand curves. In equilibrium, $Q_S = Q_D = Q^*$. Setting the *MC* equation equal to the demand equation yields

$$1Q^* = 12 - 1/2Q^*$$
$$3/2Q^* = 12$$
$$Q^* = 8$$

To solve for the equilibrium price (*P**), substitute Q^* into the demand (or into the *MC*) equation.

$$P^* = 12 - 1/2Q^*$$
$$P^* = 12 - 1/2 (8)$$
$$P^* = 8$$

b In order to achieve efficiency, *MSC* must equal marginal social benefit (*MSB*). Since there are no external benefits, the demand curve is also the *MSB* curve. In equilibrium, $Q_S = Q_D = Q^*$. To find the equilibrium quantity, set the *MSC* equation equal to the demand equation.

$$3/2Q^* = 12 - 1/2Q^*$$
$$2Q^* = 12$$
$$Q^* = 6$$

To solve for the equilibrium price (P^*), substitute Q^* into the demand (or into the *MSC*) equation.

$$P^* = 12 - 1/2Q^*$$
$$P^* = 12 - 1/2 \ (6)$$
$$P^* = 9$$

c Compared with the efficient outcomes, the unregulated market produces too much Flatulost (8 units versus 6) and the product sells at too low a price ($8 versus $9).

d The tax should be equal to the cost differential (*MSC* – *MC*) at the optimum output of 6 units. Since the *MSC* curve = 1.5 × *MC* curve, the tax should be 50 percent.

6 Government subsidizes education heavily. The economic argument is that education generates external benefits. When individuals are educated, society at large receives benefits beyond the private benefits that accrue to those choosing how much education to obtain.

7 a Figure 18.5 is a graphical representation of the data in Table 18.2. The demand for education is given by the marginal private benefit curve (labelled *MB*), the marginal private cost curve is labelled *MC* and the marginal social benefit curve is labelled *MSB*. Ignore the other curves for now.

FIGURE **18.5**

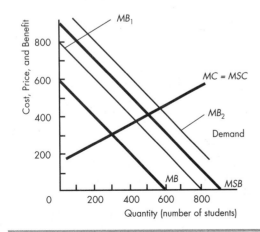

b In an unregulated market, equilibrium price and quantity are determined by the intersection of the *MB* and *MC* curves. The equilibrium price is $300 and the equilibrium quantity is 300 students.

c Since there are no external costs, the efficient quantity is determined by the intersection of the *MC* and *MSB* curves. Efficiency is attained at a quantity of 500 students.

8 a The voucher increases the marginal private benefit to each student by the amount of the voucher, $200. The new *MB* curve, labelled MB_1, is included in Figure 18.5.

b The new equilibrium after the $200 voucher is at the intersection of the *MC* and MB_1 curves. The price of a unit of education is approximately $370 and there are approximately 430 students.

9 a With a voucher of $400 per student, the *MB* curve shifts to MB_2 in Figure 18.5.

b With this voucher the equilibrium is at the intersection of the *MC* and MB_2 curves. The corresponding price of a unit of education is approximately $430 and the number of students is approximately 570.

c In order to achieve an efficient outcome, the voucher must make the *MB* curve coincide with the *MSB* curve. This requires a voucher of $300 per student.

10 Intellectual property rights create incentives for individuals to create new knowledge by granting the inventor a limited monopoly to benefit from the application of her idea. Without the property right, anyone could freely use the idea and there would be little profit to the inventor. The limited monopoly, although necessary as an incentive to produce knowledge, has a social cost—the restriction of knowledge-based output below the efficient, competitive quantity.

Understanding Market Failure and Government

PROBLEM

The Canadian Radio-television and Telecommunications Commission (CRTC) is holding public hearings on renewing the licence of Cretin's Choice Cable TV Company. You have been hired to help the CRTC evaluate the contradictory claims made by different interest groups in testimony to the commission. Figure P6.1 shows the best available information about costs and revenues for Cretin's Choice.

FIGURE **P6.1**   CRETIN'S CHOICE

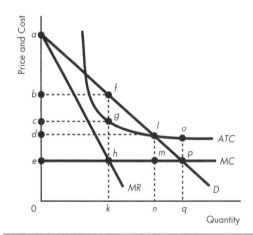

a   On the basis of Figure P6.1, explain why there is market failure and a potential role for government regulation.

b   Cretin's Choice would like to maximize its profits. Identify the firm's profit-maximizing rule and explain the outcome (price, quantity, economic profit, consumer's surplus, deadweight loss) on Figure P6.1.

c   Consumer groups are pushing for a regulatory rule that maximizes consumer surplus. Identify the rule and explain the outcome (price,

quantity, economic profit, consumer's surplus) on Figure P6.1. If the CRTC adopts the rule, what options might you suggest that would keep the cable company in business?

d   Any CRTC regulation rule has to appear to meet the public interest goal of maximum allocative efficiency. Identify the rule (other than marginal cost pricing) that comes closest to achieving this goal and explain the outcome (price, quantity, economic profit, consumer's surplus, deadweight loss) on Figure P6.1.

e   While Cretin's Choice wants maximum profits, it recognizes the CRTC's need to *appear* to use the regulatory rule in part **d**. What argument can you expect to hear from Cretin's Choice? Use Figure P6.1 to explain.

f   If, despite your advice to the contrary, the CRTC accepts the industry argument in part **e**, what theory of regulation is supported?

g   After years of the type of regulation in part **f**, the CRTC deregulates Cretin's Choice's market. If rates of return increase, what theory of regulation is supported?

MIDTERM EXAMINATION

You should allocate 32 minutes for this examination (16 questions, 2 minutes per question). For each question, choose the one *best* answer.

1   Refer to Figure P6.2. Producer surplus lost from the tax (not including tax paid) is equal to triangle

a   *abc.*
b   *dbc.*
c   *dac.*
d   *dij.*
e   *gdi.*

FIGURE **P6.2**

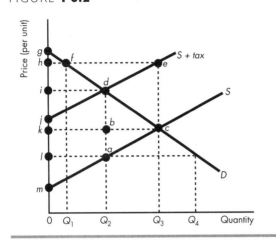

FIGURE **P6.3**

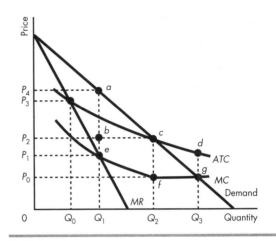

2 Refer to Figure P6.2. Consumer surplus lost from the tax (not including tax paid) is equal to triangle

a *abc.*
b *dbc.*
c *dac.*
d *dij.*
e *gdi.*

3 Total surplus is the sum of

a the gain from trade accruing to consumers and the gain from trade accruing to producers.
b the gain from regulation and the gain from anti-combine laws.
c revenues received by firms and government subsidies.
d consumer payments and producer profit.
e none of the above.

4 Consider the natural monopoly in Figure P6.3. Producer surplus is a maximum when quantity is

a Q_0 and price is P_3.
b Q_1 and price is P_1.
c Q_1 and price is P_4.
d Q_2 and price is P_2.
e Q_3 and price is P_0.

5 According to the economic theory of bureaucracy, bureaucrats

a aim to maximize the budget of their bureau.
b aim to maximize total surplus.
c aim to privatize Crown corporations.
d will operate Crown corporations to underproduce compared to private firms.
e will be rationally ignorant.

6 The demand for government regulation in a market depends on

a consumer surplus per buyer.
b number of buyers.
c producer surplus per firm.
d number of firms.
e all of the above.

7 Refer to Figure P6.4. The unregulated outcome in the paper market is

a quantity = 40, price = 11.
b quantity = 40, price = 13.
c quantity = 50, price = 12.
d quantity = 50, price = 14.
e quantity = 60, price = 13.

FIGURE **P6.4** PAPER MARKET

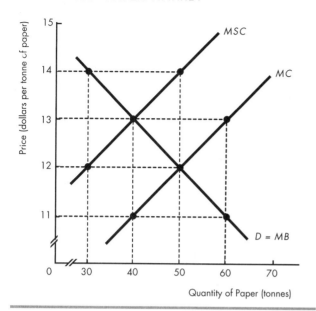

8 Refer to Figure P6.4. A tax of _____ per tonne is necessary to achieve the efficient output of _____ tonnes of paper.

a $14; 50
b $14; 30
c $13; 40
d $2; 50
e $2; 40

9 Public interest theory predicts the political process minimizes

a producer surplus.
b consumer surplus.
c total surplus.
d deadweight loss.
e allocative efficiency.

10 The factor of production least likely to display diminishing marginal productivity is

a land.
b labour.
c capital.
d entrepreneurship.
e knowledge.

11 According to the Coase theorem, if transactions costs are low and property rights exist,

a negative externalities cause deadweight losses.
b positive externalities cause deadweight losses.
c private transactions are efficient.
d public transactions are efficient.
e the efficient level of pollution will be zero.

12 If the marginal tax rate decreases as income increases, the income tax is defined as

a progressive.
b proportional.
c negative.
d regressive.
e redistributive.

13 Marketable permits for polluting the air

a give firms a pollution limit that can be bought and sold.
b overcome the need for the regulator to know firms' own costs and benefits of pollution.
c will be priced in a competitive market to yield efficient pollution outcomes where $MSC = MSB$.
d can potentially achieve the same pollution outcome as Pigovian taxes.
e are all of the above.

14 The *total benefit* of a given level of provision of a public good can be obtained by

a adding the marginal benefit of each level of provision up to the given level.
b adding the marginal benefit of each level of provision and then subtracting the marginal cost of each level of provision.
c adding the net benefit of each level of provision up to the given level.
d multiplying net benefit by the quantity of the public good provided.
e none of the above methods.

15 Voters are asked to vote for either proposition *A* or proposition *B*. Proposition *A* will win if it

a is closer to allocative efficiency.
b is supported by bureaucrats.
c is preferred by the median voter.
d generates greater social benefits than social costs.
e generates the fewest negative externalities.

16 Policies for correcting problems of positive externalities include

a emission charges.
b vouchers.
c marketable permits.
d Pigovian taxes.
e all of the above

ANSWERS

Problem

a Market failure is the inability of an unregulated market to efficiently allocate resources. Cretin's Choice is a natural monopoly with economies of scale. While only a monopoly can achieve the economies of scale, in the absence of regulation, it will restrict output, increase price, and create a deadweight efficiency loss.

b The profit-maximizing rule is to choose the quantity of output where $MC = MR$ and charge the highest possible price. On Figure P6.1, price is b, quantity is k, economic profit is $bcgf$, consumer's surplus is abf, and deadweight loss is fhp.

c The marginal cost pricing rule (set price equal to MC) maximizes consumer surplus. On Figure P6.1, price is e, quantity is q, loss per unit is op, and consumer's surplus is aep. The firm is making a loss and will not voluntarily stay in business. You could suggest that the company be allowed to price discriminate or that it receive a government subsidy (financed by taxes that would create a deadweight loss elsewhere).

d An average cost pricing rule sets price equal to ATC. On Figure P6.1, price is d, quantity is n, economic profit is zero, consumer's surplus is adl, and deadweight loss is lmp. If this deadweight loss is less than the deadweight loss associated with subsidizing the marginal cost pricing rule in part **c**, then the average cost price rule comes closest to achieving allocative efficiency.

e Cretin's Choice will argue that their costs are much higher than those reflected in the ATC curve of Figure P6.1. The company will inflate its costs and argue that its real ATC curve is higher and just tangent to the demand curve at point f. If the CRTC accepts this argument and applies the average cost pricing rule, the regulated price and outcome will be the same as the monopolist's own profit-maximizing rule in part **b**.

f If the CRTC accepts the industry argument in part **e**, the capture theory of regulation is supported.

g If, after deregulation, rates of return increase, the public interest theory of regulation is supported.

Midterm Examination

1 **a** See text discussion. (386–387)
2 **b** See text discussion. (386–387)
3 **a** Consumer surplus plus producer surplus; see Chapter 17, Helpful Hint **1**, page 244. (394–396)
4 **c** Private monopoly outcome. (397–398)
5 **a** See text discussion. (403–405)
6 **e** See text discussion. (394–395)
7 **c** Where $D = MB$ intersects MC. (417–418)
8 **e** $2 per tonne tax (vertical distance between MC and MSC) makes firm's MC equal to MSC. Output where $D = MB$ intersects MSC. (418–420)
9 **d** Or maximize total surplus (allocative efficiency). (381)
10 **e** Because of external benefits. (425)
11 **c** There are no externalities. Level of pollution where $MB = MSC$. (418–419)
12 **d** Definition. (382–384)
13 **e** See text discussion. (420–421)
14 **a** **b–d** involve irrelevant costs. (377–378)
15 **c** 50 percent of votes plus 1. (384)
16 **b** Others for negative externality problems. (423–425)

Chapter 19

A First Look at Macroeconomics

KEY CONCEPTS

Origins and Issues of Macroeconomics

Modern macroeconomics was born during the **Great Depression** (a decade of high unemployment).

◆ Keynes' focus was the short-term problems of the depression, which he thought were caused by too little spending.

◆ Once out of depression, long-term problems of inflation, etc. become central, implying government spending must be moderated. The events of the 1960s–70s showed the importance of these long-term problems.

◆ Recently, macroeconomics has merged the short-term and long-term issues to study unemployment, economic growth, inflation, and deficits.

Economic Growth

Economic growth increases economy's capacity to produce goods and services, measured by rise in real domestic product (real GDP).

◆ **Real GDP**—value of total production, measured in the prices of a single year.

◆ **Potential GDP**—real GDP when labour, capital, land, and entrepreneurial ability are fully employed.

◆ Economic growth in Canada has had two features.

• Long-term economic growth—this grew rapidly in the 1960s, but has grown much less rapidly since then due to a **productivity growth slowdown**.

• Business cycles—the periodic but irregular fluctuation of real GDP around potential.

◆ Each cycle is irregular, but has two turning points (a **peak** and a **trough**), and two phases (a **recession** when real GDP decreases for two or more quarters, and an **expansion** when real GDP increases).

◆ The recession of 1990–91 was mild but long compared to earlier recessions, much milder than the Great Depression of the 1930s.

◆ Compared to the world's largest economies, Canada has
• similar business cycles and **growth recessions** (slowdowns in the economic growth rate).
• faster growth of potential GDP than United States or Germany, but slower growth than Japan.

◆ Benefit of economic growth includes increased consumption possibilities of individuals and governments.

◆ Costs of economic growth include lost consumption due to resources devoted to growth rather than consumption, perhaps more rapid resource depletion and environmental pollution, more frequent job changes.

Jobs and Unemployment

Each year in Canada, many jobs are created and destroyed. Average net effect is 200,000 new jobs, but when aggregate production is falling, then more jobs destroyed than created, and vice versa when production is rising.

◆ **Unemployment** occurs when qualified workers seeking jobs cannot find any.

• **Unemployment rate**—percentage of labour force unemployed.

- **Labour force**—sum of unemployed and employed.
- Measured unemployment is flawed due to exclusion of **discouraged workers** (those who wish to work but give up searching) and part-time workers who desire full-time work.

◆ Unemployment has fluctuated greatly in Canadian history, with peaks occurring in 1930s, early 1980s, and early 1990s.

◆ Unemployment rises in recessions and falls in expansions.

◆ Costs of unemployment are lost production and income of unemployed and deterioration of job prospects due to lost human capital.

Inflation

Inflation is an increase in average level of prices (or **price level**), measured by the inflation rate (percentage change in price level).

◆ **Deflation**—inflation rate is negative.

◆ Inflation in Canada was low in the 1960s, rose through the 1970s, and is down since then due to the actions of the Bank of Canada.

◆ Canada's inflation rate is historically similar to that of other industrial countries, but recently is lower.

◆ Unpredictable inflation

- creates winners/losers by creating unpredictable changes in the value of money.
- leads to resources getting diverted from productive activities to predicting inflation.

◆ Getting rid of inflation is costly, since it usually involves more unemployment.

Surpluses and Deficits

◆ **Government budget surpluses** occur when tax revenues exceed spending.

◆ **Government budget deficits** occur when government spending exceeds tax revenues.

◆ Canada's international deficit occurs when our imports exceed our exports.

- The international deficit is often measured by the **current account**, which includes exports minus imports and net interest payments.

◆ Deficits of either kind mean governments and nations must borrow, and pay interest on debts. This borrowing is a problem if it is for consumption purposes.

Macroeconomic Policy Challenges and Tools

Five main policy challenges are to reduce unemployment, increase economic growth, stabilize the business cycle, keep inflation low, lower government and international deficits.

◆ Two main policy tools are

- **fiscal policy**—the government changing its taxes and spending programs.
- **monetary policy**—the Bank of Canada changing interest rates and the amount of money in the economy.

HELPFUL HINTS

1 Note that to be unemployed, as officially measured by the Canadian Labour Force Survey, it is not enough to be without a job. One must also be "actively" seeking a job. Most university students are without jobs, but they are not counted as unemployed since they are not looking for jobs while they are attending school.

2 The variables we study in this chapter are interdependent—they affect and are affected by each other in economic interrelationships that we will learn about in subsequent chapters.

   The most important relationship is the effect of the business cycle on other variables. Business cycles significantly affect the unemployment rate. In a recession, the unemployment rate rises, reaching its highest level when the economy is in the trough of the cycle. In an expansion, the unemployment rate falls, reaching its lowest level at the peak.

   Government deficits are also affected strongly by business cycles. In a recession, real GDP falls and taxes collected fall, while government payments such as employment insurance and social assistance rise, creating a larger deficit. The opposite effects occur during an expansion.

   There is also a strong relationship between business cycles and the current account. When exports are rising and we have a current account surplus, the surplus creates expansionary pressures on real GDP. On the other hand, as the economy expands, Canadians tend to buy more imported goods, pushing the current account towards a deficit.

3 The inflation rate is calculated as the percentage change in prices using the formula

$$\text{Inflation rate} = \frac{\text{Current year's price level} - \text{Last year's price level}}{\text{Last year's price level}} \times 100$$

For example, the average 1997 price level was 107.6, and the average 1996 price level was 105.8, allowing us to calculate the inflation rate for 1997:

$$\text{Inflation rate} = \frac{107.6 - 105.8}{105.8} \times 100 = 1.7\%$$

4 Inflation creates problems because it creates unpredictable changes in the value of money. The *value of money* is the quantity of goods and services that can be bought with a given amount of money. When an economy experiences inflation, the value of money falls—you cannot buy as many goods with a dollar this year as you could last year.

To illustrate this point, consider the data in Table 19.1 on the price of a chocolate bar in Canada over the past 52 years:[1]

TABLE **19.1**

Year	Price of Chocolate Bar (¢)	Number of Bars $1 Buys
1950	10	10.00
1966	15	6.67
1976	30	3.33
1986	75	1.33
2002	100	1.00

The table shows us the strong cumulative impact of inflation over this time period, as well as the result that the value of a dollar has fallen enormously over this time period—it buys about 1/10th as many chocolate bars as it did in 1950. When your grandfather tells you "A dollar ain't worth what it used to be," he's telling the truth!

<hr>

[1] *Source:* Statistics Canada, *The Consumer Price Index*, with calculations and extrapolation from 1989 by H. King.

<hr style="border-top: 3px double;">

SELF-TEST

True/False and Explain

Origins and Issues of Macroeconomics

1 Macroeconomics focuses only on short-term problems such as unemployment.

Economic Growth

2 Higher economic growth is always good for an economy.

3 Potential GDP is the level of real GDP when labour, capital, land and entrepreneurial ability are fully employed.

4 A growth recession is when real GDP growth turns negative.

Jobs and Unemployment

5 In the recession phase of a business cycle, the unemployment rate is rising.

6 Discouraged workers are counted as unemployed but probably should not be.

7 Canadian unemployment is virtually identical to U.S. unemployment.

8 A university student seeking a job is counted as unemployed.

Inflation

9   If the price level was 130 in 1998 and 110 in 1997, the inflation rate in 1998 was 20 percent.

10   Since inflation is costly, getting rid of it is always a good idea.

11   If the rate of inflation becomes more unpredictable, people will hold less money on average.

Surpluses and Deficits

12   If Canada sells more to the rest of the world than it buys from the rest of the world, Canada will have an international deficit.

13   A government budget deficit will always create problems for the government.

Macroeconomic Policy Challenges and Tools

14   In Canada, fiscal policy is implemented by the federal government.

15   One of the five main policy challenges is to increase inflation.

Multiple-Choice

Origins and Issues of Macroeconomics

1   Modern macroeconomics
a   was born during the 1960s–70s.
b   initially focused on long-term problems.
c   focuses only on short-term problems.
d   now merges both short-term and long-term problems.
e   focuses only on long-term problems.

2   Which of the following statements about long-term economic problems is *true*?
a   Keynes ignored them.
b   Keynes said they could be cured by increased government spending.
c   Economists consider them much less important than short-term problems.
d   They include inflation and slow economic growth.
e   The biggest one is business cycles.

Economic Growth

3   Comparing Canada's economic growth with the major industrial economies' growth shows that
a   Canada experienced a productivity growth slowdown, but they did not.
b   Canada and the United States experienced a productivity growth slowdown, but Japan and Germany did not.
c   Canada did not experience the productivity growth slowdown that the others did.
d   Canada always had a lower level of economic growth.
e   all four countries experienced a slowdown in economic growth at about the same time.

4   Increasing potential GDP is
a   always beneficial since living standards rise.
b   always too costly since pollution and resource depletion rise.
c   beneficial only if pollution rises at 5 percent a year.
d   beneficial if the benefits of rising living standards outweigh the costs of higher pollution and resource depletion.
e   none of the above.

5   Which of the following politicians is talking about the business cycle?
a   "Canadian unemployment is falling due to the upturn in the economy."
b   "Crime rates increase every spring as the school year ends."
c   "An average of 200,000 new jobs are created each year in Canada."
d   "More capital investment will create more jobs."
e   "Business always rises just before Christmas."

6 Real GDP is defined as the yearly value of

a all goods produced in an economy.
b all goods and services produced in an economy.
c the goods and services produced in households.
d production when resources are full employed.
e all goods and services produced in an economy, measured in the prices of a single year.

7 The correct order of the sequence of business cycle phases is

a expansion, peak, recession, trough.
b expansion, peak, trough, deviation.
c expansion, trough, recession, peak.
d expansion, recession, trough, peak.
e expansion, deviation, recession, trough.

8 In New Adanac, the percent change in real GDP went from 5% in 2003 to 2% in 2004. What would an economist call this change in the growth rate?

a A growth recession
b A recession
c An expansion
d A trough
e A slowdown recession

Jobs and Unemployment

9 Compared to the U.S. unemployment rate, the Canadian unemployment rate moves

a independently of the U.S. rate.
b with the U.S. rate, but at a lower level recently.
c in the opposite direction to the U.S. rate.
d with the U.S. rate, but at a higher level recently.
e with the U.S. rate, and at the same level.

10 The economic costs of unemployment include

a workers quitting and going to university.
b political problems for government.
c lost job prospects of the unemployed.
d the fast pace of job changes.
e the diversion of resources from productive activities to predicting unemployment.

11 In which of the following years was the unemployment rate in Canada almost 20 percent?

a 1982
b 1976
c 1959
d 1933
e 1926

12 In a country with a population of 20 million, there are 9 million employed and 1 million unemployed. What is the labour force?

a 20 million
b 10 million
c 9 million
d 8 million
e 1 million

13 In a country with a population of 20 million, there are 9 million employed and 1 million unemployed. What is the unemployment rate?

a 11 percent
b 10 percent
c 8 percent
d 5 percent
e 1 percent

14 Including discouraged workers in the measured unemployment rate would

a not change the measured unemployment rate.
b lower the measured unemployment rate.
c lower the labour force.
d raise the measured unemployment rate only if there are no part-time workers.
e raise the measured unemployment rate.

Inflation

15 If the inflation rate is positive, the price level in an economy is

a falling rapidly.
b rising.
c constant.
d falling slowly.
e zero.

16 How does an unpredictable inflation cause problems?

a It increases the variability of business cycles
b The stock market falls in value
c The value of money starts rising
d Resources are diverted from productive activities to tax evasion
e Resources are diverted from productive activities to forecasting inflation

17 Which of the following statements about Canada's inflation rate is *false*?

a It is currently lower than that of most other industrial countries.

b It was low in the 1960s.

c It rose in the 1970s.

d It fell in the 1980s due to the actions of the Bank of Canada.

e Historically, it has always been around that of other industrial countries.

18 If a price index was 128 at the end of 1987 and 136 at the end of 1988, what was the rate of inflation for 1988?

a 4.2 percent

b 5.9 percent

c 6.25 percent

d 8 percent

e 9.4 percent

19 If the price index in 1997 is equal to 130, and the inflation rate between 1997 and 1998 is 5 percent, what is the price index in 1998?

a 136.5

b 135

c 125

d 123.5

e 105

Surpluses and Deficits

20 The government deficit will rise if

a we buy more from other countries than we sell to them.

b we sell more to other countries than we buy from them.

c government revenues rise.

d unemployment rises.

e the baby boomers continue to run the country.

21 Most of the time since 1970, the current account

a deficit has been large.

b surplus has been large.

c deficit has been small.

d surplus has been small.

e has had alternating surpluses and deficits.

22 Deficits are a problem

a if they are caused by economic growth.

b only if they are international deficits, not government budget deficits.

c only if they are government budget deficits, not international deficits.

d only when they are caused by borrowing for consumption purposes.

e only when they are caused by borrowing to buy income-generating assets.

23 Which of the following will *increase* the Canadian current account deficit?

a Japan buys wheat from farmers in Canada.

b Japan buys wheat from farmers in Australia.

c Japan buys Canada Savings Bonds.

d Canada buys Hondas from Japan.

e Canada sells coal to Japan.

Macroeconomic Policy Challenges and Tools

24 An example of fiscal policy is changing the

a interest rate.

b money supply.

c exchange rate.

d tax rate.

e all of the above.

25 Which of the following is *not* a policy challenge?

a lowering unemployment

b stabilizing the business cycle

c keeping inflation low

d stopping economic growth

e lowering government deficits

Short Answer Problems

1 What are the economic costs of unemployment?

2 Go to the Statistics Canada World Wide Web site (**http://www.statcan.ca**) or the Statistics Canada publication *The Consumer Price Index*, and find out the price level in December of the most recent year available, as well as the previous year, and calculate the inflation rate over that year.

3 What is meant by the value of money? Why does the value of money fall when there is inflation?

4 The federal government gives full-time students a tax credit per month of studies. In 1980, Tracy received this credit, which was worth $50 per month, whereas in 2001 Jennifer received a credit worth $200 per month. In 1980, the price level was 52.4, and in 2001 it was 116.5. Was the value of the tax credit money worth more to Jennifer or Tracy? (Ignore any changes in taxes, tuition, etc.)

5 What is the current account? What has its recent history been like?

6 During each of the four parts of the business cycle, what happens to real GDP compared to potential GDP, and to the unemployment rate?

7 Workers and managers in the ABC Company have negotiated a wage agreement under the expectation that the inflation rate will be zero over the period of the contract. In order to protect workers against unpredictable inflation, however, the contract states that at the end of each year, the wage rate will increase by the same percentage as the increase in the consumer price index (CPI). At the beginning of the contract the CPI is 214 and the wage rate is set at $10 an hour. At the end of the first year the CPI is 225, and at the end of the second year the CPI is 234. What will the new wage rate become at the end of the first year? the second year?

8 Consider the following information about an economy: Population—25 million, employment—10 million, unemployment— 1 million.
a What is the labour force in this economy?
b What is the unemployment rate?

9 Consider the following data on unemployment and the growth rate of real GDP from the country of Dazedland:

Year	Percentage Change in Real GDP	Unemployment Rate
1	2.0	7.0
2	3.0	6.0
3	1.0	7.8
4	0.0	9.0
5	–2.0	11.5
6	–0.3	9.5
7	3.0	6.5
8	1.5	7.5

a Identify the peaks and troughs of the business cycle for this economy.
b In what years is this economy in recession?
c In which years did this economy have growth recessions?

d What is the relation between unemployment and the business cycle for this economy?

10 Is more economic growth good or bad for a society?

ANSWERS

True/False and Explain

1 F Recently macroeconomics has merged the short-term and long-term issues into a broad study. (438)
2 F It depends on the benefits versus the costs of the higher growth. (443)
3 T Definition. (439)
4 F When real GDP growth is still positive, but has fallen from the previous year. (439)
5 T As economy moves in recession, real GDP growth becomes negative, some workers become unemployed. (446)
6 F They are not counted as unemployed, but probably should be. (445)
7 F Canadian and U.S. unemployment move together, but recently Canadian unemployment > U.S. unemployment. (446)
8 F Counted as out of the labour force (not actively seeking work). (444)
9 F Inflation = [(130 – 110)/110] × 100 = 18.2%. (447)
10 F Inflation is costly, but so is getting rid of it, which increases unemployment. It depends on the relative size of the costs. (449–450)
11 T Unpredictable changes in the value of money lead to individuals holding less money. (449)
12 F Sales > purchases implies international *surplus*. (449)
13 F It depends whether or not the government borrows to increase consumption (bad) or investment (good). (450)
14 T It chooses spending, taxation, and deficit which is fiscal policy. (451)
15 F *Decrease* inflation. (451)

Multiple-Choice

1 d It was born during the Great Depression, when it focused on short-term problems, but recently it has merged studies of both. (438)
2 d Keynes did worry about them, noting they could be caused by too much government spending. Economists now study them and short-term problems together. **e** is short-term. (438)

3 e See Text Figure 19.4—all four countries had a substantial fall in their growth rates around 1970. (442–443)

4 d To decide, must weigh both costs and benefits and see which is higher. (443–444)

5 a Upturn implies expansion implies unemployment falls. **b** and **e** are irrelevant, **c** is the average over the cycle, **d** is growth in potential GDP. (440)

6 e Definition. (439)

7 a Definition. (440)

8 a Definition. (440)

9 d See Text Figure 19.7 and its discussion. (446)

10 c **a** is a gain, **b** is cost to government, **d** is cost of growth, **e** is not a cost, just an outcome. (446–447)

11 d During the Great Depression of the 1930s. (445)

12 b Labour force = unemployed + employed. (444–445)

13 b Unemployment rate = unemployed/labour force = 1/10. (444–445)

14 e It would add extra unemployed workers to the measured rate. (445)

15 b Positive inflation implies current price level – past price level > 0 by definition. (447)

16 e Forecasting inflation becomes important because unpredictable inflation leads to unpredictable winners and losers because the value of money *falls*. (448)

17 a See Text Figure 19.9. (447–448)

18 c 6.25% = [(136 – 128)/128] × 100. (447)

19 a Solve by inverting formula inflation rate = $((P_{1998} - P_{1997})/P_{1997}) \times 100$. (447)

20 d **a**, **b**, **e** are irrelevant, while **c** lowers deficit. Unemployment increasing implies more government spending and less tax revenues. (447)

21 a See Text Figure 19.10. (450)

22 d Both types of deficits can be problems, if they are for consumption, because they do not generate profits/income to help repay the resulting debts. **a** is irrelevant. (450)

23 d **a** and **e** lower the deficit, **b** and **c** are irrelevant. (449–450)

24 d **a** and **b** are monetary policy, **c** is neither. (451)

25 d Raising economic growth is a policy challenge. (451)

Short Answer Problems

1   The biggest cost of unemployment is the lost production and income. In addition, when workers are unemployed for long periods of time, their skills and abilities deteriorate, and so do their future job prospects.

2   You should have used the following formula:

$$\text{Inflation rate} = \frac{\text{Current year's price level} - \text{Last year's price level}}{\text{Last year's price level}} \times 100.$$

3   The value of money is the quantity of goods and services that can be purchased with one unit of money. Since inflation means that prices are rising on average, it means that one unit of money will buy less. Thus the value of money falls when there is inflation.

4   There are two ways to answer this question. First, between 1980 and 2001 the tax credit has risen in value by 300 percent (= 150/50 × 100), while the price level has risen by 122 percent (= (116.5 – 52.4) × 100). Clearly prices have risen less than the dollar value of the credit, raising the value of this money, so Jennifer gains more from it. Second, you could calculate the purchasing power of the tax credit in terms of how many goods it can purchase (remember the price index measures the cost of a typical family's purchases). For Tracy the credit purchased 0.96 of a typical family's purchases (= 50/52.4), whereas for Jennifer it purchased 1.72 (= 200/116.5). Clearly Jennifer gained more from the credit.

5   The current account includes our exports minus our imports and also takes interest payments paid to and received from the rest of the world into account. As Text Figure 19.10 shows, Canada's current account had been fluctuating (but usually negative) since 1970 to the late 1990s, but since the late 1990s it has been rising as a percent of GDP.

6   During the recession phase of the business cycle, the rate of growth of real GDP slows down and becomes negative, and real GDP falls below potential GDP. During this phase the unemployment rate is rising. At the trough, real GDP reaches its lowest point below potential GDP, and the unemployment rate is at its highest point over the cycle. The trough is a turning point between the recession phase and the expansion phase during which the rate of growth of real GDP increases and the unemployment rate falls. At the end of an expansion, the economy reaches the peak of the business cycle. The peak is characterized by real GDP at its highest point above potential GDP and the rate of unemployment is at its lowest point over the business cycle.

7 In order to determine the new wage rate at the end of the first year, we must determine the percentage increase in the CPI and apply that percentage change to the initial wage rate of $10 an hour. The percentage change in the CPI is [(225 − 214)/214] × 100, or 5.1 percent. Therefore the new wage rate at the end of the first year will be $10 × 1.051 = $10.51. During the second year, the increase in the CPI is 4 percent. Thus the new wage rate at the end of the second year will be $10.51 × 1.04 = $10.93.

8 a The labour force is 11 million, the sum of employment and unemployment.

  b The unemployment rate is 9.1 percent, the number of unemployed as a percentage of the labour force.

9 a Peaks occur when the percentage change in real GDP turns from positive to negative, year 4. Troughs occur when the percentage change in real GDP turns from negative to positive, between years 6 and 7.

  b The economy is in recession when the growth rate of real GDP is negative, years 5 and 6.

  c A growth recession occurs when economic growth is positive, but declining from the previous year. In Dazedland, this occurs in years 3, 4, and 8.

  d There is a rough inverse relationship between the two variables—when real GDP is rising, the unemployment rate is falling (between years 1 and 2), and when real GDP is falling, the unemployment rate is rising (between years 4 and 5).

ct 10 There is no correct answer to this question, since it depends on the balance of the costs versus the benefits of more growth—it is a normative question. However, a society would need to weigh the costs (lost consumption because of resources devoted to growth rather than consumption, potentially more rapid resource depletion and environmental pollution, and an increase in the frequency of job changes) against the benefits (an increase in consumption possibilities of individuals and governments) and make a judgement.

Chapter 20

Measuring GDP and Economic Growth

KEY CONCEPTS

Gross Domestic Product

Gross domestic product (GDP) is the market value of all final goods and services produced within a country in a given time period.

- Total production is measured by the market value of each good.

- Only **final goods** (those bought by their final users) are measured, not **intermediate goods** (those bought by firms from each other and used as inputs in production).

- GDP measures total production *and* total income *and* total expenditure.

The *circular flow* of expenditure and income shows four economic sectors (firms, households, governments, rest of world) operating in three key markets (goods markets, factor markets, financial markets).

- Households sell factor services to firms in return for income—total household income = aggregate income (Y).

- Household income is spent on taxes (to government), on **consumption expenditure** (C) on goods and services, and on **saving** (S = income – net taxes – consumption) in financial markets.

- Firms produce goods and services, and sell C to households, **investment** (I = purchase of *new* capital) to other firms, **government expenditures** (G) to governments, and **net exports** = (exports (X) – imports (M)) to the rest of world.

- Governments buy goods and services, collect taxes from households and firms, give them transfer payments (**net taxes** [NT] = taxes – transfer payments – government debt interest payments), and borrow (to cover budget deficits).

- The rest of world buys our **exports** and sells us **imports**, and borrows and lends to us in financial markets.

Circular flow shows that aggregate income = aggregate production = aggregate expenditure
($Y = C + I + G + X - M$).

- Circular flow also shows how I is financed by private saving (S) + government saving ($NT - G$) + borrowing from rest of world ($M - X$):
$I = S + (NT - G) + (M - X)$.

- If $NT > G$, the government can lend some of its surplus.

- If foreigners sell Canadians more goods than they buy from us ($M > X$), we must borrow this amount from them to finance it, so part of their savings flows to us for investment purposes.

- I is financed by **national saving** (= $S + (NT - G)$) + foreign borrowing.

GDP is a **flow** (quantity per unit of time). A **stock** is a quantity at a point in time.

- A key stock is **wealth** (value of all things people own), and Δ wealth = saving.

- The capital stock is plant, equipment, buildings, and inventories used to produce goods and services.

  - Investment (I) = purchase of *new* capital.
  - **Depreciation** = fall in stock of capital because of wear and tear = **capital consumption**.
  - **Gross investment** = net investment + replacing depreciated capital.
  - Δ capital stock = **net investment** = gross investment – depreciation.

Measuring Canada's GDP

Statistics Canada measures GDP two ways on the basis of the following equality: income = production = expenditure.

- *Expenditure approach* measures $C + I + G + X - M$.

- *Income approach* adds up all incomes paid from firms to households, and makes adjustments.
  - Net domestic income at factor cost = wages, etc. + profits + interest/investment income + farmers' income + nonfarm unincorporated business income.
  - Net domestic product at market prices = net domestic income + indirect taxes − subsidies.
  - GDP = net domestic product + depreciation.

Real GDP and the Price Level

GDP can increase due to production of more goods and services, or higher prices for goods and services.

- The change in production is measured by **real GDP** (the value of final goods and services produced in a given year when valued at constant prices).

- **Nominal GDP** is the value of final goods and services produced in a given year when valued at that year's prices = the sum of expenditures on goods and services.

- Real GDP is calculated using the **chain-weighted output index** method:
  - First, calculate the value of the current year's quantities and the previous year's quantities using the prices of the previous year, and calculate the resulting increase in value from the previous year.
  - Second, calculate the value of the current year's quantities and the previous year's quantities using the prices of the current year, and calculate the resulting increase in value from the previous year.
  - Third, take the average of the two increases in value—this is the increase in real GDP from the previous year.

The average level of prices is the **price level**.

- The **GDP deflator** is an average of current year prices expressed as a percent of base-year prices =
$$\frac{\text{Nominal GDP}}{\text{Real GDP}} \times 100$$

Measuring Economic Growth

Economic growth rate = percentage change in quantity of goods and services produced =

$$\frac{\text{Real GDP this year} - \text{Real GDP last year}}{\text{Real GDP last year}} \times 100$$

- Real GDP is used to assess **economic welfare** (measure of economic well-being), make international comparisons and assess business cycles.

- Real GDP as a measure of economic welfare is flawed because price indexes overadjust for inflation, and because real GDP does not include some items that increase economic welfare, and also does not adjust for some items that lower economic welfare.

- Comparing real GDP per capita between countries can be difficult due to price variation.

- Despite flaws, real GDP reasonably accurate indicator of recessions/expansions, but it probably overstates fluctuations in economic welfare by ignoring household production and leisure time.

HELPFUL HINTS

1 Studying the circular flow and the national accounts may seem boring, but it is useful for several reasons. First, they provide crucial equalities that are the starting point for our economic model—studying this material will help you pass the course! Second, many current debates involve tradeoffs between economic growth and environmental damage. Understanding what GDP does and does not measure is crucial to this debate. Third, in macroeconomics we study how several markets operate simultaneously in a joint, interrelated equilibrium—the circular flow gives us our first taste of this interrelation.

2 One of the key equations in this and future chapters is the identity:

$$Y = C + I + G + X - M$$

which underlies Chapters 23 and 24.

This equation can be understood by carefully examining the circular flow. The circular flow shows a stylized view of the economy, which the equation attempts to measure. Macroeconomics tries to understand what affects GDP, and we start in this chapter by measuring production (GDP). However, we cannot directly measure production that easily. The circular flow helps us measure it indirectly. In the circular flow, production is purchased by the four economic decision makers (measured by expenditure), and the money earned from these sales is used to pay incomes. Therefore, production can be measured in three equivalent ways: income = expenditure = value of production (GDP). Therefore:

$$Y \text{ (income)} = C + I + G + X - M \text{ (expenditure)}$$

3   Be sure to distinguish carefully between intermediate goods and investment goods. Both are goods sold by one firm to another, but they differ in terms of their use. Intermediate goods are processed and then resold, while investment goods are final goods. Also note that the national income accounts include purchases of residential housing as investment because housing, like business capital stock, provides a continuous stream of value over time.

4   Note the difference between government expenditures on goods and services (G) and government transfer payments. Both involve payments by the government, but transfer payments are not payments for currently produced goods and services. Instead, they are simply a flow of money, just like taxes. Think of transfer payments as negative taxes. We define net taxes (NT) as taxes minus transfer payments minus interest payments on government debt.

5   It is very important to understand the difference between real and nominal GDP. Nominal GDP is the value, *in current prices*, of the output of final goods and services in the economy in a year. Real GDP evaluates those final goods and services *at the prices prevailing in a base year (constant prices)*.

Nominal GDP can rise from one year to the next either because prices rise or because the output of goods and services rises. A rise in real GDP, however, means that the output of goods and services has risen.

If we had a simple economy that produced only pizzas, this rise in real GDP would be easy to measure—are there more pizzas to eat? In a multiple-good economy, we have a more complex task, and must turn to a weighted average of the goods and services we produce. The chain-weighted output index method is the method Statistics Canada uses to measure real GDP. It is a difficult concept, and is worth summarizing:

1   Calculate the value of the current year's quantities and the previous year's quantities using the *previous* year's prices, and calculate the percentage change in the value of the quantities from last year to this year.
2   Calculate the value of the current year's quantities and the previous year's quantities using the *current* year's prices, and calculate the percentage change in the value of the quantities from last year to this year.
3   Take the average of these two percentage changes, and this is the percentage change in real GDP.
4   Apply this percentage change to last year's real GDP to get this year's real GDP.
5   By applying this method to each year's quantities, we can link each year's real GDP back to the base year.

S E L F - T E S T

True/False and Explain

Gross Domestic Product

1   Wage payments to households are an example of a real flow from firms to households.

2   A higher government deficit lowers investment, other things being equal.

3   Net investment gives the net addition to the capital stock.

4   In the aggregate economy, income is equal to expenditure and to GDP.

5   If currently exports equal imports, then GDP must equal consumption plus investment plus government expenditures.

6 Net exports are positive if expenditures by foreigners on goods and services produced in Canada are greater than the expenditure by Canadian citizens on goods and services produced in other countries.

Measuring Canada's GDP

7 If there were only households and firms and no government, market price and factor cost would be equal for any good.

8 Net exports are used in the income approach to measuring GDP.

9 Profits are part of the income approach to measuring GDP.

Real GDP and the Price Level

10 If you are interested in knowing whether the economy is producing more output, you would look at real GDP rather than nominal GDP.

11 The GDP deflator is real GDP divided by nominal GDP, multiplied by 100.

12 The chain-weighted output index method for measuring real GDP calculates the changes in value of the quantities produced using only the previous year's prices.

13 If real GDP this year is $116 billion, and last year it was $113 billion, then the economic growth rate was 3 percent.

Measuring Economic Growth

14 If underground economic activity was included in GDP calculations, measured GDP levels would be higher.

15 If two economies have the same real GDP per person, then the standard of living must be the same in each economy.

Multiple-Choice

Gross Domestic Product

1 The capital stock in the year 2003 would equal the capital stock in the year 2002
a minus depreciation.
b plus net investment plus depreciation.
c plus gross investment.
d plus net investment.
e plus net investment minus depreciation.

2 Which of the following is a *real* flow from households to firms?
a goods and services
b factor services
c payments for goods and services
d payments for factor services
e loans

3 For the aggregate economy, income equals
a expenditure, but these are not generally equal to GDP.
b GDP, but expenditure is generally less than these.
c expenditure equals GDP.
d expenditure equals GDP only if there is no government or foreign sectors.
e expenditure equals GDP only if there is no depreciation.

4 Which of the following is *false*?
a $Y = C + I + G + M - X$
b $I = S + (NT - G) + (M - X)$
c $Y = C + S + NT$
d $Y + M = C + I + G + X$
e $Y = C + I + G + X - M$

5 The capital stock does *not* include the

a inventory of raw cucumbers ready to be made into pickles by the Smith Pickle Company.

b Smith family holdings of stock in the Smith Pickle Company.

c pickle factory building owned by the Smith family.

d pickle-packing machine in the pickle factory building owned by the Smith family.

e pickle inventories in the pickle factory building owned by the Smith family.

6 Saving can be measured as income minus

a taxes.

b transfer payments.

c net taxes minus consumption expenditure.

d consumption expenditure.

e net taxes plus subsidies.

7 Investment is financed by

a $C + I + G + X - M$.

b $C + S + NT$.

c $S + NT + M$.

d $S + (NT - G) + (X - M)$.

e $S + (NT - G) + (M - X)$.

8 Which of the following would be an example of a consumption expenditure?

a More spending by the CBC on children's programs.

b An increase in welfare payments to single mothers.

c The purchase of a new car by the IPSCO steel company.

d The purchase of a new car by the Singh household.

e The purchase of a computer by the IPSCO steel company.

9 Which of the following will happen if the government sector's deficit increases?

a There will be more funds available to lend to the rest of the world.

b There will be more funds available to finance investment.

c In the circular flow, consumption expenditure will fall.

d GDP will be higher.

e There will be less funds available to finance investment.

Measuring Canada's GDP

10 To obtain the factor cost of a good from its market price

a add indirect taxes and subtract subsidies.

b subtract indirect taxes and add subsidies.

c subtract both indirect taxes and subsidies.

d add both indirect taxes and subsidies.

e subtract depreciation.

11 Interest plus miscellaneous investment income is a component of which approach to measuring GDP?

a income approach

b expenditure approach

c injections approach

d output approach

e opportunity cost approach

12 From the data in Table 20.1, what is net investment in Eastland?

a −$160

b $160

c $240

d $400

e $500

TABLE **20.1** DATA FROM EASTLAND

Item	Amount ($)
Wages, salaries, and supplementary labour income	800
Farm income	80
Government expenditures on goods and services	240
Capital consumption	240
Gross private domestic investment	400
Personal income taxes net of transfer payments	140
Corporate profits	80
Indirect taxes	120
Net exports	80
Consumption expenditures	640
Interest and miscellaneous investment income	100

13 From Table 20.1, what additional data are needed to compute net domestic income at factor cost?

a income of nonfarm unincorporated businesses

b transfer payments

c subsidies

d depreciation

e net taxes

14 From the data in Table 20.1, what is GDP in Eastland?

a $1,120

b $1,180

c $1,360

d $1,420

e Not calculable with the given information

Real GDP and the Price Level

15 From the data in Table 20.2, compute Southton's nominal GDP in the current year.

a $197

b $208

c $209

d $226

e It cannot be calculated given the data.

TABLE **20.2** DATA FROM SOUTHTON

Item	Price ($) Base	Current	Quantity Base	Current
Rubber ducks	1.00	1.25	100	100
Beach towels	7.00	6.00	12	14

16 From the data in Table 20.2, compute Southton's nominal GDP in the base year.

a $184

b $197

c $209

d $226

e It cannot be calculated given the data.

17 From the data in Table 20.2, compute Southton's real GDP in the base year.

a $184

b $197

c $209

d $226

e It cannot be calculated given the data.

18 What is the correct definition of the chain-weighted output index method of calculating real GDP in 2003?

a The value of the final goods and services produced in 2003 valued at the prices that prevailed in 2003.

b The value of the final goods and services produced in 2003 valued at the prices that prevailed in the base year.

c Nominal GDP in 2003 multiplied by the GDP deflator.

d The value of final goods and services produced in the base year valued at the 2003 prices.

e Take the base year GDP and add the average of the increases in real GDP calculated using the 2002 prices and the 2003 prices.

19 From the data in Table 20.3, what is Northton's GDP deflator in 2003?

a 250

b 200

c 160

d 125

e 80

TABLE **20.3** DATA FROM NORTHTON

Year	Nominal GDP	Real GDP	GDP Deflator (1996 = 100)
1996	125	125	100
2003	250	200	
2004	275		122.22

20 Use the Northton data in Table 20.3. What is real GDP in 2004?

a 336.2

b 275

c 225

d 220

e 110

Measuring Economic Growth

21 Consider the data in Table 20.3. What is the growth rate of real GDP between 2003 and 2004?

a −2.8%

b 12.5%

c 22.2%

d 25%

e 100%

22 Underground economy is all economic activity that

a produces intermediate goods or services.
b is not taxed.
c is legal but unreported or is illegal.
d has negative social value.
e is conducted underground.

23 Given that pollution is a by-product of some production processes,

a GDP accountants adjust GDP downward.
b GDP accountants adjust GDP upward.
c GDP accountants do not adjust GDP unless pollution is a serious problem, as in the former East Germany.
d GDP tends to overstate economic welfare.
e GDP tends to understate economic welfare.

24 Which of the following is *not* a reason for GDP incorrectly measuring the value of total output?

a leisure time
b household production
c underground economic activity
d capital consumption
e environmental quality

25 Which of the following is the major reason China's measured GDP might be underestimated?

a It includes replacement of depreciated capital stock.
b It includes of production processes that create pollution as a side-effect.
c It ignores decreases in health and life expectancy.
d It does not use purchasing power parity prices.
e It ignores human rights and political freedoms.

Short Answer Problems

1 How can we measure Gross Domestic Product by using either the expenditure or the income approach, when neither of these approaches actually measures production?

2 Suppose nominal GDP rises by 75 percent between year 1 and year 2.
a If the average level of prices has also risen by 75 percent between year 1 and year 2, what has happened to real GDP?
b If the average level of prices has risen by less than 75 percent between year 1 and year 2, has real GDP increased or decreased?

3 What *productive* activities are *not* measured and thus are *not* included in GDP? Is this lack of measurement a serious problem?

4 Use the data for Northland given in Table 20.4 to compute the following:

TABLE **20.4** DATA FROM NORTHLAND

Item	Amount (billions of $)
Consumption expenditure (C)	600
Taxes (Tax)	400
Transfer payments (TR)	250
Exports (X)	240
Imports (M)	220
Government expenditure on goods and services (G)	200
Gross investment (I)	150
Depreciation (Depr)	60

a GDP
b net investment
c net exports
d after-tax income
e saving
f the value of each of the three sources of financing for investment

5 Use the data for the same economy given in Table 20.5 to compute:

TABLE **20.5** DATA FOR NORTHLAND

Item	Amount (billions of $)
Wages, salaries, and supplementary labour income	550
Indirect taxes	120
Subsidies	20
Farmers' income	20
Corporate profits	80
Interest and miscellaneous investment income	90
Depreciation	60
Income of nonfarm unincorporated businesses	70

a net domestic income at factor cost
b net domestic product at market prices
c GDP

6 Table 20.6 gives data for Easton, where there are three final goods included in GDP: pizzas, beer, and CDs.
a Calculate nominal GDP in 2003 and 2004.
b What is real GDP in 2003?
c Using the chain-weighted method, what is real GDP in 2004?
d What is the GDP deflator in 2004?

TABLE **20.6**

	2004		2003 (Base Period)	
Goods	Output	Price ($)	Output	Price ($)
Pizza	110	8	105	6
Beer	50	10	55	8
CDs	50	9	40	10

7 Table 20.7 gives data for the country of Weston.

TABLE **20.7** DATA FOR WESTON

Year	Nominal GDP	Real GDP	GDP Deflator
2002	3,055		94
2003		3,170	100
2004	3,410	3,280	
2005		3,500	108

a Complete Table 20.7.
b What is the base year for the GDP deflator?
c Calculate the percentage change in nominal GDP, real GDP, and the GDP deflator between 2004 and 2005. Was the increase in nominal GDP due mostly to an increase in real GDP or to an increase in the price level?

8 Figure 20.1 shows the circular flow for Northweston. All amounts are in thousands of dollars.

FIGURE **20.1**

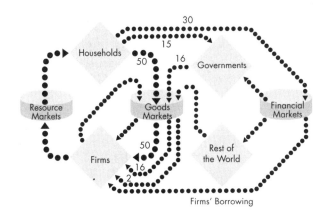

Use Figure 20.1 to calculate for Northweston:
a GDP
b aggregate expenditure
c investment
d aggregate income
e household saving
f government borrowing or saving
g foreign borrowing or saving
h firms' borrowing

9 Consider the following list of economic activities. Identify which of the three markets in the circular flow that each activity belongs to. Give a one-line reason for your answer in each case.

a Fred of the Forest buys a new loincloth in preparation for his date with Angela.
b Fred goes back to school at the University of Sandhurst to get his BA in Vine Swinging.
c While in school, Fred receives student loans.
d Fred has graduated, and is getting paid to knock down trees by Treetop City.
e Fred pays income taxes on his income from his new job.
f Fred goes on a holiday in the United States.

10 Consider the list of economic activities in Short Answer Problem **9** above. Identify whether the activity involves expenditures or not, and if so, which component of expenditures each activity belongs to (*C, I, G, X, M*).

ANSWERS

True/False and Explain

1 **F** It is an example of money flow in payment for real flow. (459)
2 **T** Higher deficit implies lower ($NT - G$), which implies lower $I = S + (NT - G) + (M - X)$. (461)
3 **T** Net investment nets out depreciation (replacement of worn-out capital), leaving only new capital additions. (461)
4 **T** From circular flow, firm production is sold (expenditure) and earnings used to pay out incomes. (460)
5 **T** If $X = M$, then $X - M = 0$, and $Y = C + I + G + 0$. (460)
6 **T** By definition of exports (goods and services sold to the rest of the world) and imports (goods bought from the rest of the world), and net exports = exports – imports. (460)
7 **T** Market price = factor cost + taxes – subsidies. (464)
8 **F** They are an expenditure, and are used in the expenditure approach. (463)
9 **T** Definition. (463–464)
10 **T** Real GDP measures the quantity of goods and services, while nominal measures current dollar value and includes price level increases. (465)
11 **F** GDP deflator = [(nominal GDP)/(real GDP)] × 100. (466)

12 F It calculates the average of this change *and* the changes using the current year's prices. (466)

13 F Economic growth = ((real GDP this year – real GDP last year)/(real GDP last year)) × 100 = ((116 – 113)/113) × 100 = 2.7%. (468)

14 T Since they are omitted, and they are a productive activity, real GDP would be higher if they were included. (469)

15 F Real GDP is imperfect measure of standard of living; answer depends on factors such as prices in each country. (470–471)

Multiple-Choice

1 d Definition. (461)

2 b **a** is in opposite direction, others are money flows. (459)

3 c Expenditure = money earned by sales of produced goods which is used to pay incomes (including profits). (460)

4 a Should be $X – M$ and not $M – X$. (459–460)

5 b Equity is financial asset, not capital. (461)

6 c From $S = (Y – NT) – C$. (460)

7 e Definition. (460)

8 d **a** is government expenditure, **b** is transfer payment, **c** and **e** are investment. (459–460)

9 e A higher deficit means $NT – G$ is smaller, so $I = S + (NT – G) + (M – X)$ is smaller. (460–461)

10 b Market price = factor cost + indirect taxes – subsidies, so factor cost = market price – indirect taxes + subsidies. (464)

11 a Definition. (464)

12 b Net investment = gross investment – capital consumption. (461)

13 a Table lists the other four components of factor incomes. (464)

14 c $Y = C + I + G + X – M = 640 + 400 + 240 + 80 = 1,360$. (463)

15 c Nominal GDP = sum of dollar value (= current price × current quantity) of all goods = ($1.25 × 100) + ($6.00 × 14) = 209. (465–466)

16 a Nominal GDP = sum of current price × current quantity of all goods = ($1.00 × 100) + ($9.00 × 12) = 184. (465–466)

17 a In base year, real GDP = nominal GDP. (465–466)

18 e Definition. (465–466)

19 d GDP deflator = [(nominal GDP)/(real GDP)] × 100. (466–467)

20 c Real GDP = [(nominal GDP)/(GDP deflator)] × 100. (466–467)

21 b Growth rate of real GDP = ([real GDP in 2004] – (real GDP in 2003)]/(real GDP in 2003)) × 100. (468)

22 c Definition. (469)

23 d No such adjustment occurs, so GDP overstates economic welfare. (469)

24 d Capital consumption is depreciation and is part of GDP. (468–470)

25 d See text discussion. (470–471)

Short Answer Problems

1 The analysis of the circular flow showed that firms produce goods and services (what we wish to measure), sell them (what the expenditure approach measures), and then use the proceeds to pay for factor incomes, rents, profits, etc. (what the income approach measures). Therefore expenditure = production = income.

2 a Real GDP is unchanged. The increased value of goods and services is only because of increased prices.

b The fact that prices have risen less in proportion to the increase in nominal GDP means that real GDP has increased.

3 Activities that produce goods and services that are not included in GDP are underground economic activity and household production. The first of these is not reported because the activities themselves are illegal or are legal but are not reported to circumvent taxes or government regulations. The second includes productive activities that households perform for themselves. Because they do not hire someone else to mow the lawn or wash the car, it is not included in GDP. The seriousness of the problem depends on the actual size of activity. The underground economy is usually estimated as about 5 to 15 percent of the Canadian economy.

4 a GDP = $C + I + G + (X – M)$ = $970 billion.

b Net $I = I – Depr$ = $90 billion.

c Net exports = $X – M$ = $20 billion.

d After-tax income = GDP + $TR – Tax$ = $820 billion.

e Saving = after-tax income – C = $220 billion.

f $I = S + (NT – G) + (M – X)$ or 150 = 220 + (150 – 200) + (220 – 240). Saving contributes $220 billion, the government budget deficit reduces investment by $50 billion, and the net export surplus reduces investment by $20 billion.

5 a Net domestic income at factor cost = wages, salaries, and supplementary labour income + interest and miscellaneous investment income +

corporate profits + farmers' income + income of nonfarm unincorporated business = $810 billion.

b Net domestic product at market prices = net domestic product at factor cost + indirect taxes – subsidies = $910 billion.

c GDP = net domestic product at market prices + depreciation = $970 billion.

6 a Nominal GDP is the sum of the expenditures on all goods in the year in question. For 2003, nominal GDP = ($6 × 105) + ($8 × 55) + ($10 × 40) = $1,470. For 2004, nominal GDP = ($8 × 110) + ($10 × 50) + ($9 × 50) = $1,830.

b Since 2003 is the base period, nominal GDP = real GDP = $1,470.

c First, calculate real GDP in 2004 by using the 2003 prices and the 2004 quantities: ($6 × 110) + ($8 × 50) + ($10 × 50) = $1,560. The percentage change in real GDP = [(1,560 – 1,470)/1,470] × 100 = +6.1%.

Second, calculate the value of the 2003 quantities using 2004 prices: ($8 × 105) + ($10 × 55) + ($9 × 40) = $1,750. At 2003 prices, the value of production increased from $1,750 to $1,830, an increase of +4.6% (= [(1,830 – 1,750)/1,750] × 100).

Finally, average the two increases: (6.1 + 4.6)/2 = 5.35%. Real GDP in 2004 is 5.35% higher than in 2003. Real GDP in 2003 was $1,470, so real GDP in 2004 is $1,548.65 (= $1,470 × 1.0535).

d The GDP deflator = [(nominal GDP)/(real GDP)] × 100 = (1,830/1,548.65) × 100 = 118.

7 a Table 20.7 is completed here as Table 20.7 Solution. The following equation is used: GDP deflator = (nominal GDP/real GDP) × 100.

TABLE **20.7** SOLUTION

Year	Nominal GDP	Real GDP	GDP Deflator
2002	3,055	3,250	94
2003	3,170	3,170	100
2004	3,410	3,280	104
2005	3,780	3,500	108

b The base year is 2003—GDP deflator is 100.

c Percentage change in nominal GDP = [(3,780 – 3,410)/3,410] × 100 = 10.9%. Percentage change in real GDP = [(3,500 – 3,280)/3,280] ×

100 = 6.7%. Percentage change in GDP deflator = [(108 – 104)/104] × 100 = 3.8%. Since the percentage change in real GDP is higher than the percentage change in the GDP deflator, most of the increase in nominal GDP is due to an increase in real GDP.

8 a GDP can be calculated from how households spend their income: $Y = C + S + NT = 50 + 30 + 15 = \$95,000$.

b Aggregate expenditure = GDP = $95,000.

c Investment is the only missing component of aggregate expenditure, and can be deduced from the equation $Y = C + I + G + X - M$ or 95 = 50 + I + 16 + 2, implying $I = \$27,000$. (Note that the components of aggregate expenditure must all flow through the goods market.)

d Aggregate income paid to households must equal aggregate expenditure earned by firms, so it equals $95,000.

e Household saving goes from households to financial markets, and equals $30,000.

f Government borrowing or saving = $NT - G$ = 15 – 16 = –$1,000, borrowing.

g From examining the goods market, foreign borrowing or saving = $X - M$ = $2,000 of borrowing.

h Firms' borrowing comes from the fact that saving = firms' borrowing + government borrowing + foreign borrowing, or 30 = firms' borrowing + 1 + 2, so that firms' borrowing = $27,000.

9 a Goods and service market—purchase of a good.

b Goods and service market—purchase of an educational service.

c Financial market—household borrowing.

d Factor market—Fred is working for wage income.

e Not part of any market, a direct flow to the government.

f Goods and services market—import expenditure, since the money flows to the United States.

10 a Expenditure (C).

b Expenditure (C).

c Not an expenditure, a financial flow.

d Not an expenditure, a factor service purchase.

e Not an expenditure, a flow to the government.

f Expenditure (M).

Chapter 21

Monitoring Cycles, Jobs, and the Price Level

KEY CONCEPTS

The Business Cycle

The business cycle is the periodic, irregular up-and-down movement in production and jobs.

- Each cycle has a peak of activity, followed by a recession (a significant decline in economic activity) which ends in a trough. The trough is followed by an expansion when real GDP increases.

- A **growth rate cycle downturn** is a persistent decline in the growth rate of aggregate economic activity.

Jobs and Wages

Employment is a key feature in determining the onset of recession. Statistics Canada surveys households to estimate job status.

- **Working-age population** = number of people 15 years and over.

- **Labour force** = employed + unemployed
  - Employed = those with full-time and part-time jobs.
  - Unemployed = without work, actively seeking within last 4 weeks, waiting to be called back after layoff, or waiting to start new job within 4 weeks.

- **Unemployment rate** = percentage of labour force who are unemployed. It increases in recessions, but has no trend recently.

- Involuntary part-time rate = percentage of labour force who are part-time but want full-time. It increases in recessions.

- **Labour force participation rate** = percentage of working-age population who are in labour force. It has strong upward trend, but decreases in recessions because of **discouraged workers** (people who temporarily leave labour force in a recession).

- **Employment-to-population ratio** = percentage of working-age population with jobs. It has increased overall since 1960s (many new jobs created), but decreases in recessions.

- Participation and employment rates down for men and up (strongly) for women since 1960s, creating increase in overall rate.

- To see quantity of labour employed, examine **aggregate hours** = total hours worked.
  - Has upward trend, decreases in recessions.
  - Hours per worker decreased until earlier 1990s, with faster decreases in recessions.

- **Real wage rate** = quantity of goods an hour's work can buy = **money wage rate** (dollars per hour)/price level. Has upward trend, but at a slower rate since early 1970s.

Unemployment and Full Employment

- People become unemployed when they
  - are laid off (**job losers**).
  - voluntarily quit (**job leavers**).
  - enter (**entrants**) or re-enter (**re-entrants**) the labour force.

- People end unemployment when they are hired, recalled, or withdraw from the labour force.

- Primary source of unemployment is job loss, which fluctuates strongly with business cycle.

- There is a wide range in duration of unemployment. Duration is higher in recessions.

◆ Unemployment rate higher for younger people.

The types of unemployment are frictional, structural, seasonal, and cyclical.

◆ **Frictional unemployment** is due to normal turnover and is a healthy part of a dynamic economy. It depends on the number of entrants/re-entrants and job creation/destruction. It is higher in Canada than in the United States due to Canada's employment insurance generosity.

◆ **Structural unemployment** is job losses in industries/regions declining due to technological change, and tends to last longer than frictional unemployment.

◆ **Seasonal unemployment** occurs when number of jobs decreases in certain seasons.

◆ **Cyclical unemployment** is the fluctuations in unemployment over the business cycle. It increases in recession, decreases in expansion.

Full employment—only frictional, structural, and seasonal unemployment occurring (no cyclical unemployment).

◆ Unemployment rate at full employment is called the **natural rate**.

◆ Actual unemployment rate fluctuates around the natural rate, as real GDP fluctuates around **potential GDP** (quantity of real GDP at full employment).

• When real GDP < potential GDP, unemployment rate > natural rate.
• When real GDP > potential GDP, unemployment rate < natural rate.

The Consumer Price Index

The **Consumer Price Index (CPI)** measures the average of the prices paid for a fixed basket of consumer goods and services.

◆ The CPI = 100 for the **base period**.

◆ The CPI basket is constructed from surveys of consumers' spending habits, with prices surveyed monthly.

◆ $\text{CPI} = \dfrac{\text{Cost of CPI basket at current prices}}{\text{Cost of CPI basket at base-period prices}} \times 100.$

◆ The **inflation rate** = the percentage change in the price level.

◆ The CPI overstates the inflation rate (biased upwards) because:

• new goods replace old goods.
• quality improvements create some part of price rises.
• consumers change consumption towards cheaper goods not reflected in fixed-basket price index.
• consumers substitute towards discount outlets not covered in CPI surveys.

◆ Magnitude of bias probably low in Canada, but it will lead to distorted contracts, more government outlays, and incorrect wage bargaining.

HELPFUL HINTS

I In a dynamic economy, some unemployment is efficient. There are economic benefits of frictional unemployment to the individual and to society. Younger workers typically experience periods of unemployment trying to find jobs that match their skills and interests. The benefit of the resulting frictional unemployment is a more satisfying and productive work life. Society benefits because the frictional unemployment that accompanies such a job-search process allows workers to find jobs in which they are more productive. As a result, the total production of goods and services in the economy increases. (Compare this case with the case for graduates in the Republic of China up until the 1990s. They were assigned jobs upon graduation, with very little personal input about type of job or location.)

On the other hand, structurally unemployed workers will not get a new job without retraining or relocation. This fact means a much greater cost to the worker and society—for example, structurally unemployed workers are typically unemployed for much longer time periods. These workers bear the brunt of the cost of restructuring industries in our economy, although society gains in the long run from the shift of labour and other productive resources to the new industries.

2 The term "full employment," or its equivalent "the natural rate of unemployment," does not mean that everyone has a job. Rather, it means that the only unemployment is frictional, structural, and seasonal—there is no cyclical unemployment. (Note this definition implies the natural rate is higher in the wintertime!)

It is possible for the actual rate of unemployment to be less than the natural rate of unemployment, because it is possible for the level of employment to exceed full employment. In these situations, people are spending too little time searching for jobs, and therefore less-productive job matches are being made.

3 There are four different types of unemployment, but defining these types does not explain them. Explanations of how unemployment occurs is a goal of the remaining chapters in the textbook!

S E L F - T E S T

True/False and Explain

The Business Cycle

1 A recession is a persistent decline in the growth rate of aggregate economic activity.

2 The correct order of a business cycle is expansion, peak, recession, trough.

Jobs and Wages

3 The employment-to-population ratio is the percentage of working-age population in the labour force.

4 If the employment-to-population ratio increases, unemployment always decreases.

5 If the number of discouraged workers decreases, the employment-to-population ratio decreases as they begin to look for jobs.

6 George was laid off last month, and is waiting to be recalled to his old job, so he is not actively seeking work. George is *not* counted as unemployed.

7 The real wage rate has an upward trend since the 1970s.

Unemployment and Full Employment

8 Being unemployed for a few months after graduating from university always hurts the graduate.

9 A decline in the number of jobs in the automobile sector matched by an equal increase in the number of jobs offered in the banking sector will not alter the unemployment rate.

10 At full employment, there is no unemployment.

11 Bill has just graduated from high school and is looking for his first job. Bill is frictionally unemployed.

12 Fluctuations in unemployment over the business cycle create frictional unemployment.

The Consumer Price Index

13 The CPI overstates the inflation rate because it ignores substitution towards higher-quality goods by households.

14 The market basket used in calculating the CPI changes each year.

15 The magnitude of the CPI bias in Canada is quite high.

Multiple-Choice

The Business Cycle

1 In 2005, real GDP growth was +4% in the first quarter, +3% in the second quarter, +2% in the third quarter, and +1% in the fourth quarter of the year. In 2005, this economy

a suffered a recession.
b reached a trough in the final quarter.
c reached a peak in the final quarter.
d suffered a growth rate cycle downturn.
e showed no evidence of a business cycle.

2 During a recession, real GDP _____ and employment _____.

a increases; increases
b increases; decreases
c decreases; increases
d decreases; decreases
e decreases; stays constant

Jobs and Wages

3 Including discouraged workers in the measured unemployment rate would

a not change the measured unemployment rate.
b lower the measured unemployment rate.
c raise the natural rate of unemployment.
d raise the full employment rate.
e raise the measured unemployment rate.

4 In a country with a working-age population of 20 million, 13 million are employed, 1.5 million are unemployed, and 1 million of the employed are working part-time, half of whom wish to work full-time. The size of the labour force is

a 20 million.
b 15.5 million.
c 14.5 million.
d 13 million.
e 11.5 million.

5 In a country with a working-age population of 20 million, 13 million are employed, 1.5 million are unemployed, and 1 million of the employed are working part-time, half of whom wish to work full-time. The labour force participation rate is

a 75.5 percent.
b 72.5 percent.
c 65 percent.
d 57.5 percent.
e none of the above.

6 In a country with a working-age population of 20 million, 13 million are employed, 1.5 million are unemployed, and 1 million of the employed are working part-time, half of whom wish to work full-time. The unemployment rate is

a 10 percent.
b 10.3 percent.
c 11.5 percent.
d 15.4 percent.
e none of the above.

7 Who of the following would be counted as unemployed in Canada?

a Doris only works five hours a week but is looking for a full-time job.
b Kanhaya has stopped looking for work since he was unable to find a suitable job during a two-month search.
c Sharon is a college student with no job.
d Maurice has been laid off from his job for 20 weeks but expects to be called back soon.
e Bogdan has been laid off from his job but does not expect to be called back, and is not looking.

8 If the number of discouraged workers increases, all else unchanged, then the

a unemployment rate will increase.
b employment-to-population ratio will decrease.
c labour force participation rate will increase.
d labour force participation rate will decrease.
e employment-to-population ratio will increase.

9 Initially the money wage rate is $10 per hour, and the price level is 100. If the money wage rate increases to $20 per hour and the price level increases to 125, what happens to the real wage rate?

a It stays the same.
b It doubles in value.
c It decreases in value.
d It increases in value, but by less than double.
e It increases in value, by more than double.

10 If the employment-to-population ratio increases, then

a the unemployment rate *must* decrease.
b the labour force participation rate *must* increase.
c the labour force participation rate will be unaffected.
d aggregate hours worked *must* increase.
e none of the above.

11 The increase in the Canadian labour force participation rate since the 1960s is largely due to the

a increase in female labour force participation.
b increase in male labour force participation.
c decrease in the number of baby boomers.
d increase in youth labour force participation.
e decrease in the number of discouraged workers.

Unemployment and Full Employment

12 Which of the following events would raise cyclical unemployment?

a real GDP growth slows down or turns negative
b an increase in unemployment benefits
c an increase in the pace of technological change
d an increase in both job destruction and job creation
e all of the above

13 Unemployment will increase if there is an increase in the number of people

a retiring.
b withdrawing from the labour force.
c recalled from layoffs.
d leaving jobs to go to school.
e leaving school to find jobs.

14 Who of the following would be considered structurally unemployed?

a a Saskatchewan farmer who has lost her farm and is unemployed until retrained
b a Nova Scotia fishery worker who is searching for a better job closer to home
c a steelworker who is laid off but who expects to be called back soon
d an office worker who has lost her job because of a general slowdown in economic activity
e none of the above

15 Who of the following would be considered cyclically unemployed?

a a Saskatchewan farmer who has lost her farm and is unemployed until retrained
b a Nova Scotia fishery worker who is searching for a better job closer to home
c a steelworker who is laid off but who expects to be called back soon
d an office worker who has lost her job because of a general slowdown in economic activity
e none of the above

16 Who of the following would be considered frictionally unemployed? A steelworker who

a loses her job because of technological change.
b is laid off but expects to be called back within a week.
c gives up her job because she retires.
d decides to leave the labour force and become a full-time ballet student.
e becomes discouraged and stops looking for a job.

17 In a recession, what is the largest source of the increase in unemployment?

a job leavers
b job losers
c new entrants to the labour force
d re-entrants to the labour force
e involuntary part-time workers

18 At full employment, there is no

a natural unemployment.
b unemployment.
c cyclical unemployment.
d structural unemployment.
e frictional unemployment.

19 Unemployment caused by permanently decreased demand for horse-drawn carriages is an example of

a cyclical unemployment.
b seasonal unemployment.
c frictional unemployment.
d structural unemployment.
e discouraged unemployment.

20 The natural rate of unemployment is

a the rate at which unemployment equals 0 percent.
b the same as cyclical unemployment.
c the rate at which cyclical unemployment equals 6 percent.
d the rate at which cyclical unemployment equals 0 percent.
e none of the above.

21 The duration of a spell of unemployment typically

a decreases in a recession and increases in an expansion.
b decreases in a recession and in an expansion.
c increases in a recession and in an expansion.
d increases in a recession and decreases in an expansion.
e does not change during recessions and expansions.

The Consumer Price Index

TABLE **21.1** DATA FROM SOUTHTON

Item	Price ($) Base	Price ($) Current	Quantity Base	Quantity Current
Rubber ducks	1.00	1.25	100	100
Beach towels	9.00	6.00	12	14

22 From the data in Table 21.1, what is Southton's consumer price index for the current year?

a 112
b 105.6
c 100.5
d 100
e 94.7

23 Refer to the data in Table 21.1. Between the base year and the current year, the relative price of rubber ducks

a remained unchanged.
b fell.
c rose.
d cannot be determined with the amount of information given.
e depends on whether overall inflation was positive or not.

24 Which of the following is *not* a reason the consumer price index overstates inflation?

a New goods of higher quality and prices replace old goods.
b Quality improvements create some part of price rises in existing goods and services.
c Consumers change their consumption basket towards cheaper goods not reflected in the fixed-basket price index.
d Consumers substitute towards using discount outlets not covered in CPI surveys.
e It does not measure the underground economy.

25 The technique used to calculate the CPI implicitly assume that consumers buy

a relatively more of goods with relative prices that are increasing.
b relatively less of goods with relative prices that are decreasing.
c the same relative quantities of goods as in a base year.
d goods and services whose quality improves at the rate of growth of real GDP.
e more computers and CD players and fewer black-and-white TVs.

Short Answer Problems

1 Explain why an economy does not have 0 percent unemployment when it has full employment.

2 Should the government try to force the unemployment rate down as close to zero as possible? Discuss some problems such a policy might create.

3 Consider the following information about an economy: working-age population—20 million; full-time employment—8 million; part-time employment—2 million (1 million of whom wish they had full-time jobs); unemployment—1 million.
a What is the labour force in this economy? What is the labour force participation rate?
b What is the unemployment rate?
c What is the involuntary part-time rate?
d What is the employment-to-population ratio?
e If 0.6 million of those unemployed are frictionally, structurally, and seasonally unemployed, what is the natural rate of unemployment?
f What is the amount of cyclical unemployment?

4 Consider the economy described in Short Answer Problem **3**. Over the next year, there is no change in the working-age population, but the number of unemployed rises to 1.5 million, while the number of full-time employed rises to 8.5 million. There are no changes in part-time employment.
a Calculate the new labour force participation rate, the new employment-to-population ratio, and the new unemployment rate.
b How is it possible that all three of these rates rose at the same time? Explain briefly. (*Hint:* what do you think has happened to the number of discouraged workers over this time period?)

5 In Chapter 19 we learned about the costs of unemployment. Are they more severe for frictional or structural unemployment?

6 Explain the difference between cyclical and structural unemployment. How would you tell a cyclically unemployed person from a structurally unemployed person?

7 Table 21.2 gives data for Southland, where there are three consumption goods: bananas, coconuts, and grapes.

TABLE **21.2** DATA FOR SOUTHLAND

Goods	Quantity in Base-Period Basket	Base Period Price ($)	Base Period Expenditure ($)	Current Period Price ($)	Current Period Expenditure ($)
Bananas	120	6		8	
Coconuts	60	8		10	
Grapes	40	10		9	

  a Complete the table by computing expenditures for the base period and expenditures for the same quantity of each good in the current period.

  b What is the value of the basket of consumption goods in the base period? in the current period?

  c What is the consumer price index for the current period?

  d On the basis of the data in this table, would you predict consumers would make any substitutions between goods between the base period and the current period? If so, what kind of problems would this create for your measurement of the CPI?

8 Examine each of the following changes in John Carter's labour market activity, and explain whether they constitute unemployment, employment, or being out of the labour force. If unemployment, which of the four types of unemployment is represented?

  a John graduates from Barsoom High and starts looking for a job.

  b John has no luck finding the full-time job he wants and takes a part-time job cleaning out the canals.

  c Canal-cleaning doesn't work out for John because of unforeseen allergies, so he quits.

  d Discouraged by the lack of work, John stops looking and stays home watching his favourite soap opera, *As Mars Turns*.

  e John sees an advertisement on TV for the Barsoom Swordfighter School, and enrolls to get his B.S.F.

  f John graduates at the top of his class and joins up with Princess Dejah Thoris' guard.

  g An inventor at Barsoom University comes up with a new laser personal defence system, and the Princess disbands her guard—John spends a long time looking for work.

  h John gets a job cleaning up after the sandstorms, but once the wet season comes along, he is laid off.

  i John sees an advertisement seeking someone to help explore the ruins of the lost city of Rhiannon and signs up as security—the six-armed tribes are particularly ferocious there.

9 Consider the data from 1995 in Table 21.3 on Canada as a whole and Newfoundland specifically.

TABLE **21.3**

Economy	Labour Force Participation Rate	Unemployment Rate	Employment-to-Population Ratio
Canada	64.8	9.5	58.6
Newfoundland	53.1	18.3	43.3

  Newfoundland has twice the unemployment of Canada, as well as a radically lower employment-to-population ratio and labour force participation rate. By examining these, can you get any insight into the impact of such a high unemployment rate on the labour market in Newfoundland? Why is the gap in the employment-to-population ratio (15.3 points) so much bigger than the unemployment gap (8.8 points)?

10 Consider the data in Table 21.4 below on the economic growth of an imaginary country.

TABLE **21.4**

Year: Quarter	2004:1	2004:2	2004:3	2004:4	2005:1	2005:2	2005:3	2005:4
Real GDP Growth	+4%	+5%	+2%	−3%	−2%	−1%	+3%	+5%

  a Identify the peak of this business cycle, any growth rate cycle downturns, the recessionary phase, the trough, the expansionary phase.

  b Are there any problems with using real GDP growth to identify the business cycle?

ANSWERS

True/False and Explain

  1 **F** This definition would be for a growth rate cycle downturn. (478–479)

  2 **T** Definition. (478–479)

  3 **F** Percentage with jobs. (481–482)

  4 **F** True if participation decreases or does not increase by much, otherwise false. (481–482)

  5 **F** This change will only change labour force participation. (481–482)

  6 **F** Since waiting for recall, he is counted. (481–482)

  7 **T** See text discussion. (484)

  8 **F** It depends on whether time unemployed leads to better job. (487–488)

9 **F** Workers retrain/relocate leading to more structural unemployment. (487–488)

10 **F** Full employment = frictional, structural, and seasonal unemployment. (487–488)

11 **T** Searching for jobs = frictionally unemployed. (487–488)

12 **F** They create *cyclical* unemployment. (489)

13 **T** See text discussion. (493)

14 **F** It is keep constant at the basket used in the base year. (491–492)

15 **F** It is low due to Statistics Canada's corrections. (493)

Multiple-Choice

1 **d** Persistent decline in the growth rate of aggregate economic activity. (478–479)

2 **d** A recession is a decline in aggregate economic activity (usually measured by real GDP), accompanied by a decline in employment. (478–479)

3 **e** It would add extra unemployed workers to the measured rate. (481–482)

4 **c** Employed + unemployed. (481–482)

5 **b** Labour force/working-age population = 14.5/20 = 72.5 percent. (481–482)

6 **b** Unemployed/labour force = 1.5/14.5 = 10.3 percent. (481–482)

7 **d** Doris is employed, Kanhaya isn't looking for work, Sharon is out of labour force, Bogdan does not expect to be called back. (481–482)

8 **d** Discouraged workers were unemployed, but stop looking and exit labour force, so unemployment rate decreases, labour force participation decreases, employment-to-population ratio unchanged. (481–482)

9 **d** Money wage doubles, but since the price level increases by 25 percent, real wage doesn't double. (481–482)

10 **e** Any of **a** to **d** *could* occur, but they do not *have* to occur. (481–484)

11 **a** See Text Figure 21.4 and discussion. (482)

12 **a** **b** to **d** raise frictional or structural unemployment, but if real GDP growth slows down, cyclical unemployment increases. (487–488)

13 **e** Others all lower unemployment. (485–488)

14 **a** Structural unemployment includes having wrong skills. Others are frictional or cyclical unemployment. (487–488)

15 **d** Cyclical unemployment is due to economy-wide slowdowns. (487–488)

16 **b** **a** is structural, rest are not officially unemployed. (485–488)

17 **b** See text discussion. (485–487)

18 **c** Definition. (488–489)

19 **d** Definition—unemployment caused by structural change. (487–488)

20 **d** Definition. (488–489)

21 **d** See Text Figure 21.9. (486)

ⓒⓣ **22** **e** CPI = [(sum of current prices × base quantities)/(sum of base prices × base quantities)] × 100. (491–492)

23 **c** Ratio P(ducks)/P(towels) has risen. (491–492)

24 **e** This problem is for real GDP. (493)

25 **c** Because it assumes a fixed basket. (493)

Short Answer Problems

ⓒⓣ **1** An economy always has some unemployment, of people searching for jobs—frictional, structural, and seasonal unemployment. We define full unemployment as when there is only frictional, structural, and seasonal unemployment.

ⓒⓣ **2** Pushing down the unemployment rate would entail stopping frictional unemployment, which would reduce the number of good job matches, and stopping structural unemployment, which would likely prevent the kind of structural readjustment the economy needs. Therefore it does not seem like a good idea to get unemployment as close to zero as possible!

3 **a** The labour force is 11 million, the sum of employment and unemployment. The labour force participation rate = percentage of working-age population who are in the labour force = 11/20 or 55 percent.

b The unemployment rate is 9.1 percent, the number of unemployed as a percentage of the labour force.

c It is 9.1 percent, the percentage of the labour force who are part-time and want full-time.

d It is 50 percent, percentage of working-age population with a job.

e The natural rate of unemployment is frictional plus structural plus seasonal unemployment. In our case, it is the rate of unemployment if unemployment were only 0.6 million. Thus the natural rate of unemployment is 5.45 percent.

f Cyclical unemployment is actual unemployment minus natural unemployment, or 0.4 million.

4 **a** The labour force participation rate = percentage of working-age population who are employed + unemployed = (1.5 + 8.5 + 2)/20 = 60 percent. The employment-to-population ratio is the percentage of the population with a job = 52.5 percent. The unemployment rate is the percentage of the labour force without a job = 12.5 percent.

b One million more people entered the labour force (participation rate increases), half of whom found a job (employment-to-population ratio increases) and half of whom did not (unemployment rate increases). It seems likely this change is due to discouraged workers now retrying to find jobs because the overall economy is improving.

5 The costs of unemployment include the lost output of the unemployed, and the deterioration of skills and abilities; in other words, human capital erodes. These costs will be higher for structural unemployment because it lasts longer, and often the workers' human capital becomes worthless in the marketplace.

6 Cyclical unemployment is caused by a downturn in the economy, when there is a decrease in demand for all products. Structural unemployment is caused by structural changes in a specific industry or region, and there is a decrease in demand for a certain type of labour whose skills are no longer desired.

Cyclical unemployment will end when the economy turns up. Structural unemployment will end when the workers retrain or move.

7 a Table 21.2 is completed here as Table 21.2 Solution. Note that the base-period quantities are evaluated at current prices to find the value of quantities in the current period.

TABLE **21.2** SOLUTION

Goods	Quantity in Base-Period Basket	Base Period Price ($)	Base Period Expenditure ($)	Current Period Price ($)	Current Period Expenditure ($)
Bananas	120	6	720	8	960
Coconuts	60	8	480	10	600
Grapes	40	10	400	9	360

b The value of the basket of consumption goods in the base period is the sum of the expenditures in that period: $1,600. The value of the basket of consumption goods in the current period is obtained as the sum of the values of quantities in that period: $1,920.

c The consumer price index is the ratio of the value of quantities in the current period to the base period expenditure, times 100:

$$CPI = (1,920/1,600) \times 100 = 120.$$

d Since the price of grapes has fallen relative to the prices of bananas and coconuts, we would expect that consumers would substitute towards the cheaper grapes and away from bananas and coconuts. This substitution means that our CPI measure will be biased upwards.

8 a He is an entrant, and is frictionally unemployed.
b He is now employed, although he is also involuntarily part-time.
c He is a job leaver, and is frictionally unemployed.
d He is a discouraged worker, but technically out of the labour force.
e He is still out of the labour force.
f He is employed.
g He is structurally unemployed.
h He is initially employed, but then is seasonally unemployed.
i He is employed again.

9 The higher unemployment rate in Newfoundland has pushed many workers out of the labour force—they have become discouraged workers and are not even attempting to find work. (We can see this in the lower participation rate.) The bigger gap in the employment-to-population ratio reflects this exiting, because it includes the measured unemployed and the discouraged workers.

10 a The peak would be at the highest *level* of real GDP, just before we move towards negative economic growth. The peak occurs in 2004:3. A growth rate cycle downturn occurs when the growth rate is positive but declining, which occurs in 2004:3. This is followed by a recessionary phase with negative real GDP growth in 2004:4 – 2005:2. The trough is the lowest *level* of real GDP, so it would be in the last quarter of negative growth in 2005:2, followed by the expansion of positive growth in 2005:3 and 2005:4.

b We are implicitly identifying our business cycle by only using real GDP growth. However, since this data is released only quarterly, the ECRI and the NBER look at a variety of monthly measures of economic activity, including employment, to try and identify the business cycle.

Chapter 22

Aggregate Supply and Aggregate Demand

KEY CONCEPTS

Aggregate Supply

The *AS-AD* model enables us to understand how equilibrium real GDP and the price level are determined.

Quantity of real GDP supplied (Y) depends on quantities of labour (*L*), capital (*K*), and technology (*T*) as described by **aggregate production function**: $Y = F(L, K, T)$.

♦ At a given time, only quantity of labour can vary.

♦ Full employment occurs at the wage rate where quantity of labour demanded = quantity of labour supplied.

♦ Even at full employment, there is some unemployment due to labour market turnover.

♦ Unemployment rate at full employment is the **natural rate of unemployment**.

♦ Potential GDP is quantity of real GDP supplied at full employment.

• Over business cycle, employment fluctuates around full employment, as real GDP fluctuates around potential GDP.

Two separate *AS* concepts: long-run (*LAS*) and short-run (*SAS*).

♦ **Macroeconomic long run** is long enough time frame so that real GDP = potential GDP. **Macroeconomic short run** is a period during which real GDP is above or below potential GDP.

♦ **Long-run aggregate supply (*LAS*)** is relationship between quantity of real GDP supplied and price level when real GDP = potential.

♦ *LAS* curve is vertical at potential GDP—increase in *P* leads to equivalent percentage increase in resource prices, which means real wages remain constant—no Δ employment, no Δ quantity supplied *Y*.

♦ **Short-run aggregate supply (*SAS*)** is relationship between quantity of real GDP supplied and price level when the money wage rates and other resource prices are held constant.

♦ *SAS* curve is upward-sloping—increase in *P* leads to an increase in employment and an increase in quantity supplied *Y*.

♦ *LAS* shifts rightward when potential GDP increases, due to increase in full employment quantity of labour, increase in capital stock, technological advance.

♦ *SAS* shifts along with *LAS*, but also shifts if Δ resource prices.

Aggregate Demand

Quantity of real GDP demanded is total amount of final goods and services produced in Canada that economic agents plan to buy. It depends on price level, expectations, fiscal/monetary policy, and world economy.

♦ **Aggregate demand (*AD*)** is total quantity real GDP (*Y*) demanded at given price level (*P*).

♦ Increase in *P* decreases quantity real GDP demanded, represented by movement up along *AD* curve because of *wealth* and *substitution effects*.

♦ Changes in other factors *shift AD* curve.

• If **fiscal policy** increases taxes (which decreases **disposable income**) or decreases government expenditure, then *AD* decreases.

- If **monetary policy** decreases interest rates or increases quantity of money, then *AD* increases.
- If exchange rate increases or foreign income decreases, then *AD* decreases.
- Increase in expectations of future disposable income or future inflation or future profits increases *AD*.

Macroeconomic Equilibrium

There are two different types of macroeconomic equilibriums—long-run equilibrium is state towards which economy is heading, short-run equilibrium occurs at each point in time along path to long-run equilibrium.

- **Long-run macroeconomic equilibrium** occurs when real GDP = potential GDP—when *AD* = *SAS* = *LAS*.
- **Short-run macroeconomic equilibrium** occurs where *AD* = *SAS*, with *P* adjusting to achieve equilibrium.
- Economic growth results from *LAS* shifting rightward on average, due to increase in underlying supply variables.
- Persistent inflation occurs when *AD* grows faster than *LAS*.
- Growth in *Y* is not steady, but goes in cycles because *AD* and *SAS* do not shift at same pace.
- Over the business cycle, short-run equilibrium may occur at
  - long-run equilibrium.
  - **below full-employment equilibrium**— *AD* = *SAS* left of *LAS*, real GDP < potential by amount of **recessionary gap**.
  - **above full-employment equilibrium**— *AD* = *SAS* right of *LAS*, real GDP > potential by amount of **inflationary gap**.
- Economy fluctuates in short run because of fluctuations in *AD* and *SAS*.
- If *AD* increases so *Y* > potential, economy does not stay in above-full equilibrium—upward pressures on the money wage rate shifts *SAS* leftward towards long-run equilibrium.
- If resource prices increase so *SAS* shifts leftward and *Y* < potential, then *stagflation* results (*P* higher, *Y* lower).

Canadian Economic Growth, Inflation, and Cycles

Levels of *Y* and *P* have changed dramatically over time in Canadian economy with economic growth, inflation, and business cycles.

- In 1970s, inflation increased and growth decreased due to massive increase in oil prices, and increase in quantity of money.
- Central banks responded by restraining *AD*, leading to deep recession in 1981–82.
- Through 1980s, steady growth and inflation as *LAS* shifted rightward.
- In 1991, decreasing *AD* led to recession. Since then, economic growth, low inflation, return to full employment.

HELPFUL HINT

1   The aggregate demand and aggregate supply model introduced in this chapter (and developed in detail throughout this book) is an insightful method of analyzing complex macroeconomic events. In order to help yourself sort out these complex events, it will be helpful if *you always draw a graph*—even if it is a small graph in the margin of a multiple-choice question. Graphs are powerful and effective tools for analyzing economic events, and you should become familiar with using them as soon as possible.

2   When using graphs, two factors often confuse students:

a   Sometimes graphs are based on explicit numerical or algebraic models, where the intercepts, slopes, sizes of shifts, etc. have explicit values. Often these numbers are based on real-world values, but sometimes they are just "made-up" numbers that the instructor has picked to illustrate the point (although they are still economically logical). Do *not* get caught up in the exact values of the numbers. Concentrate on the basic economic results—for example, an increase in *AD* leads to an increase in the price level and real GDP.

b   One common student mistake is failing to *distinguish between a shift in a curve versus a movement along a curve*. This distinction is crucial in understanding the factors that influence *AD* and *AS*, and you can be sure that your instructor will test you on it! The slope of the *AD* curve reflects the impact of a change in the price level on aggregate demand. A change in the price level produces a *movement along* the *AD* curve. A change in one of the factors affecting the *AD* curve other than price is reflected by a *shift* in the entire *AD* curve. Similarly, a change in price produces a *movement along* the *SAS* or the *LAS* curve and does not lead to a shift in the curves.

3 A change in price will not shift the *AD* or the *AS* curves. To cement the previous point, consider Figure 22.1. The initial long-run equilibrium is at the point *a*. (For the moment, ignore the SAS_1 curve.)

What happens in our model when there is a decrease in expected future disposable income and profits (such as happened in the 1990–91 recession)? This decrease in expected income and profits leads to a decrease in consumption and investment, and a decrease in aggregate demand, shown as the shift from AD_0 to AD_1.

We can best understand what happens next by imagining that the curve AD_0 can be peeled off the page, that it no longer exists—after all, the factors that created it no longer exist! This removal leaves us with the curves SAS_0 and AD_1 (remember, we are ignoring SAS_1 for the moment), and with a price level of P_0. At P_0, there is a surplus of goods and services (the quantity of real GDP supplied is equal to Y_0 [at *a*], greater than the quantity of real GDP demanded of Y_c [at *c*]), so that firms find their inventories piling up. In this case, they cut prices and decrease production. This decrease in price eliminates the surplus in two ways. First, as price decreases, firms supply fewer goods and services: a movement along the *SAS* curve from *a* to *b*. (Be careful, the price change does *not* shift the *SAS* curve.) Second, the decrease in price leads to an increase in the quantity demanded: a movement along AD_1 from *c* to *b*. (Note there is no shift in the *AD* curve as price changes.)

The end result is the new below full-employment equilibrium at *b*, with a lower price level (P_1) and a lower level of real GDP (Y_1).

4 In Figure 22.1, point *b* is a short-run below full-employment equilibrium, but it is not a long-run equilibrium since $Y_1 < Y_0$ (potential). There are two possible adjustments back from Y_1 to Y_0. First, the government or central bank could intervene with an expansionary fiscal or monetary policy, raising *AD* back to AD_0—the economy will move back to a full-employment, long-run equilibrium at *a* with $Y = Y_0$ (potential). Second, if the government does nothing, then the unemployment at *b* will lead to downward pressures on the money wage rate and other resource prices (although this adjustment can be very slow). As the money wage rates decrease, the *SAS* curve shifts slowly rightward, eventually reaching SAS_1, with a full-employment, long-run equilibrium at *d* with $Y = Y_0$ (potential).

5 On the supply side, a crucial (and often hard to understand) distinction occurs between suppliers' behaviour in the short run and the long run. The short run and long run are not lengths of calendar time, but are defined in terms of whether or not resource prices change. In the short run, the prices of productive resources do not change; in the long run, they do change.

To see what this difference implies for the supply decision, consider what happens when the price level increases. In the short run, resource prices stay unchanged. As a result, per-unit revenues are increasing, while per unit costs are unchanged. Therefore profit-maximizing firms react by hiring more productive resources and supplying more real GDP as the price level increases—the short-run aggregate supply curve is upward-sloping.

In the long run, resource prices adjust by the same amount as the price level, which means that the costs of each unit of production have increased by the same percentage as the revenue. These two effects offset each other, and firms do not change their supply decision as the price level increases—the long-run aggregate supply curve is vertical.

This distinction between the short run and the long run also applies to the influences that affect the short-run and long-run aggregate supply curves. Since prices of productive resources are held constant for the short-run aggregate supply curve but not for the long-run aggregate supply curve, a change in the prices of productive resources will shift *SAS* but not *LAS*.

FIGURE **22.1**

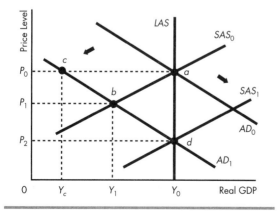

SELF-TEST

True/False and Explain

Aggregate Supply

1 As the price level increases, in the long run the aggregate quantity of goods and services supplied increases.

2 Any factor that shifts the short-run aggregate supply curve rightward will also shift the long-run aggregate supply curve rightward.

3 If there is a significant technological advance (other things remaining unchanged), the long-run aggregate supply curve will shift rightward but the short-run aggregate supply curve will not shift.

4 If the wage rate decreases (other things remaining unchanged), both the long-run aggregate supply curve and the short-run aggregate supply curve will shift rightward.

Aggregate Demand

5 An increase in the foreign exchange value of the dollar will increase aggregate demand in Canada.

6 An increase in the expected rate of inflation will decrease aggregate demand.

7 An increase in the quantity of money will increase the quantity of real GDP demanded.

8 If the price level increases, the quantity of real GDP demanded will decrease.

Macroeconomic Equilibrium

9 A shift rightward in the aggregate demand curve leads to an increase in the price level, which in turn shifts the short-run aggregate supply curve rightward in the short run.

10 If the aggregate demand curve and the short-run aggregate supply curve both shift rightward at the same time, but the aggregate demand curve shifts further rightward, then the price level increases.

11 An economy is initially in short-run equilibrium and then expected future profits decrease. The new short-run equilibrium will always be a below full-employment equilibrium.

12 If the economy is in an above full-employment equilibrium, the long-run aggregate supply curve will shift rightward until the economy is in a full-employment equilibrium.

13 If real GDP is higher than potential GDP, we would expect the money wage rate to rise.

Canadian Economic Growth, Inflation, and Cycles

14 Increases in long-run aggregate supply are the main force generating the underlying tendency of real GDP to expand over time.

15 During the 1980s in Canada, inflation rates were high and increasing.

Multiple-Choice

Aggregate Supply

I A technological improvement will shift

a both *SAS* and *AD* rightward.
b both *SAS* and *LAS* leftward.
c *SAS* rightward but leave *LAS* unchanged.
d *LAS* rightward but leave *SAS* unchanged.
e both *SAS* and *LAS* rightward.

2 An increase in the money wage rates will shift

a both *SAS* and *LAS* rightward.
b both *SAS* and *LAS* leftward.
c *SAS* leftward, but leave *LAS* unchanged.
d *LAS* rightward, but leave *SAS* unchanged.
e *SAS* rightward, but leave *LAS* unchanged.

3 Long-run aggregate supply will increase for all of the following reasons *except*

a a fall in the money wage rate.
b a rise in human capital.
c the introduction of new technology.
d more aggregate labour hours.
e more capital stock.

4 Potential GDP is the level of real GDP at which

a aggregate demand equals short-run aggregate supply.
b there is full employment.
c there is a recessionary gap.
d there is over full employment.
e prices are sure to increase.

5 The short-run aggregate supply curve is the relationship between the price level and the quantity of real GDP supplied, holding constant the

a wage rate only.
b quantities of productive resources.
c level of government expenditures.
d price level.
e prices of productive resources.

6 Consider Figure 22.2. Which graph illustrates what happens when resource prices decrease?

a (a)
b (b)
c (c)
d (d)
e none of the above

FIGURE **22.2**

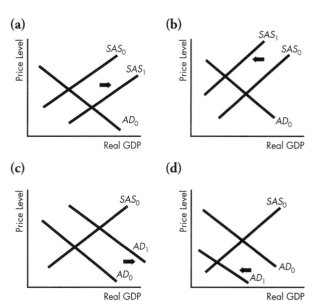

Aggregate Demand

7 Consider Figure 22.2. Which graph illustrates what happens when government expenditures increase?

a (a)
b (b)
c (c)
d (d)
e none of the above

8 Consider Figure 22.2. Which graph illustrates what happens when the quantity of money decreases?

a (a)
b (b)
c (c)
d (d)
e none of the above

9 Consider Figure 22.2. Which graph illustrates what happens when expected future disposable income increases?

a (a)
b (b)
c (c)
d (d)
e none of the above

10 Which of the following is a reason for the downward slope of the aggregate demand curve?

a the wealth effect
b the expectations effect
c the expected inflation effect
d the nominal balance effect
e none of the above

11 Which of the following will cause the aggregate demand curve to shift rightward?

a an increase in interest rates (at a given price level)
b an increase in expected inflation
c an increase in taxes
d a decrease in the price level
e an increase in the price level

Macroeconomic Equilibrium

12 We observe an increase in the price level and a decrease in real GDP. Which of the following is a possible explanation?

a The expectation of future profits has increased.
b The expectation of future disposable income has increased.
c The price of raw materials has increased.
d The stock of capital has increased.
e The money supply has increased.

13 Short-run macroeconomic equilibrium *always* occurs when the

a economy is at full employment.
b economy is below full employment.
c economy is above full employment.
d quantity of real GDP demanded equals the quantity of real GDP supplied.
e *AD* curve intersects the *LAS* curve.

14 Consider the economy represented in Table 22.1. In short-run macroeconomic equilibrium, the price level is _____ and the level of real GDP is _____ billion dollars.

a 120; 600
b 120; 500
c 125; 550
d 130; 600
e 130; 500

TABLE **22.1**

Price Level	Aggregate Demand (billions of 1997 $)	Short-Run Aggregate Supply (billions of 1997 $)	Long-Run Aggregate Supply (billions of 1997 $)
100	800	300	600
110	700	400	600
120	600	500	600
130	500	600	600
140	400	700	600

15 Consider the economy represented in Table 22.1. The economy is in a(n)

a long-run equilibrium and resource prices will not change.
b above full-employment equilibrium, and resource prices will increase.
c above full-employment equilibrium, and resource prices will decrease.
d below full-employment equilibrium, and resource prices will decrease.
e below full-employment equilibrium, and resource prices will increase.

16 Consider the economy represented in Table 22.1. There is

a an inflationary gap equal to $100 billion.
b an inflationary gap equal to $50 billion.
c a recessionary gap equal to $50 billion.
d a recessionary gap equal to $100 billion.
e no gap, the economy is at full employment.

17 The economy cannot remain at a level of real GDP above long-run aggregate supply (*LAS*) because prices of productive resources will

a decrease, shifting *LAS* rightward.
b decrease, shifting *SAS* rightward.
c increase, shifting *LAS* leftward.
d increase, shifting *SAS* leftward.
e increase, shifting *SAS* rightward.

18 Consider an economy starting from a position of full employment. Which of the following changes does *not* occur as a result of a decrease in aggregate demand?

a The price level decreases.
b The level of real GDP decreases in the short run.
c A recessionary gap arises.
d Resource prices will decrease in the long run, shifting the short-run aggregate supply curve rightward.
e The long-run aggregate supply curve shifts leftward to create the new long-run equilibrium.

19 If prices of productive resources remain constant, an increase in aggregate demand will cause a(n)

a increase in the price level and an increase in real GDP.

b increase in the price level and a decrease in real GDP.

c decrease in the price level and an increase in real GDP.

d decrease in the price level and a decrease in real GDP.

e increase in the price level, but no change in real GDP.

20 Which of the graphs in Figure 22.3 illustrates a below full-employment equilibrium?

a (a) only

b (b) only

c (c) only

d (d) only

e both (c) and (d)

FIGURE **22.3**

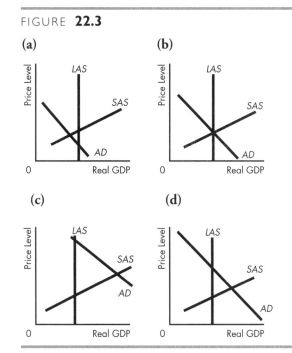

21 Which of the graphs in Figure 22.3 illustrates an above full-employment equilibrium?

a (a) only

b (b) only

c (c) only

d (d) only

e both (c) and (d)

22 If real GDP is greater than potential GDP, the economy is

a not in short-run equilibrium.

b in a recessionary equilibrium.

c in an above full-employment equilibrium.

d in a below full-employment equilibrium.

e in long-run equilibrium.

23 Which one of the following newspaper quotations best describes a movement along an *SAS* curve?

a "The decrease in consumer spending may lead to a recession."

b "The increase in consumer spending is expected to lead to inflation, without any increase in real GDP."

c "Recent higher wage settlements are expected to cause higher inflation this year."

d "Growth has been unusually high the last few years due to more women entering the workforce."

e "The recent tornadoes destroyed many factories in Calgary and Edmonton."

Growth, Inflation, and Cycles in the Canadian Economy

24 The fact that the short-run aggregate supply and aggregate demand curves do not shift at a fixed, steady pace explains why we observe

a persistent inflation.

b business cycles.

c economic growth.

d large government budget deficits.

e persistent unemployment.

25 *Persistent* inflation is caused by

a shifts rightward in aggregate demand.

b shifts rightward in short-run aggregate supply.

c the tendency for long-run aggregate supply to increase faster than aggregate demand.

d shifts rightward in short-run aggregate supply accompanied by shifts leftward in aggregate demand.

e the tendency for aggregate demand to increase faster than long-run aggregate supply.

Short Answer Problems

1 The substitution effects imply that an increase in the price level will lead to a decrease in the aggregate quantity of goods and services demanded. Explain.

2 Why is the *LAS* curve vertical?

3 Why is the *SAS* curve positively sloped?

4 What are the most important factors in explaining the steady and persistent increases in the price level over time in Canada?

5 Suppose the economy is initially in long-run equilibrium. Graphically illustrate the short-run effects of an increase in the money wage rate. What happens to the price level and the level of real GDP?

6 Consider an economy that is in above full-employment equilibrium due to an increase in *AD*. Prices of productive resources have not changed. With the help of a graph, discuss how the economy returns to long-run equilibrium, with no government intervention.

7 Table 22.2 below shows the aggregate demand and short-run aggregate supply schedule for an economy. Long-run aggregate supply is equal to 1.1 trillion 1997 $.

TABLE **22.2**

Price Level	Aggregate Demand (trillions of 1997 $)	Short-Run Aggregate Supply (trillions of 1997 $)
100	1.3	0.9
105	1.2	1.0
110	1.1	1.1
115	1.0	1.2
120	0.9	1.3

a Graph this economy's *AD, SAS, LAS* curves, and show the original macroequilibrium. What kind of equilibrium is this—below full-employment, above full employment or full employment? If there is an inflationary or recessionary gap, identify how much it is.

b Next, suppose that at every price level, the quantity of real GDP demanded falls by $200 billion. Plot the new aggregate demand curve on your graph, and show the new short-run equilibrium. What kind of equilibrium is this—below full-employment, above full employment or full employment? If there is an inflationary or recessionary gap, identify how much it is.

c Suppose that the government does not take any action and that the cause of the decrease in aggregate demand remains unchanged. What kind of adjustments occur in the long run? Explain what happens to the price level, real GDP, *AD*, and *AS* during this adjustment, illustrating the changes on your graph.

8 With the aid of a graph, illustrate the case of an economy that has persistent inflation and positive economic growth over a three-year period.

CT 9 Consider an economy where economists have estimated that last year's real GDP was $800 billion, equal to potential GDP. The price level was 105. Suppose that this year the economists estimate that potential GDP has increased by 10 percent. However, actual real GDP has decreased by 5 percent, while the price level has also decreased by 5 percent.

Draw an *AD-AS* graph that shows last year's equilibrium, as well as last year's aggregate demand, aggregate supply (short-run and long-run), price level, and real GDP level. Next, given the information above, show what has happened to the price level and the level of real GDP this year (show this year's equilibrium), plus what has happened to aggregate demand, short-run aggregate supply, and long-run aggregate supply since last year.

CT 10 In 1996, the Saguenay region of Quebec suffered some of the worst floods in memory, with many roads, towns, and buildings destroyed.

a Assuming that the economy was originally in long-run equilibrium, explain what has happened to the *LAS* and *SAS* curves in the local economy as a result of the destruction of the capital stock.

b Assuming that the *AD* curve is constant, what might happen to the price level and real GDP in the short run as a result of the changes you have described in part **a**? Show this result on an *AD-SAS* graph.

c Several observers, especially those in the construction industry, argued that the rebuilding of the destroyed capital stock would strongly stimulate the local economy. What component of aggregate demand is affected by this rebuilding? What will happen to aggregate demand as a result of this rebuilding?

d Some observers implied the local economy was better off, in a purely economic sense, as a result of the floods and the resulting rebuilding process. Do you agree?

ANSWERS

True/False and Explain

1 **F** In the long run, the money wage rates increase as well, leaving real wages and production unchanged. (500–501)

2 **F** Changes in resource prices shift only *SAS* and not *LAS*. (503–504)

3 **F** Anything that shifts *LAS* also shifts *SAS*. (503–504)

4 **F** Only the SAS shifts in response to a wage change. (503–504)

5 **F** Increase in value of dollar makes Canadian exports more expensive and imports cheaper, leading to decrease in demand for Canadian goods. (506–508)

6 **F** If individuals expect an increased inflation rate, they will spend more today to avoid higher future prices. (506–508)

7 **T** Higher quantity of money increases spending. (506–508)

8 **T** Movement along the *AD* curve due to wealth and substitution effects. (505–506)

9 **F** Increase in *P* leads to movement along *SAS* curve, not shift in it. (512–513)

10 **T** Try drawing a graph. (512–513)

⊕ 11 **F** It depends on where initial equilibrium is and on size of decrease in *AD* that results from decrease in future profits—try drawing a graph or two. (512–513)

12 **F** *SAS* shifts in this type of situation, not *LAS*. (509–513)

13 **T** Unemployment below the natural rate, upward pressure on the money wage rate. (512–513)

14 **T** Increase in population or capital stock or human capital, and new technology shift *LAS* rightward over time. (514–515)

15 **F** See text discussion. (514–515)

Multiple-Choice

1 **e** Technological improvements means same inputs can produce more output, leading to increase in quantity supplied in both short and long run. (500–508)

2 **c** Wage rates are held constant along given *SAS*; if the money wage rates increase, production is less at every price level leading to *SAS* shifting leftward. (503–504)

3 **a** Changes in the money wage rates change *SAS* only, not *LAS*. (503–504)

4 **b** Definition. (500)

5 **e** Short run is defined as time period within which resource prices are constant. (501–502)

6 **a** When resource prices decrease, firms produce more at every price level shifting *SAS* rightward. (503–504)

7 **c** Increase in government expenditures leads to increase in aggregate spending, shifting *AD* rightward. (505–508)

8 **d** Decrease in quantity of money leads to decrease in aggregate spending, shifting *AD* leftward. (505–508)

9 **c** Increase in expected future disposable income leads to increase in household consumption, shifting *AD* rightward. (505–508)

10 **a** **b** and **c** shift *AD* curve, and **d** doesn't exist. (505–508)

11 **b** Answers **a** and **c** cause it to shift leftward, while **d** and **e** are movements along *AD* curve. (505–508)

⊕ 12 **c** Answers **a**, **b**, and **e** increase *AD* leading to increase in real GDP, while **d** shifts *LAS* rightward, leading to increase in real GDP. **c** shifts *SAS* leftward leading to increase in *P*, decrease in real GDP (try drawing a graph). (512–513)

13 **d** Short-run macroeconomic equilibrium always occurs where *AD* = *SAS*; equilibrium *may* occur at answers **a**–**c** and **e**, but it doesn't *always* occur there. (512–513)

14 **c** Short-run equilibrium occurs where *AD* = *SAS*, which occurs at *P* = 125 and real GDP = 550—halfway between *P* = 120 and *P* = 130. (508–509)

⊕ 15 **d** Real GDP = 550 billion < potential GDP of 600 billion which is below full-employment equilibrium, so that unemployed workers eventually offer to work for less. (508–513)

16 **c** Actual real GDP = 550 billion, which is 50 billion less than potential GDP of 600 billion. (508–509)

17 **d** Above long-run aggregate supply, extra demand for resources leads to increase in their prices leading to increase in cost of production leading to *SAS* shifting leftward. (508–513)

18 **e** Decrease in *AD* creates recession, leading to decrease in resource prices, shifting *SAS* rightward, pushing economy back to *LAS*. (512–513)

19 **a** Increase in *AD* leads to shortages leading to increase in prices leading to increase in aggregate quantity supplied in short run, so increase in *P* and increase in real GDP. (512–513)

20 **a** Below full-employment equilibrium occurs when *AD* = *SAS* to left of *LAS*. (508–509)

21 **e** Above full-employment equilibrium occurs when *AD* = *SAS* to right of *LAS*. (508–509)

22 **c** Equilibrium is with *AD* = *SAS*; if *Y* is > *LAS* then an above full-employment equilibrium. (508–509)

ⓒ **23** **a** Decrease in consumer spending leads to shift leftward in *AD* leading to movement down an *SAS* curve in short-run leading to decrease in *P* and decrease in *Y*. (508–513)

24 **b** Sometimes curves shift leftward (creating recession) and sometimes rightward (creating boom). (514–515)

25 **e** Combination of these shifts leads to shortages leading to increase in *P*. **a**, **b**, and **c** may lead to increase in *P*, while **d** leads to decrease in *P*. (514–515)

Short Answer Problems

1 There are two substitution effects. First, if the prices of domestic goods increase and foreign prices remain constant, domestic goods become relatively more expensive, and so households will buy fewer domestic goods and more foreign goods. This decline in spending means that there will be a decrease in the quantity of real GDP demanded. Thus, an increase in the price level (the prices of domestic goods) will lead to a decrease in the aggregate quantity of (domestic) goods and services demanded.

Second, the increase in the price level increases the rate of interest, which increases saving and decreases spending. This decline in spending also means that there will again be a decrease in the quantity of real GDP demanded.

2 Long-run aggregate supply is the level of real GDP supplied when there is full employment. Since this level of real GDP is independent of the price level, the long-run aggregate supply curve is vertical. This level of real GDP is that attained when prices of productive resources are free to adjust so as to clear resource markets.

3 The short-run aggregate supply curve is positively sloped because it holds prices of productive resources constant. When the price level increases, firms see the prices of their output (revenues) increasing, but the prices of their input (costs) remain unchanged. Each firm is then induced to increase output and so aggregate output increases.

4 The price level can increase as the result of either an increase in aggregate demand or as the result of a decrease in aggregate supply. Both of these

forces have contributed to periods of an increasing price level. The steady and persistent increases in the price level, however, have been the result of a tendency for aggregate demand to increase faster than aggregate supply.

5 In Figure 22.4, the economy is initially at point *a* on the SAS_0 curve. An increase in the money wage rates will shift the *SAS* curve leftward to SAS_1. At the new equilibrium, point *b*, the price level has increased and the level of real GDP has decreased.

FIGURE **22.4**

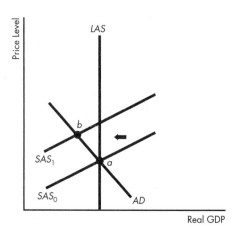

6 In Figure 22.5 shown below, the increase in *AD* from AD_0 to AD_1 results in the above full-employment equilibrium at point *b* and causes the price level to increase. Since the money wage rates have not changed, the real cost of labour to firms has decreased, and thus, output is stimulated as indicated by the movement along the SAS_0 curve from point *a* to point *b*. Furthermore, the purchasing power of workers' money wage rates has decreased.

Eventually, workers will demand higher money wage rates and firms will be willing to pay them. In a similar way, other prices of productive resources will increase as well. This long-run increase in prices of productive resources will shift the *SAS* curve leftward, which results in a new equilibrium. There will continue to be pressure for the money wage rates and other prices of productive resources to increase until the *SAS* curve shifts all the way to SAS_1, where the purchasing power of the money wage rates and other prices of productive resources has been restored and the economy is again at full employment, point *c*.

FIGURE **22.5**

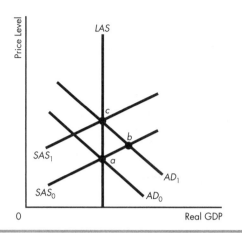

7 a The economy's AD_0, SAS_0, and LAS curves are
graphed in Figure 22.6 (ignore the AD_1 and
SAS_1 curves for now). The macroeconomic
equilibrium occurs when the AD and SAS curves
cross, at a price level of 110 and real GDP of
1.1 trillion 1997 $. Since this level of real GDP
equals the level of potential GDP, this economy
is in a full-employment equilibrium, with no
type of gap.

FIGURE **22.6**

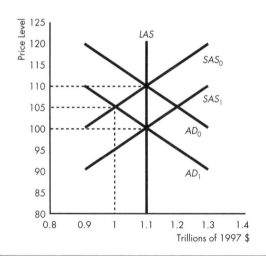

b This decrease in aggregate demand leads to a
new short-run equilibrium where the new AD_1
crosses SAS_0, at a price level of 105 and real
GDP of 1 trillion 1997 $. Since real GDP is less
than potential GDP, the economy is in a below
full-employment equilibrium, and there is a
recessionary gap equal to the difference between
real GDP and potential GDP, a gap of
$100 billion.

c Since real GDP is below potential GDP, then
unemployment is above the natural rate.
Eventually unemployed resources start offering

to work for lower resource prices, which shifts
the SAS curve rightward to SAS_1, raising
aggregate supply, lowering prices even more, and
leading to a new long-run equilibrium where
SAS_1 crosses AD_1 and LAS at the point where
the price level is 100 and real GDP is back at
potential GDP ($1.1 trillion).

8 In order to have these two events, long-run
aggregate supply is growing (shifting rightward),
and aggregate demand is shifting rightward as
well, but at a faster pace. Figure 22.7 illustrates
such a case, with the points a, b, and c showing
the three years. (The SAS curves have been
omitted from the graph for simplicity.)

FIGURE **22.7**

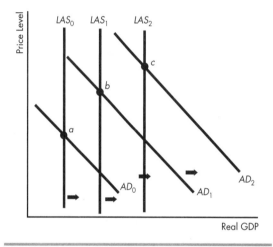

9 Figure 22.8 shows the original full-employment
equilibrium, at last year's equilibrium price level
of 105 and income level of 800.

FIGURE **22.8**

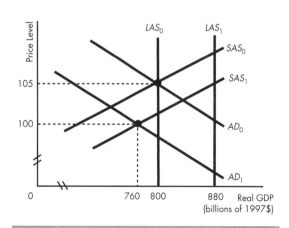

For the current year, the *LAS* curve has shifted rightward to LAS_1, a value of 880, and the *SAS* curve shifts with it to SAS_1, all else equal. The new short-run equilibrium must be along the intersection of SAS_1 and an *AD* curve. Since prices are 5 percent lower at 100, and real GDP is 5 percent lower at 760, the new *AD* curve must have shifted leftward as shown.

(*Hint:* to decide where AD_1 should be, first find the intersection of $P = 100$ and $Y = 760$ on the new *SAS* curve, and then draw in the *AD* curve to go through this point.)

⊕ **10 a** The destruction of towns, roads, etc. is a destruction of the capital stock, which would lower potential GDP, and shift the *LAS* curve leftward, shifting the *SAS* curve leftward as well.

  b Figure 22.9 shows the original long-run equilibrium at Y_0 and P_0.

The shift leftward in the long-run aggregate supply to LAS_1 and the short-run aggregate supply to SAS_1, combined with the unchanged *AD* curve leads to stagflation—a rise in the price level to P_1, accompanied by a fall in real GDP to Y_1.

  c The resulting rebuilding would stimulate investment demand, and increase aggregate demand, perhaps dramatically.

  d The region is worse off—higher inflation, and a lower level of potential GDP and real GDP. This recession is followed by higher growth once the new investment starts, *but* this investment is merely replacing lost capital, and is not adding new capital stock.

FIGURE **22.9**

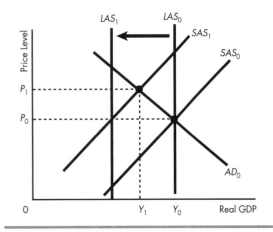

Understanding the Themes of Macroeconomics

PROBLEM

a Consider the following data for the economy of Autoland for 2003 and 2004. Calculate the value of nominal GDP for each year.

TABLE **P7.1**   2003

Item	Amount (billions of $)
Government expenditures on goods and services	60
Government transfer payments	30
Income taxes	80
Wages, etc., paid to labour	200
Export earnings	30
Consumption expenditure	180
Import payments	25
Net investment expenditure	15
Depreciation	5

TABLE **P7.2**   2004

Item	Amount (billions of $)
Wages, etc., paid to labour	200
Indirect taxes	20
Profits	20
Subsidies	5
Interest and miscellaneous investment income	5
Depreciation	10
Farmers' income	10
Income of nonfarm unincorporated business	10

b Using your data from **a**, complete the following table:

TABLE **P7.3**

Year	Nominal GDP (billions of $)	Price Level	Real GDP (billions of 1997 $)
2003		132.5	
2004		140.0	

c Draw an *AD-AS* graph that represents the Autoland economy for 2003 and 2004, based on the data in Table P7.3, and explain what has happened to the economy over this time period.

d If the economy was in long-run equilibrium in 2003, what has happened to cyclical unemployment between 2003 and 2004?

e Calculate the inflation rate, the growth rate in real GDP, and the growth rate in nominal GDP over this time period.

MIDTERM EXAMINATION

You should allocate 32 minutes for this examination
(16 questions, 2 minutes per question). For each
question, choose the one *best* answer.

1 Which of the following people would be
counted as unemployed in Canada?

a Doris only works five hours a week but is
looking for a full-time job.

b Kanhaya has stopped looking for work since he
was unable to find a suitable job during a
two-month search.

c Sharon is a college student with no job.

d Maurice is working in his garden while looking
for work.

e Taylor is a homemaker.

2 Which of the following is *not* an example of
investment in the expenditure approach to
measuring GDP? General Motors

a buys a new auto stamping machine.

b adds 500 new cars to inventories.

c buys Canadian government bonds.

d builds another assembly plant.

e replaces some worn-out stamping machines.

3 The changes represented in Figure P7.1 *must*

a not occur in the real world, because *AD* and
SAS cannot change at the same time.

b lead to an inflationary gap.

c lead to a recessionary gap.

d create inflation.

e do none of the above.

FIGURE **P7.1**

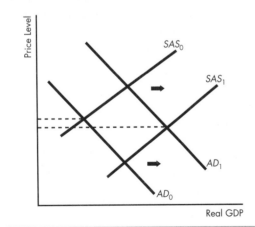

4 In a country with a working-age population of
20 million, 13 million are employed, 1.5 million
are unemployed, and 1 million of the employed
are working part-time, half of whom wish to
work full-time. The employment-to-population
ratio is

a 72.5 percent.

b 65 percent.

c 75.5 percent.

d 57.5 percent.

e none of the above.

5 Which of the following statements about
nominal and real GDP is *incorrect*?

a The chain-weighted output index is used to
calculate real GDP.

b The GDP deflator equals (nominal GDP)/(real
GDP) × 100.

c Increases in total expenditures can be due to
increases in production, or increases in prices for
goods and services.

d If total expenditures on goods and services
(measured at constant prices) is higher this year
compared to last year, this indicates positive
economic growth.

e If total expenditures on goods and services is
higher this year compared to last year, this
indicates positive economic growth.

6 Which of the following is *not* a part of the
incomes approach to GDP?

a net exports

b wages, salaries, and supplementary labour
income

c corporate profits

d farmers' income

e income of nonfarm unincorporated businesses

7 The technique used to calculate the CPI
implicitly assumes that consumers buy

a relatively more of goods with relative prices that
are rising.

b relatively fewer goods with relative prices that are
rising.

c the same relative quantities of goods as in a base
year.

d goods and services whose quality improves at the
rate of growth of real income.

e more computers and CD players and fewer
black-and-white TVs.

8 If a price index was 150 at the end of 2000 and 165 at the end of 2001, what was the rate of inflation for 2001?

a 15 percent
b 9.1 percent
c 10 percent
d 50 percent
e 65 percent

9 If the money wage rate decreases, then

a *AD* shifts rightward.
b firms hire less labour.
c only *LAS* shifts rightward.
d only *SAS* shifts rightward.
e both *SAS* and *LAS* shift rightward.

10 The aggregate demand curve illustrates that, as the price level decreases, the

a quantity of real GDP demanded increases.
b quantity of real GDP demanded decreases.
c quantity of nominal GDP demanded increases.
d quantity of nominal GDP demanded decreases.
e value of assets decrease.

11 We observe an increase in the price level and an increase in real GDP. A possible explanation is that the

a quantity of money has fallen.
b expectation of future disposable income has decreased.
c price of raw materials has increased.
d stock of capital has increased.
e expectation of future profits has increased.

12 In the circular flow, the flows of investment and saving interact with the flows of income and consumption to determine

a total production.
b aggregate income.
c aggregate expenditure.
d all of the above.
e none of the above.

13 Which of the following would be considered seasonally unemployed?

a a Saskatchewan farmer who has lost her farm and is unemployed until retrained
b a Nova Scotia fishery worker who is laid off during the winter
c a steelworker who is laid off but who expects to be called back soon
d an office worker who has lost her job because of a general slowdown in economic activity
e none of the above

14 Unemployment caused by an economy-wide decrease in the demand for goods and services is known as

a cyclical unemployment.
b seasonal unemployment.
c frictional unemployment.
d structural unemployment.
e natural unemployment.

15 Macroeconomic policy challenges include

a keeping the deficit high if borrowing is for consumption.
b stabilizing the business cycle.
c keeping inflation at the current level.
d ignoring inflation if unemployment is a problem.
e none of the above.

16 A business cycle is the

a increase in real GDP for more than 2 periods.
b decrease in real GDP for more than 2 periods.
c irregular fluctuation of potential GDP around real GDP.
d increase in the economic potential to produce goods and services.
e irregular fluctuation of real GDP around potential GDP.

ANSWERS

Problem

a For 2003, calculate nominal GDP as the sum of $C + I + G + X - M$. For G, you must use only expenditures on goods and services, and you need to calculate gross investment (= net investment + depreciation, or $20 billion). Thus nominal GDP = 180 + 20 + 60 + 30 − 25 = $265 billion for 2003.

For 2004, you need to use the incomes approach. First, calculate net domestic income at factor cost = wages, etc. + profits + interest and miscellaneous investment income + farmers' income + income of nonfarm unincorporated business = 200 + 20 + 5 + 10 + 10 = $245 billion. Next, to get net domestic product you must add indirect taxes and subtract subsidies from net domestic income, or 245 + 20 − 5 = $260 billion. Finally, to get gross domestic product, you must add depreciation to net domestic product, or 260 + 10 = $270 billion for 2004.

b Table P7.3 is completed below as Table P7.3 Solution, using the fact real GDP = nominal GDP divided by the price level.

TABLE **P7.3** SOLUTION

Year	Nominal GDP (billions of $)	Price Level	Real GDP (billions of 1997 $)
2003	265	132.5	200.0
2004	270	140.0	192.9

c Figure P7.2 shows the Autoland economy in 2003 and 2004. The exact sizes of shifts in *AD* and *SAS* depends on assumptions about their slopes, but the relative types of shifts must be as shown in order to get the simultaneous increase in the price level and decrease in real GDP that occurred from 2003 to 2004. As the graph shows, the likely changes were a shift leftward in *SAS* and a shift leftward in *AD*, with the shift leftward in *SAS* larger (it is this shift that results in the price level increasing).

FIGURE **P7.2**

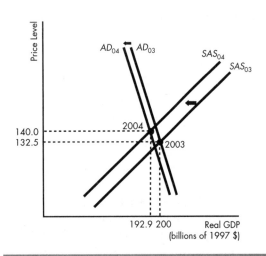

d If the economy was in long-run equilibrium in 2003, then real GDP = potential GDP and there was zero cyclical unemployment. The decrease in real GDP to below potential GDP means that unemployment must be above the natural rate, so that cyclical unemployment has increased in 2004.

e The inflation rate is equal to

$$5.7\% = \frac{140.0 - 132.5}{132.5} \times 100$$

The growth rate of real GDP is equal to

$$-3.6\% = \frac{192.9 - 200}{200} \times 100$$

The growth rate of nominal GDP is equal to

$$1.9\% = \frac{270 - 265}{265} \times 100$$

Midterm Examination

1 **d** Doris is employed part-time, Kanhaya is not looking for work (discouraged worker), Sharon and Taylor are out of labour force. (444–445)

2 **c** This is purchase of financial assets, not capital stock. (459)

3 **e** These changes can occur. Whether or not there is gap cannot be determined without *LAS* curve. (514–515)

4 **b** Employed/working-age population = 13/20 = 65 percent. (481–482)

5 **e** This definition is for nominal GDP, and it might be higher either due to higher prices or higher production of goods and services. Only the latter is positive economic growth. (465–467)

6 **a** It is part of expenditure approach. (463–464)

7 **c** Because it assumes same basket of goods used for years being compared. (491–493)

8 **c** 10% = [(165 − 150)/150] × 100. (447)

9 **d** If the money wage rates decrease, cost of production decreases, firms hire more labour, supply more goods and services, represented by (only) *SAS* shifting rightward. (508–513)

10 **a** *AD* curve is downward sloping due to three effects. It is real GDP by definition, not nominal, and asset values increase here. (505–508)

11 **e** Answer **e** shifts *AD* rightward, leading to an increase in *P* and real GDP. **a** and **b** shift *AD* leftward, while **c** shifts *SAS* leftward, leading to a decrease in *Y*, and **d** shifts *LAS* rightward, which decreases *P* (try drawing a graph). (508–513)

12 **d** Expenditure = money earned by sales of produced goods, and is used to pay incomes (including profits). (459–460)

13 **b** Job not available in winter. (487–488)

14 **a** Definition. (505–509)

15 **b** It should be reducing the deficit and keeping inflation low. (451)

16 **e** Definition. (440)

Chapter 23

Expenditure Multipliers

KEY CONCEPTS

Expenditure Plans and GDP

Components of aggregate expenditure are consumption (C), investment (I), government expenditures (G), and exports (X) – imports (M), which sum to real GDP (Y).

♦ C, M depend on real GDP (Y), so that an increase in Y increases AE, and increase in AE increases Y.

Consumption and saving depend primarily on **disposable income** (YD) = real GDP – net taxes (NT).

♦ **Consumption function** shows increase in YD leads to increase in consumption.

♦ **Saving function** shows increase in YD leads to increase in saving, with $\Delta C + \Delta S = \Delta YD$.

♦ **Marginal propensity to consume** (MPC) = fraction of ΔYD that is consumed = $\Delta C/\Delta YD$ = slope of consumption function.

♦ **Marginal propensity to save** (MPS) = fraction of ΔYD that is saved = $\Delta S/\Delta YD$ = slope of saving function.

♦ $MPC + MPS = 1$.

Influences other than ΔYD *shift* the functions.

♦ Increase in expected future disposable income shifts S function downwards, C function upwards.

♦ Increase in the real interest rate shifts S function upwards, C function downwards.

♦ Increase in wealth shifts S function downwards, C function upwards.

♦ Consumption and saving are a function of real GDP since increase in real GDP leads to increase in YD.

Import function is relationship between imports and real GDP.

♦ **Marginal propensity to import** is fraction of ΔY spent on imports = $\Delta M/\Delta Y$.

♦ Other variables, such as implementing trade agreements, also influence imports.

Equilibrium Expenditure at a Fixed Price Level

In the very short term, the price level is fixed—aggregate demand determines aggregate quantity sold.

♦ To understand AD, we study the aggregate expenditure model.

♦ **Aggregate planned expenditure** (AE) = planned C + planned I + planned G + planned X – planned M.

Components of aggregate expenditure interact to determine Y, and AE is influenced by Y.

♦ AE can be represented by graph or schedule. Increase in Y leads to increase in AE.

♦ Aggregate planned expenditure has two parts:

  • **Autonomous expenditure** (A) = part of AE that does *not* vary with income.
  • **Induced expenditure** (N) = part of AE that *does* vary with income.

♦ Actual aggregate expenditure may not equal planned expenditure if level of real GDP is not consistent with plans.

♦ **Equilibrium expenditure** occurs when AE = real GDP.

  • On graph this point occurs when AE curve crosses 45° line.

- If real GDP above equilibrium value, AE < real GDP. Firms cannot sell all their production, leading to unplanned increase in inventories. Firms lower production, leading to decrease in real GDP and convergence to equilibrium.
- If real GDP below equilibrium value, AE > real GDP. Firms sell all their production and more, leading to unplanned decrease in inventories. Firms increase production to restore inventories, leading to increase in real GDP and convergence to equilibrium.

The Multiplier

The **multiplier** is the amount by which change in autonomous expenditure is multiplied to determine change in equilibrium expenditure and real GDP.

◆ Increase in autonomous expenditure leads to primary effect of increased aggregate planned expenditure, leading to increase in real GDP, leading to further (secondary) increase in aggregate planned expenditure, leading to further increases in real GDP, etc.

◆ Secondary *induced* effects means total Δ real GDP > initial Δ autonomous expenditure.

◆ Multiplier = (Δ real GDP)/(Δ autonomous expenditure) = 1/(1 – slope of AE function) > 1 because of induced effects.

- Higher slope of AE function implies larger induced effects and larger multiplier.
- Multiplier is higher if MPC is higher, or marginal tax rate is lower or marginal propensity to import is lower.

◆ Recessions and depressions begin with expenditure fluctuations magnified by multiplier effect.

The Multiplier and the Price Level

Aggregate demand curve shows relationship between real GDP demanded and price level, other things remaining the same, and can be derived from AE curve.

◆ Increase in price level shifts AE curve downward, lowers equilibrium real GDP, shown by movement up and to left on AD curve.

◆ Δ nonprice variables shift both AE and AD curves.

◆ In short run, increase in AE leads to shift rightward in AD curve, which increases price level, which lowers AE somewhat, offsetting increase in Y somewhat, so multiplier is smaller.

◆ In long run, vertical LAS means there is large enough increase in price level to create decrease in AE that totally offsets initial increase, so that multiplier = 0.

1 The 45° line is an important concept for understanding the consumption function and equilibrium expenditure. The 45° line is a *reference line* on a graph, showing the points where the two variables on the axes of the graph have the same value.

FIGURE **23.1**

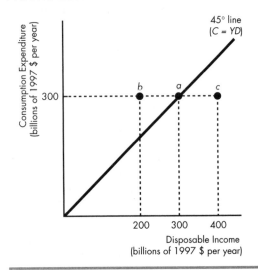

Consider the graph of consumption and disposable income illustrated in Figure 23.1. Along the 45° line, consumption equals disposable income at all points. For example, at point *a*, $C = YD = \$300$ billion.

Consider point *b*. Consumption is still equal to \$300 billion, but now disposable income is only \$200 billion. *To the left of the 45° line, variables measured on the vertical axis (here, consumption) are greater than variables measured on the horizontal axis (here, disposable income).*

Next, consider point *c*. Consumption is still equal to \$300 billion, but now disposable income is \$400 billion. *To the right of the 45° line, variables measured on the vertical axis are less than variables measured on the horizontal axis.*

To summarize, consider the consumption function (*CF*) shown in Figure 23.2. Using the 45° as our reference, any point on the consumption function that is to the left of the 45° line has consumption greater than disposable income (and therefore saving (= $YD - C$) is negative). Any point on the consumption function to the right of the 45° line has consumption less than disposable income (and saving is positive).

FIGURE **23.2**

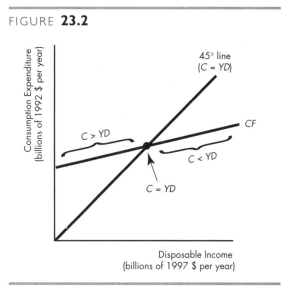

To make sure you understand, draw the graph of the aggregate expenditure function, with a 45° line, and identify the points on your graph where aggregate expenditure is greater than income, equal to income, or less than income. *Note:* For the consumption function, the 45° line is a pure reference line—it is possible in equilibrium for consumption to be greater than, less than, or equal to disposable income. However, for the aggregate expenditure function, the point on the 45° line where *AE* = *Y* is more than just a reference point, it shows the point of *equilibrium expenditure.*

2 Aggregate demand is the relationship between the price level and the quantity of goods and services demanded; in other words, it is the relationship between the price level and the level of planned aggregate expenditure. One purpose of this chapter is to help you better understand the behaviour of planned aggregate expenditure by separating and examining its individual components. In particular, consumption expenditure, investment, and net exports—the three components of private aggregate expenditure—will be examined. As you put the discussion of this chapter and the next in perspective, remember that the ultimate objective is a more complete understanding of aggregate demand (and what shifts it), which combines these expenditure components with government expenditure on goods and services. This understanding of the components such as consumption will help you in later chapters to understand the potential causes of past and future recessions.

Be sure you are able to distinguish the *AD* curve from the *AE* curve—they are based on different thought experiments. Each *AE* curve holds constant the price level, and represents only a single point on an *AD* curve, while the *AD* curve allows the price level to vary. Changing the price level will shift the *AE* curve, but create a movement along the *AD* curve.

3 Unplanned changes in inventory are an important part of the story of how equilibrium expenditure is achieved, and how it changes in the face of a shock. To help you see how this effect works, suppose that you were running a retail store—for example, selling CDs or dresses. On the basis of your normal sales and the costs versus benefits of holding inventories, you would have a target optimal planned inventory of perhaps 200 dresses. Each week you might sell an average of 40 dresses, and also reorder 40 dresses from the manufacturer who supplies you. In this simple example, production of 40 dresses equals the sales (planned expenditure) of 40 dresses on average, with week-to-week fluctuations depending on the weather, etc.

Next, suppose that there is a change in planned expenditures by consumers that leads to a decrease in your sales to only 30 dresses a week. Initially, you are still ordering 40 dresses a week because you think that this change is just a temporary fluctuation that will eventually reverse itself. However, after a few weeks there has been no reversal, and you find that your inventory of dresses in the store has had an unplanned increase. You react to this information by cutting your orders to your supplier in order to shrink your inventory. In turn, the dress manufacturer cuts production, and may lay off workers, etc.—the decrease in planned expenditures by consumers has led to a decrease in real GDP.

There are two real-world complications to this simple story. First, while initially the text holds constant the price level, in the real world (and at the end of the chapter), prices do some adjusting. For example, our dress shop might cut prices to try and move excess inventory and raise sales.

Second, there are many industries where firms cannot hold inventories, and must adjust production or prices instantly when sales decrease. Most service industries fall into this category—consider the example of a law firm. A law firm cannot maintain an inventory of legal briefs. Instead, it reacts to changes in the demand for its services by an immediate change in production. As a result, lawyers and others in various service industries have frequent periods of low workloads, followed by frequent periods of high workloads—in a sense, the inventory adjustment occurs by an adjustment of the hours of work.

4 This chapter distinguishes between *autonomous* expenditure and *induced* expenditure. Autonomous expenditure is independent of changes in real GDP, whereas induced expenditure will vary as real GDP varies. In general, a change in autonomous expenditures creates a change in real GDP, which in turn creates a change in induced expenditure. As the flow graph in Figure 23.3 illustrates, these changes are at the heart of the multiplier effect.

FIGURE **23.3**

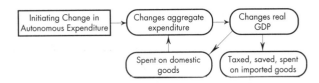

(It is important to realize, however, that even though autonomous expenditure may be independent of changes in real GDP, it will not be independent of changes in other variables, for example, the price level.)

5 The concept of the multiplier is very important. It is a result of the interaction of the components of aggregate expenditure. In particular, an initial increase in autonomous expenditure will increase real GDP directly, but that is not the end of the story. That initial increase in real GDP will generate an increase in *induced* expenditure, which further increases real GDP, and thus induces further increases in expenditure. The total effect on real GDP will be larger than the initial increase in autonomous expenditure because there is induced expenditure. You should become thoroughly familiar with both the intuition and the mathematics behind the multiplier.

6 The multiplier shows the change in equilibrium expenditure, and the change in equilibrium real GDP, price level held constant—it shows the shift rightward or leftward in the *AD* curve. However, normally the price level will change in face of a shift in the *AD* curve, with the size of the change depending on the *AS* curve. In the short run, the change in the price level creates an opposite change in aggregate expenditure, that somewhat offsets the initial change in aggregate expenditure, so that the total change in real

GDP is less than the initial shift in *AD* would indicate. In the long run, this offsetting effect is 100 percent.

7 e The mathematical note to Chapter 23 on the algebra of the multiplier will be covered by some students' instructors, and this material is worth reviewing if you are one of those students.

To start, recall that aggregate planned expenditure (*AE*) is equal to the sum of components planned levels:

(1) $AE = C + I + G + X - M$

Next, recall that consumption consists of autonomous consumption (*a*) and induced consumption (*bYD*), or

(2) $C = a + bYD$

Substituting in the definitions of disposable income ($YD = Y - NT$) and net taxes ($NT = tY$) yields:

(3) $C = a + b(Y - NT) = a + b(1 - t)Y$

Next, recall that imports also depend on real GDP.

(4) $M = mY$

Next, substitute the consumption function (equation (3)) and the import function (equation (4)) into the aggregate planned expenditure function:

(5) $AE = a + b(1 - t)Y + I + G + X - mY$

Collecting terms:

(6) $AE = [a + I + G + X] + [b(1 - t) - m]Y$

or

(6a) $AE = A + [b(1 - t) - m]Y$

A is autonomous expenditure and $[b(1 - t) - m]$ is the slope of the aggregate planned expenditure function.

Equilibrium occurs when $Y = AE$ along the 45° line:

(7) $Y^* = A + [b(1 - t) - m]Y^*$

Collecting terms and solving yields the solution:

(8) $Y^* = \dfrac{1}{1 - [b(1 - t) - m]}A$

We can use equation (8) to show the algebraic formula for the multiplier. We start with a shock to autonomous expenditure (ΔA) which creates a change in equilibrium expenditure and real GDP:

(9) $\Delta Y^* = \dfrac{1}{1 - [b(1 - t) - m]} \Delta A$

Dividing both sides of (9) by ΔA gives us the equation for the multiplier:

(10) $\dfrac{\Delta Y^*}{\Delta A} = \dfrac{1}{1 - [b(1 - t) - m]}$

$= \dfrac{1}{1 - \text{Slope of } AE \text{ function}}$

SELF-TEST

True/False and Explain

Expenditure Plans and GDP

1 The sum of the marginal propensity to consume and the marginal propensity to save is equal to 1.

2 A change in disposable income will shift the consumption function.

3 An increase in expected future disposable income will shift both the consumption and saving functions upwards.

4 Net taxes increase as real GDP increases.

Equilibrium Expenditure at a Fixed Price Level

5 When aggregate planned expenditure exceeds real GDP, inventories will increase more than planned.

6 Equilibrium expenditure occurs when aggregate planned expenditure equals real GDP.

7 Induced expenditure is that part of aggregate expenditure that varies as real GDP varies.

8 The aggregate expenditure schedule lists the level of aggregate planned expenditure that is generated at each level of real GDP.

The Multiplier

9 If the slope of the AE function is 0.75, the multiplier is equal to 3.

10 If the marginal tax rate increases, the multiplier will be higher.

11 If the marginal propensity to import decreases, the multiplier will be higher.

The Multiplier and the Price Level

12 An increase in the price level will shift the aggregate expenditure curve upward.

13 An increase in autonomous expenditure will generate an increase in equilibrium real GDP in the short run.

14 An increase in autonomous expenditure will generate an increase in equilibrium real GDP in the long run.

15 The higher the marginal propensity to consume, the higher the multiplier in the long run.

Multiple-Choice

Expenditure Levels and GDP

I The fraction of the last dollar of disposable income saved is the

a   marginal propensity to consume.
b   marginal propensity to save.
c   marginal propensity to dispose.
d   marginal tax rate.
e   saving function.

2 Consider Table 23.1. Autonomous consumption is equal to

a $0.
b $65.
c $100.
d $260
e $400.

TABLE **23.1**

Disposable Income (1997 $)	Consumption Expenditure (1997 $)
0	100
100	165
200	230
300	295
400	360

3 Consider Table 23.1. The marginal propensity to consume is

a   0.35.
b   0.65.
c   1.15.
d   1.65.
e   not calculable with the information given.

4 In Table 23.1, at which of the following level(s) of YD is there positive saving?

a   0
b   100
c   200
d   300
e   All of the above levels

5 Which of the following events would shift the consumption function upward?

a   An increase in disposable income
b   A decrease in disposable income
c   An increase in the real interest rate
d   A decrease in expected future disposable income
e   An increase in wealth

Equilibrium Expenditure at a Fixed Price Level

6 The aggregate expenditure curve shows the relationship between aggregate planned expenditure and

a   disposable income.
b   real GDP.
c   the interest rate.
d   consumption expenditure.
e   the price level.

7 If there is an unplanned increase in inventories, aggregate planned expenditure is

a   greater than real GDP and firms will increase output.
b   greater than real GDP and firms will decrease output.
c   less than real GDP and firms will increase output.
d   less than real GDP and firms will decrease output.
e   less than real GDP and firms will decrease investment.

8 If $AE = 50 + 0.6Y$ and $Y = 200$, then unplanned inventory

a   increases are 75.
b   increases are 30.
c   decreases are 75.
d   decreases are 30.
e   changes are 0 and equilibrium exists.

9 Autonomous expenditure is *not* influenced by

a   the interest rate.
b   the foreign exchange rate.
c   real GDP.
d   the price level.
e   any variable.

10 In Figure 23.4, the marginal propensity to consume is

a   0.3.
b   0.6.
c   0.9.
d   1.0.
e   none of the above.

FIGURE **23.4**

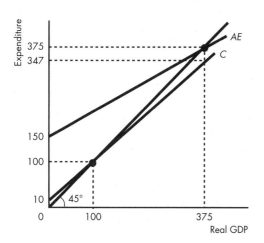

Note: There are no taxes in this economy.

11 In Figure 23.4, *autonomous* aggregate expenditure is
a 10.
b 100.
c 150.
d 347.
e 375.

12 In Figure 23.4, equilibrium expenditure is
a 10.
b 100.
c 150.
d 347.
e 375.

13 In Figure 23.4, at the equilibrium level of real GDP, *induced* expenditure is
a 28.
b 150.
c 225.
d 347.
e 375.

14 In Figure 23.4, the marginal propensity to import is
a 0.
b 0.1.
c 0.25.
d 0.3.
e 0.6.

The Multiplier

15 In Figure 23.4, the multiplier is
a 0.25.
b 1.00.
c 1.60.
d 2.50.
e 10.

16 An increase in expected future disposable income would lead to a(n)
a increase in consumption and a decrease in aggregate expenditure.
b increase in both consumption and aggregate expenditure.
c decrease in both consumption and aggregate expenditure.
d decrease in consumption and an increase in aggregate expenditure.
e increase in consumption and either an increase or a decrease in aggregate expenditure, depending on what happens to saving.

17 Which of the following quotations illustrates the idea of the multiplier?
a "The new stadium will generate $200 million in spinoff spending."
b "Higher expected profits are leading to higher investment spending by business, and will lead to higher consumer spending."
c "The projected cuts in government jobs will hurt the local retail industry."
d "Taking the grain elevator out of our small town will destroy 300 jobs."
e All of the above.

18 Which of the following will lead to an increase in the value of the multiplier?
a an increase in the marginal propensity to import
b an increase in the marginal tax rate
c a decrease in the marginal propensity to consume
d a decrease in the marginal propensity to save
e an increase in the marginal propensity to save

The Multiplier and the Price Level

19 An increase in the price level will

a shift the *AE* curve upward and increase equilibrium expenditure.

b shift the *AE* curve upward and decrease equilibrium expenditure.

c shift the *AE* curve downward and increase equilibrium expenditure.

d shift the *AE* curve downward and decrease equilibrium expenditure.

e have no impact on the *AE* curve.

20 A decrease in the price level will

a increase aggregate expenditure and thus produce a movement along the aggregate demand curve.

b increase aggregate expenditure and thus produce a rightward shift in the aggregate demand curve.

c increase aggregate expenditure and thus produce a leftward shift in the aggregate demand curve.

d have no effect on aggregate expenditure.

e increase aggregate expenditure, but produce no effect on the aggregate demand curve.

21 Suppose that investment increases by $10 billion. If the multiplier is 2, the *AD* curve will

a shift rightward by the horizontal distance of $20 billion.

b shift rightward by a horizontal distance greater than $20 billion.

c shift rightward by a horizontal distance less than $20 billion.

d not be affected.

e shift upward by a vertical distance equal to $20 billion.

22 Suppose the multiplier is 2 and the short-run aggregate supply curve is positively sloped. If investment increases by $10 billion, equilibrium real GDP will

a increase by $20 billion.

b increase by more than $20 billion.

c decrease by less than $20 billion.

d be unaffected.

e increase by less than $20 billion.

23 Suppose the multiplier is 2 and investment increases by $10 billion. In the long run, equilibrium real GDP will

a increase by $20 billion.

b increase by more than $20 billion.

c decrease by less than $20 billion.

d be unaffected.

e increase by less than $20 billion.

Mathematical Note to Chapter 23: The Algebra of the Multiplier

24 Consider Fact 23.1. What is the equation for the aggregate expenditure function of this economy?

a $AE = 16 + 0.7Y$

b $AE = 36 - 0.7Y$

c $AE = 26 + 0.8Y$

d $AE = 36 + 0.9Y$

e $AE = 36 + 0.7Y$

FACT **23.1**

The economy of Beverly Hills has a consumption function of $C = 10 + 0.8Y$, investment equal to 6, government expenditures on goods and services equal to 10, exports equal to 10, and an import function of $M = 0.1Y$.

---

25 Consider Fact 23.1. What is equilibrium real GDP in this economy?

a 36

b 120

c 130

d 360

e none of the above

Short Answer Problems

1 Explain how studying the circular flow in Chapter 20 helps us to understand the multiplier process of Chapter 23.

2 Suppose aggregate planned expenditure is greater than real GDP. Explain the process by which equilibrium expenditure is achieved.

3 Define and explain what autonomous expenditure is, and what induced expenditure is, and what role each plays in the multiplier process.

4 Explain (without algebraic expressions) why the multiplier is larger if the marginal propensity to consume is higher.

5 Explain how the effects of price level changes on the *AE* curve will generate an *AD* curve.

6 Table 23.2 illustrates the consumption function for a very small economy.

TABLE **23.2**

Disposable Income (1997 $)	Consumption Expenditure (1997 $)	Saving (1997 $)
0	3,000	
3,000	5,250	
6,000	7,500	
9,000	9,750	
12,000	12,000	
15,000	14,250	

a Compute the economy's saving at each level of disposable income by completing Table 23.2.
b Compute the economy's *MPC* and *MPS*.
c From the information given and computed, draw the economy's consumption and saving functions.
d Write out the equations of the consumption and saving functions.

7 Consider an economy with the following components of aggregate expenditure:
  • Consumption function: $C = 20 + 0.8Y$
  • Investment function: $I = 30$
  • Government expenditures: $G = 8$
  • Export function: $X = 4$
  • Import function: $M = 2 + 0.2Y$
  (There are no taxes, so $YD = Y$.)
a What is the marginal propensity to consume in this economy?
b What is the equation of the aggregate expenditure function in this economy?
c What is the slope of the *AE* function?
d Find this economy's equilibrium aggregate expenditure and real GDP by completing the columns of Table 23.3.

TABLE **23.3**

Y	C	I	G	X	M	AE
0						
30						
60						
90						
120						
150						
180						

e Using the equation of the aggregate function you derived in **b**, solve mathematically for the equilibrium aggregate expenditure and real GDP.
f What is the multiplier for this economy?

8 Consider an economy with the following characteristics:
  • Autonomous part of consumption expenditure = $10 billion
  • Investment = $5 billion
  • Government expenditures of goods and services = $40 billion
  • Exports = $5 billion
  • Slope of the *AE* function = 0.5.
  • There are no autonomous imports.
  (Assume that the price level is constant.)
a What is autonomous expenditure in this economy?
b What is the equation of the *AE* function?
c Draw a graph containing the *AE* curve for this economy (label it AE_0) as well as a 45° line.
d What is equilibrium expenditure?
e What is induced expenditure in equilibrium?

9 Return to the economy of Short Answer Problem **8**. Now suppose that the government decides to increase its expenditures on goods and services to $60 billion.
a Using the graph from Short Answer Problem **8c**, draw the new *AE* curve and label it AE_1.
b What is the new equilibrium expenditure? Solve for this value using both the graphical approach and the mathematical approach.
c What is the multiplier?
d Were there increases or decreases in autonomous expenditure, induced expenditure, consumption, imports, and investment after the increase in government expenditures?

10 Explain carefully what an increase in expected future disposable income will do to the consumption function, the saving function, the aggregate expenditure curve, and the aggregate demand curve.

ANSWERS

True/False and Explain

1 **T** Last dollar of *YD* is either spent or saved. (530–531)
2 **F** Change in *YD* leads to movement along consumption function. (528–532)
3 **F** Shifts upward the consumption function—more consumption expenditure at each level of *current YD*, but given constant current *YD*, this increase in consumption means less saving. (531–532)

4 **T** Due to induced income taxes. (532)

5 **F** *AE* > real GDP creates excess sales, leading to falling inventories. (536–537)

6 **T** Definition. (536–537)

7 **T** Definition. (535)

8 **T** Definition. (535)

9 **F** Multiplier = 1/(1 – slope of *AE* function) = 1/(1 – 0.75) = 1/0.25 = 4. (538–540)

ⓒⓣ **10** **F** A higher marginal tax rate lowers the slope of the *AE* curve and the size of the multiplier. (540–541)

11 **T** A lower marginal propensity to import increases the slope of the *AE* curve and the size of the multiplier. (540–541)

12 **F** Increase in price level lowers *AE* through wealth effect, etc. (543–545)

13 **T** The increase in *AE* shifts the *AD* curve rightward, movement along *SAS* in the short run with an increase in real GDP. (545–547)

14 **F** Same initial effect as for **13**, but given the vertical *LAS* curve, there is no increase in real GDP. (545–547)

15 **F** In the long run, the multiplier is zero due to the vertical *LAS* curve. (545–547)

Multiple-Choice

1 **b** Definition. (530–531)

2 **c** The level of consumption when disposable income is zero. (528)

3 **b** *MPC* = Δ*C*/Δ*YD* = (165 – 100)/(100 – 0) = 0.65. (530)

4 **d** Only here is *YD* > *C*. (528–529)

5 **e** **a** and **b** are movements along the curve, **c** and **d** shift it downwards. (531–532)

6 **b** Definition. (535)

ⓒⓣ **7** **d** Increase in inventories means *AE* < real GDP and decreases in firms' sales, so they decrease production in response. (536–537)

ⓒⓣ **8** **b** *Y* = 200 implies *AE* = 50 + 0.6(200) = 170. Unplanned inventories = *Y* – *AE* = +30. (536–537)

9 **c** Definition. (535)

10 **c** *MPC* = slope of consumption function = Δ*C*/Δ*Y* = 90/100 = 0.9. (530)

11 **c** Intercept of *AE* function. (535)

12 **e** From where the *AE* curve crosses the 45° line. (535–537)

13 **c** Induced = aggregate – autonomous = 375 – 150 = 225. (535–537)

ⓒⓣ **14** **d** Marginal propensity to import = *MPC* – slope of *AE* curve = 0.9 – 0.6 = 0.3, where the slope of *AE* curve = Δ*AE*/Δ*Y* = 225/375 = 0.6. (535–537)

15 **d** Multiplier = 1/(1 – slope of *AE* function) = 1/(1 – 0.6) = 1/0.4 = 2.5. (540)

16 **b** Increase in expected future disposable income leads to more consumption spending, less saving, and an increase in autonomous expenditure. (531–539)

17 **e** All of the choices discuss secondary, induced effects. (538–539)

ⓒⓣ **18** **d** This change raises *MPC* and multiplier. Others lower multiplier. (539–541)

19 **d** Increase in price level leads to decrease in aggregate expenditure due to the three effects, leading to new equilibrium at lower real GDP = equilibrium expenditure. (543–545)

20 **a** Decrease in price level leads to increase in aggregate expenditure due to three effects, leading to movement along *AD* curve. (543–545)

21 **a** Multiplier effect raises *AE* and *Y* by 2 times original Δ autonomous expenditure, which leads to shift rightward by same amount in *AD* curve. (543–545)

22 **e** Multiplier effect of Question **21** is reduced by increase in price level due to positively sloped *SAS* curve. (543–547)

23 **d** Vertical *LAS* curve means that there is no increase in real GDP after the shift rightward in *AD*. (543–547)

24 **e** *AE* = 10 + 0.8*Y* + 6 + 10 + 10 – 0.1*Y* = 36 + 0.7*Y*. (550–551)

25 **b** Solve *Y** = 36 + 0.7*Y**, which leads to *Y**(1 – 0.7) = 36, and therefore *Y** = 36/0.3 = 120. (550–551)

Short Answer Problems

1 The circular flow shows us that firms produce goods and services, sell them on the market to consumers, investors, governments, and the rest of the world, and use the money earned to pay factors of production, who in turn buy goods and services. The circular flow thus shows us the secondary, induced effects of the multiplier process in action. An initial increase in autonomous expenditure means more sales for firms, which means more household income, which means more consumption expenditure, etc.

2 If aggregate planned expenditure is greater than real GDP, inventories will decrease more than planned, and firms will increase output to replenish those depleted inventories. As a result, real GDP increases. This procedure continues as long as real GDP is less than aggregate planned expenditure. Thus it will stop only when equilibrium is attained—when real GDP equals aggregate planned expenditure.

3 Autonomous expenditure is the part of aggregate expenditure that does not vary with real GDP, but varies as a result of changes in other variables such as the real interest rate. Induced expenditure is the part of aggregate expenditure that does vary with real GDP. The multiplier process starts out with a change in autonomous expenditure that changes aggregate expenditure, which in turn changes real GDP. This change in real GDP creates secondary effects by changing induced expenditure in the same direction, which in turn changes aggregate expenditure and real GDP, leading to a total effect that is a multiple of the initial change in autonomous expenditure.

4 Any initial stimulus to autonomous expenditure will generate a direct increase in real GDP. The basic idea of the multiplier is that this initial increase in real GDP will generate further increases in real GDP as increases in consumption expenditure are induced. At each round of the multiplier process, the increase in spending, and thus the further increase in real GDP, are partially determined by the marginal propensity to consume. Since a larger marginal propensity to consume means a larger increase in real GDP at each round, the total increase in real GDP will also be greater. Thus the multiplier will be larger if the marginal propensity to consume is larger.

5 The aggregate demand curve illustrates the relationship between the price level and aggregate expenditures. The aggregate expenditure diagram shows the level of equilibrium expenditure holding the price level constant. If the price level changes, the *AE* curve will shift and a new level of equilibrium expenditure will result. Thus, for each price level, there is a different level of equilibrium expenditure. These combinations of price level and corresponding aggregate expenditure are points on the aggregate demand curve. For example, if the price level increases, autonomous expenditure will decline, and the *AE* curve will shift downward. This shift will lead to a decrease in equilibrium expenditure. Since an increase in the price level is associated with a reduction in equilibrium expenditure, the *AD* curve is negatively sloped.

6 a The answers to **a** are shown in Table 23.2 Solution, where saving = *YD* − *C*.

TABLE **23.2** SOLUTION

Disposable Income (1997 $)	Consumption Expenditure (1997 $)	Saving (1997 $)
0	3,000	−3,000
3,000	5,250	−2,250
6,000	7,500	−1,500
9,000	9,750	−750
12,000	12,000	0
15,000	14,250	+750

b The *MPC* = (change in consumption)/(change in disposable income). Using the first two entries in the table, we can see that change in consumption is 2,250, and the change in disposable income is 3,000, so that the *MPC* = 0.75 = 2,250/3,000. The *MPS* = (change in saving)/(change in disposable income). Using the first two entries in the table, we can see that change in saving is +750, and the change in disposable income is 3,000, so that the *MPS* = 0.25 = 750/3,000. Using any other two adjacent entries in the table will yield the same result.

c The consumption function is shown in Figure 23.5, and the saving function is illustrated in Figure 23.6.

FIGURE **23.5**

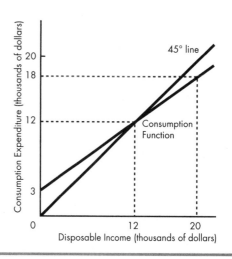

FIGURE **23.6**

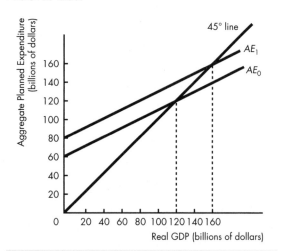

d The equation of the consumption function is based on an intercept of 3,000 and the slope (MPC) of 0.75. $C = 3,000 + 0.75\,YD$. Similarly, for the saving function, $S = -3,000 + 0.25\,YD$.

7 a From the consumption function equation we know this value is $0.8 = \Delta C/\Delta Y$.

  b Substitute the various equations into $AE = C + I + G + X - M$: $AE = 20 + 0.8\,Y + 30 + 8 + 4 - 2 - 0.2\,Y = 60 + 0.6\,Y$.

  c The slope of the AE function comes from the equation and equals $\Delta AE/\Delta Y = 0.6$.

  d The answer is presented in Table 23.3 Solution below. The table is constructed by substituting the various values of Y into the equations. Note that equilibrium occurs when $AE = Y$ at a value of 150.

TABLE **23.3**   SOLUTION

Y	C	I	G	X	M	AE
0	20	30	8	4	2	60
30	44	30	8	4	8	78
60	68	30	8	4	14	96
90	92	30	8	4	20	114
120	116	30	8	4	26	132
150	140	30	8	4	32	150
180	164	30	8	4	38	168

  e Equilibrium occurs when
$$Y = AE, \text{ or}$$
$$Y^* = 60 + 0.6\,Y^*, \text{ or}$$
$$Y^*(1 - 0.6) = Y^*(0.4) = 60, \text{ or}$$
$$Y^* = 60/0.4 = 150$$

  f The multiplier $= 1/(1 - \text{slope of } AE \text{ function}) = 1/(1 - 0.6) = 1/0.4 = 2.5$.

8 a Autonomous expenditure is the sum of the autonomous part of consumption expenditure, investment, government expenditure on goods and services, and exports. This sum is $60 billion.

  b The equation is of the form $AE = A + eY$, where A is autonomous expenditure and e is the slope of the AE function. In this case, the equation is $AE = 60 + 0.5\,Y$, where units are billions of dollars.

  c See the curve labelled AE_0 in Figure 23.7. The curve was drawn by noting that the amount of autonomous expenditure ($60 billion) gives the vertical intercept and that the slope of the AE function is 0.5.

FIGURE **23.7**

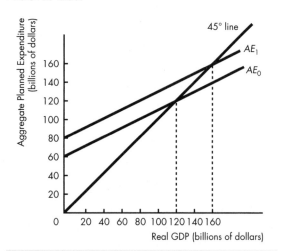

  d Equilibrium expenditure can be solved one of two ways. Equilibrium expenditure occurs at the intersection of the AE_0 curve and the 45° line. Equilibrium expenditure is $120 billion. Secondly, it can be calculated by solving the $AE = Y$ equation:
$$Y^* = 60 + 0.5\,Y^*, \text{ or}$$
$$Y^*(1 - 0.5) = 60, \text{ or}$$
$$Y^* = 60/0.5 = 120$$

  e Induced expenditure = total expenditure − autonomous expenditure = $120 - 60 = 60$ in this case.

9 a See the curve labelled AE_1 in Figure 23.7. The new curve reflects the fact that autonomous expenditure increases by $20 billion but the slope of the AE function remains unchanged.

  b The new equilibrium expenditure is $160 billion. This answer is given by the intersection of the AE_1 curve with the 45° line, or by solving the new equilibrium condition:

$$Y^* = 80 + 0.5\,Y^*, \text{ or}$$
$$Y^*(1 - 0.5) = 80, \text{ or}$$
$$Y^* = 80/0.5 = 160$$

c Since a $20 billion increase in autonomous expenditure generated a $40 billion increase in equilibrium expenditure, the multiplier is 2. This value can be obtained by using the formula that the multiplier $= 1/(1 - e)$ where e is the slope of the *AE* function.

d The total change in real GDP is $40 billion. First, we can note that the change in autonomous expenditure is just the increase in government expenditures of $20 billion, and we can further note:

$$\Delta \text{ total expenditure} = \Delta \text{ autonomous expenditure}$$
$$+ \Delta \text{ induced expenditure}$$

or

$$+\$40 \text{ billion} = +\$20 \text{ billion} + \$20 \text{ billion}$$

so that the change in induced expenditure is also $20 billion.

Second, since real GDP has increased, this will have increased both consumption and imports, since they are part of induced expenditure. However, investment is autonomous, and is therefore not affected by the change in real GDP.

10 An increase in expected future disposable income leads to less saving (so that the saving function shifts downward at each level of disposable income) and more consumption out of current disposable income (so that the consumption function shifts upward). This change is an increase in autonomous consumption, and is therefore an increase in aggregate expenditure, and leads to a shift upward in the aggregate expenditure function. This shift creates multiplier effects and a shift rightward in the aggregate demand curve at the current price level.

Chapter 24

Fiscal Policy

Government Budgets

The **federal budget** is annual statement of revenue and outlays of government of Canada (**provincial budget** is for provincial governments).

- Budgets finance government activities and achieve macroeconomic policy objectives (**fiscal policy**).

- Fiscal policy is made by government and Parliament, in consultation with bureaucrats, provincial governments, and business and consumer groups.

- Budgetary revenues—personal income taxes, corporate income taxes, indirect taxes (GST), investment income.

- Budgetary outlays—transfer payments, expenditures on goods and services, debt interest payments.

- Budget balance = revenues – outlays.

  - **Budget surplus** when revenues > outlays.
  - **Budget deficit** when revenues < outlays.
  - **Balanced budget** when revenues = outlays.

- **Government debt** = total borrowing by governments = sum of past deficits – sum of past surpluses.

  - Persistent deficits of the 1980s increased borrowing, which increased interest payments and increased deficit, etc.
  - Balanced budget of 1998 stopped this cycle— government debt is falling.

- Provincial government outlays are almost as large as federal, focused on hospitals, schools, and colleges/universities.

- Canada's budget surplus is unusual compared to other industrial nations.

Fiscal Policy Multipliers

Fiscal policy actions can either be **discretionary** (initiated by Parliament, involves Δ government outlays, taxes), or **automatic** (triggered by state of economy).

- Initially, assume a model economy with only **autonomous taxes** (do *not* vary with real GDP), and no exports or imports.

- **Government expenditures multiplier**
  = (Δ real GDP)/(Δ government expenditures)
  = $1/(1 - MPC) > 1$.

- Initial increase in G increases real GDP, which leads to secondary, induced effects.

- **Autonomous tax multiplier** = (Δ real GDP)/ (Δ taxes) = $-MPC/(1 - MPC) < 0$.

  - Increase in NT decreases YD, decreases C, and therefore decreases real GDP, which leads to secondary, induced effects.
  - Since some of tax change affects saving, initial $\Delta C = -MPC \times \Delta$ taxes.

- Autonomous transfers multiplier = $MPC/(1 - MPC)$ since transfers are negative taxes.

Induced taxes, transfer payments and imports are **automatic stabilizers**—mechanisms that reduce fluctuations in real GDP automatically.

- **Induced taxes** and induced transfer payments vary with real GDP.

  - The larger the marginal tax rate, the smaller the multipliers.

- Higher marginal propensity to import also reduces multiplier effects.

Budget deficits fluctuate with business cycle due to cyclical fluctuations in net taxes.

◆ **Structural surplus or deficit** is budget balance when real GDP = potential.

◆ **Cyclical surplus or deficit** = actual deficit – structural balance.

◆ Cyclical deficit is due only to fact that real GDP ≠ potential.

Fiscal Policy Multipliers and the Price Level

Price level adjustments change outcome of fiscal policy.

◆ **Expansionary fiscal policy** (increased G or decreased NT) shifts AD curve rightward.

◆ **Contractionary fiscal policy** (decreased G or increased NT) shifts AD curve leftward.

◆ In short run, expansionary policy has positive but reduced effects because increase in AD increases price level, which decreases AE, creating movement along AD, partially offsetting initial effect.

◆ If real GDP at potential, the increase in the price level fully offsets initial effect.

◆ Even short-run fiscal policy is limited by:

 • Slowness of the legislative process.
 • Difficulties in telling if real GDP is above or below potential GDP.

Supply-Side Effects of Fiscal Policy

Cutting tax rates might increase potential GDP and shift LAS rightward.

◆ Higher income taxes decrease incentives to work and save, which decreases labour supply and capital supply.

◆ Tax cut shifts AD curve rightward *and* shifts SAS rightward due to increased incentives.

◆ Size of rightward SAS shift is controversial.

H E L P F U L   H I N T S

I It is crucial to distinguish between two types of autonomous shocks. One type adds to the instability of the economy; it includes changes in autonomous consumption, investment, and exports. The other is planned in order to (hopefully) reduce the instability of the

economy; it includes fiscal policy—changes in government expenditures and taxes. Because both shocks work through the same multiplier process, the same process that creates instability can also help to reduce instability.

2 In this chapter, as in Chapter 23, we first derive fiscal policy multipliers for a case where there are no induced taxes, and no foreign sector. In this case, the size of the MPC is crucial in determining the size of the multiplier.

 We then add the more realistic case of induced taxes, and an import sector where the level of imports rises if real GDP rises. The multiplier is smaller than in the first case, and the higher the marginal tax rate or the higher the marginal propensity to import, the smaller the multiplier. Figure 24.1 below shows why. A crucial part of the multiplier process is the changes in induced expenditure in the second round of the multiplier. With induced taxes and imports, these induced expenditures are reduced as income is siphoned off to pay for taxes and buy imported goods!

FIGURE **24.1**

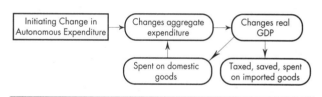

3 Helpful Hint **4** in Chapter 20 emphasized the difference between government expenditure on goods and services and government transfer payments. The difference is crucial once again in understanding why the government expenditures multiplier (= $1/(1 – MPC)$) is larger than the autonomous transfer payments multiplier (= $MPC/(1 – MPC)$).

 A \$1 increase in government expenditures on goods and services directly raises autonomous expenditure by \$1 in the first round of the multiplier. However, a \$1 increase in spending on autonomous transfer payments raises consumers' disposable income by \$1, and some of this extra income is saved, so that only \$1 × MPC is consumed, and autonomous expenditure increases by \$$MPC$ < \$1 in the first round of the multiplier.

4 The mathematical note on the algebra of fiscal multipliers will be covered by some students' instructors, and is worth reviewing if you are one of those students.

First, aggregate planned expenditure (AE) is defined as in (1) below:

(1) $AE = C + I + G + X - M$.

Second, net taxes (NT) are defined as autonomous taxes (T_a) – autonomous transfer payments (T_r) + induced taxes (tY):

(2) $NT = T_a - T_r + tY$

Consumption depends on disposable income:

(3) $C = a + b(Y - NT)$

Substituting (2) into (3):

(4) $C = a - bT_a + bT_r + b(1 - t)Y$

Imports depend on real GDP:

(5) $M = mY$

Substitute (4) and (5) into (1):

$AE = a - bT_a + bT_r + b(1 - t)Y + I + G + X - mY$

Collecting terms:

$AE = [a - bT_a + bT_r + I + G + X] + [b(1 - t) - m]Y$

We can rewrite this as:

(6) $AE = A + [b(1 - t) - m]Y$

A is autonomous expenditure (= $[a - bT_a + bT_r + I + G + X]$) and $[b(1 - t) - m]$ is the slope of AE curve. Equilibrium occurs when $Y = AE$ along the 45° line.

(7) $Y^* = A + [b(1 - t) - m]Y^*$

This equation can be solved for equilibrium real GDP:

(8) $Y^* = \dfrac{A}{1 - [b(1 - t) - m]}$

An increase in government expenditures affects A directly ($\Delta A = \Delta G$):

$\Delta Y = \dfrac{1}{1 - [b(1 - t) - m]}\Delta G$

Dividing both sides by ΔG yields the government expenditures multiplier:

(9) $\dfrac{\Delta Y}{\Delta G} = \dfrac{1}{1 - [b(1 - t) - m]}$

An increase in autonomous taxes affects A indirectly ($\Delta A = -b\Delta T_a$):

$\Delta Y = \dfrac{-b}{1 - [b(1 - t) - m]}\Delta T_a$

Dividing both sides by ΔT_a yields the autonomous tax multiplier:

(10) $\dfrac{\Delta Y}{\Delta T_a} = \dfrac{-b}{1 - [b(1 - t) - m]}$

Similarly, the autonomous transfer payments multiplier can be solved for:

(11) $\dfrac{\Delta Y}{\Delta T_r} = \dfrac{b}{1 - [b(1 - t) - m]}$

SELF-TEST

True/False and Explain

Government Budgets

1   The federal deficit is the total amount of borrowing that the federal government has undertaken.

2   Only government expenditures on goods and services, not transfer payments, are crucial in analyzing the federal deficit.

3   A government starts out with a balanced budget. In the next year, the percentage growth in outlays is higher than the percentage growth in revenues. It will now have a deficit.

4   Government investment income is an example of a budgetary outlay.

Fiscal Policy Multipliers

5   An increase in autonomous transfer payments matched by an increase in autonomous taxes will lead to an increase in real GDP equal to the size of the increase in transfer payments.

6 Taxes and transfer payments that vary with income act as automatic stabilizers in the economy.

7 The autonomous transfer payments multiplier is smaller than the government expenditures multiplier.

8 If real GDP increases, so do autonomous taxes.

9 If an economy has a structural deficit, then the budget balance at potential GDP is negative.

Fiscal Policy Multipliers and the Price Level

10 If the price level is variable, an increase in government expenditures will never lead to an increase in real GDP.

11 A cut in autonomous taxes will increase equilibrium real GDP in the short run.

12 An increase in autonomous taxes will decrease equilibrium real GDP in the long run, if there are no incentive effects.

13 An increase in government expenditures will shift the *AE* curve upward and shift the *AD* curve to the right.

Supply-Side Effects of Fiscal Policy

14 Cutting income taxes will shift the *AD* curve rightward, but shift the *SAS* curve leftward.

15 An increase in income taxes will decrease potential GDP.

Multiple-Choice

Government Budgets

1 Provincial government outlays
a are small and irrelevant to the economy.
b are an important source of fiscal policy.
c are always equal to provincial government revenues.
d are focused on transfer payments to individuals, such as employment insurance.
e tend to fluctuate with federal outlays.

2 Which of the following would *not* increase the budget deficit?
a an increase in interest on the government debt
b an increase in government expenditures on goods and services
c an increase in government transfer payments
d an increase in indirect business taxes
e a decrease in government investment income

3 The budget deficit grew as a percentage of GDP after 1974 because
a government expenditures on goods and services rose, while tax revenues remained constant.
b government expenditures on goods and services remained constant, while tax revenues fell.
c debt interest payments rose, while tax revenues remained constant.
d debt interest payments rose, while tax revenues fell.
e none of the above.

4 Which of the following groups does *not* influence federal fiscal policy?
a government bureaucrats
b provincial governments
c Parliament
d business and consumer groups
e government unions

5 Which of the following is a budgetary outlay?
a personal income taxes
b government investment income
c debt interest payments
d indirect taxes
e corporate income taxes

Fiscal Policy Multipliers

6 Which of the following happens *automatically* if the economy goes into a recession?

a Only government outlays increase.

b Only net taxes increase.

c The deficit increases.

d The deficit decreases.

e Both government outlays and net taxes increase, and the deficit stays the same.

7 During an expansion, tax revenue

a and government outlays decline.

b declines and government outlays increase.

c increases and government outlays decline.

d and government outlays increase.

e stays constant and government outlays increase.

8 Consider the economy of NoTax, where the *MPC* is 0.6, and where there are no induced taxes and no imports. If the government desires to shift the *AD* curve rightward by $5 billion, the correct increase in government expenditures is

a $2 billion.

b $2.5 billion.

c $3 billion.

d $7.5 billion.

e $8.33 billion.

9 How does an increase in the marginal tax rate affect the size of the multiplier?

a It has no impact.

b It makes the multiplier larger.

c It makes the multiplier smaller.

d It makes the multiplier smaller, but only if the new tax rate is larger than the *MPC*.

e It makes the multiplier smaller, but only if the new tax rate is smaller than the *MPC*.

10 A cyclical deficit is when

a government outlays are greater than revenues.

b government outlays are less than revenues.

c there is a deficit due to the fact real GDP is greater than potential GDP.

d there is a deficit due to the fact real GDP is less than potential GDP.

e there is a deficit even when real GDP equals potential GDP.

11 Currently the country of Ricardia has a budget plan with constant government outlays equal to $100 billion and taxes related positively to real GDP by the equation: Taxes = $25 billion + $0.1 Y$. If the structural deficit is $10 billion, what is potential GDP in this economy?

a $65 billion

b $75 billion

c $650 billion

d $750 billion

e $850 billion

12 If the *MPC* is 0.75, and there are no induced taxes or imports, what is the government expenditures multiplier?

a 0

b 0.57

c 1.33

d 3

e 4

13 If the *MPC* is 0.75, and there are no induced taxes or imports, what is the autonomous tax multiplier?

a –4

b –3

c –0.43

d 3

e 4

14 If the *MPC* is 0.75, and there are no induced taxes or imports, what is the change in *Y* if *both* government expenditures and autonomous taxes increase by $200?

a 0

b $200

c $600

d $800

e not calculable with the information given.

15 If the *MPC* is 0.75, and there are no induced taxes or imports, what is the autonomous transfer payments multiplier?

a –4

b –3

c 0.43

d 3

e 4

Fiscal Policy Multipliers and the Price Level

16 An *expansionary* fiscal policy leads to a(n)

a rightward shift in the *AD* curve equal to the multiplier times the policy change.

b leftward shift in the *AD* curve equal to the multiplier times the policy change.

c leftward shift in the *SAS* curve.

d increase in *Y* equal to the multiplier times the policy change, in the short run.

e increase in *Y* equal to the multiplier times the policy change, in the long run.

17 Short-run fiscal policy is limited by the fact that

a the *LAS* curve is vertical.

b the legislative process is slow.

c real GDP is typically not equal to potential GDP.

d the policy might shift the *SAS* curve to the right.

e the policy might shift the *SAS* curve to the left.

18 Which of the following is an example of an *expansionary* fiscal policy?

a increasing debt interest payments

b increasing taxes

c decreasing transfer payments

d increasing transfer payments

e decreasing government expenditures on goods and services

19 Which of the following policies will *not* shift the *AD* curve rightward?

a increasing government expenditures on goods and services

b decreasing autonomous taxes

c increasing autonomous transfer payments

d increasing government expenditures on goods and services *and* increasing autonomous taxes by the same amount

e decreasing government expenditures on goods and services *and* decreasing autonomous taxes by the same amount

Supply-Side Effects of Fiscal Policy

20 Which of the following quotations correctly refers to the effects of fiscal policy in the *long run*?

a "The increase in taxes will increase real GDP."

b "The increase in taxes will raise prices only."

c "A change in the budget has no impact on real GDP unless it changes aggregate supply."

d "A change in the budget has no impact on real GDP."

e "An increase in government expenditures on goods and services will increase real GDP."

21 Which of the following quotations correctly refers to the effects of fiscal policy in the *short run*?

a "The increase in taxes will increase real GDP."

b "The increase in taxes will raise prices only."

c "A change in the budget has no impact on real GDP unless it changes aggregate supply."

d "A change in the budget has no impact on real GDP."

e "The increase in government expenditures on goods and services will increase real GDP."

22 Suppose that the autonomous tax multiplier is –2. If autonomous taxes decrease by $4 billion and incentives to work and save are affected, then in the long run real GDP will

a decrease by $8 billion.

b increase by $8 billion.

c be unaffected.

d increase, but by how much is unclear.

e decrease, but by how much is unclear.

Mathematical Note to Chapter 24: The Algebra of the Fiscal Policy Multipliers

23 The formula for the tax function is

a $G = G_a + gY$.

b $M = mY$.

c $NT = T_a - T_r + tY$.

d $NT = 1/(1 - [b(1 - t) + m])$.

e none of the above.

FACT **24.1**

The economy of New Estevan has the following consumption and tax functions:

Consumption: $C = a + 0.5(Y - NT)$

Net taxes: $NT = T_a - T_r + 0.5Y$

This economy has no exports or imports.

---

24 Consider Fact 24.1. The government expenditures multiplier for this economy is

a 0.25.
b 0.5.
c 1.33.
d 2.0.
e not calculable with the given information.

25 Consider Fact 24.1. The autonomous tax multiplier for this economy is

a −0.667.
b −1.0.
c −1.33.
d −2.0.
e 0.667.

Short Answer Problems

1 What changes in the components of the federal government budget after 1974 were the principal causes of continuing large government deficits?

2 During the summer of 1995, Saskatchewan had a provincial election. A central plank of the Saskatchewan Liberal Party's election strategy was a promise to cut taxes dramatically, stating that these cuts would create 50,000 new jobs (about 10 percent of the labour force) over the next 5 years. Critics claimed that this policy would have only a small effect in Saskatchewan, that most of the new jobs from the tax cuts would show up in other provinces.
a What economic concept underlies the Liberals' promise?
b What economic concept underlies the critics' argument?
c The Liberals lost the election, so we do not get to see if the tax cuts would have had the promised effect, but what do you think would have happened?

3 Suppose you are visiting the town of Elbow, Saskatchewan, which is suffering a depressed economy due to low wheat prices. You spend $100 on accommodation and another $100 golfing and dining at the excellent local golf club.

a What factors will influence how much extra real GDP will be generated within Elbow by your $200 of expenditure? (Treat Elbow as if it were a separate economy.)
b What does your answer imply for the argument made by the Elbow town council that the Saskatchewan government should shift a government department to the town in order to stimulate the town's economy?

4 Explain why the multiplier of an expansionary fiscal policy is smaller once we consider the aggregate supply curve. What happens if there are incentive effects on *AS*?

5 Explain whether or not the following events will shift the *AE* curve and/or the *AD* curve and briefly explain why. (For each case, assume that the other variables are not changing.)
a an increase in the price level
b an increase in expected future profits for businesses
c a cut in autonomous taxes
d an increase in government expenditures

ⓒⓣ 6 Some politicians and economists argue tax cuts are beneficial for the economy in the short run *and* the long run. Explain their arguments, and evaluate them briefly.

ⓔ 7 You may wish to review the mathematical notes to Chapters 23 and 24 before doing this problem. Consider the expenditure functions for the following economy:

Consumption: $C = 4{,}000 + 0.7(Y - NT) - 20P$
Investment: $I = 2{,}000$
Government: $G = 5{,}000$
Exports: $X = 400$
Imports: $M = 0.1Y$
Taxes: $NT = 2{,}000$

where P is the price level.

a What is the equation of the aggregate expenditure function? What is autonomous expenditure in this economy? What is the slope of the *AE* function?
b Assume that the price level is equal to 100. Calculate equilibrium real GDP, consumption, and imports.
c If the price level is now equal to 200, what is the new equilibrium real GDP?
d Using your information from **b** and **c**, sketch the *AD* curve for this economy.
e Calculate the government expenditures multiplier, the autonomous tax multiplier, and the autonomous transfer payments multiplier for this economy.

f Suppose that the price level is equal to 100, and that government expenditures increase by 2,000. What is the resulting change in real GDP demanded, holding constant the price level?

g Suppose that the change in real GDP demanded raises the price level by 100. What is the overall change in real GDP from the two effects? What is the multiplier after the two effects have worked through the economy? Why is your answer different from **e**?

8 As finance minister for the government of Adanac, your crack team of economists has estimated the economy's *MPC* to be 0.75, price level held constant. (There are no induced taxes or imports.) You are confident that this estimate is correct, since you threatened to exile the economists to the North Pole should they err. You have decided that in order to get reelected next year, you need to raise real GDP by $200 billion.

a If you decide to change only government expenditures, how much change is required to accomplish your goal?

b If you decide to change only autonomous taxes, how much change is required to accomplish your goal?

c Having selected method **a**, you find that the increase in real GDP is less than $200 billion, jeopardizing your chance for reelection. Before you exile the poor economists to the North Pole, is there any excuse for their mistake? (In other words, what went wrong?)

9 Suppose that the economy is in equilibrium at the point where the *AD* curve crosses the *SAS* curve. (Assume that the economy stays in the short run for the rest of this question, and ignore any incentive effects.) Suppose that the government raises autonomous taxes dramatically.

a Initially, assume the price level is held constant. Carefully explain what happens to aggregate expenditure, aggregate demand, and real GDP as a result of this autonomous shock. Draw a two-part graph as part of your answer, showing aggregate expenditure and the 45° line on the top, and the *AD-SAS* curves on the bottom.

b What happens to the levels of the components of aggregate expenditure after this shock?

c Next, show on the graph from **a** what happens when the price level changes. Explain the overall effect on aggregate expenditure, aggregate demand, short-run aggregate supply, the price level, and real GDP from the combined effects of the shock and the resulting change in the price level.

10 In the economy of Paridisio, government outlays are related to the level of real GDP by the formula: Outlays = $500 - 0.6Y$, while tax revenues are related to the level of real GDP by the formula: Taxes = $100 + 0.4Y$.

a Complete Table 24.1.

TABLE **24.1**

Real GDP	Outlays	Revenues	Budget Balance
0			
100			
200			
300			
400			
500			
600			

b If potential GDP is 300, what is the structural balance for Paridisio?

c If real GDP is currently 200, what are the values of the cyclical deficit, the structural deficit, and the actual deficit?

d Is the tax structure in this economy acting as an automatic stabilizer?

ANSWERS

True/False and Explain

1 **F** Deficit is when outlays > revenues in current year. (556)

2 **F** Government expenditures on goods, transfer and interest payments are all part of outlays. (556)

3 **T** If outlays grow faster than taxes, then outlays > taxes next year and therefore there is a deficit. (556)

4 **F** Example of revenue. (556–557)

5 **F** They exactly offset each other (Δ net taxes = 0), so Δ real GDP = 0. (564–565)

6 **T** If income decreases, this leads to decrease in taxes + increase in transfers, and so an increase in disposable income, which increases aggregate expenditure, leading to increase in income, potentially offsetting initial decrease. (565–568)

7 **T** Since *MPC* < 1, government multiplier [$1/(1 - MPC)$] > transfer multiplier [$MPC/(1 - MPC)$]. (562–565)

8 **F** Autonomous is not affected by real GDP. (565)

9 **T** Definition. (566–568)

10 **F** In short run, increase in *G* leads to rightward shift in *AD*, and increase in real GDP. (568–570)

11 **T** Shifts *AD* rightward. (568–571)

12 **F** Vertical *LAS* curve means only price is affected by the shift in *AD*. (568–571)

13 **T** Increase in government expenditures = increase in autonomous expenditure, so *AE* curve shifts upward, leading to higher level of *AD*, same price level. (568–570)

14 **F** Income tax cut raises *YD* and shifts *AD* rightward, and it raises incentives to work and save, shifting *SAS* curve *rightward*. (571–572)

15 **T** Due to negative incentive effects. (571–572)

Multiple-Choice

1 **e** They may have a deficit, they are not really used for fiscal policy, they are almost as large as the federal government outlays, and *federal* government does employment insurance. (560–561)

2 **d** This effect is increase in revenue. (556–557)

3 **c** See text discussion. (558–560)

4 **e** See text discussion. (556–557)

5 **c** Others are sources of revenue. (556–557)

6 **c** In recession, decrease in *Y* leads to decrease in taxes and increase in spending on employment insurance, etc., which leads to increase in deficit. (556–558)

7 **c** Increase in real GDP leads to increase in tax revenue. Decrease in unemployment leads to decrease in transfer payments. (556–558)

⊕ **8** **a** Government expenditures multiplier = $1/(1 - MPC) = 1/(1 - 0.6) = 2.5$. Invert ΔY = multiplier $\times \Delta G$: $\Delta G = \Delta Y/$multiplier $= 5/2.5 = 2$. (562–564)

9 **c** It decreases *YD* at each stage of the multiplier process, reducing the amount of extra consumption spending. (565)

10 **d** Definition. (566–568)

⊕ **11** **c** $10 billion = $G - NT$ = $100 billion − $25 billion − 0.1 (potential GDP), therefore potential GDP = (100 − 25 − 10)/0.1 = $650 billion. (566–568)

12 **e** Multiplier = $1/(1 - MPC) = 1/(1 - 0.75) = 4$. (562–564)

13 **b** Autonomous tax multiplier = $-MPC/(1 - MPC) = -0.75/(1 - 0.75) = -3$. (564–565)

14 **b** Impact of government expenditures multiplier is $4 \times \$200 = \$800$, impact of autonomous tax multiplier is $-3 \times \$200 = -\$600$, total impact = $\$800 - \$600 = \$200$. (562–565)

15 **d** Autonomous transfer payments multiplier = $MPC/(1 - MPC) = 0.75/(1 - 0.75) = 3$. (564–565)

16 **a** Increase in government expenditures or tax cut would shift *AD* curve rightward by this amount. The *SAS* curve would shift *rightward* if there are incentive effects; and the ΔY is smaller than this amount due to the increase in the price level. (568–570)

17 **b** Others are irrelevant or not limitations. (571)

18 **d** Definition. (568–570)

19 **e** The decrease in *G* shifts *AD* leftward by the government expenditures multiplier, the decrease in taxes shifts *AD* rightward by the autonomous tax multiplier, which has a smaller impact. (562–565)

20 **c** In long run, changes in fiscal policy have an impact only if they change potential GDP (aggregate supply). (568–571)

21 **e** Shift rightward in *AD* increases real GDP in the short run. (568–570)

22 **d** Only the incentive effects on potential GDP matter, but their size is uncertain. (571–573)

23 **c** Definition. (576–577)

24 **c** Multiplier = $1/(1 - [b(1 - t) - m]) = 1/(1 - [0.5(1 - 0.5)]) = 1.33$. (576–577)

25 **a** Autonomous multiplier = $-MPC/(1 - [b(1 - t) - m]) = -0.5/(1 - 0.25) = -0.667$. (576–577)

Short Answer Problems

1 The deficit increased because the level of government outlays as a percentage of GDP increased, while taxes as a percentage of GDP fell during the late 1970s and then slowly increased. The components of spending that showed the most consistent growth were transfer payments and interest payments on government debt.

2 **a** The Liberals are counting on the autonomous tax multiplier to boost aggregate expenditure and create new jobs.

   b The critics are arguing that most of the new expenditure would be on products from outside the province—they are arguing that the marginal propensity to import for a province is very high, so that the multipliers are very low.

   c It is likely that fiscal policy multipliers are low for individual provinces due to high marginal propensities to import. For your information, imports in Saskatchewan were about 62 percent (= 15.14 billion/24.28 billion) of provincial real GDP in 1995.[1]

---

[1] *Source:* Statistics Canada, CANSIM matrices D21425 and D31874.

3 a Your $200 will trigger a multiplier process—the owners of the factors of production at the golf course will spend their extra income, for example. This spending induces second-round increases in consumption expenditure, leading to a final change in real GDP in Elbow that is a multiple of $200. The size of the multiplier effect will be determined by two things. First, the larger the marginal propensity to consume in Elbow and the smaller the marginal propensity to import (from outside Elbow), the larger the multiplier will be. In a small town, the marginal propensity to import from outside the town is likely to be quite high, making the multiplier much smaller. Second, the effect is smaller if the aggregate supply curve is steeper—the increase in aggregate demand gets reduced by an increase in the price level.

b Clearly, such a shift could stimulate the town's economy, since the annual increase in government expenditures will create multiplier effects. The usefulness of this endeavour is limited by the factors mentioned that might reduce the size of the multiplier. (This policy was actual government policy in Saskatchewan until the Conservatives were defeated in 1991, at least partially because of this policy.)

4 The multiplier tells us the size of the change in real GDP (the shift in the *AD* curve) relative to the size of an initial change in government expenditure or autonomous taxes, holding constant the price level. Once we consider the *AS* curve, we know the price level will increase as aggregate demand increases—the increase in the price level being higher, the steeper the *AS* curve. This increase in the price level lowers aggregate expenditure, shown by the movement up the *AD* curve, leading to a smaller increase in real GDP.

Incentive effects would potentially shift the *AS* curve rightward, increasing the value of the multiplier.

5 Any change that does not initiate as a change in real GDP will shift the *AE* curve. Therefore all four changes will shift the *AE* curve. Any change in autonomous expenditure that is not caused by a change in the price level will shift the *AD* curve. Therefore **a** involves a movement along an *AD* curve, while **b–d** involve shifts in the *AD* curve.

6 A cut in taxes will increase disposable income, and shift the *AD* curve rightward in the normal multiplier manner. However, supply-side economists argue that tax cuts will also increase

the after-tax returns to work and saving, which in turn will lead to an increase in labour supply and saving, shifting the *AS* curves rightward.

An evaluation is still somewhat premature. As the text points out, it is still a matter of opinion whether the *AS* effects are small or large. So far, there is no hard empirical evidence one way or the other.

7 a The equation can be found by totalling the components of aggregate expenditure:

$AE = 4,000 + 0.7(Y - 2,000) - 20P + 2,000 +$
     $5,000 + 400 - 0.1Y$, or
$AE = 10,000 - 20P + 0.6Y$

Autonomous expenditure, which does not depend on real GDP, is $10,000 + 20P$. The slope is 0.6.

b Substitute $P = 100$ into the *AE* function, and solve for $Y^* = AE$:

$$Y^* = 10,000 - 20(100) + 0.6Y^*, \text{ or}$$
$$Y^*(1 - 0.6) = 8,000, \text{ or}$$
$$Y^* = 8,000/0.4 = 20,000$$

Equilibrium consumption equals $4,000 + 0.7(20,000 - 2,000) - 20(100) = 14,600$. Imports $= 0.1(20,000) = 2,000$.

c Substitute $P = 200$ into the *AE* function from **a**:

$$Y^* = 10,000 - 20(200) + 0.6Y^*, \text{ or}$$
$$Y^*(0.4) = 6,000, \text{ or}$$
$$Y^* = 6,000/0.4 = 15,000$$

d One point on the curve is $P = 100$, $Y = 20,000$ and another point is $P = 200$, $Y = 15,000$. These points are illustrated in Figure 24.2.

FIGURE **24.2**

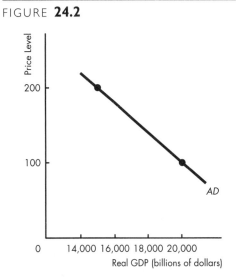

e The government expenditures multiplier =
$1/(1 - \text{slope of the } AE \text{ function}) = 1/(1 - 0.6) = 2.5$.
The autonomous tax multiplier =
$-MPC/(1 - \text{slope of the } AE \text{ function}) = -0.7/(1 - 0.6) = -1.75$.
The transfer payments multiplier =
$MPC/(1 - \text{slope of the } AE \text{ function}) = 0.7/(1 - 0.6) = 1.75$.

f The change in real GDP demanded equals the change in government expenditures times the government expenditures multiplier, or $2{,}000 \times 2.5 = 5{,}000$.

g If the price level increases by 100, then autonomous expenditure decreases by 5,000, as we saw in **d**. This decrease completely offsets the increase in real GDP due to the increase in government expenditures on 2,000. Therefore the overall change in real GDP is equal to zero, and the multiplier is equal to zero. The answer is different here compared with part **f**, because the price level is allowed to adjust, which leads to the offsetting effects.

8 a The government expenditures multiplier equals $1/(1 - MPC) = 1/(1 - 0.75) = 4$ in this case, so in order to raise real GDP by $200 billion you need to increase government expenditures by $50 billion = $200/4 billion.

b The autonomous tax multiplier equals $-MPC/(1 - MPC) = -0.75/(1 - 0.75) = -3$ in this case, so in order to raise real GDP by $200 billion you need to lower taxes by $66.6 billion = $200/3 billion.

c The multiplier effects we have been analyzing are based on the assumption that the price level is constant. In the real world, the stimulation of aggregate demand that you have carried out would raise the price level, which would lower aggregate expenditure, and partially (or completely) offset the increase in real GDP from your policy.

9 a Figure 24.3 shows what happens to aggregate expenditure (top of the graph) and to aggregate demand and supply (bottom). As taxes increase, disposable income decreases, and household consumption decreases, leading to a decrease in autonomous expenditure, shown by the shift downward in aggregate expenditure from AE_0 to AE_b. This decrease leads to a decrease in real GDP (holding constant the price level) from Y_0 to Y_b, with the new equilibrium at the point b, which is shown in the bottom graph as the shift leftward in the AD curve from AD_0 to AD_1.

FIGURE **24.3**

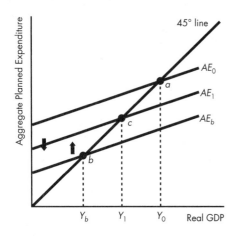

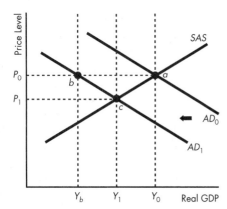

b Since the decrease in real GDP equals the decrease in aggregate expenditure, we know that the five components of aggregate expenditure have decreased in value. Since government expenditures, investment, and exports are autonomous, they are unchanged. Consumption will have decreased for two reasons—the decrease in autonomous expenditure that initiated the changes, plus a decrease in induced consumption due to the decrease in real GDP. Imports will have decreased due to the decrease in real GDP.

c At the original price level P_0, there is excess supply. This surplus leads to firms cutting their prices, leading to a decrease in the price level. This decrease gets rid of the excess supply, leading to a new equilibrium at the point c. The decrease in the price level raises aggregate expenditure back upward to the level AE_1, which also shows up as the movement along the curve AD_1 from b to c. The decrease in the price level leads to a movement along the SAS curve from point a to point c. At the new equilibrium, the overall effect of the shock is a lower level of aggregate expenditure, a lower level of aggregate demand, a lower level of aggregate supply, a lower price level, and a lower level of real GDP.

10 a Table 24.1 is completed as Table 24.1 Solution below, using the two formulas plus the fact that the budget balance = revenues – outlays.

TABLE **24.1**

Real GDP	Outlays	Revenues	Budget Balance
0	500	100	–400
100	440	140	–300
200	380	180	–200
300	320	220	–100
400	260	260	0
500	200	300	100
600	140	340	200

b The structural balance is the surplus or deficit that would exist with the existing budget structure at potential GDP, and is equal to a deficit of 100.

c The structural deficit is still 100, the actual deficit is 200 at real GDP of 200, and the cyclical deficit = actual – structural = 100.

d Yes it is, since as real GDP decreases, tax revenues decrease and outlays increase, creating upward pressure on aggregate expenditure.

Chapter 25

Money, Banking, and Interest Rates

What Is Money?

Money is something acceptable as a **means of payment** (method of settling a debt), and has three functions—medium of exchange, unit of account, store of value.

- Medium of exchange—accepted in exchange for goods and services.
  - Better than **barter** (direct exchange of goods for goods)—guarantees double coincidence of wants.
- Unit of account—agreed measure for prices.
- Store of value—exchangeable at a later date.

Money today is **currency** (coins + Bank of Canada notes) and deposits (can be converted into currency and used to pay debts).

- Cheques are only an instruction to bank.
- Debit cards are like cheques, while credit cards are ID cards for loans—neither is money.

There are two official measures of money:

- **M1**—currency outside banks + private demand deposits at banks.
- **M2+**—M1 + personal savings deposits at banks + nonpersonal notice deposits at banks + all deposits at other financial institutions.
- Currency plus some deposits are means of payments; other deposits are not, but have **liquidity** (quickly convertible into means of payments).

Depository Institutions

Depository institutions take deposits from households and firms, and make loans to others.

- Three main types are **chartered banks** (chartered under Bank Act), **credit unions** and caisses populaires, **trust and mortgage companies**.
- Bank's balance sheet shows liabilities + net worth = assets.
- Banks maximize net worth by lending out deposits.
  - Banks keep **reserves** (cash + deposits at Bank of Canada) to meet cash withdrawals.
- Depository institutions make profits by paying depositors low interest rates and lending at high rates, in return for:
  - Creating liquid assets.
  - Minimizing cost of borrowing funds.
  - Minimizing cost of monitoring borrowers.
  - Pooling risks.

How Banks Create Money

Banks create money (deposits) when they lend out excess reserves.

- If a bank gets new deposit, this creates **excess reserves** (actual reserves − desired reserves).
  - **Reserve ratio** = reserves/total deposits.
  - **Desired reserve ratio** = ratio banks wish to hold.
- Banks loan out excess reserves.
  - Borrower spends loan, recipient of money deposits it at new bank.
  - New bank has excess reserves, leading to further steps in deposit multiplier process.

- Total Δ deposits = deposit multiplier × initial Δ reserves.
  - **Deposit multiplier** = 1/desired reserve ratio > 1.
- Actual Canadian deposit multiplier smaller because some loan money held back as cash.

The Demand for Money

People choose money holdings based on price level, interest rate, real GDP, financial innovation.

- People hold money for its buying power.
  - Therefore, an increase in price level causes equal increase in nominal money demanded, so no change in real money demanded.
- Interest rate = opportunity cost of holding money.
  - Higher interest rate decreases quantity of real money demanded.
  - **Demand for money curve** (*MD*) is relationship between quantity of real money demanded and interest rate, other things remaining the same.
- Increase in real GDP shifts *MD* curve rightward.
- Recent **financial innovations** decreased demand for M1 and increased demand for M2+.

Interest Rate Determination

People divide their wealth between bonds and money.

- **Interest rate** is amount paid by borrower to lender = percentage of loan.

Bond prices are inversely related to interest rates.

- The supply of and demand for money determine the interest rate.
- Increase in *MS* creates excess money holdings, so people buy financial assets, which increases price of financial assets, and decreases interest rates.
- The level of interest rates also influence the **exchange rate** (price at which Canadian dollar exchanges for another currency).
- Increase in *MS* decreases interest rate, decreasing demand for Canadian dollar, decreasing exchange rate.

The Interest Rate and Expenditure Plans

Nominal interest rate is percentage return on an asset in terms of money.

- **Real interest rate** is percentage return in terms of what money will buy = nominal rate – inflation rate.
- Nominal interest rate is opportunity cost of holding money, real rate is opportunity cost of spending.
- The lower real interest rate, the greater autonomous consumption expenditure and investment.
- The lower real interest rate, the lower Canadian dollar's exchange rate, the greater net exports.
- Increase in real money supply decreases nominal interest rate (and therefore real interest rate) and increases **interest-sensitive expenditure**.

HELPFUL HINTS

1. What is money? In one sense, whatever meets the functions of money is money. For example, cigarettes fulfilled the functions of money in prisoner-of-war camps and similar situations. However, you should be able to answer this question on several levels. First, at the level of general definition: money is a medium of exchange. Second, at the level of classification: chequable deposits are money but savings deposits are not. Third, at the level of specific definitions: M1 and M2+ are official definitions of money.

   We often refer to our income earnings as the "money we make working." However, in economics, money means the *stock* of money we are holding in currency plus deposits (M1 or M2+). It does *not* mean the *flow* of income earnings—be careful of this distinction.

   Another important distinction is between the act of holding money and the act of consumption spending. In this situation, we are dealing with money markets, not goods and services markets. The choice for households that we model in this chapter is between holding bonds and holding money. The choice for consumer spending involves saving versus spending.[1]

2. As we work through the text, notice the important role of changes in interest rates and the exchange rate in creating shifts in aggregate demand, and therefore business cycle shocks.

[1] Thanks to David Gray for suggesting the last paragraph of this Hint.

Chapters 25 and 26 begin the process of learning what affects the values of the interest and exchange rates, showing that the money market plays a crucial role. Chapter 25 explains the demand for money, and part of the supply of money. Supply is determined by the actions of the Bank of Canada (Chapter 26) and the deposit creation process. An important concept in this chapter is the deposit multiplier process by which banks create money. Become thoroughly familiar with this process.

There are two fundamental facts that allow banks to create money. First, banks create money by creating new chequable deposits. Second, banks hold fractional reserves. Fractional reserves mean that when a bank receives a deposit, it only holds part of it as reserves and lends the rest. Note that the bank is not indulging in a scam—it is still maintaining assets (reserves plus loans) to match its liabilities (deposits). When that loan is spent, at least part of the proceeds will likely be deposited in another bank, creating a new deposit (money).

The deposit multiplier process follows from this last fact: banks make loans when they receive new deposits; these loans are spent and then return to another bank, creating another new deposit. The process then repeats itself, adding more deposits (but in progressively smaller amounts) in each round. Practise going through examples until the process becomes second nature.

3 To reinforce how the deposit multiplier process works, turn to Text Figure 25.3. We will examine the balance sheets (also known as T-accounts) for the first two banks in the multiplier process. In your analysis, note that at every step, the change in liabilities must be matched by an equivalent change in assets. All figures are in thousands.

The initial deposit by Art of $100 at Art's Bank creates the changes in its T-account shown in Table 25.1(a). This deposit leaves the bank with $100 extra reserves, but they desire only $25 extra reserves (= 25 percent of the new deposits of $100). Art's Bank therefore lends the excess reserves to Amy, crediting her account with an extra $75, shown in part (b) of Table 25.1. Amy spends her money buying a copy-shop franchise from Barb, leading to the withdrawal of $75 shown in part (c) of Table 25.1. (Barb deposits this money at Barb's Bank, discussed below.) The final (net) position of Art's Bank is shown in part (d) of Table 25.1. Note that the initial deposit has led to $100 in new deposits for Art's Bank, $25 in new reserves, and $75 in new loans.

The entire process starts anew with the deposit by Barb of the $75 she got from Amy for the franchise. This deposit in Barb's Bank is shown in part (a) of Table 25.2. Barb's Bank now has $75 in actual reserves, but only desires to hold $18.25 in reserves (= 25 percent of the $75 in new deposits), leaving Barb's Bank with $56.25 in excess reserves. These excess reserves are lent to Bob. His account is credited with the $56.25, as shown in part (b) of Table 25.2. In turn, Bob uses his money to pay off a loan from Carl, leading to the withdrawal shown in part (c) of Table 25.2. (Carl will deposit this money, leading to the further expansions shown in Text Figure 25.3, but we will examine only these two banks.) The final position of Barb's Bank is shown in part (d) of Table 25.2. Note that they have $75 in new deposits, $18.25 in new reserves, and $56.25 in new loans.

TABLE **25.1** ART'S BANK

(a) Initial New Deposit of $100

Assets		Liabilities	
Reserves	+$100	Deposits	+$100

(b) Loan Creation of $75

Assets		Liabilities	
Loans	+$75	Deposits	+$75

(c) Withdrawal of Loan Money

Assets		Liabilities	
Reserves	−$75	Deposits	−$75

(d) Final Position

Assets		Liabilities	
Reserves	+$25	Deposits	+$100
Loans	+$75		
	+$100		

TABLE **25.2**   BARB'S BANK

(a) Initial New Deposit of $75

Assets		Liabilities	
Reserves	+$75	Deposits	+$75

(b) Loan Creation of $56.25

Assets		Liabilities	
Loans	+$56.25	Deposits	+$56.25

(c) Withdrawal of Loan Money

Assets		Liabilities	
Reserves	−$56.25	Deposits	−$56.25

(d) Final Position

Assets		Liabilities	
Reserves	+$18.75	Deposits	+$75
Loans	+$56.25		
	+$75		

The crucial point that drives this multiplier process is the desire of the banks to make profits, by turning reserves, which earn no revenues, into loans, which earn revenues.

S E L F - T E S T

True/False and Explain

What Is Money?

1 Money is anything that is generally acceptable as a medium of exchange.

2 A notice deposit at a chartered bank is part of M1.

3 If the public shifts their deposits from their chequing accounts to their savings accounts, M1 will decrease and M2+ will increase.

Depository Institutions

4 Individual households are generally better at pooling risk than are depository institutions.

5 Liabilities plus assets equal net worth.

How Banks Create Money

6 Bank reserves consist of cash in the bank's vault plus its deposits at the Bank of Canada.

7 If a depositor withdraws currency from a bank, that bank's actual reserve ratio declines.

8 The deposit multiplier is equal to 1 divided by the desired reserve ratio.

The Demand for Money

9 If the price level increases, there will be an increase in the quantity of real money people will want to hold.

10 If interest rates increase, the quantity of real money demanded decreases.

11 The development of near-money deposits and growth in the use of credit cards in the 1980s caused the demand for M2+ to shift rightward.

Interest Rate Determination

12 If households or firms have more money than they want to hold, they will buy financial assets, causing asset prices to increase and the interest rate to decrease.

13 If the price of a bond increases, the interest rate earned on the bond decreases.

The Interest Rate and Expenditure Plans

14 The opportunity cost of holding money is the real interest rate.

15 An increase in the real interest rate will increase the exchange rate.

Multiple-Choice

What Is Money?

1 Which of the following is a function of money?
a medium of exchange
b measure of liquidity
c pooling risk
d store of exchange
e reducing transactions costs

2 Which of the following is a component of M2+ but *not* of M1?
a currency in circulation
b personal demand deposits at chartered banks
c personal savings deposits at chartered banks
d currency in bank vaults
e Canada Savings Bonds

3 Which of the following is *most* liquid?
a demand deposits
b real estate
c government bonds
d savings deposits
e cheques

4 Which of the following is *not* a store of value?
a credit cards
b demand deposits
c term deposits
d other chequable deposits
e savings deposits

Depository Institutions

5 Which of the following statements about depository institutions is *false*?
a They maximize net worth, ignoring all else.
b They keep reserves to meet cash withdrawals.
c A credit union is an example of a depository institution.
d They pool and therefore reduce risk.
e They borrow at low interest rates and lend high.

6 Which of the following is a liability of a depository institution?
a vault cash
b loans
c securities
d demand deposits
e its deposits at the Bank of Canada

7 Which of the following is an economic service provided by a depository institution?
a borrowing low and lending high
b keeping cash reserves
c pooling liquidity
d minimizing the cost of borrowing funds
e creating liquid liabilities

How Banks Create Money

8 Consider Fact 25.1. Based on the Bank of Speedy Creek's initial balance sheet, what is their desired reserve ratio?
a 4 percent
b 8 percent
c 12.5 percent
d 25 percent
e 40 percent

FACT **25.1**

The Bank of Speedy Creek is one of many banks in the economy, and has chosen the following initial balance sheet:

Assets		Liabilities	
Reserves	$40	Deposits	$500
Loans	$460		
	$500		

9 Consider Fact 25.1. Huck Finn comes along and deposits $10. After Huck's deposit, but before any other actions have occurred, the total amount of money in the economy has

a   stayed the same, with its components unchanged.
b   stayed the same, with currency falling and deposits rising.
c   decreased, with currency falling and deposits staying the same.
d   increased, with currency unchanged and deposits rising.
e   decreased, with currency falling and deposits unchanged.

10 Consider Fact 25.1. Huck Finn comes along and deposits $10. After Huck's deposit, but before any other actions have occurred, the Bank of Speedy Creek will have excess reserves of

a   zero.
b $9.
c $9.20.
d $10.
e $40.

11 Consider Fact 25.1. Huck Finn comes along and deposits $10. After Huck's deposit, given that the Bank of Speedy Creek is profit-seeking, what is the amount of new loans it will make?

a   zero
b $9
c $9.20
d $10
e $40

12 Consider Fact 25.1. Huck Finn comes along and deposits $10. After Huck's deposit, and after the Bank of Speedy Creek has lent the amount it wishes to lend, the total amount of reserves in the bank will be $_____, the total amount of loans will be $_____, and the total amount of deposits will be $_____

a   40.80; 469.20; 510
b   40; 460; 500
c   50; 470; 520
d   41; 469; 510
e   42.50; 467.50; 510

13 Consider Fact 25.1. Huck Finn comes along and deposits $10. If all the banks in the banking system had the same desired reserve ratio as the Bank of Speedy Creek, what would be the total change in deposits within the system resulting from Huck's initial deposit?

a $125
b $100
c $80
d $40
e $12.50

The Demand for Money

14 Consider Figure 25.1. Which of the following best describes the response of this household to an *increase* in their annual income?

a   movement from *a* to *f*
b   movement from *a* to *c*
c   movement from *e* to *a*
d   movement from *b* to *a*
e   movement from *a* to *e*

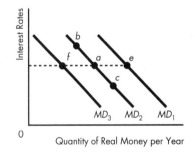

FIGURE **25.1** THE DEMAND FOR REAL MONEY BALANCES BY AN INDIVIDUAL HOUSEHOLD

15 Consider Figure 25.1. Which of the following best describes the response of this household to a *decrease* in the market price of bonds?

a   movement from *a* to *b*
b   movement from *a* to *c*
c   movement from *a* to *f*
d   movement from *a* to *e*
e   movement from *e* to *a*

16 Which of the following will cause the demand curve for real money to shift leftward?

a   an increase in real GDP
b   a decrease in interest rates
c   the expanded use of credit cards
d   an increase in the quantity of money supplied
e   an increase in the price level

17 Real money is equal to nominal money

a divided by real GDP.

b minus real GDP.

c divided by the price level.

d minus the price level.

e divided by velocity.

Interest Rate Determination

18 If the interest rate is above the equilibrium rate, how is equilibrium achieved in the money market?

a People buy goods to get rid of excess money, lowering the price of goods, and lowering the interest rate.

b People sell goods to get rid of excess money, lowering the price of goods, and lowering the interest rate.

c People sell bonds to get rid of excess money, lowering the price of bonds, and lowering the interest rate.

d People sell bonds to get rid of excess money, raising the price of bonds, and lowering the interest rate.

e People buy bonds to get rid of excess money, raising the price of bonds, and lowering the interest rate.

19 If households and firms find that their holdings of real money are less than desired, they will

a sell financial assets, which will cause interest rates to increase.

b sell financial assets, which will cause interest rates to decrease.

c buy financial assets, which will cause interest rates to increase.

d buy financial assets, which will cause interest rates to decrease.

e buy goods, which will cause the price level to increase.

20 Money market equilibrium occurs

a when interest rates are constant.

b when the level of real GDP is constant.

c when quantity of real money supplied equals real money demanded.

d only under a fixed exchange rate.

e when bond prices are constant.

21 An increase in the quantity of real money supplied will

a increase interest rates and decrease the exchange rate.

b have no impact on interest rates, but increase the exchange rate.

c have no impact on interest rates nor on the exchange rate.

d decrease interest rates and increase the exchange rate.

e decrease interest rates and the exchange rate.

The Interest Rate and Expenditure Plans

22 If the inflation rate increases by 3 percent and the nominal interest rate increases by 2 percent, then the

a real interest rate increases.

b opportunity cost of holding money increases.

c opportunity cost of holding money decreases.

d opportunity cost of spending increases.

e autonomous consumption expenditure decreases.

23 An increase in the real interest rate will

a decrease consumption expenditure.

b increase investment.

c decrease the exchange rate.

d increase net exports.

e decrease the nominal interest rate.

24 A decrease in the quantity of real money supplied will

a decrease the real interest rate, the inflation rate held constant.

b decrease nominal interest rates.

c decrease aggregate expenditure.

d increase aggregate expenditure.

e not change the nominal interest rate.

25 A higher Canadian interest rate will

a increase the demand for Canadian dollars because more people move money into Canada to take advantage of the higher interest rate.

b decrease the demand for Canadian dollars because more people move money out of Canada to take advantage of the higher interest rate.

c increase the demand for Canadian dollars because more people move money out of Canada to take advantage of the higher interest rate.

d decrease the demand for Canadian dollars because more people move money into Canada to take advantage of the higher interest rate.

e not affect the demand for Canadian dollars.

Short Answer Problems

1 Banks can no longer issue their own paper money, but can create money by creating deposit money by crediting people's deposits. Since there is no paper money deposited to back up this creation, is this created money real? Is it acceptable in society? Why or why not?

2 Carefully explain how and why banks create new money during the deposit multiplier process (in a multibank system).

3 Why do people care about the quantity of real money they hold rather than the quantity of nominal money?

4 Suppose an individual sells $1,000 worth of government securities to the Bank of Canada and deposits the proceeds ($1,000) in bank 1. Note that this new deposit initially increases the quantity of money by $1,000. (In the next chapter we will see how such a new deposit arises.) Assume that the desired reserve ratio for all banks in the multibank system is 20 percent (0.2). There is no currency drain. Table 25.3 gives information for the first round of the money expansion process that will be generated by this new deposit.
a Follow the first six rounds of the money creation process by completing Table 25.3.

TABLE **25.3** MONEY CREATION PROCESS— NO CURRENCY DRAIN

Bank Number	New Deposits	New Loans	New Reserves	Increase in Deposits	Cumulative Increase in Deposits
1	1,000	800	200	1,000	1,000
2					
3					
4					
5					
6					

b What is the total increase in the quantity of money after six rounds?
c What is the deposit multiplier?
d After all rounds have been completed, what will be the total increase in deposits?

5 For the first two banks in Short Answer Problem **4**, show their balance sheets for each stage of the process (initial deposit, loan creation, borrower's withdrawal, final position).

6 For the entire banking system in Short Answer Problem **4**, what do the final balance sheet changes look like? (Assume that banks have only reserves, loans, and deposits.)

7 Assume that the changes in the banking system in Short Answer Problems **4–6** are economically significant. Explain what they will do to
a the quantity of real money supplied.
b the nominal interest rate.
c the real interest rate, the inflation rate held constant.
d each of the components of interest-sensitive expenditure.

8 There is only one chartered bank in Gondor, and it has the following assets and liabilities (none is missing from the list except as indicated):

Currency reserves	$20 million
Reserves held at the Bank of Gondor	$10 million
Loans	?
Securities	$25 million
Demand deposits	$150 million
Notice deposits	$600 million

a Construct the balance sheet for this bank. What is the amount of loans?
b Assuming that the bank has freely chosen its reserves, what is its desired reserve ratio? What is the deposit multiplier?
c If the amount of currency in circulation is $50 million, what is M1? M2+?

9 Show on a graph and briefly explain what each of the following will do (in sequence) to the demand for real money (defined as M1) and therefore the equilibrium interest rate. Assume that the real money supply remains constant.
a The price level rises.
b There is a financial innovation (the widespread adoption of electronic funds transfers) that reduces the need to use chequing accounts.
c Real GDP falls during a recession.

10 In each of the cases in Short Answer Problem **9**, explain what happens to each component of interest-sensitive expenditure.

ANSWERS

True/False and Explain

1 **T** Basic function of money. (582–583)
ct 2 **F** See definition of M1. (583–584)
3 **F** M1 will decrease as chequing accounts (demand deposits) decrease, but since chequing and saving accounts are part of M2+, there is no change in M2+. (583–584)
4 **F** Large size allows banks to pool risk. (586–587)
5 **F** Liabilities + net worth = assets. (585)
6 **T** Definition. (587)
ct 7 **T** Withdrawal leads to decrease in reserves = decrease in deposits, which leads to decrease in reserve/deposit ratio—do a balance sheet. (587–590)
8 **T** Definition. (588)
9 **F** Real money demand independent of price level. (591–592)
10 **T** Increase in interest rate leads to increase in opportunity cost of holding money, leading to decrease in quantity money demanded. (592–594)
11 **T** Shifts towards notice accounts—see text discussion. (593–594)
12 **T** Agents substitute towards bonds, leading to increase in bond demand, leading to increase in bond price, which implies decrease in bond interest rate. (594–596)
13 **T** Price of bond and its interest rate are inversely related. (594)
14 **F** Nominal interest rate—see text discussion. (597)
15 **T** It will increase the demand for the Canadian dollar, and therefore the value of the exchange rate. (598)

Multiple-Choice

1 **a** See text discussion. (582–583)
2 **c** Definition. (583–584)
3 **a** Most readily changed into currency. (584)
4 **a** Credit cards cannot necessarily be used for purchases in the future, the credit card company could refuse to honour your card. (584)
5 **a** Must be prudent about risk too. (585–587)
6 **d** Others are all assets = claims on someone else. (585)
7 **d** See text discussion. (586–587)
8 **b** Desired reserve ratio = chosen reserves/deposits = 40/500 = 0.08. (587)

9 **b** Decrease in currency as deposit made = increase in deposits. (587–590)
10 **c** Excess = actual ($50) – desired ($40.80 = 0.08 × $510). (587)
11 **c** Banks will lend the amount of excess reserves. (589–590)
ct 12 **a** Work through balance sheet changes as shown in Helpful Hint **3**. (589–590)
ct 13 **a** Δ deposits = (1/(desired reserve ratio)) × Δ reserves = (1/0.08) × $10 = $125. (587–590)
14 **e** *a* to *f*, *e* to *a* are decreases in income, others are Δ interest rates. (592)
15 **a** Decrease in price of bonds leads to increase in interest rates. *a* to *f*, *a* to *e*, *e* to *a*, are income changes, *a* to *c* is decrease in interest rates. (592–596)
16 **c** Financial innovation means people use less money. (592)
17 **c** Definition. (591)
ct 18 **e** If interest rate > equilibrium, this implies too much money, which implies buying bonds, leading to increase in price of bonds and therefore decrease in interest rates. (595–596)
19 **a** They substitute money for bonds, extra sales leads to decrease in price of bonds and increase in interest rates. (595–596)
20 **c** Definition. (595)
21 **e** Increase in money supply leads to excess supply of money, creating excess demand for financial assets, which leads to increase in price of financial assets and decrease in interest rates, which leads to decrease in demand for Canadian dollar and therefore decrease in exchange rate. (596)
ct 22 **b** Nominal interest rate increases, opportunity cost of money increases. Real interest rate decreases since increase in inflation rate > increase in nominal interest rate, so opportunity cost of spending decreases and spending increases. (597–599)
23 **a** Higher cost of borrowing decreases borrowing and spending. (597–599)
24 **c** Less money means increased interest rates and therefore decreased consumption, investment and net exports. (597–599)
25 **a** People are trying to earn more on their money, and must buy Canadian assets to do so and must buy Canadian dollars to buy the Canadian assets. (598)

Short Answer Problems

1 This created money is real because it is backed by the assets of the bank, which consist of the bank's reserves, loans, and holdings of securities.

Deposit money is generally accepted in society (you can buy goods, pay debts, etc., with it) because people know that the banks will provide currency upon demand.

2 Banks create money by making new loans. When banks get a new deposit, this deposit leaves them with excess reserves. Their desire to make profits (maximize net worth) leads banks to lend out the excess reserves, creating a matching deposit, which is new money. When the proceeds of these loans are spent, the person receiving the money will deposit much of it in a bank deposit, which is also new money.

3 Nominal money is simply the number of dollars, while real money is a measure of what money will buy. Real money will decrease if the price level rises, and if the number of dollars is constant. What matters to people is the quantity of goods and services that money will buy, not the number of dollars. If the price level rises by 10 percent, people will want to hold 10 percent more dollars (given a constant real income and interest rates) in order to retain the same purchasing power.

4 a Table 25.3 is completed here as Table 25.3 Solution. Note that 80 percent of each new deposit will be lent and 20 percent will be held as reserves. When a new loan is deposited in the next bank, it becomes a new deposit.

TABLE **25.3** SOLUTION

Bank Number	New Deposits	New Loans	New Reserves	Increase in Deposits	Cumulative Increase in Deposits
1	1,000	800	200	1,000	1,000
2	800	640	160	800	1,800
3	640	512	128	640	2,440
4	512	410	102	512	2,952
5	410	328	82	410	3,362
6	328	262	66	328	3,690

b After six rounds, the total (cumulative) increase in the quantity of money is $3,690 (the last number of Table 25.3 Solution).
c The deposit multiplier in this case is equal to 1/(desired reserve ratio). Since the desired reserve ratio is 0.2, the deposit multiplier is 5.
d The total increase in money will be $5,000 after all rounds are completed. This value is obtained by multiplying the initial increase in deposits ($1,000) by the deposit multiplier (5).

5 Bank 1's balance sheets are shown in Table 25.4, and Bank 2's are shown in Table 25.5.

TABLE **25.4** BANK 1

(a) Initial New Deposit of $1,000

Assets		Liabilities	
Reserves	+$1,000	Deposits	+$1,000

(b) Loan Creation of $800

Assets		Liabilities	
Loans	+$800	Deposits	+$800

(c) Withdrawal of Loan Money

Assets		Liabilities	
Reserves	−$800	Deposits	−$800

(d) Final Position

Assets		Liabilities	
Reserves	+$200	Deposits	+$1,000
Loans	+$800		
	+$1,000		

TABLE **25.5** BANK 2

(a) Initial New Deposit of $800

Assets		Liabilities	
Reserves	+$800	Deposits	+$800

(b) Loan Creation of $640

Assets		Liabilities	
Loans	+$640	Deposits	+$640

(c) Withdrawal of Loan Money

Assets		Liabilities	
Reserves	−$640	Deposits	−$640

(d) Final Position

Assets		Liabilities	
Reserves	+$160	Deposits	+$800
Loans	+$640		
	+$800		

ᶜᵗ **6** The total change in reserves in the system must be equal to the initial new reserves of +$1,000. Total new deposits have been calculated as +$5,000. For the balance sheet to balance therefore, loans must be +$4,000, and the balance sheet is as shown in Table 25.6.

TABLE **25.6**

Assets		Liabilities	
Reserves	+$1,000	Deposits	+$5,000
Loans	+$4,000		
	+$5,000		

7 a The increase in deposits increases the quantity of real money supplied.
  b This increase will lead to an excess supply of money, so that people buy bonds, bidding up bond prices and lowering the nominal interest rate.
  c If the inflation rate is held constant, the real interest rate = nominal rate − inflation rate will decrease as the nominal rate decreases.
  d The lower real interest rate will decrease the opportunity cost of spending. First, for consumption expenditure, the lower real interest rate will encourage more borrowing and less saving, and therefore more current consumption. Secondly, the lower real interest rate lowers the opportunity cost of investment, and therefore raises investment spending by firms. Third, the lower interest rate encourages money to flow out of Canada, depressing the Canadian dollar exchange rate, and therefore encouraging net exports. Putting these all together, aggregate expenditure will increase.

8 a The balance sheet is shown in Table 25.7 (all values are in millions). Since assets must equal liabilities in the balance sheet, loans = $750 − $30 − $25 = $695.

TABLE **25.7**

Assets		Liabilities	
Reserves	+$30	Demand Deposits	+$150
Securities	+$25	Notice Deposits	+$600
Loans	+$695		
	+$750		+$750

b The desired reserve ratio = desired reserves/deposits = 30/750 = 0.04. The deposit multiplier = 1/(desired reserve ratio) = 1/0.04 = 25.
  c M1 = currency in circulation + demand deposits = $200 million. M2+ = M1 + notice deposits = $800 million.

9 a A change in the price level will have no impact on real money demand, and therefore no impact on the equilibrium interest rate (r). In Figure 25.2, demand for real money remains at MD_0, and the interest rate remains at r_0.

FIGURE **25.2**

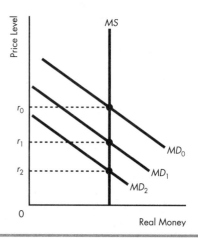

b This financial innovation would reduce the need to use chequing accounts, which are part of M1. Therefore the demand for real money falls to MD_1, and the equilibrium interest rate falls to r_1 in Figure 25.2.
  c The decrease in real GDP lowers the demand for real money to MD_2, and the equilibrium interest rate falls to r_2 in Figure 25.2.

10 In part **a**, the fact that there is no impact on the interest rate means no impact on interest-sensitive expenditure. In part **b**, the lower interest rate will mean a lower real interest rate, and higher consumption, investment and net exports as detailed in the answer to Short Answer Problem 7. Similarly, in part **c**, the lower real interest rate also means higher consumption, investment and net exports.

Chapter 26

Monetary Policy

KEY CONCEPTS

The Bank of Canada

The **Bank of Canada** (Canada's **central bank**) supervises financial institutions and conducts monetary policy.

◆ **Monetary policy** attempts to control inflation and business cycle by Δ quantity of money and by adjusting interest rates and the exchange rate.

◆ Canada's central bank is somewhat subordinate to the federal government.

- An independent central bank determines monetary policy with no government interference.
- A subordinate central bank must follow government directions.

Bank of Canada balance sheet shows

- liabilities = Bank of Canada notes + deposits (reserves) of chartered banks + government deposits
- assets = government securities + loans to banks
- **monetary base** = Bank of Canada notes outside . bank + chartered bank deposits at the Bank + coins in circulation

Monetary policy is difficult to execute because current tools create delayed, future effects.

◆ **Monetary policy indicators** are current features of economy that help predict future course.

◆ Main indicator is **overnight loans rate** (interest rate on loans banks make to each other).

Bank of Canada attempts to Δ bank reserves, which leads to Δ overnight rate, which leads to Δ quantity of money, etc., by manipulating four main policy tools:

◆ Δ required reserve ratio will Δ minimum reserves banks must hold (currently = 0).

◆ Δ **bank rate**—the rate it charges to chartered banks in lending them reserves.

- Increase in bank rate increases costs of borrowing reserves, which increases reserves held by banks, who decrease loans to public.
- Increase in banker's deposit rate (= rate earned by banks' deposits at Bank of Canada = bank rate − 0.5%) increases overnight loans rate.

◆ **Open market operations**—buying/selling government bonds.

◆ **Government deposit shifting**—transferring government funds between Bank of Canada and chartered bank deposits.

- If shift deposits out of Bank of Canada into chartered banks, banks' deposits and reserves increase, so more loans and money created.

Controlling the Quantity of Money

The major policy tool of the Bank is an open market operation.

◆ Bank of Canada carries out open market operations with banks or public.

◆ Bank of Canada buying government bonds increases chartered bank reserves = increase in excess reserves.

- The excess reserves are used to make new loans, which when spent, lead to new deposits and further second-round or multiplier effects.
- Overall result: increase in quantity of money = increase in currency held by households (**currency drain**) + increase in deposits.
- *Bank of Canada buying government bonds increases the quantity of money.*

◆ Bank of Canada selling government bonds decreases chartered bank reserves, which leads to loans called in, which decreases deposits, leading to further second-round effects and a decrease in quantity of money.

  • *Bank of Canada selling government bonds decreases the quantity of money.*

◆ **Money multiplier** = amount Δ monetary base (*MB*) is multiplied by to get resulting Δ in quantity of money = $\Delta M / \Delta MB$.

◆ Size of Δ quantity of money depends on size of second-round effects, which are larger if

  • currency drain is smaller.
  • desired reserve ratio is smaller.

The Ripple Effects of Monetary Policy

Δ quantity of money affects aggregate demand (*AD*), real GDP and price level through several channels.

◆ Buying securities increases quantity of money, which decreases interest rate (*r*) which

  • decreases exchange rate, increasing net exports and *AD*.
  • increases consumption and investment, increasing *AD*.

◆ With unemployment, increased quantity of money increases *AD*, which increases real GDP and price level, leading to a faster convergence to full employment.

◆ If real GDP > potential (inflationary pressure), decrease in quantity of money decreases *AD*, lowering pressure.

◆ Monetary policy is sometimes wrong due to time lags before policy takes effect.

◆ Historical evidence shows that actual Canadian interest rates move inversely with Δ*MB*, but in a manner not completely predictable.

The Bank of Canada targets the interest rate rather than the quantity of money due to worries about fluctuations in money demand (*MD*).

◆ If the Bank targeted quantity of money, Δ*MD* would create Δ*r* that affects economy.

The exchange rate responds to changes in Canadian interest rate relative to world rates.

◆ Historical evidence shows increase in interest rate gap between Canada and United States leads to upward pressure on exchange rate.

Historical evidence shows that when the Bank stimulates *AD* (lowers short-term interest rates), real GDP growth speeds up, but with a lag.

The Bank of Canada in Action

Strong downward pressure on money growth rates in early 1980s sharply increased *r*, which created recession, slowed inflation.

◆ Similar policy in late 1980s decreased inflation some more, but contributed to 1990–91 recession.

◆ Since then, the Bank of Canada has used a more balanced approach.

HELPFUL HINTS

I Open market operations are the most important policy tool of the Bank of Canada, and it is important to understand how they affect the quantity of money. To understand the effect of open market operations on the monetary base and thus the quantity of money, remember that one liability of the Bank of Canada is banks' deposits at the Bank of Canada that serve as bank reserves. These deposits, combined with currency in circulation (the other major liability of the Bank of Canada), constitute the monetary base. The largest class of assets of the Bank of Canada is its holdings of government securities. Finally, recall that if total assets increase, due to the conventions of double-entry bookkeeping, total liabilities must increase by the same amount.

An open market purchase of government securities is an increase in the assets of the Bank of Canada (government securities) paid for by an increase in its liabilities, principally an increase in the deposits of banks at the Bank of Canada. This increase in liabilities of the Bank of Canada is an increase in the monetary base, which will have a multiplied effect on the quantity of money.

2 Here are some further notes on open market operations:

a To remember whether an open market purchase will lead to a decrease or an increase in money, think of open market operations as an exchange of government securities for cash. For example, think of an open market purchase as the Bank of Canada acquiring government securities by giving cash to the public. The purchase increases the quantity of money.

Be careful to avoid making a very common error when working through open market operations. When the Bank of Canada buys or sells securities, chartered bank reserves at the Bank of Canada change. Many students automatically place the changed bank reserves at the Bank of Canada under assets in the Bank's balance sheet, because they are an asset on the chartered bank balance sheet. However, this placement is an error—the reserves are a deposit at the Bank of Canada, and therefore a *liability* to the Bank of Canada.

b Remember that government securities are assets to the Bank of Canada, just as they are to members of the public who hold them. They are liabilities of the government of Canada.

c Government securities are traded in two markets: the primary market in which the Treasury sells newly issued government securities, and the secondary market in which government securities previously purchased in the primary market are bought and sold. This secondary market is the open market in which *open market* operations take place.

d To understand how an open market operation changes interest rates, consider the changes in the banking sector. For example, an open market purchase of government securities (which will increase the quantity of money) leaves the banking sector with excess reserves. Profit-seeking banks attempt to lend these excess reserves. At the original interest rate, loan demand (borrowing) equaled loan supply. To convince economic agents to borrow more money, banks must decrease interest rates. The result is that as the quantity of money increases, interest rates decrease. Therefore we can see intuitively how an open market purchase leads directly to decreased interest rates.

e The text does not work through an open market sale, so for the extra practice let's try one. Suppose that the Bank of Canada wishes to decrease the quantity of money and decides to decrease the monetary base by $100 million. It decides to do so by selling $100 million worth of securities to the Royal Bank. The Royal Bank pays for the securities out of its reserves held at the Bank of Canada. Table 26.1 shows the changes in the two balance sheets. The Royal Bank now has a decrease in its reserves, and if desired reserves are too low, must call in some loans to increase reserves. This action will trigger a decrease in deposits and the overall quantity of money, as desired by the Bank of Canada.

TABLE **26.1**

Bank of Canada

Assets		Liabilities	
Securities	−100	Deposits (reserves) of Royal Bank	−100

Royal Bank

Assets		Liabilities
Reserves	−100	
Securities	+100	
	0	

SELF-TEST

True/False and Explain

The Bank of Canada

1 Increasing the bank rate will increase the amount of lending by chartered banks.

2 Chartered bank deposits at the Bank of Canada are an asset of the Bank of Canada and a liability of the chartered bank.

3 The main monetary indicator is the bank rate.

4 The monetary base = Bank of Canada notes in circulation + coins in circulation.

Controlling the Quantity of Money

5 If the Bank of Canada sells government securities in the open market, chartered bank reserves increase.

6 The higher the banks' desired reserve ratio, the larger the money multiplier.

7 The presence of a currency drain increases the size of the money multiplier.

8 The Bank of Canada buying government securities will increase the quantity of money.

The Ripple Effects of Monetary Policy

9 If real GDP is increasing and the quantity of money is increasing, interest rates must also be increasing.

10 An increase in the quantity of money shifts the aggregate demand curve rightward.

11 An increase in the quantity of money decreases the exchange rate.

12 If the Bank of Canada wants to decrease interest rates, it should sell government securities in the open market.

13 A decrease in the quantity of money will reduce inflationary pressures.

The Bank of Canada in Action

14 Historical evidence for Canada shows that lowering the money supply growth rate lowers inflation.

15 In the 1990s, the Bank of Canada carried out a strong anti-inflationary policy.

Multiple-Choice

The Bank of Canada

1 Which of the following is one of the policy tools of the Bank of Canada?
a prime rate
b exchange rate
c currency ratio
d bank rate
e none of the above

2 The bank rate is the interest rate
a banks charge their very best loan customers.
b banks pay on term deposits.
c the Bank of Canada pays on reserves held by banks.
d the Bank of Canada charges when it lends reserves to banks.
e received for holding Government of Canada Treasury bills.

3 The bank rate is an effective signal of monetary policy because it is
a a measure of the return on keeping reserves.
b useful for predicting monetary policy.
c equal to the prime rate.
d a rough approximation of the value of the money multiplier.
e changed by chartered banks.

4 Which of the Bank of Canada's policy tools is the most important?
a choosing exchange rate regimes
b setting reserve requirements
c changing the bank rate
d paying for the government's deficit
e open market operations

5 The Bank of Canada
a is totally controlled by the federal government.
b is totally independent of the federal government.
c has always been subordinate to the federal government.
d was originally independent of the federal government, but after 1967 became subordinate.
e was originally subordinate to the federal government, but after 1967 became independent.

Controlling the Quantity of Money

6 Which of the balance sheets in Table 26.2 shows the initial impact on the banking sector of an open market purchase by the Bank of Canada of $100 worth of government securities from the banking sector?

a (a)
b (b)
c (c)
d (d)
e none of the above

TABLE **26.2** CHARTERED BANKS' BALANCE SHEETS

(a)

Assets	Liabilities
Reserves +100	
Securities −100	

(b)

Assets	Liabilities
Reserves −100	
Securities +100	

(c)

Assets	Liabilities
Reserves +100	Deposits +100

(d)

Assets	Liabilities
	Deposits +100
	Securities −100

7 Which of the balance sheets in Table 26.2 shows the initial impact on the banking sector of an open market sale by the Bank of Canada of $100 worth of government securities to a private individual?

a (a)
b (b)
c (c)
d (d)
e none of the above

8 Which of the following would *not* affect the size of the monetary base?

a A bank exchanges government securities for a deposit at the Bank of Canada.
b A bank exchanges vault cash for a deposit at the Bank of Canada.
c The Bank of Canada buys government securities from a bank.
d The Bank of Canada buys government securities from someone other than a bank.
e The Bank of Canada sells government securities to a bank.

9 The monetary expansion process continues until

a required reserves are eliminated.
b the Bank of Canada eliminates required reserves.
c the discount rate is lower than the prime rate.
d the prime rate is lower than the discount rate.
e excess reserves are eliminated.

10 In an expansionary open market operation, the Bank of Canada

a sells government bonds, decreasing bank reserves, decreasing lending, decreasing the quantity of money.
b sells government bonds, decreasing bank reserves, decreasing lending, increasing the quantity of money.
c sells government bonds, decreasing bank reserves, increasing lending, increasing the quantity of money.
d buys government bonds, increasing bank reserves, increasing lending, decreasing the quantity of money.
e buys government bonds, increasing bank reserves, increasing lending, increasing the quantity of money.

11 If there is a *decrease* in the currency drain, then the

a deposit multiplier will decrease.
b deposit multiplier will increase.
c money multiplier will decrease.
d money multiplier will stay constant.
e money multiplier will increase.

12 The money multiplier will increase if either the fraction of deposits that households and firms want to hold as currency

a increases or the desired reserve ratio increases.
b decreases or the desired reserve ratio decreases.
c decreases or the desired reserve ratio increases.
d increases or the desired reserve ratio decreases.
e none of the above.

The Ripple Effects of Monetary Policy

13 Why is the exchange rate a key monetary variable?

a It is one of the four main policy tools.
b It is a key policy objective.
c It is a barometer of monetary policy.
d It shows how much the monetary base must be multiplied in order to measure the resulting increase in the quantity of money.
e It is part of the channel by which a change in quantity of money affects aggregate demand.

14 The headline "The Bank of Canada Has Cut the Bank Rate" suggests that the Bank of Canada is trying to

a lower inflationary pressures.
b increase the overnight loans rate.
c stimulate aggregate expenditure.
d raise the value of the Canadian dollar.
e help banks make profits.

15 In a situation of unemployment, an increase in the quantity of money will lead to a(n)

a increase in real GDP and the price level.
b increase in real GDP, but a decrease in the price level.
c increase in real GDP, but no change in the price level.
d increase in the price level, but no change in real GDP.
e decrease in the price level and real GDP.

16 Consider Figure 26.1. Which graph represents an anti-inflationary monetary policy?

a (a)
b (b)
c (c)
d (d)
e none of the above

FIGURE **26.1**

(a)

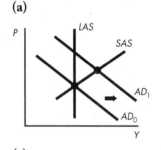

(b)

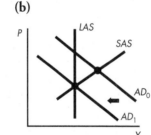

(c)

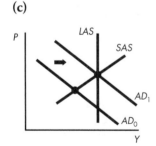

(d)

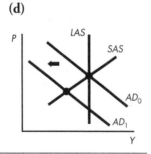

17 Consider Figure 26.1. Which graph shows an example of an attempt to lower unemployment with monetary policy?

a (a)
b (b)
c (c)
d (d)
e none of the above

18 An expansionary monetary policy will

a increase interest rates and decrease the exchange rate.
b have no impact on interest rates, but increase the exchange rate.
c have no impact on interest rates nor on the exchange rate.
d decrease interest rates and increase the exchange rate.
e decrease interest rates and the exchange rate.

19 If the Bank of Canada buys government securities in the open market, the money supply curve will shift

a leftward, and the interest rate will increase.
b leftward, and the interest rate will decrease.
c rightward, and the interest rate will increase.
d rightward, and the interest rate will remain constant as money demand will shift rightward as well.
e none of the above.

20 If the Bank of Canada targets the level of the quantity of money,

a the interest rate will be constant.
b real GDP will be constant.
c there will be no inflation.
d the interest rate will fluctuate.
e the quantity of money will fluctuate.

21 If the Bank of Canada wishes to raise the exchange rate, they should

a target the quantity of money.
b buy government bonds.
c lower Canadian interest rates.
d sell government bonds.
e target the interest rate.

22 Which of the following statements about historical evidence on monetary policy is *true*?

a Canadian interest rates move positively with the monetary base.

b Canadian interest rates are not related to the monetary base.

c When the Bank of Canada lowers short-term interest rates, real GDP rises immediately.

d When the gap between Canadian and U.S. interest rates increases, the exchange rate tends to decrease in value.

e When the gap between Canadian and U.S. interest rates increases, the exchange rate tends to increase in value.

23 Which of the following statements *correctly* describes an anti-inflationary monetary policy?

a "The Bank of Canada's recent purchases of government securities is stimulating the housing sector."

b "The Bank of Canada's recent moves to lower interest rates are behind the recent decreases in the value of the Canadian dollar."

c "The Bank of Canada's recent moves to increase the overnight loans rate are leading to less lending and less consumer spending."

d "The Bank of Canada's recent sales of government securities are stimulating the housing sector."

e "The Bank of Canada's recent moves to decrease the value of the Canadian dollar are leading to more spending in the economy."

The Bank of Canada in Action

24 The Bank of Canada's anti-inflationary policy of the early 1980s resulted in

a an increase in the quantity of money.

b lower interest rates as the policy was carried out.

c higher chartered bank reserves.

d a strong increase in aggregate demand.

e a recession.

25 Which of the following statements best describes the goals of the Bank of Canada in the early 2000s?

a Keep inflation low at all costs.

b Maintain low inflation, but moderate the business cycle.

c Keep unemployment low at all costs.

d Moderate the business cycle, but not worry about inflation.

e Keep the exchange rate fixed.

Short Answer Problems

1 The Bank of Canada often uses monetary policy to increase interest rates, in order to offset downward pressure on the exchange rate. Explain briefly how this policy works.

2 How does an open market purchase of government securities lead to an increase in the monetary base? What are the ripple effects of this policy on the different components of aggregate expenditure?

3 How does the currency drain affect the size of the money multiplier?

4 Figure 26.2 illustrates the current equilibrium in the money market where *MD* is the demand curve for real money and *MS* is the money supply curve.

a Suppose that the Bank of Canada wants to stimulate aggregate expenditure by decreasing the interest rate to 6 percent. By how much must the Bank of Canada increase the quantity of money?

FIGURE **26.2**

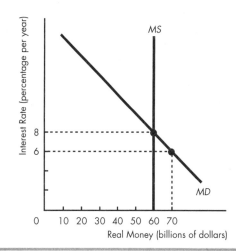

b Having determined the amount by which the Bank of Canada must increase the quantity of money, we now want to determine the open market operation that will be necessary if the money multiplier is 4. Will the Bank of Canada need to buy or sell government securities in the open market and in what amount? (Assume the Bank of Canada deals directly with chartered banks.)

5 Consider the following balance sheets for the Bank of Canada and the Bank of Speedy Creek:

TABLE **26.3**

Bank of Speedy Creek

Assets		Liabilities	
Reserves	60	Deposits	1,000
Securities	100		
Loans	840		
	1,000		

Bank of Canada

Assets		Liabilities	
Government securities	9,000	Bank of Canada notes	10,000
Loans to banks	500	Chartered banks' deposits	1,000
Other net assets	2,000	Government deposits	500
	11,500		11,500

a The Bank of Speedy Creek has chosen this balance sheet position—what is their desired reserve ratio? Explain.

b Suppose that the Bank of Canada buys all $100 of securities from the Bank of Speedy Creek. Show what happens to the balance sheets of the Bank of Speedy Creek and the Bank of Canada as a result of this action, explaining as you go. What does this action do to the monetary base?

c What will the Bank of Speedy Creek do next? Assuming no currency drain, what does this action do to the overall level of deposits in the banking sector? (Calculate the size of the deposit multiplier as part of your answer.)

6 Explain what the open market operation in Short Answer Problem **5** does to the quantity of money, the interest rate, aggregate demand, real GDP, and the price level. Be sure to explain the channels by which the monetary policy affects aggregate demand.

7 Suppose there is a decrease in the quantity of money. Using an aggregate demand–aggregate supply model, show what happens to the price level and the level of real GDP in the short run and in the long run.

8 Given the following data from the Canadian economy, graph the money market, showing the initial equilibrium in 1988 and the new equilibrium in 1989 with the changes in *MD* and *MS*. Briefly explain why you decided *MD*

and *MS* would be placed where you placed them in the graph.

Interest rate (1988) = 10.8%
Interest rate (1989) = 13.4%
Inflation rate (1988–89) = 5.0%
Nominal money growth (1988–89) = 4.6%
Real GDP growth (1988–89) = 2.3%

9 Consider the following data, from the imaginary country of Sarconia:

Current inflation rate	8% per year
Current growth rate of real GDP	3% per year
Current unemployment rate	5%
Estimate of natural unemployment rate	7%
Current growth rate of nominal quantity of money	12% per year

a Is Sarconia suffering from an inflationary gap, is it suffering from a recessionary gap, or is it right at potential GDP? How do you know?

b In part **a**, if you thought Sarconia was suffering from a problem, explain the correct monetary policy to deal with this problem.

10 Briefly explain the argument for using interest-rate targeting over money targeting.

ANSWERS

True/False and Explain

1 **F** Higher bank rate increases cost of borrowing reserves, so chartered banks wish to hold more reserves, so they *decrease* loans. (608–610)
2 **F** Asset of chartered bank (part of reserves) and liability of Bank of Canada (deposit at Bank). (607)
3 **F** Main indicator is the overnight loans rate. (608)
4 **F** Monetary base also includes chartered bank deposits at the Bank of Canada. (607)
5 **F** If securities are sold, people buy them with their deposits, leading to decrease in reserves. (611–612)
6 **F** Higher desired reserve ratio means more deposits kept back, less lent out, at each stage of money multiplier process. (613–614)
7 **F** Makes it smaller due to more withdrawals of cash at each round of the multiplier process. (615)
8 **T** The Bank buying government bonds increases chartered bank reserves, leading to new loans and new deposits = new money. (611–613)

9 F Increase in real GDP shifts *MD* rightward. Since *MS* shifting rightward too, impact on *r* uncertain. (615–618)

10 T Increase in *MS* decreases *r*, which decreases exchange rate, which increases *NX, C, I,* which together shift *AD* rightward. (615–616)

11 T Increase in *MS* decreases *r*, which decreases demand for Canadian dollar and exchange rate. (619–620)

12 F Selling government bonds decreases reserves, which decreases loans and deposits, so *MS* decreases, creating *increase* in interest rates. (615–616)

13 T The decrease in *MS* will increase interest rates and decrease *AD*. (616–617)

14 T See text discussion. (621)

15 F It carried out a balanced approach—see text discussion. (621)

Multiple-Choice

1 d Definition. (608–610)

2 d Definition. (608–610)

3 b Because bank rate is barometer of open market operations. (608–610)

4 e See text discussion. (608–610)

5 d See text discussion. (606)

6 a Bank of Canada credits banking sector's reserves at central bank and in return gets securities from banking sector. (611–612)

7 e Open market sale would look like (c), except both values would be –100. (611–612)

8 b Others are all examples of open market operations. (611–613)

9 e Until this event occurs, banks will keep lending out excess reserves. (611–613)

10 e Buying bonds increases reserves to pay for them, which creates excess reserves, leading to increase in lending to make profits, leading to increase in spending and in deposits, which increases quantity of money. (611–613)

11 e Deposit multiplier does not depend on currency drain. Decrease in currency drain will result in more loan creation and more deposit (= money) creation at each stage of the multiplier. (613–614)

12 b Both decreases mean there is more reserves to create new loans at each stage of the multiplier process. (613–614)

13 e Δ*MS* leads to Δ*r*, which Δ demand for Canadian dollar and exchange rate, which Δ*NX* and *AD*. (619–620)

14 c Lowering the bank rate lowers costs of borrowing to replenish reserves, so chartered banks will maintain lower reserves, and lend out more money, lowering interest rates (which lowers exchange rate) and stimulating *AE*. (615–616)

15 a Increase in quantity of money shifts *AD* rightward, increasing real GDP and price level if initial equilibrium is left of full employment (draw a graph). (615–616)

16 b Here, output is above natural rate (inflationary gap), and policy is attempting to reduce *AD* to reduce the gap. (616–617)

17 c Here, output is below the natural rate (recessionary gap) and policy is attempting to increase *AD* to reduce the gap. (615–616)

18 e Increase in quantity of money leads to excess supply of money, which decreases interest rates, which decreases demand for Canadian dollar and therefore exchange rate. (619–620)

19 e Buying bonds increases reserves, leading to increase in deposits and quantity of money, creating excess supply of money, which leads to excess demand for financial assets, creating increased price of financial assets and therefore decreased interest rates. (617–618)

20 d Due to fluctuations in *MD*. (618–619)

21 d This action will lower the quantity of money and raise interest rates and the demand for the Canadian dollar. (619–620)

22 e See text discussion. (619–620)

23 c All other changes lead to lower interest rates and higher aggregate expenditure, shifting *AD* rightward. (615–617)

24 e See text discussion. (621)

25 b See text discussion. (621)

Short Answer Problems

1 Increasing interest rates will increase the interest rate gap between Canada and other countries, increasing the demand for the Canadian dollar. This increase in turn will tend to increase the exchange rate, offsetting the initial downward pressure.

2 An open market purchase of government securities by the Bank of Canada increases the monetary base by increasing one of its components—banks' deposits at the Bank of Canada. The process depends on whether the securities are purchased from banks or from the nonbank public.

   If the purchase is from banks, the process is direct—the Bank of Canada pays for the securities by crediting the bank's deposit at the Bank of Canada, which directly increases the monetary base. If the purchase is from the nonbank public, the Bank of Canada pays by writing cheques on itself which the sellers of the securities deposit in their banks. The banks, in turn, present the cheques to the Bank of Canada, which credits the banks' deposits at the Bank of Canada. Thus, in either case, the monetary base increases by the amount of the open market purchase.

With the extra reserves, banks now have excess reserves. They will seek to lend out these reserves, creating an increase in the quantity of money via the money multiplier process. The extra money pushes down interest rates, which increases consumption and investment spending. The lower interest rates lower the demand for the Canadian dollar, which lowers the value of the exchange rate, and increases net exports.

3 During each round of the money multiplier process new loans are used for payments. Some of these payments are redeposited (triggering further loan and deposit expansion), and some are held back as currency. The higher the currency drain, the higher the amount held back, the smaller the amount redeposited, the smaller the amount available for further loan and deposit expansion, the smaller the overall deposit expansion, and the smaller the multiplier.

4 a The current equilibrium interest rate is 8 percent and the Bank of Canada would like to increase the quantity of money sufficiently to decrease the interest rate to 6 percent. Since the quantity of real money demanded at an interest rate of 6 percent is $70 billion, the Bank of Canada will want to increase the money supply by $10 billion.

   b To increase the quantity of money, the Bank of Canada will need to buy government securities in the open market, which will increase bank reserves and the monetary base. Given the money multiplier is 4, if we want a total increase in money of $10 billion, we need a $2.5 billion increase in the monetary base. This increase would require an open market purchase of $2.5 billion in government securities.

5 Desired reserve ratio = chosen reserves/deposits = 60/1,000 = 0.06 or 6 percent.

TABLE 26.4

(a) Changes in Balance Sheets

Bank of Speedy Creek

Assets		Liabilities	
Reserves	+100	Deposits	0
Securities	−100		
Loans	0		
	0		

Bank of Canada

Assets		Liabilities	
Government securities	+100	Bank of Canada notes	0
Loans to banks	0	Ch. banks' deposits	+100
Other net assets	0	Government deposits	0
	+100		+100

(b) Positions After the Open Market Operation

Bank of Speedy Creek

Assets		Liabilities	
Reserves	160	Deposits	1,000
Securities	0		
Loans	840		
	1,000		

Bank of Canada

Assets		Liabilities	
Government securities	9,100	Bank of Canada notes	10,000
Loans to banks	500	Ch. banks' deposits	1,100
Other net assets	2,000	Government deposits	500
	11,600		11,600

b The Bank of Canada increases its securities by 100, and pays for it by increasing the Bank of Speedy Creek's deposits by 100, which is an increase in this bank's reserves by 100 (matching the decrease in security holdings). The balance sheets in Table 26.4 show the changes, and then the new positions.

The increase in chartered banks' deposits of 100 will also increase the monetary base (= notes in circulation + chartered banks' deposits) by 100.

c The Bank of Speedy Creek now has excess reserves of 100, since deposits are unchanged by the operation. They will lend out these excess reserves, creating a multiplier process that will result in an increase in loans and deposits throughout the entire system. The deposit multiplier is 1/(desired reserve ratio) = 1/0.06 = 16.67, so that the total increase in deposits is 1,667.

6 Clearly there is an increase in the quantity of money, which creates an excess supply of money at the original interest rate. People spend their excess supply of money on bonds, driving up the price of bonds, and therefore decreasing the interest rate. The lower interest rate will increase consumer spending (e.g., more borrowing, less saving) and investment spending. In addition, the lower interest rate will lower the value of the exchange rate leading to more net exports. Therefore, the aggregate demand curve shifts rightward, increasing real GDP and the price level in the short run, as shown in Text Figure 26.6.

7 The consequences of a decrease in the quantity of money are illustrated in Figure 26.3. The economy is initially in long-run equilibrium at point *a*, the intersection of AD_0 and SAS_0 (and *LAS*). The price level is P_0 and GDP is at potential, Y^*. A decrease in the quantity of money will shift the *AD* curve leftward, from AD_0 to AD_1. The new short-run equilibrium is at point *b*. The price level decreases to P_1 and real GDP decreases to Y_1. In the long run, however, input prices will also decrease, which will shift the *SAS* curve rightward, from SAS_0 to SAS_1. A new long-run equilibrium is achieved at point *c*. Thus in the long run, the price level decreases further to P_2, while real GDP returns to potential, Y^*.

FIGURE **26.3**

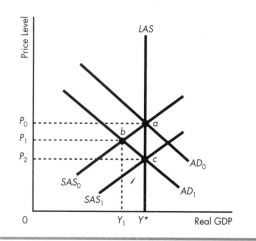

8 The initial 1988 equilibrium is indicated in Figure 26.4 at the intersection of MD_{1988} and MS_{1988}, with an interest rate of 10.8 percent. The increase in real GDP from 1988 to 1989, *ceteris paribus*, will mean an increase in real money demanded, shown by the shift rightward from MD_{1988} to MD_{1989}. The inflation rate is higher than the growth rate of the nominal money supply, so that the real quantity of money shrinks by a small amount from 1988 to 1989, shown by the shift leftward from MS_{1988} to MS_{1989}. The net result of these two changes is an increase in the interest rate from 1988 to 1989.

FIGURE **26.4**

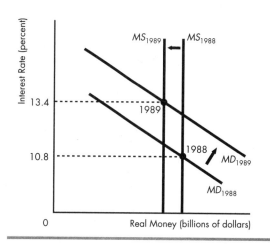

9 a Since unemployment is below the natural rate, real GDP is above potential GDP and there is an inflationary gap.

b The problem is that inflation is likely to start rising, so the correct policy is to shrink the quantity of money to lower aggregate demand, and relieve the inflationary pressure.

10 If a central bank pursues money targeting, they keep the quantity of money constant at a level that they hope will affect the economy appropriately. However, if the demand for money fluctuates, then the rate of interest will fluctuate and therefore affect the economy undesirably. On the other hand, if the central bank picks an interest rate target that is aimed at an average quantity of money (where the interest rate target crosses the average demand for money curve), there will not be undesirable fluctuations in the rate of interest.

Chapter 27

Fiscal and Monetary Interactions

Macroeconomic Equilibrium

This chapter explores how real GDP and interest rate are simultaneously determined.

- ◆ *AD-SAS* equilibrium is where *AD* = *SAS*.

  - *AD* depends on *r*.
  - Higher *r* creates lower expenditure ($IE = C + I + NX$), and lower level of *AD*, lower *Y* and *P*.

- ◆ Money market equilibrium is where *MD* = *MS*.

  - *r* depends on *AD*.
  - Higher *AD* creates higher *Y* (and higher *MD*) and higher *P* (lower *MS*), and therefore higher *r*.

- ◆ There is only one value of *Y* and one value of *r* that give simultaneous or joint money market equilibrium and *AD-SAS* equilibrium.

Fiscal Policy in the Short Run

Expansionary fiscal policy is an increase in government expenditures, increase in transfer payments, or decrease in taxes which increases *AD*.

- ◆ First-round effects: increase in government expenditure creates multiplier effects and increases quantity of real GDP demanded.

- ◆ Second-round effects: increase in real GDP demanded increases real GDP and price level.

  - Increase in *Y* shifts *MD* rightward, which increases *r* and decreases *IE*, shifting *AD* curve leftward somewhat.
  - Increase in *P* shifts *MS* leftward, which increases *r* and decreases *IE* and quantity of real GDP demanded (movement along *AD* curve).

- ◆ Tendency for expansionary fiscal policy to increase *r* and decrease *I* is called **crowding out**.

- ◆ Expansionary fiscal policy may increase *I* (**crowding in**).

- ◆ Increase in *r* may cause **international crowding out** by increasing exchange rate, which leads to decrease in $X - M$.

Monetary Policy in the Short Run

Expansionary monetary policy is an increase in quantity of real money which increases *AD*.

- ◆ First-round effects: increase in quantity of real money leads to a decrease in the interest rate, which leads to an increase in expenditure, which leads to a shift rightward in *AD*.

- ◆ Second-round effects: identical to second-round fiscal policy effects.

- ◆ The overall decrease in the interest rate decreases the demand for the Canadian dollar, which decreases the exchange rate, which increases net exports.

Relative Effectiveness of Policies

- ◆ Fiscal policy is more powerful if

  - money demand *responsive* to interest rates (ΔMD leads to small Δr).
  - interest-sensitive expenditure *unresponsive* to interest rates (given Δr leads to small Δ expenditure).

- ◆ Monetary policy is more powerful if

  - money demand *unresponsive* to interest rates (ΔMS leads to large Δr).
  - interest-sensitive expenditure *responsive* to interest rates (given Δr leads to large Δ expenditure).

◆ **Keynesians** in the 1950s believed economy was inherently unstable; fiscal policy more effective due to little crowding out.

◆ **Monetarists** in the 1950s believed economy was inherently stable; monetary policy more effective due to lots of crowding out.

◆ Empirical evidence showed both policies were effective.

Policy Actions at Full Employment

If the economy starts at full employment, an expansionary fiscal policy shifts *AD* rightward, and creates above full-employment equilibrium (inflationary gap).

◆ Labour shortage puts upward pressure on money wages.

◆ This pressure creates third-round effects— increasing wages shift *SAS* leftward.

◆ As *SAS* shifts leftward, *Y* decreases and *P* increases as economy moves to long-run equilibrium.

◆ Result is complete crowding out—*IE* decreases by amount *G* increases.

An expansionary monetary policy at full employment creates third-round effects identical to fiscal policy third-round effects.

◆ These effects create the **long-run neutrality proposition**—in the long run, a change in the quantity of money changes the price level only, and leaves all real variables unchanged.

Policy Coordination and Conflict

Government and Bank of Canada can work together to achieve common goals (**policy coordination**), or pursue conflicting goals (**policy conflict**).

◆ Monetary and fiscal policy both alter *AD*, but have opposite effects on interest and exchange rates.

• Expansionary fiscal policy increases *r* and increases exchange rate, leading to decrease in *C, I, NX.*

• Expansionary monetary policy decreases *r* and decreases exchange rate, leading to increase in *C, I, NX.*

• Coordination allows an increase in *AD* with desired Δ*r* by correctly mixing monetary and fiscal policy.

◆ One crucial conflict is about financing deficit.

• If government borrows from Bank of Canada, it avoids interest costs, but resulting increase in *MS* leads to inflationary pressures.

• In Canada, only small part of deficits are financed by Bank of Canada.

H E L P F U L   H I N T S

1 Chapters 23 and 24 examined the goods and services markets in isolation using the *AD-SAS* model and assuming that the interest rate was given. When the interest rate changed, aggregate demand changed, resulting in a new equilibrium level of real GDP.

Similarly, Chapters 25 and 26 examined the money market in isolation by using the money supply and money demand model and assuming that the level of real GDP was given. When the level of real GDP changed, the demand for real money changed, resulting in a new equilibrium. The equilibrium value of real GDP was determined assuming a value for the interest rate, and the equilibrium interest rate was determined assuming a value for real GDP.

This chapter puts the two models of these markets together and simultaneously determines equilibrium real GDP and the equilibrium interest rate. Examining the simultaneous equilibrium reveals important *second round* effects of fiscal and monetary policy that did not appear in the partial analysis of earlier chapters. One example of these second-round effects is crowding out. Because of crowding out, the fiscal policy multipliers in the full model are smaller than the multipliers examined in the partial model of Chapter 24.

2 The major focus of this chapter is on channels of monetary or fiscal policy—how an initial change in monetary or fiscal policy is transmitted through the economy to its eventual effect on aggregate demand. The graphical analysis in the text is valuable in studying these channels.

The economy initially starts out in equilibrium, then a change in either monetary or fiscal policy throws a market out of equilibrium. As this market changes and moves towards a new equilibrium, changes are triggered in other markets. Eventually a new, simultaneous equilibrium is achieved in all markets.

It is helpful to augment the graphical analysis with simple "arrow diagrams" that show the *sequence* of changes as the economy adjusts to an initial policy change. For example, the interest rate transmission channel of monetary policy is represented by the following arrow diagram:

(i) First round:

$$\uparrow M \rightarrow \uparrow MS$$
$$\uparrow MS \rightarrow \downarrow r \text{ (link 1)}$$
$$\downarrow r \rightarrow \uparrow IE \text{ (link 2)}$$
$$\uparrow IE \rightarrow \uparrow AD$$
$$\uparrow AD \rightarrow \uparrow \text{ real GDP}, \uparrow P$$

Second round:

$$\uparrow \text{ real GDP} \rightarrow \uparrow MD$$
$$\uparrow P \rightarrow \downarrow MS$$
$$\downarrow MS, \uparrow MD \rightarrow \uparrow r$$
$$\uparrow r \rightarrow \downarrow IE$$
$$\downarrow IE \rightarrow \downarrow AD$$
$$\downarrow AD \rightarrow \downarrow \text{ real GDP}, \downarrow P$$

This diagram indicates that an expansionary monetary policy (an open market purchase of government securities by the Bank of Canada) will cause the quantity of money to increase ($\uparrow M$), which leads to an increase in the quantity of real money ($\uparrow MS$). This increase in turn will result in a decrease in the interest rate ($\downarrow r$) that will increase expenditure ($\uparrow IE$), which is a part of aggregate demand ($\uparrow AD$). This increase will cause real GDP and the price level to begin increasing ($\uparrow$ real GDP, $\uparrow P$), the end of the first round effects.

However, the increase in real GDP and the price level cause second round effects—the higher real GDP leads to a rightward shift in the demand for real money ($\uparrow MD$), the higher price level shifts the money supply curve leftward ($\downarrow MS$). The increase in the demand for real money and the decrease in the quantity of real money will cause the interest rate to increase ($\uparrow r$) and thus expenditure ($\downarrow IE$) and aggregate expenditure ($\downarrow AD$) will decrease, which will lead to a decrease in real GDP and the price level ($\downarrow$ real GDP, $\downarrow P$). This crowding-out effect offsets somewhat the initial changes, but the economy still eventually converges to a new equilibrium. (Ignore link 1 and link 2 in the arrow diagram for the moment.)

An arrow diagram can be a convenient way of summarizing the more detailed graphical analysis. Arrow diagrams can also be useful to reveal effects that can weaken or strengthen the ability of policy to change aggregate demand.

3 The transmission channel of fiscal policy (for example, an increase in government expenditures on goods and services), is represented by the following arrow diagram:

(ii) First round:

$$\uparrow G \rightarrow \uparrow AD$$
$$\uparrow AD \rightarrow \uparrow \text{ real GDP}, \uparrow P$$

Second round:

$$\uparrow \text{ real GDP} \rightarrow \uparrow MD$$
$$\uparrow P \rightarrow \downarrow MS$$
$$\downarrow MS, \uparrow MD \rightarrow \uparrow r \text{ (link 1)}$$
$$\uparrow r \rightarrow \downarrow IE \text{ (link 2)}$$
$$\downarrow IE \rightarrow \downarrow AD$$
$$\downarrow AD \rightarrow \downarrow \text{ real GDP}, \downarrow P$$

The amount of government expenditures on goods and services is represented by G. Otherwise the notation is the same as used above. (Once again, ignore link 1 and link 2.)

4 The text indicates that the strength of the effect of a change in the quantity of money on aggregate demand depends on the responsiveness of the demand for real money to changes in the interest rate, and the responsiveness of expenditure to changes in the interest rate.

The arrow diagram given by (i) illustrates how these factors affect the strength of monetary policy. The link between the increase in the quantity of real money and the subsequent decrease in the interest rate is indicated as link 1. If the demand for real money is very sensitive to interest rate changes (the MD curve is very flat or interest-elastic), then this link is quite weak—a given increase in the quantity of real money will have only a small effect on the interest rate. This small effect in turn means a relatively small effect on expenditure. Link 2 captures the effect of a change in the interest rate on expenditure. If expenditure is very sensitive to interest rate changes (the interest-sensitive expenditure curve is very flat or interest-elastic), then this link is quite strong—a given decrease in the interest rate will have a very large effect on expenditure.

We can also examine the factors that determine the strength of the effect of fiscal policy on aggregate demand. Links 1 and 2 of (ii) are the relevant links; indeed they are the same as links 1 and 2 for monetary policy. If the demand for real money is very sensitive to interest rate changes (the MD curve is very flat), then link 1 is quite weak, the amount of crowding out is small, and fiscal policy is strong. Similarly, if expenditure is very sensitive to interest rate changes (the interest-sensitive expenditure curve is very flat), then link 2 is quite strong, the amount of crowding out is large, and fiscal policy is weak.

Links 1 and 2 are critical in the transmission process and the focus of the Keynesian-monetarist controversy. It is interesting to think about the extreme Keynesian and monetarist positions in terms of these links. The existence of a liquidity trap (horizontal *MD* curve assumed by an extreme Keynesian) makes monetary policy ineffective because it completely breaks link 1—an increase in the quantity of real money will have no effect on the interest rate. It also makes fiscal policy very strong, because there is no crowding out (an increase in real GDP has no impact on interest rates and expenditure).

The existence of a vertical interest-sensitive expenditure curve (assumed by an extreme Keynesian) makes monetary policy ineffective because it completely breaks link 2. Similarly, the existence of a horizontal interest-sensitive expenditure curve or a vertical *MD* curve (assumed by an extreme monetarist) implies complete crowding out and therefore ineffective fiscal policy.

Note that the same effects that create a strong fiscal policy create a weak monetary policy, and vice versa.

5   The effect of changes in monetary policy or fiscal policy on the exchange rate are very important in economies with large foreign sectors such as Canada. Changes in interest rates change the demand for the Canadian dollar in the same direction. This change in turn causes an appreciation in the Canadian dollar if the interest rate increases, and a depreciation in the exchange rate if the interest rate decreases. However, there is a crucial difference between fiscal and monetary policy for this effect, because of the fact the two policies have opposite effects on interest rates.

An expansionary fiscal policy will *increase* interest rates, *increasing* the exchange rate, *decreasing* net exports, thus *offsetting* the expansionary policy. However, an expansionary monetary policy *decreases* interest rates, *decreasing* the exchange rate, *decreasing* net exports, thus *augmenting* the expansionary policy.

True/False and Explain

Macroeconomic Equilibrium

1   An increase in the interest rate will cause the interest-sensitive expenditure curve to shift leftward.

2   An increase in the demand for money will cause the interest rate to rise.

3   An increase in real GDP will shift the demand curve for real money leftward.

Fiscal Policy in the Short Run

4   Crowding in is always more powerful than crowding out.

5   If aggregate demand is increased by an increase in government expenditures on goods and services, interest rates decrease and investment increases.

6   An increase in government expenditures will lower the exchange rate.

Monetary Policy in the Short Run

7   If aggregate demand is increased by an increase in the quantity of real money, interest rates decrease and investment increases.

8   An increase in the quantity of money will cause the interest rate to increase.

9 An increase in the quantity of money will cause the exchange rate to increase.

Relative Effectiveness of Policies

10 Other things equal, a change in the quantity of money will have a larger effect on aggregate planned expenditure the more responsive expenditure is to the interest rate.

11 Crowding out will be greater if the interest-sensitive expenditure curve is very steep.

12 Keynesians consider the economy to be relatively unstable.

Policy Actions at Full Employment

13 In the *AD-AS* model at full employment, in the long run an expansionary monetary policy leads only to an increase in price, not an increase in real GDP.

14 Crowding out is 100% if the economy starts out in a long-run equilibrium.

Policy Coordination and Conflict

15 Coordination of monetary and fiscal policy means that an expansionary policy can be carried out without any crowding out.

Multiple-Choice

Macroeconomic Equilibrium

1 Which of the following best describes how the level of aggregate demand affects the interest rate?

a An increase in the level of aggregate demand increases the price level, which in turn increases money demand and therefore increases the interest rate.

b An increase in the level of aggregate demand decreases the price level, which in turn increases the supply of real money and therefore increases the interest rate.

c A decrease in the level of aggregate demand decreases the price level, which in turn increases money demand and therefore increases the interest rate.

d An increase in the level of aggregate demand increases real GDP, which in turn increases money demand and therefore increases the interest rate.

e An increase in the level of aggregate demand increases real GDP, which in turn decreases the quantity of real money and therefore increases the interest rate.

2 Which of the following best describes how the interest rate affects aggregate demand?

a A lower interest rate increases investment demand, which in turn increases aggregate demand.

b A higher interest rate increases investment demand, which in turn increases aggregate demand.

c A higher interest rate decreases investment demand, which in turn increases aggregate demand.

d A higher interest rate increases consumption, which in turn increases aggregate demand.

e A higher interest rate increases net exports, which in turn increases aggregate demand.

3 Consider Figure 27.1. Why is the situation depicted *not* a consistent equilibrium?

a The level of aggregate demand is inconsistent with the interest rate.

b The money market and the *AD-AS* graph are not individually in equilibrium.

c The *AD-AS* equilibrium occurs at a different level of real GDP than the level of real GDP assumed when the demand curve is drawn for real money.

d The level of expenditure in part (b) is inconsistent with the level of expenditure in part (c).

e Aggregate demand is greater than aggregate supply.

4 Suppose Figure 27.1 depicts the actual current position of an economy. When this economy moves to equilibrium, real GDP will be

a less than $800 billion and the interest rate will be higher than 4 percent.

b less than $800 billion and the interest rate will be lower than 4 percent.

c more than $800 billion and the interest rate will be higher than 4 percent.

d more than $800 billion and the interest rate will be lower than 4 percent.

e none of the above.

5 A change in interest rates (price level held constant) affects aggregate demand through which one of the following changes?

a a shift of the interest-sensitive expenditure curve and movement along the aggregate demand curve

b a shift of the demand for real money curve and the interest-sensitive expenditure curve

c a shift of both the interest-sensitive expenditure and the aggregate demand curves

d movements along both the interest-sensitive expenditure and the aggregate demand curves

e a movement along the interest-sensitive expenditure curve and a shift of the aggregate demand curve

FIGURE **27.1**

(a)

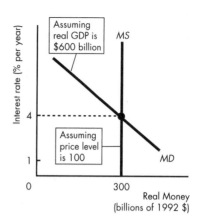

(b)

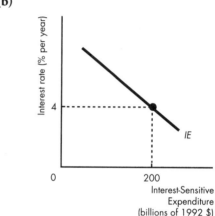

(c)

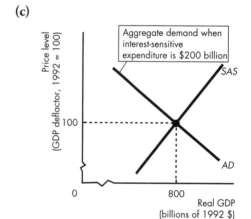

Fiscal Policy in the Short Run

6 Which of the following sequences best describes an expansionary fiscal policy? Government expenditures increase, therefore aggregate demand

a increases, leading to an increase in real GDP, leading to an increase in money demand, leading to a decrease in the interest rate, leading to a further increase in real GDP.

b increases, leading to an increase in the price level, leading to an increase in quantity of real money, leading to a decrease in the interest rate, leading to a further increase in real GDP.

c decreases, leading to an increase in real GDP, leading to an increase in money demand, leading to a decrease in the interest rate, leading to a further increase in real GDP.

d increases, leading to a decrease in the price level, leading to an increase in money demand, leading to a decrease in the interest rate, leading to a partially offsetting increase in real GDP.

e increases, leading to an increase in real GDP, leading to an increase in money demand, leading to an increase in the interest rate, leading to a partially offsetting decrease in real GDP.

7 Crowding in refers to the tendency for an increase in government expenditures on goods and services to

a induce an increase in money demand, leading to an increase in interest rates and a decrease in investment.

b induce a decrease in money demand, leading to a decrease in interest rates and an increase in investment.

c induce an increase in the quantity of money.

d raise interest rates, which leads to an increase in the exchange rate, leading to a decrease in net exports.

e raise profit expectations in the private sector, leading to an increase in investment demand.

8 Crowding out is the effect of expansionary fiscal policy on

a the exchange rate and therefore the quantity of real money.

b the exchange rate and therefore the level of imports.

c the exchange rate and therefore investment.

d the interest rate and therefore investment.

e the interest rate and therefore money demand.

9 The total impact of a *contractionary* fiscal policy is to decrease real GDP,

a reduce the interest rate, and reduce investment.

b reduce the interest rate, and increase investment.

c increase the interest rate, and reduce investment.

d increase the interest rate, and increase investment.

e none of the above.

10 Overall, a tax cut will

a increase aggregate demand by causing consumption to increase.

b increase aggregate demand by causing the interest rate to decrease.

c decrease aggregate demand by causing consumption to decrease.

d decrease aggregate demand by causing the interest rate to increase.

e decrease aggregate demand by causing investment to decrease.

11 Which of the following effects could offset fiscal policy?

a The crowding-in effect

b The exchange rate effect

c The import effect

d The consumption effect

e The bond rate effect

Monetary Policy in the Short Run

12 Which of the following describes the start of a *second-round* effect of an expansionary monetary policy?

a Interest rates decrease, Canadian dollar depreciates, prices of exports decrease, and prices of imports increase

b Interest rates increase, Canadian dollar depreciates, prices of exports increase, and prices of imports decrease

c Interest rates decrease, Canadian dollar appreciates, prices of exports increase, and prices of imports decrease

d Interest rates increase, Canadian dollar depreciates, prices of exports decrease, and prices of imports increase

e Interest rates decrease, expenditure increases, aggregate expenditure increases, real GDP increases, and demand for real money increases

13 The stimulative effects of fiscal and monetary policy on aggregate demand are reduced when the resulting increase in the price level increases interest rates, that in turn decrease

a just investment, but not net exports nor consumption.

b just net exports, but not investment nor consumption.

c just consumption, but not investment nor net exports.

d both consumption and investment, but not net exports.

e all three of consumption, investment, and net exports.

14 Consider the *AD-AS* model with unemployment. After an expansionary monetary policy has increased aggregate demand, the overall effect on real GDP is

a a decrease because of the increase in the price level.

b an increase even more than the initial aggregate demand effect because of the increase in the price level.

c zero due to the increase in the price level.

d zero due to the decrease in the price level.

e an increase, but by a smaller amount than the initial aggregate demand effect because of the increase in the price level.

15 The total impact of a contractionary monetary policy is to decrease real GDP,

a reduce the interest rate, and reduce investment.

b reduce the interest rate, and increase investment.

c increase the interest rate, and reduce investment.

d increase the interest rate, and increase investment.

e none of the above.

16 An increase in the quantity of money will eventually lead to an increase in real GDP, which will shift the demand curve for real money

a leftward, causing the interest rate to decrease.

b leftward, causing the interest rate to increase.

c rightward, causing the interest rate to decrease.

d rightward, causing the interest rate to increase.

e rightward, causing the quantity of real money to increase.

Relative Effectiveness of Policies

17 Monetary policy will have the *smallest* effect on aggregate demand when the sensitivity of the demand for real money to the interest rate is

a large and the sensitivity of expenditure to the interest rate is large.

b large and the sensitivity of expenditure to the interest rate is small.

c small and the sensitivity of aggregate supply to the interest rate is large.

d small and the sensitivity of expenditure to the interest rate is small.

e small and the sensitivity of expenditure to the interest rate is large.

18 Consider an economy where the demand for real money is very sensitive to changes in the interest rate. The problem with monetary policy in this economy is that

a there will be a high level of crowding out.

b monetary policy will create changes in the exchange rate that offset the monetary policy.

c a change in the interest rate creates only a small change in expenditure.

d a change in the quantity of real money creates too large a change in the interest rate.

e a change in the quantity of real money creates only a small change in the interest rate.

19 Statistical evidence from a variety of historical and national experiences suggests that

a fiscal policy affects aggregate demand and monetary policy does not.

b monetary policy affects aggregate demand and fiscal policy does not.

c both fiscal policy and monetary policy affect aggregate demand.

d neither fiscal policy nor monetary policy affect aggregate demand.

e fiscal policy affected aggregate demand only during the Great Depression of the 1930s.

20 A Keynesian believes the economy is inherently

a unstable, and fiscal policy is more important than monetary policy.

b unstable, and monetary policy is more important than fiscal policy.

c stable, and fiscal policy is more important than monetary policy.

d stable, and monetary policy is more important than fiscal policy.

e stable, and crowding out is strong.

Policy Actions at Full Employment

21 If the aggregate supply curve was vertical, expansionary fiscal policy would cause all of the following *except*

a an increase in investment.

b a decrease in the quantity of real money.

c an increase in interest rates.

d an increase in the price level.

e a decrease in investment.

22 Which of the following is the long-run neutrality proposition?

a Changes in the quantity of money change the price level only, not real variables.

b Changes in the quantity of money change real variables only, not the price level.

c In the long run, fiscal policy is 100 percent crowded out.

d In the long run, expenditure is completely unresponsive to changes in the interest rate, so monetary policy does not work.

e In the long run, money demand is completely unresponsive to changes in the interest rate, so fiscal policy does not work.

23 If there is an expansionary fiscal policy at full employment, which of the following effects does *not* occur in the long run?

a Crowding out.

b Higher price.

c International crowding out.

d Labour shortages increase the wage rate.

e Increases in money demand permanently increase the interest rate.

Policy Coordination and Conflict

24 Coordinating fiscal and monetary policy is better for the economy because it

a allows cheap financing of the deficit.

b allows the desired change in interest rates by appropriately mixing monetary and fiscal policy.

c has the opposite effects on the interest rate and the exchange rate.

d can stop inflation.

e none of the above.

25 Aggregate demand can be increased by either expansionary monetary policy or expansionary fiscal policy. Which of the following is a correct comparison?

a The interest rate will increase under the monetary policy and decrease under the fiscal policy, while consumption will increase under both.

b The interest rate will decrease under the monetary policy and increase under the fiscal policy, while consumption will increase under both.

c Consumption will increase under the monetary policy and decrease under the fiscal policy, while the interest rate will increase under both.

d Consumption will increase under the monetary policy and decrease under the fiscal policy, while the interest rate will decrease under both.

e Consumption will decrease under both the monetary policy and fiscal policy, while the interest rate will increase under both.

Short Answer Problems

1 Trace the main steps following an increase in the quantity of real money.

2 Why does an increase in the quantity of real money have a smaller effect on aggregate demand if the demand for real money is very sensitive to changes in the interest rate?

3 Explain how an increase in the quantity of real money leads to an increase in aggregate demand through a change in the exchange rate.

4 How does crowding out take place?

5 Consider an economy that has real GDP less than potential, and needs an expansionary policy. Evaluate an expansionary fiscal policy versus an expansionary monetary policy, on the basis of the following four considerations:

a the empirical evidence on the relative effectiveness of each policy

b the impacts of each on expenditure

c the impacts of each on potential GDP

d the impacts of each on the deficit

6 Figure 27.2 depicts an economy. Note that MD_0 corresponds to real GDP = $400 billion, MD_1 corresponds to real GDP = $500 billion, and MD_2 corresponds to real GDP = $600 billion. MS_0 corresponds to a price level of 110, and AD_0 corresponds to an expenditure level of 100.

a What are the equilibrium values for real GDP, the interest rate, and expenditure?

b Is this equilibrium a consistent equilibrium? Why or why not?

FIGURE **27.2**

(a)

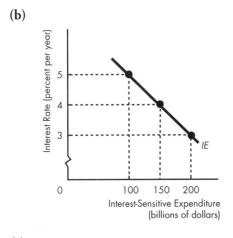

(b)

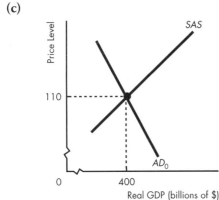

(c)

7 Consider again the economy depicted by Figure 27.2. Suppose that the Bank of Canada increases the quantity of real money from $300 billion to $400 billion.

a What is the initial effect on the interest rate? Illustrate this effect on Figure 27.2.

b What effect will this change in the interest rate have on expenditure?

c As a result of this change in expenditure, what happens to the quantity of real GDP demanded if the multiplier is 2? Illustrate this change on Figure 27.2.

d As best as you can (not worrying too much about exact numbers), show on Figure 27.2 what the final equilibrium is after this change, explaining what has happened to the interest rate, expenditure, real GDP, and the price level as a result of the increase in the quantity of real money.

8 Suppose that as a result of the increase in real GDP in Short Answer Problem **7**, firms' expectations of future profits increase.

a What happens to expenditure as a result? What is this effect called?

b What will be the first- and second-round results of this increase in firms' profit expectations? Specifically, what happens to *AD*, *IE*, *MD*, *r*, real GDP, and the price level? (A written explanation is sufficient.)

9 Suppose the economy in Short Answer Problem **7** was initially at full employment. Describe what would happen in the *AD-SAS* equilibrium in the long run after the increase in the quantity of real money.

10 When Canada had a large debt in the early 1990s, some analysts called for the Bank of Canada to erase the debt by printing money and buying up all the outstanding government bonds. Explain why the Bank of Canada strongly resisted this policy suggestion.

ANSWERS

True/False and Explain

1 F Increase in *r* leads to movement along *IE* curve. (628)

2 T Draw a graph. (628)

3 F More real GDP means more spending, which increases desired inventory holdings, shift *rightward* in demand curve. (628)

4 F Depends on relative strength of each effect, which is unknown. (633)

5 F Increase in *G* leads to an increase in real GDP and *P*, which leads to an increase in *MD* and a decrease in *MS*, creating an increase in *r* and therefore a decrease in *I*. (630–633)

6 F Increase in government expenditures increases real GDP, which increases money demand, which increases the interest rate, which increases the demand for the Canadian dollar, which increases the exchange rate. (633)

7 T Increase in *MS* leads to a decrease in *r*, which leads to increase in *I*, which shifts *AD* rightward. (634–635)

8 F Increase in *MS* creates an excess supply of money, which leads to a decrease in interest rates. (634–637)

9 F Increase in *MS* leads to a decrease in *r*, which leads to a decrease in demand for Canadian assets, leading to decrease in demand for Canadian dollar and therefore a decrease in the exchange rate. (637)

10 T Δ*MS* works by Δ*r* creating Δ*IE* and therefore Δ*AD*, so if impact of *r* on *IE* is larger, impact of Δ*MS* on *AD* is larger. (638)

11 F Steep *IE* curve is not responsive to an increase in *r*. Crowding out happens due to expansionary fiscal policy creating an increase in *r*, and the smaller the impact of the increase in *r*, the smaller the crowding out. (637)

12 T See text discussion. (638–639)

ⓒⓣ **13 T** In the long run, the economy returns to a full-employment equilibrium. (640–641)

14 T The increase in government expenditures shifts *AD* curve rightward, but net effect is zero for real GDP. (640)

15 T By picking the appropriate mixture of fiscal policy (which tends to increase *r*) and monetary policy (which tends to decrease *r*), the authorities can have no change in *r*, and therefore no crowding out. (642–643)

Multiple-Choice

1 d Increases in aggregate demand increase the price level (and therefore lower the quantity of real money and raise the interest rate). (628)

2 a See text description. (628)

ⓒⓣ **3 c** The higher equilibrium real GDP will shift money demand—therefore current money demand is inconsistent. (628–629)

ⓒⓣ **4 a** The current real GDP of $800 billion will raise money demand, which leads to increase in interest rate, and therefore a decrease in expenditure, which leads to decrease in aggregate demand and in equilibrium real GDP. (628–629)

5 e By definition of *IE* curve and components of *AD*. (628–629)

6 e An increase in *G* leads to an increase in *AD*, which creates an increase in real GDP, and therefore an increase in *MD*, which creates an increase in *r*, and therefore a decrease in *IE*, resulting in a decrease in *AD* and in real GDP. (630–633)

7 e Definition. (633)

8 d Definition. (633)

9 b Decrease in real GDP and *P* leads to decrease in money demand and increase in *MS*, which leads to decrease in interest rate and therefore increase in expenditure. (630–633)

10 a Decrease in taxes increases disposable income, leading to increase in consumption and aggregate demand. (630–633)

11 b Increase in real GDP leads to an increase in money demand, which leads to an increase in *r* and therefore the exchange rate, as well as a decrease in expenditure. (633)

12 e The increase in *AD* increases *MD*, which leads to an increase in *r* and a decrease in expenditure, a decrease in *AD*, which leads to a decrease in real GDP, moderating the increase in real GDP. (634–637)

13 e Increase in price level creates an increase in *r*, which leads to an increase in cost of borrowing, lowering *C* and *I*; increase in *r* leads to an increase in demand for Canadian dollar, which leads to increase in exchange rate and a decrease in *NX*. (634–637)

14 e Shift rightward in *AD* curve leads to an increase in price level leads, which leads to an increase in *r* and a decrease in aggregate demand. (634–637)

15 c Decrease in real GDP and *P* leads to decrease in money demand and increase in *MS*, which leads to decrease in interest rate (somewhat offsetting original increase), which leads to increase in expenditure but not enough to overcome initial decrease in expenditure. (634–637)

16 d Money demand depends positively on real GDP, so higher real GDP leads to increase in money demand and increase in interest rate. (634–637)

17 b Sensitive *MD* implies a Δ*MS* leads to small Δ*r*, and insensitive *IE* implies Δ*r* leads to small Δ expenditure. (638)

18 e Because with sensitive money demand, Δ interest rate needed to get money market in equilibrium after Δ quantity of real money is small. (638)

19 c See text discussion. (638–639)

20 a See text discussion. (638–639)

21 a Expansionary policy creates crowding out (decrease in *I*). (640–641)

22 a Definition. (641)

ⓒⓣ **23 e** Real GDP is unchanged, so money demand is unchanged. (640–641)

24 b Monetary and fiscal policy have opposite effects on interest rates—using both at same time in different strengths means can get Δ*r* at desired level. (642)

25 b Under both, increase in real GDP leads to increase in consumption. Under fiscal policy, crowding out leads to increase in interest rate. Under monetary policy, increase in quantity of real money leads to decrease in interest rate. (642)

Short Answer Problems

1 An increase in the quantity of real money
- will shift the money supply curve rightward and decrease the interest rate.
- the lower interest rate will cause expenditure to increase.
- the increase in expenditure means that aggregate demand increases.
- the increase in aggregate demand increases real GDP and the price level.
- increasing real GDP causes the demand curve for real money to shift rightward and the increasing price level causes the money supply curve to shift leftward, causing the interest rate to increase.
- the higher interest rate will cause expenditure to decrease.
- the decrease in expenditure means that aggregate demand decreases somewhat, but the economy converges to a new equilibrium with higher real GDP.

2 If the demand for real money is very sensitive to changes in the interest rate, the demand curve for real money is very flat. Thus when the quantity of money increases and the money supply curve shifts rightward, the resulting change in the equilibrium interest rate will be small. *Ceteris paribus*, a small interest rate change will lead to a small change in expenditure and a small change in aggregate demand.

3 An increase in the quantity of money will shift the money supply curve rightward and decrease the interest rate. The lower interest rate (relative to interest rates in other countries) will cause people to want to sell low-interest Canadian financial assets and buy relatively high-interest foreign financial assets. Therefore the demand for dollars decreases and the demand for foreign currencies increases, which results in a lower exchange rate relative to foreign currencies. This decrease in the exchange rate will cause net exports to increase as foreigners can now buy Canadian goods for less (in terms of their currencies) and Canadians must pay more (in dollars) for foreign goods. The increase in net exports creates an increase in aggregate demand.

4 Crowding out is the tendency for expansionary fiscal policy to cause the interest rate to increase and thus investment to decline. Expansionary fiscal policy "crowds out" investment. An increase in government expenditure on goods and services increases real GDP and the price level, causing the demand curve for real money to shift rightward, and the money supply curve to shift leftward. Thus the equilibrium interest rate will increase.

5 a The empirical evidence is that both policies work with a fair degree of strength, so you could pick either.
b An expansionary fiscal policy raises interest rates, and therefore will decrease investment, while an expansionary monetary policy decreases interest rates and will raise investment. On these grounds, you would tend to pick monetary policy.
c The fiscal policy decreases investment, which means in the long run less capital stock and less growth of potential GDP, while the monetary policy has the opposite effect. On these grounds, you would tend to pick monetary policy.
d Expansionary fiscal policy usually means some combination of more spending and lower taxes, which leads to a higher deficit. Expansionary monetary policy has no impact on the deficit, so you would tend to pick it.

6 a The equilibrium value for real GDP is at the intersection of the AD_0 and SAS curves—$400 billion. The equilibrium value for the interest rate is 5 percent, since the relevant MD curve is MD_0 when real GDP is $400 billion. At an interest rate of 5 percent, expenditure is $100 billion (part (b)).
b This equilibrium is a consistent equilibrium because equilibrium real GDP is $400 billion when the interest rate is 5 percent and the equilibrium interest rate is 5 percent when real GDP is $400 billion. In other words, it is a consistent equilibrium because the values of real GDP and the interest rate that give money market equilibrium and AD-SAS equilibrium are the same.

7 a The initial effect of an increase in the quantity of real money from $300 billion to $400 billion is to decrease the interest rate from 5 percent to 3 percent. This shift is illustrated in part (a) of Figure 27.2 Solution as the shift from MS_0 to MS_1.
b The decrease in the interest rate from 5 percent to 3 percent will increase expenditure from $100 billion to $200 billion.

c If the multiplier is 2, the $100 billion increase in expenditure translates into a rightward shift of the *AD* curve by $200 billion (quantity of real GDP demanded rises by $200 billion), as shown.

d The increase in the quantity of real GDP demanded will raise real GDP and the price level. The rise in real GDP will shift the *MD* curve rightward, and the rise in the price level will shift the *MS* curve leftward, as shown in Figure 27.2 Solution. Your graph might have different numerical values, but the final value of the interest rate should be between 3 percent and 5 percent, etc. The result is a shift leftward in the *AD* curve to AD_2, and a movement along this new *AD* curve to the new equilibrium with real GDP = $500 billion and the price level = 120.

FIGURE **27.2** SOLUTION

(a)

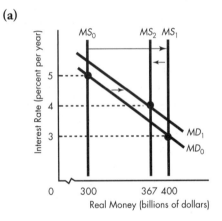

(b)

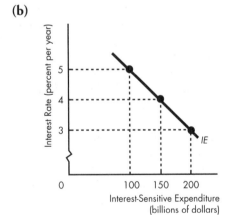

(c)

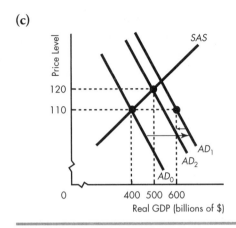

8 a The higher profit expectations leads firms to raise their investment demand, shifting the *IE* curve rightward. This effect is called crowding in.

b The higher investment demand leads to an increase in the quantity of real GDP demanded—the *AD* curve shifts rightward. The shift in the *AD* curve leads to higher real GDP and a higher price level, which leads to the second-round effects—real money demand increases as a result of the higher real GDP and the quantity of real money decreases due to the higher price level, leading to higher interest rates, which in turn lead to lower expenditure, decreasing aggregate demand and lower real GDP, which somewhat crowds out the first-round effects.

9 If the economy was initially at full employment, after the move to the new equilibrium at the intersection of AD_2 and *SAS*, the economy is in an above-full-employment equilibrium. As a result, there will be a shortage of labour, which will lead to an increase in the wage rate. This increase in the wage rate increases the costs of production, and aggregate supply decreases—the *SAS* starts shifting leftward, until the economy goes back to full employment at the original level of real GDP, with a higher price level.

10 If the Bank of Canada buys up the debt, this is equivalent to an enormous open-market purchase of government securities. The result will be a large rise in the quantity of money, which will lower interest rates, increase interest-sensitive expenditure, and shift the *AD* curve rightward, creating strong inflationary pressure. Since the Bank of Canada considers resisting inflation as its primary objective, it would strongly resist such a proposal.

Chapter 28

Inflation

Inflation and the Price Level

Inflation is the ongoing increase in the price level (P) with money losing value.

♦ Inflation rate = annual percentage change in price level = $\dfrac{P_1 - P_0}{P_0} \times 100$

Demand-Pull Inflation

Demand-pull inflation arises from increasing aggregate demand due to increases in quantity of money or government expenditures or exports.

♦ In short run, result is increase in P (inflation), increase in Y, decrease in unemployment to below natural rate.

♦ Unemployment less than the natural rate creates labour shortage, which leads to increase in wages and costs, so that SAS shifts leftward, and price level increases even more, but real GDP is back to the original level.

♦ If AD shifts rightward again, and wages increase again, a *price-wage spiral* may result.

♦ Persistent inflation requires persistent increases in quantity of money.

Cost-Push Inflation

Cost-push inflation arises from decreasing aggregate supply, due to increase in costs (increase in money wage rates and money prices of raw materials).

♦ Firms decrease production, so that SAS shifts leftward creating stagflation (increase in price level, decrease in real GDP).

♦ If government or Bank of Canada shifts AD rightward in response, price level increases again, so that input owners raise input prices again, and a cost-push inflation spiral may result.

♦ If there is no government or Bank response— economy remains below full employment.

The Quantity Theory of Money

Quantity theory of money predicts increase in quantity of money leads to increase in price level by same percentage.

♦ Quantity theory starts with definition of **velocity of circulation** ($V = PY/M$), which leads to the equation of exchange ($MV = PY$).

• Assumes velocity and potential GDP are unaffected by Δ quantity of money.
• Then, in long run $\%\Delta P = \%\Delta M$.

♦ Historical evidence suggests money growth rate strongly influences inflation.

Effects of Inflation

Incorrect inflation forecasts are costly in labour markets.

♦ If inflation > anticipated, then money wages set too low and employers gain, workers lose income, but firm has trouble keeping workers as a result.

♦ If inflation < anticipated, then money wages set too high and employers lose, workers gain income, but firm lays off workers as a result.

Incorrect forecasts in capital markets lead to incorrect borrowing/lending and income redistribution.

♦ If inflation > anticipated, then interest rates set too low, and borrowers gain at expense of lenders, but both wished to have made different decisions.

◆ If inflation < anticipated, then interest rates set too high, lenders gain at expense of borrowers, but both wished to have made different decisions.

People forecast inflation in different ways, including hiring specialists, who make best possible forecast on the basis of all available relevant information (a **rational expectation**).

◆ If increase in *AD* correctly anticipated, then money wages adjust to keep up with anticipated inflation, Δ price level only, no Δ real GDP or employment.

◆ If increase in *AD* more than expected, then increase in money wage only reflects expected part, and the result is new above full-employment equilibrium to right of potential GDP, which leads eventually to increase in money wages and *SAS* leftward again.

◆ If increase in *AD* less than expected, then increase in money wage to reflect expected change results in a new below full-employment equilibrium to left of potential GDP.

Anticipated inflation decreases potential GDP and lowers economic growth due to higher transactions costs, tax effects, and increased uncertainty.

Inflation and Unemployment: The Phillips Curve

Phillips curve shows relationship between inflation and unemployment.

◆ **Short-run Phillips curve** (*SRPC*) shows relationship between inflation and unemployment for a given expected inflation rate and natural rate of unemployment. It is negatively sloped.

◆ In short run, if actual inflation > expected, then movement up and leftward along *SRPC*.

◆ **Long-run Phillips curve** (*LRPC*) shows relationship between inflation and unemployment when actual inflation = expected. It is vertical at the natural rate of unemployment.

◆ A decrease in expected inflation rate shifts *SRPC* downward.

◆ An increase in natural rate of unemployment shifts both *LRPC* and *SRPC* rightward.

Interest Rates and Inflation

A large part of changes in nominal rate of interest are due to changes in expected inflation.

◆ Real interest rate determined by global investment demand and saving supply plus national risk differences.

◆ Nominal interest rate determined by money demand and quantity of money.

◆ An increase in expected inflation leads to an increase in nominal interest rate by equivalent amount, keeping real rate of interest constant.

HELPFUL HINTS

1 An important concept introduced in this chapter is that of a *rational expectation*—the best possible forecast based on all available relevant information. Text Fig. 28.9 applies this concept to forecasting the price level. We know the *actual* price level is found in the short run at the intersection of the *AD* curve and the *SAS* curve, and in the long run at the intersection of the *AD* curve and the *LAS* curve. Thus in Fig. 28.9, when *AD* is expected to increase to AD_1, the best *forecast* of the new price level (the forecast most likely to be correct) is at the intersection of AD_1 and *LAS*, yielding a wage demand that in turn leads to SAS_1.

Note that the rational expectation of the price level will be at the intersection of the *expected* aggregate demand curve and the *expected short-run* aggregate supply curve in the short run, and the *expected long-run* aggregate supply curve in the long run. The *actual* equilibrium, which determines the *actual* price level, is at the intersection of the *actual* aggregate demand curve and the *actual short-run* aggregate supply curve.

2 An important equation in this chapter is the equation of exchange:

$$\text{Quantity of money} \times \text{Velocity of circulation} = \text{Price level} \times \text{Real GDP}$$

This equation simply says that the quantity of money times the average number of times each dollar is spent (equalling total expenditure) is equal to the dollar value of the goods and services on which it was spent. The equation is always true by definition—it is an identity. If we further assume that the velocity of circulation and potential GDP are independent of the quantity of money, we get the quantity theory of money. These assumptions imply that when the quantity of money increases by 10 percent, the price level must increase by 10 percent in order to maintain equality between the two sides of the equation.

3 Students (and politicians and commentators!) are often confused by the fact that sometimes a decrease in the growth rate of money leads to an *increase* in the interest rate, and sometimes it leads to a *decrease* in the interest rate. The key to understanding this difference is to focus on the time frame—short- or long-run. Figure 28.1 illustrates the changes in the nominal rate of interest over time when the growth rate of money is lowered. Initially, the rate of interest is r_0, and then there is an unanticipated decrease in the growth rate of the money at time T*, which leads to an unexpectedly low level of the money supply. As we saw in Chapter 27, in the short run this decrease in the money supply will lead to an increase in the rate of interest (to the level r_1), which in turn leads to a decrease in investment demand and aggregate demand. If this change is unexpected, it leads to lower inflation and lower real GDP. In the long run, once economic agents realize that the lower inflation is going to remain in place, they lower their forecast of inflation, which in turn lowers the nominal rate of interest to a level such as r_2.

FIGURE **28.1**

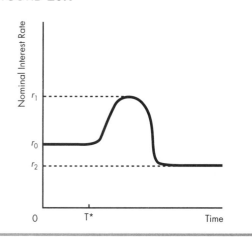

SELF - TEST

True/False and Explain

Inflation and the Price Level

1 If the price level at the beginning of 2000 is 120 and the price level at the beginning of 2001 is 130, the rate of inflation is 8.3 percent.

Demand-Pull Inflation

2 Increases in government expenditures alone can create persistent inflation.

3 An increase in exports cannot create demand-pull inflation.

Cost-Push Inflation

4 The inflation resulting from expansionary monetary policy is an example of cost-push inflation.

5 Stagflation occurs when real GDP decreases and the price level increases.

The Quantity Theory of Money

6 If the quantity of money is $50 billion and nominal GDP is $200 billion, the velocity of circulation is 1/4.

Effects of Inflation

7 When inflation is unanticipated there are no negative effects on the economy.

8 If people expect aggregate demand to increase but it does not, the price level will increase and real GDP will decrease.

9 If an increase in aggregate demand is correctly anticipated, inflation will not occur.

10 If there is an unexpected increase in the rate of inflation, employers will gain at the expense of workers.

11 A rational expectation is a forecast that is always correct.

Inflation and Unemployment: The Phillips Curve

12 The short-run Phillips curve shows that if there is an increase in the inflation rate, unemployment will decrease.

13 The long-run Phillips curve shows a tradeoff between inflation and unemployment.

14 If there is an increase in the expected rate of inflation, then the long-run Phillips curve shifts rightward.

Interest Rates and Inflation

15 An increase in expected inflation will lead to an equivalent increase in the nominal interest rate.

Multiple-Choice

Inflation and the Price Level

1 The current year's price level is 180, and the rate of inflation over the past year has been 20 percent. What was last year's price level?

a 100
b 144
c 150
d 160
e 216

Demand-Pull Inflation

2 Demand-pull inflation occurs when

a aggregate demand increases.
b aggregate supply decreases.
c input costs increase.
d people incorrectly forecast inflation.
e unemployment is above the natural rate.

3 Which of the following would cause the aggregate demand curve to keep shifting rightward year after year?

a a one-time tax cut
b a one-time increase in government expenditures on goods and services
c inflation
d excess wage demands
e a positive rate of money growth

Cost-Push Inflation

4 An increase in the price level due to an increase in the price of oil

a will create a stagflation in the short run and *will* trigger a price-wage spiral.
b will create a stagflation in the short run and *may* trigger a price-wage spiral.
c will raise output above potential GDP.
d must lead to an increase in the wage rate.
e must lead to a decrease in the wage rate.

5 Figure 28.2 illustrates an economy initially in equilibrium at point *a*. What would cause the short-run aggregate supply curve to shift from SAS_0 to SAS_1?

a an increase in the price of oil
b an increase in the price level
c an increase in the marginal product of labour
d an increase in the demand for money
e a decrease in wages

FIGURE **28.2**

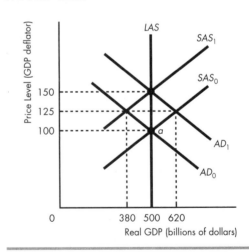

The Quantity Theory of Money

6 The quantity theory of money begins with the equation of exchange—$MV = PY$—and then adds the assumptions that

a velocity varies inversely with the rate of interest, and the price level is independent of the quantity of money.

b velocity and the price level are independent of the quantity of money.

c potential GDP and the quantity of money are independent of the price level.

d potential GDP and the price level are independent of the quantity of money.

e velocity and potential GDP are independent of the quantity of money.

7 According to the quantity theory of money,

a V/M is constant.

b Y/M is constant.

c Y/P is constant.

d M/P is constant.

e M/V is constant.

8 According to the quantity theory of money, an increase in the quantity of money will lead to an increase in the price level

a but have no effect on real GDP or the velocity of circulation.

b as well as increasing both real GDP and the velocity of circulation.

c as well as increasing real GDP but decreasing the velocity of circulation.

d as well as decreasing real GDP but increasing the velocity of circulation.

e but have no effect on real GDP while decreasing velocity.

Effects of Inflation

9 If the AD curve in Figure 28.2 is correctly expected to shift from AD_0 to AD_1, what will be the new equilibrium real GDP and price level?

a $380 billion and price level = 125

b $500 billion and price level = 150

c $500 billion and price level = 100

d $620 billion and price level = 125

e $500 billion and price level = 125

10 If the AD curve in Figure 28.2 is expected to shift from AD_0 to AD_1 but, in fact, remains at AD_0, what will be the new equilibrium real GDP and price level?

a $380 billion and price level = 100

b $500 billion and price level = 150

c $500 billion and price level = 100

d $620 billion and price level = 125

e $380 billion and price level = 125

11 If the AD curve in Figure 28.2 is expected to remain at AD_0 but, in fact, shifts to AD_1, what will be the new equilibrium real GDP and price level?

a $380 billion and price level = 125

b $500 billion and price level = 150

c $500 billion and price level = 100

d $620 billion and price level = 125

e $500 billion and price level = 125

12 Which of the following business quotes illustrates costs associated with an anticipated inflation?

a "The bank is losing money on its loans, given the current rate of interest."

b "Wage increases were low last year, but I am having trouble keeping workers."

c "I find I have to send invoices out to customers twice a month now, because of the higher inflation."

d "The low inflation rate means my borrowing costs are too high."

e None of the above.

13 If the rate of inflation is lower than anticipated,

a lenders will gain at the expense of borrowers, and workers will gain at the expense of employers.

b borrowers will gain at the expense of lenders, and workers will gain at the expense of employers.

c lenders will gain at the expense of borrowers, and employers will gain at the expense of workers.

d borrowers will gain at the expense of lenders, and employers will gain at the expense of workers.

e lenders will gain at the expense of borrowers, and whether employers or workers will gain is uncertain.

14 In an economy with the price level greater than expected and output above the natural rate, which of the following is a possible explanation, *ceteris paribus*?

a Potential real GDP has increased by more than expected.
b Potential real GDP has increased by less than expected.
c Aggregate demand has decreased by more than expected.
d Aggregate demand has increased by less than expected.
e Aggregate demand has increased by more than expected.

15 A fully anticipated increase in the rate of inflation

a is not costly because contracts can be adjusted.
b benefits both workers and employers.
c is costly because it increases the value of money.
d is costly because it encourages an increase in the frequency of transactions that people undertake.
e is costly because it redistributes from lender to borrower.

16 Which of the following is *not* true of a rational expectation forecast?

a It uses all available information.
b It can be wrong.
c It is always correct.
d It is the best possible forecast.
e Sometimes economic agents purchase their forecasts from specialists.

17 The price level is expected to decrease because of an expected decrease in aggregate demand. If aggregate demand remains unchanged, then the actual price level will

a stay the same and real GDP will stay the same.
b decrease and real GDP will decrease.
c increase and real GDP will increase.
d increase and real GDP will decrease.
e decrease and real GDP will increase.

Inflation and Unemployment: The Phillips Curve

18 The short-run Phillips curve shows the relationship between

a the price level and real GDP in the short run.
b the price level and unemployment in the short run.
c unemployment and real GDP in the short run.
d inflation and unemployment, when inflation expectations can change.
e inflation and unemployment, when inflation expectations do not change.

19 Figure 28.3 illustrates an economy's Phillips curves. What is the natural rate of unemployment?

a 9 percent
b 6 percent
c 4 percent
d depends on the actual inflation rate
e cannot be determined without more information

FIGURE **28.3**

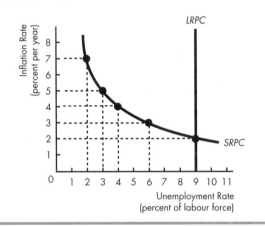

20 Figure 28.3 illustrates an economy's Phillips curves. What is the expected inflation rate?

a 9 percent
b 4 percent
c 2 percent
d depends on the actual inflation rate
e cannot be determined without more information

21 Figure 28.3 illustrates an economy's Phillips curves. If the current inflation rate is 4 percent, what is the current unemployment rate?

a 9 percent
b 6 percent
c 4 percent
d 3 percent
e cannot be determined without more information

22 If the inflation rate is lower than the expected inflation rate,

a unemployment will be above the natural rate.
b the natural rate of unemployment will increase.
c the expected inflation rate will increase.
d unemployment will be below the natural rate.
e the economy must off the *SRPC*.

23 If there is an increase in the inflation rate that is fully anticipated, then

a unemployment will be below the natural rate.
b unemployment will be above the natural rate.
c the natural rate of unemployment will increase.
d the economy must be off the *LRPC*.
e the economy must be on the *LRPC*.

Interest Rates and Inflation

24 Suppose that initially the nominal rate of interest is 8 percent and the expected rate of inflation is 5 percent. If the expected rate of inflation increases to 8 percent, what will the new nominal rate of interest be?

a 3 percent
b 8 percent
c 11 percent
d 13 percent
e 16 percent

25 A correctly anticipated increase in the rate of growth of the quantity of money will cause nominal interest rates to

a decrease and real interest rates to decrease.
b decrease and leave real interest rates unchanged.
c increase and real interest rates to increase.
d increase and leave real interest rates unchanged.
e increase and real interest rates to decrease.

Short Answer Problems

I What will happen to the price level and real GDP if the government increases its expenditures on goods and services and that increase is not anticipated (the price level is not expected to change)?

2 Explain how the events in Short Answer Problem **1** could lead to a price-wage spiral.

3 What is the relationship between the expected rate of inflation and nominal interest rates?

4 Explain carefully the difference between the short-run Phillips curve and the long-run Phillips curve.

5 Sometimes politicians or other commentators make the following type of statement: "Unemployment is a more serious economic and social problem than inflation. Increasing inflation by a small amount in order to lower unemployment is therefore worthwhile." Briefly evaluate this statement.

6 Why does inflation start? Why does it persist?

7 Table 28.1 gives the initial actual aggregate demand and short-run aggregate supply schedules for an economy in which the expected price level is 80, and potential real GDP is 500.

a What is actual real GDP and the actual price level?

TABLE **28.1** AGGREGATE DEMAND AND SUPPLY

Price Level	Real GDP Demanded	Real GDP Supplied
60	600	400
80	500	500
100	400	600
120	300	700
140	200	700

b In year 1 the economy is in the equilibrium characterized in **a**. It is *expected* that in year 2, aggregate demand will be as given in Table 28.2. (Assume that the long-run aggregate supply curve is not expected to shift, and does not shift.) What is the *vertical* amount of the expected shift in the aggregate demand curve when real GDP is $500 billion?

TABLE **28.2** AGGREGATE DEMAND AND SUPPLY

Price Level	Real GDP Demanded	Real GDP Supplied
60	800	
80	700	
100	600	
120	500	
140	400	

c What is the (long-run) rational expectation of the price level for year 2?

d The expected shift in aggregate demand will cause the short-run aggregate supply (*SAS*) curve to shift. What will the new *SAS* curve be? For each price level, give the new values of real GDP supplied in the last column of Table 28.2.

8 According to the quantity theory of money, what is the effect of an increase in the quantity of money? What assumptions of the theory are crucial for this effect to occur? Why?

9 We observe an economy in which the price level is 1.5, real GDP is $240 billion, and the quantity of money is $60 billion.

a What is the velocity of circulation?

b According to the quantity theory of money, what will be the result of an increase in the quantity of money to $80 billion?

10 The country of Colditz has an expected inflation rate of 8 percent, and its recent inflation and unemployment history is summarized in Table 28.3. Originally both unemployment and inflation are each 8 percent.

TABLE **28.3**

Inflation (% per year)	Unemployment (%)
12	4
10	6
8	8
6	10
4	12

a What is Colditz's natural rate of unemployment?

b Draw a diagram of Colditz's short-run and long-run Phillips curves.

c If inflation unexpectedly increases to 12 percent per year, explain what happens to unemployment.

d Return to the original situation. If the expected inflation rate increases to 10 percent, and the actual inflation rate increases to 10 percent, explain and show on your graph what happens, *ceteris paribus*, to inflation and unemployment.

A N S W E R S

True/False and Explain

1 **T** Inflation rate = $[(P_1 - P_0)/P_0] \times 100 = [(130 - 120)/120] \times 100 = 8.3$. (650)

2 **F** Persistent inflation requires persistent increases in quantity of money. (652–653)

3 **F** Increase in exports creates shift rightwards in *AD*, which can create demand-pull inflation. (652–653)

4 **F** Cost-push inflation is due to increase in input costs. (651–655)

5 **T** Definition. (653–655)

6 **F** $V = PY/M = 200/50 = 4$. (656)

7 **F** It makes payments from long-term contracts unpredictable, hurting one side or other. (658–661)

8 **T** If expected increase in aggregate demand, then there is an increase in wage demands,

which leads to leftward shift *SAS* curve, but no Δ *AD* curve, resulting in stagflation. (658–661)

9 **F** *AD* shifts rightward, *SAS* shifts leftward due to higher wage demands, so that price level increases. (658–661)

10 **T** Wage increases will be based on expected inflation, and so are too low, resulting in a drop in real wages. (658–659)

11 **F** Correct on *average*. (659)

12 **T** Movement up and leftward along the *SRPC*. (662–664)

13 **F** It is vertical at the natural rate of unemployment. (664)

14 **F** Movement upward along the *LRPC*. (662–665)

15 **T** Lenders demand compensation for expected inflation, borrowers are willing to pay it. (666–667)

Multiple-Choice

1 **c** Inflation rate = $[(P_1 - P_0)/P_0] \times 100$, or $20 = [(180 - P_0)/P_0] \times 100$—solve this for P_0. (650)

2 **a** Definition. (651)

3 **e** **a** and **b** have one-time effects, **c** is caused by Δ*AD*, and **d** is a supply-side effect. (652–653)

4 **b** Increase in price of oil leads to shift leftward in *SAS* curve, creating cost-push inflation (stagflation), which *may* trigger price-wage spiral if government raises aggregate demand. (653–655)

5 **a** Increase in price of crucial input leads to increase in costs of production, and shift leftward in *SAS*. (653–655)

6 **e** See text discussion. (656–657)

7 **d** Because theory assumes $Y/V (= M/P)$ is constant. (656–657)

8 **a** Due to assumption that neither is affected by Δ quantity of money. (656–657)

9 **b** Expected *P* found from intersection of $EAD = AD_1$, and actual new *SAS* is set here, and new equilibrium is where actual *AD* and new *SAS* cross. (659–660)

10 **e** Expected *P* found from intersection of $EAD = AD_1$, and actual new *SAS* is set here, and new equilibrium is where actual *AD* and new *SAS* cross. (659–660)

11 **d** Expected *P* found from intersection of $EAD = AD_0$, and actual new *SAS* is set here, and new equilibrium is where actual *AD* and new *SAS* cross. (659–660)

12 **c** Example of higher transactions costs, the others are unanticipated inflation costs. (658–661)

13 a Because interest rates and wage rates too high given actual inflation rate. (658–661)

14 e Draw a graph. (659–660)

15 d Higher inflation decreases value of money, so people decrease money holdings, which leads to increase in transactions. (658–661)

16 c It is correct on *average*. (659)

17 e Decrease in expected price level leads to shift rightward *SAS*, so new equilibrium to the right of *LAS* along original *AD* curve. (659–660)

18 e Definition. (662–663)

19 a *LRPC* is at natural rate. (664)

20 c Expected inflation rate is where *SRPC* crosses *LRPC*. (664)

21 c Found by reading off the *SRPC*. (662–663)

22 a Draw a Phillips curve. (662–665)

23 e Economy just moves up the *LRPC*. (662–665)

24 c Initially, real rate = 8 − 5 = 3 percent. New nominal rate = real rate + expected inflation = 3 + 8 = 11 percent. (666–667)

25 d Increase in growth rate of quantity of money leads to increase in inflation rate, which leads to increase in nominal rate by same amount (since anticipated). No change in real rate, which is determined on world capital markets. (666–667)

Short Answer Problems

1 An increase in government expenditures on goods and services will shift the aggregate demand curve rightward. If the price level is not expected to change, the short-run aggregate supply curve remains unchanged, and the increase in aggregate demand will cause the price level to increase and real GDP to increase.

2 The higher price level leads to demands for higher wages, which push up the costs of production and shift the *SAS* curve leftward, leading to a further increase in the price level and a decrease in real GDP. A price-wage spiral could result *if* the government once again raises the level of their purchases or if the government continues to run a deficit (financed by printing money), then *AD* will continue to shift rightward, triggering leftward shifts in *SAS*, leading to the price-wage spiral.

3 When the rate of inflation is expected to increase, the nominal interest rate will also increase to compensate for the increased rate at which the purchasing power of money is eroding. The essential point is that lenders and borrowers are interested in the quantity of goods and services that a unit of money will buy. Lenders will insist on the higher interest rate, to compensate for the loss of purchasing power of money, and borrowers will agree because they realize that the dollars they repay will buy fewer goods and services.

4 The short-run Phillips curve is constructed assuming that the expected inflation rate is constant, and is therefore downward-sloping. As a result, if there is an increase in the inflation rate (and therefore a decrease in real wages), there will be a decrease in unemployment to a rate below the natural rate. The long-run Phillips curve is constructed assuming that the expected inflation rate adjusts fully to reflect changes in the actual inflation rate, and is therefore vertical at the natural rate of unemployment. If there is an increase in the actual inflation rate, there is an equivalent increase in the expected inflation rate (so that the real wage rate stays constant), and the rate of unemployment stays constant at the natural rate.

5 Partially this statement is a value judgement, based on the tradeoff of a higher cost to society from the higher inflation versus the gain to society from a lower inflation rate. In this case, we would need to evaluate the costs of inflation vis-à-vis the costs of unemployment. However, there is also an objective (normative) problem with this statement. In the short run, such a tradeoff does exist, represented by the downward-sloping short-run Phillips curve. In the long run, there is no such tradeoff. As a result, a higher inflation rate will lead to a lower unemployment rate in the short run, but eventually inflation expectations will increase, represented by a shift upward in the short-run Phillips curve, and unemployment will return to the natural rate. Therefore in the long run, increasing inflation will have no impact on the unemployment rate, but will increase the costs to society that come from the higher inflation.

6 Inflation is an increase in the price level, and starts with either a shift rightward in the *AD* curve due to an increase in the quantity of money, government spending, or exports (demand-pull inflation), or with a shift leftward in the *SAS* curve due to an increase in wages or raw materials prices (cost-push inflation). However, the increase in the price level in either case can only persist if a price-wage spiral results from the initial shock. A price-wage spiral starts when increases in aggregate demand and shifts

leftward in *SAS* chase each other up the long-run aggregate supply curve.

7 a Actual real GDP and the actual price level are determined by the intersection of the aggregate demand curve and the short-run aggregate supply curve. Real GDP is $500 billion and the price level is 80, because at a price level of 80, the quantity of real GDP demanded equals the quantity of real GDP supplied ($500 billion).

  b The price level associated with $500 billion of real GDP demanded for the original aggregate demand curve (Table 28.1) is 80. The price level associated with $500 billion of real GDP demanded for the new expected aggregate demand curve (Table 28.2) is 120. Therefore the aggregate demand curve is expected to shift upward by 40.

  c The rational expectation of the price level is given by the intersection of the expected aggregate demand curve (Table 28.2) and the expected long-run aggregate supply curve. Long-run aggregate supply is equal to $500 billion and is not expected to change. Since the price level associated with $500 billion of real GDP demanded is 120, the rational expectation of the price level is 120.

  d The quantities of real GDP supplied for the new *SAS* curve are shown in completed Table 28.2 Solution. The original expected price level is 80. From part **b** we know that the new expected price level is 120, which implies that the *SAS* curve shifts up by 40. Thus at each quantity of real GDP supplied, the price level on the new *SAS* curve is 40 points higher than on the original *SAS* curve (Table 28.1).

  For example, real GDP supplied of $500 billion now requires a price level of 120 rather than 80. Similarly, real GDP supplied of $400 billion now requires a price level of 100 rather than 60. (*Note*: The values in parentheses in this table are inferred by extrapolation rather than calculated from Table 28.1.)

TABLE **28.2** SOLUTION
AGGREGATE DEMAND AND SUPPLY

Price Level	Real GDP Demanded	Real GDP Supplied
60	800	(200)
80	700	(300)
100	600	400
120	500	500
140	400	600

8 According to the quantity theory of money, an increase in the quantity of money will cause the price level to increase by an equal percentage. The required assumptions are that velocity and potential GDP are independent of changes in the quantity of money, so that the change in the quantity of money affects only the price level.

9 a The velocity of circulation is defined by

$$\text{Velocity of circulation} = \frac{\text{Price level} \times \text{Real GDP}}{\text{Quantity of money}}$$

With the values for the price level, real GDP, and the quantity of money given in this problem, we have

$$\text{Velocity of circulation} = \frac{1.5 \times 240}{60} = 6$$

  b The quantity theory of money predicts that an increase in the quantity of money will cause an equal percentage increase in the price level. An increase in money from $60 billion to $80 billion is a one-third (33 percent) increase. Thus the quantity theory of money predicts that the price level will increase by a third (33 percent). Since the initial price level is 1.5, the predicted price level will be 2.0. (This value can also be confirmed by using the equation of exchange.)

10 a The natural rate of unemployment is the rate of unemployment that occurs when the actual rate of inflation equals the expected rate of inflation—in this case, the natural rate of unemployment is 8 percent.

  b See Figure 28.4. The long-run Phillips curve is vertical at the natural rate of unemployment. The current short-run curve is $SRPC_0$ (ignore the other short-run curve for the moment).

FIGURE **28.4**

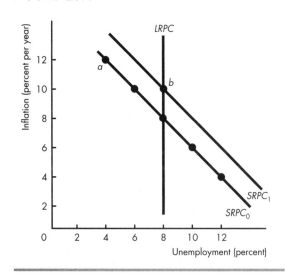

c In this case, the relevant short-run Phillips curve is $SRPC_0$, the curve for an expected inflation rate of 8 percent. From the curve (or Table 28.3), it can be seen that with inflation equal to 12 percent, unemployment is 4 percent at the point *a*.

d An increase in the expected inflation rate will shift the short-run Phillips curve to a new curve, with the new curve crossing the long-run Phillips curve at the new expected inflation rate of 10 percent. (The actual shape of the curve is not clear without further information, so it has been assumed that the new curve is parallel to the old curve.) If the actual inflation rate is 10 percent, the unemployment rate will be 8 percent, at the natural rate, at the point *b*.

Part 8 Wrap Up

Understanding Aggregate Demand and Inflation

PROBLEM

The Canadian economy is originally in a full-employment equilibrium. Suppose that the U.S. economy *unexpectedly* goes into recession.

a Holding constant the price level, carefully explain (and show on a graph) what these changes do to aggregate expenditure and aggregate demand. Explain what happens to each component of aggregate expenditure and real GDP.

b Next, show on your graph and explain what happens to aggregate expenditure and aggregate demand in the short run when the price level adjusts.

The Bank of Canada decides to redress the economy's problems by carrying out an expansionary monetary policy.

c Give an example of the type of open market operation the Bank of Canada would carry out in such a circumstance. Show what happens to the balance sheets of the Bank of Canada and the banking sector as a result of the initial impacts of the operation. What is the overall impact of such an operation on chartered bank reserves, loans, deposit, and the quantity of money?

d Explain what this policy will do to the money supply curve, money demand, the interest rate, investment, net exports, and aggregate demand, holding constant the price level.

e Next, with the price level adjusting, explain what this policy does to the *AD-SAS* equilibrium in the short run.

f Does the quantity theory of money hold in this economy?

MIDTERM EXAMINATION

You should allocate 48 minutes for this examination (24 questions, 2 minutes per question). For each question, choose the best answer.

1 The consumption function shows the relationship between consumption expenditure and
a the interest rate.
b the price level.
c disposable income.
d saving.
e nominal income.

2 A *contractionary* fiscal policy leads to
a a rightward shift in the *AD* curve equal to the multiplier times the policy change.
b a leftward shift in the *AD* curve equal to the multiplier times the policy change.
c a leftward shift in the *SAS* curve.
d an increase in *Y* equal to the multiplier times the policy change, in the short run.
e an increase in *Y* equal to the multiplier times the policy change, in the long run.

3 The Bank of Canada and the government have a potential conflict about the government borrowing from the Bank of Canada because the borrowing will have an impact in the money market. It will

a increase money demand and increase interest rates, lowering investment too much.

b increase money demand and increase interest rates, which puts too much upward pressure on aggregate demand.

c lower the quantity of money and increase interest rates, lowering investment too much.

d increase the quantity of money, creating deflationary pressures.

e increase the quantity of money, creating inflationary pressures.

4 A rise in the natural rate of unemployment is shown as a

a rightward shift in the long-run Phillips curve only.

b leftward shift in the long-run Phillips curve only.

c rightward shift in the short-run Phillips curve only.

d leftward shift in both the short-run and long-run Phillips curves.

e rightward shift in both the short-run and long-run Phillips curves.

5 Which of the following quotations *correctly* describes the impact of monetary policy on the economy?

a "House sales are down a lot, due to the higher money growth."

b "The extra money pumped into the economy by the central bank is creating less exports."

c "The tightening of money growth is helping sell goods abroad."

d "Businesses are investing more, now that monetary policy has become less expansionary."

e "The extra money pumped into the economy by the central bank is creating more jobs."

6 International crowding out refers to the tendency for an increase in government expenditures on goods and services to induce a(n)

a decrease in interest rates, leading to a decrease in the exchange rate, leading to an increase in net exports.

b decrease in interest rates, leading to a withdrawal of foreign funds from Canada.

c increase in interest rates, leading to a decrease in the exchange rate, leading to an increase in net exports.

d increase in interest rates, leading to an increase in the exchange rate, leading to an increase in net exports.

e increase in interest rates, leading to an increase in the exchange rate, leading to a decrease in net exports.

7 If real GDP is less than aggregate planned expenditure,

a aggregate planned expenditure will increase.

b real GDP will decrease.

c the price level must decrease to restore equilibrium.

d imports must be too large.

e aggregate planned expenditure will decrease.

8 Which of the following is *not* a source of budgetary revenues?

a personal income taxes

b transfer payments

c corporate income taxes

d indirect taxes

e investment income

9 Suppose OPEC unexpectedly collapses, leading to a decrease in the price of oil. This is a positive aggregate supply shock. As a result, in the short run the price level will

a increase and real GDP will increase.

b increase and real GDP will decrease.

c decrease and real GDP will increase.

d decrease and real GDP will decrease.

e increase and real GDP will stay the same.

10 A chartered bank can create money by

a selling some of its investment securities.

b increasing its reserves.

c lending its excess reserves.

d printing more cheques.

e converting reserves into securities.

11 According to the quantity theory of money, a decrease in the quantity of money will cause

a both the price level and real GDP to decline in the short run, but, in the long run, only the price level will decrease as real GDP returns to its initial level.

b both the price level and real GDP to increase in the short run, but, in the long run, only the price level will increase as real GDP returns to its initial level.

c the price level to decrease in the short run, but, in the long run, the price level will return to its initial level.

d the price level to decrease and real GDP to increase in both the short run and the long run.

e the price level to decrease and real GDP to decrease in both the short run and the long run.

12 The introduction of induced taxes compared to a situation with only autonomous taxes means

a fiscal policy multipliers are made stronger.

b discretionary fiscal policy is eliminated.

c there is always a structural deficit.

d there is always a cyclical deficit.

e fluctuations in aggregate expenditure are reduced.

13 An open market purchase of government securities by the Bank of Canada will

a increase bank reserves and thus increase the monetary base.

b decrease bank reserves and thus decrease the monetary base.

c increase bank reserves and thus decrease the monetary base.

d decrease bank reserves and thus increase the monetary base.

e decrease bank reserves but increase the quantity of money if banks have excess reserves.

14 When is there complete crowding out of an expansionary fiscal policy?

a if the economy was originally in an under full-employment equilibrium

b if the economy was originally in a full-employment equilibrium

c when there is policy conflict with the Bank of Canada

d when there is policy coordination to ensure the resulting change in the interest rate is zero

e if there is a liquidity trap in the money market

15 An expansionary monetary policy will lead to a decrease in interest rates, which will lead to a(n)

a increase in the demand for the dollar, leading to an increase in the exchange rate, which leads to a decrease in net exports.

b increase in the demand for the dollar, leading to an increase in the exchange rate, which leads to an increase in net exports.

c increase in the demand for the dollar, leading to a decrease in the exchange rate, which leads to an increase in net exports.

d decrease in the demand for the dollar, leading to a decrease in the exchange rate, which leads to an increase in net exports.

e decrease in the demand for the dollar, leading to a decrease in the exchange rate, which leads to a decrease in net exports.

16 Suppose that investment increases by $10 billion. Which of the following would *reduce* the effect of this increase in autonomous expenditure on equilibrium real GDP?

a an increase in the marginal propensity to consume

b a decrease in the marginal propensity to import

c a decrease in the marginal tax rate

d a steeper aggregate supply curve

e a flatter aggregate supply curve

17 An increase in expected inflation raises the nominal interest rate because

a borrowers require compensation for the inflation eroding the value of money.

b lenders require compensation for the inflation eroding the value of money.

c the inflation creates higher transactions costs.

d the real rate of interest rises by an amount equal to the increase in expected inflation.

e none of the above.

18 In a recent study, the University of Underfunded argued that it created four times as many jobs as people it hired directly. This argument illustrates the idea of

a the marginal propensity to consume.

b the multiplier.

c government spending.

d the tax multiplier.

e universities wasting taxpayers' dollars.

19 If the *MPC* is 0.6, and there are no induced taxes or imports, what is the autonomous tax multiplier?

a −1.50
b −1.67
c −2.50
d 2.50
e impossible to calculate without further information

20 Consider the following data on the economy of Adanac:

Currency reserves of private banks	$5 billion
Currency in circulation	15 billion
Demand deposits of banks	40 billion
Demand deposits of other financial institutions	50 billion
Personal savings deposits at other financial institutions	125 billion
Nonpersonal notice deposits at banks	200 billion

What is the value of M1 and the value of M2+ in this economy in billions of dollars?

a 105; 230
b 110; 235
c 55; 430
d 55; 230
e 60; 430

21 Which of the following statements about depository institutions is *false*?

a They aim to maximize net worth without other considerations.
b They take deposits from households and firms, and lend to other households and firms.
c They minimize the cost of borrowing.
d They pool and reduce risk.
e They hold a variety of assets, not just loans.

22 An attempt to stimulate the economy by using the bank rate would work by

a lowering the bank rate, resulting in more excess reserves, resulting in more loans, resulting in more deposits and money.
b raising the bank rate, resulting in more excess reserves, resulting in more loans, resulting in more deposits and money.
c raising the bank rate, resulting in less excess reserves, resulting in less loans, resulting in less deposits and money.
d lowering the bank rate, resulting in less excess reserves, resulting in less loans, resulting in less deposits and money.
e lowering the bank rate, resulting in more excess reserves, resulting in more loans, resulting in less deposits and money.

23 There will be no crowding out if

a the demand for real money is totally unresponsive to changes in the price level.
b the money supply is totally unresponsive to changes in the interest rate.
c investment is very responsive to changes in the interest rate.
d investment is totally unresponsive to changes in real GDP.
e the demand for real money is totally unresponsive to changes in real GDP.

24 The amount of real money people want to hold will increase if either real income increases or the

a price level increases.
b price level decreases.
c interest rate increases.
d interest rate decreases.
e price of bonds decreases.

ANSWERS

Problem

a The U.S. recession leads to a decrease in their imports of Canadian goods, which means a decrease in our exports. This decrease in exports leads to a decrease in aggregate planned expenditure, represented by a shift downward in the *AE* curve to AE_b in Figure P8.1. The decrease in aggregate expenditure leads to an increase in inventories, which leads to firms lowering production, leading to a decrease in real GDP that is a multiple of the initial decrease in aggregate expenditure—the new equilibrium is at *b*, compared with the original equilibrium at *a*. The shift down in aggregate expenditure is also shown as a shift leftward in aggregate demand in part (b) of the graph.

Consumption is lower because of the decrease in real GDP. Investment is unchanged. Government purchases are unchanged. Exports are lower because of the shock, and imports are also lower because of the decrease in real GDP.

FIGURE **P8.1**

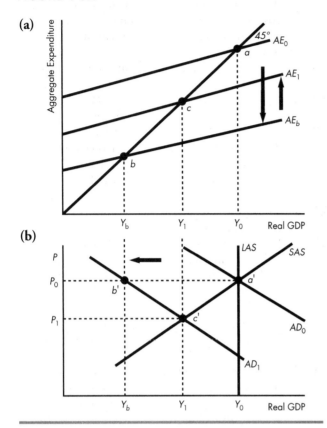

(a)

(b)

TABLE **P8.1**

Bank of Canada		Chartered Banks	
Assets	**Liabilities**	**Assets**	**Liabilities**
Government securities (+)	Bank deposits (+)	Reserves (+)	
		Government securities (−)	

This operation will lead to a deposit multiplier effect, leading to more reserves, more loans, more deposits, and a higher quantity of money.

d The higher quantity of money will shift the money supply curve rightward. This in turn creates a surplus of money, which leads to an increase in the demand for financial assets, which leads to an increase in the price of these assets, which leads to a decrease in the interest rate. The lower interest rate leads to an increase in investment expenditure and aggregate demand, as well as a decrease in the demand for Canadian dollars and therefore a decrease in the value of the Canadian dollar and an increase in net exports and aggregate demand.

e The higher aggregate demand translates into a shift rightward in the aggregate demand curve, which leads to an increase in the price level, which triggers a movement along the short-run aggregate supply curve, leading to an increase in real GDP.

f No, it does not because one of the crucial assumptions of the quantity theory does not hold—since the economy is in the short run, real GDP is not independent of changes in the quantity of money.

Midterm Examination

1 c Definition. (528–533)

2 b Multiplier calculation holds constant the price level. (568–571)

3 e If government borrows from Bank of Canada, the Bank prints money to give to government, which leads to increase in quantity of money which leads to increase in *AD*, creating inflation. (642–643)

4 e *LRPC* is vertical at new higher natural rate, and *SRPC* shifts with it since it crosses *LRPC* at natural rate. (664–665)

5 e Increase in *MS* leads to decrease in *r*, which leads to increase in *C* (so **a** wrong), increase in *I* (so **d** wrong), increase in *NX* (so **b** and **c** wrong), and they all lead to increase in *AD*, which creates more jobs. (615–620)

b After the shock, at the original price level aggregate demand is less than aggregate supply ($Y_b < Y_0$). This surplus leads to a decrease in the price level. *Since the decrease in AD was unexpected, so is the decrease in the price level—there is no shift in the SAS curve.* This decrease in the price level in turn leads to a decrease in the real quantity supplied in the short run (the movement from a' to c'), as well as an increase in the real money supply, which leads to a decrease in the interest rate, an increase in investment and aggregate expenditure (from AE_b to AE_1), and a movement along the aggregate demand curve from b' to c'.

c The Bank of Canada wants to increase the quantity of money, and will do so by purchasing government securities. If, for example, they buy these securities directly from the chartered banks, they will pay for them by crediting the chartered banks' deposits at the Bank of Canada (which are reserves). The result of such a purchase is shown in Table P8.1.

6 **e** Definition. (633)

7 **a** Firms' sales > production leads to decrease in inventories, which leads to increase in production. New equilibrium has higher real GDP = higher *AE*. (533–537)

8 **b** Outlay. (556–557)

9 **c** This will lead to a fall in the cost of production and a rightward shift in *SAS*. (653–655)

10 **c** Lending its reserves is done by crediting borrowers' deposits, creating more deposits = more money. (587–590)

11 **a** In long run, real GDP is independent of Δ quantity of money. (656–657)

12 **e** Induced taxes act as automatic stabilizer. Multipliers are weaker, can still do discretionary policy, and there may or may not be a cyclical/structural deficit depending on other factors. (566–568)

13 **a** Bank of Canada pays for securities by crediting banks' reserves, which are part of monetary base. (611–613)

14 **b** At full employment, shift in *SAS* offsets shift in *AD*. (640)

15 **d** Decrease in interest rates leads to Canadian assets being less desirable, which leads to decrease in demand for these assets and for Canadian dollars, which leads to decrease in exchange rate, etc. (615–620)

16 **d** This effect leads to more Δ*P*, less Δ*Y*. All others make effect larger. (543–547)

17 **b** Borrowers are paying the money, so are happy if its value erodes, the higher transactions costs do not affect interest rates, and the real rate is set independently of inflation. (666–667)

18 **b** University spending creates multiplier effects. (538–541)

19 **a** Autonomous tax multiplier = $-MPC/(1 - MPC) = -0.6/(1 - 0.6) = -1.5$. (564–565)

20 **c** M1 = currency in circulation + banks' demand deposits, M2+ = M1 + (personal savings and nonpersonal notice deposits at banks) + deposits at other financial institutions. (583–584)

21 **a** They must also balance off various risk considerations. (585–587)

22 **a** Decrease in bank rate leads to decrease in cost of borrowing from central bank, which leads to decrease in desired reserves, creating excess reserves, which leads to increase in loans, etc. (608–615)

23 **e** Because then Δ real GDP due to fiscal policy has no impact on real money demand or on interest rates. (630–633)

24 **d** Real money demand is not affected by Δ price level, decrease in price of bonds leads to increase in interest rate, which lowers quantity of real money demanded. (594–596)

Chapter 29

The Economy at Full Employment

Real GDP and Employment

The production possibility frontier is the boundary between combinations of goods that can be produced and those that cannot.

◆ Such a relationship exists between real GDP and leisure—more real GDP requires less leisure and more time spent working.

◆ The **production function** (*PF*) shows the relationship between real GDP and quantity of labour employed, all other influences constant.

  • Increase in quantity of labour employed creates movement along *PF*.

Labour productivity is real GDP per hour of labour, which is influenced by three factors:

◆ More physical capital increases labour productivity.

◆ More **human capital** (people's knowledge and skills) increases labour productivity. Human capital can increase from **learning-by-doing** (on-the-job education from experience).

◆ Technological advances increase labour productivity.

◆ An increase in labour productivity shifts *PF* upward.

Labour Market and Aggregate Supply

The labour market determines the quantity of labour hours employed and real GDP supplied.

◆ **Quantity of labour demanded** = number of labour hours hired by all firms.

◆ **Demand for labour** (*LD*)—quantity of labour demanded at each real wage rate.

◆ **Real wage rate** = **money wage rate** (in current dollars)/price level.

◆ **Marginal product of labour** = Δ real GDP per hour additional labour.

  • As labour used increases there is a decrease in marginal product (law of diminishing marginal returns).

◆ Firms hire labour as long as the marginal product of labour > real wage rate—*LD* curve is the marginal product curve.

◆ Increase in real wage, movement up *LD* curve.

◆ *LD* curve shifts rightward if marginal product of labour increases.

Quantity of labour supplied = number of hours labour services households plan to work.

◆ **Supply of labour** (*LS*)—quantity of labour supplied at each real wage rate.

◆ Increase in real wage rate will increase quantity labour supplied because

  • hours per person increase (if effect of increasing opportunity cost of leisure outweighs effect of desire for more leisure).
  • labour force participation rate increases.

Real wage rate adjusts to create full-employment labour market equilibrium where *LD* = *LS*.

◆ The level of real GDP at full employment is potential GDP.

◆ Vertical **long-run aggregate supply curve** is relationship between quantity of real GDP supplied and price level when real GDP = potential GDP.

  • When *P* changes, money wage rate also changes to keep real wage rate at the level that makes *LD* = *LS*, so that employment is unchanged and therefore *LAS* curve is vertical at potential GDP.

◆ Upward-sloping **short-run aggregate supply**
(**SAS**) **curve** is relationship between quantity of
real GDP supplied and price level, money wage
and all other influences constant.

  • Along *SAS*, if *P* increases the money wage stays
  constant, so real wage falls, and therefore
  quantity of labour demanded increases and real
  GDP increases.

Changes in Potential GDP

Real GDP increases if economy recovers from recession
or potential GDP increases.

◆ Potential GDP increases if population or labour
productivity increase.

◆ Increasing population increases labour supply.

  • As a result, real wage rate decreases, which
  increases hiring and potential GDP.

◆ An increase in labour productivity increases
demand for labour.

  • As a result, real wage rate increases, so more
  labour supplied, and potential GDP increases.

Unemployment at Full Employment

The unemployment rate at full employment is the
natural rate of unemployment.

◆ Two broad reasons for unemployment—job search
and job rationing.

◆ **Job search** is the activity of looking for an
acceptable job.

  • Constant change in labour market implies there
  is always job search.
  • Normal job search generates the natural rate of
  unemployment.
  • If real wage rate > equilibrium, job search high.
  • Job search increases if proportion of working-
  age population increases, if unemployment
  compensation increases, or if technological
  change increases structural change.

◆ **Job rationing** is paying an above-equilibrium
wage that creates a surplus of labour and frictional
unemployment. Two reasons:

  • Firms pay **efficiency wages**—higher wages
  designed to maximize profits by increasing work
  effort, decreasing labour turnover rate (therefore
  lowering recruiting costs), and increasing
  quality of labour.
  • **Minimum wage** legally keeps wages above
  equilibrium value for covered workers.

◆ Job rationing creates a surplus of labour that adds
extra job search.

HELPFUL HINTS

1 The purpose of this chapter is to deepen our
understanding of aggregate supply: the
relationship between the price level and the
quantity of real GDP supplied. Chapter 22
introduced the basic *AD-AS* model, and showed
some of its usefulness in exploring the economy.
The next part of the text examined aggregate
demand in detail (Chapters 23–28), while
Chapters 29 and 30 examine aggregate supply in
detail in order to explore its composition, and
the variables that affect it. As we will see in
Chapters 31 and 32, aggregate supply is a crucial
variable in understanding macroeconomic
problems and policy.

2 Our work at understanding aggregate supply is
broken down into two constituent issues—the
production function and the labour market.

   The first issue is: How is the quantity of real
GDP supplied determined in general? When the
capital stock and the state of technology are
given, the maximum amount of real GDP that
can be produced depends on the quantity of
labour employed. This relationship between
employment and the quantity of real GDP
supplied is captured by the production function.

   To understand the determination of the
quantity of real GDP supplied, it is necessary to
pursue the second issue: How is the level of
employment determined? The answer is in the
labour market. The demand for labour is
determined by firms, and the supply of labour is
determined by households. If money wages
continuously adjust to clear the labour market,
the level of employment will always be the
equilibrium level with full employment. If, on
the other hand, money wages are fixed in the
short run, the level of employment can deviate
from its equilibrium level.

   Since our interest is in aggregate supply, we
want to know how the quantity of real GDP
varies as the price level varies. This desire brings
us to a third issue: How do changes in the price
level affect employment and real GDP? It turns
out that if money wages continuously adjust, the
level of employment, and thus the quantity of
real GDP supplied, is independent of the price
level. Whatever the price level, the wage rate will
adjust so that the unique equilibrium level of

employment is achieved. This adjustment implies a long-run aggregate supply curve that is vertical at potential GDP.

On the other hand, if wages are constant, the level of employment, and thus the quantity of real GDP supplied, depends on the actual value of the price level relative to the expected value of the price level. If the price level turns out to be equal to its expected value, the equilibrium level of employment (full employment) results. If the price level is higher than expected, the level of employment turns out to be higher than the equilibrium value and thus real GDP supplied will be larger than potential GDP. If the price level is lower than expected, employment will be less than equilibrium and real GDP supplied will be less than potential GDP. This result implies a positively sloped short-run aggregate supply curve.

3   As Chapter 21 explained, there are four different *types* of unemployment—frictional, structural, seasonal, and cyclical. The first three of these make up the natural rate of unemployment.

Defining the types of unemployment does not *explain* them. This chapter advances two basic explanations of unemployment to help us to see the origin of the three types of natural unemployment.

Frictional unemployment comes from job search (there is always job search in the economy because of changes in the fortunes of individual firms, people searching for good matches), and from job rationing leading to a wage above the equilibrium wage, with queuing for jobs as a result. It is often the result of a downturn in one firm.

Structural unemployment comes from excessive job search in times of structural change due to technological change. It is due to a downturn in a specific industry or region.

Seasonal unemployment is due to job search in specific seasons when certain types of jobs do not exist.

SELF-TEST

True/False and Explain

Real GDP and Employment

1   The production possibilities frontier is the relationship between real GDP and the quantity of labour employed.

2   More human capital creates a movement along the production function.

3   The only way labour productivity can increase is if there is more physical capital.

Labour Market and Aggregate Supply

4   If the real wage rate decreases, the opportunity cost effect implies that households will increase the time spent working.

5   The diminishing marginal product of labour implies that the demand for labour curve is negatively sloped.

6   As the real wage rate increases, the quantity of labour demanded decreases, other things remaining constant.

7   If the marginal product of each unit of labour increases, the demand for labour curve shifts rightward.

8   In the short run, an increase in the price level will increase the quantity of real GDP supplied.

Changes in Potential GDP

9 Increasing population decreases the real wage rate and potential GDP.

10 An increase in labour productivity will decrease real wages and increase potential GDP.

11 Japan's population is shrinking and its labour productivity is increasing. The net effect of these two effects will definitely be an increase in potential GDP.

Unemployment at Full Employment

12 Job rationing keeps real wages too high and creates cyclical unemployment.

13 Equilibrium in the labour market is when labour demand equals labour supply and unemployment is zero.

14 Full employment is when there is 0 job search unemployment.

15 Efficiency wages are when firms pay wages lower than the equilibrium wage in order to get higher profits.

Multiple-Choice

Real GDP and Employment

1 The production function shows
a how much real GDP changes as the capital stock changes, all else remaining the same.
b how much real GDP changes as the price level changes, all else remaining the same.
c how much labour demand changes as the real wage rate changes, all else remaining the same.
d how much labour demand changes as the money wage rate changes, all else remaining the same.
e none of the above.

2 Which of the following would shift the production function upward?
a a decrease in the stock of capital
b a decrease in the real wage rate
c an increase in labour employed
d an increase in the price level
e a technological advance

3 An increase in an economy's stock of human capital would lead to
a a shift outward in the leisure hours—real GDP *PPF* and a movement along the production function.
b a movement along the leisure hours—real GDP *PPF* and a shift upward in the production function.
c a shift outward in the leisure hours—real GDP *PPF* and a shift upward in the production function.
d a movement along the leisure hours—real GDP *PPF* and a movement along the production function.
e no change in the leisure hours—real GDP *PPF* and a movement along the production function.

4 An increase in the quantity of labour supplied (driven by a fall in leisure consumed) would lead to
a a shift outward in the production possibilities frontier and a movement along the production function.
b a movement along the production possibilities frontier and a shift upward in the production function.
c a shift outward in the production possibilities frontier and a shift upward in the production function.
d a movement along the production possibilities frontier and a movement along the production function.
e no change in the production possibilities frontier and a movement along the production function.

5 Which of the following is an example of learning-by-doing?
a The use of a laptop instead of pen and paper to keep class notes.
b A student being better at note-taking at the end of the fourth year of university, compared to their first year of university.
c A student with five economics classes doing better in a third-year business class, compared to a student with only one economics class.
d A student installing a software upgrade on their computer.
e Falling asleep on your economics text while studying.

Labour Market and Aggregate Supply

6 Which one of the following quotations describes a rightward shift in the labour demand curve?

a "Recent higher wage rates have led to more leisure being consumed."

b "The recent lower price level has induced people to work more hours."

c "The recent higher real wage rate has induced people to work more hours."

d "The recent high investment in capital equipment has raised hiring by firms."

e "Adding extra workers leads to lower productivity of each additional worker."

7 If tacos sell for $2 each at the Burning Belly Taco Stand, and the wage rate of a taco maker is $60 per day, the real wage rate faced by the Burning Belly manager is equivalent to:

a 2 tacos per day.

b $60 per day.

c 120 tacos per day.

d $2 per day.

e 30 tacos per day.

8 Initially, tacos sell for $2 each at the Burning Belly Taco Stand, and the wage rate of a taco maker is $60 per day. Suppose that the price of a taco increases to $2.50 after a *National Inquisitor* story linking tacos to baldness cures. The profit-maximizing Burning Belly manager will

a employ more taco makers because the real wage rate has increased to $2.50 per day.

b employ fewer taco makers because the real wage rate has increased to $2.50 per day.

c employ the same number of taco makers because the wage rate is unchanged.

d employ more taco makers because the real wage rate has decreased to 24 tacos per day.

e start advertising "I'm the owner, but I'm a customer too."

9 The labour demand curve is

a positively sloped and shifts when there is a change in the capital stock.

b positively sloped and shifts when there is a change in the quantity of labour employed.

c negatively sloped and shifts when there is a change in the capital stock.

d negatively sloped and shifts when there is a change in the quantity of labour employed.

e negatively sloped and shifts when there is a change in the real wage rate.

10 The demand for labour curve shows that, as the

a price level increases, the quantity of labour demanded decreases.

b real wage rate increases, the quantity of labour demanded increases.

c money wage rate increases, the quantity of labour demanded decreases.

d money wage rate increases, the quantity of labour demanded increases.

e real wage rate increases, the quantity of labour demanded decreases.

11 In the short run, if the price level decreases, the real wage rate will be

a lower than the equilibrium real wage rate, and employment will decrease.

b lower than the equilibrium real wage rate, and employment will increase.

c higher than the equilibrium real wage rate, and employment will decrease.

d higher than the equilibrium real wage rate, and employment will increase.

e equal to the equilibrium real wage rate, and employment will stay constant.

12 In the long run, if the price level decreases, the real wage rate will be

a less than the equilibrium real wage rate, and employment will decrease.

b less than the equilibrium real wage rate, and employment will increase.

c higher than the equilibrium real wage rate, and employment will decrease.

d higher than the equilibrium real wage rate, and employment will increase.

e equal to the equilibrium real wage rate, and employment will stay constant.

13 If the money wage rate is $12 per hour and the GDP deflator is 150, what is the real wage rate per hour?

a $18

b $15

c $12

d $8

e $6

14 A profit-maximizing firm will hire additional units of labour up to the point at which

a workers are no longer willing to work.

b the marginal product of labour is zero.

c the marginal product of labour is a maximum.

d the marginal product of labour is equal to the real wage.

e the marginal product of labour is equal to the money wage.

15 Which one of the following quotations describes the upward-sloping labour supply curve?

a "Recent higher wage rates have led to more leisure being consumed."

b "The recent lower price level has induced people to work less hours."

c "The recent higher real wage rate has induced people to work more hours."

d "The recent high investment in capital equipment has raised hiring by firms."

e "Adding extra workers leads to lower productivity of each additional worker."

16 Which one of the following variables is *not* held constant in deriving the short-run aggregate supply curve?

a The level of wages.

b Raw material prices.

c Climate.

d Price level.

e Technology.

Changes in Potential GDP

17 The demand for labour and the supply of labour are both increasing over time, but the demand for labour is increasing at a faster rate. Over time we expect to see the

a real wage rate rising and employment decreasing.

b real wage rate and employment increasing.

c real wage rate decreasing and employment increasing.

d real wage rate and employment decreasing.

e long-run aggregate supply curve shifting leftward.

18 An increase in potential GDP would be shown as

a a shift outward in the production possibilities frontier and a movement along the production function.

b a movement along the production possibilities frontier and a shift upward in the production function.

c a shift outward in the production possibilities frontier and a shift upward in the production function.

d a movement along the production possibilities frontier and a movement along the production function.

e either a shift in the production possibilities frontier and the production function, or a movement along each curve, depending on the source of the change.

19 *Ceteris paribus*, an increase in labour productivity results in

a a higher real wage rate and higher potential GDP per hour of work.

b a lower real wage rate and higher potential GDP per hour of work.

c a higher real wage rate and lower potential GDP per hour of work.

d a lower real wage rate and lower potential GDP per hour of work.

e a constant real wage rate in the long run.

20 *Ceteris paribus*, an increase in the population results in

a a higher level of labour employed and higher potential GDP per hour of work.

b a lower level of labour employed and higher potential GDP per hour of work.

c a higher level of labour employed and lower potential GDP per hour of work.

d a lower level of labour employed and lower potential GDP per hour of work.

e a constant level of labour employed and constant potential GDP per hour of work.

Unemployment at Full Employment

21 Which of the following quotations best describes job search unemployment?

a "Wages are so good at the factory, they always have enough applicants to pick whomever they want for the job."

b "Professors with tenured jobs are refusing to take pay cuts to help hire new professors."

c "Wages have failed to fall in the current economic downturn, creating extra unemployment."

d "People are taking too long to find jobs, because unemployment insurance is so generous."

e All of the above.

22 Which of the following is *not* a possible explanation for unemployment?

a job search

b efficiency wages

c minimum wages

d job market turnover

e part-time searches

23 Job search unemployment increases if

a the proportion of working-age population decreases.

b unemployment compensation becomes less generous.

c technological change slows down.

d unemployment compensation becomes more generous.

e none of the above.

24 An efficiency wage refers to wages

a paid below the equilibrium wage rate in order to increase the firm's efficiency.

b set to generate the efficient level of employment.

c paid above the equilibrium wage rate in order to increase worker productivity.

d being too high because of minimum wage laws.

e off of the production possibilities frontier.

25 Which of the following government policies would *lower* the unemployment rate?

a increasing unemployment benefits

b raising the minimum wage

c closing down employment agencies

d reducing unemployment benefits

e decreasing aggregate demand

Short Answer Problems

1 Explain why the labour force participation rate increases as the real wage rate increases. Why does this factor help explain the positive slope of the labour supply curve?

2 What determines the demand for labour?

3 Table 29.1 gives information about the production function for the country of Orania, where L = units of labour per day (measured in the millions) and Y = units of output per day (real GDP, millions of constant dollars per day).

TABLE **29.1** PRODUCTION FUNCTION

L	Y	MP_L
0	0	
1	8	
2	15	
3	21	
4	26	
5	30	
6	33	

a There are a total of 6 units of labour available for leisure or labour supply in Orania. Graph Orania's production possibilities frontier.

b Complete the last column of Table 29.1 by computing the marginal product of labour (MP_L). Remember to place the marginal product halfway between the two rows.

c How much labour will be demanded if the money wage rate is $6 and the GDP deflator is 150?

d Draw a graph of the demand for labour.

4 Table 29.2 gives the supply of labour schedule for Orania.

TABLE **29.2** SUPPLY OF LABOUR

Real Wage Rate	Quantity of Labour Supplied
8	7.5
7	6.5
6	5.5
5	4.5
4	3.5
3	2.5

a On the graph from Short Answer Problem **3d**, draw the supply of labour curve.

b What is the equilibrium real wage rate?

c What is the equilibrium level of employment?

d What is the level of output at this level of employment?

ⓒⓣ **5** a If the natural rate of unemployment in Orania is 10 percent, calculate the labour force and the units of labour unemployed in equilibrium.

b Since labour demand equals labour supply in Orania, how can there be any unemployment?

6 Now suppose that a technological advance gives Orania a new production function summarized in Table 29.3.

TABLE **29.3** NEW PRODUCTION FUNCTION

L	Y	MP_L
0	0	
1	10	
2	19	
3	27	
4	34	
5	40	
6	45	

a On your *PPF* graph from Short Answer Problem **3a**, graph Orania's new *PPF*.

b Complete the last column of Table 29.3 by computing the marginal product of labour. Remember to place the marginal product halfway between the two rows.

c On the graph from Short Answer Problems **3c** and **4a**, draw the new demand for labour curve.

d In the long run, what will be the new equilibrium real wage rate, level of employment, and level of output? (The supply of labour curve is unchanged.)

7 In Short Answer Problem **6**, what happened to potential GDP and the *SAS* and *LAS* curves? Have they shifted?

8 "The theory of job rationing tells us firms keep real wages too high and therefore create extra unemployment. Real wages should be forced downward to create more employment." Discuss this statement in light of efficiency wages.

9 Consider the following statement. "A major source of unemployment is job search due to employment insurance. It would be better for the economy if we eliminated employment insurance." What would eliminating employment insurance do to job search and unemployment levels? Is it clearly better for the economy if we eliminate employment insurance? Explain briefly.

10 Is the natural rate of unemployment constant? Briefly explain what factors can change the natural rate of unemployment.

ANSWERS

True/False and Explain

1 F Definition given is for production function. (680)
2 F Creates shift in *PF*. (682)
3 F Technological advances or increases in human capital raise labour productivity too. (681–682)
4 F Decrease in real wage rate leads to decrease in opportunity cost of leisure, which leads to increase in leisure. (685–686)
5 T If hire more labour, diminishing marginal returns imply decrease in marginal product. Therefore firms will hire more labour only if real wage rate decreases. (683–685)
6 T Definition of labour demand curve. (683–685)

7 T Increase in marginal product leads to increase in output per worker and therefore increase in number desired at a constant real wage rate. (683–685)
8 T Upward-sloping *SAS* curve. (687–688)
9 F Increasing population increases labour supply, and decreases real wage, but more labour is hired so potential GDP increases. (688–689)
10 F It will shift *LD* curve rightward, and increase real wage rate. (690–691)
11 F Shrinking population will lower potential GDP, increasing labour productivity will increase it, net effect is ambiguous. (689–691)
12 F It creates frictional unemployment, since it is independent of the cycle. (694–695)
13 F Even in equilibrium there is natural unemployment. (693–694)
14 F There is always some job search and job rationing unemployment. (693)
15 F They pay wages higher than the equilibrium wage. (694–695)

Multiple-Choice

1 e Definition: how much real GDP changes as the labour hired changes. (680)
2 e Technological advance leads to increase in productivity of labour. (681–682)
3 c The change increases labour productivity, which shifts both curves. (680–682)
4 d Decreasing leisure creates move along *PPF* (more real GDP, less leisure), and the increase in labour supply creates move along *PF*. (680–682)
5 b The student has learned by repetition. (681–682)
6 d This change leads to higher productivity and more labour demand. **a**, **b**, and **c** are *LS* effect, **e** movement along curve. (683–685)
7 e Real wage rate = money wage rate/price of good = $60/$2 = 30. (683–685)
8 d Real wage = $60/$2.50 = 24 < 30 leads to hire more labour since cheaper. (683–685)
9 c Negatively sloped due to diminishing marginal product. **d** and **e** imply movements along the curve. (683–685)
10 e Demand for labour depends inversely on real wage rate. (683–685)
11 c Lower actual price level leads to higher real wage (since money wage constant), so labour demanded decreases. (687–688)
12 e Money wage adjust to any price level changes, so real wage constant, and therefore no change in labour hired. (687–688)

13 d Real wage = (money wage/price level) × 100. (683–685)

14 d Here profits maximized. (683–685)

15 c Higher wages, higher quantity of labour supplied. **a**, **b** are opposite relationships, **d** and **e** refer to labour demand. (685–686)

16 d This variable is on the vertical axis. (687–688)

17 b Draw a graph. (691–692)

18 e If labour productivity is the original change, then there is a shift in the curves. If the change is due to a change in labour force participation rates, then there is a movement along the curves. If it is due to a population change, then there is a shift in the *PPF* and a movement along the *PF*. (688–691)

19 a Productivity increase creates an increase in labour demand, which raises real wage rate. Potential GDP per hour of work = productivity, so it must have increased. (690–691)

20 c Labour supply shifts right, real wage falls, more people are hired, but due to diminishing marginal productivity potential GDP per hour of work falls. (689–690)

21 d **a** and **b** are job rationing unemployment, **c** is cyclical unemployment. (693–695)

22 e These workers are employed while searching. (693–695)

23 d Individuals can afford to spend more time in job search. (693–694)

24 c Definition. (694–695)

25 d This change will reduce length of job search. (693–694)

Short Answer Problems

1 Individuals compare the value of working (the real wage) to the value of activities outside the labour force (for example, education, taking care of children). If the real wage rate is too low, an individual will not even enter the labour force. As the real wage rate increases, it will exceed the value of alternative activities of an increasingly larger group of people; thus the labour force increases relative to the size of the working age population; the labour force participation rate increases.

As this rate increases, more individuals offer to supply labour; thus, the quantity of labour supplied increases. Because the original impetus was an increasing real wage rate, the real wage rate and the quantity of labour supplied are positively related.

2 The demand for labour is set where the real wage rate equals the marginal product of labour.

The marginal product of labour is affected by the physical and human capital stock, and the technology. Therefore in the short run the demand for labour is affected by the real wage rate, physical and human capital stock, and level of technology.

3 a The *PPF* graph is labelled as *PPF*₀ in Figure 29.1 below.

FIGURE **29.1** ORANIA'S *PPF*

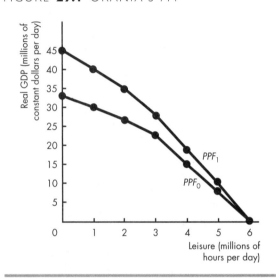

b Completed Table 29.1 is shown here as Table 29.1 Solution. The marginal product of labour is the additional output produced by an additional unit of labour.

TABLE **29.1**   SOLUTION

L	Y	MP$_L$
0	0	
		8
1	8	
		7
2	15	
		6
3	21	
		5
4	26	
		4
5	30	
		3
6	33	

c The real wage rate is computed as follows: real wage rate = (money wage rate × 100)/GDP deflator.

In this case, the money wage rate is $6 per unit and the GDP deflator is 150. Therefore the real wage is $4. Since a profit-maximizing firm will hire labour until the marginal product of labour is equal to the real wage rate, we can see that the quantity of labour demanded at a real wage rate of $4 is 4.5 units.

d The graph of the demand curve for labour (labelled LD_0) is given in Figure 29.2. The demand curve for labour is the same as the marginal product of labour curve (see Table 29.1 Solution).

FIGURE **29.2**

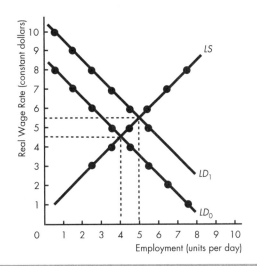

4 a Figure 29.2 illustrates the supply curve of labour (labelled LS) on the same graph with the LD_0 curve from Short Answer Problem **3**.

b The equilibrium real wage rate is $4.50 since the quantity of labour demanded and supplied are both equal to 4 units per day. This result can be seen from the graph or the tables.

c The equilibrium level of employment is 4 units.

d From the production function in Table 29.1, we can see that 4 units of labour will yield 26 units of output per day.

ct 5 a If the unemployment rate is 10 percent, then
  • 0.10 = (labour force – employed)/labour force, or
  • labour force × 0.10 = labour force – 4, or
  • labour force × 0.9 = 4, or
  • labour force = 4/0.9 = 4.44
  Therefore, there are 0.44 units unemployed.

b Even at full employment, there is always some job search and job rationing unemployment, equal to the natural rate of unemployment.

6 a The new production possibilities graph is graphed in Figure 29.1 as PPF_1.

b Completed Table 29.3 is shown here as Table 29.3 Solution. Note that the marginal product

of each unit of labour has increased as a result of the technological advance.

TABLE **29.3** SOLUTION

L	Y	MP_L
0	0	
		10
1	10	
		9
2	19	
		8
3	27	
		7
4	34	
		6
5	40	
		5
6	45	

c Figure 29.2 gives the graph. Notice that the new labour demand curve, LD_1 (which comes from the new MP_L relationship), lies rightward of LD_0.

d It can be seen from Figure 29.2 or Tables 29.2 and 29.3 that the quantity of labour demanded equals the quantity of labour supplied at a real wage rate of $5.50. The level of employment is now 5 units of labour per day, which implies an output of 40 units per day (from Table 29.3).

7 Since labour productivity has increased, we have seen the resulting increase in potential GDP. This increase in potential GDP shifts the LAS curve rightward from 26 to 40, and the SAS curve moves with it.

ct 8 Yes, firms keep real wages too high, but the result is higher productivity. Forcing real wages down might create more employment, but it would also create lower productivity and lower potential GDP. It is not clear that this change is desirable.

ct 9 Eliminating employment insurance will mean unemployed workers receive no government payments while job searching. They will therefore accept job offers much faster, and search less. This reduction in searching will reduce the level of unemployment. However, this reduction in unemployment is not clearly good, because workers may settle for poor job matches because they cannot afford to keep searching, which will reduce productivity in the economy.

10 The natural rate of unemployment is determined by the amount of job search and job rationing. Job search is affected by the proportion of working-age population, by unemployment compensation, and by technological change. Job rationing is affected by the use of efficiency wages and the level of the minimum wage. Changes in any of these underlying factors will change the level of the natural rate of unemployment.

Appendix: Deriving the Aggregate Supply Curves

Deriving the Long-Run Aggregate Supply Curve

LAS curve is vertical at potential GDP.

◆ When price level increases, real wage rate falls and there is excess demand for labour.

  • As a result, money wage rate also increases until the real wage rate returns to the level that makes *LD* = *LS*.
  • Result: full employment and real GDP produced = potential GDP.

◆ When the price level falls, the money wage rate also falls, *LD* = *LS*, and employment and real GDP produced are unchanged.

◆ *LAS* shifts rightward if

  • population grows so that *LS* shifts rightward, real wage decreases.
  • labour productivity increases, so that *LD* shifts rightward, real wage rate increases.

Short-Run Aggregate Supply

SAS curve shows the relationship between quantity of real GDP supplied and price level, holding money wage, etc. constant.

◆ It is assumed in the short run employment is set by firms hiring, given the real wage—*LD* may not equal *LS*.

◆ In the short run, increase in *P* decreases real wage rate, so that labour demand increases and so does employment, leading to increase in real GDP produced.

◆ Overall result: price level increases, quantity of real GDP supplied increases in the short run—the *SAS* is upward-sloping.

◆ If the *LAS* shifts, so does the *SAS*.

◆ If the money wage increases,

  • *LAS* unaffected.
  • Real wage rate increases, quantity of labour demanded decreases, employment and production decrease.
  • *SAS* shifts leftward.

◆ A shift in *AD* creates a price change and a movement along *SAS*.

True/False and Explain

Deriving the Long-Run Aggregate Supply Curve

1 A decrease in the price level will lead to a decrease in employment in the long run.

2 After an increase in the price level, the real wage rate will be lower in the long run.

3 The *LAS* shifts rightward if labour productivity increases.

Short-Run Aggregate Supply

4 A decrease in the price level will lead to a decrease in employment in the short run.

5 An economy is initially in macroeconomic equilibrium and then expected future profits decrease. Real GDP will fall in the short run.

6 After an increase in the price level, the real wage rate will be lower in the short run.

7 An increase in the money wage rate will shift the *SAS* curve and the *LAS* curve rightward.

Multiple-Choice

Deriving the Long-Run Aggregate Supply Curve

1 Which one of the following quotations describes a movement along a long-run aggregate supply curve?
a "The recent higher price levels have lowered production in the country."
b "The recent higher price levels have raised production in the country."
c "The recent higher price levels have led to compensating increases in wages, with no changes in labour hired or production."
d "The recent lower price levels have led to lower production in the country."
e None of the above.

2 The aggregate supply curve is vertical at full-employment real GDP if
a the real wage rate adjusts continually so as to leave the labour market always in equilibrium.
b the money wage rate is fixed but the real wage rate changes due to changes in the price level.
c employment is determined by the quantity of labour demanded.
d employment is determined by the quantity of labour supplied.
e employment is determined by the money usage.

3 The *LAS* curve shifts rightward if
a the money wage rate increases.
b the money wage rate decreases.
c the real wage rate increases.
d the real wage rate decreases.
e the population increases.

4 Figure A29.1 depicts the labour market. The price level, measured by the GDP deflator, is 150. What is the money wage rate in equilibrium?
a $8
b $12
c $15
d $18
e $24

FIGURE **A29.1**

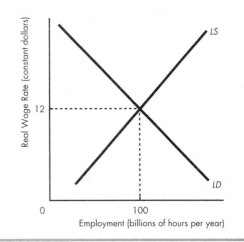

Short-Run Aggregate Supply

5 Refer to Figure A29.1 and assume that when the money wage was set, the GDP deflator was expected to remain constant at 150. If the GDP deflator actually turns out to be 200 in the short run, the real wage rate will be
a $9, and employment will be less than 100 billion hours per year.
b $9, and employment will be more than 100 billion hours per year.
c $24, and employment will be less than 100 billion hours per year.
d $24, and employment will be more than 100 billion hours per year.
e $6, and employment will be more than 100 billion hours per year.

6 Which one of the following quotations describes a shift rightward in a short-run aggregate supply curve?

a "The recent higher price levels have lowered production in the country."
b "The recent higher price levels have raised production in the country."
c "The recent higher price levels have led to compensating increases in wages, with no changes in labour hired or production."
d "The recent lower price levels have led to lower production in the country."
e None of the above.

7 In the short run, employment is determined by the

a quantity of labour demanded at the actual real wage rate.
b quantity of labour supplied at the actual real wage rate.
c intersection of the demand for labour and supply of labour curves.
d intersection of the aggregate demand and aggregate supply curves.
e price level.

8 In the long run, an increase in real GDP implies that

a potential GDP has increased.
b aggregate demand has increased.
c the economy has moved up its short-run aggregate supply curve.
d the price level has increased.
e real wages have fallen.

Short Answer Problems

1 Consider the labour market for Orania derived earlier in Chapter 29, at the end of Short Answer Problem **4**. Suppose Orania is operating on its long-run aggregate supply curve.
  a If the GDP deflator is 100, what is the equilibrium money wage rate, the level of employment, and the level of output?
  b If the GDP deflator is 80, what is the equilibrium money wage rate, the level of employment, and the level of output?
  c If the GDP deflator is 120, what is the equilibrium money wage rate, the level of employment, and the level of output?
  d Draw Orania's long-run aggregate supply curve.

2 Now suppose Orania has a fixed money wage, set at $4.50. Assuming Orania is in the short run, answer the following questions.

a If the actual value of the GDP deflator is 100, what is the real wage rate, the level of employment, and the level of output?
b If the actual value of the GDP deflator is 82, what is the real wage rate, the level of employment, and the level of output?
c If the actual value of the GDP deflator is 128, what is the real wage rate, the level of employment, and the level of output?
d On the graph from Short Answer Problem **1d**, indicate three points on the short-run aggregate supply curve for Orania. Draw part of that curve by connecting the points.

3 Suppose the price level increases unexpectedly. In the short run, what will happen to the money wage rate, the real wage rate, employment, and real GDP?

ANSWERS

True/False and Explain

1 F In the long run, real wage rate stays constant and so does employment. (698–700)
2 F In the long run, money wage adjusts equivalently, and the real wage rate stays constant. (698–700)
3 T *PF* shifts upward, movement along it too, increase in potential GDP. (698–700)
4 T In the short run, the decrease in price level will lead to an increase in the real wage rate and a decrease in employment. (700–703)
5 T Fall in expected future profits will shift *AD* curve leftward, movement along *SAS* curve leads to new short-run equilibrium will lower real GDP. (700–703)
6 T In short run, money wage is constant. (700–703)
7 F Changes in money wage rate shift *SAS* only, not *LAS*. (700–703)

Multiple-Choice

1 c No Δ employment leads to no Δ production—vertical *LAS*. (698–700)
2 a Vertical *AS* implies *LAS* implies real wage adjusts. (698–700)
3 e Δ money wage change *SAS* only, Δ in real wage rate may be part of another change that shift the *LAS*, but cannot tell for sure. (698–700)
4 d Real wage set where *LD* = *LS* at $12, money wage = real wage × price level/100. (698–700)

5 b Actual real wage = (money wage/price level) ×
100, and lower real wage leads to more labour
demanded. (700–703)

6 e a is nonsense, **b**, **c**, and **d** are movements
along curves. (700–703)

7 a Firms select labour hired given actual real
wage rate. (700–703)

8 a Fluctuations in real GDP are due to Δ *LAS*.
(700–703)

Short Answer Problems

1 Regardless of the value of the GDP deflator, in
the long run, the equilibrium real wage rate is
$4.50, the level of employment is 4 units per
day, and the level of output is 26 units per day.
If we know the real wage rate and the GDP
deflator, the money wage rate can be found as
follows:

$$\frac{\text{Money}}{\text{wage rate}} = \frac{\text{Real}}{\text{wage rate}} \times \frac{\text{GDP deflator}}{100}$$

a If the GDP deflator is 100, a real wage rate of
$4.50 implies a money wage rate of $4.50.

b If the GDP deflator is 80, a real wage rate of
$4.50 suggests a money wage rate of $3.60.

c If the GDP deflator is 120, a real wage rate of
$4.50 suggests a money wage rate of $5.40.

d The long-run aggregate supply curve (labelled
LAS) is given in Figure A29.2. Parts **a**, **b**, and **c**
indicate that at every price level output is 26
units per day.

FIGURE **A29.2** SOLUTION

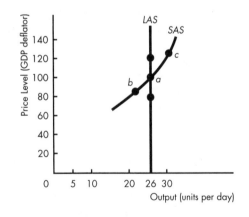

2 a If the actual value of the GDP deflator is 100,
since the money wage rate is fixed at $4.50, the
real wage rate is $4.50. This real wage rate
implies that employment is 4 units and output is
26 units.

b If the actual value of the GDP deflator is 82,
since the money wage rate is fixed at $4.50, the
real wage rate is $5.50 (4.5/82 × 100 = 5.5).
Employment is determined by the demand for
labour which, at a real wage of $5.50, is 3 units
per day. This employment level means that
(from Table 29.1) output is 21 units per day.

c If the actual value of the GDP deflator is 128,
since the money wage rate is fixed at $4.50, the
real wage rate is $3.50. Employment is
determined by the demand for labour and is 5
units per day. From Table 29.1, this employment
level implies a daily output of 30 units.

d Figure A29.2 indicates three points on the short-
run aggregate supply curve in the sticky-wage
economy: point *a* corresponds to output = 26,
GDP deflator = 100; point *b* corresponds to
output = 21, GDP deflator = 82; point *c*
corresponds to output = 30, GDP deflator =
128. The points are connected to give a portion
of the short-run aggregate supply curve (labelled
SAS).

3 In the short run, an increase in the price level
will, at the constant money wage rate, reduce the
real wage rate. Because the money wage rate
does not adjust in the short run, this lower real
wage rate will remain and, since the level of
employment is determined by the demand for
labour, the level of employment will increase.
This, of course, implies that the quantity of real
GDP supplied will increase via the aggregate
production function.

Chapter 30
Economic Growth

KEY CONCEPTS

Long-Term Growth Trends

Canada's growth rate was low in the 1950s, higher in the 1960s, slower in the 1970s and 1980s, and faster in the late 1990s.

◆ Internationally, between 1960 and 1990, Canada caught up to the United States, but Japan and other Asian countries have been catching up to both countries.

◆ Since 1990 Canada has fallen behind somewhat.

The Causes of Economic Growth: A First Look

Growth requires the essential precondition of an appropriate *incentive* system.

◆ Three institutions are crucial to an incentive system: markets, property rights, and monetary exchange.

This source of growth eventually runs its course—for further growth to continue we need

◆ saving and investment in new capital, which increases capital per worker

◆ investment in human capital (including by learning and repetitively doing tasks)

◆ discovery of new technologies

Growth Accounting

Growth accounting calculates how much of economic growth is due to growth of labour and capital or to technological change.

◆ Real GDP supplied (Y) depends on quantity of labour (N), quantity of capital (K), and state of technology (T)—summarized in **aggregate production function** $Y = F(N, K, T)$.

◆ **Labour productivity** is real GDP per hour of labour (Y/N).

Productivity growth comes from growth in capital per hour of labour and technological change (which includes human capital).

◆ **Productivity curve** (PC) is relationship between real GDP per hour of labour and capital per hour of labour, holding constant technology.

• Increase in capital per hour of labour creates movement up PC function.
• Technological change creates upward shift of PC function.
• Increase in one input, other inputs held constant, increases output at a diminishing rate—**law of diminishing returns**.

◆ **One-third rule** says, on average, one percent increase in capital per hour of labour (with no change in technology) leads to 1/3 of 1 percent increase in output per hour of labour.

◆ The one-third rule can be used to calculate contribution of capital growth to real GDP growth, and to study reasons for changes in productivity growth:

• 1961–73—high productivity growth due to high technological change and strong capital accumulation.
• 1973–96—lower productivity growth due to slowdown in technological change and lower capital accumulation.
• 1996–2001—speedup in technological change.

Main suggestions for increasing economic growth rates:

◆ Stimulate saving by tax incentives.

◆ Subsidize research and development.

◆ Target high-technology industries.

◆ Encourage international trade.

◆ Improve education quality.

Growth Theories

Classical growth theory argues real GDP growth is temporary, because it leads to population explosions.

◆ Advances in technology increase real GDP per hour of labour.

◆ Since real GDP per hour > **subsistence real GDP per hour** (minimum needed to maintain life), population grows, which lowers capital per hour of labour, and therefore output per hour of labour back to subsistence.

Neoclassical growth theory says real GDP per person grows due to technological change inducing growth in capital per person.

◆ The theory argues that population growth rate is roughly independent of economic growth.

◆ The driving force of economic growth is technological change, and its interaction with capital accumulation.

◆ Ongoing *exogenous* technological advances increases the rate of return on capital, increasing saving and investment, which increases capital per person and leads to real GDP growth.

◆ As capital per hour of labour increases, the rate of return on capital decreases to the target rate, and capital accumulation and growth end.

◆ Neoclassical growth theory predicts growth rates and income levels per person in different countries should converge, but this convergence doesn't happen empirically.

New growth theory attempts to overcome this shortcoming by explaining technological changes as a profit-maximizing choice.

◆ New discoveries are sought for (temporary) profits, but once made, discoveries are copied and benefits dispersed through economy, *without* diminishing returns.

◆ Knowledge is a special kind of capital not subject to diminishing returns.

◆ Inventions increase rate of return to knowledge capital until > target saving rate, resulting in increased capital per person and real GDP growth.

◆ Rate of return > target rate, which increases saving and capital per person and real GDP growth with *no automatic slowdown* because rate of return to capital does not diminish.

HELPFUL HINTS

1 Economic growth is a powerful force in raising living standards. Countries become rich by achieving high rates of growth in per person GDP and maintaining them over a long period of time. The role of compounding of income can create startling effects in this regard. We can see this effect by examining the post-1973 productivity growth slowdown. Growth between 1947 and 1973 was 3.2 percent per year, but after 1973 only 1.8 percent per year. This slowdown means that between 1973 and 1995, real GDP per person rose by about 48 percent $(= [(1.018)^{22} - 1] \times 100)$. However, if economic growth had continued at the pre-1973 rate of 3.2 percent, real GDP per person would have increased by about 100 percent $(= [(1.032)^{22} - 1] \times 100)$. Even the worst recession over this time period only lowered real GDP per person by about 5 percent. Avoiding the productivity growth slowdown would clearly have had a big payoff!

2 The key to understanding the different theories of growth is understanding the role of "the law of diminishing returns" in each theory. This law states that adding more of one input, other inputs held constant, eventually leads to a situation of diminishing returns to adding extra inputs.

In neoclassical theory, the discovery of a new technology increases the rate of return on capital above the target rate for savers, which increases saving and investment, increasing the amount of capital used. However, the increase in capital eventually leads to diminishing returns. As an example, we might think of the introduction of new and more powerful computers. As the number of computers increases, holding constant the number of workers, the extra output of the nth computer will not be as high as the productivity of the first computer. Eventually, the productivity of the extra capital must decrease (so that the rate of return decreases), and economic growth automatically slows down.

New growth theory has a different idea of technology and capital, with no diminishing returns, and no slowdown in economic growth. New growth theory examines "knowledge capital," a concept of technology that is not embodied so much in capital, but in ideas. These ideas might include new management techniques, or new processes of production (such as the assembly line) that can be copied from business to business without encountering diminishing returns. As an example, consider the introduction of new and better software (such as the first word processing package). As more copies of the software are introduced into different businesses around the country, we do not run into diminishing returns, at least not until the entire country has access to the new knowledge. Even then, new software will be continually developed and introduced without diminishing returns (so that the rate of return does *not* decrease), and economic growth need not automatically slow down.

SELF-TEST

True/False and Explain

Long-Term Growth Trends

1 Canada's recent growth speedup is quite unusual in Canadian history.

2 Asian countries are catching up with Canada's real GDP per person.

The Causes of Economic Growth: A First Look

3 Specialization is the crucial source of current growth.

4 Higher levels of average human capital, but with the same level of physical capital per person, will not raise per person income.

5 The three preconditions for economic growth are markets, property rights, and the discovery of new technologies.

Growth Accounting

6 When a country adopts a better technology, its productivity curve will shift upward.

7 Rapid changes in technology create growth without need for new capital.

8 High economic growth has typically been accompanied by high saving rates.

9 The slowdown in productivity growth after 1973 was due to a slowdown in the growth of capital per hour of labour, with a constant rate of technological change.

10 The most dramatic economic growth success stories have almost always involved rapid expansion of international trade.

11 The productivity curve shows the relationship between real GDP and labour inputs.

Growth Theories

12 Neoclassical growth theory argues economic growth will eventually slow down because the rate of return on capital begins to diminish as the amount of capital increases.

13 Classical growth theory argues economic growth leads to a smaller population growth rate.

14 Neoclassical growth theory requires ongoing technological change to get ongoing economic growth.

15 In new growth theory, diminishing returns do not occur for knowledge capital.

Multiple-Choice

Long-Term Growth Trends

1 Canada's economic growth rates were highest in which of the following decades?

a the 1930s
b the 1960s
c the 1970s
d the 1980s
e the 1990s

2 Compared to the growth in other countries, between 1960 and 1990 Canada

a fell behind most other countries.
b dramatically caught up to and passed other countries.
c worsened versus the United States, but did better versus other countries.
d did as well or better than most countries except certain Asian countries.
e none of the above.

3 Which of the following statements about Canada's long-term growth trends is *false*?

a Economic growth has tended to be steady, except for the business cycle.
b Economic growth shows periods of slow and high growth.
c Economic growth has been faster since 1996.
d Economic growth has been generally faster in Japan than in Canada.
e African countries have fallen further behind Canada in recent years.

The Causes of Economic Growth: A First Look

4 Which of the following is *not* a source of economic growth?

a increasing stock market prices
b better educated workers
c growing stock of capital equipment
d an appropriate incentive system
e advances in technology

5 Markets are an essential precondition to growth because

a they suffer from diminishing returns.
b they allow countries to benefit from high saving rates.
c prices send signals that create incentives.
d people have an assurance that their income and savings will not be confiscated.
e they discourage consumer spending.

6 The basic sources of economic growth include all of the following *except*

a saving and investment in new capital.
b investment in human capital.
c discoveries of new techniques.
d discoveries of new management processes.
e discouraging market systems.

7 A good incentive system

a leads to specialization and exchange, with higher GDP per person.
b is all that is needed to have continuous growth.
c solves the problem of diminishing returns.
d has no role for government.
e can have the rate of return on capital above the target rate of savers for an extended period of time.

Growth Accounting

8 Suppose that productivity increased 20 percent last year. Capital per hour of labour increased by 12 percent as well. The increase in capital was responsible for

a all of the increase in productivity.
b 80 percent of the increase in productivity.
c 60 percent of the increase in productivity.
d 40 percent of the increase in productivity.
e 20 percent of the increase in productivity.

9 Suppose that productivity increased 20 percent last year. Capital per hour of labour increased by 12 percent as well. An increase in technology was responsible for

a all of the increase in productivity.
b 80 percent of the increase in productivity.
c 60 percent of the increase in productivity.
d 40 percent of the increase in productivity.
e 20 percent of the increase in productivity.

10 Which of the following was one of the causes of Canada's post-1973 growth slowdown?

a higher population pressures
b lower amounts of saving
c diminishing returns
d slowdowns in technological change
e too-rapid increases in technological change

11 If there were significant technological advances last year, and the capital stock per hour of labour grew by 9 percent,

a the rate of return on capital must have decreased.
b economic growth would have been significantly less than 3 percent.
c economic growth would have been significantly more than 3 percent.
d economic growth would have been about 3 percent.
e the target rate of savers must have fallen.

12 Which of the following is a suggestion for increasing Canadian economic growth rates?

a Stimulate saving by taxing consumption.
b Reduce the time period for patents to increase replication.
c Put less public research funds into universities.
d Protect our industries from foreign competition.
e Tax education.

13 One of the reasons technological change slowed down after 1973 was the

a energy-inefficiency of the new capital stock.
b lack of new capital stock.
c one-third rule.
d law of diminishing returns.
e introduction of new environmental protection laws and regulations.

14 It is argued that governments must subsidize research and development

a because there is too little private saving.
b it is too expensive for small firms.
c there are external benefits to research and development that firms ignore.
d in order to take advantage of the gains from specialization and exchange.
e in order to overcome diminishing returns.

15 The aggregate production function shows the relationship between

a real GDP supplied and the quantity of labour, the quantity of capital, and the state of technology.
b real GDP per hour of labour and capital per hour of labour, technology level constant.
c real GDP per hour of labour, and knowledge capital per hour of labour, technology level constant.
d real GDP supplied and the quantity of labour and the quantity of capital.
e real GDP per hour of labour and capital per hour of labour.

Growth Theories

16 The law of diminishing returns

a holds only for knowledge capital.
b states that if capital increases by 1 percent, real GDP increases by about 1/3 of a percent.
c states that if capital increases by 1 percent, real GDP increases by about 3 percent.
d holds for both physical and knowledge capital.
e does not hold for knowledge capital.

17 In neoclassical growth theory, if the rate of return on capital exceeds the target rate of savers, then

a the rate of return on capital will eventually decline.
b capital per hour of labour will decrease.
c real GDP per hour of labour will decrease.
d the rate of return on capital will never decline.
e population growth will explode.

18 In new growth theory, if the rate of return on capital exceeds the target rate of savers, then

a the rate of return on capital will eventually decline.
b capital per hour of labour will decrease.
c real GDP per hour of labour will decrease.
d the rate of return on capital will never decline.
e population growth will explode.

19 Which theory of economic growth argues that growth always slows down unless there are new technological inventions?

a classical theory
b neoclassical theory
c new growth theory
d old growth theory
e none of the theories

20 Which theory of economic growth concludes that technological advances are influenced by the profit motive?

a classical theory
b neoclassical theory
c new growth theory
d old growth theory
e none of the theories

21 Incentives are important in the new growth theory because they

a imply there are no diminishing returns.
b lead to higher rates of saving.
c imply that economic growth does not lead to population growth.
d create specialization and exchange.
e lead to profit-seeking searches for new discoveries.

22 In the classical growth theory, economic growth eventually stops after a technological advance because of

a diminishing returns.
b knowledge capital being easily replicated.
c the rate of return on capital decreasing back down to the target rate of savers.
d real GDP per person becoming too high.
e high population growth resulting from the increase in real GDP per person.

23 The important difference between knowledge capital and physical capital is that knowledge capital

a can be replicated without diminishing returns.
b cannot be held in your hand.
c leads to an automatic slowdown in growth.
d cannot be replicated without diminishing returns.
e none of the above.

24 The rate of return on capital does not decline in new growth theory because

a the productivity of capital diminishes as more capital is employed per hour of labour.
b technological advances occur frequently due to profit-seeking activities.
c discoveries can be replicated without diminishing their marginal productivity.
d the target rate of savers is constant.
e population growth in response to high real GDP per person keeps the rate of return on capital high.

25 The key difference between neoclassical growth theory and new growth theory is that

a capital is not subject to diminishing returns under new growth theory.
b capital is subject to diminishing returns under new growth theory.
c increases in technology increase population which drives workers' incomes back down to the subsistence level in neoclassical theory.
d technological advances are exogenous in new growth theory.
e the one-third rule only holds in new growth theory.

Short Answer Problems

1 Why is an appropriate incentive system a precondition to growth?

2 Why does this source of growth eventually run its course?

3 Explain what happens in classical growth theory when advances in technology increase real GDP per person.

4 Some economists speculate that the Asian miracle economies have achieved such fast growth at least partially due to their adeptness at replicating new technology from other countries. Explain how and why this replicating is such a good source of growth.

5 Paul Krugman and others have argued that in fact the Asian miracle economies' extra-high economic growth is mostly due to the mobilization of capital and labour resources that were previously underutilized, and that therefore North American worries that these countries will catch up to and surpass Canada and the United States are unfounded. Assuming his argument is true, explain why this argument implies that these worries are unfounded.

6 Use the concept of a productivity function curve to explain why an increase in the amount of capital per hour of labour will lead to economic growth.

7 You are given the data in Table 30.1 on the economy of Erehwon where the one-third rule holds, and the labour supply and population is unchanging over these three years. Do the calculations needed to show the contributions of changes in capital per hour of labour (as a fraction of the total change) and technological change to productivity growth, and fill in the rest of the table.

TABLE **30.1**

Year	1998	1999	2000
Capital per hour of labour ($)	125	150	200
Productivity ($)	35	40	44.4
Contribution of capital	—	?	?
Contribution of technological change	—	?	?

8 On a graph, sketch the productivity curves from Short Answer Problem 7 for the three years, showing the production points for each of the three years.

9 Consider the following productivity curve:

TABLE **30.2**

Capital per Hour of Labour	Real GDP per Hour of Labour
100	60
120	64
156	70

The economy is originally producing 60 units of real GDP per hour of labour in year 1.

a Does this productivity curve roughly meet the one-third rule?

b Graph this function, and the current point of production. Suppose that there is a technological advance that increases real GDP per hour of labour by 20 percent, holding constant the capital per hour of labour. Show the impact of this change in a new table and on your graph.

c In year 2, real GDP per hour of labour is now 84 units. Show this point on your graph. How much (if any) of the increase in real GDP was due to the technological advance, and how much (if any) was due to an increase in the capital per hour of labour?

10 Some commentators have argued that Japan has had a higher growth rate than countries like Canada or the United States because the Japanese care more about the future and less about present consumption, reflected in a lower target interest rate for savers. Explain within the context of growth theory whether or not this argument seems likely to be true.

ANSWERS

True/False and Explain

1 **F** Growth was higher in the 1960s. (708)
2 **T** See text discussion. (709–710)
3 **F** It is the initial source of growth, but once specialization is high, growth slows down. (711–712)
4 **F** Human capital growth is part of advances in technology. (712)
5 **F** Third precondition should be monetary exchange. (711–712)
6 **T** Technological advance increases productivity, capital per hour of labour unchanged. (714)
7 **F** Rapid technological change is embodied in new human and physical capital. (715)
8 **T** See discussion of East Asian economies. (716)
9 **F** Due to slowdown in both—see text discussion. (715)
10 **T** See text discussion. (715)
11 **F** Relationship between real GDP per hour of labour and capital per hour of labour, technology level constant. (714)
12 **T** Due to the law of diminishing returns. (719–721)
13 **F** Economic growth increases real GDP per hour, which increases population growth. (717–718)
14 **T** A technological advance increases rate of return on capital, which is now > target rate, which increases savings and investment, and therefore capital per hour of labour, which leads to more economic growth, but rate of return on capital down due to diminishing returns, which means growth eventually stops, unless there is more technological change. (719–721)
15 **T** Because knowledge capital can be duplicated at essentially zero marginal cost. (721–723)

Multiple-Choice

1 **b** See text discussion. (708)
2 **d** See text discussion. (709)
3 **a** Growth rates have fluctuated. (708–711)
4 **a** This factor has no impact on productivity, others increase it. (711–712)
5 **c** Incentives to specialize, trade, save, and invest. (711–712)
6 **e** See text discussion. (711–712)
7 **a** It eventually no longer contributes to growth, does not solve diminishing returns, government is needed to allocate property

rights, and has little to do with rate of return on capital. (711–712)

℗ **8 e** By one-third rule, capital increase of 12 percent leads to real GDP per hour of labour increase in 4 percent, or 20% of increase in productivity. (714–715)

℗ **9 b** From **8**, 80% is left over for technology to explain. (714–715)

10 d See text discussion. (715)

11 c One-third rule says capital growth leads to real GDP per hour of labour of about 3 percent, but technological growth will add to this amount. (714–715)

12 a b would lower return to and number of inventions, **c** would lower research and number of inventions, and trade and education should be encouraged. (716)

13 e See text discussion. (716)

14 c See text discussion. (716)

15 a Definition. (714)

16 e Holds for ordinary capital, but not for knowledgeable capital. (714–723)

17 a If rate of return on capital > target rate, saving increases supply of capital, which leads to more capital per hour of labour (and more real GDP per hour of labour), decreasing rate of return on capital due to law of diminishing returns. (719–721)

℗ **18 d** If rate of return on capital > target rate, saving increases supply of capital, leading to increase in capital per hour of labour (and in real GDP per hour of labour), but no change in rate of return on capital since the law of diminishing returns doesn't hold for knowledge capital. (721–723)

19 b Due to diminishing returns to capital. (717–723)

20 c This is a core assumption of the theory. (721–723)

21 e This assumption makes technological change endogenous, and continuous. (721–723)

22 e This growth leads to decrease in real wages. (717–718)

23 a Due to its nature—see text discussion. (721–723)

24 c Therefore as increase in capital stock, rate of return on capital does not diminish. (721–723)

25 a Due to the different nature of knowledge capital. (721–723)

Short Answer Problems

1 The incentive system includes
- markets to send signals and enable people to specialize, exchange, save, and invest (all of which increase growth)
- property rights to ensure income and savings are not confiscated and hence encourage people to work and save
- monetary exchange to facilitate transactions and encourage trade

2 This source creates growth by increasing specialization. Eventually the level of specialization is so high, there is little left to be gained from further specialization.

3 Technology advances imply increases in the demand for labour, and real GDP per hour of labour. As real GDP per hour goes up, the rate of population growth increases, increasing the supply of labour, decreasing real GDP per hour back down to the subsistence wage rate, so workers are no better off than at the beginning.

4 Knowledge capital can be replicated without running into diminishing returns, so that the rate of return on capital increases after the replication, which in turn brings more saving and investment, and therefore capital per hour of labour can increase without limit, implying that growth can increase without limit.

5 If the growth is due to increasing the amounts of capital and labour, then eventually these countries will run into diminishing returns to each of these inputs, which means that the increases in productivity will slow down, meaning that economic growth will also slow down.

6 The productivity curve illustrates how output per hour increases as the stock of capital per hour increases, given the state of technology. If the amount of capital per hour of labour increases, then the productivity of workers is increasing, which means that output per hour of labour is increasing—that is, there is faster economic growth. This effect is illustrated graphically by movements up along the graph of the productivity curve.

℗ **7** Table 30.1 is reproduced below as Table 30.1 Solution, with the calculations in place.

TABLE **30.1**   SOLUTION

Year	1998	1999	2000
Capital per hour of labour ($)	125	150	200
Productivity ($)	35	40	44.4
Contribution of capital	—	46.6%	100%
Contribution of technological change	—	53.4%	0

The percentage change in capital from 1998 to 1999 was 20 percent ((25/125) × 100), implying a resulting percentage change in productivity of 6.67 percent. The total change in productivity was 14.3 percent ((5/35) × 100), leaving 7.63 percent due to technological change. Capital's contribution was (6.67/14.3) × 100 = 46.6 percent, and technology's contribution was 53.4 percent.

The percentage change in capital from 1999 to 2000 was 33 percent ((50/150) × 100), implying a resulting percentage change in productivity of 11 percent. The total change in productivity was 11 percent ((4.4/40) × 100), leaving no contribution due to technological change. Capital's contribution was 100 percent.

8 The graphs are shown in Figure 30.1. Note that from Table 30.1 the three yearly points must be where shown, and given our result about technological change in 1999 and 2000, the shift in 1999 and no shift in 2000 must be so.

FIGURE **30.1**

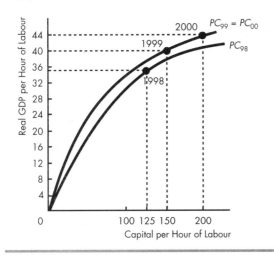

9 a Between 100 and 120, the percentage change in capital per hour is (20/100) × 100 = 20 percent, while the percentage change in real GDP per hour is (4/60) × 100 = 6.67 percent. One-third of 20 percent is 6.67 percent. Between 120 and 156, the percentage change in capital per hour is (36/120) × 100 = 30 percent, while the percentage change in real GDP per hour is (6/64) × 100 = 9.4 percent. One-third of 30 percent is 10 percent, a little bit higher than 9.4 percent. The one-third rule roughly holds.

b Figure 30.2 shows the original productivity curve as PC_0, with the three points from the table graphed on it, with the current production point marked as year 1. A 20 percent increase in productivity would lead to a shift upwards in the

productivity curve to PC_1, shown in Table 30.3, and graphed as PC_1, with the new production point marked as year 2.

TABLE **30.3**

Capital per Hour of Labour	Real GDP per Hour of Labour
100	72
120	76.8
156	84

FIGURE **30.2**

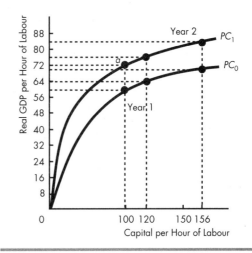

c The point is labelled as year 2 on the graph. We can see that the increase in real GDP per hour of labour from 60 to 84 units is broken down into two components. The technological change is shown as the movement from the point Year 1 to the point *a*, a total change of 12 units or 50 percent (= (12/24) × 100) of the total change. The increase in capital per hour must be from 100 to 156 units to get production up to 84 units, and is shown as the movement from the point *a* to the point Year 2. This change is a total of 12 units or 50 percent (= (12/24) × 100) of the total change.

10 The lower the target interest rate for savers, the more willing a person or country is to forgo current consumption and save for the future. Since Japan has a lower target rate, in any given situation Japan's saving rate will be higher. This higher saving in turn means the increase in the supply of capital in Japan is higher in any situation. Therefore, in general, Japan will have a higher capital stock per person than Canada, and it will generally be increasing each year at a higher rate, which in turn leads to a higher growth rate of real GDP per person in Japan than in Canada. Thus this argument seems to be true.

Chapter **31**

The Business Cycle

Cycle Patterns, Impulses, and Mechanisms

All theories of the business cycle emphasize initiating *impulses*, cycle mechanisms, and especially the role of investment.

◆ In an expansion, investment is high and capital stock increases quickly, leading to diminishing returns to capital and therefore decreased investment, and recession begins.

◆ In a recession, investment is low and capital stock increases slowly, leading to increased marginal product of capital, increasing investment, and recession ends.

Aggregate Demand Theories of the Business Cycle

Keynesian theory of the business cycle regards volatile expectations as the main cycle source.

◆ Keynesian impulse is Δ expected future sales/profits, which leads to Δ investment.

◆ Initial change in investment has a multiplier effect, which creates strong shifts in *AD* curve.

◆ *SAS* curve is assumed flat to left of potential GDP—therefore decrease in *AD* leads to long-term unemployment equilibrium.

◆ Above full employment, *LAS* curve vertical—prices adjust quickly, economy stays near full employment.

Monetarist theory of the business cycle regards Δ quantity of money as main source of the cycle.

◆ Decrease in money growth increases interest rates (and exchange rate), *AD* shifts leftward.

◆ *SAS* curve upward-sloping, so decrease in *AD* decreases both real GDP and price level.

◆ Unemployment equilibrium decreases money wage rate, and *SAS* adjusts rightward, with movement to full-employment equilibrium.

Rational expectations theories of cycle claim money wages set by **rational expectation** of price level (forecast based on all available, relevant information).

New classical theory of the business cycle regards unanticipated fluctuations in *AD* as main source of cycle.

◆ Unanticipated decrease in *AD* decreases price level, so real wage increases (since money wage constant), increasing unemployment.

◆ Money wages adjust quickly, economy moves to full employment.

◆ Anticipated Δ*AD* is fully built into money wages—no change real GDP.

New Keynesian theory of the business cycle regards unanticipated *and* anticipated fluctuations in *AD* as sources of the cycle.

◆ Effects of unanticipated Δ*AD* the same as in new classical.

◆ If anticipated Δ*AD*, because current wages built on past expectations due to long-term contracts, money wages cannot adjust to anticipated change, so both real GDP and employment affected.

Real Business Cycle Theory

Real business cycle (RBC) theory regards random fluctuations in productivity (due to Δ pace of technological change) as main source of the cycle.

◆ RBC recession starts with technological change that makes existing capital obsolete—temporary decrease in productivity.

◆ Fall in productivity decreases demand for labour and capital (which decreases real rate of interest).

◆ Decreasing real rate of interest decreases labour supply (intertemporal substitution effect), leading to small decrease in real wage rate, large decrease in employment.

◆ Decrease in investment demand decreases *AD*, and decrease in employment decreases *LAS*, resulting in decreased real GDP.

Critics of RBC theory argue that money wages are sticky, intertemporal substitution is weak, and technological shocks are *caused by AD* fluctuations.

◆ Defenders of RBC theory reply that it is consistent with facts (explains both growth *and* cycles) and microeconomic theory.

Recessions During the 1990s

The 1990–91 Canadian recession was caused by the Bank of Canada's anti-inflationary policy, the U.S. recession, and the Canada–United States Free Trade Agreement.

◆ The first two causes shifted *AD* leftward, while the third shifted both *AD* and *SAS* leftward.

◆ In labour market, slowdown in inflation not anticipated, so real wages increased and employment decreased.

The Japanese recession of the 1990s started with a collapse in overvalued asset prices in 1990, leading to lowered consumption, investment, and therefore *AD* and potential GDP growth.

◆ Japan's fiscal policy was usually expansionary, while monetary policy had little impact.

◆ Some of the Japanese problem is due to delayed structural change slowing productivity growth.

The Great Depression

In the Great Depression, real GDP fell 30 percent, unemployment went from 2.9 percent to 20 percent.

◆ Primary cause was increased uncertainty and pessimism, creating decreased investment and consumer spending.

◆ These unexpected shocks shift *AD* more than *SAS*, resulting in decreased real GDP and price level.

◆ Depression prolonged by further unexpected shifts leftward in *AD*, driven by collapse of the financial system and the quantity of money in the United States, and by an international tariff war.

◆ Great Depression unlikely to occur again due to the presence of Bank of Canada acting as a lender of last resort, deposit insurance, a higher government presence, and multi-income families.

HELPFUL HINTS

1 This chapter should be very rewarding to those who have worked hard to understand the previous chapters. It introduces no new analytical structure, but instead demonstrates the power of the fully developed aggregate demand and aggregate supply model by analyzing some interesting macroeconomic episodes, including the Great Depression. You should be pleased that you have mastered this powerful analytical tool.

2 As you examine various macroeconomic episodes, focus on these key factors: Are changes primarily in aggregate demand, aggregate supply, or both? As you follow the changes, be sure you understand what is going on in the labour market that underlies the goods and services market. The labour market will tell you what is happening to the key variables of employment and unemployment.

3 This chapter contains competing theories that explain real-world events. There is no dispute over the facts such as the level of prices or real GDP. The dispute centres around what changes in the economy created the facts, and touches on what government policies might affect the economy.

To help you remember and understand these theories, use Table 31.1. It highlights the similarities and differences between the theories, and it helps to highlight how radically different real business cycle theory is.

Theories differ based on two primary factors: the source of the cycle (*AD* versus *AS*), and the responsiveness of the labour market (sticky versus flexible wages). Be sure you can catalogue and understand these theories.

Remember, these are theories, *not* statements of facts, and their explanations could be incorrect. Only proper empirical investigation over time will cast light on their validity.

TABLE **31.1**

Labour Market Structure		Theory	Primary Source of the Cycle
Wages are sticky	U above natural rate for long time periods	Keynesian and New Keynesian	AD Shocks
Wages are flexible	U above natural rate for short time periods	New classical and Monetarist	
	U = natural rate always	Real business cycle	AS Shocks

SELF-TEST

True/False and Explain

Cycle Patterns, Impulses, and Mechanisms

1 During the early stages of a recession, interest rates tend to decrease but later they typically increase.

Aggregate Demand Theories of the Business Cycle

2 Unanticipated decreases in aggregate demand cause recessions only in new Keynesian theory, not in new classical theory.

3 A decrease in aggregate demand will cause a recession in Keynesian theory.

4 An anticipated decrease in aggregate demand will create a recession in new classical theory.

5 An anticipated decrease in aggregate demand will create a recession in new Keynesian theory.

6 A rational expectation is always correct.

Real Business Cycle Theory

7 Monetarists and real business cycle theorists tend to believe that wages are flexible and adjust quickly.

8 In real business cycle theory, most fluctuations in real GDP are the best possible responses of the economy to the uneven pace of technological change.

9 In order for the RBC theory to explain the behaviour of the labour market (real wages and employment), it must assume that the natural rate of unemployment increases in a recession.

Recessions During the 1990s

10 The reduction in the growth rate of the quantity of money by the Bank of Canada in 1988 and 1989 was generally anticipated by households and firms.

11 According to real business cycle theory, the unemployment of the 1990–91 Canadian recession could have been avoided by an expansionary monetary or fiscal policy.

12 The expansionary fiscal policy carried out by Japan in the 1990s was effective in battling the Japanese stagnation.

The Great Depression

13 A recession today is likely to be less severe than during the 1930s because the government sector is larger today.

14 The stock market crash of 1929 was the cause of the Great Depression.

15 The existence of the Canadian Deposit Insurance Corporation increases the likelihood that another Great Depression will occur.

Multiple-Choice

Cycle Patterns, Impulses, and Mechanisms

1 Recessions tend to begin when
a consumption expenditure decreases.
b investment decreases.
c investment increases.
d government purchases decrease.
e net exports decrease.

2 Typically in a recession, investment
a is low at the start, but eventually increases as the recession ends.
b is high at the start, but eventually decreases as the recession ends.
c has the same pattern as in an expansion.
d is constant.
e moves around, but with no distinct pattern.

Aggregate Demand Theories of the Business Cycle

3 If the Bank of Canada unexpectedly decreases the quantity of money during a recession,
a nothing will happen since the recession is already occurring.
b the recession will deepen, as higher interest rates discourage investment.
c the recession will deepen, because the value of the Canadian dollar will decrease.
d the recession will end, as higher interest rates encourage more saving.
e interest rates will decrease, since the change in the quantity of money was unexpected.

4 Which of the following news quotes *best* describes a *Keynesian* view of a recession?
a "Rapid computerization is creating obsolete workers and higher unemployment."
b "The unexpectedly tight fiscal policy is raising spending and lowering unemployment."
c "The promised anti-inflationary policy of the Bank of Canada is increasing spending."
d "The promised cuts in government spending have helped lower consumer spending and created unemployment."
e "Businesses are very worried about future sales and have lowered their purchases of capital equipment."

5 Which of the following news quotes *best* describes a *new classical* view of a recession?
a "Rapid computerization is creating obsolete workers and higher unemployment."
b "The unexpectedly tight fiscal policy is lowering spending and creating unemployment."
c "The promised anti-inflationary policy of the Bank of Canada is lowering spending as promised."
d "The promised cuts in government spending have helped lower consumer spending and created unemployment."
e "Businesses are very worried about future sales and have lowered their purchases of capital equipment."

6 What is the key impulse in the *Keynesian* theory of the business cycle?
a changes in expected future sales and profits
b changes in the quantity of money
c unanticipated changes in aggregate demand
d anticipated changes in aggregate demand
e changes in the pace of technological change

7 Consider Figure 31.1. Which graph(s) represent(s) an economy that is recovering from a recession without any government involvement?
a (a)
b (b)
c (c)
d (d)
e (b) and (d)

FIGURE **31.1**

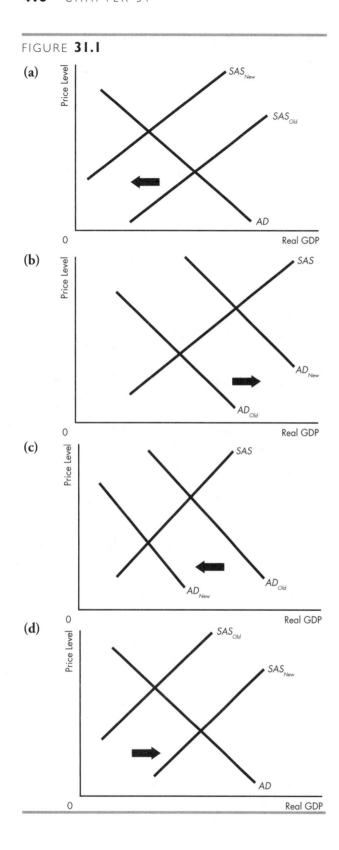

8 In Figure 31.1, which graph(s) represent(s) an economy where the government is helping it recover from a recession?

a (a)
b (b)
c (c)
d (b) and (a)
e none of the graphs

9 In Figure 31.1, which graph(s) represent(s) an economy entering a recession due to worsening consumer and investor expectations?

a (a)
b (b)
c (c)
d (b) and (d)
e none of the graphs

Real Business Cycle Theory

10 In Figure 31.1, which graph(s) represent(s) an economy entering a recession according to real business cycle theory?

a (a)
b (b)
c (c)
d (b) and (d)
e none of the graphs

11 An increase in aggregate demand causes GDP to increase by the least amount in the

a Keynesian theory.
b monetarist theory.
c new Keynesian theory.
d new classical theory.
e real business cycle theory.

12 In which theory of the business cycle is government policy likely to be *most* effective (has the strongest impact)?

a Keynesian
b monetarist
c new classical
d new Keynesian
e real business cycle

13 If the intertemporal substitution effect is weak, then the RBC theory of the business cycle would have problems explaining

a a large decrease in employment in a recession.
b how a recession begins.
c why aggregate demand decreases in a recession.
d the automatic adjustment to full employment.
e what creates technological change.

14 The intertemporal substitution effect states that

a in a recession, investment is low and the capital stock increases slowly, leading to a rising marginal product of capital.

b money wages are based on a rational expectation of the price level.

c a decrease in productivity leads to a decrease in the demand for capital, and a decrease in the real interest rate.

d when current real wages and real interest rates are high, people decrease their labour supply strongly.

e when current real wages and real interest rates are high, people increase their labour supply strongly.

15 According to the real business cycle theorists, the increase in the unemployment rate during a recession is due to an increase in the

a deviation of the unemployment rate from the natural rate of unemployment resulting from a real wage rate that is too high to clear the labour market.

b deviation of the unemployment rate from the natural rate of unemployment resulting from an increase in job market turnover.

c natural rate of unemployment resulting from a real wage that is too high to clear the labour market.

d natural rate of unemployment resulting from an increase in job market turnover.

e rate of new entries into the labour market.

16 Which of the following news quotes *best* describes a *real business cycle* view of a recession?

a "Rapid computerization is creating obsolete workers and higher unemployment."

b "The unexpectedly tight fiscal policy is lowering spending and creating unemployment."

c "The promised anti-inflationary policy of the Bank of Canada is lowering spending as promised."

d "The promised cuts in government spending have helped lower consumer spending and created unemployment."

e "Businesses are very worried about future sales and have lowered their purchases of capital equipment."

Recessions During the 1990s

17 The cause of the 1990–91 Canadian recession was an aggregate

a supply shock, accompanied by a rightward shift in aggregate demand.

b demand shock, accompanied by a leftward shift in aggregate supply.

c demand shock alone.

d demand shock, accompanied by a rightward shift in aggregate supply.

e supply shock alone.

18 During the 1990–91 Canadian recession, the real wage rate

a decreased and employment decreased.

b decreased and employment increased.

c stayed constant and employment decreased.

d increased and employment increased.

e increased and employment decreased.

19 Which of the following statements about the Japanese recession of the 1990s is *false*?

a Negative wealth effects lowered consumption expenditures.

b Potential GDP growth slowed down.

c Fiscal policy was very expansionary.

d Monetary policy was very expansionary.

e One cause of the recession was structural change lowering productivity growth.

The Great Depression

20 Fill in the blanks in the following sentence. During the Great Depression, which was caused by an aggregate _____ shock, the rate of inflation _____.

a supply; increased

b supply; decreased

c demand; increased

d demand; decreased

e demand; became negative

21 Once the Great Depression started, aggregate demand was expected to

a decrease, but it did not decrease as rapidly as expected.

b decrease, but it decreased faster than expected.

c increase, but it actually decreased.

d increase, which it did due to an increase in the quantity of money.

e increase, but it increased less than expected.

22   The Great Depression was prolonged by

a   a massive increase in confidence following the stock market crash.

b   extended bank failures in the United States leading to a large decrease in the quantity of money.

c   structural reorganizing of the economy.

d   governments increasing their spending and cutting taxes.

e   expansionary monetary policy.

23   According to Friedman and Schwartz, the Great Depression was caused by

a   the stock market crash of 1929.

b   a decrease in the quantity of money leading to higher interest rates and lower investment.

c   an increase in the quantity of money leading to higher inflation.

d   decreases in business and consumer confidence.

e   imports decreasing.

24   The initial cause of the Great Depression was

a   a dramatic increase in the prices of raw materials during 1929.

b   a decrease in the quantity of money during 1929.

c   a decrease in investment and consumer spending because of uncertainty about the future.

d   the stock market crash of 1929.

e   none of the above.

25   Multi-income families reduce the probability of another Great Depression by

a   reducing the probability of everyone in the family being simultaneously unemployed.

b   investing more in the economy.

c   paying more taxes.

d   increasing fluctuations in consumption.

e   none of the above.

Short Answer Problems

1   What was the cause of the 1990–91 Canadian recession? What was the cause of the Great Depression?

2   What is the basic controversy among economists about the behaviour of the labour market during recession? Why is the controversy important for designing an appropriate anti-recessionary economic policy?

3   List the four important features of the Canadian economy that make severe depression less likely today.

4   How do government transfer payments in Canada help to reduce the severity of a recession?

5   Suppose that you have been selected to be the economic advisor to the prime minister, on the basis of your sterling performance in macroeconomics. You have been asked to evaluate the new Keynesian theory of the business cycle, and the real business cycle theory of the business cycle, and to explain what each theory argues should be the optimal government policy for a recession.

a   What does each theory argue is the likely cause of a recession, and why?

b   What does each theory argue is the best response to a recession? Why do the two theories differ? That is, what crucial differences in their approach to the economy leads to the different policy conclusions?

6 a   If an individual was politically conservative and tended to distrust the government, which theory or theories of the business cycle do you think they would support?

b   If an individual was politically leftist and tended to trust the government, which theory or theories of the business cycle do you think they would support?

7   Table 31.2 gives data for a hypothetical economy in years 1 and 2.

TABLE **31.2**

	Year 1	Year 2
Real GDP (billions of dollars)	800	750
Price level (GDP deflator)	100	105

a   If the real business cycle theory is true, what happened to aggregate demand and aggregate supply in this economy?

b   If the new Keynesian theory is true, what happened to aggregate demand and aggregate supply in this economy?

8   Consider the labour market in the economy from Short Answer Problem 7.

a   If the real business cycle theory is true, what happened in the labour market? Is the unemployment natural or not?

b   If the new Keynesian theory is true, what happened in the labour market? Is the unemployment natural or not?

ⓒ **9** Consider the economy from Short Answer Problem 7 again.

a Suppose instead that you knew that the expected price level in year 1 was 100 and that in year 2 it was 110. Would this information allow you to decide which theory was correct?

b Suppose instead that you knew that the expected price level in year 1 was 100 and that in year 2 it was 105. Would this information allow you to decide which theory was correct?

ⓒ **10** Some economists argue that real business cycle theory is false because it is unable to explain the events of the Great Depression, especially the events in the labour market. Briefly evaluate this argument.

ANSWERS

True/False and Explain

1 F Reverse occurs. (730)
2 F In both theories, unanticipated decrease means wages set too high, creating unemployment and recession. (731–736)
3 T Due to flat *SAS* curve. (731–732)
4 F *SAS* will shift with anticipated change, so no change in real GDP. (734–736)
5 T *SAS* will not shift fully due to long-term contracts. (734–736)
6 F Uses all relevant, available information, but might be missing some information. (734)
7 T See text discussion. (731–741)
8 T See text discussion. (737–740)
9 T All unemployment natural in RBC theory. (737–740)
10 F It was unanticipated, so unexpectedly low inflation led to recession. (741–743)
11 F All changes in unemployment are natural. (741–743)
12 F It was too erratic, and the stagnation did not end. (743–745)
13 T Larger government sector leads to larger automatic stabilizers. (748–749)
14 F It was a symptom of uncertainty about future that was initial cause. (747–748)
15 F It reduces chance of banking collapses. (748–749)

Multiple-Choice

1 b See text discussion. (730)
2 a See text discussion. (730)

ⓒ **3 b** Decrease in quantity of money increases interest rates, which decreases investment demand and aggregate demand. (732–734)
4 e Key impulse in Keynesian theory is Δ expected sales/profits. (731–732)
5 b Key impulse in new classical theory is unexpected change in *AD*. (734–736)
6 a See text discussion. (731–732)
7 d Recession leads to unemployment, which decreases real wages and shifts *SAS* rightward. (731–736)
8 b Expansionary policy shifts *AD* rightward. (731–736)
9 c Decrease in expectations decreases consumption and investment and shift leftward in *AD*. (731–736)
10 e In RBC theory, negative productivity shock shifts *LAS*, there is no *SAS*. (737–740)
11 e Vertical *AS* curve. (731–740)
12 a Flat *SAS* curve implies biggest swings in *Y* for a given Δ *AD*. (731–740)
13 a Intertemporal substitution means Δ current real wage or real interest rate leads to big Δ labour supply. (738–740)
14 e Definition. (738–740)
15 d All unemployment is natural, and real wage rate is always correct. (738–740)
16 a Key impulse is Δ pace of technological change. (737)
17 b Decrease in consumer and investor confidence shifts *AD* leftward, and increase in wages plus restructuring shifts *SAS* leftward. (741–743)
18 e See text discussion. (741–743)
19 d See text discussion. (743–745)
20 e Decrease in consumer and investor confidence shifts *AD* leftward so much it decreases price level. (746–748)
21 b See text discussion. (746–748)
22 b See text discussion. (746–748)
23 b They argue that monetary forces are most important. (746–748)
24 c See text discussion. (746–748)
25 a This arrangement leads to smaller decrease in consumer confidence when one member becomes unemployed. (748–749)

Short Answer Problems

1 The cause of the 1990–91 Canadian recession was an unanticipated reduction in the rate of growth of aggregate demand. This reduction resulted from the Bank of Canada's decision to reduce the rate of money growth, the U.S. recession lowering exports, and uncertainty lowering investment. Thus the aggregate demand curve did not shift rightward by as much as expected—it actually shifted leftward.

The major cause of the Great Depression was an unanticipated decrease in aggregate demand, which was the result of reduced investment and reduced consumer expenditure (especially on durable goods) due to uncertainty and pessimism. For several years (1930–32), aggregate demand decreased by more than expected. This change caused real GDP to decrease and the rate of inflation to decrease.

2 Economists disagree about the speed with which money wage rates adjust to clear the labour market. Some economists (Keynesians and new Keynesians) believe that money wages are sticky and adjust only slowly. As a consequence, when a recession occurs, the real wage does not decrease sufficiently to clear the labour market in the short run and there is an excess supply of labour (unemployment). Other economists (monetarists, new classical theorists, and real business cycle theorists) believe that wages are flexible. According to monetarists and new classical theorists, any recession is temporary in nature, because wages adjust downward quickly and the *SAS* shifts rightward, moving the economy towards full employment. According to RBC theorists, when a recession occurs, real wages adjust instantly. Any increase in unemployment is thus interpreted as an increase in natural unemployment.

These issues have significant implications for the design of an appropriate policy as a response to recession. If the Keynesians and new Keynesians are correct, then it may be useful to consider expansionary monetary or fiscal policies to counteract recession. If the others are correct, since the short-run aggregate supply adjusts quickly, or only the vertical *LAS* is relevant, expansionary monetary or fiscal policy will simply increase the rate of inflation and have no effect on real GDP or unemployment.

3 The four important features of the Canadian economy that make severe depression less likely today are: (1) bank deposits are insured; (2) the Bank of Canada is prepared to be the "lender of last resort"; (3) taxes and government spending play a stabilizing role; and (4) multi-income families are more economically secure.

4 When a recession arises, unemployment increases and disposable income declines. This decline in disposable income leads to a decline in consumption expenditure, which has a multiplied negative effect on real GDP. Transfer payments, however, reduce these secondary effects of a recession by moderating the decline in disposable income. As incomes decrease and unemployment increases, government transfer payments increase in the form of higher unemployment benefits or other welfare payments. As a result, the decline in consumption is less.

5 a The new Keynesian theory argues the likely source of a recession is a negative shock to aggregate demand, most likely due to unanticipated, and possibly anticipated, changes in one or more of the underlying variables. The RBC theory argues that the key impulse is a change in the pace of technological change, leading to a negative shock to the *LAS*.

b The new Keynesian theory also argues that money wages are sticky, so that the labour market and the *SAS* adjust slowly—the economy is in the recession for some time unless the government increases *AD*. The RBC theory argues that the labour market has already adjusted instantly, and output is at potential GDP. Any government policy will affect *AD*, but have no impact on real variables, so no policy should be carried out.

The crucial difference is due to the impulse variable that starts the recession—in one case it is an *AD* variable and can be counteracted by increasing *AD*, and in the other case it is a *LAS* variable, and increasing *AD* has no beneficial effect.

6 a The monetarist, new classical, and RBC theories all argue government intervention to offset the business cycle is unneeded—a conservative person is most likely to support one of these.

b The Keynesian and new Keynesian theories all argue that government intervention can offset the business cycle, so a leftist is more likely to support one of these.

7 a Since real GDP has decreased, the *LAS* curve must have shifted leftward, since the only *AS* curve is a vertical *LAS* in a RBC world. For the price level to have increased, it must be the case that either the *AD* curve increased, or decreased so little that in combination with the *LAS* curve shift, the price level has increased.

b In order to get both the price level rising, and real GDP decreasing, it must be the case that the *SAS* curve shifted leftward by more than the shift rightward in the *AD* curve (if there was one), indicating that people anticipated an increase in *AD* (leading to an increase in wages and a shift leftward in the *SAS*), but the actual increase was less than anticipated.

8 a A real business cycle recession starts with a temporary decrease in productivity, which leads to a decrease in the marginal product of capital, and a decrease in the demand for capital (and therefore a decrease in the real interest rate), a decrease in the demand for investment, and a shift leftward in the *AD* curve. In addition, there is a decrease in the demand for labour because of the decrease in productivity, and a shift leftward in the supply of labour because of the lower real interest rate. These two shifts lead to a decrease in employment and a shift leftward in the *LAS* curve. All the unemployment is natural.

b In the new Keynesian labour market, money wages are based on wrong expectations, so that real wages are too high since the increase in money wages is more than the increase in the price level. Labour supply is greater than labour demand, creating the unemployment. All the extra unemployment is cyclical, not natural.

9 a Since the actual price level was lower than the expected price level, the decrease in real GDP must have been due to an increase in aggregate demand that was less than expected. Therefore actual real GDP must be less than potential GDP—the new Keynesian theory is most likely to be correct.

b Since the actual price level is equal to the expected price level, then actual real GDP must equal potential GDP—the RBC theory is most likely to be correct.

10 In the Great Depression, the real wage rate stayed roughly constant, but the level of unemployment increased from about 3 percent to about 20 percent. If the RBC theory is correct, all of this unemployment is natural. This argument would require either an enormous negative productivity shock, or a huge intertemporal substitution effect in response to a large decrease in the real rate of interest. The real interest rate actually increased during the Great Depression, due to the large decrease in the quantity of money. It would seem unlikely that the RBC theory can explain the behaviour of the labour market in the Great Depression.

Chapter 32

Macroeconomic Policy Challenges

Policy Goals

Four main domestic macroeconomic goals:

◆ *Achieve highest sustainable rate of potential GDP growth.*

◆ *Smooth out avoidable business fluctuations.*

◆ *Maintain low unemployment at the natural rate.*

◆ *Maintain low inflation.*

The goals of increasing real GDP growth, smoothing business cycle, and keeping unemployment at natural rate are complementary.

◆ Concentrating on real GDP growth is one core policy target, and inflation is the other.

◆ Real GDP growth goal conflicts with the inflation goal in the short run.

Policy Tools and Performance

Federal government uses fiscal policy (Δ tax rates, benefit rates, government expenditures), and Bank of Canada uses monetary policy (Δ money growth, interest rates) to achieve macroeconomic policy goals.

◆ Fiscal policy expansionary under Trudeau and contractionary under Mulroney—followed a cycle similar to business cycle.

◆ Monetary policy expansionary in late 1970s and anti-inflationary in early and late 1980s.

Long-Term Growth Policy

Long-term growth comes from accumulation of physical and human capital, and new technology— government policy can affect these somewhat.

◆ National saving = private saving + government saving.

◆ National saving was relatively constant between 1971 and 2001, due to offsetting changes in private and government saving.

◆ Decrease in government deficits leads to decrease in government dissaving, which leads to increase in national saving.

◆ Decrease in specific taxes, decrease in inflation rate creates increase in private saving.

◆ Social returns to human capital > private returns— so government subsidizes schooling and health care.

◆ Investments in new technologies increase growth—governments fund and provide tax incentives for research and development.

Business Cycle and Unemployment Policy

Three alternative policies to stabilize business cycle, and minimize cyclical unemployment:

◆ **Fixed-rule policy** is independent of state of the economy, such as always balancing budget.

◆ **Feedback-rule policy** specifies responses to changes in state of economy, such as cutting tax rates in a recession.

◆ **Discretionary policy** responds to state of economy in unique manner—learning from past mistakes in similar situations.

Fixed and feedback rules react differently to aggregate demand shocks.

◆ **Monetarists** advocate fixed rule of doing nothing—recession eventually ends when *AD* increases again (temporary shock), or *SAS* shifts rightward as wages decrease (permanent shock).

◆ **Keynesian activists** advocate feedback rule of expansionary fiscal and monetary policy to try to counter swings in *AD*—returns economy to full employment more quickly.

◆ In theory, feedback rules seem superior, but some economists argue that in practice they are flawed because potential GDP is not known, there are time lags in policy, and feedback rules are less predictable.

Fourth argument against feedback rules is that they fail in face of aggregate supply shocks, such as productivity slowdowns emphasized by RBC theory.

◆ Feedback rule raises *AD*, leading to further increases in the price level, output unchanged.

◆ Fixed rule does nothing, leading to no further increases in price level, output unchanged.

Governments can also try to reduce natural rate of unemployment, by decreasing unemployment compensation and minimum wage.

Anti-Inflation Policy

Cost-push inflation arises from increase in resource prices shifting *SAS* leftward.

◆ Feedback rule raises *AD*, which further increases price level, output back to full employment. This rule *accommodates* inflation, encouraging further increases in resource prices.

◆ Fixed rule does nothing, no further increases in price level, eventually resource prices and *SAS* return to original levels.

In theory, inflation can be tamed by reducing the growth of aggregate demand in a credible and predictable manner, which reduces expectations and wage demands without creating recession.

◆ In practice, anti-inflationary policy leads to recession.

◆ The Taylor rule attempts to balance real GDP and inflation concerns, by targeting an interest rate based on inflation and real GDP growth.

1 This chapter introduces only a few new concepts, and uses the model developed in previous chapters to analyze the effects of policy. This is the payoff for all your effort mastering that model.

However, this chapter asks the most important macroeconomic question: Can the government and the Bank of Canada carry out successful fiscal and monetary policies to reduce the problems of the business cycle?

2 Many complications arise in real-world use of the aggregate demand and aggregate supply models to make policy decisions. In previous chapters these complications were set aside. Here, we present a more realistic perspective of problems that confront a policymaker. Among the most important problems is the inability to predict the *magnitude* or the *timing* of factors that affect aggregate demand or aggregate supply.

a Our macroeconomic model is a good guide to the *qualitative* effects of changes in factors that affect aggregate demand and aggregate supply. For example, we know that an increase in the quantity of money will shift the aggregate demand curve rightward. When conducting policy, however, qualitative knowledge is not sufficient. We must also have *quantitative* knowledge. We must know *how much* a given increase in the quantity of money will increase aggregate demand.

While we may have an understanding of the direction of the effect, knowledge of the magnitude of the effect is much more difficult to obtain and much more limited. This problem reduces the potential to use policy to "fine-tune" the economy.

b In addition to direction and magnitude, we must also know *timing*. The full effect on aggregate demand of policy changes made today will not be immediate. Much, if not most, of that effect will occur only with considerable time lags. Thus it is important that policymakers be able to predict these time lags in order to be confident that the future effect of a policy change made today will be appropriate when the effect actually occurs.

Unfortunately, that is extremely difficult. Lags are often long, vary in length, and are unpredictable. As a result, policymakers may initiate a policy today which, when it has its effect sometime in the future, turns out to shift aggregate demand in the "wrong" direction because circumstances have changed. In such a case, policy will actually turn out to be destabilizing and therefore worse than doing nothing at all.

Consider the analogy of driving a car from your house to the house of a friend. The policy goal is to get the car from here to there. Suppose there is a single policy tool: the steering wheel. If you want the car to turn rightward, you turn the steering wheel clockwise. To turn leftward, you turn the steering wheel counterclockwise. Note that the direction in which the steering wheel turns is important, but so is the magnitude of the turn in order that the car can change direction without accident. Most of us can steer a car rather well because there is essentially no lag between the time we turn the steering wheel and the turning of the front wheels of the car. Now, consider how the task would be complicated if there is a time lag of one minute. In this case, a much better prediction of where the car will be one minute hence is required. Consider how the task would be complicated further if there is not only a time lag but the length of that time lag is variable, and thus unpredictable.

In the real world, cars do not operate with this type of lag, but policymakers do.

3 This chapter presents two opposing views of the usefulness of countercyclical policy. These views come partially from differing assumptions about one crucial factor—the speed with which the private sector reacts to macroeconomic shocks relative to the speed with which the government sector reacts.

The advocates of fixed rules (real business cycle theorists, monetarists, new classical theorists) believe on the whole that the private sector reacts quickly—people have rational expectations, process new information quickly because there are economic incentives to do so, sign flexible wage contracts that allow wages to react quickly to changes in the price level. They also believe that the government sector reacts slowly because of lags in recognizing problems, implementing policy, and carrying out policy. Fixed-rule advocates therefore arrive logically at the conclusion that feedback rules are doomed at best to impotence, and at worst can harm the economy.

The advocates of feedback rules (Keynesians, new Keynesian theorists) believe that the private sector reacts slowly—people sign long-term contracts that prevent wages from reacting quickly to changes in the price level. They also believe that the government sector can react

more quickly than the private sector and, therefore, arrive logically at the conclusion that feedback rules can make the economy better off by speeding up the recovery from recession.

As of yet, no clear-cut empirical evidence favours either viewpoint.

4 Many students (and policymakers!) fall into the trap of thinking that feedback rules must obviously be better than fixed rules, since theoretically feedback rules seem to be able to do everything fixed rules can, plus more. Do not fall into this trap! There are many problems with the actual implementation of feedback rules in the real world: they require very good knowledge of the economy (for example, the level of full employment); they introduce unpredictability into the economy; they can generate *bigger* fluctuations in aggregate demand, due to the lags mentioned previously; they do not work for aggregate supply shocks. These reasons make it far from obvious that feedback rules are better than fixed rules.

SELF-TEST

True/False and Explain

Policy Goals

1 One of the goals of economic policy is to reduce the unemployment rate below its natural rate.

Policy Tools and Performance

2 In Canada, fiscal policy is implemented by the federal government.

3 The Department of Finance conducts monetary policy.

Long-Term Growth Policy

4 Increasing private saving will increase the economic growth rate.

5 The government may subsidize education because the social return to human capital is less than the private return.

6 Increasing the government deficit will increase the economic growth rate.k

Business Cycle and Unemployment Policy

7 Aggregate supply shocks are more frequent than aggregate demand shocks.

8 The use of feedback rules cannot make the business cycle worse.

9 A feedback policy rule is superior to a fixed rule.

10 The statement "allow the money supply to grow at the constant rate of 3 percent per year" is an example of a feedback policy rule.

11 The use of fixed rules can increase the degree of unpredictability in the economy.

Anti-Inflation Policy

12 The use of a feedback rule rather than a fixed rule increases the likelihood of cost-push inflation.

13 Recent Canadian monetary experience suggests that anti-inflationary monetary policy does not work.

14 Cost-push inflation cannot persist unless it is accommodated by the central bank.

15 The Taylor rule is an example of a feedback rule.

Multiple-Choice

Policy Goals

1 Which of the following is a core macroeconomic policy target?
a unemployment constant at 6 percent
b steady growth in real GDP
c steady growth in nominal GDP
d a flexible exchange rate
e inflation at the natural rate

2 Which of the following is *not* a policy goal?
a achieving the highest sustainable growth rate of potential GDP
b smoothing out avoidable business fluctuations
c maintaining unemployment at the natural rate
d maintaining low inflation
e accommodating inflation

Policy Tools and Performance

3 Over the late 1980s in Canada, fiscal policy featured
a constantly rising deficits.
b constantly decreasing deficits.
c an expansionary policy.
d a somewhat contractionary policy.
e small surpluses.

4 Over the late 1980s in Canada, monetary policy featured
a rising growth of M2+.
b decreasing growth of M2+.
c rising inflation.
d zero inflation.
e a cycle in the growth of M2+ that tended to counter fiscal policy.

Long-Term Growth Policy

5 If the marginal tax rate _____, the returns to saving _____.
a increases; are unchanged
b decreases; decrease
c decreases; increase
d decreases; are unchanged
e increases; increase

6 Which of the following is *not* a determinant of long-term growth?

a national saving

b investment in human capital

c investment in consumer durables

d investment in new technologies

e government deficits

7 From 1971 to 2001, national saving averaged

a 10 percent.

b 15 percent.

c 20 percent.

d 25 percent.

e 30 percent.

8 Government deficits tend to lower economic growth because they

a lower aggregate demand.

b increase private investment and lower private saving.

c are typically used to increase education spending.

d lower expenditure on research and development.

e crowd out national saving by using up some of private saving.

9 Canada's private saving rate declined in the 1990s. Which of the following statements correctly explains the likely long-term effects of this decline?

a This decline will create inflationary pressures.

b This decline will create recessionary pressures.

c The decline will increase long-term economic growth.

d The decline will lower long-term economic growth.

e This decline will have no impact on long-term growth.

Business Cycle and Unemployment Policy

10 Which of the following is *true*? Monetary policy affects the economy

a immediately, and fiscal policy affects it immediately.

b immediately, and fiscal policy does not affect it at all.

c immediately, and fiscal policy affects it after a lag.

d after a lag, and fiscal policy affects it immediately.

e after a lag, and fiscal policy affects it after a lag.

11 An economy is initially in full-employment equilibrium when consumer confidence decreases. This is an example of an aggregate _____ shock and a _____ rule will raise real GDP back to its original value.

a demand; fixed

b demand; feedback

c supply; monetary

d demand; fiscal

e supply; fixed

12 Which of the following is an example of a fixed policy rule?

a Wear your boots if it snows.

b Leave your boots home if it does not snow.

c Wear your boots every day.

d Take your boots off in the house if they are wet.

e Listen to the weather forecast and then decide whether to wear your boots.

13 Which of the following is an argument *for* a feedback rule?

a Feedback rules require greater knowledge of the natural rate than we have.

b Feedback rules introduce unpredictability.

c Aggregate supply shocks cause most economic fluctuations.

d Aggregate demand shocks cause most economic fluctuations.

e Feedback rules generate bigger fluctuations in aggregate demand.

14 Economists who favour fixed rules over feedback rules argue that policy lags are

a shorter than the forecast horizon and that potential GDP is known reasonably well.

b shorter than the forecast horizon and that potential GDP is not known.

c longer than the forecast horizon and that potential GDP is known reasonably well.

d longer than the forecast horizon and that potential GDP is not known.

e equal to the forecast horizon and that full-employment real GDP is constant.

15 According to real business cycle theories,

a any decline in real GDP is a decline in long-run real GDP.

b wages are flexible but labour market equilibrium does not necessarily imply full employment.

c fluctuations in aggregate demand change long-run real GDP.

d fluctuations in aggregate demand cannot affect the price level.

e feedback rules are best.

16 Which of the following would *lower* the natural rate of unemployment?

a a feedback rule
b a fixed rule
c more unemployment compensation
d reducing the minimum wage
e accommodating inflation

17 If the Bank of Canada uses the Taylor rule, this is an example of

a a fixed rule.
b a feedback rule.
c a monetarist rule.
d a discretionary rule.
e a fiscal rule.

Anti-Inflation Policy

18 Cost-push inflation is best met by a

a fixed rule.
b feedback rule.
c discretionary policy.
d political business cycle.
e socialist approach.

19 Taming inflation is difficult because

a the Bank of Canada is too independent.
b the Phillips curve shows that unemployment always increases in the long run when inflation decreases.
c the natural rate of inflation is equal to 6 percent.
d surprise anti-inflationary policies work well.
e central banks have credibility problems.

20 In practice, inflation reduction in Canada

a worked in 1982 without any additional unemployment.
b worked in 1990 without any additional unemployment.
c never works.
d works well due to its surprise nature.
e none of the above.

21 Fighting inflation by using contractionary policy is

a generally endorsed by politicians in election years.
b generally unpopular with politicians in election years.
c a zero-cost way to reduce inflation.
d easily accepted by workers.
e an example of a fixed rule.

22 Fixed-rule monetary policies are intended to

a bring long-run inflationary pressures under control.
b counteract temporary increases in aggregate demand.
c counteract temporary decreases in real output.
d offset supply shocks.
e keep real GDP growth high.

23 If the Bank of Canada announces its intention to reduce the rate of money growth, but it lacks credibility, the short-run Phillips curve will

a shift leftward.
b shift rightward.
c not move.
d become vertical.
e become flatter.

24 If the Bank of Canada announces its intention to slow the rate of money growth and has full credibility, the short-run Phillips curve will

a quickly shift leftward.
b quickly shift rightward.
c not shift.
d become horizontal.
e become vertical.

25 A fixed rule for monetary policy

a requires considerable knowledge of how changes in the quantity of money affect the economy.
b would be impossible for the Bank of Canada to achieve.
c generates bigger fluctuations in aggregate demand.
d would result in constant real GDP.
e lowers the threat of cost-push inflation.

Short Answer Problems

1 The Bank of Adanac is attempting to lower inflation in Adanac from 8 percent, but the policy is leading to higher real interest rates and real wage rates.

a What do the high real interest rates and real wage rates indicate about expectations and this policy?
b Some business observers are objecting to this policy, arguing that the high real interest rates are choking off investment and future growth. Comment on the validity of this argument.

2 The prime minister of Adanac has made the following statement: "We are reducing government expenditure to reduce the deficit and create more jobs." How can this statement be true? Won't reducing government expenditure reduce aggregate demand and create unemployment?

3 In 1994, the personal saving rate by households was 7.5 percent of disposable income, but by 1998 it had fallen to 1.2 percent.[1]

 a Explain how this fall in the personal saving rate might hurt the economy.

 b What other factors might offset the damage created by this fall in the personal saving rate? (*Hint:* focus on the national saving rate.)

4 One purpose of policy is to stabilize aggregate demand. How can feedback rules result in even greater variability in aggregate demand?

5 If the Bank of Canada announced its intention to reduce the rate of inflation by reducing the rate of money growth, in theory expected inflation would decline accordingly, and thus a reduction in the actual rate of inflation could be achieved without a recession. Why doesn't this result seem to occur in practice?

6 Assume that the Bank of Canada knows exactly how much and when the aggregate demand curve will shift, both in the absence of monetary policy and when the Bank of Canada changes the quantity of money.

 In this environment, compare the effects on real GDP and the price level of a temporary decline in aggregate demand that returns gradually to its previous level over several periods under fixed and feedback policy rules. Assume the economy is initially at long-run real GDP and that long-run real GDP is constant. Illustrate each of the following rules on a separate graph.

 a First, assume that the Bank of Canada follows the fixed rule: Hold the quantity of money constant.

 b Now, assume that the Bank of Canada follows the feedback rule: Increase the quantity of money whenever aggregate demand decreases and decrease the quantity of money whenever aggregate demand increases.

7 Consider an economy that experiences a temporary increase in aggregate demand. The Bank of Canada follows a feedback rule similar to the one given in Short Answer Problem **6b**, but now we assume that the Bank of Canada does not have perfect knowledge of how much and when aggregate demand will shift.

 In year 1, the economy is in macroeconomic equilibrium at long-run real GDP, but, as the year ends, there is a burst of optimism about the future, which initiates a (temporary) increase in aggregate demand. As a result, in year 2, real

GDP increases, and the rate of unemployment decreases below its natural rate. Given its feedback rule, the Bank of Canada reduces the quantity of money "to keep the economy from overheating." The effect on aggregate demand, however, takes place only after a time lag of one year. In year 3, this burst of optimism returns to its previous level, and thus so does aggregate demand. In addition, the monetary policy implemented in year 2 finally has its effect on aggregate demand in year 3. Analyze the behaviour of real GDP and the price level using three graphs: one each for years 1, 2, and 3. Assume that all changes in aggregate demand are unanticipated and that long-run real GDP is constant. Did a feedback monetary policy rule stabilize aggregate demand?

8 Assume that real business cycle theories are correct. There is a decrease in long-run real GDP due to droughts on the Prairies. First, graph the effect on real GDP and the price level if the Bank of Canada follows the fixed rule: Hold the quantity of money constant. Then, on the same graph, illustrate the effect on real GDP and the price level if the Bank of Canada follows the feedback rule: Increase the quantity of money whenever real GDP decreases and decrease the quantity of money whenever real GDP increases.

9 Consider a central bank that decides to start an anti-inflationary policy. Figure 32.1 shows the initial state of the economy (point *a*) and the expected state next period (point *b*). The bank decides to carry out a gradual policy of inflation reduction. In year 1, it will reduce the growth in *AD* to 5 percent; in year 2 it will reduce the growth in *AD* to 2.5 percent. If the policy is unexpected initially, show on the graph what will occur over the next few years.

FIGURE **32.1**

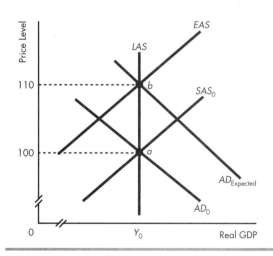

10 You are an economic advisor to the governor of the Bank of Adanac. Recently the economy has slid into a recession—unemployment has increased from 7 percent to 11 percent, the price level has increased from 125 to 135, and real GDP has decreased from 200 billion 1997 dollars to 180 billion 1997 dollars. Two other advisors are attempting to persuade the governor of the validity of their arguments. Ms. F. Ixed argues that there is an *LAS* shock, with full-employment real GDP decreasing and the natural rate of unemployment rising. Therefore, she insists, the optimal policy is to do nothing. Mr. F. E. Edback argues that this recession is due to an unexpectedly low *AD*, and that the optimal policy is to carry out an expansionary monetary policy.

a The governor, Jane Raven, has asked you to draw an *AS-AD* graph for each argument, to test its veracity. No explanation is necessary other than to indicate where the original and new equilibriums are. Are both arguments theoretically possible?

b Ms. Ixed also argues that even if it is an *AD* shock that has caused the current recession, using a feedback policy will just make the economy worse. She argues that timing lags in the implementation of monetary policy mean that the stimulation to aggregate demand will come too late to do any good and will just do harm. Explain and illustrate her argument on the graph you have drawn for Mr. Edback's explanation of the recession.

c Governor Raven wants your advice. Should she order an expansionary monetary policy? Why or why not?

ANSWERS

True/False and Explain

1 **F** One goal is to keep unemployment at natural rate. (756–757)

2 **T** It chooses spending, taxation, and deficit—fiscal policy. (758–759)

3 **F** Bank of Canada does. (759–760)

4 **T** Growth is positively affected by national saving = private saving + government saving. (760–762)

5 **F** Because social return > private return. (762)

6 **F** It will lower government saving and national saving, and decrease investment. (760–762)

7 **F** There is no strong economic evidence either way. (763–769)

8 **F** If there are timing lags, then feedback policy can arrive too late, which makes cycle worse. (763–767)

9 **F** It depends on which theory you think is best. (763–767)

10 **F** Example of a fixed rule—independent of the state of the economy. (763)

11 **F** It is feedback rules that create this problem. (763–767)

12 **T** Feedback rules accommodate wage increases. (769–771)

13 **F** Inflation was lowered both in 1982–85 and in 1990–92, at the cost of increase in unemployment. (772–773)

14 **T** If not accommodated increase in unemployment leads to decrease in resource prices, which shifts *SAS* rightward, so price level returns to original level. (769–771)

15 **T** Dependent on the state of the economy, but in a mathematical manner. (763, 773)

Multiple-Choice

1 **b** See text discussion. (757)

2 **e** See text discussion. (756–757)

3 **d** See text discussion. (758–759)

4 **e** See text discussion. (759–760)

5 **c** Lower marginal tax rate leads to more after-tax earnings from saving. (760–761)

6 **c** See text discussion. (760–761)

7 **c** See text discussion. (760)

8 **e** Since national saving = private saving + government saving. (760–761)

9 **d** Lower national saving, less capital accumulation. (760–762)

10 **e** Due to policy lags and a short forecast horizon. (763–767)

11 **b** Decrease in consumer confidence leads to decrease in consumption, so *AD* shifts leftward. A feedback rule will raise *AD* and counter shock. (763–767)

12 **c** Same choice regardless of circumstances. (763)

13 **d** Others are reasons *against* feedback rules. (763–767)

14 **d** Therefore policy arrives too late, and is often incorrect. (763–767)

15 **a** Because aggregate supply curves are all vertical at long-run real GDP. (767–768)

16 **d** See text discussion. (769)

17 **b** Dependent on the state of the economy, but in a mathematical manner. (763, 773)

18 **a** Keeping *AD* constant does not accommodate inflation and reduces chances of future cost-push inflation. (769–771)

19 e Actual anti-inflationary policies in the past were not always carried out, so it is hard to promise credibly to reduce inflation—expectations do not decrease easily, so that unemployment results when anti-inflationary policy is carried out. (772–773)

20 e In both 1982 and 1990, unemployment resulted due to credibility problems, but inflation was reduced. (772–773)

21 b Because it generally means unemployment, which voters weigh as being more important than inflation fighting. (772–773)

22 a They ignore short-run pressures. (771–773)

ct **23 c** Expectations will not change. (771–773)

ct **24 a** As inflation expectations are reduced. (771–773)

25 e Because it would not accommodate cost-push inflation, reducing likelihood of future cost-push inflation. (769–771)

Short Answer Problems

1 a The fact that real interest rates and real wage rates have shot up indicates that this policy is an unexpected policy—if it was expected and working, the rates would be constant.

b The higher real interest rates will indeed lower investment, meaning a lower capital stock and less growth of potential GDP in the long run. However, the lower inflation will also raise growth, as we saw in Chapter 28. The net effect is probably less growth in the short run, and more growth in the long run, once real interest rates come back down.

ct **2** Indeed, in the short run, reducing government expenditures will reduce aggregate demand and create unemployment. However, in the long run, the lower government deficit will raise national saving, raise economic growth, and presumably create more jobs.

3 a A fall in the personal saving rate, *ceteris paribus*, will lead to a fall in the national saving rate. This fall will reduce capital accumulation, and therefore potentially reduce long-term economic growth.

b The national saving rate = private saving + government saving. Private saving includes personal saving by households and saving by firms. Therefore, the fall in personal saving might be offset by higher firm saving, or higher government saving. In Canada over this time period, the overall government deficit fell from about 6 percent of real GDP to near 0 percent. This sharp rise in government saving completely offsets the fall in personal saving.

4 Policy actions, for example, an open market operation, will affect aggregate demand only after a time lag. Therefore, a policy action taken today will have its intended effect sometime in the future. Therefore it is necessary to forecast the state of the economy for a year or two to be confident that the effect of today's policy action will be appropriate when the effect occurs. It is very difficult to do so, since the lags are long (one to two years) and unpredictable. As a result, there is a very good chance that today's policy action will have a future effect opposite to what originally seemed appropriate; in other words, policy could destabilize rather than stabilize aggregate demand.

ct **5** The problem is that expected inflation may not decline as a result of the announcement by the Bank of Canada. There may be a credibility problem because expectations are much more strongly affected by the Bank's record of actions than by its announcement to take action. If people do not believe the Bank of Canada, they will not adjust expectations. Then if the Bank of Canada carries out the policy, a recession will result in spite of the fact that an announcement was made. In addition, sticky wages could slow down the adjustment of the labour market.

6 a The behaviour of real GDP and the price level under the fixed rule is illustrated in Figure 32.2(a). The economy is initially at point *a* on the aggregate demand curve AD_0: the price level is P_0, and real GDP is at its long-run value denoted Y_0. The temporary decline in aggregate demand shifts the aggregate demand curve downward to AD_1.

Since the quantity of money is held constant under the fixed rule, the new equilibrium is at point *b*: the price level has decreased to P_1, and real GDP has decreased to Y_1. The economy is in recession. As the aggregate demand curve gradually returns to AD_0, the price level gradually increases to P_0 and real GDP gradually returns to Y_0.

FIGURE **32.2**

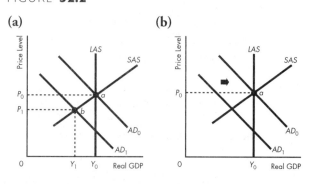

b The behaviour of real GDP and the price level under the feedback rule is illustrated in Figure 32.2(b). Once again the economy is initially at point *a* on the aggregate demand curve AD_0. The temporary decline in aggregate demand temporarily shifts the aggregate demand curve to AD_1. Given the Bank of Canada's feedback rule, it will increase the quantity of money sufficiently to shift the AD_1 curve back to AD_0. Thus the Bank of Canada offsets the decline in aggregate demand and equilibrium remains at point *a*: the price level remains at P_0 and real GDP remains at Y_0.

As the temporary causes of the decline in aggregate demand dissipate, the aggregate demand curve will begin gradually shifting upward. The Bank of Canada will then decrease the quantity of money just enough to offset these shifts. As a result, the aggregate demand curve will remain at AD_0 and equilibrium will remain at point *a*. In these circumstances, the feedback rule is superior to the fixed rule—the recession is shorter in duration.

7 The state of the economy in years 1, 2, and 3 is illustrated in Figure 32.3, parts (a), (b), and (c) respectively. The initial equilibrium (point *a*) in year 1 is illustrated in part (a). The economy is producing at long-run real GDP (Y_1) and the price level is P_1.

In year 2, the aggregate demand curve shifts to AD_2 in part (b) because of the burst of optimism. The Bank of Canada also reduces the quantity of money, but there is no immediate effect on aggregate demand. Therefore the equilibrium in year 2 occurs at the intersection of the AD_2 and SAS curves; at point *b* in part (b). Real GDP has increased to Y_2, which is above long-run real GDP, and the price level has increased to P_2.

In year 3, there are two effects on aggregate demand. First, the burst of optimism expires, pushing the aggregate demand curve back from AD_2 to AD_1. But, in addition, the Bank of Canada's reduction in the quantity of money initiated in year 2 finally has its effect on aggregate demand in year 3. As a result, the aggregate demand curve shifts all the way down to AD_3, and the new equilibrium is at point *c* in part (c). The price level has decreased to P_3, and real GDP has decreased to Y_3, which is below its long-run value. The Bank of Canada's feedback policy in year 2 has caused a recession in year 3 even though it looked like the rightward policy when it was implemented. Note that if the Bank of Canada had been following a fixed rule it would not have changed the quantity of money

in year 2 and as a result, in year 3, the equilibrium would have been at point *a* and real GDP would have been at capacity. Because of imperfect knowledge on the part of the Bank of Canada and the delayed effect of policy changes, the feedback rule has resulted in destabilizing aggregate demand; policy has increased the *variability* of aggregate demand.

FIGURE **32.3**

(a)

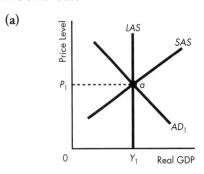

(b)

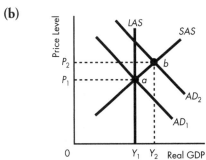

(c)

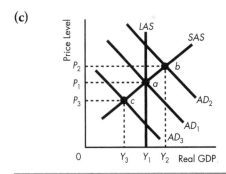

8 The effects on real GDP and the price level are illustrated in Figure 32.4. Because we *assume* that real business cycle theories are correct, the only aggregate supply curve is the potential GDP curve. The economy is initially in equilibrium at the intersection of the AD_0 and LAS_0 curves, point *a*. Real GDP is Y_0, and the price level is P_0. Then long-run real GDP decreases, and the aggregate supply curve shifts leftward from LAS_0 to LAS_1.

If the Bank of Canada follows the fixed policy rule, it will hold the quantity of money constant, and the aggregate demand curve will remain at AD_0. Thus the new equilibrium is at point *b*: real GDP will decrease to Y_1 (the new capacity), and the price level will have increased to P_1. If, on the other hand, the Bank of Canada follows the feedback rule, the decrease in real GDP will lead the Bank of Canada to increase the quantity of money, which will shift the aggregate demand curve rightward from AD_0 to AD_1. Note that monetary policy will have no effect on long-run real GDP and thus no effect on the (long-run) aggregate supply curve. Therefore, under the feedback policy rule, the new equilibrium is at point *c*: real GDP has remained at Y_1, but the price level has increased to P_2. The consequence of a feedback rule is a larger increase in the price level (higher inflation) with no effect on real GDP.

FIGURE **32.4**

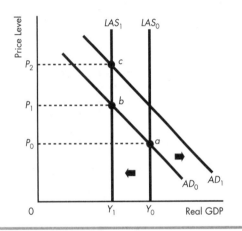

ct **9**   The anti-inflationary policy is illustrated in Figure 32.1 Solution. It will reduce the growth of aggregate demand to a (vertical) distance of 5 percent, at AD_1. However, the actual *SAS* will be based on the expected inflation rate of 10 percent, and therefore SAS_1 is the relevant curve, yielding an equilibrium in year 1 at the point *c*, with a decrease in real GDP, and an increase in inflation of (say) 7.5 percent, less than expected.

In year 2, the central bank allows aggregate demand to increase a further 2.5 percent, or a vertical increase to 107.625 (105×102.5), crossing the potential GDP curve at the point *d*, where AD_2 and *LAS* cross. The actual impact on the economy depends on how much adjustment of expectations occurs. If the policy is now credible, and if wages can adjust sufficiently, there will be a decrease in the short-run aggregate supply curve to SAS_2, and the equilibrium will be at the point *d*, with a very small inflation, and with real GDP back to the natural rate.

FIGURE **32.1** SOLUTION

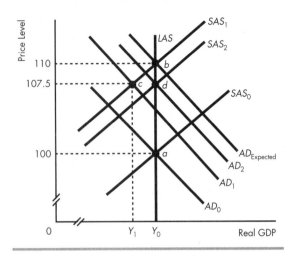

10 a   Ms. Ixed's argument is shown in Figure 32.5(a), and Mr. Edback's in Figure 32.5(b). The original equilibrium is at point *a*, and the new equilibrium is at point *b*. As the graphs show, both arguments are theoretically possible.

FIGURE **32.5**

(a)

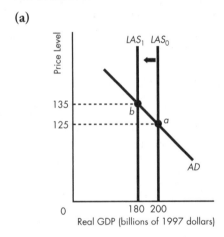

(b)

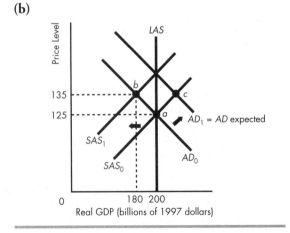

b She is arguing that the stimulation to aggregate demand (shown as the shift from AD_0 to AD_1) arrives after wages start to adjust downward (shown by SAS_1 shifting to SAS_0). Therefore the new equilibrium is at the point c, with the economy overheating due to the expansionary monetary policy.

c Which policy you pick is a matter of choice. However, your choice should be based on an economic argument. You would support a feedback rule if you thought (a) it was an AD shock, and (b) the central bank could successively and quickly implement the appropriate stimulation. You would pick a fixed rule of doing nothing if you thought (a) it was an AS shock, or (b) even if it was an AD shock, the Bank of Adanac reacts too slowly or incorrectly when carrying out the policy.

Part 9 Wrap Up

Chapters
29–32

Understanding Aggregate Supply and Economic Growth

PROBLEM

You have been hired as an economic consultant for the premier of the country of Nova Calenia. The economy of Nova Calenia is experiencing a recession, reflected in the data in Table P9.1.

TABLE **P9.1**

	Year 1	Year 2
Price Level (GDP deflator)	125	130
Real GDP (billions of constant dollars)	200	190
Real wages (billions of constant dollars)	15.00	15.45
Employment (billions of hours)	100	90
Unemployment (%)	8	11

One set of advisors (new Keynesians) have told the premier that the recession has been caused by an unexpected decrease in aggregate demand (due to an unexpected decrease in exports), combined with sticky wages (inflation was expected to remain constant at 7 percent).

a Explain briefly to the premier what these advisors think is happening to the market for goods and services (draw an *AD-AS* graph as part of your answer), and in the labour market (just describe what is going on, do not draw a graph).

    Another set of advisors (real business cycle theorists) have argued that the above events are due solely to an aggregate supply shock, driven by technological change.

b Explain briefly to the premier what these advisors think is happening to the market for goods and services (draw an *AD–AS* graph as part of your answer), and in the labour market (just describe what is going on, do not draw a graph of the labour market).

c After this explanation, and your sorry admission that there is no clear consensus on which view is correct, the premier wants to know what happens if
    i he believes the new Keynesian argument, and follows the appropriate policy, *but* the real business cycle argument turns out to be correct, or if
    ii he believes the real business cycle argument, and follows the appropriate policy, *but* the Keynesian argument turns out to be correct.

d The premier has decided to pick an expansionary policy, but cannot decide between raising government spending and cutting taxes. He wishes to know which policy is better if he is concerned about economic growth as well as the business cycle.

MIDTERM EXAMINATION

You should allocate 32 minutes for this examination (16 questions, 2 minutes per question). For each question, choose the one *best* answer.

1 Given that the use of all other factor inputs are held constant, a diminishing marginal product of labour might best be described as when the total number of hours worked in the economy

a increases and total output increases.
b increases and total output increases at a decreasing rate.
c increases and total output decreases.
d decreases and total output increases.
e increases and total output increases at an increasing rate.

2 New Keynesians would attribute the increase in unemployment during the 1990–91 Canadian recession to a(n)

a increase in the natural rate of unemployment.

b sharp decrease in real wages.

c increase in labour force participation.

d increase in real wages.

e increase in structural unemployment.

3 To _____ government saving, the government deficit must _____.

a decrease; decrease

b decrease; be zero

c increase; be zero

d increase; decrease

e increase; increase

4 Which one of the following quotations describes a shift rightward in an *LAS* curve?

a "The recent higher price levels have lowered production in the country."

b "The recent higher price levels have raised production in the country."

c "The recent higher price levels have led to compensating rises in wages, so that there have been no changes in labour hired or production."

d "The recent lower price levels have led to lower production in the country."

e None of the above.

5 Suppose that productivity has increased by 15 percent over last year. Capital per hour of labour increased by 9 percent as well. The increase in capital was responsible for

a all of the increase in productivity.

b 80% of the increase in productivity.

c 60% of the increase in productivity.

d 33% of the increase in productivity.

e 20% of the increase in productivity.

6 Suppose that productivity has increased by 15 percent over last year. Capital per hour of labour increased by 9 percent as well. An increase in technology was responsible for

a all of the increase in productivity.

b 80% of the increase in productivity.

c 60% of the increase in productivity.

d 33% of the increase in productivity.

e 20% of the increase in productivity.

7 How did monetary policy affect interest rates during the Great Depression?

a High real interest rates resulted from a decrease in the quantity of money.

b Low real interest rates resulted from a decrease in the quantity of money.

c High real interest rates resulted from an increase in the quantity of money.

d Low real interest rates resulted from an increase in the quantity of money.

e High real interest rates resulted from the positive inflation.

8 Which of the following supports the claim that feedback rules exaggerate fluctuations in aggregate demand? Policymakers

a use the wrong feedback rules to achieve their goals.

b must take actions today that will not have their effects until well into the future.

c do not really want to stabilize the economy.

d try to make their policies unpredictable.

e have enough knowledge of the economy.

9 Which theory of economic growth concludes that in the long run, people do not benefit from growth?

a classical theory

b neoclassical theory

c new growth theory

d old growth theories

e none of the theories

10 Which of the following quotations describes job rationing unemployment?

a "Wages are so good at the factory, they always have enough applicants to pick whomever they want for the job."

b "Professors with tenured jobs are taking pay cuts to help hire new professors."

c "Wages have failed to fall in the current economic downturn, creating extra unemployment."

d "People are taking too long to find jobs, because employment insurance is so generous."

e None of the above.

11 What is the key impulse in the RBC theory of the business cycle?

a changes in expected future sales and profits

b changes in the money supply

c unanticipated changes in aggregate demand

d anticipated changes in aggregate demand

e changes in the pace of technological change

12 Which of the following would tend to create the *worst* problems with persistent inflation?

a the Taylor rule
b fixed rules
c feedback rules
d credible policies
e promoting more saving

13 What is the key impulse in the new Keynesian theory of the business cycle?

a changes in expected future sales and profits
b changes in the money supply
c unanticipated changes in aggregate demand
d anticipated changes in aggregate demand
e changes in the pace of technological change

14 Which one of the following quotations describes a movement along the labour demand curve?

a "Recent higher wage rates have led to more leisure being consumed."
b "The recent lower price level has induced people to work more hours."
c "The recent higher real wage rate has induced people to work more hours."
d "The recent high investment in capital equipment has raised hiring by firms."
e None of the above.

15 The key difference between neoclassical growth theory and classical growth theory is that

a capital is not subject to diminishing returns under classical growth theory.
b capital is subject to diminishing returns under classical growth theory.
c increases in technology lead to increases in population that drive workers' incomes back down to the subsistence level in classical theory.
d technological advances are exogenous in classical growth theory.
e the one-third rule only holds in the neoclassical growth theory.

16 According to real business cycle theories, if the Bank of Canada increases the money supply when real GDP declines, real GDP

a will increase, but only temporarily.
b will increase permanently.
c and the price level will both be unaffected.
d will be unaffected, but the price level will increase.
e will decrease due to the inefficiencies introduced into production as a result.

ANSWERS

Problem

a The new Keynesian graph of the market for goods and services is shown in Figure P9.1. Note the decrease in aggregate demand combined with the shift leftward in short-run aggregate supply (due to the rising wages).

The labour market has rising real wages, decreasing employment, and rising unemployment, implying that the real wage is too high (nominal wages were based on the expected inflation of 7 percent, but since *AD* was unexpectedly low, the actual inflation is only 4 percent, creating high real wages), creating (cyclical) unemployment above the natural rate.

FIGURE **P9.1**

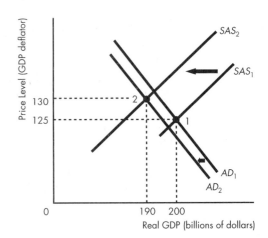

b The real business cycle graph of the market for goods and services is shown in Figure P9.2. Note that aggregate demand is assumed constant, and that a shift leftward in long-run aggregate supply causes all the changes. This shift is due to a decrease in productivity, due to the technological change, which lowers the demand for labour and capital (lowering the real interest rate). There is also a decrease in the supply of labour, due to the lower real interest rate, creating a big decrease in labour hired, and therefore a shift leftward in the *LAS* curve. The extra unemployment is due to a rise in natural unemployment—the turnover rate has risen in the labour market.

FIGURE **P9.2**

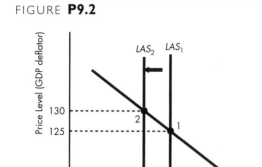

Midterm Examination

1   **b**   Definition. (683–685)

2   **d**   Unexpectedly low inflation leads to unexpectedly high real wages and unemployment above the natural rate. (734–736)

3   **d**   Because government saving = taxes – expenditures = – government deficit. (760–761)

4   **e**   **a** is nonsense, **b**, **c**, and **d** are movements along curves. (698–700)

5   **e**   By one-third rule, capital increase of 9 percent leads to increase in real GDP per hour of work of 3 percent, or 20% of increase in productivity. (713–716)

6   **b**   Capital's effect was one-third of 9 percent or 3 percent, leaving 12 percent or 80 of the total increase due to technology. (713–716)

7   **a**   Banking failures led to a decrease in the real money supply, and even though nominal interest rates decreased, the negative inflation created higher real interest rates. (746–748)

8   **b**   Therefore fluctuations in *AD* are exaggerated. (763–767)

9   **a**   In long run, technological advances increase demand for labour and real GDP per capita, so population increases which lowers real GDP per capita. (717–723)

10   **a**   This describes efficiency wages, a form of job rationing. (694–695)

11   **e**   See text discussion. (737)

12   **c**   Accommodates inflation. (769–771)

13   **c**   Anticipated changes are not as important—see text discussion. (734–736)

14   **e**   **a**, **b**, **c** are *LS* effect, **d** shift in *LD* curve. (683–685)

15   **c**   In neoclassical theory, population growth is not driven by economic growth. In both theories, capital is subject to diminishing returns, technology is exogenous, and the one-third rule holds. (717–723)

16   **d**   Because *LAS* is vertical. (767–768)

c   **i**   According to the new Keynesian theory, the right policy is to stimulate aggregate demand by an expansionary policy, attempting to raise the price level, lower real wages, and raise employment and real GDP. If, however, the real business cycle theory is correct, this stimulation of aggregate demand will just lead to extra inflation, with its costs, with no change in real GDP.

    ii   According to the real business cycle theory, the correct policy is to do nothing. If, however, the Keynesian theory is correct, this will result in the recession lasting longer than necessary.

d   Both policies will raise the deficit, lowering national saving (= private saving + government saving), which lowers economic growth. However, cutting taxes on savings might raise private saving, and counter this effect.

Chapter 33

Trading with the World

Patterns and Trends in International Trade

Imports are goods and services we buy from other countries, **exports** are what we sell to them.

◆ Canada's major exports and imports are motor vehicles and capital goods, our major trading partner is the United States.

◆ Trade includes trade in services, such as tourism.

◆ **Net exports** = value of exports – value of imports.

The Gains from International Trade

Countries can produce anywhere on or inside production possibilities frontier (*PPF*).

◆ Slope of *PPF* = Δ *y*-axis variable/Δ *x*-axis variable = opportunity cost of one more *x*-axis variable.

◆ A country has comparative advantage in production of good for which it has lowest opportunity cost.

A country gains from trading by buying goods from countries with lower opportunity costs and selling the goods for which it has lower opportunity cost.

◆ **Terms of trade** = quantity need to export to buy 1 unit of imports.

◆ Countries pay for their imports with their exports—the value of exports = the value of imports.

◆ Countries react to new terms of trade by producing more exported good and less imported good.

◆ *Both* countries gain by specializing—both can therefore *consume outside* their PPF.

◆ Most trade can be explained by comparative advantage, but much trade is trade in similar goods, due to diversified tastes and economies of scale.

International Trade Restrictions

Governments protect domestic industries by restricting trade with tariffs and nontariff barriers.

◆ Tariffs have been decreasing due to **General Agreement on Tariffs and Trade** (international treaty to limit trade restriction), its successor the **World Trade Organization**, and the **North American Free Trade Agreement**.

Tariffs are taxes on imported goods.

◆ Tariffs increase import price, decreasing imports, increasing domestic production.

◆ Net losses to importing country because new price > original import price.

◆ Tariffs lower imports in home country and exports to foreign country.

Nontariff barriers restrict supply of imports, which increases domestic price and domestic production.

◆ **Quotas** set import quantity restriction, with quota licences distributed by home country.

◆ **Voluntary export restraints** (VERs) set export quantity restrictions, with foreign distributors having export licences.

The Case Against Protection

Trade restrictions are used despite losses of gains from trade for three somewhat credible reasons—to protect **infant industries**, prevent foreign companies from **dumping** their products on world markets at prices less than cost, and to save jobs in import-competing industries.

A country may restrict trade for the following less credible reasons:

◆ Protect strategic industries to help national security.

◆ To compete with cheap foreign labour.

◆ To bring diversity and stability.

◆ To penalize lax environmental standards.

◆ To protect a national culture.

◆ To prevent rich countries from exploiting developing countries.

The biggest problem with protection is that it invites retaliation from other countries.

Why Is International Trade Restricted?

There are two reasons for trade restrictions:

◆ Tariff revenue is an attractive tax base for governments in developing countries.

◆ To protect groups/industries that suffer disproportionately under freer trade.

◆ In Canada, employment insurance and interprovincial transfers provide some compensation for losses due to free trade.

The North American Free Trade Agreement

Despite protectionism pressures, Canada has a free trade agreement with the United States and Mexico.

◆ This agreement involves
  • reducing common tariffs to zero in phases
  • reducing nontariff barriers
  • freer trade in energy and services
  • future negotiations on subsidies
  • a dispute-settling mechanism

◆ Total effects of the agreement are unknown at the moment, but they do include large increases in the total volume of trade, with significant changes in some sectors.

HELPFUL HINTS

1 This chapter applies the fundamental concepts of opportunity cost and comparative advantage discussed in Chapter 2 to the problem of trade between nations. The basic principles are the same for trade between individuals in the same country and between individuals in different countries.

Many people involved in debates about trade seem confused by the concept of comparative advantage, partially because they implicitly consider *absolute advantage* as the sole reason for trade. A country has an absolute advantage if it can produce all goods using less inputs than another country. However, such a country can still gain from trade. Consider California and Saskatchewan. California has a better climate and, with widespread irrigation, has an absolute advantage in the production of all agricultural products. Indeed, California frequently has more than one harvest a year! This absolute advantage would seem to imply that California has no need to trade with Saskatchewan. Saskatchewan, however, has a *comparative advantage* in the production of wheat. Therefore California will specialize in fruits and trade them for wheat. California could easily grow its own wheat, but the opportunity cost would be too high—the lost fruit crops. By specializing and trading, both California and Saskatchewan can gain.

2 One of the most crucial results of this chapter is that both countries can gain from trade. This gain occurs because the post-trade price is between the two countries' pre-trade opportunity costs. We can see this gain illustrated in Text Figure 33.3, where the equilibrium price of a car is 3 tonnes of grain, between the pre-trade opportunity costs of 1 tonne and 9 tonnes.

Students are often puzzled by where to put the price when working through these types of examples. How did the authors come up with the value of 3? In a sense, it is an arbitrary value, one they just plucked out of a hat. Given the logic of voluntary trade, it must be between the two pre-trade values of 1 and 9. However, by redrawing the export supply and the import demand curves with different slopes, the authors might have arrived at a value of 6 tonnes. This result would have been equally logical, and equally valid.

In the real world, the strength of the demand for specific products by the consumers of each country will determine the slopes of the export supply and import demand curves, and determine just where the equilibrium price is set. In your examples, either you will be able to pick where you want the price to be (given that it must be between the two pre-trade opportunity costs) or you will be given some specific information telling you where the price is.

3 An important economic effect of trade restrictions is that a tariff and a quota have the same effects. A voluntary export restraint (VER) is also a quota, but it is a quota imposed by the exporting country rather than by the importing country.

All trade restrictions raise the domestic price of the imported goods and reduce the volume and value of imports. They also reduce the value of exports by the same amount as the reduction in the value of imports. The increase in price that results from each trade restriction produces a gap between the domestic price of the imported good and the foreign supply price of the good.

The difference between the alternative trade restrictions lies in which party captures this excess. In the case of a tariff, the government receives the tariff revenue. In the case of a quota imposed by the importing country, domestic importers who have been awarded a licence to import capture this excess through increased profit. When a VER is imposed, the excess is captured by foreign exporters who have been awarded licences to export by their government.

4 The major point of this chapter is that gains from free trade can be considerable. Why then do countries have such a strong tendency to impose trade restrictions? The key is that while free trade creates overall benefits to the economy as a whole, there are both winners and losers. The winners gain more in total than the losers lose, but the losers tend to be concentrated in a few industries.

Given this concentration, free trade will be resisted by some acting on the basis of rational self-interest. Even though only a small minority benefit while the overwhelming majority will be hurt, it is not surprising to see trade restrictions implemented. The cost of a given trade restriction to *each* of the majority will be individually quite small, while the benefit to *each* of the few will be individually large. Thus the minority will have a significant incentive to see that restriction takes place, while the majority will have little incentive to expend time and energy in resisting trade restriction.

5 To understand the source of pressures for trade restrictions, let us summarize those who win and lose from trade restrictions.

Under the three forms of restrictions (tariffs, quotas, and VERs) *consumers* lose, because the price of the imported good increases. *Domestic producers* of the imported good and their factors of production gain from all three, because the price of the imported good increases. *Foreign producers* and their factors of production lose under all three schemes, because their export

sales decrease. Under quotas and VERs, the *holders of import licences* gain from buying low and selling high (they may be foreign or domestic). *Government* gains tariff revenue under tariffs and, potentially, votes under other schemes.

Given this list, it is hardly surprising that the main supporters of trade restrictions are domestic producers and their factors of production.

SELF-TEST

True/False and Explain

Patterns and Trends in International Trade

1 When a Canadian citizen stays in a hotel in France, Canada is exporting a service.

The Gains from International Trade

2 If a country can produce all goods cheaper than other countries, it will not benefit from trade.

3 Trading according to comparative advantage allows all trading countries to consume outside their *PPF*.

4 If Atlantis must give up 3 widgets to produce 1 watch and Beltran must give up 4 widgets to produce 1 watch, Atlantis has a comparative advantage in the production of watches.

5 Countries may exchange similar goods with each other due to economies of scale in the face of diversified tastes.

International Trade Restrictions

6 When governments impose tariffs, they are increasing their country's gain from trade.

7 A tariff on a good will raise its price and reduce the quantity traded.

8 A quota will cause the price of the imported good to decrease.

9 The excess revenue created by a voluntary export restraint is captured by the seller.

The Case Against Protection

10 Japan is dumping steel if it sells steel in Japan at a lower price than it sells it in Canada.

11 International trade increases net employment in Canada.

12 Since Mexican labour is paid so much less than Canadian labour, entering in to a free trade agreement with Mexico guarantees Canada will lose jobs to Mexico.

Why Is International Trade Restricted?

13 Elected governments are slow to reduce trade restrictions because there would be more losers than gainers.

14 Developing nations often favour tariffs because they are a stable source of tax revenue.

The North American Free Trade Agreement

15 The impact of the North American Free Trade Agreement has been significant changes in some sectors, but no overall change in the total volume of trade.

Multiple-Choice

Patterns and Trends in International Trade

1 If we import more than we export,
a we will be unable to buy as many foreign goods as we desire.
b we will make loans to foreigners to enable them to buy our goods.
c we will have to finance the difference by borrowing from foreigners.
d our patterns of trade, including the direction of exports and imports, will be different than if exports equal imports.
e none of the above.

2 Which of the following is a Canadian service export?
a A Canadian buys dinner while travelling in Switzerland.
b A Swiss buys dinner while travelling in Canada.
c A Canadian buys a clock made in Switzerland.
d A Swiss buys a computer made in Canada.
e A Canadian buys a Canadian computer in Switzerland.

The Gains from International Trade

3 In Atlantis, 1 unit of capital and 1 unit of labour are required to produce 1 watch, and 2 units of capital and 2 units of labour are required to produce 1 widget. What is the opportunity cost of producing one watch?
a the price of 1 unit of capital plus the price of 1 unit of labour
b 1 unit of capital and 1 unit of labour
c 2 units of capital and 2 units of labour
d 1/2 widget
e 2 widgets

4 Refer to Figure 33.1. The opportunity cost of 1 beer in Partyland is _____, and the opportunity cost of 1 beer in Cowabunga is _____.
a dependent on where on the *PPF* we measure it; dependent on where on the *PPF* we measure it
b 100 pizzas; 25 pizzas
c 3 pizzas; 1 pizza
d 1 pizza; 1 pizza
e 1 pizza; 1/3 pizza

FIGURE **33.1** PARTYLAND AND
COWABUNGA—*PPF* FOR BEER
AND PIZZA

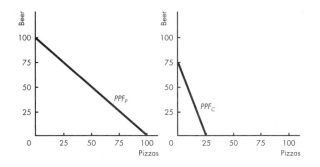

5 Refer to Figure 33.1. The opportunity cost of
1 pizza in Partyland is _____, and the
opportunity cost of 1 pizza in Cowabunga is
_____.

a dependent on where on the *PPF* we measure it;
dependent on where on the *PPF* we measure it

b 100 beers; 25 beers

c 3 beers; 1 beer

d 1 beer; 1 beer

e 1 beer; 3 beers

6 Refer to Figure 33.1. If trade occurs between
Partyland and Cowabunga,

a there will be a lot of drunk turtles.

b Partyland will supply both pizza and beer,
because it has a comparative advantage in both.

c Cowabunga will supply both pizza and beer,
because it has a comparative advantage in both.

d Partyland will supply pizza, and Cowabunga will
supply beer.

e Partyland will supply beer, and Cowabunga will
supply pizza.

7 Refer to Figure 33.1. If trade occurs between
Partyland and Cowabunga, the trade price for
beer will be

a 1 beer for 1 pizza.

b 1 beer for 1/3 pizza.

c 1 beer for 3 pizzas.

d somewhere between 1 beer for 1 pizza and
1 beer for 3 pizzas.

e somewhere between 1 beer for 1 pizza and
1 beer for 1/3 pizza.

8 If Atlantis can produce everything cheaper than
can any other country,

a no trade will take place because Atlantis will
have a comparative advantage in everything.

b no trade will take place because no country will
have a comparative advantage in anything.

c trade will probably take place, and all countries
will gain.

d trade will probably take place, but Atlantis will
not gain.

e trade will probably take place, but Atlantis will
be the only one to gain.

9 How does international trade change the
consumption possibilities of each country?

a It allows each country to consume more of the
goods it exports, but less of the goods it imports
than without trade.

b It allows each country to consume more of the
goods it imports, but less of the goods it exports
than without trade.

c It allows each country to consume more of the
goods it exports and imports than without trade.

d It allows each country to consume less of the
goods it exports and imports than without trade.

e It allows each country to consume more of
either the good it exports or the good it imports,
but not both.

10 We often observe countries trading virtually
identical goods—for example, Canada exports
cars to the United States and imports cars from
them. This pattern of trade

a indicates that the theory of comparative
advantage is incorrect.

b indicates most trade is due to absolute
advantage.

c reflects the presence of demand for only a few
types of products.

d reflects the presence of demand for a diversified
set of products.

e reflects the presence of diseconomies of scale.

International Trade Restrictions

11 Consider Table 33.1. Under free trade, the
international price of donut holes would be
$_____ per hundred donut holes, and _____
million holes would be exchanged.

a 0.75; 6

b 1.00; 3

c 1.25; 4

d 1.25; 5

e 1.50; 4

TABLE **33.1** INTERNATIONAL TRADE IN
DONUT HOLES

International Price (dollars per 100 holes)	Glazeland's Export Supply of Holes (millions)	Snorfleland's Import Demand for Holes (millions)
0.50	1	10
0.75	2	8
1.00	3	6
1.25	4	4
1.50	5	2
1.75	6	0

12 Consider Table 33.1. Snorfleland's donut hole producers manage to convince their government that there is a need to protect the domestic industry from Glazeland's cheap imports. (They argue that holes are a crucial food group.) In response, Snorfleland's government sets an import quota of 3 million donut holes. The resulting price of a donut hole in Snorfleland will be $_____ per hundred holes, and domestic production of donut holes will _____.

a 0.75; decrease
b 0.75; increase
c 1.25; remain unchanged
d 1.38; increase
e 1.38; remain unchanged

13 Canada has an import quota of one million pairs of shoes per year, and is currently importing this amount. An increase in the domestic demand for shoes will result in

a no change in the domestic prices of shoes, but an increase in the quantity of shoes imported.
b no change in the domestic prices of shoes or in the quantity of shoes imported.
c an increase in the domestic prices of shoes and in the quantity of shoes imported.
d an increase in the domestic prices of shoes and no change in the quantity of shoes imported.
e an increase in the domestic prices of shoes and an uncertain change in the quantity of shoes imported, depending on whether the increase in demand is greater than one million pairs or not.

14 A tariff on watches which are imported by Atlantis will cause the

a demand curve for watches in Atlantis to shift leftward.
b demand curve for watches in Atlantis to shift rightward.
c supply curve of watches in Atlantis to shift leftward.
d supply curve of watches in Atlantis to shift rightward.
e demand and the supply curve of watches in Atlantis to shift leftward.

15 When a *quota* is imposed, the gap between the domestic price and the export price is captured by

a consumers in the importing country.
b the domestic producers of the good.
c the government of the importing country.
d foreign exporters.
e the person with the right to import the good.

16 When a *voluntary export restraint* agreement is reached, the gap between the domestic import price and the export price is captured by

a consumers in the importing country.
b the person with the right to import the good.
c the government of the importing country.
d foreign exporters.
e the domestic producers of the good.

17 When a *tariff* is imposed, the gap between the domestic price and the export price is captured by

a consumers in the importing country.
b the person with the right to import the good.
c the domestic producers of the good.
d foreign exporters.
e the government of the importing country.

18 Which of the following statements about international trade is *true*?

a Tariffs will increase jobs in our export industries.
b Quotas are better than tariffs because they do not raise prices.
c Tariffs are needed to allow us to compete with cheap foreign labour.
d No one gains from free trade between a poor and a rich country.
e VERs raise prices as much as equivalent tariffs do.

19 Atlantis and Beltran are currently engaging in free trade. Atlantis imports watches from Beltran and exports widgets to Beltran. If Atlantis imposes a *quota* on watches, Atlantis' watch-producing industry will

a expand, and its widget-producing industry will contract.
b expand, and its widget-producing industry will expand.
c contract, and its widget-producing industry will contract.
d contract, and its widget-producing industry will expand.
e expand, and its widget-producing industry will be unchanged.

The Case Against Protection

20 Which of the following is *not* an argument for protectionism?

a to protect strategic industries
b to save jobs in import-competing industries
c to gain a comparative advantage
d to allow infant industries to grow
e to prevent rich nations from exploiting poor nations

21 Which of the following is a relatively *credible* argument for protectionism?

a national security
b helping infant industries grow up
c to prevent exploitation of poor countries
d to compete with cheap foreign labour
e to save jobs in export industries

22 The biggest problem with protection is that

a it invites retaliation from trading partners.
b losers are not compensated.
c it worsens environmental standards.
d it can worsen national security.
e it lowers wages.

Why Is International Trade Restricted?

23 Why is international trade restricted?

a because government revenue is costly to collect via tariffs
b in order to get higher consumption possibilities
c to realize the gains from trade
d due to rent-seeking
e because free trade creates economic losses on average

The North American Free Trade Agreement

24 Which of the following is *not* part of the North American Free Trade Agreement?

a reducing common tariffs to zero in phases
b reducing nontariff barriers
c freer trade in energy and services
d future negotiations on subsidies
e raising common tariffs against countries outside the agreement

25 Examining the implementation of the North American Free Trade Agreement has revealed that

a Canada has been severely damaged by the agreement.
b Canada has been helped enormously by the agreement.
c free trade does not work.
d all losers from free trade will be compensated.
e there has been a large increase in the volume of international trade, benefiting consumers, but at the cost of a high rate of job destruction in the late 1980s and early 1990s.

Short Answer Problems

1 Why can *both* parties involved in trade gain?

2 How does a tariff on a particular imported good affect the domestic price of the good, the export price, the quantity imported, and the quantity of the good produced domestically?

3 How does a tariff on imports affect the exports of the country?

4 It is often argued by union leaders that tariffs are needed to protect domestic jobs. In light of your answers to Short Answer Problems **2** and **3**, evaluate this argument.

5 Consider a simple world in which there are two countries, Atlantis and Beltran, each producing food and cloth. The *PPF* for each country is given in Table 33.2.

a Assuming a constant opportunity cost in each country, complete the table.
b What is the opportunity cost of food in Atlantis? of cloth?
c What is the opportunity cost of food in Beltran? of cloth?
d Draw the *PPFs* on separate graphs.

TABLE **33.2** ATLANTIS AND BELTRAN—*PPF* FOR FOOD AND CLOTH

Atlantis		Beltran	
Food (units)	Cloth (units)	Food (units)	Cloth (units)
0	500	0	800
200	400	100	600
400		200	
600		300	
800		400	
1,000		—	—

6 Suppose that Atlantis and Beltran engage in trade.

a In which good will each country specialize?

b If 1 unit of food trades for 1 unit of cloth, what will happen to the production of each good in each country?

c If 1 unit of food trades for 1 unit of cloth, draw the consumption possibility frontiers for each country on the corresponding graph from Short Answer Problem **5**.

d Before trade, if Atlantis consumed 600 units of food, the most cloth it could consume was 200 units. After trade, how many units of cloth can be consumed if 600 units of food are consumed?

7 Continue the analysis of Atlantis and Beltran trading at the rate of 1 unit of food for 1 unit of cloth.

a If Atlantis consumes 600 units of food and 400 units of cloth, how much food and cloth will be consumed by Beltran?

b Given the consumption quantities and the production quantities from Short Answer Problem **6b**, how much food and cloth will Atlantis and Beltran import and export?

8 Figure 33.2 gives the import demand curve for shirts for Atlantis, labelled *D*, and the export supply curve of shirts for Beltran, labelled *S*.

a What is the price of a shirt under free trade?

b How many shirts will be imported by Atlantis?

FIGURE **33.2**

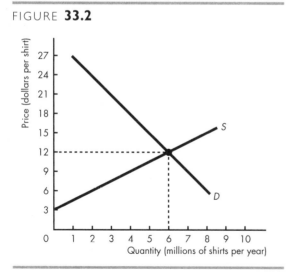

9 Suppose the shirtmakers in Atlantis of Short Answer Problem **8** are concerned about foreign competition and, as a result, the government of Atlantis imposes a tariff of $9 per shirt.

a What will happen to the price of a shirt in Atlantis?

b What is the price the exporter will actually receive?

c How many shirts will be imported by Atlantis?

d What is the revenue from the tariff? Who captures it?

10 Suppose that instead of a tariff, Atlantis imposes a quota of 4 million shirts per year.

a What will be the price of a shirt in Atlantis?

b What price will the exporter actually receive?

c How many shirts will be imported by Atlantis?

d What is the difference between the total amount paid by consumers and the total amount received by exporters—the "excess profit"? Who captures it?

ANSWERS

True/False and Explain

1 **F** Canada is importing (using) a service. (786)

2 **F** If comparative advantage exists, then gains from trade exist. (787–792)

3 **T** Countries will specialize and trade to consume outside *PPF*. (787–791)

4 **T** Atlantis has a lower opportunity cost (3 widgets < 4 widgets) = lost widgets per unit of gained watches. (788–789)

5 **T** Diversified tastes implies many products demanded. Economies of scale implies cheaper method of production, but requires specialization and trade. (791–792)

6 **F** Trade restrictions reduce gains from trade. (794–796)

7 **T** Tariff shifts export supply curve leftward, which increases price and decreases quantity traded. (793–796)

8 **F** Quota decreases supply, which increases price. (796)

9 **F** Captured by whoever has the export permit. (796)

10 **F** Dumping would be selling in Canada at lower price than in Japan. (798)

11 **F** It increases jobs in export industries, decreases jobs in import-competing industries, net result is unclear. (797)

12 **F** We must also examine the productivity of workers in each country, and Canadian workers are more productive. (798)

13 **F** They will be slow because losers' losses are individually much greater than winners' gains. (800–801)

14 **T** See text discussion. (800)

15 **F** There has been a large increase in the total volume of trade. (802–803)

Multiple-Choice

1 **c** Necessary in order to get foreign exchange. General patterns of trade unchanged, once we have enough dollars. (786)

2 **b** **a** and **c** are imports, **d** and **e** are exports of a *good*. (786)

3 **d** Inputs required to make one watch could make 1/2 widget. (787–788)

4 **e** Opportunity cost of 1 more beer = lost pizza. For Partyland, going from 0 beer to 25 beers costs 25 pizzas (one for one). Do same calculation for Cowabunga. (787–788)

5 **e** Same type of calculation as in **4**. (787–788)

6 **d** Each specializes where they have comparative advantage (lowest opportunity cost). (787–789)

7 **e** Trade price is between the opportunity costs in each country at the pre-trade equilibrium. (787–789)

8 **c** Even if Atlantis can produce everything cheaper, it probably has comparative advantage in only some goods. (787–789)

9 **c** Consumption possibilities frontier is outside *PPF*. (789–791)

10 **d** See text discussion. (789–792)

11 **c** Equilibrium is where export supply = import demand. (794–796)

12 **d** Equilibrium is where quota = import demand increases price. Higher domestic price increases domestic production. (796)

13 **d** Given quotas, increase in demand leads only to increase in price. (796)

14 **c** Tariff increases domestic price = export price + tariff, or a shift leftward in supply curve. (794–795)

15 **e** Under quota, domestic government allocates the licence to import. (796)

16 **d** Because they have right to export. (796)

17 **e** They collect tariff revenue = import price – export price. (794–795)

18 **e** Tariffs decrease exports and jobs in export industries, quotas restrict supply and increase prices, cheap foreign labour doesn't necessarily hurt us, poor and rich countries can have comparative advantage and gain from trade. VERs restrict supply and raise prices just like tariffs. (793–796)

19 **a** Quota decreases imports, which increases domestic price of watches, which increases domestic production. Decrease in imports = decrease in Beltran's exports, which decreases its income and therefore its imports = decrease in Atlantis' exports, which decreases widget production in Atlantis. (793–796)

20 **c** See text discussion. (797–800)

21 **b** See text discussion. (797–800)

22 **a** See text discussion. (797–800)

23 **d** See text discussion. (800–801)

24 **e** Not part of agreement. (802–803)

25 **e** See text discussion. (802–803)

Short Answer Problems

1 For two potential trading partners to be willing to trade, they must have different comparative advantages; that is, different opportunity costs. Then they will trade and both parties will gain. If the parties do not trade, each will face its own opportunity costs. A price at which trade takes place must be somewhere between the opportunity costs of the two traders. This result means that the party with the lower opportunity cost of the good in question will gain because it will sell at a price above its opportunity cost. Similarly, the party with the higher opportunity cost will gain because it will buy at a price below its opportunity cost.

2 A tariff on an imported good will *raise its price to domestic consumers* as the export supply curve shifts leftward. The export price is determined by the original export supply curve. As the domestic price of the good increases, the quantity of the good demanded decreases, and thus the relevant point on the original export supply curve is at a lower quantity and a *lower export price*. This lower quantity means that the quantity imported decreases. The increase in the domestic price will also lead to an *increase in the quantity of the good supplied domestically*.

3 When Atlantis imposes a tariff on its imports of watches, not only does the volume of imports shrink, but the volume of exports of widgets to Beltran will shrink by the same amount. Thus a balance of trade is maintained. As indicated in the answer to Short Answer Problem **2**, the export price of watches received by Beltran and the quantity exported decreases when a tariff is imposed. This decrease in the price and the quantity exported means that the income of Beltran has decreased. This result implies that the quantity of widgets (Atlantis' export) demanded by Beltran will decrease and thus Atlantis' exports decline.

4 This argument has some truth to it. As Short Answer Problem **2** shows, the tariff will lead an increase in domestic production of the protected good, which will lead to an increase in jobs in that industry. However, as Short Answer Problem **3** shows, the same tariff will reduce foreign income, and reduce foreign purchases of our goods, reducing our exports and our export production, reducing jobs in the export industry. The net effect on jobs is unclear, but it is definitely not large.

5 a Completed Table 33.2 is shown here as Table 33.2 Solution. The values in the table are calculated using the opportunity cost of each good in each country. See **b** and **c** below.

TABLE **33.2** SOLUTION
ATLANTIS AND BELTRAN—*PPF* FOR FOOD AND CLOTH

Atlantis		Beltran	
Food (units)	Cloth (units)	Food (units)	Cloth (units)
0	500	0	800
200	400	100	600
400	300	200	400
600	200	300	200
800	100	400	0
1,000	0	—	—

b To increase the output (consumption) of food by 200 units, cloth production (consumption) decreases by 100 units in Atlantis. Thus the opportunity cost of a unit of food is 1/2 unit of cloth. This opportunity cost is constant as are all others in this problem, for simplicity. Similarly, the opportunity cost of cloth in Atlantis is 2 units of food.

c In Beltran a 100-unit increase in the production (consumption) of food requires a reduction in the output (consumption) of cloth of 200 units. Thus the opportunity cost of food is 2 units of cloth. Similarly the opportunity cost of cloth in Beltran is 1/2 units of food.

d Figure 33.3, parts (a) and (b) illustrate the production possibility frontiers for Atlantis and Beltran, respectively labelled PPF_A and PPF_B. The rest of the diagram is discussed in the solutions to Short Answer Problems **6** and **7**.

FIGURE **33.3**

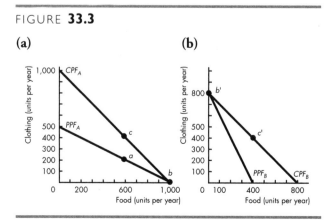

(a)   **(b)**

6 a We see from the solution to Short Answer Problems **5b** and **c** that Atlantis has a lower opportunity cost (1/2 unit of cloth) in the production of food. Therefore Atlantis will specialize in the production of food. Beltran, with the lower opportunity cost for cloth (1/2 unit of food), will specialize in cloth.

b Each country will want to produce every unit of the good in which they specialize as long as the amount they receive in trade exceeds their opportunity cost. For Atlantis, the opportunity cost of a unit of food is 1/2 unit of cloth, but it can obtain 1 unit of cloth in trade. Because the opportunity cost is constant, Atlantis will totally specialize by producing all of the food it can: 1,000 units per year, point *b* in Figure 33.3(a). Similarly, in Beltran, the opportunity cost of a unit of cloth is 1/2 unit of food but a unit of cloth will trade for 1 unit of food. Since the opportunity cost is constant, Beltran will totally specialize in the production of cloth and will produce 800 units per year, point *b′* in Figure 33.3(b).

c The consumption possibility frontiers for Atlantis and Beltran, labelled CPF_A and CPF_B, are illustrated in Figure 33.3, parts (a) and (b) respectively. These frontiers are straight lines that indicate all the combinations of food and cloth that can be consumed with trade. The position and slope of the consumption possibility frontier for an economy depend on the terms of trade between the goods (one for one in this example) and the production point of the economy.

The consumption possibility frontier for Atlantis (CPF_A), for example, is obtained by starting at point *b* on PPF_A, the production point, and examining possible trades. For example, if Atlantis traded 400 units of the food it produces for 400 units of cloth, it would be able to consume 600 units of food (1,000 units produced minus 400 units traded) and 400 units of cloth, which is represented by point *c*.

d If Atlantis consumes 600 units of food, trade allows consumption of cloth to be 400 units, 200 units more than possible without trade. The maximum amount of cloth that can be consumed without trade is given by the production possibility frontier. If food consumption is 600 units, this outcome is indicated by point *a* on PPF_A. The maximum amount of cloth consumption for any level of food consumption with trade is given by the consumption possibility frontier. If food consumption is 600 units, this outcome is indicated by point *c* on CPF_A.

7 a Since Atlantis produces 1,000 units of food per year (point *b* on PPF_A), to consume 600 units of food and 400 units of cloth (point *c* on CPF_A) it must trade 400 units of food for 400 units of cloth. This outcome means that Beltran has traded 400 units of cloth for 400 units of food. Since Beltran produces 800 units of cloth, this result suggests that Beltran must consume 400 units of food and 400 units of cloth (point c' on CPF_B).

b Atlantis exports 400 units of food per year and imports 400 units of cloth. Beltran exports 400 units of cloth per year and imports 400 units of food.

8 a The price of a shirt under free trade will occur at the intersection of Atlantis' import demand curve for shirts and Beltran's export supply curve for shirts. This result occurs at a price of $12 per shirt.

b Atlantis will import 6 million shirts per year.

9 a The effect of the $9 per shirt tariff is to shift the export supply curve (*S*) leftward. This outcome is shown as a shift from *S* to *S'* in Figure 33.2 Solution. The price is now determined by the intersection of the *D* curve, which is unaffected by the tariff, and the *S'* curve. The new price of a shirt is $18.

FIGURE **33.2** SOLUTION

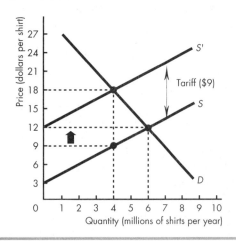

b Of this $18, $9 is the tariff, so the exporter only receives the remaining $9.

c Atlantis will now import only 4 million shirts per year.

d The tariff revenue is $9 (the tariff per shirt) × 4 million (the number of shirts imported), which is $36 million. This money is received by the government of Atlantis.

10 a The quota restricts the quantity that can be imported to 4 million shirts per year regardless of the price and is represented by a vertical line in Figure 33.4 (which corresponds to Figure 33.2). The market for shirts will thus clear at a price of $18 per shirt.

FIGURE **33.4**

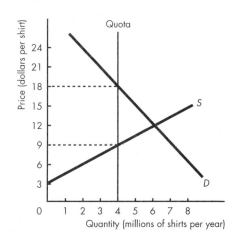

b This $18 price is received by the people who are given the right to import shirts under the quota. The amount received by the exporter is $9, given by the height of the *S* curve at a quantity of 4 million shirts per year.

c Atlantis will import 4 million shirts per year, the quota limit.

d The "excess profit" is $9 per shirt (the $18 received by the importer minus the $9 received by the exporter) × 4 million shirts, which is $36 million. This profit is captured by the importers who have been rewarded by the government of Atlantis because they have been given the right to import under the quota. This licence is essentially a right to make an "excess profit."

Chapter 34

International Finance

Financing International Trade

The **balance of payments** accounts measure Canada's international transactions.

♦ **Current account**—net exports + net interest payments + net transfers.

♦ **Capital account**—foreign investment in Canada – Canadian investment abroad.

♦ **Official settlements account**—net changes in Canada's **official international reserves** (government's holdings of foreign currency)

  • If official reserves increase, official settlement balance is negative.

♦ Current account balance + Capital account balance + Official settlements balance = 0

♦ To pay a current account deficit we must borrow from abroad or decrease official reserves.

A country that in current year is borrowing more from rest of world than it is lending is a **net borrower**.

♦ **Net lender** lends more to rest of world than it borrows.

♦ **Debtor nation** has borrowed more than lent to rest of world over its history.

♦ **Creditor nation** has lent more over its history to rest of world than it has borrowed.

♦ Being a net borrower is not a problem if it is to finance investment that generates higher income to pay debts, as has been recent case in Canada.

Current account balance (*CAB*) is primarily determined by **net exports** ($NX = X - M$).

♦ Via circular flow, net exports = **private sector balance** ($S - I$) + **government sector balance** ($NT - G$).

♦ Government deficit and current account deficit move together (**twin deficits**).

The Exchange Rate

Foreigners and Canadians exchange dollars for foreign currency in the **foreign exchange market**.

♦ **Foreign exchange rate** = price at which one currency exchanges for another (number of U.S. cents per Canadian dollar).

♦ **Currency depreciation** is decrease in value of Canadian dollar in terms of another currency, **currency appreciation** is increase.

The quantity of Canadian dollars demanded in the foreign exchange market = amount traders plan to buy at a given price—a *derived demand* based on demand for Canadian exports and Canadian assets.

♦ Decrease in exchange rate increases quantity demanded of Canadian dollars (movement down to the right along demand curve), because

  • exports become cheaper for foreigners, increasing demand for exports and therefore demand for dollars.
  • expected profits increase from buying Canadian dollars and holding them until they appreciate.

♦ The demand curve shifts *rightward* if

  • **Canadian interest rate differential** (Canadian interest rate – foreign interest rate) increases, increasing demand for Canadian assets.
  • expected future exchange rate increases, increasing expected profits from buying Canadian dollars and holding them until they appreciate.

Quantity of Canadian dollars supplied in foreign exchange market = amount traders plan to sell at a given price in order to buy other currencies to buy imports and foreign assets.

◆ Increase in exchange rate increases quantity supplied of Canadian dollars (movement up to the right along supply curve), because

- imports become cheaper for Canadians, increasing demand for imports and therefore demand for foreign currency = increase in supply Canadian dollars.
- expected profits increase from buying foreign currency and holding it until it appreciates, increasing demand for foreign currency = increase in supply Canadian dollars.

◆ The supply curve shifts *leftward* if

- Canadian interest rate differential increases, decreasing demand for foreign assets = decrease in supply of Canadian dollar.
- expected future exchange rate increases, decreasing expected profits from selling Canadian dollars, buying foreign currency and holding it until Canadian dollar depreciates.

Market equilibrium determined by demand and supply, with exchange rate adjusting as required.

◆ Exchange rate is often volatile, because supply and demand often move together, creating big swings in value of exchange rate.

Expectations of Δ exchange rate are due to the forces of **purchasing power parity** (two currencies have the same value or purchasing power) and **interest rate parity** (two currencies earn the same interest rate, adjusted for expected depreciation).

◆ If purchasing power parity does not hold, and Canadian dollar buys more than the U.S. dollar, then people expect it to appreciate, which increases demand for Canadian dollar, decreases supply—it does appreciate.

◆ Interest rate parity always holds (adjusted for risk), but if returns are higher in Canada, increased demand for Canadian dollar instantly increases exchange rate.

Bank of Canada can affect exchange rate in two ways:

◆ Use monetary policy to Δ interest rates, which leads to Δ exchange rate.

◆ Buy or sell Canadian dollars directly. Buying dollars increases demand, which increases exchange rate.

◆ Such interventions Δ official international reserves, which limits amount of intervention.

HELPFUL HINTS

1 There is an important difference between trade within a single country and trade between countries—currency. Individuals trading in the same country use the same currency, and trade is straightforward. International trade is complicated by the fact that individuals in different countries use different currencies. A Japanese vendor selling goods will want payment in Japanese yen, but a Canadian buyer will likely be holding only Canadian dollars. This chapter addresses this trade complication by looking at the balance of payments of a country, as well as the relation of the balance of payments to the foreign exchange rate.

2 It is important to understand foreign exchange rates as prices determined by supply and demand. They are prices of currency determined in markets for currency. The demand for Canadian dollars in the foreign exchange market arises from the desire on the part of foreigners to purchase Canadian goods and services (which requires dollars) and Canadian financial or real assets.

The supply of Canadian dollars is a special type of supply, because the offer to sell a Canadian dollar is equivalent to an offer to buy foreign currency. Therefore it depends on the desire of Canadians to buy foreign goods and services (which requires foreign currency), and to buy foreign assets. Remembering that the supply of Canadian dollars equals the demand for foreign currency will help you to understand many of the shifts in the supply of Canadian dollars.

As an example of this effect in action, think about what happens if currency speculators learn new information that makes them think the Canadian dollar will appreciate next month (which also implies foreign currencies will depreciate next month). They will plan to buy Canadian dollars *this* month, and sell foreign currencies this month, in order to make a profit. Thus, the demand for the Canadian dollar shifts rightward this month, and the supply of foreign exchange shifts leftward.

3 The exchange rate is often volatile because supply and demand often shift in a reinforcing manner, since they are both affected by the same changes in expectations. These changes in expectations are driven by two forces: purchasing power parity and interest rate parity. Each of

these is a version of the law of one price, which states anytime there is a discrepancy in the price of the same good in two markets, natural economic forces (unless restricted) will eliminate that discrepancy and establish a single price. Suppose that the price in market 1 increases relative to the price in market 2. Individuals will now buy in the market with the lower price and not in the market with the higher price. This increase in the demand in market 2 and decrease in demand in market 1 will cause the two prices to come together. This principle applies to international markets as well: natural market forces will result in a single world price for the same good.

Suppose that purchasing power parity does not hold. For example, suppose that the wholesale price of a portable MP3 player in Canada is $200, and in Japan it is 20,000 yen, and that the exchange rate is currently 125 yen per dollar. The dollar price of the player in Japan is $160 (20,000 yen/125 yen per dollar). People expect the demand for the player in Canada to decrease (= a decrease in the demand for Canadian dollars), and the demand for the player in Japan to increase (= supply of dollars rising), which would lead to the exchange rate depreciating towards 100 yen per dollar (the purchasing power parity level). Their expectations will lead to a decrease in the demand for the Canadian dollar and an increase in the supply of the Canadian dollar, so that the exchange rate will depreciate even before the demand for the player adjusts!

The law of one price also holds for the price of assets such as bonds. If we recall that bond prices are inversely related to interest rates, we can see that interest rate parity is a version of the law of one price. For example, consider a situation where, taking into account the expected depreciation of the Canadian dollar, the Canadian interest rate was higher than the U.S. rate (which implies the price of bonds is lower in Canada). Buyers would demand Canadian bonds, raising their price and lowering Canadian interest rates. In addition, they would be selling U.S. bonds, lowering their price and raising U.S. interest rates. These actions occur until the interest differential between the two countries has shrunk to a level where it just reflects the expected depreciation of the Canadian dollar—interest parity holds.

4   In Chapter 26, we saw how monetary policy influenced the economy via changes in the interest rate, and changes in the exchange rate. This chapter fills in the details of the exchange rate channel. A change in the quantity of money leads to a change in the interest rate, which changes the demand and supply of the Canadian dollar, and therefore the exchange rate, and therefore net exports and aggregate demand, and therefore inflation, real GDP, and unemployment.

There is also another international effect that the Bank of Canada often worries about. Imported goods play an important role in the production process, so that a depreciation of the Canadian dollar will increase the cost of production (Canadian dollar price of imports = foreign price/exchange rate). This depreciation in turn can create cost-push inflation. The Bank of Canada often works to offset temporary fluctuations in the exchange rate, or to smooth permanent changes in the exchange rate, in order to reduce fluctuations in the price level.

SELF-TEST

True/False and Explain

Financing International Trade

1   There can be no such thing as a balance of payments surplus/deficit, because by definition a *balance* of payments must always *balance*.

2   A larger government sector deficit always leads to a higher current account deficit.

3   If a nation is a net borrower from the rest of the world, it must be a debtor nation.

4   If a country has a large government budget deficit and the private sector deficit is small, the balance of trade deficit must be large.

5   If investment is greater than saving, the private sector has a deficit.

6 If Canada borrows more from the rest of the world than it lends to the rest of the world, Canada has a capital account surplus.

7 An increase in the government sector deficit must lead to an increase in a current account deficit.

The Exchange Rate

8 An increase in Canadian interest rates will lead to an increase in the demand for the Canadian dollar.

9 The demand and supply of Canadian dollars tend to move independently of each other.

10 Countries with currencies that are expected to appreciate will have higher interest rates than countries with currencies that are expected to depreciate.

11 If the yen price of the dollar is 100 yen per dollar and the price of a traded good is $10 in Canada, purchasing power parity implies that the price in Japan will be 1,000 yen.

12 If the exchange rate between the Canadian dollar and the Japanese yen changes from 130 yen per dollar to 140 yen per dollar, the Canadian dollar has appreciated.

13 If the foreign exchange value of the dollar is expected to increase, the demand for dollars increases.

14 If the Bank of Canada has a target exchange rate in mind, then if the demand for the Canadian dollar increases, the Bank of Canada will sell the Canadian dollar.

15 If the exchange rate is expected to depreciate in value in the future, the demand for the U.S. dollar will increase today.

Multiple-Choice

Financing International Trade

1 Which of the following statements is *true*? A high and persistent current account deficit implies Canada is
a a net borrower only.
b a net lender only.
c a debtor nation only.
d a creditor nation only.
e both a net borrower and a debtor nation.

2 $NX =$
a $C + I + G$
b $(S + I) - (NT + G)$
c $(G - NT) + (I - S)$
d $(S - I) + (G - NT)$
e none of the above.

3 Which of the following is one of the balance of payments accounts?
a current account
b borrowing account
c official lending account
d net interest account
e public account

4 Suppose Canada initially has all balance of payments accounts in balance (no surplus or deficit). Then Canadian firms increase their imports from Japan, financing that increase by borrowing from Japan. There will now be a current account
a surplus and a capital account surplus.
b surplus and a capital account deficit.
c deficit and a capital account surplus.
d deficit and a capital account deficit.
e deficit and a capital account balance.

5 The country of Mengia came into existence at the beginning of year 1. Given the information in Table 34.1, in year 4 Mengia is a
a net lender and a creditor nation.
b net lender and a debtor nation.
c net borrower and a creditor nation.
d net borrower and a debtor nation.
e net lender and neither a creditor nor a debtor nation.

TABLE **34.1**

Year	Borrowed from Rest of World (billions of dollars)	Lent to Rest of World (billions of dollars)
1	60	20
2	60	40
3	60	60
4	60	80

6 Assuming that Mengia's official settlement account is always in balance, in which year or years in Table 34.1 did Mengia have a current account surplus?

a year 1
b year 2
c years 1, 2, and 3
d years 1 and 2
e year 4 only

7 If Mengia's official settlement balance was in deficit every year, for which year or years in Table 34.1 can you say *for sure* there was a current account surplus?

a year 1
b year 2
c years 2 and 3
d years 1 and 2
e years 3 and 4

8 Suppose that a country's government expenditures are $400 billion, net taxes are $300 billion, saving is $300 billion, and investment is $250 billion. This country has a government budget

a surplus and a private sector surplus.
b surplus and a private sector deficit.
c deficit and a private sector surplus.
d deficit and a private sector deficit.
e surplus and a private sector balance.

9 Suppose that a country's government expenditures are $400 billion, net taxes are $300 billion, saving is $300 billion, and investment is $250 billion. Net exports are in a

a surplus of $150 billion.
b surplus of $50 billion.
c deficit of $150 billion.
d deficit of $50 billion.
e deficit of $250 billion.

10 The distinction between a debtor or creditor nation and a net borrower or net lender nation depends on

a the distinction between the level of saving in the economy and the saving rate.
b the distinction between the level of saving in the economy and the rate of borrowing.
c the distinction between the stock of net borrowing and the flow of net borrowing.
d the distinction between exports and imports.
e nothing really; they are the same.

11 If the current account is in deficit, and the capital account is also in deficit, then the *change* in official reserves is

a negative.
b positive.
c probably close to zero, but could be either negative or positive.
d zero.
e not affected.

The Exchange Rate

12 Suppose that the dollar-yen foreign exchange rate changes from 140 yen per dollar to 130 yen per dollar. Then the yen has

a depreciated against the dollar, and the dollar has appreciated against the yen.
b depreciated against the dollar, and the dollar has depreciated against the yen.
c appreciated against the dollar, and the dollar has appreciated against the yen.
d appreciated against the dollar, and the dollar has depreciated against the yen.
e neither appreciated nor depreciated, but the dollar has depreciated against the yen.

13 Suppose the exchange rate between the Canadian dollar and the British pound is 0.5 pounds per dollar. If a radio sells for 38 pounds in Britain, what is the dollar price of the radio?

a $19
b $26
c $38
d $57
e $76

14 The market in which the currency of one country is exchanged for the currency of another is called the

a money market.
b capital market.
c foreign exchange market.
d forward exchange market.
e international trading market.

15 If the Bank of Canada wishes to increase the exchange rate, it should

a lower interest rates.
b increase the quantity of money.
c buy foreign exchange.
d sell Canadian dollars.
e buy Canadian dollars.

16 Which of the following quotations best describes the purchasing power parity effect in action?

a "The recent high Canadian interest rate has increased the demand for the Canadian dollar."
b "The market feeling is that the Canadian dollar is overvalued and will likely depreciate."
c "The price of bananas is the same in Canada and the United States, adjusting for the exchange rate."
d "The expected depreciation of the Canadian dollar is currently lowering demand for it."
e None of the above.

17 If you think that the exchange rate will depreciate over the next month, you can expect to make money by

a only buying Canadian dollars.
b only buying U.S. dollars.
c only selling Canadian dollars.
d only selling U.S. dollars.
e both buying U.S. dollars and selling Canadian dollars.

18 Consider Table 34.2. Between 1994 and 1995, the Canadian dollar has _____ versus the mark and _____ versus the yen.

a appreciated; depreciated
b appreciated; appreciated
c depreciated; depreciated
d depreciated; appreciated
e not changed; not changed

TABLE **34.2**

Currency	1994 Exchange Rate	1995 Exchange Rate
German mark	2 marks/dollar	3 marks/dollar
Japanese yen	120 yen/dollar	90 yen/dollar

19 Consider Table 34.2. Between 1994 and 1995, the yen

a must have depreciated in value versus the mark.
b must have appreciated in value versus the mark.
c may or may not have appreciated in value versus the mark.
d will have appreciated in value versus the mark if the mark has a higher weight in the Canadian trade index.
e will have appreciated in value versus the mark if the mark has a lower weight in the Canadian trade index.

20 The Bank of Canada cannot just set the exchange rate at any level it desires because

a such intervention violates international law.
b the foreign exchange market is unregulated.
c doing so would make Canada a debtor nation.
d doing so would require constant changes in international reserves.
e interest rate parity forbids it.

21 When would the exchange rate decrease in value the most?

a When the supply and demand of dollars both increase.
b When the supply of dollars increases, and the demand decreases.
c When the supply of dollars decreases, and the demand increases.
d When the supply and demand of dollars both decrease.
e When there is intervention by the Bank of Canada.

22 Which of the following will shift the supply curve of Canadian dollars rightward?

a An increase occurs in the demand for foreign goods by Canadian citizens.
b A decrease occurs in the demand for Canadian goods by foreigners.
c The dollar is expected to appreciate next year.
d U.S. interest rates decrease.
e None of the above.

23 Which of the following will shift the demand curve for Canadian dollars rightward?

a an increase occurs in the demand for foreign goods by Canadian citizens
b a decrease occurs in the demand for Canadian goods by foreigners
c the dollar is expected to appreciate
d the dollar is expected to depreciate
e U.S. interest rates increase

24 If the interest rate in Canada is greater than the interest rate in Japan, interest rate parity implies that

a the inflation rate is higher in Japan.

b Japanese financial assets are poor investments.

c the yen is expected to depreciate against the dollar.

d the yen is expected to appreciate against the dollar.

e Canadian financial assets are poor investments.

25 The exchange rate is volatile because

a government intervention always make things worse.

b the demand curve is very flat.

c the demand curve is very steep.

d shifts in demand and supply are independent of each other.

e shifts in demand and supply are not independent of each other.

Short Answer Problems

1 What is the relationship between a country's trade deficit, its government budget deficit, and its private sector deficit?

2 What determines the value of the exchange rate?

3 What is purchasing power parity?

4 Consider the following headline from the December 12, 1997 issue of *The Globe and Mail*: "Dollar hits new 11½-year low: Interest rate hike expected after recurrence of Asian flu forces Bank of Canada to intervene." Clearly the Canadian dollar's exchange rate was decreasing in value during December 1997. Explain briefly but carefully why an increase in interest rates by the Bank of Canada would help to reverse this decrease.

5 Over its lifetime as a country, Canada has tended to be a net borrower more than a net lender. Is this outcome good or bad?

6 The international transactions of a country for a given year are reported in Table 34.3.

TABLE **34.3**

Transaction	Amount (billions of dollars)
Exports of goods and services	100
Imports of goods and services	130
Transfers to the rest of the world	20
Loans to the rest of the world	60
Loans from the rest of the world	?
Increases in official reserves	10
Net interest pyaments	0

a What is the amount of loans from the rest of the world?

b What is the current account balance?

c What is the capital account balance?

d What is the official settlements balance?

7 The information in Table 34.4 is for a country during a given year.

TABLE **34.4**

Variable	Amount (billions of dollars)
GDP	800
Net taxes	200
Government budget deficit	50
Consumption	500
Investment	150
Imports	150

a What is the level of government expenditure on goods and services?

b What is the private sector surplus or deficit?

c What is the value of exports?

d What is the balance of trade surplus or deficit?

8 Suppose that the exchange rate between the Canadian dollar and the German mark is 2 marks per dollar.

a What is the exchange rate in terms of dollars per mark?

b What is the price in dollars of a camera selling for 250 marks?

c What is the price in marks of a computer selling for 1,000 dollars?

9 You are trying to decide whether to buy some laptaps for your business in either Canada or the U.S. Looking at identical machines on the Dell Canada and the Dell U.S. Web sites, you find that they sell for US$2,000 in the United States and C$3,000 in Canada.

a Where would you buy the laptop if the exchange rate between the Canadian dollar and the U.S. dollar was US$0.80 per C$?

b If there is a profit opportunity, where would you resell it if you wanted to make a profit? (Ignore any taxes, tariffs, transportation costs, and differences in quality.)

c Does purchasing power parity hold?

d If many Canadian *and* American businesses acted like you, and if the exchange rate was flexible, what would happen to the value of the exchange rate? What would be the new equilibrium exchange rate that would make purchasing power parity hold for laptops, if the U.S. dollar price and the Canadian dollar price stayed constant?

10 Go to the Government Documents Section of your library, or to the Bank of Canada Review, or to the Statistics Canada Web site (**http://www.statcan.ca**). Find data for the years 1985–95 on the value of the exchange rate in terms of U.S. cents, and data on Canadian and U.S. interest rates (use the prime interest rate banks charge to their best businesses). Construct a table of the Canadian interest rate differential versus the exchange rate, and discuss what kind of relationship you find.

ANSWERS

True/False and Explain

1 F Overall flow of money in/out of country = sum of the three balances of payment must balance. Individual balances may be in deficit/surplus/balance. (810–812)

2 F Depends on reaction of private sector surplus/deficit. (813–814)

3 F May or may not be true. Net borrower implies *current* net borrowing > 0. Debtor nation implies sum of *all* net borrowing > 0. (812)

4 T Balance of trade (negative) = government balance (large negative) + private balance (small negative). (813–814)

5 T Definition. (813)

6 T Definition—note which way the money is flowing. (810–812)

7 F It may lead to it, *if* the private sector balance remains unchanged. (814)

8 T Other things remaining the same, this increase will increase interest rate differential. (816–817)

9 F They are both affected by expected future exchange rate and interest rates, and so move together. (821–822)

10 F If expected to appreciate, this expected appreciation implies increased earnings in foreign currency terms, which increases demand for their bonds, which decreases interest rates until interest rate parity holds. (821–822)

11 T Under purchasing power parity, yen price identical in each country. 10×100 yen/$ = 1,000 yen. (821–822)

12 T Dollar is more valuable—takes more yen to buy one dollar. (815)

13 T Increase in foreign exchange value of dollar implies a profit opportunity, which increases demand for dollars. (816–817)

14 T Shifts supply curve of Canadian dollars rightward, offsetting shift in demand. (822–823)

15 T Expected profit motive. (816–817)

Multiple-Choice

1 a High current account deficit implies likely capital account surplus. It is unclear about debtor versus lender. (810–812)

2 e $(S - I) + (NT - G)$ by definition. (813–814)

3 a Definition. (810–812)

4 c Imports > exports implies current account deficit. Borrowing > lending implies capital account surplus. (Think about which direction money is flowing.) (810–812)

5 b Current lending > borrowing implies net lender. Sum of past borrowing > sum of lending implies debtor nation. (810–812)

6 e Official settlements balance = 0 implies current account surplus = capital account deficit, which occurs only when lending > borrowing. (810–812)

7 e Since current account + capital account + official settlements account = 0, when official settlements is a deficit, to be sure current is a surplus, it must be the case that capital is 0 or a deficit. (810–812)

8 c Government sector deficit = $NT - G$ = 300 – 400 = –100. Private sector surplus = $S - I$ = 300 – 250 = + 50. (813–814)

9 d Net exports = $(NT - G) + (S - I)$ = 300 – 400 + 300 – 250 = –50. (813–814)

10 c Net lender implies stock of investments rising. Debtor nation implies negative flow of interest payments on investments. (812)

11 a Official settlements balance = –(capital account + current account) = surplus, which implies change in official reserves < 0. (810–812)

12 d It takes less yen to buy dollar, which implies the dollar depreciated. Via inverse relationship, yen has appreciated. (815)

13 e $76 = £38 × ($2 per £). (815)

14 c Definition. (815)

15 e This increases demand for Canadian dollars. **a** decreases demand, **b–d** increase supply. (822–823)

16 c Two currencies have same purchasing power. (821–822)

17 e You will wish to buy foreign currency, since it will increase in value, which also requires you to sell Canadian dollars. (821–822)

18 a It takes more marks to buy $1 (increase in value), and less yen (decrease in value). (815)

ⓒⓣ **19 b** 1994:
1/60 mark/yen = (2 marks/$)/(120yen/$).
1995:
1/30 mark/yen = (3marks/$)/(90 yen/$).
Takes more marks in 1995 to buy 1 yen, so yen has appreciated. (815)

20 d Such intervention requires buying/selling Canadian dollars, which changes official reserves, which cannot occur forever. (822–823)

21 b Draw a graph. (820)

22 a Increased demand for foreign currency increases supply of Canadian dollars. (819)

23 c **a** has no impact on demand, **b, d**, and **e** shift it leftward. (816–817)

24 d Therefore Canadian dollar expected to depreciate, offsetting the interest rate differential. (821–822)

25 e They are both affected by the same expectations. (820–822)

Short Answer Problems

1 The national income accounting identities show that a country's balance of trade deficit is equal to the sum of its government budget deficit and its private sector deficit.

2 The value of the exchange rate is determined by supply and demand. The supply of the Canadian dollar is affected by two things—changes in the Canadian interest rate differential and changes in the expected future exchange rate. The demand for the Canadian dollar is also affected by the same two things.

3 Purchasing power parity follows from arbitrage and the law of one price. It means that the value of money is the same in all countries. For example, if the exchange rate between the dollar and the yen is 120 yen per dollar, purchasing power parity says that a good that sells for 120 yen in Japan will sell for 1 dollar in Canada. Thus, the exchange rate is such that money (dollars or yen) has the same purchasing power in both countries.

ⓒⓣ **4** An increase in Canadian interest rates increases the Canadian interest rate differential, which increases the desirability of Canadian assets relative to foreign assets. This increase in turn increases the demand for Canadian dollars by foreigners, and decreases the demand for foreign exchange by Canadians, which decreases the supply of the Canadian dollar. These shifts in supply and demand will increase the value of the exchange rate.

ⓒⓣ **5** Being a net borrower is fine if the country is borrowing for investment purposes, and creating earnings to pay off what it owes. This situation has mostly been the case for Canada; so being a net borrower is good—it has allowed a resource-rich but capital-poor country like Canada to develop its resources.

6 a Current account balance + capital account balance + official settlements balance = 0, or (100 − 130 − 20) + (loans from rest of world − 60) + (−10) = 0, so loans from the rest of the world = 120.

b The current account balance is a $50 billion deficit: exports minus imports minus transfers to the rest of the world plus net interest payments to the rest of the world.

c The capital account balance is a surplus of $60 billion: loans from the rest of the world minus loans to the rest of the world.

d Because official reserves increased, the official settlements balance is −10.

7 a Since we know that the government budget deficit is $50 billion and net taxes are $200 billion, we can infer that government expenditure on goods and services is $250 billion.

b The private sector surplus or deficit is given by saving minus investment. Investment is given as $150 billion, but we must compute saving. Saving is equal to GDP minus net taxes minus consumption: $100 billion. Thus there is a private sector deficit of $50 billion.

c We know that GDP is consumption plus investment plus government expenditure on goods and services plus net exports (exports minus imports). Since we know all these values except exports, we can obtain that value by solving for exports. The value of exports equals

GDP plus imports minus consumption minus investment minus government expenditure on goods and services; the value of exports equals $50 billion.

d There is a balance of trade deficit of $100 billion. This result can be obtained in two ways. First we can recognize that the balance of trade surplus or deficit is given by the value of exports ($50 billion) minus the value of imports ($150 billion). The alternative method is to recognize that the balance of trade deficit is equal to the sum of the government budget deficit ($50 billion) and the private sector deficit ($50 billion).

8 a If 1 dollar can be purchased for 2 marks, the price of a mark is 1/2 dollar per mark.

b At an exchange rate of 2 marks per dollar, it takes 125 dollars to obtain the 250 marks needed to buy the camera.

c At an exchange rate of 2 marks per dollar, it takes 2,000 marks to obtain the 1,000 dollars needed to buy the computer.

9 a The Canadian laptop costs US$2,400 = C$3,000 × US$0.80 per C$. Therefore, it is cheaper from the U.S. Web site.

b It is profitable to buy it in the United States for US$2,000 and sell it in Canada for US$2,400.

c No, the two currencies do not have the same purchasing power—U.S. dollars buy more.

d The extra demand for U.S. laptops would tend to push up the demand for U.S. dollars, leading to an appreciation of the U.S. dollar (and a depreciation of the Canadian dollar). The value of the exchange rate that makes purchasing power parity hold would be the value A that solves US$2,000 = C$3,000 × US$$A$ per C$, which is a value of 0.667.

10 The data is listed in Table 34.5. Your data may be slightly different, due to rounding errors, etc. in your data source.

TABLE **34.5**

Year	Differential	U.S. $/C$
1985	0.7	0.732
1986	2.27	0.72
1987	1.31	0.754
1988	1.43	0.813
1989	2.45	0.845
1990	4.06	0.856
1991	1.55	0.873
1992	1.23	0.827
1993	−0.07	0.775
1994	−0.38	0.732
1995	−0.17	0.729

Source: Bank of Canada *Review,* various issues.

We can see that there is a rough positive relationship between the differential and the value of the exchange rate. As the differential rose through the middle of the time period, so did the value of the exchange rate, driven by an increase in the demand for Canadian dollars and a decrease in the supply of Canadian dollars. As the differential fell towards the end, so did the exchange rate. The relationship is not exact, but it does meet the rough predictions of our theories.

Chapter **35**

Global Stock Markets

KEY CONCEPTS

Stock Market Basics

Firms raise some financial capital by selling **stock** (tradable security indicating partial ownership).

- Value of stock = **equity capital**.
- **Dividend** is a share of profits, paid in proportion to stock holdings.

Sales of stock from one individual to another are carried out on a **stock exchange**.

- **Stock price** = price one share trades for on an exchange.
- **Return** = stock's dividend + **capital gain** (increase in price) or – **capital loss**.
- **Dividend yield** = dividend as a percent of price; **rate of return** = return as percent of price.
- A firm's accounting profits are its **earnings**.
  - **Price-earnings ratio** = price/current earnings.

Stock price indexes such as the S&P Composite Index or the Dow Jones Industrial Average track average stock prices.

- In real terms, stock price indexes have risen on average over long time periods, but with many strong fluctuations.
- One of the biggest increases in stock prices occurred in the late 1990s.
- Price-earnings ratios fluctuate lots too, with recent strong increases.

How Are Stock Prices Determined?

The market fundamentals theory argues that the amount people are willing to pay for a stock is based on the sources of value of that stock.

- Average willingness to pay depends on future expected dividend.
- People dislike uncertainty, and will pay less for a stock with an uncertain rate of return.
  - In such cases, people discount the uncertain future amount by the **discount factor**.
- The price of a stock will move towards the average willingness to pay by demand and supply pressures.
- Result: price = expected value of [discount factor × (dividend + future price)].
- Forecast of future price is a **rational expectation** (uses all available information).
- Given that future price depends on future dividends, market fundamentals price depends only on the stream of expected future dividend payments.

An alternative theory is that of **speculative bubbles**—prices rise and fall sharply based on people expecting them to rise and fall.

- Bubbles occur as people try and forecast each others' forecasts, leading to herdlike behaviour.
- Some economists believe the late 1990s stock market boom was a bubble, others think that market fundamentals had changed—true answer is still not known.

Risk and Return

Stock prices fluctuate in an unpredictable or risky manner, and some stocks fluctuate more than others.

◆ Investors will not hold riskier stocks unless they are compensated by an additional return known as the **risk premium**—riskier stocks generally have higher rates of return.

◆ People have a higher discount rate for riskier stock, yielding a lower current price (expected dividend and future price held constant), and therefore a higher expected rate of return.

◆ Risk can be reduced by portfolio diversification—holding a number of different stocks.

The Stock Market and the Economy

Over time, real stock earnings have trended upwards, although with lots of fluctuations.

◆ Stronger-than-usual growths in real stock earnings in 1890s, 1950s/1960s, and the 1990s.

◆ Each period involved the spread of new technologies.

◆ It is not clear yet if the 1990s involved the spread of a "new economy" based on the spread of the Internet.

Monetary policy affects interest rates, which in turn affect the stock market.

◆ Higher interests rates lead to lower stock prices because they create:

• higher saving and lower spending on goods and services and lower revenue for firms.
• higher returns on bonds, so some people switch from stocks to bonds.

◆ It is profitable for people to try and anticipate policy changes—if interest rates are expected to rise, stock prices will fall *before* they rise.

Higher capital gains taxes lower the **realized capital gain** people make by selling stocks at a higher price, so they lower the demand for stocks and the price.

◆ Higher taxes on corporate profits also lower stock prices.

Rising stock prices lead to a rise in **wealth** (the market value of assets).

◆ Via the **wealth effect**, consumption increases and the **saving rate** (saving as a percent of disposable income) decreases.

◆ The rising stock prices of the late 1990s primarily affected the wealth of those earning $100,000 or more.

HELPFUL HINTS

1 One part of the stock market that sometimes confuses students is the difference between the *primary* market and the *secondary* market.

The primary market involves the initial sale of newly issued stock by a firm to investors. At that stage, the firm can use the money earned for the reason they raised it, typically investment in new technology or physical capital, or to expand markets.

The secondary market is the resale market of the above primary issues, the market in already existing stocks. Transactions in the stock market are typically the secondary kind, involving trades from one person to another, without involving the original firm in the transaction.

2 The price of a stock is determined by demand and supply. Specifically, on any given day, some holders of the stock will be trying to sell it, and some others will be trying to buy it. The interaction of supply and demand (aided by the stock exchange in matching buyers and sellers) will determine the price at any given moment, and the size of the volume of sales.

We can use these concepts of demand and supply to help us understand the various factors that create different prices for stocks. As an example, suppose people find out that stock in company A is riskier than they previously thought. Holding constant the current price, expected future price, and expected future dividends, this stock is now less desirable. As a result, the demand for the stock decreases, and therefore the price will decrease as well. With the lower current price, the expected capital gain (= expected future price – current price) is higher. Given this, the rate of return (= (expected dividend + expected capital gain)/current price) must be higher. There is now a risk premium included in the rate of return.

S E L F - T E S T

True/False and Explain

Stock Market Basics

1 A dividend is the expected change in the price of a stock.

2 Glitzsoft shares paid a dividend of $10 per share last year, and the stock rose in value from $20 per share to $25 per share. The rate of return was 60%.

3 If a stock price is expected to increase over the next year, the expected return will be higher.

4 Over the last 50 years, price-earnings ratios for the S&P/TSX index have risen steadily.

5 Sales of stock from one individual to another are carried out on a stock index.

How Are Stock Prices Determined?

6 In the market fundamentals view, people are willing to pay for a stock based on the sources of value of that stock.

7 In the market fundamentals view, the price of a stock fundamentally depends only on the stream of expected future dividend payments.

8 People will pay less for a stock with more uncertainty.

9 In the speculative bubbles view, if stock prices rise, it is because people expected them to rise.

Risk and Return

10 The riskier the stock, the lower its current price (expected dividend and future price held constant), and the higher its expected rate of return.

11 Risk can be reduced by holding a number of different stocks.

The Stock Market and the Economy

12 Strong than usual growths in real stock earnings are usually in periods that involve the spread of new technologies.

13 Higher interest rates raise stock prices.

14 Higher corporate taxes will lower stock prices.

15 Rising stock prices can lead to a decrease in the saving rate.

Multiple-Choice

Stock Market Basics

1 Stock is
a a tradable security that a firm issues to certify the stockholder owns a share in the firm.
b a proportional share of profits.
c an entitlement to be paid first before any debtors of the firm.
d not related to the right to vote in the selection of the firm's directors.
e an organized market where people buy and sell shares.

2 Table 35.1 below shows some information on the earnings, dividend payments and stock prices on a yearly basis for Glitzsoft stock. What is the capital gain on Glitzsoft stock between 1999 and 2000?

a $10.00
b $90.00
c $100.00
d –$10.00
e –$12.00

TABLE **35.1** GLITZSOFT STOCK

Year Ending	Earnings per Share	Dividend Payments	Stock Price
1999	$10.00	$5.00	$100.00
2000	$5.00	$3.00	$90.00

3 Table 35.1 above shows some information on the dividend payments and stock prices on a yearly basis for Glitzsoft stock. In 2000, what was the return on Glitzsoft Stock?

a $3.00
b $7.00
c $90.00
d –$7.00
e –$10.00

4 Table 35.1 above shows some information on the earnings, dividend payments and stock prices on a yearly basis for Glitzsoft stock. What is the rate of return on Glitzsoft stock in 2000?

a 12%
b 13.33%
c –7%
d –10%
e –12%

5 Table 35.1 above shows some information on the earnings, dividend payments and stock prices on a yearly basis for Glitzsoft stock. What is the dividend yield on Glitzsoft stock in 2000?

a 60%
b 5.55%
c 3.33%
d 3%
e –3.33%

6 Table 35.1 above shows some information on the earnings, dividend payments and stock prices on a yearly basis for Glitzsoft stock. What is the price-earnings ratio on Glitzsoft stock in 2000?

a 0.033
b 0.055
c 18
d 20
e 30

7 Which of the following statements about stock market indexes is *false*?

a Real stock prices have had a positive trend over the last 50 years.
b Real stock prices tend to move smoothly upwards or downwards.
c Stock prices boomed in the 1990s.
d U.S. stock prices climbed more than Canadian stock prices in the 1990s.
e Stock prices crashed at the start of the Great Depression.

8 Which of the following indexes has the broadest set of stock prices in it?

a the Dow Jones Industrial Average
b the NASDAQ
c the FTSE 100
d the S&P Composite Index
e the New York Stock Exchange Index

9 Which of the following statements about stock markets is *correct*?

a When a company goes bankrupt, only its common stockholders must pay its debt.
b When a company goes bankrupt, only its preferred stockholders must pay its debt.
c Companies distribute all of their earnings as dividends.
d When you buy a share of Bombardier stock, Bombardier receives the funds.
e If a stock decreases in price after you buy it, you have a capital loss on the stock.

How Are Stock Prices Determined?

10 Which of the following quotations is consistent with the market fundamentals view of stock prices?

a "Since Glitzsoft is paying such good dividends now and in the future, I think it is a good buy."
b "Since Glitzsoft's future dividends stream is so uncertain, I think it is a good buy."
c "Since everyone else in the market seems to think Glitzsoft's stock price will rise, I am *not* going to buy it."
d "Since everyone else in the market seems to think Glitzsoft's stock price will rise, I am going to buy it."
e "I think that Glitzsoft stock will rise in value next year, so I am not going to buy now, since the dividend payments are low."

11 Which of the following quotations is consistent with the speculative bubbles view of stock prices?

a "Since Glitzsoft is paying such good dividends now and in the future, I think it is a good buy."
b "Since Glitzsoft's future dividends stream is so uncertain, I think it is a good buy."
c "Since everyone else in the market seems to think Glitzsoft's stock price will rise, I am *not* going to buy it."
d "Since everyone else in the market seems to think Glitzsoft's stock price will rise, I am going to buy it."
e "I think that Glitzsoft stock will rise in value next year, so I am *not* going to buy some now, since the dividend payments are low."

12 You are considering buying a share of stock. The company is expected to earn $40 per share next year, but is expected to only pay a dividend of $20. You expect the value of the share to be $100 next year. Your discount factor is 0.75. What is the most you will be willing to pay for the share?

a $120
b $105
c $100
d $90
e $75

13 If news comes out that the IPSCO Steel Company unexpectedly failed to get the contract to manufacture the pipeline for the Alaskan Pipeline starting in 3 years, which of the following statements describes what will happen according to the market fundamentals view?

a Nothing will happen.
b The price of IPSCO stock will fall in 3 years.
c The price of IPSCO stock will fall in 2 years.
d The price of IPSCO stock will fall immediately.
e The price of IPSCO stock will rise now, so that it can fall in 3 years.

14 Which of the following activities most closely resembles stock-picking decisions in the speculative bubble view?

a Trying to decide which person is going to be voted off the island by the other people.
b Deciding which person to vote off the island.
c Carefully calculating which person has the best survival skills on the island.
d Checking out the TV Guide to find out when the next episode comes on.
e Eating bugs to get immunity.

15 Which of the following statements best describes why people discount future payments?

a People prefer current consumption to future consumption and they discount uncertain future payments.
b People prefer future consumption to current consumption and they discount uncertain future payments.
c People prefer current consumption to future consumption and they discount stock market bubbles.
d People prefer future consumption to current consumption and they discount stock market bubbles.
e Rational expectations require them to discount the future.

Risk and Return

16 What happens if people discover that a stock's prices are going to fluctuate even more than usual in the future?

a People discount the stock more, leading to a lower current price and a higher expected return.

b People discount the stock less, leading to a lower current price and a higher expected return.

c People discount the stock more, leading to a higher current price and a higher expected return.

d People discount the stock more, leading to a lower current price and a lower expected return.

e People discount the stock less, leading to a higher current price and a lower expected return.

17 What is the cost of using portfolio diversification?

a Your risk goes up.

b You are more likely to get caught in a speculative bubble.

c You are ignoring market fundamentals, and will likely earn a negative return.

d You expected return is lower.

e You must borrow to carry out the diversification.

18 Which of the following statements about stock market risk is *false*?

a Portfolio diversification reduces risk.

b People discount riskier stocks more.

c Riskier stocks usually pay a risk premium.

d Riskier stocks usually sell for a higher price.

e People will accept lower expected returns to avoid risk.

The Stock Market and the Economy

19 Which of the following statements best describes the timepath of real stock earnings in the last 140 years?

a Real stock earnings had no distinct upward or downward trend, but fluctuate a lot.

b Real stock earnings had no distinct upward or downward trend, except for burst of high earnings growth in the 1890s, 1950s/1960s and 1990s.

c Real stock earnings had a distinct upward trend, with lots of fluctuations.

d Real stock earnings had a distinct upward trend, with almost no fluctuations.

e Real stock earnings had a distinct downward trend, with lots of fluctuations.

20 Which of the following does *not* affect real stock earnings?

a New technologies.

b Taxes.

c Interest rates.

d Monetary policy.

e Inflation.

21 Which of the following best describes how interest rates affect stock prices?

a Higher interest rates mean more risk, and therefore lead to lower stock prices.

b Higher interest rates encourage stockholders to buy more shares, seeking the higher returns.

c Higher interest rates make borrowing more expensive, and this leads to less spending and lower earnings for firms.

d Higher interest rates encourage bondholders to switch to stocks.

e Higher interest rates raise wealth, and therefore encourage people to buy fewer shares.

22 Which of the following best describes how taxes affect stock prices?

a Taxes make stocks riskier, and therefore lead to lower stock prices.

b Taxes reduce firms' earnings, and lead to lower stock prices.

c Taxes increase capital gains, and lead to higher stock prices.

d Taxes reduce capital gains, and lead to higher stock returns and higher stock prices.

e Taxes reduce the number of transactions, and therefore reduce the demand for stocks.

23 How do investors profit by anticipating the central bank's monetary policy?

a If they expect expansionary monetary policy, they will sell stocks before the stock prices fall.

b If they expect expansionary monetary policy, they will buy stock before the stock prices rise.

c If they expect contractionary monetary policy, they will buy stock before the stock prices rise.

d If they expect contractionary monetary policy, they will sell stock before the stock prices rise.

e If they expect an increase in taxes, they will buy stock before the stock prices rise.

24 Why do increases in the value of the stock market lead to a lower saving rate?

a With more wealth, people wish to buy more stocks, and take the money out of their savings.

b With more wealth, people spend less, leading to lower saving.

c With more wealth, people are less worried about risk, and spend more on stocks and save less.

d With more wealth, people spend more on consumption, and save less.

e With more wealth, firms find their earnings increasing, and save less.

25 Which of the following statements is correct?
   1 During the 1990s, the saving rate excluding capital gains decreased in Canada.
   2 During the 1990s, the saving rate including capital gains increased in Canada.

a 1 only.
b 2 only.
c Both 1 and 2.
d Neither 1 nor 2.
e 1 is true, 2 is not measurable.

Short Answer Problems

1 Consider the information in Table 35.2 on Glitzsoft Stock.
   a Fill in the remainder of the table.
   ⓒ **b** Why did Glitzsoft still pay a dividend, even when its earnings were negative?
   c Why did investors still keep the stock price high in 2001, when Glitzsoft had negative earnings?

2 Explain how and why riskier stocks pay higher expected returns.

ⓒ **3** The stock market rose dramatically in value in Canada and especially in the United States in the 1990s. Do you think this was due to a speculative bubble, or to a change in market fundamentals due to the introduction of new technologies. Explain your reasoning briefly.

4 Morgan's discount rate is 0.8. Lubaba's discount rate is 0.75. They are each considering buying the stocks listed in Table 35.3 below, which also shows each person's evaluation of the expected dividend and price of the stock. Each stock sells for $100 per share. Explain whether or not they will buy each stock, and explain why you know.

TABLE **35.3** STOCK DIVIDEND AND FUTURE PRICE ESTIMATES

	Bobbie's Dolls'n'Toys		Maxwell's MP3 Mart	
	Estimated Dividend	Estimated Future Price	Estimated Dividend	Estimated Future Price
Morgan	$10	$120	$4	$110
Lubaba	$12	$125	$2	$140

5 With respect to your answers to Short Answer Problem **4**, how would your answers change if you found out Morgan and Lubaba lived in a province with a capital gains tax?

6 Microsoft announced in January of 2003 that it would pay a dividend. It has never paid a dividend before then. Why would people want to hold a stock that pays no dividend?

7 According to the market fundamentals view, the price of a stock depends only on the stream of expected future dividend payments. Explain briefly why.

8 When James Tobin won the Nobel Prize in Economics, he was asked to explain in simple words the theory of risk diversification that won him the Nobel Prize. His answer "Don't put all your eggs in one basket." In terms of buying stocks, why shouldn't you put all your eggs in one basket?

9 Your granny maintains a large portfolio of stocks. She has heard that she should be following monetary policy in order to properly

TABLE **35.2** GLITZSOFT STOCK

Year Ending	Earnings per Share	Dividend Payments	Stock Price	Price-Earnings Ratio	Dividend Yield	Rate of Return
1999	$8.00	$4.00	$100.00			—
2000	$5.00	$3.00	$90.00			
2001	−$5.00	$7.00	$100.00			
2002	$12.00	$10.00	$110.00			

look after her portfolio. She would like you to explain *why* she should follow monetary policy.

10 Why did the measured saving rate (excluding capital gains) collapse in Canada and the United States in the late 1990s?

A N S W E R S

True/False and Explain

1 **F** It is a share of profits. (831)
2 **F** 75% = (10 + (25 − 20))/20 × 100. (831)
3 **T** Expected return = expected dividend + expected capital gain. (831)
4 **F** They have risen, but with many fluctuations up and down. (832–833)
5 **F** Carried out on a stock market. (830–832)
6 **T** Definition. (836–837)
7 **T** Individuals look at the expected value of the discounted dividend and future price, and since the future price depends on future dividends, then they are really looking only at the stream of expected future dividends. (838)
8 **T** People dislike uncertainty, so their willingness to pay is lower. (836–838)
9 **T** Defined by self-fulfilling expectations. (838–839)
10 **T** Riskier stock means lower demand, which leads to a lower price holding constant future price, which means a higher expected capital gain and higher expected return. (840)
11 **T** Portfolio diversification reduces range of possible outcomes. (840)
12 **T** See text discussion. (841–842)
13 **F** Higher interest rates lead to lower spending by consumers, lower earnings by firms, lower stock prices. (842–843)
14 **T** Higher taxes mean lower net earnings for firms, lower return for stockholders, lower demand for stock. (843)
15 **T** Capital gains mean rising wealth, and less need to save. (843–845)

Multiple-Choice

1 **a** Definition. (830)
2 **d** Change in price. (831)
3 **d** Dividend − capital loss. (831)
4 **c** Return as a percent of 1999 price. (831)
5 **c** Dividend as a percent of 2000 price. (831)
6 **c** 90/5. (831)
7 **b** They fluctuate a great deal. (832–835)

8 **d** See text discussion. (832–833)
9 **e** Stockholders have limited liability, companies frequently reinvest earnings, and Bombardier only gets the sale price for the initial sale. (830–835)
10 **a** **b** is nonsense, **c** or **d** would be speculative bubble views, and **e** is wrong, might buy. (838–838)
11 **d** Herd behaviour. (838–839)
12 **d** Willingness to pay = 0.75 × ($20 + $100). (836–838)
13 **d** Since future earnings/dividends expected to be lower, current willingness to pay falls, current price falls. (836–838)
14 **a** Trying to pick who other people think is a winning stock, as opposed to picking the best stock. (838–839)
15 **a** See text discussion. (836)
16 **a** React to extra uncertainty by increasing discount rate, lowering willingness to pay and current price, raising expected returns. (840)
17 **d** See text discussion. (840)
18 **d** Sell for lower price. (840)
19 **c** See Text Figure 35.6. (841)
20 **e** Real earnings control for inflation effects. (841–845)
21 **c** Lower earnings for firms means lower dividends, and lower willingness to pay, lower price. (842–843)
22 **b** Taxes do lower capital gains, but this leads to lower current stock prices. (843)
23 **b** Expansionary policy will lead to lower interest rates, higher stock prices in the future. (842–843)
24 **d** Capital gains are part of wealth, and spending depends on wealth. (843–845)
25 **a** See text discussion around Text Figures 35.7 and 35.8. (844–845)

Short Answer Problems

1 **a** Table 35.2 is filled in on the next page as Table 35.2 Solution.
  b It paid a dividend to keep its stockholders happy, and to keep them holding the stock.
  c The investors were expecting that the future stream of earnings would be positive.

2 Investors do not like risk, so they will show a lower willingness to pay, by discounting a riskier stock by more than a less risky stock with the same expected dividend payments and future price. This extra discounting will mean a lower current price for the stock. Since the current price is lower, but the future expected price is the same, the riskier stock will pay an higher expected capital gain and higher expected return.

TABLE **35.2** GLITZSOFT STOCK

Year Ending	Earnings per Share	Dividend Payments	Stock Price	Price-Earnings Ratio	Dividend Yield	Rate of Return
1999	$8.00	$4.00	$100.00	12.5	4%	—
2000	$5.00	$3.00	$90.00	18	3.33%	–7%
2001	–$5.00	$7.00	$100.00	—	7%	18.9%
2002	$12.00	$10.00	$110.00	9.17	9.1%	20%

3 Any answer to this question is a value judgement, but should be based on an argument. In favour of the speculative bubbles view, we see a strong rise and decline in stock prices, the strongest rise in history, out of proportion to the changes in earnings. In favour of the market fundamentals view, we see that earnings were strong in the 1990s, and we see there was an unusual technological revolution going on, just as in previous situations where stocks rose sharply. The big unresolved question is whether or not the earnings rise is strong and permanent enough to justify the higher prices.

4 Each person will calculate their willingness to pay based on the formula:

P_1 = expected value of [discount rate × (dividend + future price)]

For Morgan, Bobbie's Dolls'n'Toys is worth $104 = 0.8 × [$10 + $120] to her. Maxwell's is worth $91.20 = 0.8 × [$4 + $110] to her. She will buy a share of Bobbie's, but not of Maxwell's stock.

For Lubaba, Bobbie's Dolls'n'Toys is worth $102.75 = 0.75 × [$12 + $125] to her. Maxwell's is worth $106.50 = 0.75 × [$2 + $140] to her. She will buy a share of both stocks.

5 If either person has to pay capital gains taxes, we would have to use the after-tax value of the capital gain in our calculations, and this would reduce the potential return on any stock. Morgan and Lubaba would not start buying one of the stocks they have already rejected, and they may reject buying one of those they have accepted, if the tax rate is high enough to reduce the willingness to pay below $100.

6 The investors anticipated that future earnings or future capital gains would give them the return they are looking for.

7 Individuals prefer current consumption to future consumption, and they dislike uncertainty. For these two reasons, they discount future payments. Buying a stock entitles you to a share of future dividends, and to the right to sell the stock in the future. Combining discounting, dividends and the right to sell, we can logically see that

P_1 = expected value of [discount rate × (dividend + future price)]

The expected future price, by logic, will also depend on the expected future dividend. Substituting in all these expected future prices tells us that the current price will depend on the stream of expected future payments.

8 Putting all your eggs in one basket (investing everything in one stock) is riskier than holding a mixture of stocks in your portfolio—portfolio diversification. Holding the mixture of stocks means that the actual potential range of your earnings is smaller then if you held only one type of stock.

9 Monetary policy affects interest rates, which in turn affect stock prices. For example, if interest rates fall in value, then stock prices will be affected via two routes. First, the lower interest rates will encourage more borrowing (and less saving) and more spending by consumers and business, which in turn will lead to more earnings for firms, and higher future dividends. As a result, the expected return on stocks is higher, and your granny should buy more.

Secondly, the lower interest rates will lower the return on stocks, and individuals (including your granny) will switch from bonds to stocks. This increase in demand will also increase the price of stocks, so your granny might like to anticipate this increase by buying stocks now.

10 The strong rise in the value of stock markets in Canada and the United States added to the wealth of households—the change in wealth was positive due to the paper capital gains they earned. As a result of the higher wealth, households spent more and saved less out of their current disposable income—the saving rate plummeted.

Another way to think of this is to note that their savings rate including capital gains did not plummet—they did indeed save (accumulate wealth).

Understanding the Global Economy

PROBLEM

You are an advisor to the prime minister, specializing in exchange rate considerations. The Canadian dollar is suffering from a crisis of nonconfidence on world markets, sparked by an economic crisis in Asia. Foreign investors are afraid that Canada's economy will be hurt by the Asian economic crisis, since Asia buys many commodities from Canada. The investors are afraid that profits and returns at Canadian companies will decrease dramatically. Foreigners start a selloff of Canadian assets.

a Explain to the prime minister (with the aid of a graph showing the demand and supply of dollars) what this will imply for the value of the Canadian dollar, as well as for interest rates, the value of the monetary base and the money supply, and the three balance of payments accounts. (The Bank of Canada is operating under a rule of trying to stabilize the exchange rate.)

b Another advisor to the prime minister has told her that the Bank of Canada should be ordered to increase the money supply to try and lower interest rates. What will this do to the value of the exchange rate and to foreign holdings of Canadian assets? Can the Bank of Canada do this and still maintain a managed exchange rate?

c The prime minister has received a phone call from the owner of Big Importer Company, complaining that the change in the value of the Canadian dollar has hurt his ability to sell imported whatzits in Canada. With the aid of a graph of the market for whatzits in Canada (with the vertical axis measuring the price of whatzits in Canadian dollars), explain to the prime minister what has happened to the price and quantity imported in this market. What has happened to exports? to the balance of trade?

d The prime minister has been considering asking the Bank of Canada to defend the dollar more strongly, but is worried about the impact on the stock market. Briefly explain to her the impact of defending the Canadian dollar on the stock market.

e The prime minister asks you whether she should ask the Bank of Canada to defend the dollar even more strongly, or not. What do you think?

MIDTERM EXAMINATION

You should allocate 24 minutes for this examination (12 questions, 2 minutes per question). For each question, choose the one *best* answer.

I The short-run adjustment costs in Canada associated with reducing the level of tariffs under a North American Free Trade Agreement will be borne principally by

a taxpayers, whose higher taxes provide the generous retraining programs.

b employers and workers in those sectors in which Canada has a comparative advantage.

c employers and workers in those sectors in which Canada has a comparative disadvantage.

d Canadian consumers of imported goods.

e Canadian producers of exported goods.

2 Table P10.1 below shows some information on the dividend payments and stock prices on a yearly basis for Present Shop Inc. What is the capital gain on Present Shop stock between 2001 and 2002?

a $20.00

b $32.00

c $45.00

d −$20.00

e $0.00

TABLE **P10.1** PRESENT SHOP STOCK

Year Ending	Earnings per Share	Dividend Payments	Stock Price
2001	$15.00	$12.00	$125.00
2002	$20.00	$12.00	$145.00

3 Which of the following quotations best describes the interest rate parity effect?

a "The recent high Canadian interest rate has increased the demand for the Canadian dollar."

b "The market feeling is that the Canadian dollar is overvalued and will likely appreciate."

c "The price of bananas is the same in Canada and the United States, adjusting for the exchange rate."

d "The expected appreciation of the Canadian dollar is currently lowering demand for it."

e None of the above.

4 Which of the following statements with regard to stock market risk is *true*?

a Portfolio diversification increases risk.

b People discount riskier stocks less.

c Riskier stocks usually pay a risk premium.

d Riskier stocks usually sell for a higher price.

e People need lower expected returns to accept risk.

5 Atlantis imports watches from Beltran and exports widgets to Beltran. Why would Atlantis prefer arranging a voluntary export restraint rather than a quota on watches?

a to not hurt Beltran's imports

b to prevent Beltran from retaliating by restricting Atlantis' exports

c to keep the domestic price of watches low

d to increase government revenue

e to help domestic producers

6 Which of the following would cause the dollar to depreciate against the yen?

a an increase in the Canadian monetary supply

b an increase in interest rates in Canada

c a decrease in interest rates in Japan

d an increase in the expected future exchange rate

e a decrease in the current exchange rate

7 You are considering buying a share of stock. The company is expected to earn $50 per share next year, but is expected to only pay a dividend of $25. You expect the value of the share to be $200 next year. Your discount factor is 0.8. What is the most you will be willing to pay for the share?

a $250

b $225

c $200

d $180

e $160

8 If Fullofland is currently a net lender and a debtor nation,

a it has loaned more capital than it borrowed abroad this year, but borrowed more than it loaned during its history.

b it has borrowed more capital than it loaned abroad this year and also borrowed more than it loaned during its history.

c it has loaned more capital than it borrowed abroad this year and has loaned more than it borrowed during its history.

d its accounting system must be in error if it shows this nation to be a net lender and a debtor nation at the same time.

e its debts must be currently growing.

9 Suppose Musicland and Videoland produce two goods—CDs and videos. Musicland has a comparative advantage in the production of CDs if

a fewer CDs must be given up to produce one unit of videos than in Videoland.

b less labour is required to produce one unit of CDs than in Videoland.

c less capital is required to produce one unit of CDs than in Videoland.

d less labour and capital are required to produce one unit of CDs than in Videoland.

e fewer videos must be given up to produce one unit of CDs than in Videoland.

10 Which of the following changes is likely to increase real stock earnings?

a Introduction of new technologies.

b Higher corporate profits taxes.

c Higher interest rates.

d Contractionary monetary policy.

e Higher capital gains taxes.

11 Acadia and Breton are currently engaged in free trade. Acadia imports cheese from Breton and exports sheep to Breton. If Acadia imposes a tariff on cheese, Acadia's cheese-producing industry will

a expand, and its sheep-producing industry will contract.

b expand, and its sheep-producing industry will expand.

c contract, and its sheep-producing industry will contract.

d contract, and its sheep-producing industry will expand.

e expand, and its sheep-producing industry will be unchanged.

12 Canada has a trade deficit when the

a value of Canadian exports of goods and services exceeds the value of Canadian imports of goods and services.

b value of Canadian exports of goods and services is exceeded by the value of Canadian imports of goods and services.

c value of Canadian exports of goods exceeds the value of Canadian imports of goods.

d value of Canadian exports of goods is exceeded by the value of Canadian imports of goods.

e current account balance is less than zero.

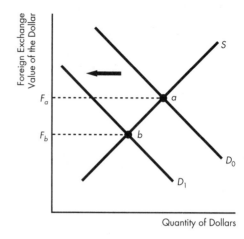

FIGURE **P10.1**

Quantity of Dollars

ANSWERS

Problem

a The fear of lower future returns leads to a decrease in the demand for Canadian dollar assets, leading to a decrease in the demand for Canadian dollars. In Figure P10.1, this decrease, in turn, leads to a decrease in the value of the exchange rate from F_a to F_b. To keep it from decreasing even further, the Bank of Canada intervenes and buys Canadian dollars, supplying foreign exchange from official reserves. They also might shrink the money supply, which will tend to increase Canadian interest rates. (There are also potential supply effects not shown here.)

   Foreigners are lending us less, so the capital account will move towards a smaller surplus or a deficit. The decrease in the foreign exchange value of the Canadian dollar will lead to an increase in exports and a decrease in imports (see part **c** below), so that the current account will move towards a surplus. Since the Bank of Canada is supplying foreign exchange, this is a decrease in reserves, or a movement towards a surplus.

b A lower interest rate would spark a further decrease in the demand for the Canadian dollar, as foreigners buy fewer Canadian assets, given the lower Canadian interest rate differential. This would tend to push down the Canadian dollar's value, which would conflict with the Bank of Canada's attempts to stabilize the exchange rate.

c The market for whatzits is shown in Figure P10.2. The new, lower exchange rate of fewer U.S. dollars per Canadian dollar means more Canadian dollars per U.S. dollar, and acts like a tariff—it increases the Canadian dollar price of the imported whatzits, shown as the shift leftward in the supply curve. This change leads to a new equilibrium, with a higher price, and a lower quantity imported and sold.

   The market for Canadian exports would be acting in an opposite manner, with lower prices and more exports. The higher exports and lower imports will mean the balance of trade (and hence the current account) is moving towards a surplus.

d Defending the Canadian dollar involves shrinking the money supply, and raising interest rates. Higher interest rates lead to a) less borrowing, less consumption and investment expenditure and less revenue earning by firms, and lower demand for stocks, as well as b) stock holders selling their stock and shifting to bonds. The net effect is lower stock prices.

e The answer is a value judgement, and depends on the value you place on defending the Canadian dollar (for example, helping the importer) versus the damage the defense might do to the Canadian economy. Defending the Canadian dollar will entail buying Canadian dollars (which will shrink the domestic money supply), and raising Canadian interest rates. Both of these actions will depress aggregate demand and put downward pressure on real GDP and jobs. It is your call.

FIGURE **P10.2**

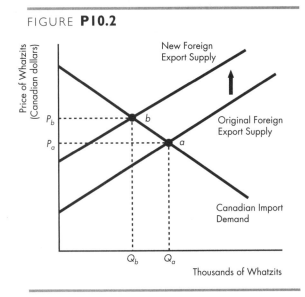

Midterm Examination

1   c   Because decrease in U.S. or Mexican prices implies decrease in Canadian production. (802–803)

2   a   Change in market price of stock. (831)

3   a   If two currencies do not have the same interest rate, market conditions will change the demand for assets and the dollar. (821–822)

4   c   Because people do not like riskier stocks, they discount them more, leading to a lower price, and a higher return. (840)

5   b   Under a VER, exporting country gains excess revenue, which means it is less likely to retaliate, since hurt less. (794–796)

6   a   **a** decreases interest rates, which decrease demand for Canadian dollars. **b–d** are increase in demand, **e** move along, not a shift. (820)

7   d   Price = discount rate × (expected dividend + expected future price). (836–838)

8   a   Definitions of net lender and debtor nation. Debts are shrinking. (812)

9   e   Definition. (787–788)

10   a   It leads to higher earnings for firms. (841–845)

11   a   Tariff increases domestic price of cheese, which decreases imports, which increases domestic production. Decreased imports = decreased exports in Breton, which decreases its income, which decreases its imports = decrease in Acadia's exports, decreasing Acadia's sheep production. (794–795)

12   b   Definition of balance of trade. (810)